MUSSOLINI UNLEASHED
1939–1941

Mussolini Unleashed
1939–1941
Politics and Strategy in Fascist Italy's Last War

MACGREGOR KNOX

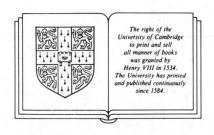

The right of the
University of Cambridge
to print and sell
all manner of books
was granted by
Henry VIII in 1534.
The University has printed
and published continuously
since 1584.

CAMBRIDGE UNIVERSITY PRESS

CAMBRIDGE

LONDON   NEW YORK   NEW ROCHELLE

MELBOURNE   SYDNEY

Published by the Press Syndicate of the University of Cambridge
The Pitt Building, Trumpington Street, Cambridge CB2 1RP
32 East 57th Street, New York, NY 10022, USA
10 Stamford Road, Oakleigh, Melbourne 3166, Australia

First published 1982
First paperback edition 1986

Printed in the United States of America

Library of Congress Cataloging in Publication Data
Knox, MacGregor.
Mussolini unleashed, 1939–1941.
Includes bibliographical references and index.
1. Italy – Foreign relations – 1922–1945.
2. Fascism – Italy – History.   3. World War,
1939–1945 – Italy.   4. World War, 1939–1945 –
Diplomatic history.   5. Mussolini, Benito,
1883–1945.   I. title.
DG572.K56   327.45   81-38508 AACR2
ISBN 0 521 23917 6 hard covers
ISBN 0 521 33835 2 paperback

Quotations from Crown copyright records in the Public Record Office, London,
appear by permission of the Controller of H. M. Stationery Office.

For my parents

BIANCA VANORDEN
BERNARD M. W. KNOX

Contents

Preface

I wrote this book to try to explain to myself what actually happened. When I had finished, I realized that I had quite unintentionally produced a work with something in it likely to annoy most people connected with Italian history. In mitigation, I can only plead that I have attempted to fulfill the historian's duty to call things by their right names. As an outsider born in 1945 (who has nevertheless lived in Italy for a number of years and speaks the language) and as a historian with training and experience in a variety of fields, I think I can claim some degree of detachment from my subject. That does not mean I believe "historical objectivity" demands abstention from judgment. I hope those who read this book will take it as I intended it, as a small contribution to the far from complete task of understanding the Fascist past.

One pleasant side of finishing a project is that it brings the opportunity to acknowledge one's debts. I could not have done research in Europe without grants both from Yale University's Concilium on International and Area Studies and from the American Council of Learned Societies. A Yale University Whiting Fellowship in the Humanities supported me while I wrote much of the text. I owe a great deal to Mrs. Marian Johnson, who shared with me her profound knowledge of Italy, and opened a number of important doors for me during my stay in Rome in 1973–4. Colonel and Mrs. John Weaver of Chelsea welcomed me warmly, and generously put me up during my work at the Public Record Office in London. A number of people at the various archives I worked at were especially helpful: Messrs. George Wagner, John Mendelsohn, Harry Riley, Timothy P. Milligan, and Robert Wolfe of the U.S. National Archives; Drs. Carucci and Nicola Gallerano of the Archivio Centrale dello Stato; Generale di Brigata Rinaldo Cruccu of the Archivio dell'Ufficio Storico dell'Esercito; Contr'ammiraglio Gino Galuppini of the Archivio dell'Ufficio Storico della Marina Militare; and Dr. Maria Keipert of the Politisches Archiv des Auswärtigen Amts.

I have learned a great deal from the published works of other scholars, above all those of Alberto Aquarone, Lucio Ceva, F. W. Deakin, Renzo De Felice, Andreas Hillgruber, Klaus Hildebrand, and Giorgio Rochat. I am deeply indebted to Henry A. Turner, Jr., for arousing my interest in the Fascist regime and "fascism." I have had pleasant and useful conversations with Alberto Aquarone, Jens Petersen, David D. Roberts, and Michael Geyer. Geoffrey Warner offered great encouragement at an early stage, and generously allowed me to consult a chapter of his unpublished work on Italy in World War II. Brian R. Sullivan has been ever generous with time, advice, copies of documents, and chapters from his outstanding dissertation, "A Thirst for Glory: Mussolini, the Italian Military, and the Fascist Regime, 1922–1940." Williamson Murray, Isabel Hull, and Tina Isaacs, whose careful reading and criticism of the manuscript was indispensable, helped me at every turn. Bianca VanOrden, Frank M. Snowden, and Piotr S. Wandycz read the part of the book I submitted as a dissertation, and offered invaluable suggestions. Stanley Engerman helped me avoid statistical gaffes. Eugene D. Genovese and Perez Zagorin have been liberal with comments, counsel, and support. Above all, my *Doktorvater* Hans W. Gatzke has watched over the project throughout. Without his acute criticism, unfailing encouragement, and friendship I would have been lost.

All of those I have mentioned have contributed in one way or another to whatever merits this book may possess: sins of omission or commission and errors of fact or judgment are mine alone.

December 1980

MacGregor Knox
Rochester, New York

Maps

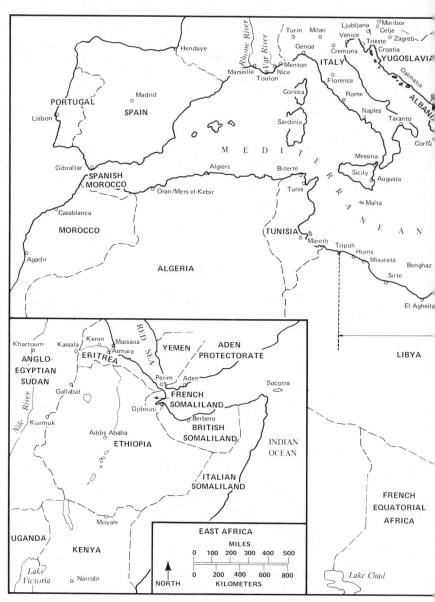

Map 1. The Mediterranean and Africa. *Source:* United States Military Academy, *A Military History of World War II: Atlas* (West Point, New York, 1956), map 73.

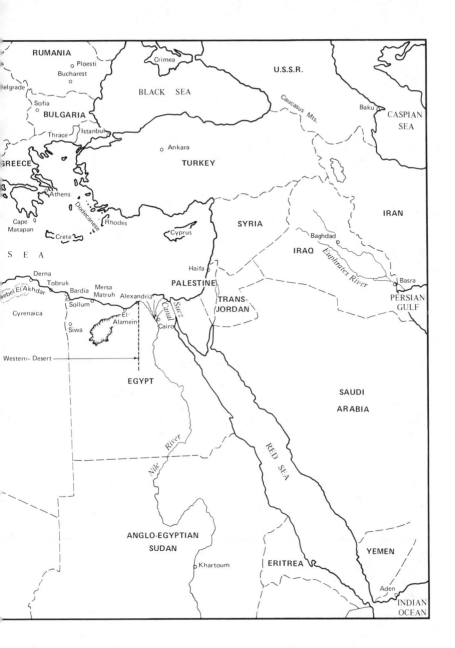

Introduction

Failure, as Hitler put it in December 1940 with a touch of racialist contempt, had the "healthy effect of once more compressing Italian claims to within the natural boundaries of Italian capabilities."[1] The Fascist regime, which Mussolini and many contemporaries believed had at last made Italy a great power of sorts, had failed the only test its founder recognized as valid, the test of war. That failure has dominated later interpretations of the regime, which have tended to underestimate its brutality, the vigor and extent of its expansionist ambition, and the degree of domestic support its aims enjoyed until their price became fully apparent.

The sources of this underestimation are various. Professional historians have no direct experience of wielding power, except in academic politics. They tend, perhaps naïvely, to underrate the degree of unwisdom prevalent in the world of action, and too often expect political leaders to behave rationally – as men of goodwill with the advantage of hindsight define rationality. Mussolini's outwardly erratic course and irresponsible decisions, and above all his failure, have therefore aroused widespread contempt, which in turn has inhibited analysis of his intentions and activities on their own terms.

Italian liberals from the philosopher Benedetto Croce downward have tended, once they ceased to support Fascism, to dismiss it as "antihistorical" and condemn it as the "anti-*Risorgimento.*"[2] The regime's success until 1940 affronted their tidy vision of civilization and progress, and the Fascist movement's not entirely illegitimate claim to the heritage of Mazzini and Garibaldi outraged their sense of propriety. From a more dispassionate point of view, Renzo De Felice has in his awe-inspiring multi-volume biography of Mussolini conjured up a fundamentally humane dictator, "far from the cold fanaticism and the ferocious determination of a Hitler, of a Stalin, or, on the other hand, of a Churchill" – an interpretation not entirely free of apologetic nationalism. De Felice has done a great service in emphasizing the popular support the regime enjoyed in the early and middle 1930s. But he has also implied that Mussolini's later foreign policy was a Nordic import that increasing German preponderance forced upon a fundamentally opportunistic Duce, and has suggested that Mussolini merely "tended" toward certain unspecified "general objectives" he allegedly sought through a policy of balance between European power groupings.[3]

Some British scholars, and even anti-Fascists of the stature of Gaetano Salvemini, have exchanged analysis for sarcasm, and given us a Mussolini operating "from hand to mouth" as an "artist in propaganda" whose sole driving force was "egotism and self-justification."[4] Political scientists have attempted to define and confine the regime within the abstract categories of "mass society," "totalitarianism," or "fascism" (the last a generic phenomenon characteristic of those of whom one disapproves). Such terms either encourage static analysis of a system inexplicable except through its ultimate goals, or dissolve its uniqueness in a morass of transnational generalities.[5]

Italian Marxists, whose struggle against the regime has led them to underestimate it less than others, have done more justice to Mussolini's brutality and seriousness of purpose. Nevertheless, they have too often assumed that the "stage of capitalism" Lenin defined as "imperialism" explains both Mussolini's expansionist foreign policy and the context in which he operated. Some Leninist accounts have considerable descriptive merit, but the theory that underlies them does not face the sad truth that in relations between states and in much else, "the strong do as they will, and the weak suffer what they must,"[6] regardless of historical epoch or economic system. Internally, the usual Marxist counterpart to "imperialism" has been the characterization of Fascism as a "class dictatorship of the bourgeoisie," or, in embarrassed tribute to its popular support, as a "reactionary mass regime."[7] Even against the will of the historian, such formulas reduce Mussolini and his associates to mere agents of shadowy malefactors of great wealth.

The regime was far more than a "class dictatorship." Unfortunately for Italy its leader aspired to more than self-justification or even self-preservation – as his goals and his policies in the years from 1936 to 1941 demonstrate. In those years, which historians of the regime have yet to explore fully, the growing power of a resurgent Germany gave Italy unprecedented leverage and freedom of action. In 1940, that freedom unleashed Mussolini's long-meditated assault on the West's Mediterranean position. That assault, its motives, preparation, objectives, execution, and consequences, is the subject of this book.

CHAPTER I

"There has been much bluff"

". . . tutt'i profeti armati vinsono e li disarmati ruinorono."

Machiavelli

Duce politics. It is a commonplace among educated Italians that "Mussolini was indeed a dictator, but no bloody-handed murderer [*sanguinario*] like Hitler." Scholarly sources tell us that he was a "realist," unlike Hitler, who "was gripped by a delusion which he made from the purely personal into a collective organic delusion shared by thousands of his fellow-countrymen."[1] Finally, "far from possessing the gifts of intelligence and character of a truly great and creative statesman," Mussolini had a hidden weakness in dealing with individuals, and was incapable of choosing or retaining competent subordinates.[2]

Mussolini was certainly no *sanguinario* on Hitler's scale. He did not have millions of people murdered in the service of a racialist pseudoscience. Italian political prisoners generally ended up in desolate corners of the South and the Islands rather than in concentration camps of the German type. The regime's systematic persecution of the Jews did not end in their extermination until Italy's collapse in 1943 brought German occupation.[3] But Mussolini was hardly squeamish, nor was his brutality free of racialist motivation even before the adoption of an anti-Jewish policy. The imposition of what the regime pleased to call a "Roman peace" upon the Arabs of Libya required mass shootings, large-scale population transfers, and concentration camps.[4] In Ethiopia, Italian forces employed mustard gas systematically in accordance with Mussolini's own directives, issued eight months before the campaign opened.[5] The telegrams with which he bombarded his viceroy, Marshal Rodolfo Graziani, vividly render the Duce's conception of what he called a "radical house-cleaning" of the newly conquered *Impero:*

H[is] E[xcellency] GRAZIANI — ADDIS ABABA
6496 — 5 JUNE 1936 — ALL REBELS MADE PRISONER ARE TO
BE SHOT.

MUSSOLINI

H. E. GRAZIANI — ADDIS ABABA
6595 — SECRET — 8 JUNE 1936. TO FINISH OFF REBELS AS
IN CASE AT ANCOBER USE GAS.

MUSSOLINI

H. E. GRAZIANI — ADDIS ABABA
8103 — SECRET — 8 JULY 1936. I REPEAT MY AUTHORIZA-
TION TO YOUR EXCELLENCY TO INITIATE AND SYSTEMATI-
CALLY CONDUCT POLICY OF TERROR AND EXTERMINATION
AGAINST REBELS AND POPULATIONS IN COMPLICITY WITH
THEM. WITHOUT THE LAW OF TEN EYES FOR ONE WE CAN-
NOT HEAL THIS WOUND IN GOOD TIME. ACKNOWLEDGE.

MUSSOLINI

H. E. GRAZIANI — ADDIS ABABA
54000 — 21 FEBRUARY 1937. AGREED THAT MALE POPULA-
TION OF GOGGETTI OVER 18 YEARS OF AGE IS TO BE SHOT
AND VILLAGE DESTROYED.

MUSSOLINI

H. E. GRAZIANI — ADDIS ABABA
93980 PERS[ONAL] — 21 FEBRUARY 1937. NO PERSONS
ARRESTED ARE TO BE RELEASED WITHOUT MY ORDER. ALL
CIVILIANS AND [Coptic] CLERICS IN ANY WAY SUSPECT ARE
TO BE SHOT WITHOUT DELAY. ACKNOWLEDGE.

MUSSOLINI[6]

These directives were not merely isolated examples of frightfulness. The entire thrust of Fascist colonial policy was to eliminate the native ruling classes and create an undifferentiated mass of disarmed, terrorized, and submissive subjects who would eventually make way for the massive influx of Italian colonists the regime intended to promote. While not strictly analogous to the "final solution of the Jewish question" or Germany's racial war of annihilation against the Soviet Union, such methods hardly testify to a lack of fixity of purpose or an absence of bloody-mindedness on Mussolini's part. Nor do they bear out the suggestion of one belated anti-Fascist that the regime "kept an incorrigibly clownlike appearance even in the crimes it committed."[7]

Mussolini did not mellow with age. At the end of the Spanish Civil War, he ordered the killing of all Italian "reds" captured — justifying the action with the motto, "the dead tell no tales." During the Italo-German occupation of Yugoslavia, he detected a lack of ruthlessness in some of his generals, and praised the example of one officer who reportedly harangued his troops in these terms: "I have heard that you are all good fathers of families. That's fine in your own home, but not here. Here you will never be thieves, assassins, and rapists enough." Mussolini demanded "steel and fire," and initiated a series of massacres and population transfers that rivaled in brutality the actions of his German ally.[8]

As for Mussolini's alleged "realism," one has only to see a few of the regime's newsreels (admittedly not so well filmed as Leni Riefenstahl's satanic documentaries) to see that his "delusion" that Italy under Fascist leadership was a great power indeed inspired "thousands of his countrymen." No less an expert than Hitler testified to the genuineness of the emotions the Duce roused in the masses,[9] and Mussolini himself drew reassurance from this enthusiasm. In private, while he did not have the "sleepwalker's self-assurance" of the Führer, he did lay claim to an "animal instinct" that he asserted never failed him.[10]

His "hidden weakness in dealing with individuals" was not entirely imaginary. He often agreed with the last of his advisers spoken to, a practice that resulted in mutually contradictory decisions and frequent administrative paralysis.[11] But this characteristic was not peculiar to Mussolini. It is more or less inherent in any system of personal rule. Mussolini shared it with Franklin D. Roosevelt, and with Adolf Hitler, who "was likely to avoid conflict, postpone unpleasant decisions, and delay solutions," while issuing "oral orders based on impulse" that produced unending confusion.[12] This "Führungschaos" exacted a price, and contemplating it has led one scholar to conclude that it stemmed from weakness on Hitler's part.[13] The Führer's regrettable genius for political and military decision making, without which his rise is inexplicable, is answer enough to such suggestions. Actually, madness — social Darwinism run amok — was method. In both Germany and Italy it enabled the dictator to play off subordinates against one another and remain above the battle as supreme arbiter of their disputes. Paradoxically, competition was not entirely disadvantageous, at least in Germany. It contributed to the regime's expansionist dynamism; Hitler's foreign policy and military subordinates rushed about like eager spaniels, each bearing the Führer a bone. The shared values and objectives of the National Socialist bureaucracies also mitigated the effects of competition, and Germany's economic strength and military leadership tradition made it affordable. The feuds of Ribbentrop and Goebbels, Göring and Raeder, Himmler and the Army, Party and state bureaucracy, did not keep the Reich from conquering Western Europe and almost crushing the Soviet Union. But in Fascist Italy, given its economic weakness and the disparate origins and lack of cohesion of its elites, the conflicts the dictator required to maintain his position were more immediately damaging than in Germany.

Italy's weakness and Germany's strength explain the disparity between the two dictators' performances better than the usually alleged differences between their personalities. Mussolini's tenacity during the Ethiopian crisis suggests that the claim he lacked "nerve"[14] is arbitrary. His performance compares favorably with Hitler's during the Rhineland affair or the crucial last days of August 1939, when news of Italian nonbelligerence, on top of the announcement of the Anglo–Polish alliance, caused the Führer to waver before taking the final plunge. Hitler too was not immune to vanity, as his vindictiveness after foreign press reports that he had "backed down" in the face of Czech partial mobilization of 20 May 1938 suggests. But Mussolini nevertheless had serious drawbacks as a leader. His vanity, even more than Hitler's, took the form of constant attention to the figure he was cutting. This vanity was not the origin of his expansionism. Certainly, less-dangerous activities could have assuaged it. It did, however, influence his moods and short-term policy choices.

Mussolini's methods of finding out what others thought of him varied from the foreign press, of which he was a voracious reader, to the reports of his chief of police. During the prewar years, Italian military intelligence (the Servizio Informazioni Militari or SIM) systematically photographed the contents of the British Embassy safe, decrypted the diplomatic and military traffic of most of Italy's smaller neighbors, and, in 1935, read communications between the British Home Fleet and the Admiralty. The information these methods produced, as Mario Toscano has pointed out, did not usually lead to a more realistic appreciation of the motives and intentions of the other side, but produced furious outbursts by the dictator.[15] Thus his grudge against the Greeks, latent since his brief but violent occupation of Corfù in 1923,[16] reached new heights after SIM purloined the record of a December 1937 conversation between British Foreign Secretary Anthony Eden and the King of Greece. The King's hope that Britain would one day "put [the Italians] in their place" and his remark that while in Rome "it had been difficult to resist the temptation to tell [Mussolini's son-in-law and foreign minister] Count [Galeazzo] Ciano that, if Italy were really so great a power, it was not necessary to say so quite so often," produced fury at Palazzo Venezia.[17] But the incident did not cause new departures. Ciano, reflecting his master's preoccupations, had concluded weeks before that "destiny" would take the Serbs, with whom Ciano was at that point attempting to arrange an alliance, "to Salonika, and us to Tirana and Corfù."[18]

More important than the gleanings of the SIM was the foreign press, summaries of which Mussolini received twice daily,[19] along with a number of newspapers, principally French. Despite, or because of, his journalistic origins, Mussolini paid great attention to what journalists wrote about him and the regime. Slurs upon his private life routinely produced threats of "cannon fire and bombs."[20] Even more vulnerable was Italian military prowess, upon the exaltation of which the regime's propaganda rested. Unfortunately, the performance of Mussolini's military experts failed to support his propaganda. In March 1937, the four "volunteer" divisions with which the regime had intervened in the Spanish Civil War launched a drive on Madrid through the outlying town of Guadalajara. The Republicans held, then counterattacked with a battalion of Italian anti-Fascists at their head, and routed Mussolini's troops. The military consequences were grave enough: the swift and glorious end to the war that Mussolini, Ciano, and their generals had promised themselves was clearly far off. But British press mockery of the "new Caporetto," including an article by Lloyd George on "The Italian Skedaddle," turned a question of military prestige into a major Anglo-Italian confrontation.[21] The immediate effects of the battle did not die down until the summer, when Franco victories with Italian participation soothed Mussolini somewhat. Despite the relaxation of tension, Guadalajara played a major part in pushing Italy closer to its partner in the Rome–Berlin Axis that Mussolini had announced with fanfare the previous November.[22]

While Guadalajara was the most conspicuous single incident in which the dictator's vanity, though not exclusively personal, influenced policy, his tenacity in holding to the Axis once committed to it stemmed at least partly from the precedent of 1914–15. Italy had entered World War I alongside the West after abandoning its Triple Alliance partners, Germany and Austria-Hungary. German and Austrian failure to consult Italy before unleashing war in July-August 1914 fully justified Italian neutrality, despite vociferous Austro-German claims of betrayal. But subsequent Italian belligerence, which the Allies purchased in the April 1915 Treaty of London with lavish though later partly repudiated promises of territory, reinforced the Germans in their views. It left an enduring taint of betrayal and of what one Italian statesman had unwisely called *"sacro egoismo."* Consequently, the new, Fascist Italy, while aggressively proud of its egotism, must of necessity keep faith, must pursue "a policy as straight as a sword blade." However, more mundane, Machiavellian considerations often overshadowed this laudable aspiration. If, after the surprise German move on Prague in March 1939, Mussolini told Ciano that "we cannot change our policy because we are not whores," his first thought was of the danger of falling between two stools, of rendering himself, like the cowards in the *Inferno, "a Dio spiacenti ed ai nimici sui."* German power was now overwhelming – and at the Brenner.[23]

More dangerous than vanity was Mussolini's deep-seated distrust of his subordinates. Particularly in the later years, he delighted in sudden "changes of the guard": the removal, without warning or explanation, of most of his ministers. All too frequently these reshuffles replaced experienced administrators with unqualified nonentities. Perhaps Mussolini was not a good judge of men.[24] More likely, as Alberto Aquarone has suggested, he felt competence and excessive zeal threatened his own position. "Don't be-plume your subordinates too much," Gabriele D'Annunzio, prophet of the "national rebirth" and virtual poet laureate of the regime, had advised shortly after Italo Balbo's great publicity flight to Chicago in 1933.[25] The advice was congenial, and Mussolini followed it systematically. He prized the reliability of discreet apolitical functionaries from the old administrative elite, men like Arturo Bocchini, chief of police from 1925 until his death in 1940. Hitler, by contrast, was fiercely loyal to his Party associates (with the conspicuous exceptions of Gregor Strasser and Ernst Röhm) and found Mussolini's changes of the guard unfortunate. Evidently the Duce could not "find amongst his advisers the sort of collaboration he need[ed]."[26]

Given his ambitions, Mussolini's most serious defect was his military dilettantism, which contributed to his downfall in no uncertain measure. Like Hitler, Mussolini had served in the infantry in the World War, though without the former's distinction. He had none of Hitler's obsessive interest in military machinery. Mussolini could thunder that "words are a beautiful thing, but rifles, cannon, warships and aircraft are still more beautiful,"[27] but he best understood the external "Prussianization" of Italy. A hearty manner in dealing with his generals masked a secret inferiority complex that inhibited him from much questioning of their technical advice.[28] He generally concentrated "on questions of form," and called down "the wrath of God if a 'present arms' [was] done badly or an officer [was] unable to get his leg up high enough for the *passo romano* [the Italian goose step, introduced in 1938]."[29] Unlike Hitler, Mussolini initially had little conception of the industrial requirements of modern war. He confused numbers with technological superiority, *élan* with careful staff work, and form with substance. Writing in his diary of Mussolini's June 1940 visit to the troops after the abortive Alpine battles, a high officer noted that "the Duce made the visit more as a journalist than as a commander: no word to his staff; no visits to the subordinate commands . . . ; not a single conference with the officers, but only rapid review of the troops in formation, often carried out without even descending from his automobile."[30] Hitler, if he was not (in the phrase of General Wilhelm Keitel of the *Wehrmacht* staff) "the greatest general of all time," was at least responsible for the initial German run of victories. By contrast, Mussolini's journalistic streak rendered him incapable of effectively commanding the Italian armed forces, while his insistence on personally conducting the war prevented anyone else from doing so until too late.

The limits of Mussolini's power. Mussolini's personal deficiencies, however, were far from the sole cause of military failure or short-term policy vacillation. He labored under a number of crippling restrictions. First of all, Italian society was still largely traditional. Over half the population of roughly 43 million were peasants. In the South, prefect, *Carabiniere,* landlord, overseer, parish priest, and Mafia or Camorra presided over human misery almost without parallel north of Africa and west of the Adriatic. Agrarian overpopulation was endemic even in the North. By the 1906–10 period, over 650,000 emigrants were leaving Italy each year; the movement culminated in 1913, when over 872,000 departed. Thereafter the outflow declined, thanks to war and to United States immigration restrictions in the early 1920s. By the 1930s, internal migration from countryside to city had largely replaced emigration, despite police measures and the regime's much-trumpeted agricultural expansion in search of national self-sufficiency.[31]

Mussolini made demographic catastrophe a virtue. He enthusiastically promoted further population increase both to justify territorial expansion and to provide the bayonet-wielding hordes appropriate to his 1914–18 vision of warfare. As late as September 1940, he proclaimed his faith in "courageous illiterates" over literary generals; an apt choice, for the former were in far greater supply than the latter. Even in 1951, almost 13 percent of Italy's population could neither read nor write, and only slightly over 10

8

percent of the population had better than a primary school education. Germany, by contrast, had an official illiteracy rate of half a percent in 1900.[32] Nor do the statistics do full justice to Italy's problems. The small educated elite gravitated overwhelmingly to the law and the state bureaucracy, rather than technical institutes and industry. Despite the enviable record of individual Italian scientists and engineers, the country's pool of technological talent was exceedingly small in proportion to the population as a whole.

Above all, Italian social mores and "political culture" resisted – as effectively as they have retarded change under the postwar Republic – the regime's attempts to mobilize the masses. Centuries of semicolonial Bourbon rule (which Gladstone once described as "the negation of God erected into a system of government") in the South and of autocratic, aristocratic, and clerical domination in the North had produced a combination of apathy and systematic corruption – *"clientelismo"* – that still bedevils the country. Distrust of the state, which admittedly appeared to most Italians only in the form of the tax collector, the *Carabiniere,* and the Army in which young men compulsorily served, was and remains the dominant political emotion. National patriotism was strong, particularly among the educated, but local pride (*"campanilismo"*) was stronger, and the mutually incomprehensible dialects most Italians spoke as their first language, before learning Tuscan "official" Italian, impeded growth of a national civic consciousness. The basic institution of Italian society remained the patriarchal family, the focus of individual loyalties to a degree unheard of in western and northern Europe.[33] To move such a society in any direction whatsoever was a Sisyphaean task, and one the regime largely lacked the tools to accomplish. Mussolini and his associates did promote economic development in some respects, particularly in the 1930s. But inability to diagnose Italy's weaknesses fully, fear of increasing the often hostile urban work force, a chronic lack of capital, and above all the unsteady foundation of Mussolini's own authority inhibited action.[34]

The Fascist regime bore throughout its existence the marks of its birth in 1922. It rested on uneasy compromise of Duce and Party with monarchy, military, state bureaucracy, Church, and agrarian, industrial, and financial interests. The Italian establishment never let Mussolini forget that it had acquiesced in his "March on Rome" not to promote revolution, but to prevent it. He operated within a web of group and institutional interests that he dominated but could not fully control. In Rome, Mussolini once explained to Heinrich Himmler, there were "three of us; [my]self, the King, and the Pope."[35] Constitutionally, Italy was a "diarchy." Mussolini could not dispense with that "acid and untrustworthy little man,"[36] Victor Emmanuel III. The King clung jealously to his remaining prerogatives and intruded, in his capacity as head of state, on such eminently party-political occasions as Hitler's Italian visit in May 1938.

Mussolini used every opportunity to undermine the monarchy. As early as 1928 he elevated the highest Party organ, the Grand Council of Fascism, to governmental status, and attributed to it the right to propose his eventual successor and sanction the royal succession. In March 1938, Mussolini promoted his own proclamation and that of the King as "First Marshals of the Impero" – thus formalizing his parity with and prospective dominance over the monarchy.[37] But this was not enough. Mussolini frequently expressed frustration: "If Hitler had been stuck with this dolt of a King, he could never have taken Austria and Czechoslovakia." Actually, Victor Emmanuel was not entirely hostile to foreign adventure. He hated the French, and coveted the southern part of Switzerland. He harbored an almost pathetic belief in Mussolini's luck (*"lo stellone"*) that had held through many difficult moments since 1922. But the King was too cautious for the dictator, and remained a major impediment and potential threat. Mussolini repeatedly made clear to Ciano that he intended to "liquidate" the monarchy at the first appropriate moment.[38]

However, the monarchical loyalties and caste spirit of the military and the conservative civil bureaucracy – the basic structures of the Italian state that survived both Fascism and monarchy – stood in the way of any such revolution. Mussolini himself had helped perpetuate this situation. From the beginning he had deferred to establishment pressure and to his Nationalist allies' ideal of a "strong state." He had even used that state to curb the tumultuous Party barons and the discontented remnants of *squadrismo*. Fascist infiltration into the bureaucracy and compulsory Party membership for its functionaries failed to change the character of the state machine. The armed forces, particularly the Army and Navy, were even more successful than the bureaucracy in resisting absorption. Although scarcely charismatic, and mortally compromised with Duce and regime, the King still commanded the first loyalty of the officer corps. Indoctrination and even Party membership did not prevent junior officers from feeling the pull of monarchical esprit de corps.[39] Political connections and Fascist sentiment played a role in advancement at the higher levels, as the careers of Mussolini or Ciano protégés such as Graziani, Roatta, Soddu, and Gambara (of whom more later) demonstrate. But the Army remained the main potential danger to the regime.

Hitler faced many of the same problems, but from a position of greater strength than Mussolini. After the death of Reichspräsident Hindenburg in August 1934, Hitler's authority, according to a leading contemporary expert on German constitutional law, was "all-encompassing and total."[40] In practice, despite Party and SS, Hitler had to defer to his generals to some degree even after taking command of the armed forces in the Blomberg–Fritsch purge of January–February 1938. But German military opposition lacked both nerve and the sort of legitimacy and leadership Victor Emmanuel II reluctantly provided the generals who overthrew Mussolini in July 1943.[41] Not surprisingly, Hitler was sensitive to the plight of "the poor Duce." The German Social Democrats, the Führer once remarked, had despite their faults at least disposed of the German monarchy in 1918 and thus unwit-

:ingly cleared the way for the creation and consolidation of National Socialism.[42]

Moreover, Hitler did not confront the Vatican on its own territory, as
Mussolini did. The relations between Catholic Church and Fascist state had
not always been as strained as they became in the late 1930s. At the time of
the Lateran Pacts between Church and state in 1929, Pius XI had hailed
Mussolini as the man "Providence has placed in Our path," words he did not
repudiate despite struggles over Italy's youth, the regime's racial policies,
and the Axis. Pius XII, who succeeded to the pontificate in early 1939,
expressed on occasion an "explicit appreciation for the beneficent effects and
the successes of Fascism."[43] The Church enthusiastically supported the
Ethiopian enterprise, and was not displeased over the occupation of Albania;
its representative in Tirana smoothly excused it to his British colleague with
the remark that it was "lawful to rejoice in the good consequences of an
event regardless of its character."[44] But a European war, especially with
Italian participation, was clearly excessive. It could place Rome itself, and
with it such independence as the Church enjoyed, in jeopardy. Victory
would shift the internal balance in favor of Mussolini, and could prove as
dangerous as defeat, which would place the Lateran Pacts in question. The
Vatican therefore used its considerable leverage to restrain Mussolini.[45]

The barons of agriculture, industry, and finance were a different sort of
power than monarchy, state machine, or Church. Landowning elites in
North and South exercised appreciable local power through the Party, which
they had helped found in the North and had opportunistically joined in the
South, and through close relations with the bureaucracy. But Italy had no
Junkers, no compact, self-conscious, and ruthless landed aristocracy with a
tradition of service to and control of Army and state. The agricultural interests lacked centralized leadership and decisive influence at the national level.
Industry and finance, although well organized in the General Confederation
of Italian Industry (or Confindustria), were similarly neither so unified nor
so wedded to the regime as Marxist or para-Marxist treatments suggest.[46]
By 1938, year of *passo romano,* racial laws, and "antibourgeois" campaign,
the businessmen had sunk to what one of them mournfully described as an
"exgoverning class," whom Mussolini "hate[d]."[47] The Great Depression
had led to state holding company control of entire sectors of heavy industry,
and war in Ethiopia and Spain consolidated that control.[48] "Autarchy," a
product of League of Nations sanctions in 1935 and the regime's consequent
drive to reduce import dependence, was "too tight a shirt" for powerful
export industries such as textiles and the great FIAT automobile complex of
Turin.[49] Other sectors, particularly chemicals, hydroelectric power, and
armaments profited mightily from increased demand, lavish government
contracts, state guarantees, and, in the case of firms manufacturing artillery
and aircraft, outright gifts. But profits depended largely upon a firm's usefulness to the regime, not on the power of the industrialists themselves.

The *"padroni del vapore,"* men like Giovanni Agnelli (FIAT), Guido Donegani (Montecatini chemical complex), Alberto Pirelli (rubber and chemicals), Giorgio Falck (Milanese steel), Vittorio Cini (hydroelectric power, shipping) and his close associate, Count Giuseppe Volpi di Misurata (uncrowned king of Venice and of the *terra ferma* chemical and manufacturing center of Port Marghera) came to dominate the economy[50] – but only with the sufferance of the state. Industry and finance ensured the orderly conduct of economic life and armament production, and generated funds to finance the regime's wars through taxes and through devices such as the 10 percent levy in 1937 on corporate capital assets that aroused dismay from Confindustria to Vatican.[51] In return, the regime lowered labor costs, guaranteed the industrialists against unrest, and curbed Fascist unions (in 1925–8) and the corporative experiment (in the early 1930s) in the face of the industrialists' displeasure.

In the realm of foreign policy, the industrialists had minimal influence. Theories of "industrial imperialism" no more explain Fascist expansionism than they do that of Liberal Italy.[52] Some industrialists profited from government contracts and from the 1941 Balkan loot, but some would have profited from almost any state policy. Fewer gained from Fascist expansionism than would have under a system more open to the world economy, as postwar Italy has demonstrated. Even the 1939 annexation of Albania (where Ciano, his business associates, and even FIAT had important mining and oil interests) was a political and strategic thrust, not a response to business pressures. Mussolini made policy, and from 1934–5 on lightheartedly risked state bankruptcy in pursuit of empire. To more than one doubting magnate, he insisted that economics had never "halted the march of history."[53] As the 1930s drew to a close, the dictator found the industrialists' preference for financial stability and modest profits over aggrandizement increasingly irritating.

A further obstacle to the untrammeled exercise of Mussolini's authority was the National Fascist Party (PNF) itself. After 1922, he had coldly and resolutely curbed the Party's independence (except in time of need – as when the furor in 1924 over his subordinates' murder of a Socialist deputy, Giacomo Matteotti, caused Mussolini to crush the opposition parties, fascistize the Chamber, and openly assume dictatorial power). After experimenting with a variety of Party secretaries, including Roberto Farinacci, lord of Cremona and voice of the violent, factious old guard of Po Valley agrarian Fascism, Mussolini had in 1932 appointed Achille Starace, an Apulian who owed his career entirely to the Duce. Starace had neither the ambition nor political skill to challenge Mussolini. The Party lost what little remained of its political character. It became a mere "ministry" charged with indoctrinating Italy's youth and enforcing the increasingly baroque "Fascist style" upon the public. Correspondingly, the Party's composition changed radically. The more uncouth and volatile elements of the old guard departed, willing or not. Beginning with the fusion with the Nationalists in 1923, the

PNF's allies and "flankers" increasingly merged with it, bringing respectability but diluting its original membership. Starace's PNF was increasingly a party of "well-adjusted state servants and parasitic . . . functionaries."[54]

Despite this progressive political nullity, which paradoxically went hand-in-hand with its invasion of ever broader areas of Italian life, the Party influenced Mussolini. Its bureaucratic structure continued to harbor a multiplicity of cliques: clienteles of individual chieftains such as Farinacci, the "moderates," such as Balbo, Giuseppe Bottai, and Dino Grandi (ambassador to London and former foreign minister), the functionaries under Starace, and the Fascist *haut monde* around the regime's heir apparent, Galeazzo Ciano. Mussolini had of necessity to consider the effects of policies, even foreign policies, on the factional balance, on Party opinion, and on the Party's assigned role of forging a new, truly Fascist ruling class from Italy's youth. Survival as dictator required the maintenance of Party prestige. Even more than in Germany, where the SS was the ultimate guarantor of the regime, the Party was Mussolini's power base; the Army had succeeded in reducing the Fascist Militia to a position of dependence. Mussolini relied on the legitimacy, however spurious, that supreme leadership of the "movement" conferred. Without it, he would be a mere "constitutional dictator" serving at the King's pleasure.

An even more serious source of restraint upon Mussolini was the state of Italian public opinion. By the late 1930s the soundings of the police authorities, who provided the most accurate picture of the popular mood, had begun to cause Mussolini increasing displeasure. The hoped-for transformation of the Italians, the molding of the younger generation in the Fascist image upon which he had counted since the 1920s,[55] was obviously not succeeding, despite the appeal of Fascist expansionism to youth and to the land hunger of the peasantry. The troops in Ethiopia fraternized too freely with the natives, necessitating draconian legislation against what the Germans would have described as "race defilement." Mussolini fulminated against Italian "racial immaturity," an immaturity he saw at the root of the regime's difficulty in pacifying the *Impero*.[56] At home, he discovered the "intellectual and bourgeois class" rotten with "cowardice, laziness, [and] love of the quiet life." The Duce resolved to "keep them on their feet 'to the tune of kicks in the shins.'" To Ciano, he announced that when the Spanish war was over he would "think up something else" to instill "character" into the Italians by combat.[57]

However, after the end of the Ethiopian adventure the regime's propaganda was less and less successful in keeping the nation "on its feet," despite the genuine appeal of Fascist expansionism to national and personal self-esteem. Intervention in Spain was not popular, the anti-Jewish campaign Mussolini mounted in 1938 to symbolize his commitment to Germany even less so, and the Axis least of all. Increasing economic difficulties caused distress and complaint. The prospect of general war, both in 1938 and 1939, horrified Italian opinion.[58] Mussolini therefore devoted a great deal of effort during the period of nonbelligerence in 1939–40 to "cleaning out the corners" where defeatists lurked (as he put it in a speech).

But deeds rather than words were the most effective influence on public opinion, and the last and most important restriction on his freedom of action, the weakness of the Italian armed forces and economy, lamed Mussolini's capacity for deeds. The reasons for this weakness are important, because the acid test of the earnestness of his expansionism, of the substance behind imperial rhetoric, is the effort put into armaments. If his foreign policy was a "tissue of incoherencies and perpetual contradictions"[59] based on bombast and bluff, then purposeful military preparation would be largely superfluous. The regime would only require internal security forces and adroit public relations – at least until the outbreak of a European war.

According to the foremost authority on Fascist military policy, Giorgio Rochat, that was indeed the situation. Mussolini "subordinated Italian military policy to the maintenance of his personal position as leader . . . the successes of the Duce (and of the regime) were always sought on a short-term basis, aiming at the momentary crowd-pleasing propaganda triumph, and never the real military preparedness of the nation."[60] The poor performance of 1940–3 was not "the result of the ambitions or the incompetence of some men, but the logical consequence of a gradual renunciation of the use of the armed forces as an instrument of imperialistic conquest."[61] Rochat is not content with a claim that this was "objectively" the case. Rather, he has argued on the basis of the events of 1935 that Mussolini and his senior military advisers were conscious of the situation but did nothing about it. When the Italo-Ethiopian crisis of 1935 turned into a confrontation between Italy and Great Britain, the Italian service chiefs met, and the chairman of the meeting, Marshal Pietro Badoglio, wrote to Mussolini at least twice in order to impress on him the seriousness of the situation. In the second letter he almost implored him to avoid a war with Britain that "would reduce us to a Balkan level."[62] Rochat has concluded that "Italian imperialism was weak, knew it, and did not delude itself that it could any longer resolve its problems by force of arms. The solution was entrusted to diplomatic action or, in other words, to the 'genius' of Mussolini, to systematic bluff based on the continuous and conscious deception of national public opinion."[63] Rochat has also argued that the internal deficiencies of the armed forces themselves, of which more later, were also a consequence of Fascism. The absence of free debate, informed criticism, and openness to new ideas was primarily the product of a tacit political bargain between Mussolini and the generals, a bargain that exchanged military efficiency for the maintenance of both parties' hegemony in their respective spheres.[64]

Despite its status as the only comprehensive interpretation of Fascist military policy, Rochat's framework has serious weaknesses. First, neither Mussolini nor his military authorities were quite as resigned to defeat in 1935 as Rochat suggests. Mussolini had gone forward in September–October 1935 with the expectation, gleaned from SIM's decrypts, that the British show of force was bluff. But once London's position hardened in the wake of the collapse of the Hoare–Laval scheme for a compromise settlement, Mussolini prepared to fight. "In the long run, of course, British superiority was indisputable," he admitted to the German ambassador in January 1936, but he also terrified his subordinates with threats to unleash Navy, Air Force, and land forces in Libya against the British.[65] Leaving aside Mussolini's own views, it is not even clear that the Navy fully concurred in Badoglio's dire predictions. Naval plans during the crisis included a number of offensive projects: a dawn cruiser raid on Alexandria at the outbreak of hostilities, the use of blockships to bottle up the British at Malta, and (although they were not combat-ready in 1935–6, or for a long time thereafter) the use of torpedolike frogman-guided devices to attack enemy capital ships in harbor.[66] At least one senior admiral, named in early 1936 to command the fleet, had favored an attack on the as yet unprepared British forces in July 1935.[67]

A second major flaw in Rochat's interpretation is its insistence that bluff was the basis of Italian military policy from 1935 to 1940. Even before the Ethiopian war, Army and Navy had begun rearmament programs that accelerated and expanded after the Mediterranean confrontation of 1935–6. Between 1935 and 1938 Italy spent roughly 11.8 percent of its national income on military preparations and operations, compared with 12.9 percent for Germany, 6.9 percent for France, and 5.5 percent for Britain.[68] A large if not precisely identifiable portion of Italian expenditure went for actual warfare, and Italian armament programs were ill conceived and worse coordinated. But bluff scarcely accounts for either spending-level or outcome.

Finally, Rochat's suggestion that the political bargain between regime and military inhibited debate and paralyzed innovation is unconvincing. The military indeed received a measure of internal autonomy in return for its support of the regime, even if this autonomy suffered inroads such as the acceptance of Party membership by the officer corps or the adoption of "racial discharges" for Jewish officers in 1938.[69] But the efficiency of the individual services, as distinguished from the highly political question of their coordination, hardly depended in any direct sense on public debate – which in any case continued to exist, as a glance at *Nuova Antologia* or the Air Force's *Rivista Aeronautica* demonstrates. Extensive publicity for armored warfare doctrines made little impression on the conservative establishments of the British and French armies. In Germany, to cite a counterexample, the power vacuum of Weimar conferred on General Hans von Seeckt practically unlimited authority in military questions, but the reverse of intellectual stagnation resulted. Finally, the relative autonomy Hitler accorded his generals, at least until 1938, scarcely led to the sort of leadership the *Regio Esercito* displayed at Guadalajara or in Albania in the winter of 1940–1. No schematic explanation of the regime's military policy can do justice to the complexity of the subject, as a glance at the armed forces will show.

Military elite and high command. Mussolini had to take his generals as he found them: even the replacement of obvious incompetents was fraught with potential risk, given the monarchy's jealous special relationship with the military. The rigidity of the armed forces' seniority system ensured that replacements could come only from the topmost ranks, and nothing guaranteed such men would improve on the incumbents. The fundamental problem was the Italian general staff tradition: Custoza, Lissa, Adua, Caporetto. On those occasions the military, as yet uncontaminated by contact with Fascism, distinguished itself by the absence of the study, planning, and attention to detail that characterized the Germans, and by a tendency to intrigue and confusion of responsibilities among senior officers.[70] These vices were sometimes almost comical in their manifestations, though not in their effects. The troops, particularly in World War I, performed heroically under almost unimaginable hardships. They deserved better than generals who, in the harsh words of a former prime minister, Giovanni Giolitti, were products of an age when Italian families sent to the military only "boys they didn't know what to do with – black sheep and half-wits."[71] The situation had no easy remedy. The inadequacies of the Army officer corps, in particular, were a reflection of the relative shortage of modern technical and intellectual talent from which the entire society suffered, a shortage the literary formalism of most secondary and university instruction only accentuated. Recruitment of talent was difficult, given the military's relatively low pay and prestige and the absence of a genuine national military tradition, of a "military culture." One of the few eminent academics to interest himself in military history has lamented that after thirty years "of teaching in this warrior nation I could count on my fingers the young students who have shown a real interest in military affairs." Rochat himself has written of the "lack of interest that has almost always surrounded military problems in Italy, encouraged equally by left and right, anti-militarist circles and generals."[72]

Mussolini's own contribution was to render impossible the intelligent coordination of the armed forces. Despite his fundamental diffidence in military affairs, he nevertheless aspired to direct the military in person. By 1926 he had made himself minister of each of the three services, and he remained so, with short interruptions, until 1943. The preservation of his own power required that he personally supervise, and divide and rule, his chief military subordinates. A genuine tri-service general staff capable of coordinating the services would challenge his position in several ways. It might damp down otherwise fierce interservice rivalries, and give the service chiefs a collegial voice in defense matters. It would give the monarchy an opportunity to exercise its military prerogatives, which in theory included the supreme command in war, exercised in 1914–18 through a chief of general staff. Finally, the chief of any tri-service staff would capture the Napoleonic role Mussolini claimed for himself.

Mussolini had two rivals for the role of supreme commander: Marshal Pietro Badoglio and Italo Balbo, the young and dynamic Fascist chieftain of

Ferrara and Air Force chief. Badoglio, a stolid Piedmontese with little military imagination but a remarkable talent for political survival, was nominally responsible for the coordination of the armed forces.[73] He had dexterously evaded his heavy responsibilities as commander of the first corps to crack at Caporetto, and had ended World War I as deputy chief of the supreme command. In 1922, he had imprudently boasted that a few Army machine-gun bursts would sweep the Fascists away, then retreated into semiexile as ambassador to Brazil. Mussolini recalled him in 1925 and placed him at the head of the high command as chief of general staff (*Capo di Stato Maggiore Generale*). The position involved concurrent service as Army chief of staff, responsibility for "the coordination of the defensive organization of the state" and of war plans, the right to issue directives to the Navy and Air Force chiefs, and control over the Army's force structure. Badoglio's uncertain reputation and bad relations with the Party may have seemed a guarantee of malleability, but Mussolini evidently found Badoglio not malleable enough. In 1927 the director exploited Badoglio's rivalry with the undersecretary of war, General Ugo Cavallero, to cut Badoglio's powers drastically by splitting the positions of Army chief of staff and chief of general staff. Badoglio continued to hold the latter position, but with the prerogatives of a mere "technical consultant to the head of government," with vague war-planning responsibilities.[74]

Badoglio was temporarily content with this position of eminence but little direct power. From 1929 to 1933 he served concurrently as governor of Libya, supervising Graziani's massacre of the Arabs between trips to Rome to catch up on general staff business. Mussolini himself directed the next war, in Ethiopia, riding high over the bitter rivalries of his subordinates. But Badoglio also profited. When the Italian advance bogged down in November 1935, Mussolini found it necessary to turn over the East African theater command to Badoglio. The ensuing victories through artillery and mustard gas made Badoglio the regime's preeminent military figure. It was now more difficult for Mussolini to ignore his advice in moments of crisis. This advice was consistently defensive, and pessimistic about Italy's prospects in a general war – he once wrote that war against France and Yugoslavia combined would be "a genuine case of suicide on our part."[75] Badoglio offered no remedies, and tended to inhibit Mussolini's pursuit of his ambitions.

Balbo was easier to dispose of. Mussolini packed him off to Libya in 1933–4 to replace Badoglio as governor after Balbo proposed major military reforms, and himself as chief of general staff. Balbo's personal popularity and the fame his propaganda flights had brought put Mussolini in the shade. Worse, Balbo's appointment would have broken the political and interservice equilibrium upon which the regime rested. Army, Navy, and King, a ground soldier by training and temperament, would never have accepted the appointment. Balbo was not merely a Fascist: he was also head of the Air Force. In the fall of 1936, a last attempt to reorganize the high command took place. Rearmament and the increasing likelihood of war with the West made interservice coordination seem imperative. Badoglio was now the only possible candidate for chief of a genuine tri-service staff, but his covert objections to intervention in Spain, the mistrust in which Party extremists such as Farinacci held him, the resistance of Ciano, newly appointed foreign minister and Mussolini's heir apparent, and fierce Navy opposition to subordination to a general killed the project by early 1937.[76]

The Ethiopian victory had made Mussolini more avid than ever to run the military establishment himself with a minimum of technical assistance; he publicly claimed the role of supreme commander in a speech to the Senate in March 1938. Nor did Mussolini lack a vision of the nature of war, a vision that shaped his military policies and imposed on the Italian armaments effort what direction it possessed. Mussolini's theory apparently derived from his own experiences in World War I, from the crackpot air warfare theories of Giulio Douhet, from a too assiduous reading of the French press, and from the advice of generals like Badoglio. Demonstrations of German armored techniques during his visit to Germany in September 1937, and the enthusiasm of his Army chief of staff and undersecretary of war, General Alberto Pariani, for a *Blitzkrieg* with truckborne infantry hordes did not wean Mussolini from the notion that a new land war between first-class European powers would resemble the previous one. "Walled nations" in arms would face one another in enforced immobility behind casemates. Such a war would of necessity be long. Decisive action would be possible only at sea, in the air, in North Africa, and in the Balkans.[77]

Since Italy's aspirations lay principally in those very areas, this strategic concept necessarily led Mussolini to assign priority to a first-rate Navy and a powerful Air Force to dominate the Mediterranean and secure Italy's objectives in the teeth of English and French opposition. The Army, through its size, senior status, closeness to the monarchy, and traditional importance in the maintenance of public order and of Mussolini's own power, commanded the major portion of military appropriations. Nevertheless, its share dropped from almost 60 percent during the Ethiopian war to about 45 percent for 1937–9.[78] This was not enough to cope with the aftermath of Ethiopia, with the Spanish Civil War, and with modernization. In response to a plea from Pariani in 1937 for funds with which to renovate the Army's artillery, Mussolini exhorted patience: "I have my program. First I must bring the Navy up to full efficiency, then we will provide for the Army and Air Force."[79] The Army's poor performance later was in part a consequence of these priorities.

Ironically, but not coincidentally, the only service that offered Mussolini a war plan commensurate with his ambitions was the Army. The 1935–6 Mediterranean crisis produced a general turning against Britain among Italian planners, and from 1937 on Italy's preeminent offensive project was a drive from Libya on Egypt to "defeat the main enemy at a *vital point and open one of the doors* that close off Italy from free access to the oceans."[80] General

Pariani was the principal backer of the operation, which also enjoyed the support of Balbo in Libya. Pariani was in Ciano's words "convinced of the inevitability of [Axis] war with the Western powers. . . . He believes in the success of a lightning war of surprise. Attack on Egypt, attack on the [British and French] fleets, invasion of France. The war will be won at Suez and Paris."[81] Pariani coupled this vision with a claim that the Army must dictate the supporting services' force structures and war plans – a challenge both to Badoglio and to Navy and Air Force.[82] Badoglio nevertheless did his best to assert control over planning, and in 1937 and 1938 supervised interservice discussions about transporting and supporting Pariani's expeditionary force.[83] The major prewar Navy planning document, the D.G. 10/A2 memorandum of December 1938, was primarily concerned with supporting the Army plan, although it also considered a landing at Suez from East Africa, and the conquest of Malta. The latter operation would remove a major threat to the North African supply lines, and would strike a deadly blow to British prestige.[84] Nothing came of this planning. As will emerge, Badoglio's skepticism and Mussolini's increasing hostility to France in early 1939 temporarily killed both the Egyptian plan and thoughts of Malta. Italy consequently faced war in the summer of 1939 without a coherent war plan, and Mussolini's later efforts failed to elicit one from his high command. Even intelligent planning, however, could not have entirely overcome the deficiencies of the three services themselves.

Ruling the Mediterranean. In the 1920s Mussolini already conceived of his Navy as offensive in function, even if it could not reach the theoretical parity with France in capital ships the 1922 Washington Naval Treaty allowed: "the goal is to construct a navy that will represent for France what the German Navy represented and will, in good time, [again] represent for England: a nightmare and a menace. 'Communist cells' in France, and the aggressive and tenacious 'Fascist spirit' in Italy will do the rest."[85] Despite occasional inspirations, such as his 1932 proposal to construct seven heavy cruisers simultaneously (his undersecretary of the Navy warily pointed out that the result would be an arms race not only with France but with the oceanic powers as well),[86] Mussolini refrained from major rearmament until 1933. But he did construct enough new units to raise Italian fleet tonnage from 400,000 tons in 1926 to 550,000 tons in 1933.[87] In that year he ordered the renovation of two of Italy's pre-World War battleships, *Cesare* and *Cavour*. In 1934 he laid down *Littorio* and *Vittorio Veneto,* which secretly exceeded the 35,000-ton maximum displacement permitted under the Washington and London treaties. Also in 1934, the Navy took the first step inexplicable in terms of rivalry with France. "In view of the probable Ethiopian conflict" (the official history guardedly explains), Italy increased the number of submarines laid down from the planned ten to the remarkable figure of twenty-seven. In May 1935 the Navy Ministry began preparation of a five-year plan that included four battleships, three aircraft carriers, four cruisers, twenty frigates, twelve corvettes, and fifty-four submarines, for a total of 300,000 additional tons.[88]

The turning point in Fascist naval policy had come. When the British Home Fleet redeployed in the Mediterranean in mid-September 1935, the Italian Navy had not a single modern battleship in service. To the chief of staff, Admiral Domenico Cavagnari, the moral was obvious: "If the ships of the line *Littorio, Vittorio Veneto, Cesare* and *Cavour* had been ready to take to sea, British arrogance would have been lowered in tone. . . ." The British were now the enemy: they were *"fundamentally* inclined to oppose" Italy's Mediterranean and African aspirations. Italy must therefore arm to secure "[its] existence and the respect of [its] rights."[89] In December 1935 Cavagnari consequently proposed to Mussolini renovation of the two remaining old battleships, *Duilio* and *Doria,* the construction of two more *Littorio*-class ships, of an aircraft carrier, and of a large number of submarines and small surface units.[90] Mussolini apparently postponed decision until the critical raw material shortage League sanctions produced could ease. Also, as the plans department of the naval staff noted in January 1936, "the increase in size of the fleet should take place in a not excessively visible manner, and therefore in a gradual one,"[91] if Italy wanted to avoid stirring up an armaments race in which it could not compete.

In the early summer of 1936, despite a continuing shortage of raw materials that forced a slowdown in all armaments production,[92] Mussolini approved an impressive program of small units. But to Cavagnari's disappointment he reserved decision on further battleships, and disapproved the admiral's request that work on an aircraft carrier start immediately.[93] Cavagnari did not insist, and in 1938 swallowed his earlier views and publicly protested his service had no need of carriers; none of his fellow admirals dissented. Of the major navies, only the Germans were as retrograde in carrier development and air cooperation. The Italian decision was the consequence of Mussolini's sympathy for the Air Force and his espousal of its thesis that Italy was itself an aircraft carrier – an unsinkable one at that. The result in 1940 was that the Navy had no effective air cover, for interservice rivalry prevented adequate coordination of the fleet and of the Air Force's land-based bombers.

The battleship program nevertheless went forward. In January 1937, Mussolini authorized detailed planning for the transformation of the *Doria* and *Duilio,* and for the two additional *Littorio*-class ships.[94] In the spring, he ordered the modernizations to begin, and by early December he had formally approved and found money for the new *Littorios,* which were to bear the proud names of *Roma* and *Impero.*[95] As important as the capital ship program was the submarine fleet, which Mussolini continued to increase at a significant rate throughout the late 1930s. The Navy entered the war in June 1940 with a total of 113 boats, the largest submarine force in the world except perhaps that of the Soviet Union. Mussolini had the highest hopes for his underwater arm. At a naval display in June 1937 he proudly exclaimed o the German military attaché, General Enno von Rintelen, "This is the weapon for the Mediterranean. With this we will rule the Mediterranean."[96] To this tune, the Italian Navy launched by the end of 1937 a building program that by 1941–2 would theoretically give it control of the central Mediterranean and an excellent fighting chance against the combined British and French fleets, especially if the Germans and Japanese drew off sizable Allied forces, as Cavagnari already hoped.[97]

That the Navy failed in its task was not primarily the result of deficient equipment, even though the new battleships were not quite ready when Italy moved in June 1940. The submarine fleet was a disappointment. The boats lacked attack computers, their air-conditioning systems gave off poisonous gases when tubing ruptured under depth-charge attack, and they were relatively slow in diving, which proved embarrassing when enemy aircraft approached. Many of the cruisers sacrificed protection for speed, and disintegrated suddenly and spectacularly under fire.[98] But unit for unit the fleet was fully comparable and in some ways superior to its adversaries. Its problem was doctrine and frame of mind. Cavagnari was a battleship admiral. He had prepared the Italian Navy for a Mediterranean Jutland. In his conception of war, two battle fleets would thunder toward one another at twenty-five knots while the opposing admirals surveyed the enemy line through clouds of cordite smoke and the spray of near misses. But neither technology nor the enemy cooperated; the Mediterranean in World War II was not the North Sea in World War I. The weapons of coastal warfare – mine, submarine, light torpedo craft, and land-based aircraft, properly used, could almost dominate that inland sea – as Göring's X Air Corps and the German navy's U-boats were to demonstrate in 1941.

The Italians had all these weapons, but had given little thought to their coordinated use. The Regia Marina neglected night operations, always a resource of weaker navies, and of some strong ones, as the Japanese demonstrated brilliantly at Savo Island. The Navy staff so procrastinated in developing frogman-guided torpedoes that the weapon only came into its own in 1941, although the history of its development suggests that it could have been ready by September 1939 had Rome regarded it as more than an interesting toy. The Navy failed to anticipate wolf-pack operations and the submarine night surface attack, despite access to German training establishments. Even fleet training was unrealistic. In the summer of 1939, the German naval attaché praised Italian skill at fair-weather formation drill, but noted a tendency to avoid "difficult conditions of the kind we deliberately create in combat-type maneuvers," and a tactical rigidity that discouraged initiative in junior commanders.[99]

A paralysis of will, which German observers almost invariably diagnosed as an inferiority complex in the face of the British, also crippled the Navy in 1940.[100] Cavagnari's foremost concern was not to close with and destroy the enemy, but to avoid arriving at the peace table "without a fleet."[101] The Navy merely aspired to keeping the supply lanes to Libya open. The head of the German liaison staff to the Italian Admiralty, Admiral Eberhard Weichold, commented acidly in September 1940 to his superiors in Berlin:

The Italian Naval Staff has [produced] many different kinds of justifications for holding back its forces, as it has done up to now, justifications that change according to their momentary applicability. Usually it is the as yet insufficient operational readiness of the new battleships, the great distances [of the enemy] from the Italian ports, or the inadequate equipment of the Libyan bases, above all for oiling. When none of these reasons can be alleged, the blame for failure to attack enemy forces reported at sea is placed on inadequate air reconnaissance.

Although the above reasons have, at least partially, some foundation, . . . [I see] the real reason for holding back in an inner lack of dash [*Schwunglosigkeit*] on the part of the operational leadership, in a lack of eagerness for combat, in a fear of incurring risk, and in a striving for the greatest possible security.[102]

On the night of 11–12 November 1940 Royal Navy torpedo aircraft took full advantage of this *Schwunglosigkeit* to sink *Littorio, Cavour,* and *Duilio* in harbor at Taranto.

The Air Force's private wars. While the Navy had a vaguely Anglophile flavor and a penchant for afternoon tea, the Air Force, as in Germany, was the service the public mind associated with the regime. During the 1920s, under Balbo, it was efficient enough to earn the admiration of the head of the German army office dealing clandestinely with air matters.[103] But the Air Force had a major defect that was unquestionably a direct result of the regime's interest in propaganda triumphs. The breaking of speed and altitude records, demonstration formation flights across the Atlantic, the accumulation of "firsts," took priority over preparation for war. Balbo's departure for gilded exile in Libya in 1934 hardly improved matters, although wars in Ethiopia and Spain took the place of propaganda flights. Balbo's successor, General Giuseppe Valle, had been chief of staff since 1929, and proved even less able than his predecessor to distinguish appearance from reality.

The *Regia Aeronautica*'s early concentration on propagandistic coups at the expense of combat efficiency lends a certain superficial plausibility to Rochat's suggestion that bluff was the foundation of Fascist military policy. However, the ambitious nature of Italy's late 1930s armaments programs do not suggest that those in charge conceived of their efforts solely in terms of public relations. The Ethiopian crisis, which caught Valle almost as unprepared as it did Cavagnari, prompted preparation of an intensive rearmament scheme. The production of over 2,000 fighters and bombers would bring Italian line forces up to a total of 3,000 modern aircraft. Unfortunately, the Spanish war required the commitment of over 700 aircraft. The consequent attrition and expenditure, along with administrative confusion and vacillation over aircraft types, delayed intensive rearmament until 1938–9. Nevertheless, between 1935 and 1939 the *Regia Aeronautica* ordered about 8,700 warplanes and almost 3,000 trainers – a sizable figure by international standards. The first serious British air armament plan, "Scheme F" of February

1936, provided for the production of 8,000 aircraft in three years.[104] Given Italy's small industrial and financial base, air appropriations were "indeed notable," according to the service's semiofficial historian, who concedes the Air Force did not always use the money to best advantage.[105]

Italian aircraft compared favorably with those of the French in 1939–40, but did not come up to British or German standards. The mainstay of the Italian fighter force throughout 1940 was the FIAT CR 42 biplane. Despite quite exceptional maneuverability, it had less armament than its British counterpart, the Gloster Gladiator. The Hurricane and Spitfire outclassed it in all respects, although neither reached the Mediterranean in significant numbers in 1940. In North Africa, the only active Italian ground theater between the fall of France in June and the attack on Greece in late October, an inexplicable shortage of engine sand filters grounded large numbers of CR 42s. That such difficulties persisted despite a generation of *Regia Aeronautica* experience in Libya could only have been the result of ineptitude.[106] The CR 42's successors, the FIAT G.50 and Macchi MC 200, were at least monoplanes and had adequate filters, but again fell far short of their British contemporaries.

The Italian bomber force was better off. Its mainstay, the Savoia-Marchetti S.79, was, in the postwar judgment of a leading British aeronautical expert, "an extremely efficient machine and perhaps the most successful land-based torpedo-bomber of the war." It nevertheless had flaws — the chief of which was extreme instability in rough air; according to Valle's successor, the Germans "considered it so dangerous that they dared not set foot in it."[107]

The most serious single shortcoming of the Italian air armaments program was the lack of a good basic water-cooled engine in the 1500 horsepower class, like the Daimler-Benz DB 601 or the Merlin, the powerplants of many of the aircraft with which *Luftwaffe* and RAF began the war. FIAT and other Italian firms had amassed considerable experience with in-line water-cooled engines by the early 1930s. But in 1934–5 the Air Force decided in favor of radial engines, apparently because they were simpler to maintain, less prone to battle damage, and provided enough power for the highly maneuverable lightly armed fabric-covered biplanes the service favored. Consequently, when developments abroad compelled transition to all-metal monoplane fighters, no suitable power plants were on hand.[108] The radials' broad frontal cross-section produced excessive drag, and the engines available lacked the power to operate well with sand filters, or drive duraluminum aircraft laden with multiple heavy machine guns and cannon, cockpit armor, and self-sealing fuel tanks through the sky at speeds exceeding 400 miles per hour. Until the adoption of Daimler-Benz engines in the course of 1940, Italy had no truly modern fighters.

Tactically and organizationally, the Air Force was equally weak. Its considerable combat experience in Ethiopia and Spain fostered the illusion of the "easy war." In the judgment of Hermann Göring's *Luftwaffe* staff the *Regia*

Aeronautica neglected unit tactical training, and bad weather and night flying.[109] Nor was the officer corps entirely up to the complexities and stresses of modern warfare. In the course of the 1940 campaign the commander of air units in North Africa, General Felice Porro, bombarded Valle's successor, Francesco Pricolo, with lamentations about the quality of his subordinates. One was "a good office colonel, but is easily discouraged [*Si perde in un bicchiere d'acqua*] and has neither initiative nor energy." Another, presumably a reserve officer, was perhaps "a good teacher of history, but no commander"; many of his officers seemed preoccupied with securing transfers to safe billets in Italy. In less than two months of war Porro relieved for incompetence or excessive caution in action twelve of his senior subordinates, including four squadron commanders and a number of high maintenance and supply officers. The problem was not peculiar to Libya. In replying to Porro's complaints and requests for replacements, Pricolo reminded his colleague that the difficulties of the Air Force's personnel situation made it "far from easy to ensure that only officers fully up to their tasks receive unit commands."[110]

If these difficulties were not enough, the Air Force's dominant ideology – it was scarcely a strategic concept – was utterly fallacious, and contributed substantially to failure in 1940. The *Regia Aeronautica,* like other major air forces in the 1930s, espoused strategic air warfare as the perfect defense against what air officers viewed as jealous efforts of armies and navies to throttle or reabsorb their younger rivals. Balbo, Valle, and their subordinates reverently invoked General Giulio Douhet, the foremost interwar airpower theorist. Douhet ridiculed as indecisive and irrelevant all forms of military activity other than the unproven and largely unworkable formula of independent air warfare against enemy population centers and industrial resources.[111] Even in Ethiopia, where tactical air support was vital to the Army, Valle initially proposed a wildly extravagant and totally autonomous air war aiming at "the destruction of Addis Ababa, of Gondar, of Harrar, and the systematic burning off of the entire Somali bush."[112]

In the event, Army requirements prevented Valle from putting this apocalyptic vision into effect. The Air Force nevertheless continued to demand the right to conduct its own wars independent of the other services, while paradoxically building only medium and light bombers equipped with small-caliber bombs of quite remarkable ineffectiveness. The bombs were small because the high-altitude level bombing the *Regia Aeronautica* favored required a pattern in order to maximize hit probability; few seem to have realized that the point was to destroy the target, not simply to hit it. Some officers, notably General Amedeo Mecozzi, defied orthodoxy and demanded close interservice cooperation with emphasis on ground attack aircraft and doctrine.[113] The Air Force did develop a large fighter arm, in defiance of Douhet's precepts. But Valle persevered in denying the pleas of the other services for support. He starved the Navy of maritime reconnaissance aircraft, and steadfastly refused Cavagnari's requests to form aerial torpedo units, even though the Whitehead works at Fiume had by 1938 developed a first-rate torpedo for the S.79. The weapon was indeed so superior that the *Luftwaffe,* itself involved in a similar feud with the German navy, immediately ordered a lot of 300. In 1941, after the torpedo bomber had proven itself in combat, Valle's successor admitted to Mussolini that Air Force opposition had resulted above all from fear of the potential "subordination to the naval forces" of any such units.[114] This fear was the source of other problems — most notably the procedure by which the fleet called for air support. All requests, however urgent, had to go to the Air Ministry in Rome before passing slowly down the entire chain of command to airfields in Southern Italy, Sicily, and Sardinia. The system did not change until 1941, after defeat at Cape Matapan. By then the autonomous Italian war was over, and the Mediterranean had long since become a strategic backwater as Hitler readied his forces for the assault on the Soviet Union.

The Army's "war of rapid decision". The senior service, the Army, was slower to modernize than the others. Its leaders failed to recognize that they had to choose between numbers and effectiveness. The *Regio Esercito's* time-hallowed structure of thirty-odd infantry divisions was more than Italian industry could equip with modern weapons, or the Army itself provide with well-trained and experienced junior officers and NCOs. But instead of a cutback in size to free money for mechanization and cadres for a smaller force of well-trained and instantly ready units, the Army sought to improve its equipment piecemeal while keeping its original framework.

The area the Army's leaders sought most consistently to modernize was the artillery, the dominant weapon of World War I. In 1929 Mussolini agreed to the proposals of the then minister of war, General Pietro Gazzera, for the replacement of the Army's current inventory of relics. However, the financial strains of the Depression apparently precluded the necessary expenditure of 8,000,000,000 lire, three times the Army's annual budget. The Army did produce in the next years a series of excellent light and medium artillery prototypes.[115] In addition, General Federico Baistrocchi, who became undersecretary for war and Army chief of staff in 1933–4, initiated a program of general modernization. But the Ethiopian war, which Baistrocchi initially opposed, but then skillfully organized, intervened. In the summer of 1936, while Mussolini plunged into Spain, Baistrocchi again pressed for thoroughgoing modernization and new artillery. He also informed Mussolini with unheard-of frankness that attempts to save money by repatriating equipment sent to Ethiopia would mean that in the event of European war, "You, Duce, will lose the Empire you have created."[116] This bluntness and Baistrocchi's adamant opposition to the Spanish commitment were uncongenial. Mussolini therefore replaced Baistrocchi with the general's immediate subordinate, Alberto Pariani. Less forceful than his predecessor, and bound by a promise of Baistrocchi's not to ask for new supplementary appropriations until 1938, Pariani made little headway.

Nonetheless, despite Mussolini's decision to give the Navy priority and the drain of Spanish war and Ethiopian pacification, the Army apparently put into effect in 1937 a ten-year plan for artillery replacement, and ordered small numbers of new guns. From early 1938 Badoglio and the King prodded both Pariani and Mussolini to accelerate the program. At a meeting with Pariani and the minister of finance in July 1938, Mussolini ordered a provisional appropriation of 5,000,000,000 lire for the production of the new generation of cannon and their auxiliary vehicles. But shortages of foreign exchange, machine tools, and special steels, and difficulties in rebuilding or retooling industrial plants delayed the beginning of quantity production until 1940–1.[117]

If industrial inadequacies and the low priority Mussolini had assigned the Army helped prevent the reequipment of the artillery, the other major deficiency — in armored fighting vehicles — was the consequence of deliberate choice. The older generation of Italian generals were fully comparable to their French counterparts. Formed in the bitter battles on the Carso and in the Carnic Alps, in a war of rifle and bayonet, mule and mountain gun, they regarded the tank without enthusiasm. While chief of staff of the Army in 1926, Marshal Badoglio had written that "the nature of our terrain limits considerably the use of tanks, and thus the lack, and even the total absence of them, does not have the same consequences which it would have for other nations, for example for France and Germany. We can thus wait calmly."[118]

This the Army proceeded to do, while chauvinistically proclaiming its rejection of "exotic doctrines."[119] The need for tracked vehicles in Libya and the other colonies was indisputable, but no tank especially designed for the desert appeared. The Army's intention of reinforcing Libya rapidly with troops from the homeland in case of war resulted in a fruitless search for a vehicle that would perform equally well in the Julian Alps and in North Africa.[120] Production of armored fighting vehicles in the interwar years consisted almost exclusively of the 3½-ton FIAT L.3, armed with two machine guns. This was the main battle tank of Italy's "armored divisions," and by 1940 roughly 1,300 of the machines were in service. The next heavier tank was the M11/39, with a fixed 37-mm gun and a tendency to mechanical unreliability.[121] It required a direct order from Mussolini in the summer of 1940 to start work on a 75-mm-gun tank.[122] The Army staff remained skeptical. Its deputy chief, General Mario Roatta, who had commanded the "volunteers" at Guadalajara, was in his own words "decisively opposed" to the abolition of horse cavalry — this in the *fall* of 1940. Badoglio, serving that summer as chief of the *Comando Supremo* under Mussolini, was so incurious about the techniques that shattered the French, and so confident of a quick peace settlement, that he annotated an Italian intelligence report on German use of armor with a contemptuous "We'll study it when the war is over."[123]

The Army's substitute for the serious development of armored forces was the *Blitzkrieg* Italian style, the "war of rapid decision." The doctrine apparently originated with Baistrocchi, who was no Guderian, but had organizational ability and commonsense. Baistrocchi's successor Pariani, however, was (in the words of the Nationalist notable Luigi Federzoni) "a cold-blooded maniac [*un esaltato a freddo*]" who despite many admirable qualities was "totally divorced from reality."[124] Pariani's visions of lightning campaigns prompted him to take a leaf from Balbo's 1933 reorganization project for the armed forces, which had provided for an elite twenty-division army and an amphibious force.[125] In early 1937, Pariani reportedly made a speech in the Supreme Defense Commission, a body Mussolini chaired that included the ministers and service chiefs, calling for "motorized and armored shock troops" to "attack, break through, advance, and deliver the deathblow to the enemy." He began planning a 14-division motorized force to put these ideas into practice. But Pariani apparently believed that 3½-ton tanks and truck-mounted infantry alone could deliver the deathblow. He passionately defended the L.3 against the slurs ("tin cans") of the uninitiated.[126] He also failed to recognize that Italy could arm and pay for a small, mobile, hard-hitting army, or a large, ponderous, and ill-equipped one, but not both.

Pariani instead proceeded without choosing. In the autumn of 1938 he established the "Po" Army, which consisted by early 1939 of three infantry divisions, three light (*"celere"*) divisions, two motorized infantry divisions and two armored divisions.[127] This formation was in theory able to move at any time on six hours' notice, but it never reached that state of readiness. Its missions were to provide a mobile counteroffensive against France, and operations of a "preeminently offensive character" in the direction of Ljubljana.[128] But the "Po" Army was far from impressive in practice. Its 1939 maneuvers prompted the King to comment that it was in "a sad state of unpreparedness," and the German military attaché later remarked that the Italian *"Panzerwaffe"* was still "in children's shoes."[129]

Pariani's other recipe for "rapid decision" was more within Italy's grasp: massive use of mustard and nerve gas, sprayed from aircraft as in Ethiopia or delivered by cluster bomb system. As the general explained to the Germans, chemical warfare was "easier for Italy to prepare and carry out [than more conventional methods] because Italy has all the necessary raw materials, while iron and other ores are lacking." In early 1939, he considered an attack on the Maginot Line practical "either through surprise or through the intensive use of chemical agents," and thought gas attacks on a front of forty to fifty kilometers feasible.[130]

But Pariani's chief innovation was tactical rather than technological. As a result of the "lessons learned" in the Ethiopian war, in which he had taken part from behind a desk in Rome, he proposed and more or less single-handedly imposed a far-reaching change in the Army's organization. Experience had shown that the standard three-regiment division, if motorized, became a road-bound, cumbersome, vulnerable, serpentine confusion. Badoglio, in his best-selling Ethiopian war memoirs, had suggested lightening the divisional organization, at least for service in Africa.[131] The removal of one regiment to produce what Pariani called a *"divisione binaria,"* would render it more "svelte and manageable" while retaining the larger formation's firepower. In theory, one binary division would make contact and use its superior firepower to break through. Another division would then leapfrog it to "deliver the deathblow."

In private, Pariani was willing to concede that his new formations were no more than mixed brigades, but "today, everybody estimates the strength of a country by the number of divisions it is able to mobilize; thus it is a question . . . of morale – it is better to talk about divisions than about mixed brigades." Some generals and even Mussolini himself were skeptical, but failed to voice resolute opposition. Pariani briefed the senior commanders in November 1937 on plans to transform the entire Army into binary divisions.[132] After limited testing at the summer maneuvers of 1937, the actual reorganization began in December 1938, and by 1940 had produced seventy-three anemic "mixed brigades" instead of the preexisting thirty-eight fairly solid mule and mountain gun infantry divisions, or the ten to fifteen modern armored and motorized divisions the funds and industrial capacity available to the Army could have yielded if intelligently employed.

The absence of adequate artillery and armored fighting vehicles and the dubious innovation of the binary division were important causes of the *Regio Esercito's* dismal record in 1940 and subsequent years. But they were merely aspects of a more general failure of doctrine, leadership, and imagination. The Army had destroyed Haile Selassie's tribal levies not through numbers, but through a crushing technological and material superiority that had deluged the enemy with fire, steel, and mustard gas. Well-founded embarrassment, and the complacency that quintessential "easy war" produced, inhibited analysis of the causes of Italian victory, and ultimately cast the *Regio Esercito* itself, in World War II, in the role of the Ethiopians.

Defeat at Guadalajara – the consequence of abominable staff work and worse tactical leadership – was no more conducive than East African victory to a rethinking of doctrine. Roatta and his associates commanded the four divisions of the *Corpo Truppe Volontarie* from a 1:400,000 Michelin road map, with easily imaginable results. At unit level, his officers failed to redeem their commander's failings. Serious tactical errors led to unnecessary casualties and contributed to the precipitateness of the Italian retreat in the face of Republican counteroffensive. Roatta of course lost his command, though without prejudice to his later career, which Mussolini and Ciano saved. Pariani, who had "carefully checked" the operational plans beforehand, as had Mussolini, presumably felt a few minor adjustments would suffice. The dictator himself was content to ascribe Guadalajara to inadequate ideological motivation among the volunteers; Roatta had excused defeat by reporting that the "reds" had fought "with fanaticism and hatred."[133] Actually, the International Brigades had merely fought effectively: both troops and cadres knew what they were doing. The Italian forces, by contrast, lacked both leadership and training. Army and Fascist militia had thrown the force together on an ad hoc basis from the unemployed of the South and the islands, and shipped it to Spain in ill-advised haste.[134] In the end, the Army and Mussolini apparently convinced themselves that peculiar and nonrecurring circumstances had produced the fiasco; in fact, Guadalajara provided an accurate preview of *Regio Esercito* performance in the next war.

Whatever conclusions Italy's leaders drew from the Spanish experiment, methods did not change. The cost of Pariani's modernization programs, of the transition to the binary division, and the Army's' overblown structure made it impossible to keep more than 150,000–160,000 men under arms during the long annual off-season between September and April – in remarkable contrast to the projected war strength of over 1.7 million.[135] Tactical training was in any case not part of the *Regio Esercito*'s barracks army style. Pariani himself made a virtue of necessity, and jocularly exhorted a subordinate transferring to Libya not to do "too much training." Even Roatta's former chief of staff at Guadalajara, General Emilio Faldella, concedes in a semiofficial postwar work that the Army neglected training "from an absence of doctrine, exercise areas, and equipment, but also because of the widespread assumption that in battle, intuition and individual valor counted for more than training."[136]

Fortunately for Pariani, the Army's Albanian expedition in April 1939 met no serious opposition. Had King Zog's troops or the numerous tribal armed bands shown much fight, an almost total breakdown of radio communication and logistical chaos might well have exposed General Alfredo Guzzoni's dash for Tirana to serious setbacks.[137] In 1940, during the Italian advance on Sidi el Barrani, a general experienced in fighting Libyans and Ethiopians got himself and his motorized brigade task force utterly lost while making his approach march. Despite two months of preparation for the offensive, he had neglected to secure adequate maps or navigational instruments. At the last moment he inexplicably failed to pick up Arab guides detailed to lead him around the British desert flank. Such lack of attention to detail was not unusual. Advancement depended almost exclusively on seniority. Baistrocchi introduced accelerated promotion for merit, but the Army establishment bitterly resented it, and privately denounced it as an attempt to "fascistize" the service. As Faldella has remarked, the system brought "to high rank even the mediocre" while discouraging initiative and "innovative fervor." Even prolonged war failed to weed out incompetents. As late as 1942, Badoglio's rival Ugo Cavallero, by then chief of general staff, felt it necessary to insist to the Army chief of staff that general officer replacements for North Africa be "up to operational requirements and not simply chosen from the seniority list."[138]

Pariani also failed to find effective remedies for the desperate shortage of trained junior leaders. Indeed, to save money and guarantee the few career officers regular promotion, he further accentuated the Army's policy that almost all lieutenants and most captains should be reservists who had received only the sketchiest sort of training in the peacetime barracks army.

The majority of Italian company officers therefore had almost no opportunity to learn their jobs — except wastefully, in combat. Even the King failed to deflect Pariani from this policy; a royal complaint to Mussolini after Guadalajara that the Army had a desperate need for "numerous junior career officers, carefully trained and conscientiously prepared for the exercise of command" had no noticeable effect.[139] The Army's professional NCO corps was also disastrously weak in numbers, tradition, and prestige.[140] The social conditions of Southern Italy and the islands, where many NCOs originated, hardly encouraged general knowledge, technical aptitude, and initiative. The *Regio Esercito*'s deficiencies in armament, doctrine, organization, staff work, training, and leadership were mutually reinforcing. Efforts to remedy the situation in the fall and winter of 1939–40 were too little too late. The consequence was generally poor performance in war and numerous episodes of collapse under fire. Only the fine record of a few elite units and the good humor and immense capacity for suffering of the troops redeemed the picture.

A poor man's war economy. Weight of fire and steel might have partially compensated for absence of strategic insight, operational expertise, and tactical training. But Italian industry and the Italian economy were inadequate.[141] The country was still predominantly agricultural. Shortages of materials and foreign exchange, the absence of alternate sources for the seaborne raw materials which war with the West would cut off, and the weakness of the country's industrial and scientific base all made detailed and extraordinarily precise planning necessary to provide the armed forces with adequate quantities of modern equipment and ammunition.

Shortages dominated the rearmament program. The only strategic raw material in adequate supply was aluminum. Almost everything else had to come from abroad. In the market conditions of the late 1930s this required cash on the barrelhead in hard currency. In 1934–5 Mussolini imposed import quotas to prevent an excessive drain on currency reserves and cut down inessential imports. In 1936, with much fanfare, he introduced an "autarchy" campaign. Synthetic wool, coffee, and leather became the order of the day. But import substitution was only part of the solution; without extensive exports, Italy could not buy the oil, scrap iron, copper, nickel, chrome, and rubber indispensable for rearmament. The aircraft industry alone sold over 4,000,000,000 lire worth of machines, engines and accessories abroad between 1937 and 1943,[142] with easily imaginable effects on Air Force procurement. Exports were not enough to save the reserves of the Bank of Italy from shrinking from over 20,000,000,000 lire in 1927 to under 3,000,000,000 at the end of 1939. Felice Guarneri, minister for exchange and currency, was increasingly pessimistic. "We are bankrupt," he exclaimed after a meeting of the Supreme Defense Commission in 1938.[143] The Ethiopian war and subsequent pacification campaign, along with intervention in Spain, drained the budget. From 1934–5 to 1939–40 over 51 percent of Italy's state expenditure of 249,500,000,000 lire went to Ethiopia, Spain, Albania, other colonies, and the military.[144]

If budgetary strain and the bottleneck in foreign exchange were dangers in peacetime, the prospective total loss of seaborne imports was paramount in war. Of Italy's raw materials and foodstuff imports in peacetime, 80 percent came past Gibraltar and Suez. Some exceptions existed. With enormous effort, the rail systems of Italy, Germany, and Switzerland could move the twelve million tons of imported coal Italy required annually, but transport on this scale did not seem feasible until it became necessary in 1940. Scrap iron and oil were far less available, particularly if Italy had to compete for them with Germany in the closed market of continental Europe. The only answer was to stockpile, and hope that the war would be indeed one of "rapid decision." Perhaps something would turn up. But the available foreign exchange did not cover even current needs in the late 1930s, and precluded accumulating stockpiles for the future.

When the German attack on Poland faced Italy with war in September 1939, supplies of industrial raw materials, including coal, were short or entirely lacking.[145] As for the armed forces, only the Navy had adequate stocks even of fuel. The Army had gasoline and diesel for perhaps a month of war. The *Regia Aeronautica* had roughly a month and a half's supply of aviation gasoline, following ill-advised experimentation with tin-lined concrete storage tanks, which leaked, in place of steel.[146] In addition, Italy's industrial base and supply of skilled labor were narrow — both literally, and in relation to the demands placed upon them. The vulnerable Turin–Milan–Genoa triangle contained practically all Italian industrial plant and skilled labor. Steel production in 1939 was roughly 2.4 million tons — in contrast with Germany's 22.5 million and Great Britain's 13.4 million tons.[147] Government subsidies and German technical help built synthetic rubber plants, but at the outbreak of war production had yet to begin. "Autarchic" substitutes for materials such as wool and leather proved less than satisfactory in the field. Machine tool production, which regulated the pace of setting up new plants or adapting old ones to new requirements, was utterly inadequate. Industry relied largely on machines imported against hard currency, or extracted from the reluctant Germans, who had the strongest machine tool industry in Europe but preferred to keep its products for themselves, or exchange them for more vital commodities than the fruits and vegetables Italy could offer.

Nevertheless, Italian industry could probably have supplied the Navy, Air Force, and a mechanized Army of ten to fifteen divisions if some central authority had imposed an end to administrative confusion, jurisdictional conflict, and dispersal of effort. No such authority existed. A "Supreme Defense Commission" charged with military–economic coordination had vegetated since the 1920s under Mussolini's chairmanship. It met once a year, and its permanent secretariat possessed no powers of note. Badoglio, among his other duties, headed a National Research Council for military and "autarchic" research, but he had no executive powers and his organization failed to keep the armaments industry abreast of developments abroad. In the 1935 crisis, Mussolini had created a General Commissariat for War Production to handle raw material allocation on a rational, centralized basis. But the service undersecretaries kept control of procurement, thus institutionalizing delay and interservice competition for plant and skilled workers. Instead of concentrating on mass production by semiskilled labor of relatively few standardized types, as the Soviet armaments industry did with conspicuous success, the Italian effort exhausted itself in piecemeal output of a bewildering variety of weapons from numerous small and inefficient plants manned by skilled artisans. Inadequate materials, deficient research and testing, and unrealistic and constantly changing specifications from the military resulted in long lead-times and unreliable or even unusable equipment.[148]

Mussolini himself was partly responsible for these economic weaknesses, and for the more general deficiencies of the armed forces, most of which he was aware of in his sober moments. He had neglected the armaments industry during the 1920s in favor of balancing the budget, despite warnings such as the forceful report of the Army chief of staff, General Giuseppe Ferrari, who insisted in January 1928 that military expenditures, equipment, and interservice coordination were inadequate.[149] The Great Depression, the Ethiopian and Spanish forays, and the decision to give Navy and Air Force priority had kept the Army short of funds and raw materials for modernization, despite the protests of Baistrocchi and Pariani. By December 1938, after belatedly launching the artillery program, Mussolini had begun to lament disingenuously the Army's sad state to the Council of Ministers. In April 1939 he complained that "this Army bureaucracy doesn't work; one can never be sure of it. Its figures are never exact. On the question of cannon we have been fooled. Our artillery is old and insufficient in number." As Bottai commented, these were indeed "surprising confessions from the mouth of the minister of war." Ciano noted that there had been "much bluff in the military sector, and they have fooled even the Duce himself; but it has been a tragic sort of bluff."[150] The Army's "bluff" took place with Mussolini's partial connivance, even if he preferred to pose as the innocent victim of his subordinates' incompetence or duplicity. But in the case of the Air Force, the bluff was clearly directed at the political leadership. Valle insisted to Ciano in mid-1939 that Italian aircraft were comparable to German types, and that their armament was superior. His claims of 3,000 ready aircraft apparently carried conviction until April 1939, when a secret naval intelligence survey failed to find even 1,000.[151] This sort of malfeasance, although remarkable, is not evidence that the armed forces had no purpose other than propaganda. The generals themselves had difficulty distinguishing appearance from reality, and Pariani was even willing to fight. In the last days of August 1939, when general war seemed imminent, he reported the Army ready in the face of crushing evidence to the contrary.[152]

As for the economy, Mussolini was almost ostentatiously unconcerned:

Guarneri's fears were "exaggerated." As late as February 1940 he still did "not believe in the Cassandras of the Ministry of Exchange and Currency: . . . Guarneri for six years constantly announced that we were on the verge of bankruptcy and instead we have done rather well." But as Ciano commented, "the Duce does not add that during Guarneri's tenure we ate up a whole 12,000,000,000 lire in foreign stocks and bonds and 5,000,000,000 in gold. Our resources are now reduced to 1,400 miserable millions, and when they are finished we will have nothing left but our eyes to cry with."[153] Nevertheless, Mussolini paid a great deal of attention to Guarneri's technical advice — and when the minister insisted on throttling back imports, Mussolini generally resigned himself. The dictator partially recognized the limits the economy set, but did not allow them to deflect him from his imperial aims.

The road to non-belligerence. Mussolini's quest for Mediterranean hegemony was not without precedent in the history of unified Italy. Giuseppe Mazzini, prophet of Italian nationalism as well as of "Europe of the Peoples," turned at the end of his long career to celebrating Roman imperialism and proclaiming Italy's mission in the Mediterranean and North Africa.[154] Not by chance or without good reason did Mussolini and the regime claim him as their own. A one-time disciple of Mazzini, Francesco Crispi, led Italy as prime minister from 1887 until the mid-1890s, and launched the nation's first bid to subjugate Ethiopia. Disaster at the battle of Adua in 1896 ended that adventure and Crispi's career. But the imperial idea did not die, and Mussolini himself acknowledged Crispi as the "greatest pioneer" of Fascist empire.[155] Liberal Italy under Giovanni Giolitti seized Libya from the Ottoman Empire in 1911. In April-May 1915, a vociferous minority in which Mussolini figured prominently agitated for war against the Central Powers. Government and monarchy struck at Austria-Hungary in pursuit of the unredeemed territories of Trento and Trieste, and of immense Balkan, Near Eastern, and colonial aspirations.[156] The disappointing outcome of a war in which Italy suffered over 600,000 dead helped launch Mussolini's movement, which posed as the defender of victory against Allies, Socialists, and "renouncers" of Italy's Adriatic claims.[157] Once in power, Mussolini hardly gave evidence of that "good behavior" some historians have ascribed to the regime's first decade.[158] After an incident in 1923 in which unknown assailants killed an Italian general who was delimiting Albania's southern border, Mussolini bombarded and occupied the Greek island of Corfù. His advisers restrained him with difficulty from provoking a Mediterranean war when Britain and the League of Nations insisted on withdrawal. In the mid-1920s he began planning the conquest of Ethiopia, and seriously contemplated a war with Turkey. He intrigued with the German radical right, supplied weapons to Magyars and Croat terrorists for use against Yugoslavia, and on a number of occasions prepared to dismember that unfortunate nation. The Croats who assassinated King Alexander of Yugoslavia and French Foreign

Minister Louis Barthou in October 1934 came from Italy; the regime's complicity is likely although unproven. As for Albania, the Duce reduced it to what he described as "an Italian province without a prefect."[159]

Mussolini covered these activities by posing as guardian of order and prophet of anti-Bolshevism, a pose that at first endeared him to British Conservatives such as Winston Churchill. Then the Depression enfeebled the West, and the resurgence of Germany gave Mussolini leverage for active expansion. Fear of the Germans led Pierre Laval, prime minister of France, to offer Italy secretly a free hand in Ethiopia as early as 1931 (although Laval and Mussolini did not reach final agreement until January 1935).[160] In 1932 Mussolini set in motion preparations to strike in East Africa while fear ensured French acquiescence, but before German rearmament required a major effort in defense of Italy's Austrian buffer state.[161] He inaugurated his new policy by taking back the Foreign Ministry, which he had yielded in 1929, from his too moderate Party associate, Dino Grandi. The latter, in Mussolini's words, had "allowed himself to become prisoner of the League of Nations, had practiced a pacific and internationalist policy, had acted the ultrademocrat and League enthusiast, had diverted Italy from the straight and narrow path of an egoist and realistic policy, had compromised certain ambitions of the younger generation, had 'gone to bed with England and France, and since they were males, Italy had emerged pregnant with disarmament.' "[162]

Any such danger ended when Italian troops, without a declaration of war, crossed the Mareb into Ethiopia on 3 October 1935. British opposition was halfhearted. The Conservative government found itself wedged between public outrage over Italian aggression, its own pro-Mussolinian sentiments, and pusillanimity at the Admiralty (which chose to ignore the outspoken confidence of the British Mediterranean Fleet in its ability to crush the Italians).[163] The British leadership, and Laval, who notwithstanding his agreement with Italy followed unhappily in London's wake, succeeded in enraging Mussolini without saving Ethiopia, for which they cared nothing in any case. The crisis led Mussolini to seek German support in return for the abandonment of Austria, a process that ultimately led to the Austro-German Anschluss of March 1938. It also convinced him that Grandi, in exile as ambassador to London, had been correct in his unflattering 1934 assessment of the British: the bulldog had become "a hippopotamus . . . slow, fat, heavy, somnolent, weak in eyesight and even weaker in nerve." The French, as the Germans obligingly told Mussolini's unofficial contact man in Berlin, were a "dying nation."[164] The future belonged to the young, prolific, dynamic peoples of Italy and Germany – and possibly even to the Japanese.

Ethiopia was only the beginning. Mussolini intended to use the colony to "raise an Ethiopian force of a million soldiers, build fifty or so airfields, and a metallurgical industry, so that Ethiopia would find on its own soil everything necessary for its military development. Then we can realize the link-up with Libya and liberate ourselves of the servitude imposed by the Suez Canal."[165] Nor did he relax in Europe. Civil war erupted in Spain in July 1936, and within three weeks Italian airmen were again in combat. In the next year, an expeditionary force of roughly 50,000 combat and support troops followed. Italian objectives in Spain were both ideological and strategic: to prevent the "bolshevization" of the country, and, above all, to put pressure on the French both in the Pyrenees and in the Mediterranean.

Convergence of Italian and German policy in Spain, where Hitler also responded to the aid requests of the rebel generals Mola and Franco, followed swiftly upon Italy's African and Mediterranean quarrel with the West, and prepared the way for a formal Italo-German political agreement in October 1936. Mussolini set the seal on the bargain by announcing on 1 November that "an axis around which all European states committed to cooperation and peace may collaborate" now united Rome with Berlin.[166] Despite a brief truce with Great Britain in the winter of 1936–7 (the so-called Gentlemen's Agreement, that left untouched the key issue of Italian sovereignty over Ethiopia, which the British had not recognized), intervention in Spain continued to widen the gulf between Italy and the West. Guadalajara intensified Italian military effort, which culminated in Mussolini's response to Franco's August 1937 appeal to cut off Soviet seaborne aid to the Spanish Republic. The "unknown submarines" of the Italian Navy conducted a remarkable campaign from the Bosporus to Gibraltar. According to figures Mussolini gave the Germans, the *Regia Marina* accounted for almost 200,000 tons of merchant shipping by September.[167] This outrage produced the only resolute British stand against Mussolini since Corfù. Under Eden's leadership, the Nyon conference on "piracy" in the Mediterranean organized an international antisubmarine patrol. A hasty Italian retreat resulted, even if the West subsequently spoiled the effect by meekly inviting Italy to aid in the policing.

Nyon more or less coincided with Mussolini's long-planned September 1937 visit to Germany, which proved a triumphal celebration of the alleged common character of the Fascist and National Socialist revolutions, and led to a significant tightening of the relationship between the regimes. Mussolini chose Germany. He abandoned any genuine attempt at the more traditional Italian policy of "equidistance," of providing the "decisive weight" in an unstable European balance, in order, as Grandi elegantly put it, to "sell ourselves at a high price in the hours of the great future crisis."[168] In November 1937 Italy left the League of Nations and joined the German-Japanese Anti-Comintern Pact. Ciano was in ecstasy: three peoples "were setting out on the same road – which perhaps will lead them to battle. A necessary battle, if we want to break the crust that suffocates the energies and aspirations of the young peoples." Italy, Mussolini gloated, was "at the center of the most formidable politico-military combination that has ever existed."[169]

To maintain equilibrium within this bloc as German power and German pressure on Austria increased, Mussolini and Ciano relied not on the West, but on their own forward policy in southeastern Europe. Ciano mounted a whirlwind courtship of Italy's eastern neighbor. In March 1937 he descended dramatically on Belgrade to sign an Italo-Yugoslav treaty of friendship. The agreement officially, though temporarily, ended Italian efforts to subvert Yugoslavia through support of Ante Pavelić's Croat terrorists. It also provided for Italo-Yugoslav economic cooperation. But Ciano had wanted to go much farther. As early as November 1936 he bid for an alliance, tactfully suggesting that refusal would lead to "war to the knife."[170] The Yugoslavs, under intense British pressure and determined to avoid service as an Italian catspaw against Germany, held out successfully for mere normalization of relations. Ciano was not abashed. During his March visit he told Prince Paul, regent and ruler of Yugoslavia, that Germany was "a dangerous enemy but a disagreeable friend." The Anschluss was inevitable, and only an "Italo-Yugoslav union" with Hungarian cooperation could blunt the German thrust to the southeast. This "horizontal axis" project gave the Italians the illusion throughout 1937 that German absorption of Austria would not threaten Italy's Balkan hunting preserve.[171] In the event, Rome's ties to Belgrade were cold comfort after German troops appeared on both Italian and Yugoslav borders in March 1938. But Ciano had another string to his bow. To maintain weight within the Axis and influence in southeastern Europe, Italy would annex Albania.[172]

Although committed to the Axis, Mussolini was not averse to tactical détente with Britain. It would reinsure against the loss of leverage both within and without the Axis that was likely if the British prime minister, Neville Chamberlain, secured the comprehensive Anglo-German agreement he so assiduously sought. Détente would also isolate the French, who were in Mussolini's way in Spain and elsewhere, and seemed the weaker of Italy's western adversaries. The consequence was the Anglo-Italian agreement of 16 April 1938. Mussolini, fearing the appearance of "a trip to Canossa under German pressure" at the Brenner, and afraid that the approaching Anschluss would lessen his bargaining power with the West, began negotiations in haste. Even after Hitler swallowed Austria on 11–12 March while lavishing profuse thanks on the Duce, the Italians pressed the British to conclude before the forthcoming visit of the Führer to Italy, scheduled for early May.[173] The outcome was a curious document, hedged about with provisos and limitations. It provided for reductions of Italian troops in Spain and Libya, a cessation of anti-British propaganda in the Middle East, and a pledge to respect the Mediterranean and Red Sea *status quo*. In return, Britain would work toward League recognition of Italy's Ethiopian conquest. The coming into effect of the agreement, however, depended on Italian withdrawal from Spain, where Mussolini's troops fought on and the *Regia Aeronautica* bombed cities and British shipping until the fall of 1938.[174] Meanwhile, Mussolini looked to his Alpine defenses against Germany, and in April ordered what Badoglio described as "very serious precautions" at the

Brenner. But such activities, which persisted throughout Italy's wartime alliance with Germany, were defensive reinsurance to avoid vassalage, not preparation for a change of sides.[175]

Meanwhile Hitler redressed to some extent the painful impression the Anschluss created in Italy. As early as 1922 he had publicly proposed to sacrifice the South Tyrol in return for an Italian alliance. Now, at a state dinner on 7 May 1938 at Palazzo Venezia, he pledged as his "political testament to the German people" the inviolability of the Alpine frontier "for all time."[176] Even before this lapidary announcement, Mussolini was determined to sign an alliance with the Germans – but not yet. When the pactomaniacal German Foreign Minister Joachim von Ribbentrop produced a draft, Mussolini yielded to Ciano's pressure for postponement until he had squeezed maximum advantage out of the agreement with the British.[177]

If tactical compromise with Britain was still possible, the same was not true for France, which the Anglo-Italian agreement and German support for Italy threatened with isolation. To humor the British, who had initially hoped to include the French in the negotiations for the April agreement, Ciano talked desultorily with the French chargé, Jules-François Blondel. However, after Hitler had delivered his "political testament," a "distinct chill" entered Ciano's attitude.[178] Mussolini himself remained intransigent, then made a thunderous anti-French speech at Genoa to the accompaniment of massive demonstrations. Italy and France were "on opposite sides of the barricade" in Spain. Collaboration between the Fascist and National Socialist revolutions was "destined to set the tone for this century."[179]

Italian refusal of the German alliance proposal did not cool Hitler's desire for an early reckoning with his next victims, the Czechs.[180] Nor did Italian evasion of formal ties preclude support for Hitler's action, although Mussolini had at first apparently anticipated that the Germans would devote at least a year to digesting Austria before moving on.[181] An Italian press crescendo and a torrent of Mussolinian oratory throughout September 1938 demanded self-determination for the large Sudeten German minority along Czechoslovakia's borders. Mussolini and Ciano did not expect the effete democracies to fight for that small and faraway country, despite the long-standing military alliance between France and Czechoslovakia. But if general war did come, Mussolini assured Berlin he would fight; Axis victory was certain, by "force of arms, and irresistible force of the spirit." On 27 September, Ciano arranged a council of war at Munich between himself, Pariani, Valle, and Keitel of the *Wehrmacht* high command. The services mobilized partially and the Navy issued orders for fast convoys to transfer reinforcements to the Dodecanese and North Africa.[182]

The next day, almost miraculously, a British suggestion offered Mussolini a chance to play one of his favorite roles, that of the great mediator – even while Ciano impressed upon the slightly hysterical British ambassador, Lord Perth, that Italy's "interests, honour, and pledged word" required war at Germany's side.[183] Mussolini nevertheless prevailed on Hitler to postpone the attack on Czechoslovakia, then acted at the Munich Conference of 29–30 September 1938 as Hitler's spokesman in imposing on Chamberlain and Daladier the dissolution of France's small ally. Hitler, although he longed to test the *Wehrmacht* in action, drew back at the last moment from wiping the Czechs from the map, and settled for annexation of the Sudeten areas, which contained Czechoslovakia's border fortifications and much of its economic potential. Despite his complaint that his "entry into Prague had been spoiled," Hitler alone gained real advantages at Munich. Italy settled for a public relations triumph, and delirious crowds greeted Mussolini upon his return over the Brenner, to his secret chagrin. Peace was too popular in Italy for his taste.[184]

Mussolini followed up Munich by angling for a reward from the British: the putting into effect of the April agreement. Simultaneously he pushed himself forward as the self-appointed protector of the Hungarians, who were pressing their aspirations against rump Czecho-Slovakia, which the Germans had now temporarily adopted as a client. The Germans refused to fall in with a Ciano proposal for a new conference of the four Munich powers to settle the dispute. Ciano grumbled: "Today, for the first time, we have allowed ourselves to be taken in tow, and this greatly annoys me."[185] It was not to be the last. Next the Germans scotched a Hungarian attempt to go it alone; Budapest had secured Mussolini's support by telling him that the Reich looked benevolently on its project. If the *Regia Aeronautica* had been more proficient at instrument flight, and the weather over the Julian Alps not prevented the deployment of the hundred fighters Mussolini had promised the Hungarians, the world might have been treated to the curious spectacle of the Axis partners fighting a proxy war on the Danube. Informed of Hungarian duplicity, Mussolini rather shamefacedly fell into line and abandoned Budapest, more or less definitively, to German tutelage.[186]

He had other interests to console him. In early November, armed with an assurance that the Chamberlain government intended to put the April agreement into effect shortly, he moved to put pressure on the French, whose pusillanimity during the Czech crisis had perhaps suggested that they might swallow almost anything.[187] A campaign against France might also head off a Franco-German rapprochement, which a forthcoming Ribbentrop visit to Paris threatened. On 30 November Ciano spoke in the Chamber of Deputies. When he came to mention, though not by name, Italy's "natural aspirations," a sudden disturbance convulsed the floor. Deputies rose and chanted, "Tunis, Corsica, Nice, Savoy." That evening the Grand Council of Fascism, the regime's highest organ, met, and Mussolini delivered a secret speech:

I announce to you the immediate goals of Fascist dynamism. As we have avenged Adua, so we will avenge Valona [one of the two principal ports in Albania, evacuated by Italian troops in 1920]. Albania will become Italian. I cannot yet – and I do not wish to – tell you how or when. But it will come to pass. Then, for the requirements of our security in this Mediterranean that still confines us, we need Tunis and Corsica. The [French] frontier must move to the Var [River]. I do not aim for Savoy, because it is outside the circle of the Alps. But I have my eye on the Ticino, since Switzerland has lost its cohesive force and is destined one day, like so many small nations, to be demolished. All this is a program. I cannot lay down a fixed time-table. I merely indicate the route along which we shall march.[188]

The Italian press maintained the pressure begun with the Chamber demonstration. The French, however, did not react by inviting the Duce to a Mediterranean Munich at their own expense. Their prime minister, Edouard Daladier, replied with a defiant *"jamais"* and toured the areas Italy claimed, making enormously successful speeches. The British, as usual, hinted to the French that minor concessions would be in order once the clamor died, but could not abandon their ally publicly. On 14 December Chamberlain felt compelled to announce in the House of Commons that His Majesty's Government would regard any change in the status of Tunis as a breach of the April agreement provision on the maintenance of the Mediterranean *status quo*. However, he did not cancel the visit to Rome that he and his foreign secretary, Lord Halifax, planned for January 1939.

Mussolini's response to the French was twofold. He continued to hope for crumbs from the negotiating table, and a clandestine emissary of Daladier's soon appeared offering limited concessions.[189] But in the long run, as Mussolini told the Grand Council of Fascism on 4 February 1939, he had no doubt that war with France was unavoidable. Its initiation, he argued, should wait until Italian military and economic preparations were complete at the end of 1942 – his first enunciation of a deadline that figured prominently in the coming alliance talks with the Germans. Mussolini was characteristically less than frank to Badoglio. The marshal briefed the service chiefs on 26 January in terms that suggested Mussolini had denied any offensive intent; to a more trusted general, the dictator contemporaneously remarked that he intended "to fight France." Britain had temporarily receded as enemy and victim. Badoglio insisted to his colleagues that Pariani's attack on Egypt was out, and that defense against the French had priority.[190] An "isolated" anti-French war in the Mediterranean continued to intrigue Mussolini, and even Ciano, who boasted to the Polish ambassador that Italy would crush France in two weeks.[191] The conception also appeared in the April 1939 Italo-German staff talks. General Pariani, who raised the question on orders from Mussolini, received a sharp reminder from Keitel of the *Wehrmacht* high command that such a war would not remain isolated. Britain would undoubtedly come to France's aid.[192]

Mussolini, too, foresaw a general conflict with the West beyond the Italo-French confrontation he had summoned up. His 4 February 1939 remarks to the Grand Council were part of a document intended to "orient" Italian policy, "in the short term, in the long term, and in the very long term." It was a sort of Mussolinian *Mein Kampf*, a lapidary statement of a geopolitical vision the dictator had entertained since at least the mid-1920s:[193]

states are more or less independent according to their maritime position. In other words, states that possess coasts on the oceans or have free access to the oceans are independent. States that cannot communicate freely with the oceans and are enclosed in inland seas are semiindependent. States that are absolutely continental and have outlets neither on the oceans nor on [inland] seas are not independent.

Italy belongs to the second category of states. It is bathed by a landlocked sea that communicates with the oceans through the Suez Canal, an artificial link easily blocked even by improvised methods, and through the straits of Gibraltar, dominated by the cannons of Great Britain.

Italy therefore does not have free connection with the oceans. Italy is therefore in truth a prisoner of the Mediterranean, and the more populous and prosperous Italy becomes, the more its imprisonment will gall.

The bars of this prison are Corsica, Tunis, Malta, Cyprus. The sentinels of this prison are Gibraltar and Suez. Corsica is a pistol pointed at the heart of Italy; Tunisia at Sicily; while Malta and Cyprus constitute a threat to all our positions in the eastern and western Mediterranean. Greece, Turkey, Egypt have been ready to form a chain with Great Britain and to complete the politico-military encirclement of Italy. Greece, Turkey, Egypt must be considered virtual enemies of Italy and of its expansion. From this situation, whose geographical rigor leaps to one's eyes and which tormented, even before our regime, those men who saw beyond considerations of momentary political expediency, one can draw the following conclusions:

1. The task of Italian policy, which cannot have and does not have continental objectives of a European territorial nature except Albania, is to first of all break the bars of the prison.

2. Once the bars are broken, Italian policy can have only one watchword – to march to the ocean.

Which ocean? The Indian Ocean, joining Libya with Ethiopia through the Sudan, or the Atlantic, through French North Africa.

In either case, we will find ourselves confronted with Anglo-French opposition. . . .

Italy would deal with it. As for the Germans, Mussolini relegated them to the modest but vital function of covering "Italy's shoulders on the continent."

Unfortunately, it soon emerged that Hitler had other interests besides playing the loyal second. Once again acting without consultation, he seized Prague on 15 March, tearing up the Munich agreement, in which Mussolini took considerable paternal pride. Mussolini reacted far more severely than he had to the Anschluss. But he retained his pro-German orientation and his intention of signing the long-delayed alliance both to pressure the West further and to exert more influence over the Germans. Rumors of German intrigues in Croatia, which raised the specter of German expansion into Italy's Mediterranean and Balkan sphere of influence, restrained him from moving immediately to seize Albania, a course Ciano pressed on him as the appropriate response to the German action in Bohemia-Moravia. Albania was "a fruit that can fall into our hands when we desire it," he commented in a note to Ciano on 16 March, and made its seizure conditional on a solution to the Czech crisis, the end of the Spanish war, satisfactory clarification of the "preeminent" problem of Croatia, closer agreement with Germany on alliance terms, and progress in Italian rearmament. But renewed assurances from Ribbentrop that Croatia would remain part of Italy's exclusive sphere overcame all hesitations.[194] On Good Friday, 7 April 1939, Italian troops landed at Durazzo and Valona in the face of ineffective and short-lived Albanian resistance.

The Albanian coup was far more than an exercise in gunboat diplomacy in competition with the Germans. It was a "preliminary operation" in the program Mussolini had set for himself.[195] The significance of the action did not escape even one erstwhile proponent of the "policy of the decisive weight." The day of the landing, Dino Grandi dispatched to his master a letter of fulsome congratulation that summed up the long-term significance of the action, paid homage to Mussolini's fixity of purpose, and, by implication, attempted to make up for his own less aggressive policy in the past. The conquest of Albania immobilized Yugoslavia, opened "the ancient paths of the Roman conquests in the East to the Italy of Mussolini," and threatened Britain "with the loss in advance of its naval bases, and our complete domination of the Eastern Mediterranean."[196]

In Rome, Ciano and Mussolini entertained similar visions. To the German ambassador and to the visiting Hungarian premier and foreign minister, they announced their intention of creating in Albania a mighty "bulwark" from which to dominate the Balkans. The Duce ordered a large-scale road-building program, particularly south toward Greece. A sizable Italian garrison and the air power of the *Regia Aeronautica,* now only 140 kilometers from Salonika, would secure the total dependence of the Balkan states upon the Axis. The Albanians were "outstanding" as military material, and Mussolini proposed to employ them in support of uprisings fomented among their unredeemed cousins in the Yugoslav and Greek border provinces of Kossovo and Ciamuria. By May 1939, he was meditating "more and more about jumping upon Greece at the first opportunity," despite a British territorial guarantee extended to Athens following the Albanian coup. Should general war come, invasion of Greece would help "drive the British from the Mediterranean basin" and reduce the eastern end of that sea to an Italian lake, as the seizure of Albania had reduced the Adriatic.[197]

Albania convinced the West that the Italians were firmly in the German camp. Italy had nothing to gain by further postponement of the alliance, particularly because the Turks, in alarm over the Albanian coup, were now openly aligning themselves with France and Britain. Ciano and Ribbentrop met on 6 and 7 May 1939 in Milan. Their progress in negotiation, and infuriating suggestions in the foreign press that the Milanese were less than enthusiastic about the Germans, induced Mussolini to order immediate announcement of the alliance. Signed on 22 May in Berlin, the "Pact of Steel," as Mussolini christened it, was "absolute dynamite," an offensive military alliance with none of the usual coy references to unprovoked aggression.[198]

The Italians gave their signature on the verbal understanding that neither dictator would precipitate the inevitable war before 1943, when Italian armaments, and ostensibly German ones as well, would be ready.[199] But the new allies did not intend to rest in the intervening period. The day after the signing, Hitler secretly told his generals that "further successes cannot be achieved without bloodshed" and announced his decision to "attack Poland at the first favorable opportunity."[200] For his part, Mussolini took a renewed interest in Yugoslavia as well as Greece. Prince Regent Paul had aroused Italian anger by removing his philo-Fascist prime minister, Stoyadinović, in early February. Ciano now signed with the purported representative of the Croat leader Vladko Maček an agreement which provided for a rising against the Belgrade government in four to five months, Italian military intervention, and a Croat puppet state under Italian control.[201] Italy had acquired new "continental objectives of a European territorial nature," not to mention Switzerland, which the Duce had neglected in his February speech to the Grand Council.

In late July, the Italians began belatedly to realize that the Germans were keeping them in the dark about Poland. More perspicacious than Ribbentrop in seeing that this time the West would surely fight, Mussolini attempted to apply the remedies that had gained him laurels at Munich. The Germans were unhelpful. In early August the insistent reports of the Italian ambassador in Berlin finally alarmed Ciano and Mussolini: Hitler was intent on fighting Poland. In talks between 11 and 13 August at the Führer's mountain retreat at Berchtesgaden, near Salzburg, Ciano vainly hinted to the Germans that premature general war would result. Hitler flatly refused to reconsider, predicted the West would again back down, and invited Italy to partake of the feast by attacking Yugoslavia.[202]

The offer sorely tempted Mussolini. Ciano, who after Salzburg was determined to keep Italy out of war, recorded in his diary the "seesaw of [Mussolini's] sentiments." Mussolini oscillated between greed and fear, desire to conduct a policy "as straight as a sword blade" and knowledge that "we cannot make [war] because our [armaments] situation does not permit it." On 15 August Mussolini informed Badoglio that general war was imminent; he proposed to maintain "the strictest defensive" without committing any act that might signify support of the German move. If the Allies forced Italy to go to war, Mussolini proposed to mount "an offensive against Greece in the direction of Salonika." In addition, "situation permitting, and only after having unleashed internal disorders in Yugoslavia," he proposed to "seize Croatia to exploit the considerable resources of that area." Badoglio pointed out that the defenses of Libya, where he expected the principal Allied effort, were utterly inadequate. Mussolini agreed that the situation of the colony was "truly precarious," but nevertheless insisted on the Greek and Yugoslav offensives.[203] If Italy were to lose its African colonies, it would gain new ones in the Balkans.

The Russo-German Nonaggression Pact of 23–24 August, which aligned

Russia with Germany and seemed to preclude Western aid to Poland, momentarily dispelled this pessimism. Even Ciano prepared, as he suavely put it in his diary, "to grab . . . our part of the booty in Croatia and Dalmatia" without war with Britain or France.[204] Pariani's assurances of Army readiness pushed Mussolini in the direction he dearly preferred. But Pariani was clearly far from reliable, and the other service chiefs promised nothing. Above all, the King demanded neutrality. To Ciano, on 24 August, he was adamant. Italy was incapable of fighting; the Army was in a "pitiful" state, as the "Po" Army maneuvers earlier in the month had revealed. The frontier defenses, which he had personally inspected, were inadequate; the French could descend to the plains of Piedmont with ease. Finally, Victor Emmanuel emphasized, public opinion was firmly anti-German, and the peasants were reporting to their mobilization centers cursing Italy's ally. The King insisted that Mussolini take no "supreme decisions" without him. To add insult to injury, he requested that if war indeed came, his son, Crown Prince Umberto, should have a major command.[205]

Ciano reported all this faithfully to a still bellicose Mussolini in order to "dismount" him. Finally, after further vacillation, the dictator disengaged Italy from its Pact of Steel obligations. On the afternoon of 25 August he communicated to Hitler that Italy could only intervene in a general conflict if Germany immediately provided "the military equipment and raw materials to withstand the blow which France and Britain will direct predominantly against us." When Hitler asked for a list of Italian requirements, Mussolini and his subordinates produced a fantastic demand for 18,153,000 metric tons of coal, steel, oil, nickel, molybdenum, tungsten, and so on, along with 150 heavy antiaircraft batteries and a broad range of machine tools. Bernardo Attolico, the ambassador in Berlin, added on his own initiative that Italy needed all this delivered *before* entry into war. Hitler confessed himself unable to fulfill this last condition, and, as the Italians had hoped, released his ally from the duty of fighting at Germany's side.[206]

In the meantime, the British stood firm in support of Poland. To avoid an involuntary collision with the West, Ciano therefore convinced Mussolini to allow him to inform secretly Perth's replacement as British ambassador, Sir Percy Loraine, that Italy would not fight unless attacked. As the *Wehrmacht* rolled across the Polish frontier on 1 September, Ciano did his best to arrange another Munich at Polish expense, while Italy took up a position of "nonbelligerence" — a status unrecognized in international law, but more congenial to the dictator than that odious and degrading condition, neutrality. Mussolini was not happy, but there was little to do but attempt to whip the Italian military into shape and "dream about heroic enterprises against Yugoslavia," enterprises Badoglio informed him were impractical in the face of probable French counteraction and certain Yugoslav resistance.[207]

CHAPTER 2

Bellicose nonbelligerent

> I . . . believe – even if we march on separate paths – that Destiny will nevertheless continue to bind us together. If National Socialist Germany is destroyed by the western democracies, Fascist Italy would also face a hard future.
>
> Hitler to Mussolini, 3 September 1939

1. The limits of abstention

"Verrat!" By the morning of 1 September, despite the agitation of the preceding days, Mussolini was temporarily calm. He solicited from Hitler a message publicly releasing Italy from its obligations, then composed with Ciano the resolution declaring Italy's nonbelligerence. The Council of Ministers promulgated it that afternoon at a meeting in which Mussolini surveyed the situation in his habitual off-the-record speech.[1] Despite rumors of "fantastic" plans to descend on the Po valley prepared by "those Gascons on the French General Staff," he was nevertheless confident that for the moment, at least, the belligerents would leave Italy alone. But he was far from happy. One witness noted that for Mussolini neutrality was "a failure, a betrayal." Another recalled him muttering to himself *"Verrat! Verrat!* [Betrayal! Betrayal!]."* Mussolini had the "mortified expression of one who was doing something popular against his will." Even Starace and the minister of popular culture, Dino Alfieri, the most conspicuous war enthusiasts of the previous weeks, congratulated Ciano on his part in Mussolini's decision.[2]

The Allies were equally relieved. Earlier in the year the British had contemplated a "knock-out blow" against Italy on the assumption that it would join Germany at the outset. But despite crushing Allied naval superiority in the Mediterranean, French enthusiasm for an immediate offensive against Libya with their North African army had oscillated wildly in the months before war. In London, fear of an extended Mediterranean commitment and resulting Atlantic and Far Eastern difficulties vied with the urge to have it out with the impudent "Ice-creamers."[3] Fear eventually won. By July 1939, the intricate machinery of the Committee of Imperial Defence and its subordinate bodies had laboriously reached a tentative assessment: "Italian neutrality, if it could by any means be *assured,* would be decidedly preferable to her active hostility." Only Leslie Hore-Belisha, the nonconformist secretary of state for war, noted that a neutral Italy "would sustain Germany, whereas as an ally she would constitute a drain on German resources" and thus further Britain's fundamental strategic aim of strangling Germany economically.[4] British intelligence recognized that Italian fuel stocks were short, but neither Cabinet nor chiefs of staff made anything of that information in their deliberations.[5] Nor did British strategists understand that short of Mussolini's sudden disappearance from the scene or the unlikely contingency of immediate German collapse, the only way to "assure" Italian neutrality was the sudden and ruthless application of overwhelming force – force the Allies still possessed in September 1939.[6]

Apart from the precariousness of Italy's hold on Libya and East Africa, seven Allied battleships and battlecruisers and one aircraft carrier, subject to further reinforcement, faced two Italian battleships (*Cesare* and *Cavour*) in the Mediterranean. *Doria, Duilio, Littorio,* and *Vittorio Veneto* were not combat-ready until the summer of 1940. From Alexandria the Royal Navy's Mediterranean Fleet proposed to sweep the eastern Mediterranean free of Italian submarines, attack Italian bases in Libya, and launch carrier strikes against the fleet bases at Augusta and Taranto.[7] The French would have sallied from Bizerte and Toulon to bombard with impunity Italian coastal cities from Palermo to Genoa. While Italy would presumably have remained in the war for some time as a military and economic drag on Germany, a succession of major disasters in the fall and winter of 1939–40, before the great German victories in the West, would have had even more serious effects on the internal stability of Mussolini's regime than did the defeats of the winter of 1940–1.

However, in the last hurried and confused days of peace, the reluctance of the chiefs of staff to add to their liabilities and the secret telephone contacts between Halifax and Ciano over the Italian proposal for a Polish Munich produced a natural drift into British acquiescence to Italian nonbelligerence. Foreign Office and Cabinet did not appreciate the dangers for the future that ambiguous status might hold. When the War Cabinet belatedly considered the issue on 4 September it rejected any thought of an ultimatum. The British concluded Italy "had further to go now than she had in 1914 before she would be induced to throw in her lot with us, desirable as this ultimate object might be."[8] How much further they did not discover until September 1943.

In Paris, more enthusiasm for action against Italy apparently existed. By the end of July the French commander-in-chief, General Maurice Gamelin, had recovered from his initial pessimism about North Africa. The French announced themselves willing to attack Libya roughly twenty-five days after the beginning of mobilization.[9] But in September, the "Gascons" could not overcome the philo-Mussolinian faction in the Daladier cabinet, the desire of Gamelin – with the German wolf at the door – to avoid risk, and British pressure to let the Italians be. The French soon swung to the opposite extreme. With British encouragement, they offered in early September to discuss with Italy all issues except Corsica, Nice, and Savoy. Mussolini contemptuously left these overtures unanswered.[10]

If British and French failed to understand the precariousness of Italy's military and economic position in September 1939 and the dangers "nonbelligerence" held in store for them, the Germans hardly showed better judgment. Hitler had counted on Italian military cooperation to help deter the Western powers or keep them occupied while he crushed the Poles. Mussolini's defection on 25 August therefore had a chastening effect. Hitler postponed the attack, at that point scheduled for 0430 next morning, while he assessed the situation, which Britain's simultaneous reaffirmation of its commitment to Poland further complicated. He of course recovered from his shock, remarked caustically that the Italians were behaving "exactly as in 1914," and pressed on to destroy the Poles.[11] But he did not give up hope of eventual Italian assistance in the event of a German offensive against France. "So long as the Duce lives," Hitler affirmed to his commanders on 23 November, "one can rest assured that Italy will seize every opportunity to achieve its imperialistic aims." He added, however, that it was "too much to ask of Italy that it should intervene before Germany had grasped the initiative in the West."[12]

Despite Hitler's enthusiasm, his subordinates divided on the merits of Italian participation. The naval staff was aware of some of the Italian Navy's deficiencies, but initially overestimated Cavagnari's aggressiveness, and counted on Allied difficulties in the Mediterranean to ease the German task in the Atlantic. The army, whose opinion of its Italian counterpart was low, at least hoped that Italy would tie down fifteen French divisions in the Alps, and that war in North Africa would absorb France's colonial forces. But in the first weeks of September some German leaders, including Göring, came to agree with Italian suggestions that nonbelligerence, inevitable given Italy's weakness, was also in Germany's military and economic interests.[13] It preserved Italy's access to seaborne imports, and relieved the Germans of the need – all too evident a year and a half later – to shore up their ally after the collapse of its overseas empire under British onslaught.

The Ciano line. Despite momentary success, the solidarity of his colleagues, the connivance of the Allies, and the grudging toleration of the Germans, Mussolini's son-in-law faced an uphill struggle in keeping Italy out of war. The first days were trying: "news of the first successes of Germany against Poland [had] reawakened the bellicose spirit of the Duce," and Ciano was able to contain him only with difficulty. By the 6th, however, the immediate crisis was over: though far from happy, Mussolini was "more serene."[14]

Ciano's attempt to restrain Mussolini and the latter's reluctance to be held back are the principal theme of Italian policy from September 1939 to March 1940. Three things hampered Ciano's efforts from the start: personal loyalty to Mussolini, lack of a substantial independent power base, and, most important, inability to formulate a feasible alternative policy. Apart from the improbable contingencies of a swift and catastrophic German defeat or a peace settlement in which the West accepted the destruction of Poland, only Mussolini's removal could have prevented Italian participation in the war. Despite undeniable ambition for the succession and a tendency to adopt Mussolinian poses in public, however, Ciano was too loyal to his father-in-law to contemplate a coup d'état at this stage of the game.[15] Sumner Welles later described him as a Renaissance princeling,[16] but Ciano was not the regime's Cesare Borgia, nor even an adroit conspirator, as he and his associates amply demonstrated in July 1943, when their ambiguous vote against Mussolini at the last meeting of the Grand Council of Fascism profited only the monarchy. Ciano was fundamentally a *fils de papa;* his father had conquered as a World War I naval hero and Fascist notable the position and fortune that made the son's further ascent possible. The younger Ciano combined irresponsibility, fecklessness, vanity, and the snobbery of the newly rich with a political judgment keener in many respects than that of Mussolini, deep family feeling, apparently genuine religious conviction, and physical courage.[17]

Ciano had influence, but no power independent of Mussolini. The Foreign Ministry, which he ran in a haphazard and secretive manner reminiscent of Mussolini's own administrative method,[18] was not a bureaucracy with a great deal of influence on internal affairs. By authority of his position as "the son-in-law" he maintained close ties with the chief of police, Arturo Bocchini, and with the devious undersecretary (under Mussolini) of the Ministry of the Interior, Guido Buffarini Guidi. But these contacts gave him no direct power. When Ciano attempted to strengthen his position in the fall of 1939 by helping replace Starace as Party secretary with a nonentity he mistakenly viewed as his man, the results were disappointing.

Ciano had other actual or potential allies – the monarchy, the Church, "moderate" Fascists such as Balbo and Grandi, the fashionably Anglophile Roman *haut monde* at the Acquasanta golf club, and the "party of business," industrial and financial magnates such as Donegani, Agnelli, Cini, Volpi, and Pirelli. But the support of all these groups for neutrality was covert, ambiguous, and ineffectual. In the end, few indeed remained unimpressed as the *Wehrmacht* crushed France in May–June 1940. Balbo, in particular, displayed remarkable versatility. He told the British ambassador in January 1940 that any thought of Italian intervention alongside Germany was "rubbish," and simultaneously agitated for a march on Alexandria, despite Badoglio's protests that any such plan rested on an assessment of the situation "that did not correspond to reality."[19]

Ciano's loyalty to Mussolini and his lack of an independent power base were neither as crippling as his failure to define a convincing alternative to intervention. Under the conditions of 1939–40, neutrality was no guarantee of continued freedom of action in the face of the massive military and economic pressure both sides could wield. As Mussolini repeatedly told Ciano and his other subordinates, Italy's position as a great power, not to mention

47

the "natural aspirations" the moderates shared, required war. Ciano's concil-iatory choice for the vacant London Embassy, Giuseppe Bastianini, insisted to the British through an intermediary that Italy must have "internationali-zation" of the "doors" to the Mediterranean, and *"complete freedom"* in that sea — an objective unattainable without the collapse of Britain.[20] Italy could not change sides even if it wished. The Germans were too strong, and at the Brenner. Mussolini had long since made his choices; neither he nor his move-ment could escape their twenty years of history. Farinacci, despot of Cre-mona and voice of the old guard, saw the logic of the situation more clearly than Ciano and the moderates. In a letter to Mussolini on 13 September, Farinacci commented that:

Naturally all those, socialistoids, democratoids and cretinoids . . . who were hostile to the Axis policy that aided us in the conquest of the *Impero,* the victory in Spain, and the occupation of Albania, are beginning to say that if we are to intervene, we shall intervene at the side of France against Germany. For the sake of these individ-uals we are supposed to take up the policy of international anti-fascism, the emigrés, and the Jews. That would be a grave misfortune for Italy, since nobody would take us seriously any more and we would lose that prestige which you have secured for us in so many years of struggle.[21]

Ciano could hardly counter such arguments, though he still believed the latent strength of the West would defeat Germany in the long run, and that even if the French and British faltered, the United States would eventually intervene.[22] But he could do little more than coax Mussolini in the direction of "fat neutrality,"[23] attempt to make it as palatable as possible, and create as much friction with Berlin as he could without endangering his own posi-tion. On 13 September Ciano assured the British ambassador, Sir Percy Loraine, that "the decision which he (Loraine) would find most disagreeable and from which he had most to fear, would not be taken." Ciano implied with a certain bravado that Italy would intervene only "over his dead body," and in the ensuing months frequently hinted "disapproval of German goings on or . . . personal sympathy with [the West]."[24] But Ciano suited his views to his company, and his later attempts to tranquilize British and French about Mussolini's intentions aided intervention more than they did Ciano's increasingly half-hearted efforts to keep Italy out of war. Mussolini may have tolerated his son-in-law's independent line for precisely that reason.

Ciano initially worked hard at stabilizing Italian relations with the Allies, and at encouraging trade with the West. The war had vastly increased demand for Italian merchant shipping; this gave Mussolini "a bit of plea-sure," but in Ciano's judgment not enough.[25] The foreign minister also defended vigorously those Italian interests that did not coincide with those of Italy's ally. He tentatively sought to exploit Japanese chagrin over Rib-bentrop's unexpected collusion with the Soviets, against whom the Anti-Comintern Pact still theoretically linked Italy, Germany, and Japan. Contin-ued Japanese pressure on Russia's Far Eastern borders might restrain Stalin from adventures elsewhere that would test Italy's claim to be the greatest Balkan power by virtue of its Albanian conquest. Ciano's policy cut directly across German hopes of arranging a Russo-Japanese détente to free Russia for concerted action against Poland. On a more trivial level, Ciano protested demonstratively in early September over the "intrigues" of the ever-indiscreet Franz von Papen, at that point German ambassador in Ankara.[26]

Slightly less futile were Ciano's attempts to turn the project of an Italian-led bloc of neutrals, of which more presently, against Germany. But Ciano dared go no further. He refrained from exploiting the most explosive question in Italo-German relations, the Alto Adige, when it came to a head in late fall. A "prudent" policy was in order; even Ciano had to take into account the possibility of a German victory.[27] Finally, he undercut his own policy by enthusiastically promoting Mussolini's goal of a "new order" in southeastern Europe, a goal that could not fail to embroil Italy with the West.

Peace and neutral bloc. Once he had overcome his original impulse to enter the war regardless of consequences, Mussolini pursued four main lines of policy. He initially attempted to bring the war to a swift end in order to rescue Italy from the shame of nonbelligerence. More lastingly, he sought to preserve Italy's alliance with Germany despite the disquieting development of close ties between Berlin and Moscow. He maintained his objective of further Balkan expansion, and attempted to reduce Greece to satellite status through diplomatic means while preparing to destroy Yugoslavia at the first opportunity. Finally, he attempted to prepare the armed forces to act should the European war continue, and to ensure the expansion of Italy's empire even if it did not.

For the first six weeks of the conflict Mussolini hoped for a negotiated peace, preferably under Italian auspices. Ciano had dropped his proposal for a Polish Munich on 2 September, after London had refused to talk unless the swiftly advancing Germans withdrew. Once Polish resistance appeared broken, however, Mussolini approached the Germans through a variety of channels, urging the reestablishment of a rump Poland as a sop to the Western powers.[28] The Italian press chorused support for Hitler's triumphal 19 September speech at Danzig, which Ciano mistakenly construed as 'moderate."[29] Mussolini informed a closed assembly of Fascist leaders from Bologna on 23 September that with Poland "liquidated," the West no longer had a valid war aim. He commended support of peace initiatives, but also implied that Italy might ultimately intervene: "When and if I appear at the balcony and call together the entire Italian people to hear me, it will not be to put before them a survey of the situation, but to announce – as on 2 October 1935 [the attack on Ethiopia] or 9 May 1936 [the proclamation of the *Impero*] – decisions, I repeat, decisions, of historic importance."[30] From this point Mussolini's hopes for negotiation declined rapidly, despite a brief flurry of optimism in early October due to reports of French and British irresolution. The Italian press hailed Hitler's 6 October Reichstag speech which indicated the low limits of German forthcomingness over Poland, as evidence of a "will to peace." Mussolini himself briefly judged that "the war [was] over." But intransigent Chamberlain and Daladier replies induced him in mid-October to abandon any plan of Italian peace initiatives. Thereafter Mussolini ceased to regard compromise as a serious possibility.[31]

Interest in a negotiated peace was at least partly a consequence of Mussolini's desire to maintain the German alliance. If Italy could not fight, it could perhaps earn Berlin's gratitude by bringing the West to the negotiating table. The main threat to the Italo-German alliance was not Italy's non-belligerence or possible defection, but the danger that Berlin would find its new ally Moscow more useful than Rome. That threat became ever clearer in the days after 17 September, when Stalin moved to seize the share of Poland he had claimed in the 23–24 August Russo-German *Pakt*. On 27 September Ribbentrop flew to Moscow to formalize by border treaty the fourth partition of Poland. The step, and the "absolute silence" toward Rome that accompanied it, brought a brief though significant panic at Palazzo Venezia. Italy was still in the Axis, "but . . . things are changing," Alfieri informed his newspaper editors at a 29 September briefing. Mussolini himself, at a Council of Ministers the next morning, went as far in disassociating himself from the Germans as he was to go. He implied that Italy could choose either side once its armaments were complete. Then an unusually solicitous Ribbentrop telephoned Ciano to propose a meeting of the Italian and German leaders Ciano dissuaded Mussolini from going in person, but Ribbentrop's call reassured the dictator that Hitler was not about to desert him for Stalin.[32]

That same afternoon, Mussolini harangued the Fascist leaders of Genoa in another closed conclave at Palazzo Venezia, and warned them that Italy must exercise "merciless political realism"; "nations receive the destiny that they themselves have created." The logic of the situation implied war against the West: "Centuries-old hegemonies are tottering. We are prisoners in the Mediterranean – a large prison. Three entrances, but all well-guarded and in the hands of enemies or adversaries."[33] Ciano repaired to Berlin for a 1 October conference with Hitler and Ribbentrop, to whom he insisted that "Italy was not resigned to remaining neutral, should the war continue." He also faithfully repeated to Mussolini vehement Hitler assertions of the common destiny of Fascist Italy and National Socialist Germany. A deep-rooted and fully understandable jealousy of Hitler's successes, and faulty assessments by Italian intelligence, led Mussolini to greet the returning Ciano on 3 October with predictions of German defeat.[34] But the Axis, the vehicle of Mussolini's imperial ambitions, remained the basis of Italian policy. Soon he was to conceive an entirely different view of German prospects.

About the time Mussolini abandoned his expectations of a compromise peace, another project he had explored partly to prove his usefulness to Berlin came to grief. The possibility of creating a neutral Balkan bloc under Italian hegemony had attracted Mussolini's interest by 15 September. After Hitler's

9 September Danzig speech and the accompanying Italian press campaign failed to entice the West into negotiations, Mussolini gave Ciano permission to approach Berlin about the project. Ciano naturally favored it as a means of giving Italy "a much vaster political and diplomatic base," and of transforming nonbelligerence into neutrality.[35] The Germans welcomed the proposal gingerly, and made clear that their approval depended on whether the bloc promoted Balkan resistance to Western economic pressure, or Italian political aims. Ciano did not let the Germans deter him, and Mussolini found the plan important enough to describe it, in a report on 29 September to Victor Emmanuel III, as "under study."[36] Temporary chagrin over Ribbentrop's flight to Moscow may also have influenced Mussolini toward the plan; the bloc had potential as a weapon against Soviet Balkan aspirations, and as a means of preserving Italian ideological and political influence should the German alliance collapse.

Rome's interest proved fleeting. Ribbentrop's 30 September call, a sign of Berlin's continued devotion, coincided with advance word from the British to Ciano that they were about to formalize Turkey's connection with the West with an Anglo-Turkish defensive alliance. The Turks, Ciano had just learned, were attempting to bring into existence their own version of the Balkan bloc, one with a pro-Allied and anti-Italian twist. Ciano was therefore reticent about the project during his 1 October Berlin visit. Hitler mentioned and guardedly recommended the plan, but Ciano implied that Italy would not attempt to organize a bloc if the action would number Italy among the neutrals. Preservation of the Axis, and of Italy's freedom to intervene, came first.[37]

In the ensuing weeks, while Mussolini's expectations of a negotiated peace again rose momentarily before finally dissipating, the bloc project languished, despite a discreet prod from the Vatican and entreaties from the Rumanians, who desperately sought Italian protection against Soviets, Hungarians, and Germans.[38] Increasing Allied interest in Italian patronage of a Balkan bloc ultimately moved Mussolini to drop the plan for good. The final blow was a United Press report from London that Italy was moving away from Germany toward command of a neutral bloc. On 17 October, Ciano revealed to the German ambassador, Hans Georg von Mackensen, that Mussolini had considered the bloc project "long and thoroughly," and had rejected it. Such a tie "might one day become inconvenient." Italy's status was neither belligerent nor neutral, but "that of the most strenuous preparation, at which the Duce was working with every conceivable method in order to be ready at a given moment."[39] Rather than pursue a Balkan policy that would enhance his prestige, but inevitably drag Italy toward a position of neutrality approximating the "policy of the decisive weight" between two contending groups of powers, Mussolini reaffirmed his faithfulness to the German alliance and his decision to keep the decks clear for war against the Allies. From the Italian viewpoint the bloc was dead, although "dictatorial arrogance" and hope on Ciano's part that Mussolini would change his mind prevented Italy from taking a public position against a Balkan bloc until Ciano's 16 December foreign policy speech, of which more later.[40]

Balkan appetites. Besides fleeting promotion of a compromise peace, and continued support of the German connection and of Italy's eventual intervention if peace did not come, Mussolini stood by his intention of redrawing the Balkan map at Greek and Yugoslav expense. But Italy's current circumstances restricted his freedom of action. In the Greek case, the British guarantee of April 1939 placed the country off-limits unless Italy intervened in the wider war. Mussolini therefore welcomed a 6 September proposal by the Greek dictator, Ioannis Metaxas, for a joint reduction of troops on the Greco-Albanian border. To his minister in Athens, charged with the ensuing negotiations, Mussolini insisted for Greek consumption that "Greece is not on our path." Privately, he remarked that the country was "too poor to be coveted by us." Italy's objectives were "more in the direction of Yugoslavia," Ciano informed the Germans.[41]

Rome appears to have hoped initially that rapprochement with Greece would prove almost as rewarding as conquest. Metaxas's approach encouraged hope that Greece might be willing to move away from Britain, whose prestige, according to Ciano, was sinking. Ciano planned a nonaggression and consultative pact that would make Greece an Italian satellite – a solution similar to but more binding than the 1937 arrangement that had induced Mussolini to swallow temporarily his hostility to Yugoslavia. As Ciano told Ambassador von Mackensen on 23 September, an Italo-Greek agreement might keep the British out of the vital Greek harbors should Italy go to war.[42] In the short term, rapprochement would promote Italy's Balkan influence, and ease Mussolini's Yugoslav plans. Nor was the prospect of bringing Greece within the Italian orbit without economic attractions, despite Mussolini's disparaging remarks. As the Albanian enterprise had demonstrated, no country was "too poor to be coveted." Since early 1939, Mussolini was aware, the Italian state metal-mining concern had vied with Krupp for control of the Greek mines at Lokris, the only source of nickel – indispensable for armor plate – in southern Europe.[43] The Italo-Greek rapprochement facilitated these continuing negotiations and thus had an anti-German as well as an anti-Western thrust, as did Mussolini's reversal of policy that culminated in the attack on Greece a year later. Nor did rapprochement preclude force. While continuing to deny designs on Greece,[44] Mussolini and his son-in-law held the card of Albanian irredentism in reserve.

In the event, no durable rapprochement resulted. British distrust of close Greco-Italian ties and Metaxas's own well-founded lack of confidence in Italy led to a gradual loss of negotiating momentum after publication on 20 September of a joint communiqué announcing the border troop withdrawals.[45] The far-reaching political agreement Ciano and Mussolini had initially envisaged shrunk to a mere exchange of declarations reaffirming both governments' continued desire for good relations, in accordance with the principles f a recently expired Greco-Italian friendship treaty dating from 1928. Diplomacy had failed to lure Greece away from Britain, and for the moment Mussolini lost interest. If Italy joined Germany against the West, force would again come into its own.

As Ciano had remarked to the Germans, Italian aspirations of the moment above all involved Yugoslavia. That country had important mineral resources, it stood between Italy and Rumania's vital oilfields, it had no British guarantee, and its large discontented Croat minority had been Mussolini's hope since the 1920s. On 20 September Ciano noted in his diary that "our Croat friends are making themselves heard again." The entertaining possibility emerged of "a situation in which we might carry out the Croat action with the complicity – though perhaps with gritted teeth – of Germany, and without the hostility of France and England, which might appreciate this new barrier against the Teutonic advance." Mussolini agreed, and contributed 100,000 Swiss francs in order to intensify Italian propaganda.

Ciano's conception was a direct descendant of the Albanian operation, as he himself recognized.[46] As in April 1939, Ciano hoped to conduct a further Italian expansion as a covert anti-German move with the tacit connivance of the West. The conception betrayed a certain naïveté, for Ciano had been unable in April to convince even Chamberlain and Halifax that Italy had seized Albania to contain Germany. Nor could Rome have enlightened Western public opinion about the true motives behind the policy. Despite these weaknesses, the Ciano plan was one source of the Duce's conception, soon to emerge, of an Italian war parallel to the larger conflict. In May 1940 Mussolini's Mediterranean challenge to the British and French superseded the Yugoslav project, but the latter remained a major element in the Duce's strategy throughout the summer of 1940.

In the fall of 1939, Ciano maintained pressure on Belgrade by following an irreproachably Axis line in his conversations with the Yugoslav minister, to whom he declared Germany "invincible." Military preparations also began in late September. Pariani held a conference in Rome with Marshal Graziani, at that point commander of Army Group "E" facing Yugoslavia, and General Ambrosio of Second Army. Should "a particular Yugoslav politico-military situation extremely favorable to us" occur, the "Po" Army would dash for Zagreb by the shortest route. If, as seemed more probable, only full-scale attack would do, Italian forces would open a breach with a "devastating artillery preparation," and advance on a broad front. Pariani ordered the artillery deployed with the greatest secrecy by the end of the following April.[47]

By mid-October 1939 Serb-Croat conflicts in the Yugoslav Army appeared to confirm Ciano's faith in the efficacy of Swiss francs. Some disturbances apparently stemmed from Communist agitation, which Yugoslav authorities and Western observers uniformly ascribed to Italian machinations.[48] Evidence from the Italian side is lacking, but Communist-inspired unrest was clearly most convenient to Rome; it would provide vis-à-vis the

West a far more credible and publicly exploitable alibi for Italian interven
tion than the claim that Italy was heading off "the Teutonic advance." Nei
ther Mussolini nor Ciano had ever been squeamish about profiting from
Communist subversion of their enemies.[49] In any case, Ciano exhibited
unusual interest in the activities of the Yugoslav Communists, and implied
to the Hungarians that Italy would intervene in Yugoslavia should "Bolshe
vism" break out there, the Germans intervene, or the country collapse.[50]

With the new year of 1940, Mussolini's interest in the project rapidly
increased. By 13 January Ciano judged that the "Croat question" was
"maturing rapidly." His principal Croat contact, Baron Bombelles,[51] dis
closed that the situation was "precipitating" and proposed a meeting
between Ciano and the terrorist leader Pavelić, whom the Italians, despite
their 1937 pact with Belgrade, had continued to hold in reserve in Italy.
Ciano agreed, and conferred with Pavelić and Bombelles on 23 January.
Ciano proposed that the Croats seize Zagreb and proclaim independence.
Italian troops would then occupy Croatia and the Kossovo area of southern
Yugoslavia, where the inhabitants were primarily Albanian. The new Croat
state would be an Italian vassal, bound by personal union of the two crowns.
But Ciano insisted that "for evident reasons of an international character"
the moment was not yet ripe. It was above all important that action not
begin "prematurely."[52]

Ciano was fully aware of the difficulties of gaining tacit Western approval.
The British were favorable to an Italian role in keeping the peace in the
Balkans, but could hardly approve the dismemberment of Yugoslavia, with
whose ruler, Prince Paul, they maintained close and cordial ties. Ciano was
also not willing to disregard Western objections: "We would pay dearly for
it – and soon." But Mussolini was "unwilling to hear from that ear," as
Ciano put it. On the day Ciano met Pavelić, Mussolini announced to the
Council of Ministers that despite Italy's military weakness, "even today we
could undertake and sustain a . . . parallel war . . . ," an as yet nebulous
phrase that Bottai took to mean "a war included in and meshed with the
larger and more general one, but with its own, specifically Italian objec
tives." Graziani, who succeeded Pariani in November, confirmed the end of
April as target date for readiness against Yugoslavia, while the Navy contem
plated with relish a descent on the Dalmatian coast should Italy enter the
larger war. Cavagnari's planners judged that this action, at least, was "com
mensurate with [the] operational capabilities" of the armed forces. But the
evident reasons that made action too dangerous did not lose their force for
several months ahead, despite the Soviets' dearly bought success in their own
parallel war against Finland. In the first days of March, Ciano ordered his
Croat friends to subside for the moment.[53] Mussolini held Pavelić in reserve
and waited on events.

Change of the guard. Intervention, whether against an isolated and divided
Yugoslavia or against the West, required drastic improvements in the read

ness of the Army and Air Force. Mussolini immediately took steps to
strengthen the most vulnerable point in Italian defenses by reinforcing Libya
with 35,000 troops and a considerable amount of equipment.[54] He also
attempted to spur on the armament industry. In a series of early September
meetings with Guarneri, other economic ministers, the service chiefs, and
the head of General Commissariat for War Production, General Carlo Favagrossa, Mussolini reviewed government expenditures and the raw materials
requirements of the economy and the military programs. The "enormous
disequilibrium between needs and resources" was disheartening. Nevertheless, the armament industries received orders to increase production insofar
as shortages of raw materials, machine tools, and skilled labor would permit.
Aircraft production rose between August and October from roughly 130 to
212 per month. But the inefficiency of the military bureaucracies made it
impossible to gain any early idea of the full requirements of the services in
order to allot limited supplies on a rational basis. On 24 September, Favagrossa requested from the service ministries detailed descriptions of their
production programs, and lists of the materials required to complete Italy's
preparations, as well as a compilation of the armaments, ammunition, and
raw materials needed for a year of war. The Air Force ignored the request
until Mussolini personally telephoned Valle in late October. Not until 11
December could Favagrossa submit a more or less complete picture of armed
forces requirements.[55]

By that point, Mussolini had taken the most obvious and necessary step
toward combat-readiness. He had fired Pariani and Valle. Of the two, the
Army chief of staff had given the most spectacular and public display of
incompetence. In August and September, hundreds of thousands of reservists
had descended on the *Regio Esercito*'s depots and barracks to discover unspeakable food, severe shortages of bedding, clothing, boots, and weapons, and an
atmosphere of total administrative collapse. While Mussolini knew of the
Army's deficiencies in artillery, and was aware that its bureaucracy was ineffectual, unpunctual, and imprecise, Pariani's failure to produce even a functioning World War I fighting force seems to have come as a shock. He
shamefacedly argued at first that "one should not exaggerate." To the King,
who in his constitutional capacity as commander-in-chief was extremely well
informed on military affairs, Mussolini denied the disorganization was serious, while reporting he had sent Pariani off on a tour of "detailed inspection."[56] But it was unlikely that the general's journey contributed to Mussolini's enlightenment. Ciano noted incredulously on 15 September that
Pariani was "so optimistic and self-confident that one begins to ask oneself
if he isn't right after all."

Despite Pariani's self-assurance, the chorus of those demanding his head
grew steadily louder. The superannuated Marshal Emilio De Bono, who
sought both high Army command and the political prominence he felt due
a surviving "Quadrumvir" of the March on Rome (an honor he shared with
Balbo and Cesare Maria De Vecchi), went about denouncing Pariani as a

"traitor." Farinacci, in the same letter in which he drew Mussolini's atten
tion to the views of dissidents and "cretinoids," proclaimed the Army
"unanimous" lack of confidence in Pariani's leadership; "superficiality
improvisation, and facile irresponsibility" presided over the mobilization.[5]
The multiplication of command position through the binary division reor
ganization had produced "a sort of Mexican army, with an immense som
brero covering an emaciated body." Farinacci included in his tirade a numbe
of sensible recommendations, including the separation of the posts of under
secretary of war and Army chief of staff (both held by Pariani), review c
mobilization procedures, and an increase in junior officer recruitment. H
also urged solution of the delicate problem, "still unsolved, of the genuin
and effective coordination of the final preparation and employment of th
three armed forces."

By 18 September, Mussolini had learned from the commander of Italia
troops in Albania, General Guzzoni, that only ten of Italy's sixty-seven divi
sions were in any sense combat-ready. Privately, Mussolini gave vent to "bit
ter words."[58] But according to Ciano he still had illusions about the Ai
Force, illusions Valle had nourished with figures "of an absurd optimism.
The general had consistently claimed between 2,200 and 2,300 combat
ready aircraft. Actually, on 1 November 1939 the Air Force had in servic
with the units only 841 relatively modern bombers and fighters, of whicl
240 were down for maintenance. The remaining aircraft were either museun
pieces, or deathtraps like the Breda Ba.88 bomber, of which the Air Forc
acquired and subsequently scrapped over 100.[59]

As for the Army, Mussolini admitted on 24 September that Pariani ha
"a lot of lead in his wing." From Mussolini's private secretary, Osvald
Sebastiani, Ciano learned that Mussolini now wanted to sack Valle as well
but was as usual at a loss for a suitable replacement. Reasons of persona
prestige also restrained Mussolini from parting precipitately with thos
"whom he had kept close to himself, despite all their misdeeds," as De Bon
sarcastically put it in his diary.[60]

Criticism of Pariani naturally continued. On 7 October De Bono saw Mus
solini, who apparently allowed the marshal to vent his disgust without con
tradiction. A week later Farinacci sent Mussolini a critical study of the Ital
ian Army and its preparations in reply to a report of Pariani's that the Duc
had forwarded to Cremona. The memorandum, by Farinacci's own militar
expert, Emilio Canevari, roundly and convincingly denounced Pariani an
all his works. Italy's two armored divisions were "armored only in name."
The Army suffered from gross deficiencies of organization and personnel, an
had made appallingly inefficient use of its appropriations. Mussolini's appar
ent reaction was "a long tirade" on 16 October to Ciano, the definitive deci
sion to relieve Pariani and Valle, and recognition that he could not figh
before June or July 1940. Even at that point Italy would have only thre
months' worth of fuel and industrial raw materials. But Mussolini was stil
inclined to mistake form for substance. He railed at the "retrograde mental

ty" of the Army's senior officers – by which he meant not their ignorance of he principles of modern warfare, but their attachment to the dynasty.[61]

After his talk with Ciano, Mussolini made up the list for his most spec-acular "change of the guard." Ciano gloated that Mussolini was about to make "all of my friends ministers." Ciano's candidate for secretary of the Party was a much-decorated desperado, Ettore Muti, who would ostensibly "follow like a child."[62] Starace and Alfieri, useful lightning rods for public discontent, left Party and Ministry of Popular Culture to take lesser posts as chief of staff of the Fascist Militia and ambassador to the Vatican. Three figures replaced Pariani. Marshal Rodolfo Graziani, whose personal loyalty to Mussolini presumably served as guarantee against the "retrograde men-tality" of the officer corps, became Army chief of staff. Roatta, of Guadala-jara fame, left the post of military attaché in Berlin to become Graziani's deputy, charged with the technical side of the staff's operation; the marshal had passed most of his career in the colonies and had never attended the *Scuola di Guerra*. At the Ministry of War, General Ubaldo Soddu replaced Pariani as Mussolini's undersecretary. Soddu was a general "of the pacific appearance of a senior civil servant, mild in character, and rotund in face, body, and manner." He enjoyed an incongruous reputation as "an especially shrewd and capable officer" and a "first-class commander." His military phi-losophy was simple, and perhaps far from unique in the upper reaches of the armed forces: ". . . when you have a fine plate of *pasta* guaranteed for life, and a little music, you don't need anything more." Soddu was the perfect political general. To the British he seemed "genuinely anglophile," to the Germans *"sehr deutschfreundlich."* As Mussolini's closest military adviser and confidential agent, Soddu's influence grew throughout the period of nonbel-ligerence until, in the early days of the war, he sought to secure the succes-sion to Badoglio as chief of the general staff. Later he whiled away the eve-nings of his theater command in Albania, secured over the heads of numerous senior generals, by composing sound-track music for films while the Italian front collapsed under the Greek counteroffensive.[63]

For the Air Force, at the suggestion of both Ciano and Valle himself, Mussolini appointed General Francesco Pricolo, who had commanded the air units in northeastern Italy. Cavagnari remained at his post. The Navy had at least mobilized without organizational breakdown, and Ciano interceded for Cavagnari, with whom he had always maintained a cordial relationship. As Ciano remarked to the Germans, "if the other two" had been as competent, "many things would have taken a different course."[64] Badoglio emerged from the purge unscathed. Pariani's disgrace disposed of his principal rival within the high command. The partition of Pariani's prerogatives between Soddu, Graziani, and Roatta consolidated Badoglio's newly won ascendency. Finally, Pariani's fall eliminated the only high command figure who favored the offensive plans appropriate to Mussolini's ambitions.

On 18 November, the chiefs of staff and service undersecretaries met under Badoglio's presidency to get some idea of the real condition of the armed forces.[65] Mussolini had complained, Badoglio noted, that "things which should have been done, but had not been, had often been reported as done." For the record, Badoglio also insisted on deference to Mussolini's prerogatives in the political sphere: "whether we fight or not, whether we fight in the East or the West, is none of our business." But he also made clear that he himself would tolerate no more wide-ranging Pariani-style war planning against Egypt: "To study operations not corresponding to reality is to tire the brain and waste time." Badoglio's unspoken assumption was that the mere existence of war plans would excite Mussolini, and he did his best in the ensuing months to prevent Italy from having any.

In the remainder of the long meeting, Badoglio sought improved inter-service coordination by establishing his own prerogatives over the armed forces in the colonies, and by ending the acrimonious Navy–Air Force struggle over who should pay for the torpedo bombers Italy desperately needed. He also lamented the antediluvian nature of the antiaircraft artillery, a consequence of the Air Force's Douhet-inspired skepticism about static defenses. Asked about fuel, ammunition, and food stocks in the colonies, the services revealed that they had not been computing the time their supplies would last by uniform criteria. In any case, neither Libya, nor the Dodecanese, nor East Africa had more than six months' worth. The Army, worst provided for of the services, had a mere month of food and two months of fuel and ammunition in Libya, and perhaps three months of supplies of all types in East Africa. Badoglio established a year's self-sufficiency as the goal for the overseas territories. It was obvious to all concerned that this objective was unreachable by the spring of 1940.

While the service chiefs attempted to straighten out the tangled heritage their own and their former colleagues' sins of omission and commission had left, Mussolini continued his attack on "defeatism." Alfieri's replacement as minister for popular culture, Alessandro Pavolini, informed his editors on 14 November that the Italian press was not "the press of a neutral country, but the press of a country whose fundamental interests remain at stake."[66] The next day, Mussolini proclaimed to a Rome university student demonstration under his Palazzo Venezia window that "the peace of Fascist Italy is not a peace of weakness [una pace imbelle]; it is an armed peace." Cries of "Tunis!" and "Corsica!" inspired a grave nod of his head, and provoked consternation at the French Embassy.[67]

Mussolini also took in hand the industrial magnates and the bureaucracy in a speech to one of the regime's many decorative institutions, the Supreme Autarchy Commission, on 18 November, fourth anniversary of the League of Nations' sanctions. He reveled in Italy's "singular good fortune" in again, after twenty years, facing a major war:

Now above all, everyone, even the most obtuse, must recognize that the distinction between a war economy and a peacetime economy is utterly absurd. . . . [T]oday the tempo of the march must be accelerated beyond the limits of the possible. No

58

energy must be wasted, all wills must be coordinated, all sacrifices undertaken, all surviving laggards and skeptics, eliminated.[68]

War was inevitable, and the Italian people were going to have to get used to the idea.

2. Uneasy axis

The watch on the Brenner. While planning the "change of the guard" in late October 1939 Mussolini conceived a series of measures designed to clarify Italy's position, both for home consumption and for the benefit of his ally. He proposed to write to Hitler, emphasizing that Italy represented a "reserve" of economic and moral support, and holding out the prospect that it might subsequently play a military role as well. He also planned to summon the Grand Council of Fascism and explain to his associates exactly why Italy had taken up "nonbelligerence." Ciano would then address the same embarrassing topic before the Fascist Chamber. Mussolini himself would not make a major public speech until he could announce the "decisions of historic importance" promised in September. Ciano was delighted; he planned a speech that would "dig very deep" and cause "the definitive break" with Germany.[69]

Simultaneously, the two governments indeed faced a problem that, like the apparent threat in late September of a formal Russo-German alliance, might have caused that break: the Alto Adige–South Tyrol question. Mussolini not unnaturally regarded this sorest point in Italo-German relations as the supreme test of his ally's frontier pledge of 1938, and of German promises to respect Italy's Balkan and Mediterranean sphere. Friction over South Tyrol in the late fall of 1939, and suggestions that Hitler's underlings aspired to descend to the Adriatic and beyond, produced paroxysms at Palazzo Venezia and caused Mussolini to speak briefly of breaking with Germany.

One of the implicit conditions under which Mussolini had concluded the Pact of Steel that spring had been German implementation of suggestions Hitler had several times made for the "return to the *Reich*" of the German-speaking population of South Tyrol (thus backing Hitler's Brenner pledge with deeds). In late June 1939 Ambassador Attolico and Heinrich Himmler had reached a general understanding on population transfer. But war supervened before further negotiations produced a definitive written agreement.[70]

The Germans had much else to worry about – Himmler was busy liquidating the Polish intelligentsia – and took a relatively relaxed view. *Ortsgruppenleiter* Kaufmann of the Bolzano National Socialist organization, whom Hitler had ordered confined to a concentration camp in June for unauthorized pan-German agitation, quietly reemerged in early September. Ambassador Karl Clodius, the foreign office's flying economic negotiator, showed a singular lack of urgency when the Italians pressed him during his visit to Rome in mid-September. He succeeded in giving the impression that Germany hoped to postpone action until war's end. Repeated Italian prodding led to resumed negotiations in early October. Subsequently only a virtual ultimatum from Mussolini and an Italian undertaking to reimburse the departing *Volksdeutsche* for their property at an absurdly favorable exchange rate induced the Germans to sign the implementation agreements on 21 October.[71]

Difficulties had only begun. The populations concerned had until 31 December 1939 to choose between Italy and Germany. From the Italian point of view this was too long, especially in comparison with the alacrity with which Himmler was currently arranging the massive exodus of Baltic ethnic Germans following the Molotov–Ribbentrop agreements of 28 September. Italian pressure failed to move the Germans to admit the validity of such comparisons.[72] The National Socialist Party organ, *Völkischer Beobachter,* noted on 22 October that the *Reich* was summoning home all ethnic Germans lest their continued presence on foreign soil cause "political tensions with other powers" – but smugly added that "no open questions of any sort" existed between Germany and its ally Italy.

These honeyed words did not inhibit the National Socialist organizations on the spot from turning the option process into a sort of plebiscite for Germany, complete with covert suggestions that the South Tyrol itself, and not merely its German-speaking population, would ultimately "return to the Reich." By 9 November, these efforts had begun to provoke anti-German fulminations from Mussolini. Ciano noted wistfully in his diary that "if the British and French were on the ball [*in gamba*], it would be the right moment to produce a tremendous incident."[73] By 21 November, Mussolini had concluded that the matter might eventually lead to war with the Reich. He reinforced police, *Carabinieri,* and Army covering force, and conveyed his displeasure to his allies through the undersecretary of the interior, Buffarini Guidi, who impressed Himmler's representative in Rome with the "extraordinarily threatening" nature of the situation. Simultaneously, Mussolini expressed fear of the rumored German fall offensive in the West, which would render his position of enforced bystander intolerably humiliating. To parry the threat, he discreetly ordered the Italian consul in Prague to advise dissident Czechs to increase their nuisance value by declaring themselves Communists. Mussolini hoped thereby to exacerbate the already tense situation in Bohemia-Moravia, embroil the Germans with their Russian friends, and inhibit Hitler from acting against France.[74]

Mussolini's indignation with his allies rose to new heights on 26 November, when he learned that an important National Socialist official, the *Reichsstatthalter* of Saxony, had publicly referred to "friends who betray us" – a remark his audience, which included the Italian consul-general at Dresden, had taken as a reference to Italy's abstention from war. Ciano protested energetically to Mackensen, and judged that "the German star [was] beginning to pale" even in the Duce's mind.[75]

Mussolini was indeed alarmed over the situation in South Tyrol, and he took action. On 24 November, he summoned to Rome the commander of the Bolzano Army Corps, presumably for consultation on the state of the border defenses. In early December, Mussolini met with Soddu and General Edoardo Monti, the head of the skeleton Army command entrusted with contingency planning against Switzerland. On 15 December, Monti took over responsibility for all fortification work on the Italo-German frontier. Construction would go forward through the winter "to the extreme limits of our capabilities." This time the Duce intended to be sure of his generals. He informed Soddu that "by the *end of May* 1940, the *third* [i.e. rearmost] *defensive line* on the northern and northeastern frontier must be ready. At that time a committee of generals must assure me *in writing* that the line is impregnable [*ermetica*] in the most absolute sense of the term." Work went forward on the French and Yugoslav borders as well, but Mussolini's emphasis on the utmost speed on the northern frontier and the special appropriations of February 1940 (1,000,000,000 lire for the German border, 600 million for the French, and 300 million for the Yugoslav) made his priorities clear.[76]

Fortification of the northern border was not unprecedented. Construction had intensified after the Anschluss. Mussolini had announced to the Council of Ministers in April 1939 that he intended to "close the doors of the house, . . . even to the north." The day of his dismissal, Pariani had issued a directive proclaiming that the Tarvisio area (the other major pass into Italy from Austria, to the east of the Brenner) "must become the most formidable sector of the Italian defense."[77] But the new urgency was the direct consequence of the South Tyrol situation. In broader terms, it was an attempt by Mussolini to preserve Italian independence and bargaining power by rendering the country impervious to direct German threat, not preparation for an Italian volte-face or a sign of lack of enthusiasm for entry into the war at Germany's side.[78] That the money and steel squandered on the alpine passes would have yielded more – even for defense – in bringing the "Po" Army up to standard did not occur to Mussolini or his generals. Both believed that modern weapons made the offensive prohibitively costly. Badoglio considered the Maginot Line the last word in warfare. The attaché in Paris, General Sebastiano Visconti Prasca, whose military handiwork will be of interest later in another connection entirely, judged the French army "the best in the world."[79]

Notwithstanding the indiscretion of the *Reichsstatthalter* of Saxony and the ominous South Tyrol developments, which might foreshadow a weakening of the German commitment to resettle the *Volksdeutsche,* or even of Hitler's Brenner pledge, Mussolini stood by Germany. On 28 November, he approved without alteration the draft of Ciano's forthcoming Chamber speech, which had an anti-German thrust Ciano considered "insidious in the extreme." But Mussolini soon afterward disclosed to Mackensen the intention, earlier confided to Ciano, of writing to Hitler a letter that would "content" the Führer by promising Italian intervention in 1942 should the war continue. Mussolini also insisted on including in a draft declaration for the Grand Council of Fascism a passage affirming the continuing vitality of the Pact of Steel. In a conversation on 6 December with the visiting chief of the German Labor Front, Robert Ley, Mussolini once more proposed to enter the war as soon as possible. He bemoaned the slow pace of Italian armament production and, symptomatically, the political resistance of the monarchy. Mussolini was "ashamed" that he and Italy could not match the German "tempo."[80]

The Grand Council met on the night of 7 December 1939. Ciano spoke to justify Italy's refusal to enter the war, and read passages from documents his staff had selected to put the best light on Italian abstention.[81] Mussolini then took the floor. Formally, at least, he approved Ciano's line. A victory by either of the "two lions" locked in struggle would be a disaster for Italy. The best outcome was ". . . that the two lions tear each other to pieces, until they leave their tails on the ground – and we, possibly, can go and scoop them up." But Bottai, who noted down these remarks, also judged that Mussolini's acceptance of Ciano's policy was "only an intellectual acceptance." The Duce's heart was still full of "interventionist palpitations." Farinacci too spoke at the meeting, and urged war at Germany's side. On 13 December, Mussolini commanded Graziani to increase the Army to a million trained men by the next summer; a call-up began in February 1940 and by May brought the service as close to war strength as its depleted materiel stocks would permit. Mussolini still coveted Tunis and Corsica, and found flattering an English newspaper remark that Italy might yet fight on Germany's side "for reasons of honor." He added to Ciano's draft Chamber speech a confirmation that the Pact of Steel was still in effect, thus blocking Ciano's attempt to create a new crisis in Italo-German relations.[82]

The speech, delivered on 16 December, had "great success," although not everyone immediately caught "all the subtle anti-German venom with which it was impregnated." The Germans kept their resentment within bounds, and took steps to smooth over the South Tyrol question. Himmler came south and left a two-hour audience with Mussolini on 20 December with "radiant face." Ciano wondered despairingly: "What has Mussolini promised him?"[83]

But the last and most serious blow to Mussolini's confidence in Germany's word was still to come. A Czech lawyer passed to the Italians remarks that the Sudeten German vice-mayor of Prague, Josef Pfitzner, had purportedly made to a Party gathering. According to the stenographic record the Czech supplied, Pfitzner had declared that "not a single Alpine peak should remain in Italian hands." Germany should roll into the Po Valley, seize Trieste, and dominate the Balkans and eastern Mediterranean. The Pfitzner document brought Mussolini's mistrust and fear of his ally to a head. He ordered a copy of the speech with an appropriate anonymous letter sent to the Russian Embassy in Paris; Pfitzner had also allegedly called for the destruction of the

Soviet Union.[84] Ciano presented the German ambassador with a copy as well, and emphasized Mussolini's extreme interest. This sort of incident, Ciano informed a shaken Mackensen, left him and Mussolini "speechless," even though they had no doubt of Hitler's faithfulness to his pledged word. A "terrific flap" in Berlin followed. Ribbentrop called Mackensen home to consult, and Weizsäcker wired Prague to check the story.[85]

Mackensen's assurances that no German could possibly have given such a speech in view of the Führer's frontier pledge had little effect on Mussolini, who for the first and only time in this period, "openly hope[d]" for German defeat. Further, he took action perhaps designed to bring about this defeat, or at least, as with his earlier advice to the Czechs, to delay German victory until Italy was ready for war. On 26 December, Mussolini ordered Ciano to pass to the Dutch and Belgian ambassadors in Rome news from the Italian military attaché in Berlin that the German offensive in the West was imminent and would include a lightning invasion of the Low Countries.[86] This uncomradely step may have contributed to the Belgian and Dutch defense measures that, along with the apparent leakage in early January of the German operational plan and the persistently unsuitable weather, induced Hitler to postpone action until much later. The only permanent result of Mussolini's intrigue was to destroy what little trust in Ciano the Germans had retained after his obstructionism in August. German intelligence naturally read the diplomatic ciphers of most of the Reich's small neighbors. The report of the Belgian ambassador in Rome of his conversation with Ciano aroused extreme interest at the Führer's headquarters – although the Italians never learned that their allies had caught them in the act.[87]

"Death to Russia". While the South Tyrol simmered, Ciano did his best within certain limits to undermine the Italo-German alliance. The development of a serious crisis between Italy and the other nonbelligerent "ally" of Germany, the Soviet Union, immeasurably aided him in his task. Mussolini himself took a relatively pragmatic view of relations with the "Bolsheviks." Fascist Italy had been one of the first major European powers to recognize the Soviet regime – a shrewd blow of the Duce's at the Italian Communist Party. In 1933 Mussolini had signed a friendship and nonaggression treaty with Russia. Baku crude had fueled the Italian fleet during the conquest of Ethiopia. Despite the supposedly ideological conflict in Spain, Mussolini had by the spring of 1939 become an eager supporter of Russo-German rapprochement, which he viewed as a convenient means of preventing alliance between Russia and the West. Nor, as Mussolini had told Bottai in early September, was the internal political and ideological contrast between Fascist and Bolshevik systems so acute as formerly. Both were equally distant from the "demo-plutocratic capitalism of the western powers." In mid-October, Mussolini even contemplated a press campaign "to explain to the Italians that Bolshevism [was] dead and [had] given way to a sort of slavic

63

Fascism," to the horror of Ciano, who ultimately dissuaded his father-in-law.[88]

For Ciano, hostility to the Soviets during the period of nonbelligerence was second nature, the logical corollary of his aversion to the Germans. He sought to influence Mussolini indirectly against his ally by deliberately creating and encouraging tension with the Russians. The Soviets soon provided the foreign minister with opportunities. From September onwards they failed to deliver bunker oil the Italian Navy had contracted for, probably because German requirements took priority. Far worse, a Comintern pronouncement to the toiling masses upon the anniversary of the Bolshevik revolution gratuitously remarked (in the course of a complacent survey of the international situation since the Russo-German *Pakt*) that "the Italian bourgeoisie only awaits the appropriate moment in order to fling itself upon the vanquished and gobble up a share of the booty." Mussolini was predictably irate, and with Ciano's encouragement unleashed in reply the regime's star journalist, the unspeakable Virginio Gayda.[89]

After this preliminary skirmish, the opening of the Soviet "parallel war" against Finland on 30 November provided Ciano with an unprecedented opportunity. The news created uproar within Italy. Apparently spontaneous student demonstrations of support for Finland and hostility to Russia took place for over a week.[90] Ciano noted delightedly that "people cry 'death to Russia' and think 'death to Germany.' " Mussolini himself denounced the greed of the Russian "crooks" to Mackensen, and untruthfully asserted that Bolshevism remained Italy's "enemy number one." This vehemence was merely a tactical ploy, an accompaniment to the real message: Mussolini would not tolerate Stalin replacing him in Hitler's affections. Within a week of his outburst to Mackensen, Mussolini was proposing to add to the text of Ciano's forthcoming speech a reference to the Soviets "inspired, if not by cordiality, at least by correctness," presumably in reply to the Soviet recognition of the conquest of Ethiopia and the occupation of Albania contained in the credentials of the newly appointed Soviet ambassador. Only Gorelkin's protests against the Italian student demonstrations and his subsequent abrupt recall to Moscow kept the Duce firmly on an anti-Soviet course.[91]

In the end, Ciano received license to include several indirect barbs at the Russians in his speech. He made the most of the Soviet ambassador's recall, and withdrew his own ambassador from Moscow. Ciano also once more attempted to exacerbate German-Japanese relations. He stressed to Tokyo Italy's "clear anti-Bolshevik orientation," he cut across German efforts to secure Russo-Japanese reconciliation, and he even suggested Japanese rapprochement with the United States. But the Japanese put an end to Ciano's intrigue by disclosing his approaches to the Germans, who wisely declined to make a major issue of the matter.[92]

While attacking the Russo-German connection diplomatically, Ciano did not neglect the possibilities for action within Italy. He furthered negotiations between Quirinal and Vatican for a royal visit to the Pope and an unprecedented return visit by the pontiff. The visits, in late December, were a public reminder of the distinction between Italy and Germany in relations between Church and state, and a demonstration of solidarity between papacy and monarchy – Mussolini's twin bêtes noires – in opposition to war.[93] The editor of the *Telegrafo,* the Livorno newspaper of the Ciano family, Giovanni Ansaldo, celebrated the close relationship of Catholicism ("its Apostles followed the tracks of the Roman legions") and the imperial idea, and emphasized the convergence between Italian and papal policies in "deploring" the present war. Anti-German and monarcho-Fascist elements such as Balbo, Luigi Federzoni, and the ferociously mustachioed Count Cesare Maria de Vecchi di Val Cismon, governor of the Dodecanese and quadrumvir of the Fascist revolution, made a pilgrimage to the "knees of the Holy Father" (as Farinacci sarcastically put it in a letter to Mussolini). Ciano naturally denied to the Germans that the conversation between King and Pope had any political significance.[94]

Besides intrigue in Tokyo and covert encouragement to anti-German sentiment at home, Ciano tried to commit Italy to direct action. When Berlin held up a shipment of FIAT fighter aircraft sold to the Finns and dispatched northward over the Brenner, Ciano insisted, unsuccessfully, that the Germans relent. Meanwhile, Russian protests against the shipment caused Berlin acute embarrassment.[95] In early January 1940, Ciano even secured Mussolini's permission to send military experts under Ciano's personal pilot to Finland. But Ciano and Mussolini were unwilling to risk ground volunteers, for, despite Finnish successes, the Italians did not expect that small nation to hold out indefinitely. A Russian victory would make repatriation of Italian troops difficult.[96] Above all, the Germans would take an extremely dim view of such adventures. Intervention in such a preeminently German sphere might later provide a justification for German encroachments on Italy's own *Lebensraum.*

In southeastern Europe, where Italian interests were much greater than in the Baltic, Ciano – and Mussolini as well – undertook a potentially more serious commitment. The Rumanians, isolated and desperate after the failure of the neutral bloc, turned once more to Italy. In late December, King Carol sent the former Rumanian foreign minister, Mihai Antonescu, to Rome to seek advice and aid. In their first interview on 23 December, Ciano avoided promises, but he was willing to discourage Hungarian designs on Transylvania should the Soviets attack Bessarabia.[97] The next day, probably not entirely coincidentally, the French ambassador, André François-Poncet, broached to Ciano on a personal basis the possibility of Allied intervention should Germany and Russia attack Hungary and Rumania. The French approach was not the result of a sudden solicitude for small nations, even ones that, like Rumania, the Allies had guaranteed in April. Rather, Daladier and his associates hoped to shift the principal focus of the war from Rhine and Meuse to the Danube, or at the very least to open a second front in the place of the hapless Poles, who had proved so much less valuable as an

Eastern ally than had the Russians in 1914. The advisability of informing the Italians of Allied Balkan plans had led to long and inconclusive debate between Paris and London. As Loraine had pointed out to Halifax in mid-December, it would be "risky" to tell Ciano of Allied preparations, but even more risky to go ahead with preparations and allow the Italians to discover them on their own. François-Poncet's démarche had the merit of cutting the Gordian knot.[98]

François-Poncet emphasized that the Allies desired to act in the Balkans "with the agreement, if not with the participation, of Italy." Ciano was confident that neither Germans nor Russians would act soon; the latter were now thoroughly bogged down in Finland. But he predicted emphatically, if overoptimistically, that Italy would intervene alongside the West if Russia attacked Bessarabia. Ciano also pointed out the dangers of "arousing susceptibilities and suspicions" in Mussolini, but implied that "the natural tendency was in the right direction."[99] Ciano indeed informed Mussolini of the French approach, and the Duce, Ciano later assured François-Poncet, had appreciated "the desire of the French Government to consult him and inform him of Allied intentions." He had not "raised any particular objection."[100] At that moment Mussolini was at the height of his chagrin over Pfitzner's pan-German effusions, and of his alarm over the impending German offensive in the West. Stalin's fulsome Christmas message to Ribbentrop celebrating Russo-German friendship, "cemented by blood" in Poland, and rumors that the Russian dictator had requested German military experts to help the floundering Red Army in Finland probably did not strengthen Mussolini's faith in his German allies.[101] The first result of all these converging pressures, which came to a head on 26 December, was Mussolini's order to Ciano to warn the Dutch and Belgians. Simultaneously, Mussolini agreed to provide Rumania with military aid "along the lines of that given Franco" in years past, should the Russians attack. Ciano informed Antonescu, and pressed the Hungarians to moderate in the common interest their cravings for Transylvania. Significantly, Mussolini also experienced a sudden renewal of appetite for Yugoslavia; that state's location between Italy and Rumania perhaps destined it to be his reward for helping maintain the latter as a "bulwark of Mediterranean civilization against Bolshevism."[102]

But Mussolini presumably did not take the likelihood of Russian action all that seriously, for Soviet difficulties in the Finnish woods suggested that quiet would prevail in the southeast for some time. In any case, Italian help was conditional upon effective Rumanian resistance – and no one expected Rumania to do more than "make a great fuss" when the Russians ultimately presented their demands.[103] Finally, if it did come to fighting, Mussolini was well aware that German dependence on Rumanian oil was such that his allies could not stand aside in a full-scale Russo-Rumanian war. Italian intervention on the Danube might thus still take place within the Axis. Mussolini's willingness to help the Rumanians was above all a blow, in the manner of Italian aid for Finland, against closer German-Soviet relations. It was not a sign of Mussolinian drift into the Allied camp, despite Ciano's cautious pressure and the fantastic hint by Bastianini to the British on 8 January 1940 that "if Britain would take Germany's place in the Anti-Comintern Pact, Mussolini (who was becoming increasingly anti-German) was ready to play and that Franco was too." Mussolini summed up his policy in a memorandum for Ciano on 6 January: Italy would not denounce the alliance unless Germany "committed other irreparable errors." Italian entry into the war on the Allied side was "excluded," for it would mean "the confirmation of the [Allied] military and colonial hegemony at Italy's expense."[104] Mussolini was more determined than ever to fight the West for Mediterranean supremacy.

Epistle to the Führer. Mussolini's wrath at his ally did not last. By the last day of 1939 he was once more "Germanophile," and had revived his earlier intention of writing to Hitler, to whom he now proposed to offer advice and assurances that Italy's preparations for war continued. In the ensuing days, he drafted what he himself described as a "deplorably long" letter, which he hoped would substitute for face-to-face talk with the Führer.[105]

Mussolini took upon himself full responsibility for Ciano's Chamber speech "from first word to last," despite the unfavorable reception it had received in "certain German circles." Mussolini then turned to the unfavorable repercussions of the Russo-German pact in Spain, to Italy's relations with the Western Allies ("correct but cold"), to Finland ("Fascist Italy looks with favor upon this small but valorous nation"), and to the Polish question. Unless Hitler was "irrevocably committed to fighting this war to the bitter end," the Duce commended to his ally the establishment of "a modest, disarmed, exclusively Polish Poland – freed from the Jews, for whom your plan of concentrating them all in a large ghetto at Lublin meets with my full approval."[106] A rump Poland would utterly deflate Allied propaganda, "liquidate" the Polish government-in-exile, and open the way for negotiations. Mussolini continued expressing faith that:

Great Britain and France will never succeed in making your Germany, aided by Italy, capitulate, but neither is it certain that you will succeed in bringing the French and British to their knees, or even in dividing them. The United States would not permit a total defeat of the democracies. Empires collapse through internal instability, while external shocks can consolidate them. . . . Is it worth it . . . to risk everything – including the regime – and sacrifice the flower of German manhood in order [merely] to hasten the descent of a fruit that must inevitably fall, and that we, who represent the new forces of Europe, will harvest? The great democracies carry in themselves the causes of their own downfall.

After this prophecy, Mussolini turned to the Russian question. He conceded the temporary utility of the *Pakt,* and recalled his own early dealings with the Soviets, but warned his ally in no uncertain terms:

I, who was born a revolutionary and have not changed my ideas, tell you that you cannot permanently sacrifice the principles of your Revolution to the tactical demands of a particular political situation. I feel that you cannot simply abandon the antisemitic and anti-Bolshevist banner which you have flown in the wind for twenty years and for which so many of your comrades have died. You cannot foreswear your gospel, in which the German people has blindly believed. I have the inescapable duty of adding that a further step in your relations with Moscow would have catastrophic repercussions in Italy, where anti-Bolshevist unanimity, especially among the Fascist masses, is absolute, *granitico,* indivisible.

Germany's *Lebensraum,* Mussolini insisted, was in Russia, with its Slav and Asiatic masses under the sway of the Jews. Only after Germany and Italy had "demolished Bolshevism" would the turn of the already moribund democracies come. His warning against closer ties to Stalin delivered, Mussolini concluded:

I am accelerating the rhythm of military preparation. Italy cannot and does not wish to commit itself to a long war; its intervention must take place at the most profitable [*redditizio*] and decisive moment. . . .
In the present, Fascist Italy intends to be your reserve:
From a politico-diplomatic point of view, in the event you desire to reach a politico-diplomatic solution.
From an economic point of view, supporting you as much as possible in everything that can increase your resistance to the blockade.
From a military point of view, when Italy's help will be a relief rather than a burden.

The letter has provoked a variety of interpretations. At the time, Ciano thought it "an excellent document, full of wisdom and moderation."[107] Attolico, who delivered the letter, was not hopeful that it would produce significant changes in German policy. The Führer himself complained privately that Mussolini did not "believe in my victory," and left it unanswered for two months. Historians have tended to regard the document as the quintessential expression of a serious crisis in Italo-German relations, and have frequently taken its argumentation at face value as a genuine attempt of Mussolini's to press Hitler toward compromise peace.[108]

Actually, as Gianluca André has pointed out, the arguments Mussolini employed and the policies he advocated were hardly very Mussolinian.[109] Though the Duce continued to doubt Allied resolve, he was well aware that negotiations were not currently feasible. The day before Mussolini drafted his letter, Ciano had informed the Italian minister at the Hague that the Duce would not receive a high-level Dutch peace mission because "it was not in His intentions to take peace initiatives, given the present situation." Nor, unlike his son-in-law, did Mussolini believe that the United States (which he despised even more than his fellow dictator did), and underestimated (which Hitler on the whole did not), would intervene if the Western Allies were to falter.[110] Finally, Mussolini did not feel in the least the anti-Bolshevist fervor his remarks about the Soviet Union exuded.

The letter's real purposes were two. First, Mussolini wanted desperately to prevent Hitler from taking the offensive before Italy could participate. "Toward summer," he announced to Ciano in a memorandum written the day of the letter's dispatch, "Italy will have, under the personal command of the Duce, an array of ground and air forces capable of exerting a decisive influence on the situation."[111] Until then, Mussolini hoped Hitler would hesitate before the sacrifice of "the flower of German manhood," and shrink from the dangers to his regime a setback would entail. The second purpose of the letter was of course to safeguard Italy's position as Germany's ally, a position Mussolini considered threatened ever since Russo-German "friendship" had been "cemented by blood" in Poland that September. Hence the *Lebensraum* rhetoric, which was scarcely designed to incite Hitler to attack the Soviet Union. Italy's aspirations were after all directed against the Western powers – Tunis and Corsica, Gibraltar and Suez – not the rich black soil of the Ukraine.

The Germans were far from delighted. Hitler reserved reply until he could "get a clear view of the general situation." Ribbentrop and Göring dissected the letter paragraph by paragraph in conversations with Attolico and his staff, and reaffirmed at every conceivable opportunity their faith and that of the Führer in the crushing success of the coming offensive. Ribbentrop also assured Attolico categorically that Germany had "only *one* alliance: namely that with Italy," and expressed astonishment at Mussolini's sudden sounding of such a "sharp anti-Bolshevik note."[112]

Mussolini's eloquence had not fooled the Germans, though they obviously understood his warning against closer relations with the Soviets. Mussolini also undercut his message by indirectly approaching Mackensen's staff in the ensuing days with a plea for more intense German propaganda activities in Italy to counter Allied harping upon the Russo-German connection. The unofficial message suggested to Mackensen that Mussolini merely feared that too evident Nazi–Soviet collusion – or Soviet action in Bessarabia – would make the task of bringing Italy into the war at Germany's side more difficult. Nor, finally, did Mussolini's letter deflect Hitler from attacking the West, despite the postponement that weather and the compromise of the operational plan soon required. German confidence in Mussolini's fidelity and in his desire to enter the war – "even shortly" – was on the rise.[113]

3. Toward commitment

Coal and iron. January 1940, the month of Mussolini's letter, was also the month the economic pressures of the belligerents upon Italy began to aid him in convincing his subordinates and Italian opinion of the necessity of war. Ciano and the dictator's economic advisers had attempted to make palatable to Mussolini a period of "fat neutrality," in which Italy would fill the gaps in its currency reserves, raw materials, and armaments.[114] The premises for such a policy proved entirely lacking. At Suez and Gibraltar the Allies controlled the 80 percent of Italy's raw material and foodstuff imports normally transported by sea. They commanded the principal sources of raw materials – oil, rubber, copper, tin – without which Italian war potential would languish. They also provided roughly a fifth of Italy's monthly requirement of one million metric tons of imported coal; Poland provided another 15 percent. The remainder of Italian coal imports came from Germany, through a barter arrangement that made it unnecessary for the Italians to pay in hard currency they did not have.[115] But even Italy's supply of German coal faced Allied interference. Two-thirds of it came by sea from Bremen, and, after the outbreak of war, from neutral Rotterdam. Only the roughly 250,000 tons a month that rolled through Switzerland, the Brenner, and Tarvisio were beyond Allied reach.

These conditions condemned Italy "to dance as long as possible like an acrobat, keeping its balance toward both sides," as one of Mussolini's ministers put it to the Germans.[116] The act required toleration by both Germans and Allies, toleration forthcoming in the political field, but ultimately absent in the economic one. As Germany's nonbelligerent ally, Italy could not in the end count upon Allied indulgence. The progressive tightening of the maritime blockade raised issues of prestige dear to Mussolini's heart. Above all, it threatened to restrict Italy to extremely low levels of essential imports, and might eventually strangle it economically even if it remained out of the war. As a trading partner of the Allies Italy faced German displeasure, potentially devastating retaliation if it acceded too enthusiastically to Allied economic demands, and the indiscriminate and uncontrollable effects of Germany's "siege" of the British Isles by mine, aircraft, and U-boat. Ultimately, these pressures threatened to render vain even the most skillful balancing act, and compel Italy to choose between the belligerents in the economic sphere as it had long since chosen in the political one.

The force that ultimately precipitated that choice was the British blockade, proven in World War I and recently rechristened with the grandiose name of "economic warfare." The name summed up equally grandiose expectations. The Allies had neither the power nor the intention of attacking Germany on land in the foreseeable future, and therefore tended to place in "economic warfare" a share of their hopes for victory wholly disproportionate to the method's effectiveness in 1939–40.[117] German seaborne imports fell under the Allied ban immediately upon declaration of war. German exports were next to go, in November, in reprisal for indiscriminate German use of magnetic mines. Upon the European neutrals, all of which traded with Germany to some extent, descended the heavy mesh of the net developed in the previous war – Royal Navy "contraband control" at sea, blacklists of neutral firms and individuals "trading with the enemy," clearance certificates for goods bound for neutral ports ("navicerts"), and "war trade agreements" to restrict to prewar levels neutral imports of commodities in which the enemy was deficient and secure economic leverage by purchasing at guaranteed prices large quantities of the neutrals' staple products.

Germany hoped to escape the net by importing vast quantities of strategic raw materials from the Soviets, by intensifying exploitation of its own economic *Grossraum* in the Balkans, and by evading contraband control with the connivance of the neutrals – particularly its nonbelligerent ally, Italy. The Germans also hoped to restrict their own exports of vital materials and equipment to their ally, and perhaps take over what remained of Italy's Balkan markets. As a neutral, Italy could presumably redirect that branch of its trade onto the world market from which the Allies now excluded Germany.[118]

Initially, Italian problems were relatively manageable. Despite the heavy wartime traffic on the German railways and the disruption of the Polish Silesian coalfields, adequate if diminished coal supplies reached Italy until November.[119] The Allies, with the French in the lead as befitted holders of hard currency, attempted to harness Italian industry to their own purposes with tempting contract offers for the production of war materiel and strategic goods. The Germans sought to use Italy as a transshipment point for raw materials destined for Germany. Berlin also urged a more energetic attitude toward British control measures, but Mussolini refused to commit himself to a collision course at this point. Italy "could only enter the war at the militarily and politically correct moment, in pursuit of large objectives, . . . and should not be dragged into it at a perhaps inconvenient moment" over secondary questions.[120] This self-restraint was temporary. Mussolini set firm limits on economic ties to the Allies. Despite extreme shortages of raw materials in the armaments industries, he refused to sell weapons to the West. Sales to France of tankers and railroad tank cars in September, and of 600 aircraft engines and 500 trainers in October were short-term arrangements to bring in hard currency. When Guarneri asked Mussolini in September whether he should keep the tankers to profit from wartime shipping rate increases, or sell them to build up fuel and raw material stocks for intervention, the dictator erupted: "Sell them!" He suggested that Italy might move at any time after May 1940.[121]

Whether Italy intervened or remained an uneasy nonbelligerent, it had to find a steady coal supply. In November, German deliveries by both sea and rail dropped sharply, and imports sank to little more than half of the million tons a month needed. Worse, the British decision of 21 November to include German exports in the blockade would cut off Italy's seaborne German coal from Rotterdam, and throttle Italian industry. Ciano faced the crisis with deftness and his usual ambiguity. By early December he had secured Allied promises to exempt temporarily German coal exports to Italy from the blockade, and had succeeded with Ribbentrop's help in raising Germany's railborne quota to 500,000 tons a month, despite the strain this placed on German railroads and consumers. Nevertheless, seaborne coal remained vital, and London's forbearance was only a reprieve. The general principles of the blockade effort, the basis of British strategy, ultimately took precedence over smooth relations with Italy.[122]

London did attempt to find a way out of the approaching impasse. On 6

December the War Cabinet approved a plan of Halifax and the minister for economic warfare for a comprehensive economic agreement with Italy. Britain would offer 8,500,000 tons of coal, or 70 percent of Italy's total requirement, in 1940. To allow Italy to pay for the coal, Britain would buy from Italy £20 million worth of goods, including large quantities of armaments and munitions. Halifax was also prepared if necessary to purchase the fruit and vegetables Italy would no longer export to Germany in return for German coal. The plan would provide Italy with the means to pay for its imports of British and Empire raw materials, and would allow Britain to secure Italian armaments without paying in hard currency it did not have. The scheme would also, as Halifax put it, "bring into force our embargo on German exports without risking Italian opposition."[123]

With the benefit of hindsight it is hard to decide whether the plan's boldness or its naïveté is more striking. The British were proposing nothing less than the economic conquest of Germany's ally. They seem to have entirely missed the political implications of their scheme until too late. Chamberlain did remark in Cabinet that "Signor Mussolini was in a very embarrassing position and was sensitive in regard to his personal engagements to Germany," and Halifax commented that "it should be against this background that Anglo-Italian economic relations should be judged," but on the whole British deliberations concentrated on the economic aspects of the scheme. London sought above all to avoid paying hard currency for the badly needed antitank guns and aircraft the British services were attempting to purchase in Rome. The other major consideration in the official mind was the hope of avoiding friction over the stoppage of German seaborne coal by offering British coal in return. The need to stop German seaborne coal was a given that British strategy against Germany dictated, not a policy designed from the beginning to force Italy to choose sides.

Misgivings of Loraine's did not prevent London from ordering the plan presented to Ciano, who received it in the warm afterglow of his 16 December Fascist Chamber speech. Ciano raised no immediate objection to Britain's continued determination to cut off German seaborne coal. But he did suggest that London not set a deadline. Any appearance of an ultimatum would offend Mussolini. The next day, Ciano informed Loraine that Mussolini had accepted the British proposals "as a basis."[124] The dictator was not yet aware, however, that the sale of armaments was an indispensable part of the scheme; Loraine's memorandum for Ciano had failed to mention that significant detail.

Without armament sales, the proposal was unworkable. Italy was unable to offer enough of the other goods Britain needed. Further, notwithstanding the negotiations between Italian armament firms and British missions, Mussolini was not disposed to sell. In early December he ordered his aircraft manufacturers not to offer combat aircraft, although the insistence of the British and of his own subordinates did induce him to contemplate sale of disarmed training versions of Italian light bombers and fighters. Negotiations over the 47-mm Breda antitank guns had less result. On 18 December the British, whom the Italians had allowed to test the gun, received word no sale was possible "at least for the moment."[125]

From this point forth relations between Rome and London deteriorated. Prodding from Berlin in early December had already led to a long Italian protest about alleged chicanery by British contraband control authorities in the Mediterranean. Concurrently, Italian shipping interests deluged Palazzo Venezia with complaints. On 20 December Mussolini "blew up," and Ciano with difficulty restrained him from summoning Loraine for a tonguelashing. Loraine's reports of Mussolini's fury over British invasion of "Italy's own sea" produced a temporary loosening of restrictions at the end of December.[126] But London failed to realize that no room for agreement existed. Ciano and his colleagues prevented Mussolini in mid-January from acceding to German complaints and canceling the sales of aircraft engines to France; the currency and raw materials the arrangement brought in were indispensable to the armament industry.[127] But Mussolini regarded both contraband control, and the import rationing agreement British negotiators suggested as a less galling alternative, as intolerable affronts. He was no more willing than before to sell arms, and he further complicated the situation by canceling a major agreement his subordinates had negotiated for British charter of Italian merchant ships. By 18 January he had decided to reject the entire range of British proposals, and he informed his minister of corporations, Renato Ricci, that Italy's supply of British coal would soon cease. The break would be a healthy shock to the Italian people.[128]

On 29 January the War Cabinet decided on a last attempt. Permanent exemption of Italy's seaborne coal from the ban on German exports was out of the question; other neutrals would demand similar favors. But Chamberlain thought "that at this stage of the war, the goodwill of Italy was so important to us that we should do whatever might be necessary to secure it," and the War Office insisted the 47-mm antitank guns "might be of supreme importance."[129] Loraine still discerned an "obstinate streak of anti-British resentment" on Mussolini's part, but he also misled London: "the risk of Italy's joining up with Germany ha[d] pretty well reached the vanishing point." News that Italy was fortifying the Brenner, and perhaps also Bastianini's curious hint that Britain take Germany's place in the Anti-Comintern Pact, further encouraged the War Cabinet.[130] British negotiators therefore returned to Rome in early February to offer a further £5 million for fruits and vegetables within the framework of their earlier comprehensive proposal for coal and armaments sales.

Mussolini's response did not bear out Loraine's comforting prognostications. Absent in Romagna when Loraine presented Ciano with the latest version of the British scheme, Mussolini telephoned to confirm his refusal to sell antitank guns. He now also vetoed the sale of 400 Caproni CA 313 bomber crew trainers, an arrangement apparently approved as recently as 2 February, and he rejected the entire list of ammunition, explosives, and other war materiel the British desired to purchase.[131] Back in Rome on 7 February, Mussolini lectured Ciano on political morality: "States, like individuals, must follow a straight line of rectitude and honor." He was indifferent to warnings that the British would cut off German seaborne coal, and that the collapse of the comprehensive scheme meant Italy must pay in hard currency for coal from Britain. Austerity, Mussolini maintained, would do the masses good, would "shake [their] centuries-old mental sloth." The Italians had to be kept "in ranks and in uniform from morning to night" with liberal use of "the rod." The next day, Mussolini met Hitler's customary confidential messenger, the Prince of Hesse, and repeated forcefully the assurances, but not the warnings, of the January letter. Italy would go to war when its preparations were enough advanced that participation would assist rather than hinder Germany.[123]

The decision to reject London's proposals left Ciano desolate, despite Mussolini's derisory promise to reconsider in six months. Nothing was left except to inform the British. Mussolini, Ciano apologetically explained to Loraine on 8 February, did not wish to expose himself to "misunderstandings with [the] Germans," and Italy needed the armaments in question itself. Mussolini's alleged willingness to negotiate in six months did not mollify Loraine. By then "the fate of European man for many generations to come would have been settled." Loraine warned that nothing now stood in the way of the stoppage of German coal from Rotterdam and an Anglo-Italian crisis.[133]

London greeted the news with something approximating relief. As Halifax remarked in the War Cabinet, Loraine's report was "not altogether unsatisfactory, as at any rate freeing us of any position of obligation to Italy."[134] In the ensuing days, rumors that Mussolini might reconsider induced the War Cabinet to postpone decision briefly. But by 19 February further delay was impossible. Public pressure for the use of the blockade weapon to the full had begun to mount. Emmanuel Shinwell, gray eminence of the Labour Party left, had tabled a question in the House of Commons for 20 February challenging the government's forbearance toward German coal exports to Italy. Fear of public embarrassment induced the War Cabinet to make an end, and set the date of 1 March.[135] But neither Loraine nor the War Cabinet entirely gave up hope. They assumed Germany could not supply the entire Italian coal requirement by rail, and hoped strong internal pressures would induce Mussolini to relent. Although Loraine warned that Italian policy might now swing against Britain, he nevertheless held out some possibility of "mutiny against [the] regime."[136] This was a gross exaggeration, although Mussolini did apparently face unwelcome advice from Italian industrialists. Guido Donegani, chief of the giant Montecatini Chemical Trust, prophesied to Ciano that a coal stoppage would shut Italian industry down "with the most catastrophic consequences." Mussolini was unmoved. He would make up the difference through the regime's crash domestic coal and lignite program, in the teeth of the experts' warnings that the attempt would cripple the economy.[137]

In this atmosphere, the annual renegotiation of the Italo-German barter agreement concluded in Rome on 24 February. After much hard bargaining, Mussolini's personal intervention produced a result highly satisfactory to the Germans. Italy would fulfill German requests for copper by confiscating the cooking pots of its own civilian population. Even the sacred vessels of the Church were not exempt; what that institution needed, Mussolini quipped, was "not copper, but faith." In return, the Germans offered some petrochemicals, magnesium, and twelve million tons of coal — Italy's entire annual requirement. But they could not promise rail delivery of more than 500,000 tons per month, and experience in January had shown that even maximum effort could not guarantee delivery of that amount in unfavorable weather. Although the Germans promised to surpass the 500,000-ton figure whenever possible, Italy still faced ruin once the Allied embargo took effect. Unless rail deliveries increased further, the only recourse was greater imports of British coal, imports for which Italy would have once again to pay in hard currency it did not possess.[138]

Mussolini viewed the approaching confrontation with relish. He had preserved his "honor" and that of Italy by resisting the British. While he recognized, at least by Ciano's account, that London had approached the matter "on an economic basis" rather than a political one, he already discerned by 1 March the uses of British "blackmail" in levering subordinates, industrialists, and Italian people into war.[139]

Hannibal at the gates. While he awaited Hitler's reply to his letter, and resisted British economic pressure, Mussolini made further attempts to accelerate Italian preparations. By mid-December Favagrossa had digested the statistics the services had belatedly provided, and had presented an estimate of the time necessary to make the armed forces combat-ready. The news was discouraging. The Air Force would be ready by mid-1941, since its equipment required less production time than that of the other services. Army and Navy, however, would not have a full complement of artillery until at least 1943–4. By 11 January 1940 the figures and Badoglio's advocacy of delay impelled Mussolini to discard temporarily his hope of fighting that year. He proposed to intervene in the second half of 1941.[140]

In the meantime, he did his best to stem the continuing "defeatist trend" in public opinion. To "crack the whip" and demonstrate that Fascism was not "finished," as some in the middle classes had apparently come to believe, Mussolini drafted a bellicose speech that Muti delivered at a meeting of high Party officials on 17 January. Any "surviving tendencies to quietism, to the comfortable life, to grumbling, and to pacifism" were to be "choked off by the simplicity of life and by the example of the Party hierarchy [!], by appropriate propaganda, and by all available means." Fascist Italy might "find itself at any moment under the necessity of taking up arms."[141] At the beginning of February, Mussolini railed in his habitual manner to Ciano at the Italian "race of sheep"; even eighteen years of Fascism had failed to transform them into wolves. He then spoke at the ceremony commemorating the founding of the Fascist Militia. The regime's press did not report his words, but they were brief and intransigent: the Italian people were anxious for combat, "for that combat that shall take place."[142]

In meetings of the Council of Ministers on 20 and 23 January, Mussolini hinted at his interest in a "parallel war" in Croatia. He also maintained an "imperturbable calm" in the face of the "phantasmagorical dance of millions that we do not have" while the minister of finance, Paolo Thaon di Revel, briefed the ministers on the coming fiscal year budget. One had to take the long view of deficit spending, Mussolini announced. States did not fall from "financial problems." They collapsed only "through internal instability, or military defeat." When Thaon di Revel feebly objected that the *assignats* had contributed mightily to the disintegration of the First French Republic, Mussolini cut him off. Britain and France could "no longer win the war." Italy could not remain neutral indefinitely, under pain of falling into the "bush league" of European power politics. Mussolini's spirits had again revived, and despite Favagrossa's figures he once more insisted, as in early January, that the Army would have seventy divisions ready by the coming July. His chief hope was the *Regia Aeronautica*. Taking up a Douhetian motif that recurred later in other circumstances, Mussolini insisted that ground defenses were not enough. Air power decreed that small nations had to place themselves "under the wings of the great, or perish." Not content with harrying the weak, Mussolini also proposed with enthusiasm "terrorizing bombardments of France" and the wresting of Mediterranean hegemony from the West. His words moved his audience. Thaon di Revel and Renato Ricci immediately trimmed their sails to the prevailing wind. Only Raffaello Riccardi, Guarneri's successor as minister of exchange and currency, remained unconvinced.[143]

The direction of the wind became even clearer at the annual meeting of the regime's highest military-economic planning body, the Supreme Defense Commission, held from 8 to 14 February. The agenda covered some twenty-four topics, ranging from the "campaign against waste" to antiaircraft defense. Agencies and ministries circulated in advance a huge mass of reports and recommendations. Bottai had

never seen, in any other organization of this kind, so much paper: programs, plans, budget projections, graphs, diagrams, statistics. Mussolini circulates with nonchalance through his jungle; he shows that he knows its most out-of-the-way trails and alleyways. He touches upon the crucial point in each document, and brings it out with effectiveness, with *bravura*. But one has the sensation of a dialectical and polemical skill that fails to mesh with this massive machine. Nobody adds things up.[144]

The diagnosis was all too acute. Nevertheless, the paperwork jungle of reports and minutes gives an unparalleled picture of Mussolini's fierce determination to enter the war despite seemingly insuperable obstacles.[145]

In the long term, Mussolini hoped for a considerable degree of economic independence. By 1944 Italian production of coal from Istria and Sardinia, and of lignite, would reach ten million tons a year, over two-thirds of the projected annual requirement. Italy could then answer British and Germans that it would "make it with [its] own coal." Steel production would increase to four million tons a year, "the minimum indispensable" according to Mussolini, who erroneously assumed that that modest figure was a quarter of German production. The aluminum industry was similarly to increase production from the 40,000 tons predicted for 1940 to an ultimate target figure of 70,000 tons. Synthetic rubber plants would enter operation in 1940–1, and initially provide a fifth of Italy's annual requirement. Refinery capacity had increased to produce aviation gasoline and petrochemicals from the small amounts of oil discovered in Albania. Mussolini occasionally lamented past errors. The dismantlings of the great armaments plants by the liberal governments immediately after World War I had been "genuine crimes." His own regime's failure to recognize the need for economic independence earlier meant that in coal mining, for instance, Italy now had to do in two to four years "that which we could have done with less expense and with greater efficiency from 1925 to 1935."[146]

The crucial question for Mussolini, however, was not long-term solutions, but stop-gap measures. He once more hoped that Italy could be ready by summer.[147] The crucial economic obstacle was Italy's low stocks of hard currency, strategic raw materials, and military necessities such as fuel and ammunition. In some respects, the situation had improved since the previous September. The Navy, thanks to Cavagnari's foresight and recent imports of oil from Mexico and the United States, was well off, although the new *Littorio*-class battleships would drink up "rivers of bunker oil."[148] Air Force and Army had each accumulated about 100,000 tons of gasoline, diesel oil, and lubricants, enough along with requisitioned civilian stocks to fuel several months of combat. By the end of the year, the Air Force hoped to have 250,000 tons of fuel.

But the industrial raw material situation was little short of disastrous. Total coal stocks stood at about a million and a half tons, and in January coking coal supplies had declined to less than twelve days' worth at the normal rate of consumption. Blast furnaces, which would suffer damage if allowed to go out, had frequently operated with only a day's supply of coke in reserve.[149] Italy's currency reserves and increasing difficulties in buying strategic raw materials on the world market – even in exchange for gold – did not present an encouraging picture either. Soddu and Badoglio insisted that "without stockpiles one does not make war," and the stockpiles would have to be adequate for at least a year. In the Great War, Badoglio claimed, the Italian Army had worn through 42 million pairs of shoes.[150] Favagrossa summed up the bleak prospects in the iron and steel sector. For technical reasons, the steel industry required ore from French Morocco to mix with the Italian ore from Elba and elsewhere. Since September, shortages of shipping space and other difficulties had reduced Moroccan ore imports. Pig iron production had in turn declined drastically, and the steel industry had become even more dependent on imported scrap, which was increasingly difficult to obtain. No solution was in sight. Nonferrous metals were in similarly short supply. As Mussolini insisted, the situation was "not very comforting."[151]

Paying for strategic raw material imports remained an intractable problem, and produced the only open debate during the Commission's meetings. Riccardi, minister of exchange and currency and thus one of the major victims of Mussolini's refusal to sell arms, challenged Mussolini's policy "in a tone without precedent."[152] The experts detailed to compute Italy's annual import requirements in war had come up with an astronomical 22 million tons. That, Riccardi announced, would cost 22,000,000,000 lire. Such figures were out "in the interstellar spaces." He acidly noted that the services still refused to standardize basic issue items, and suggested that there remained "much cloth to cut" in their budgets. Italy's imports, he continued, had to drop to a point just short of that which would result in serious production slowdowns. That was "the only program practical under present conditions," and it was practical only if nonbelligerence and the current inactivity on the Western front continued. Even so, Italy simply could not find the 7,000,000,000 lire in hard currency to cover the imports Riccardi's reduced arms program called for, interest on foreign debts, and other unavoidable outflows. Riccardi concluded with a plea for fundamental policy change. The military, he urged, should limit its programs. Only increased exports could avert bankruptcy.

Before Mussolini could reply, Badoglio struck back at Riccardi's allegations of fat in the military budget. It was not Riccardi's station, or even that of the military itself, to urge reduction of the services' programs. If the Italian economy could not meet the demands made on it, that was not "the affair of the Armed Forces." For Badoglio the task of the military was "to be as sincere as Comrade Riccardi, and tell the truth, whole and complete." It must say to Mussolini, "If this is needed, then we must have that."

Mussolini now intervened to pacify his advisers. The services were indeed "taking into account the economic situation and attempting to adapt their programs to it." He himself had not fixed impossible goals. He had renounced the mobilization of four to six million men. Modern war was "a technological war," he belatedly conceded. It was useless "to mobilize great masses one would then not know how to employ." Nor could one "ask of Comrade Riccardi that which he cannot give us." Nevertheless, Mussolini insisted, he intended to obtain a certain minimum degree of "security," even "at the cost of emptying the reserves of the Bank of Italy." He did not now see the need for such a drastic step, despite Riccardi's prophecies of imminent bankruptcy. Other nations had economic problems as difficult as Italy's. Further, some of the services actually promoted exports. The Air Force, in particular, was responsible for generating aircraft sales worth more than 1,000,000,000 lire. Pricolo's service had "given so much" that it had "the right to ask as well." The ministers heard their master's voice, and no one supported Riccardi's call to throttle back military programs in favor of exports. Balbo, an old enemy of Riccardi's, openly shook hands with him — but only after Mussolini had left the room.[153]

In the final Commission meeting on 14 February, Graziani answered Riccardi with a long, baroque appeal to the overriding necessity of defending Italy's frontiers. Riccardi must have recognized that Mussolini was behind Graziani's outburst, for he did concede that "polemical fervor" had perhaps carried him away. But he stood by the substance of his earlier statement. Everything else depended on the currency question. He did not lack faith, but faith did not generate foreign exchange. The threatened frontiers were not among the Alpine peaks, but at the Bank of Italy.

Mussolini now took charge, and again put the problem in perspective:

Since 1935 we have always been in a precarious position. Guarneri gave the same speech at least twenty times from the period of sanctions onward: "We can't go on. We will end by going under." And 1935, '36, '37, and so on have passed, and now we are in 1940. I believe that at the end of the year Riccardi will tell us that the ship is still afloat.

Mussolini denied the Army's programs were "insane" in relation to Italy's economic potential. In case of necessity, he would empty even the "sacristy" of the Bank of Italy, and he "despised those Italians who, in the face of present and future difficulties, 'stand at the window' and claim that they want to wait and see how things will turn out." Italy could not "remain absent from a drama that will remake the map of the continent."

However, Mussolini still had no conception of the form the war was about to take. In the course of the Commission's meetings, he had voiced "the greatest reservations" about French and Germans meeting in the open field. France was certainly not capable of such an effort. Rumors of the impending German onslaught had subsided with the postponement of the operation in January. By mid-February Mussolini apparently felt his advice had taken effect, and that the Germans had postponed an offensive that he, like the majority of experts on both sides, still imagined would be bloody and indecisive despite German superiority in leadership and air power. The world, Mussolini insisted, was moving toward an age of "walled nations." The next months rudely awakened him and his advisers from that illusion.[154]

To the Brenner. Although he judged the German offensives not yet imminent, Mussolini maintained his objective of an Italian "parallel war." The press received initiation into the mysteries of high policy. Alessandro Pavolini,

Alfieri's replacement as minister of popular culture, confidentially urged his editors on 22 February to keep in mind that the current conflict was not one war, but several. "Within this scene a war of our own, perhaps connected either wholly or partially with the wars of others, but with its own ends and its own objectives, could find a place tomorrow." Privately, Mussolini repeatedly emphasized certainty of German victory, the urgency of Italy's aspirations against France, and the pressing need for an outlet to the oceans, "without which Italy will never truly be an empire."[155]

In Berlin, Hitler brooded over his offensive, his recently aroused interest in an attack on Scandinavia, and his belated answer to Mussolini's January letter. At this moment Franklin Delano Roosevelt chose to launch the only sort of emissary his naïvely self-absorbed compatriots would as yet permit him to send to Europe: a peace mission. The president's chosen instrument was his friend and associate, Undersecretary of State Sumner Welles. His purpose, as Roosevelt confided to another subordinate, was "to get the low-down on Hitler and get Mussolini's point of view," to split the Axis if possible, and in any case delay the German offensive.[156] The mission occasioned the last round of diplomatic maneuver before Hitler's guns spoke in the West and crushed the already quixotic hope of compromise.

Welles's first stop was Rome; erroneous belief in Italy's pivotal role in the European balance died hard. Welles charmed Ciano, whom he impressed as a "gentleman" quite unlike the Berlin "crew of presumptuous plebeians." But Ciano was less frank with Welles about Italian objectives than he had been with his German associates. At Palazzo Venezia, Welles found Mussolini "laboring under some tremendous strain," which he ascribed partly to political causes, partly to the "new and young . . . mistress" Welles breathlessly reported Mussolini had procured "only ten days ago." Welles bore a letter from Roosevelt proposing a meeting "some day soon," a suggestion that touched Mussolini's vanity. But the dictator's main interest, besides impressing on Welles the reasonableness of German war aims, was to insist on the satisfaction of Italy's just claim to "free egress from, and access to, the Mediterranean." A negotiated peace was still possible, but once the Germans launched their offensive that chance would vanish. The sole effect of the Welles mission in Rome was to increase Mussolini's already vehement contempt for the United States: the Americans judged "things superficially, whereas we judge them in depth." In the ensuing days Mussolini ordered further press attacks on the Allies, and railed at the "imbeciles and criminals who [still] believed Germany would be defeated." He also commanded Ciano to pass the Italian record of the talks on to Berlin.[157]

At this point, the application of the British embargo on seaborne German coal produced the predictable Anglo-Italian crisis. Ciano's family paper, the *Telegrafo,* had commented on 27 February that it hoped the British would not be so "ill advised" as to put the measure into effect. This hint met no response in London, but Loraine complained to Ciano of "thinly veiled threats."[158] In Rome, the Duce's economic experts apparently concluded that the embargo would now compel Italy to lean more heavily on British coal. To cover payments, they convinced Mussolini to release 1,000,000,000 lire in gold from the Bank of Italy's remaining 2,300,000,000 lire reserve. The minister of finance, Thaon di Revel, comforted his colleagues and Mussolini with the thought "that gold will soon be worth nothing, and we shall all become rich selling works of art." Like an increasing number of the Duce's subordinates, Revel had now "become an extreme interventionist in order to please the Boss."[159]

Mussolini also ordered a strenuous diplomatic protest against all aspects of British blockade policy. He personally drafted the "bitter and threatening" final sentence of the Italian note. The effect in London was predictable. The War Cabinet belatedly stiffened: any sign of British weakness would only encourage Mussolini further. If anything, Britain ought to "put on the screw." British coal deliveries through the clearing agreement would nevertheless continue until the end of the month to give Italy "a breathing space in which to reconsider her position" and to choose between selling Britain armaments to pay for coal after the end of March, paying the hard currency Britain doubted Italy could raise, or suffering "a restriction of imports of a severity that might bring Italian industry almost to a standstill." The War Cabinet thought "Signor Mussolini" would be "under considerable pressure from Italian industry, and, in particular, from the aircraft and munitions firms whose contracts with [Great Britain] had almost gone through."[160]

The matter turned out to be not so simple. Misunderstanding of Loraine's warnings and administrative confusion in Rome led to seizure by the Royal Navy of thirteen Italian coal ships leaving Rotterdam and Antwerp. Mussolini was still haranguing his subordinates about a parallel war, and was predictably livid. The blockade was making him "the laughing-stock of Europe." As soon as he was ready, he would make the British repent; for the moment, Italy was powerless. To the rescue came Halifax, "anxious to avoid getting into a serious dispute with Italy on 'sanctions' lines." With Chamberlain's support, and with the help of evidence that the Italians had not been "trailing their coats," but had been victims of a genuine misunderstanding, the foreign secretary induced the War Cabinet to release the ships already detained. Italy in return undertook not to repeat the experiment.[161]

In Rome, Ciano suffered for the first time since taking office the direct lash of Mussolini's tongue. Muttering threats, Mussolini warned his son-in-law that the British were doomed. That was "a definite truth" even Ciano "would do well to get through [his] head." Ciano was mildly shocked, and in his diary struck a pose of noble indifference to the excitement and perquisites of office.[162] But in the ensuing weeks he too began to fall into line.

Not coincidentally, what Ciano described as a *"coup de théâtre* dear to the gross tastes of the Germans" enlivened the Anglo-Italian crisis. On the morning of 8 March Mackensen announced out of the blue that Ribbentrop would arrive in Rome in two days, bearing Hitler's belated reply to Mussolini's letter. As early as the first week of January, the Germans had suggested a Ribbentrop visit in return for Ciano's two trips to Germany in August and October.[163] Mussolini's apparent lack of faith in German victory presumably made a German effort to stiffen Italy desirable. The Prince of Hesse had in his talk with Mussolini on 8 February even suggested a Brenner meeting of the dictators. The Welles mission, with its overtones of a possible United States peace initiative associating Roosevelt, Mussolini, and the Vatican, made a German step in Rome to reinforce the Axis appear advisable before Welles should return thence from Paris and London. But Hitler seems to have taken the final decision to launch Ribbentrop only on 7 March.[164] It was the Anglo-Italian coal crisis that gave the Führer the chance to send his "second Bismarck" to Rome, secretly bearing a priceless gift – a firm offer to deliver *by rail* the one million tons of coal a month promised Italy under the Italo-German economic agreement of 24 February. The Germans probably did not at this point expect more from Mussolini than political support for the coming offensive. Nevertheless, Hitler presumably hoped, as he had since September, for Italian entry into the war once the first phase of the attack had achieved success. The mission to Rome sought to prepare the ground for that decision.[165]

Mussolini welcomed the visit enthusiastically from the first, despite a Ciano attempt to convince him that the delicate state of Anglo-Italian relations made it extremely inopportune. Ciano did his best to play up the British release of the coal ships to "balance off" Ribbentrop's arrival. Such gestures, and a series of Ciano reassurances in the following days, merely hid from the Allies the true implications of events in Rome. Nevertheless, on the eve of Ribbentrop's arrival Mussolini was hardly committed to entering the war immediately. As in his January letter, he planned to ask whether Germany really needed the offensive (which Attolico once more reported was imminent, probably at the end of the month) in order to "break the French and British."[166]

Ribbentrop greeted Ciano with the sweeping promise that "in a few months the French Army will be destroyed and the only British remaining on the continent will be prisoners of war," and according to one account remarked that for Fascist Italy, it was "now or never."[167] At Palazzo Venezia, Ribbentrop presented Hitler's letter, and excused the long delay – the Führer had wanted to "gain a clear picture [of the situation] before he replied [to Mussolini's letter]; that had only been possible in the last few weeks."[168]

Ribbentrop then played his trump card. Hitler had been "utterly outraged" over the British embargo, "an unheard-of attempt by the plutocratic-democratic states to throttle Italy economically." Germany was "obviously ready and able to cover Italy's entire coal requirement." Clodius had accompanied Ribbentrop in order to convey the details to the Italian experts. Mussolini announced that Italy's requirement would be between 500,000 and 700,000 tons; presumably he did not think the Germans capable of transporting more.

Ribbentrop also conveyed Hitler's emphatic confidence in destroying the French army "in the course of the summer," and insisted at length that Italy and Germany must stand together against the implacable hostility of the Allies and the "Jewish-plutocratic clique . . . whose influence reached through Morgan and Rockefeller to Roosevelt." Toward the end of the discussion, Mussolini chimed in with a series of uncomplimentary remarks about British and French military performance and morale; the British had 24,000 conscientious objectors. He proposed to explain Italy's position to "*Kamerad* Ribbentrop" at a further meeting the next day.

It is customary to assign Mussolini's conversion to the German point of view to the interval between the two talks.[169] Immediately after the first, Mussolini told Ciano he still did not believe in the German offensive, or at least in its success. But these remarks were merely the belated traces of his earlier doubts. Hitler's promise to give independence from the hated British, and Ribbentrop's insistence that the Führer's decision to attack was immovable and the crushing success of German arms assured had already half convinced Mussolini. Further resistance would be ineffective, impolitic, and unnecessary. At the end of the first interview, he conceded Hitler's thesis that "the destiny of the German and Italian nations was the same" in the face of the enmity of the plutocratic West. This admission was the prelude to Mussolini's commitment to fight at Germany's side.

The skillful letter from Hitler that Ribbentrop conveyed drove the German case home. If Italy aspired to more than "mere survival as a modest European state," if Italy's future involved the "securing of the existence of the Italian *Volk* from the historical, geopolitical, and general moral point of view, in other words according to the standards by which one must measure the right of your people to existence," then Mussolini would have to face "those same adversaries against which Germany today fights." Hitler closed by asking for a meeting.[170]

Mussolini delivered his reply to Ribbentrop on the afternoon of 11 March.[171] "At the appropriate moment" Italy would enter the war, and fight it "with Germany and parallel to Germany" in order to resolve the nation's problems, which Mussolini explained in his customary geopolitical terms. Italy's armaments had made much progress, progress the Duce exaggerated for Ribbentrop's benefit. The Navy would soon have four 35,000-ton battleships;[172] 120 submarines would be ready by May; 150,000 naval reservists would report in April. The Army would be up to a million men by May. Italy could not survive a long war economically, but it would intervene at the decisive moment.

Ribbentrop was delighted, and proposed a Duce–Führer meeting. Mussolini accepted without hesitation, on the understanding that it would take place at the Brenner at some point after 19 March. The talks closed amid much cordiality, and repeated Mussolinian assurances of Italian intervention in the struggle between the "new *Weltanschauung*" of the populous and proletarian nations and the "old concepts and ideas." The Americans, Mussolini insisted, would never enter the war; they "doubted the victory of the Allies and did not intend to bet on a losing horse." He had made his own bet. A day and a half later, after strenuous negotiations, Clodius and his Italian counterparts signed a secret protocol to the Italo-German barter agreement of 24 February. Italy would receive one million tons of coal per month, beginning in April.[173]

In the first days after Ribbentrop's departure, Ciano appears to have hoped that Mussolini's mood would pass. He informed the Allies that Italian policy had not changed. In London, self-satisfaction reigned. Success in smoothing over the Rotterdam shipping conflict made Halifax hopeful that Ribbentrop would prove unwelcome in Rome. Behind the back of the Cabinet, Chamberlain informed Ciano of the impending arrival of a confidential agent used in earlier back-channel contacts in 1937. Chamberlain, who displayed boundless admiration for "the political genius of the Duce, and his works" to Bastianini, moved to bypass the Foreign Office to settle the Anglo-Italian trade tangle, and to "confirm personally . . . the firm sentiments of good will of the present English government towards the Fascist regime." Nor did the triumphant announcement of the Italo-German coal agreement affect the British estimate of the situation. Loraine and the experts in London considered that "it is not certain that Germany could supply [12,000,000 tons annually] and it is quite certain that the railways could not carry it."[174]

Only the Italian monarchy took the situation seriously enough to act – and its action was typically hesitant and tentative. The minister of the royal household, Duke Pietro Acquarone, who was to play a leading role in the July 1943 coup, approached Ciano at the Golf Club on 14 March. His Majesty, Acquarone explained delicately, "feels that the necessity of intervening in order to give a different shape to matters might present itself from one moment to the next." The King was "ready to do it, and with the greatest energy." The King looked upon Ciano "with more than benevolence, with true affection, and great confidence." Acquarone then attempted to "carry the discussion further." Ciano, by his own account, parried the attempt, and talked only in generalities. Despite his eagerness for American and British approval, and the hope of leading a pro-Allied *"trasformismo"* current Roman gossip plausibly ascribed to him, Ciano was unwilling to run risks. The King thought better of attempting to launch a monarcho-Fascist regime without Mussolini, and resigned himself, as usual, to dragging his feet behind the dictator's "lucky star."[175]

Mussolini himself characteristically succumbed to doubts soon after Ribbentrop's departure. He insistently asked after the minutes of the Ribbentrop talks, apparently because he thought "he [had] gone too far in pledging himself to fight against the Allies." He once more contemplated dissuading Hitler from the attack. Ciano did not think the Germans would budge, and feared the Brenner meeting would associate Mussolini with Hitler in responsibility for the "immense massacre" all expected once the offensive opened. Mussolini briefly shared some of these misgivings. But it was too late. On 13 March Ribbentrop telephoned to propose the 18th for the conference. Mussolini, annoyed that "these Germans" had given him "no time to breathe or think things over," nevertheless agreed. He had up to this point cultivated "the illusion that a real war would not be fought," Ciano noted. The prospect of an impending clash he could not join was profoundly humiliating.[176]

While Mussolini, caught between his aims and the limits military weakness imposed, ruminated over his course, Sumner Welles again appeared. On 16 March, back from Berlin, London, and Paris, he called on Ciano and Mussolini. Ciano insisted that Mussolini had no intention of changing Italian policy, and remarked disingenuously that Italy was not "stirring up trouble" in Croatia. At Palazzo Venezia Welles found that Mussolini had thrown off his earlier depression; evidently the commitment to Ribbentrop had soothed his unquiet spirit. Mussolini protested his devotion to the cause of peace, but insisted that only genuine Allied concessions could give him the leverage to hold Hitler back. However, although Welles had detected willingness to compromise behind the brave façade Allied leaders had put up, Roosevelt refused to authorize an American effort to open negotiations. In private, Ciano expressed to Welles "emphatic approval" of Roosevelt's reticence. This effusiveness, like Ciano's occasional confidences to Western ambassadors, was to some extent an attempt to establish private ties for use should Mussolini falter. But Ciano was also alive to the dangers of asking Berlin for negotiations; he noted that the "tergiversations of the democracies" were likely to confirm Hitler's resolve to attack.[177]

Mussolini had meanwhile arrived at a provisional resting place in his own tergiversations. He would confirm to Hitler his "potential solidarity," but he did not intend to enter the war yet. Ciano noted Mussolini's words: "I will act like Bertoldo.[178] He accepted the death sentence, on condition that he be permitted to select the tree from which to be hanged. Obviously, he never found the tree." Professions of opportunism did not reassure Ciano: "to push Mussolini forward is an easy task; to pull him back difficult." These were words born of long and unhappy experience. As Mussolini and Ciano departed for the Brenner on 17 March, the dictator was "serene, and, in his heart, pleased that Hitler want[ed] to see him." Mussolini's most recent theory on Italy's role in the German offensive assigned Italian forces to "the left wing, tying up an equal number of enemy forces, not acting, but nevertheless ready to commence operations at the appropriate moment."[179] This proposal Mussolini put to Hitler the next morning, to the latter's great satisfaction.

Mussolini had succeeded in his long battle to preserve the German alliance. He had done his best to convince the public that Italy was not neutral, and must eventually intervene. He had pressed rearmament up to and beyond the limits of the economy. He had rejected British attempts to secure Italian arms and ration Italy's imports, and had blocked the feeble objections of the Italian industrialists with Hitler's coal. Now, with the spring of 1940, the Germans were about to open the road to his Mediterranean war against the West.

CHAPTER 3

"The most impatient of all Italians"

What can you say to someone who doesn't dare risk a single soldier
while his ally is winning a crushing victory, and that victory can give
Italy back the remainder of its national territory and establish its
supremacy in the Mediterranean? Is it a pipe-dream? We'll see if it is.
In any case, there are Italians who believe in it, myself first of all. It
does not matter if some general or other doesn't believe; perhaps it is
better that way . . .

Mussolini, to Ciano and Anfuso, late May 1940

1. Under restraint

A war "parallel" to that of Germany. It was snowing at the Brenner on the
morning of 18 March, as Mussolini waited "with a feeling of impatient
pleasure" for Hitler's arrival. In the night, he told Ciano, a dream "had rent
the veil of the future." But Mussolini did not confide the details of that very
personal revelation to his son-in-law. At the Brenner, Hitler opened with
his usual prolix harangue, deriding the clumsiness of the British and the
"defeatist, pacifist" fortifications of the French.[1] He then came to the point.
Either the coming offensive would so shake the West that "one last push"
would bring collapse – Mussolini could then strike that blow at Germany's
side – or the offensive might lead to a struggle of attrition that would gradually wear down the Allies: "for once Germany attacked, it would never let
go." In a protracted struggle, Italian intervention at the right moment could
be "the last kilogram, that would cause the scales to tip irrevocably in favor
of Germany and Italy." Hitler was fully aware that Italy could not fight a
long war. He was "a man of reality, who did not in the least wish the Duce
to do anything contrary to the interests of the Italian people."

Mussolini replied with assurances that Italy would indeed intervene, for
its own "honor and interests." The choice of the moment nevertheless presented a problem. Mussolini pleaded for four months, until the Navy's new
battleships would be ready. Hitler did not reply to this embarrassed appeal,
but instead tentatively proposed an Italian ground operation against France
across the upper Rhine. Germany would provide logistical support and the
initial breakthrough of the Maginot Line. Italy could then exploit. Mussolini
left the offer unanswered, but assured Hitler that "as soon as Germany thrust
forward victoriously," he would act. Mussolini had said the decisive words.
He had confirmed directly and almost irrevocably his personal commitment
to Hitler and to war.

87

In the days that followed, Ciano tried to believe that the meeting had not substantially altered Italy's position. He so informed François-Poncet and Loraine, though he did tell the former that Mussolini had "doubled his bet" on the German horse. At lunch at the Golf Club on the 19th, he assured Welles that he "was determined to do everything within his power to keep Italy from getting into the war." There would be "absolutely no change in Italy's nonbelligerent attitude."[2] Hitler's seeming moderation by contrast with Ribbentrop had perhaps impressed Ciano, for he intimated to the Vatican that Hitler was far less intransigent than before, and added that he himself continued to hold to his "well-known" line of action, although "given the temperament and tendencies of the Duce" he had to "operate with prudence."[3]

In the ensuing days Ciano's adherence to the cause of nonintervention began to waver as his perception of the relative balance of forces between Germany and the Allies changed and the dictator's bellicosity increased daily. British and French hastened to propitiate Mussolini. Chamberlain sent a message through Bastianini, stressing firm conviction that "a will to peace and European reconstruction" animated the Duce. Adriano Dingli, solicitor to the Italian Embassy in London and unofficial emissary of the prime minister whom Bastianini had announced earlier, now hastened to Rome behind the back of Halifax and Loraine. The French were not far behind. But Ciano was unreceptive, and had his ambassador make clear in Paris that Italy was not interested.[4] When Dingli gave an "impression of Allied weakness" and produced a "useless and general message from the prime minister, one of those messages of goodwill destined from the beginning to remain unanswered," Ciano's attitude hardened. At Mussolini's orders, Ciano offered to mediate if the British were really interested in proposing acceptable peace terms — in other words, if they would surrender Poland and continental Europe to Germany. If not, Italy would be at Germany's side.[5]

But Mussolini had thoughts other than peace. The press, which soon showed a further "evolution" in Germany's favor, reported that the dictator's first business meeting upon return from the Brenner was with Graziani.[6] In the days that followed, Mussolini was ever more decidedly pro-German, and began to consider the strategic lineaments of an Italian war: defensive on the Alps, defensive in Libya, offensive against Djibouti and Kenya, naval and air offensive in the Mediterranean. Mussolini's war plan was not the consequence of a conviction that Italy "had to count on diplomacy and luck, rather than [force of] arms," as Giorgio Rochat and others have argued.[7] It was rather an embarrassed attempt to break free of the restraints that his "walled nations" fixation, the weakness of Italy's armed forces, and the intolerance of risk of his military subordinates imposed. Mussolini's strategic concept was a direct descendant of his vision of 1937–9, but without the Egyptian offensive, which Pariani's disgrace, Badoglio's mania for the defensive, and Allied preponderance had quashed.

A week later, on 31 March, Mussolini transferred his conception to paper in the form of directives for Italian intervention. Mussolini's memorandum followed closely his remarks to Ciano, and is the fullest surviving exposition of the dictator's intentions in the spring of 1940.[8] Mussolini began with a survey of the situation. A compromise peace was currently "to be excluded." Allied strategy was to avoid action and rely upon the gradually tightening blockade. "Logically," Germany would not choose to attack in the West, but would continue the "phony war" and intensify naval and air operations. Only in the certainty of a crushing victory, or in desperation if the blockade left no other course, would Germany launch a land offensive.

In the unlikely event of compromise peace, Italy could still have a voice. But if the war continued, it was "absurd and impossible" to think that Italy could remain out of it until the end. It was not off "in a corner of Europe like Spain, or semi-Asiatic like Russia." Nor would a change of policy and passage "bag and baggage" to the Allies avoid war. It would rather summon up immediate conflict with Germany, a conflict Italy would fight alone. Only alliance with Germany had made Italy's current position feasible. The only conceivable course was thus a war "parallel to that of Germany, to reach [Italy's] objectives," to resolve the problem of its maritime frontiers, to break free from its Mediterranean prison.

The problem, Mussolini insisted, was not whether Italy was to fight, but when and how: "It is a question of retarding as much as possible, consistent with honor and dignity, our entry into the war," in order to "prepare ourselves so that our intervention is decisive." Italy was unable to support the economic strain of a long war. These premises established, Mussolini proceeded to lay down the principal lines of his strategy, in order to "orient" the work of the service staffs. In the Alps, the Army was to remain on the defensive except "in the case, in my opinion improbable," of complete French collapse. Occupation of Corsica was possible but was perhaps not worth the effort. Toward Yugoslavia, Mussolini prescribed an attitude of "distrustful observation" and an offensive "in the case of internal collapse of that state, due to the secession, already in course, of the Croats." Dispositions in Albania against Yugoslavia and Greece depended on "what happens on the eastern [Yugoslav] front." In Libya, Balbo's forces would stand on the defensive; the strength of Marshal Weygand's French army in Syria purportedly made Balbo's plan for attack on Egypt impractical. In Ethiopia, Italian forces could mount local offensives against Kassala, other Sudanese border towns, and Kenya. The task of the Air Force was to support Army and Navy.

Mussolini reserved discussion of the principal effort for last. The Navy was to take the offensive "right down the line [*su tutta la linea*] in the Mediterranean and outside it." He did not lay down specific objectives, and left it to the service chiefs to translate general directives into detailed plans. Experience was to show that his subordinates had no intention of complying.

In a Council of Ministers of 2 April, Mussolini was more warlike than ever. He refused to act "like whores [*puttane*]" with the democracies. Neutrality "would downgrade Italy for a century as a great power and for eternity

as a Fascist Regime." On 4 April, he began distribution of his 31 March
directives to the King, Ciano, Badoglio, Soddu, the service chiefs, Muti,
and the colonial minister. Ciano's resistance was declining rapidly; he judged
it a "sober document." According to Mussolini's later testimony, the King
found its logic "geometric," although Victor Emmanuel's native caution rendered him incapable of approving any course more adventurous than entry
in order to "pick up the *pots cassés*" the belligerents left, as Mussolini contemptuously put it. Badoglio replied with a positively obsequious letter disingenuously assuring Mussolini that "studies" for all the actions proposed
were long completed; he did not mention the equally necessary training and
logistical preparation. Badoglio promised to summon a meeting of the service chiefs on 9 April to discuss plans.[9]

At the meeting, in deference to Mussolini's directives, Badoglio showed
a few flashes of offensive spirit – until his colleagues conveniently insisted
that passivity was inescapable. Badoglio's principal intent at the meeting
was to emphasize the dangers of too close cooperation with the "arrogant and
domineering" Germans. He adamantly refused to authorize Graziani to discuss with Berlin joint offensive operations or the cession of German artillery
to the Italian army. Graziani was appalled: "But we won't be able to do
anything in that case, even if France collapses." Badoglio insisted that
Franco-British collapse was precisely the contingency in which Italy would
act, and it must then act exclusively with its own forces: "If we were to have
recourse to German help, we would not only lose our dignity, but we would
expose ourselves to having to pay our debt very dearly indeed." For a long-
standing francophile, Badoglio seemed remarkably hopeful of French downfall:

Graziani: There are 150 kilometers to cover.
Badoglio: When the enemy is in rout kilometers no longer matter.
Graziani: There are fortifications to overcome.
Badoglio: Everything depends on the instinct [*sensibilità*] of the commander.

Mussolini's method of leadership had made a temporary convert. But
Graziani would not keep silent. Impending action apparently dampened the
enthusiasm he had evidenced that winter. He complained of slow progress
on the Alpine fortifications, and gloomily described the situation in Ethiopia. His replacement as viceroy, Duke Amedeo of Savoia-Aosta, had
impressed on all the precariousness of Italy's position there during meetings
in Rome in the previous days.[10] Badoglio retreated; he had only associated
himself with Mussolini's offensive directives for East Africa in order to provide mental exercise for the staffs!

Next came the Navy. Badoglio proceeded to interpret the "offensive right
down the line" until it was merely, as Soddu observed, a *"guerre de course* in
the Mediterranean, without objectives." Cavagnari lamented: "One [enemy]
fleet will place itself at Gibraltar and the other at Suez, and we shall
asphyxiate inside." All agreed that no offensive was possible from Libya.

Toward the end Pricolo observed that "too many illusions [were] being entertained" about chances for Mediterranean air and naval operations, which he judged "slim indeed." But no decision resulted. Badoglio closed, as in November, with the need to keep Mussolini informed of "our real capabilities." With characteristic vagueness he directed his colleagues to "study" and report.[11] The service chiefs had proved even less willing than Badoglio to contemplate the sort of offensive preparations Mussolini had requested, and that alone could make Italian intervention effective.

The April crisis. While Mussolini's military authorities engaged in futile deliberation, the *Wehrmacht* launched one of the most brilliantly successful amphibious operations in history. Despite a command structure at least as disjointed as that of Fascist Italy, a commander-in-chief who at a critical moment suffered an almost total loss of nerve, and a navy only one-third the size of that of Britain, the Germans stormed into Denmark and Norway in the early hours of 9 April. Ciano, whom Mackensen awakened at 0630 with a letter from Hitler, was not enthusiastic: "The usual letter, in the usual style, to announce a stroke already carried out."[12] Ciano told Mackensen he had expected a different announcement – the opening of the German offensive in the West, and warned that occupation of two neutral capitals would have strong repercussions in the United States. Mussolini did not share these misgivings: "That is the way to win wars. Whoever gets there first is right." Mussolini also announced that he was ordering press and people to "applaud without reservations Germany's action." Alone with Ciano, Mussolini spoke of Croatia. "His hands itch," Ciano noted; "he intends to speed things up, taking advantage of the disorder that reigns in Europe." But Mussolini did not yet act, although he was "convinced that an attack on Yugoslavia [would] not bring France and England down on [Italy]."[13]

On the home front, the German coup was the first substantial blow against public aversion to war. The press received orders to "raise the temperature of the Italian people gradually," but without giving the impression of "the imminence of the warlike act, or of popular clamor for war," which, if premature, might produce an undesirable sense of anticlimax. Mussolini nevertheless personally informed the provincial newspaper editors on 10 April that intervention was "inevitable."[14] Even before the Ministry of Popular Culture's machinery was fully in motion, Ciano noted that the German action in the North has "had a favorable repercussion among the populace, which, as Mussolini says, 'is a whore who goes with the conquering male.'" To Ciano, as to the public, the surprising thing was "the nonexistent reaction of the Allies," whose initial answer had been "an offensive of speeches and press articles," and whose subsequent intervention in Norway swiftly turned into fiasco. Ciano confided in his diary the belief that "the last word [had] not yet been said." But François-Poncet detected a complete change in his judgment of the probable outcome. To the Germans, Ciano was naturally fulsome: the Allied situation was "simply *pitoyable.*" Full of "bitter words" against the British, Ciano disclosed to Mackensen that he had assembled, for publication "at the appropriate moment," an entire dossier on their "encroachments."[15]

Mussolini, in replying to Hitler's letters – a second one, with further details of the Scandinavian action, had arrived on 10 April – left little doubt that the "appropriate moment" was drawing steadily closer. The tightening blockade was producing a strong "anti-Allied *Stimmung*" in the Italian people. The Italian dictator pointed out, with particular reference to Rumania and its oil, that it was important to avoid dragging the Balkans into war. Nevertheless, the Axis must strike first, as in Norway, if the Allies seemed about to move. From the morning of 12 April, the Italian Fleet would be fully mobilized. He was also increasing the tempo of the other services' preparations.[16]

Mussolini's mobilization of the fleet had immediate repercussions. He clearly did not intend to move against Yugoslavia at this point, but the Yugoslavs could not know this. In the late hours of 12 April, evidently fearing a Norwegian-type coup complete with Italian troops hiding below the hatches of seemingly innocent merchant vessels, the Yugoslav navy went on full alert. It also ordered an immediate no-notice search of all ships arrived from Italy during the day.[17] Meanwhile, in Rome, the most extraordinary rumors began to circulate. Italy planned to strike at Corfù, Dalmatia, and even Rumania. Mussolini and Ciano had quarreled violently because the latter refused to accept "the axiomatic certainty of British defeat." Ciano had taken to his bed after the scene, but was "not really ill." As late as 17 April, the Yugoslav minister in Rome considered Italian action imminent.[18]

These lurid tales created consternation in the Allied camp. On the 14th, under prodding from his professional advisers, Halifax raised in Cabinet the question of what the Allies should do if Italy attacked Yugoslavia. Churchill, in his capacity as First Lord of the Admiralty, was against immediate counteraction. Halifax was nevertheless concerned about the "unfavourable effect" in the Balkans of British passivity in such an event, and he ultimately recommended, along with the chiefs of staff, that Britain should go to war with Italy whether or not Yugoslavia resisted. But a series of consultations with the French produced no clear decision. Some in Paris seem to have contemplated buying the Italians off by giving them a free hand in Dalmatia. Paul Reynaud, now French prime minister in place of Daladier, was willing to contemplate war in the event of an Italian move, but only if the Balkan nations cooperated – a proviso that rendered Allied action improbable. In the final discussions on the subject, the Allies agreed to prepare naval and air bombardments of North Italy's industry as a fit reply to an Italian attack on the Allies themselves, or to an "act of aggression committed by Italy that they might consider themselves bound to oppose." With this ambiguous formula, the matter rested. Soon the Allies would have more urgent concerns than fear of Mussolinian forays to the southeast.[19]

Reality in Rome was considerably less dramatic than the rumors reaching

London and Paris. On 11 April Mussolini had a heated discussion with the King, who was still unwilling to risk war until the Allies were utterly prostrate. Mussolini was incensed:

It is humiliating to stand with one's hands in one's pockets while others are making history. Who wins counts for little. To make a people great one must take them into combat even if one has to boot them in the ass [*magari a calci in culo*]. That is what I shall do. . . . If we do not seize this moment to measure our Navy with that of the Allies why should we maintain 600,000 tons of warships? All we would need would be coastguard cutters and pleasure boats to take the *signorine* on excursions.[20]

Mussolini was still unable to fire his military advisers with this spirit, however. Badoglio forwarded the minutes of the 9 April meeting to Mussolini with a covering letter that emphasized "lively preoccupation" for Libya, the likelihood of full-scale tribal revolt in East Africa if Italy went to war, and the deep pessimism of Cavagnari, Graziani, and Pricolo. Badoglio therefore concluded that Italian intervention would not be "profitable" unless "a *puissant* German action . . . should have truly prostrated the enemy forces to such an extent that every audacity would be justified." "That decision," he announced comfortingly, "is reserved for You, Duce: Our task is to execute Your orders."[21] Badoglio's obsequiousness scarcely concealed his refusal to cooperate. After a further conference on 13 April with the viceroy of East Africa, Badoglio reiterated his message. No offensives in East Africa were possible; all Italy's land fronts would thus be defensive ones. Mediterranean naval and air action offered no prospect of decisive success. Badoglio summed up in phrases that left no doubt of the outlines of his own war plan:

Nothing is left to us, then, but to continue our military preparations as best we can, and await the decisive collision between the belligerents in order to intervene when the state of prostration of our adversaries gives us a chance of success. This is a supremely delicate line of action. But You, O Duce, have guided the fate of the Nation with a steady hand in other circumstances of equal difficulty, and You will do the same in the present tragic situation.[22]

Cavagnari also committed his "uncertainties" to paper in a memorandum delivered to Badoglio on 11 April and to Mussolini on the 14th. The directives for an "offensive right down the line" had to be "interpreted and defined with precision." Cavagnari assumed that no combined operation against an "important strategic objective" was in the cards. This assumption was an expression of the Navy's preference. Malta was the most important such objective, but the Navy overestimated the strength of its defenses, and unlike the Germans lacked the self-confidence to plan amphibious operations in the face of Allied naval superiority. The fleet's other objective could only be the enemy naval forces. In that contest, Cavagnari insisted, all the advantages lay with the enemy, organized in "two huge fleets" in eastern and western Mediterranean. The Allies were already mobilized, and surprise attack was thus allegedly impossible. The planned mine barrage across the Sicily–Tunisia strait would serve little purpose. In neither eastern nor western Mediterranean would the Navy be strong enough to attack. Submarines would not tip the balance. If the enemy were to initiate "a decisively aggressive conduct of the war against Italy," a full-scale naval battle soon after the opening of hostilities was likely. Losses on both sides would be "immense." The Allies, with their superior forces and industrial capacity, could make good their losses. Italy could not. Cavagnari concluded that "in the absence of the possibility of achieving important strategic objectives or the defeat of the opposing naval forces, entry into the war of our own initiative, with the prospect of remaining on the defensive even by sea, does not seem justified." He ended with the depressing prediction that Italy "could arrive at the peace negotiations not only without territorial bargaining counters, but also without a fleet and possibly without an air force."[23]

Mussolini's military subordinates simply refused to contemplate a genuine war, and luxuriated in what the semiofficial historian of the Italian war effort, General Emilio Faldella, has described as "supine acceptance of the situation of the moment." In the Navy's case, more than acceptance was probably involved. Cavagnari later claimed the merit of having tried to slow Italy's "slide toward war."[24] In any case, the persistent tendency of all three services to gross overestimates of enemy strength, of which more later, paralyzed Italian planners. However, as will emerge, Mussolini proved equal to the task of convincing his generals and admirals that they need not fight — while concealing a passionately held intention of taking the Italian people "into combat."

On top of the remonstrances of the military came a further complication, this time from the Germans. Since Hitler had returned from the Brenner meeting "beaming with joy and highly contented," he had apparently proceeded on the assumption that his ally had wholeheartedly accepted the subordinate role offered on the upper Rhine.[25] Mussolini undoubtedly fostered this impression by approving in principle a German suggestion in late March that Roatta go to Berlin for staff talks "over the concrete preparation of a coalition war in either joint or separate theaters."[26] But Mussolini's lack of response at the Brenner, and above all his "parallel war" directives of 31 March, make clear he never seriously considered Hitler's suggestion.

When General Enno von Rintelen, the German military attaché, approached the Italian army staff on 10 April with a detailed proposal and the request that Roatta be in Berlin by the 16th, the Italians were surprised. Rintelen reported that "[a] concrete plan for Italian participation in the war . . . seems hardly to have existed, and if one did, it was certainly not along the lines of that proposed from the German side."[27] Graziani informed Mussolini that from a purely technical viewpoint Italian participation required certainty that the French would not attack across the Alps. Yugoslav neutrality was also indispensable. Graziani concluded that the German plan cut across Mussolini's strategic directives, and suggested confining the forthcoming Berlin talks to a "general exchange of ideas."[28]

Badoglio followed up with a letter to Mussolini designed to clarify his own position in the event of war; the law of 1927 that governed the powers of the chief of general staff merely provided he would "exercise the powers to be established for his post by the government." Badoglio had already raised the question of the high command in his 4 April letter. He now insisted that he would not serve as a mere consultant, nor allow Graziani to use the direct channel to Mussolini that Pariani had possessed. Graziani, and by implication Cavagnari and Pricolo as well, must be in operational matters the direct subordinates of the chief of general staff; any other solution would risk the "personal feuds and unsatisfactory functioning of the high command" that Badoglio recognized were "lamentably" common in Italian military history.

Badoglio also attacked the upper Rhine operation: "We would be going [there] to act the part of second echelon troops." He did not think that Mussolini, "who had felt so keenly and had held so high Italian prestige in 1935 and 1936 against the threats of the entire world, could possibly consent to the employment of our armed forces in this manner."[29] Badoglio was preaching to the converted. A conference of Mussolini, Badoglio, Soddu, and the service chiefs on 15 April apparently brought Graziani back into line. That evening, Soddu informed Rintelen that before sending Roatta to Berlin, Mussolini desired to "clarify the politico-military side" of the question directly in a letter to Hitler. The German proposal was "clearly understandable," but Mussolini had ostensibly not yet reached a decision. Soddu expressed hope that the talks would begin in about ten days. That was the end of the matter. Mussolini never wrote the letter, and by early May the Germans concluded they could mount the lower Rhine attack themselves.[30]

Toward a new geography. After 9 April, Mussolini mobilized press and propaganda services as well as the fleet. The clamor mounted. On 14 April Ciano's unofficial spokesman, Giovanni Ansaldo, delivered a radio address to the armed forces. It was the first public and authoritative statement that Italy's entry into the war in the next months was inevitable. The press did not report the speech, and the state broadcasting network and Ministry of Popular Culture showed "a rather curious reticence" when asked for a transcript. Pavolini, the minister, told his editors that "we are persuaded that there has been and continues to be a decisive turning point in the course of the war." This fact was not to "produce a sensation of imminence" as far as Italy was concerned. The British chargé put it more succinctly: "The Italian press has become completely Goebbelized."[31]

Another letter from Hitler arrived with a further lengthy report on the situation in Norway, where the German landing force hung on at Narvik despite Allied counteraction and Hitler's own panicky evacuation order, which he neglected to mention in the letter. Hitler concluded with words which "went straight to the heart" of the Duce:[32]

What these operations mean for us, and especially for me, is understood by one man in the whole world outside myself, and that man is You, Duce. You had the courage to conduct your action in Abyssinia under the cannons of the British. My situation up to now has not been much different, but I, too, have decided not to listen in the most difficult hours to the voice of so-called common sense, but instead appeal to . . . honor, . . . duty, and ultimately to my own heart.

Ciano, back from a week in bed with influenza, found Mussolini "more warlike and Germanizing" than ever. In a short appearance at Palazzo Venezia on 21 April he was "sober and moderate," contenting himself with recommending "labor and arms" to the assembled populace. Inside, to the representatives of the Fascist labor and management organizations, he was "100 percent extremist and pro-Axis."[33] With an enraged expression, and an occasional blow on the table for emphasis, Mussolini rhythmically stressed each syllable. He asked his audience "Are we independent?" Confused cries of "Yes!" and "No!" answered. After a gesture to indicate that the "No's" were fundamentally correct, Mussolini continued. Both answers were in some sense right – for to be independent was above all a matter of will. But in the realm of fact rather than of intention, Italy was not independent. "For eight months, for eight long months, I have felt a secret torment which makes me suffer physically – though from my appearance you would not know it – eight long months during which not one, I repeat, not one ship of ours has escaped the Allied controls." Though the time had not yet come to enlighten the Italian people about the full heinousness of the blockade, it was clear Italy was indeed a prisoner. It was useless, the Duce continued, to bemoan the possibility of German hegemony on the continent, for Italy faced a more dangerous fact: the maritime hegemony of the Allies that was depriving it of the raw materials without which it could not live. In any case, as he had announced in the past, Italy kept its word. Allied to the West, Italy would long since have had to go to war to pull Allied chestnuts from the fire for the same paltry recompense as in 1918 – whereas Germany, having no need of aid, had asked for nothing. The ills of the present stemmed from the Italians of former generations, who had cultivated the idyllic pastoral life while the Portuguese, the French, and the British had conquered entire continents.

From his "long meditations on history," Mussolini had derived a governing law – and here he explained to his audience the geopolitics of independence in his usual terms. These truths, he added, were ones upon which the Italian people would do well to meditate at length. According to one version of the speech, Mussolini authorized his audience to repeat what he had told them, then closed with the order to push ahead "full throttle," but without dramatizing the situation. Italy must prepare to face events "of which we cannot forever remain spectators."[34]

After this effusion, Mussolini directed Ciano to damp down alarm in the diplomatic corps, because he did not, at this point, intend to move until August.[35] Mussolini also had another bout with the King, whose caution

Mussolini reportedly answered with the assertion that Italy was *"de facto* a British colony, and that . . . *some* Italians would like to see it become one *de jure* as well."* Royal opposition had some effect; Mussolini once more contemplated putting Italian intervention off until 1941. The campaign in Scandinavia, he now theorized, had postponed the decisive moment in the West. Ciano therefore attempted to reassure the French and British representatives, with considerable success.[36]

Meanwhile, Mussolini received a series of peace appeals from Allies and neutrals, appeals he contemptuously passed on to Hitler, along with Italy's replies. A private letter from Reynaud received a "bold, acrid, contemptuous" rebuff, much to the amusement of Ciano, whose dislike of the French was ever more in evidence. Mussolini countered an unctuous papal message with a history lesson: the Church had never subscribed to "peace without justice." Roosevelt's appeal was more robust than the others: if the conflict widened, other nations, "however determined they may today be to remain at peace, might yet eventually find it imperative in their own defense to enter the war." Mussolini was furious. He urged on U.S. Ambassador William Phillips, and on Roosevelt, "the necessity of a 'new geography.' " Italy's situation as a prisoner in the Mediterranean was "intolerable," and no peace was possible "unless the fundamental issues of Italian freedom are resolved." Italy had avoided involvement in the affairs of the New World; it expected the United States to stay out of those of the Old.[37]

The propaganda crescendo designed to raise the temperature inside Italy continued. A Fascist of the first hour, Francesco Giunta, spoke fulsomely in the Chamber of German successes.[38] Grandi, hope of those in Italy and abroad who still had faith in the "moderates," followed:

There is but one watchword, today as yesterday and as always: absolute loyalty to You, Duce; blind faith in the goals indicated by You, silent virile obedience of Your orders and of the guiding lines that You have laid down, in keeping with Italy's honor and great historical interests.[39]

Diplomatically, the temperature also needed raising. Hitler, upon his return to Berlin from the Brenner, had pointedly refused to allow the Italian Embassy staff to greet him. In late April he requested the recall of Attolico, whose attitude, well known to the Germans through their decryption of Italian diplomatic traffic, was unsuitable to the new climate. Ciano, who had "lately become acute of hearing," was most forthcoming to Mackensen's cautious approach. Ciano judged Hitler's preferred candidate, Farinacci, "out of the question," but promised to put forward the Germans' second choice, Alfieri, along with his own "right hand," Anfuso. Ciano originally told Mackensen that he would retire Attolico forthwith, but then secured the ambassador's appointment to replace Alfieri at the Holy See. It would be unwise "to give the Germans the impression that their 'thumbs down' is enough to liquidate one of our people, who has done his duty well. Otherwise who knows where we will end up or who will be the next victim immolated upon the Nazi altar."[40] After a month of rumors of his own impending replacement, Ciano was extremely sensitive on this point – Attolico's report upon his return to Rome of Ribbentrop's open detestation of his Italian counterpart came as no surprise.

From Mussolini's point of view, the situation was developing well. He announced triumphantly to the Council of Ministers on 1 May that the "revolution" would triumph over Anglo-French "conservatism." News of the hurried British evacuation of central Norway rendered him "literally exultant" on 3 May.[41] A further incitement, a report from Major Giuseppe Renzetti, Mussolini's longtime confidential agent in Berlin, arrived the same day. On 27 April Göring, who had up to now alternated between approval and bumptious resentment of Italian nonbelligerence, for the first time sought to influence the Italians to enter the war. He warmly recommended the upper Rhine operation. Italy should go to war even if it were not completely prepared. Temporary loss of North Africa, the field marshal remarked lightheartedly, would be insignificant beside crushing Axis victory on the continent. Göring also felt that "at the beginning of the conflict Italy should immediately occupy Greece and block the Adriatic in order to take from Yugoslavia any inclination to enter the war at the side of the Allies."[42] All this was probably no more than the jovial field marshal's usual loose talk, but it came on top of a 25 April message from Hitler that "if the Duce believed it necessary or even opportune to improve his strategic position as he [Hitler] had done in Denmark and Norway, the Führer saw no inconvenience and would always be found at the Duce's side." The Germans, including Hitler, at this point apparently valued Italian cooperation enough to be ready – as in August 1939 – to purchase it with an Italian Balkan foray, despite the possibility that this would encourage the Russians to move against Rumania.[43] But Graziani, "worried by the responsibility," as Ciano put it, now advised against even the Croatian project, much less Italian intervention in the larger war.[44] When the chiefs of staff again met on 6 May at Mussolini's orders to consider the military situation in Libya and coordinate the sending of reinforcements, Badoglio reassuringly noted that "it is true that an offensive against Yugoslavia has been mentioned, but that doesn't mean that we are going to do it." Italy would move in that direction "if the situation require[d] it."[45]

The principal purpose of the chiefs' meeting of 6 May was to discuss the alleged need for massive reinforcement of Libya. Badoglio had agitated for reinforcement since the beginning of the preceding month, and had claimed that Italian forces were inadequate "even for a simple defensive." He now produced a grotesquely inflated Allied order of battle. 314,000 French and French colonials, 100,000 British and Egyptians, and the 200,000 men of General Weygand's French Syrian army faced a mere 140,000 Italian troops, or 230,000 after full mobilization.[46] Badoglio's figures were absurd: Weygand's army was ill equipped and immobile, and the 80,000 Egyptians were more of a threat to the British than to the Italians. Many of the French units were reserve divisions left behind after the transfer of the best North African troops to France in the fall of 1939. The threat from Spanish Morocco and internal security needs left the French only six divisions to deploy in Tunisia.[47] Badoglio's figures were either the consequence of intelligence error and exaggerated worst-case analysis, or were deliberate fabrications to keep Mussolini in his place. Political calculation may have played some role, given the anti-German convictions of the chief of the Servizio Informazioni Militari (SIM), General Giacomo Carboni. But Carboni was also incapable of correctly reading French strength even after Italy's entry into war; error rather than design was presumably the main source of the inflated figures.[48] SIM proved equally blind in southern France, where it discerned on 10 June twelve first-line divisions when the French had six at best, while air intelligence credited the *Armée de l'Air* with 2,060 aircraft in the Mediterranean theater when the actual figure by early June was perhaps 200 combat-ready bombers and fighters.[49]

Whatever the cause of the North African error, its effect was to reinforce further the defensive inclinations of Badoglio and colleagues, who were as yet unaware that numbers were an impediment in the desert, where mobility, firepower, armor, and hard-driving independent leadership were all-important. The service chiefs decided to bring Libya up to full war strength immediately. This well-intentioned measure merely strained the supply system, and ultimately swelled the British "bag" in December 1940–February 1941. Balbo, at least, was well aware that equipment was more important than mere numbers of *"uomini."* He pointed out in a letter to Mussolini of 11 May that "the finest of Caesar's legions would collapse if faced with a machine gun platoon." But despite vehement requests for equipment, he failed to define the simple choice he – and the Army as a whole – faced: either a small, relatively well-equipped mobile force, or a large, ill-equipped, sessile one.[50] In any case, Balbo's equipment requests did not receive the wholehearted cooperation of Mussolini's subordinates. Soddu insisted that the pressing requirements of other theaters meant the Army could only fill Balbo's needs to a very limited extent; he also demanded that Balbo keep to channels, and address Mussolini only through Badoglio.[51] Soddu and colleagues continued to pursue the unimaginative and unfeasible ambition of safety on all fronts.

Despite the apparently difficult situation in Libya, however, Italy's position was scarcely as desperate as in the previous September. A Favagrossa report to Mussolini on 13 May made clear that Italy could survive a short war, even though raw material stocks were still generally low, and many military production programs were in their beginnings.[52] The Germans were no help either in machine tools or materiel; in mid-April Hitler had secretly ruled out supplying arms to Italy.[53] But in other respects the Italian situation had considerably improved. The Navy was combat-ready, and expected four new or modernized battleships to join the fleet that summer. The Air Force, under Pricolo's supervision, now possessed 1,609 reasonably modern bombers and fighters, of which about 1,032 were fully combat-ready with line units – an increase of 768 and 463 respectively since November 1939. The Army, by the end of May, numbered 1,634,950 officers and men in Italy and the colonies, organized in seventy-three divisions, of which twenty-four were "complete," thirty "effective" but short of personnel and equipment, and nineteen "incomplete."[54] Notwithstanding this improvement, intervention remained a gamble – though Mussolini was less and less inclined to listen to the eternal difficulties of the experts and "the voice of so-called common sense." The state of prostration of Italy's adversaries was in any case soon to satisfy even the fastidious Badoglio and the ever-cautious Victor Emmanuel III.

Through the front door. On 10 May 1940, at 0535 German summer time, the *Wehrmacht* struck at Holland and Belgium with wave upon wave of bombers, gliders, and paratroops. On the ground, infantry and armor drove forward across the Dutch and Belgian canal lines. Seven panzer and three motorized infantry divisions plunged into the hills and woods of the Ardennes, and emerged on 12 May to seize the Meuse crossings and sweep across northern France in one of the greatest strategic surprises in modern history. As with Norway, Hitler was unwilling to trust the Italians with details, date, or time of the operation. His letter, delivered to the hastily awakened Duce at 0500, announced that "when you receive this letter, I [shall] have already crossed the Rubicon." Hitler tactfully promised to keep Mussolini fully informed in order to permit him to take "in full freedom" whatever decisions the Duce might feel necessary "in the interest of [his] people." Mussolini thanked Hitler warmly and declared that by the end of May he would have two army groups ready facing France and Yugoslavia. He did not promise action.[55]

Ciano tried to convince François-Poncet, Loraine, and Phillips that no Italian move was imminent. To Loraine, Ciano was remarkably explicit: "the whole face of things would be changed if the Germans broke through and smashed France," or if they failed to do so. Ciano wanted to believe Loraine's assurances that the Allies would hold, but clearly could not. Nor did he confine his conversations on that day to the corps diplomatique. He summoned the terrorist leader Pavelić from cold storage and prepared to "pass to the executive phase" in Croatia. Further delay would permit "sympathies to orient themselves toward Germany," and once more raise the specter of a German presence on the Adriatic. The Italian consul general in Zagreb had just reported pro-German stirrings within the Croat Peasant Party. Mussolini dramatically marked a date in early June on his calendar, and ordered the recall from Madrid of the ambassador, General Gastone Gambara, the most successful Italian commander of the Spanish war and a particular favorite of the Duce and Ciano. Gambara was to take command of the forces spearheading the attack on Yugoslavia.[56]

On the home front, thousands of anti-British posters appeared mysteriously on the walls of Rome and other Italian cities on 11 May. A group of Party activists, possibly including plainclothes policemen, administered "various beatings" in Via Veneto, "even including foreigners (a Dutchman and several Englishmen) who had dared to tear the posters down," as Muti reported to Mussolini in his characteristic tone of casual brutality. Muti's enthusiasts had set upon the British naval attaché and another member of the embassy staff, and had also manhandled Noel Charles, Loraine's second-in-command, when he arrived to protest. Charles, again according to the PNF's report to Mussolini, had "provocatively refused to return to the embassy unless protected by the police, but subsequently came around." Ciano was actively hostile when Loraine remonstrated the next day. He compared the anti-British posters to "free speech" in England, and refused to explain the activities of the Party.[57]

As well as unleashing Muti's *squadristi,* Mussolini released the dossier on the British blockade that Ciano had assembled. Drafted in the form of a memorandum to Mussolini by Ambassador Luca Pietromarchi, the Foreign Ministry's chief troubleshooter and current head of the economic warfare section, it was a withering indictment of British methods. Pavolini went through the memorandum paragraph by paragraph for the benefit of his editors. The morning papers were to publish it "with the greatest emphasis [*sensibilizzazione*]," following up with "clear, firm, and even violent" commentaries. The press also received orders to take up German accusations that Holland and Belgium had pursued the grossly unneutral policy of defending their neutrality solely against Germany. Pavolini also ordered a counterattack on papal messages of sympathy to the invaded states.[58] In extreme irritation, Mussolini dispatched a diplomatic protest to Pius XII, and loosed Farinacci's *Regime Fascista* and the *Resto del Carlino* of Bologna against the Vatican's *Osservatore Romano,* which persisted in carrying Allied news bulletins. The Vatican also aroused Mussolini's wrath by choosing this moment to place on the Index the works of Alfredo Oriani, a late nineteenth-century nationalist philosopher-historian the regime considered a precursor of Fascism.[59] The Pope was part of that old order that victory would permit Mussolini to sweep away. Ciano noted on 12 May:

In these [last] days [Mussolini] often repeats that the Papacy is a cancer gnawing at our national life, and that he intends – if necessary – to liquidate this problem once and for all. He added: "The Pope had better not think he can seek alliance with the Monarchy because I am ready to blow up both institutions together. The seven cities of the Romagna are enough to do in Pope and King simultaneously."[60]

The next morning, 13 May, Mussolini made up his mind. The Allies had "lost the war," he announced to Ciano. Italy was already dishonored enough, and further delay "inconceivable." He would declare war within the month, and "attack France and England by sea and air." He no longer planned action

against Yugoslavia: it would be "a humiliating comedown." Ciano immediately trimmed his sails. He could no longer attempt to restrain Mussolini:
"He has decided to act, and act he will."

The Yugoslav minister visited Ciano the next day "in a state of great
agitation" to complain of street demonstrations demanding the annexation
of Dalmatia and rumors that Italy would enter the war by attacking Yugoslavia while avoiding battle with the Allies. Ciano answered with hauteur
that "when Italy entered the war against France and England, it would do it
through the front door – rather than through the servants' back entrance."[61]
Mussolini now had bigger game than Yugoslavia in mind. Despite Hitler's
explicit approval of any moves that might improve Italy's "strategic position," and the disarray of the Allies, which at last guaranteed that an Italian
Balkan action would meet no Western opposition, Mussolini deliberately
chose a Mediterranean war even before the magnitude of German triumph
became apparent. It was more than a question of prestige or "honor," or of
fulfilling Italy's Pact of Steel commitments. Mussolini had after all signed
that agreement with certain objectives in mind. From his Grand Council
remarks of November 1938 ("for the requirements of our security in this
Mediterranean that still confines us") to the eve of war and beyond, his goals
were consistent in nature, massive in scope, and pursued with tenacity
within the limits Italy's military and economic weaknesses imposed. Mussolini, as he told Ciano and Anfuso at the end of May, indeed "believed"
that Italy must "establish its supremacy in the Mediterranean," and he was
prepared to act on that belief. Nor, despite the military's refusal to cooperate
in offensive planning, were the Italian armed forces in so desperate a condition that Mussolini could not contemplate genuine fighting. As he had
remarked to Ciano after the German coup in Scandinavia, if Italy did not
intend to measure its Navy against the Allies, why should it maintain
600,000 tons of warships? By mid-May, Mussolini did not intend to let
opportunity slip.

Mussolini also entered the war in pursuit of a domestic political program.
As his repeated and ever more vehement outbursts to Ciano in March, April,
and May demonstrate, he would no longer suffer the restrictions under which
he labored at home. The anticipated war "of a few months" would enable
him to prove, "once and for all," not merely to the world but to the Italians
themselves that they were indeed a warrior nation.[62] Victory would not only
secure Mediterranean hegemony and mastery of the Middle East, it would
also give the dictator the prestige to at last sweep away monarchy, Church,
and "bourgeoisie" enamored of the comfortable life. Mussolini's war was to
be a war of internal as well as foreign conquest, a war of revenge on the
Italian establishment.[63]

Ciano, caught amidst doubts, loyalty, and territorial appetite, fell into
line. His private doubts were now predominantly tactical: "a mistake in
[choosing] the moment to come in would be fatal." To Mackensen, who
delivered another message from Hitler on 14 May, Ciano spoke "for the first

time positively about the active intervention of Italy." He excused himself for not having used his influence before; now, however, "the moment had come." Italy would move in ten to fourteen days. Hitler's message, which proclaimed the Dutch broken, and announced that the swastika flew over the citadel at Liège, deeply impressed Mussolini. He judged correctly that the uncontested air superiority of the *Luftwaffe*, which Hitler announced as the principal result of the first day's action, would prove decisive. He foresaw a large-scale battle of movement *west* of the Maginot Line, and planned to reply immediately, informing Hitler of the steps Italy proposed to take. While Mussolini conferred with Ciano and Mackensen, a crowd composed primarily of students chanted outside Palazzo Venezia. The day before, the first street demonstrations for intervention had occurred in Rome: groups of students had marched through the city shouting "we want war."[64]

Mussolini refused to receive Ambassador Phillips when he arrived on 15 May bearing a new message from Roosevelt – this one full of what Ciano contemptuously dismissed as "Christian-sentimental meditations." The president's melodramatic dating ("midnight, 14 May") gave Ciano further cause for mirth. Churchill, now in the saddle in London, had better luck. His message sought to place the moral burden of a Mediterranean war on the Italians, and struck Ciano as "dignified and noble." Even Mussolini appreciated its tone. But his reply was a harsh denunciation of the "state of genuine slavery in which Italy finds itself in its own sea."[65]

Unfortunately, the military situation was still uncertain enough so that Mussolini could not hope to carry Badoglio, King, and military chiefs with him. Badoglio believed that to break through the Maginot Line would take four months and a million lives. Soddu thought the French defense in Flanders would be "absolutely unbreachable." On 18 May, he still considered Allied defeat not yet decisive, and asked for two more weeks before venturing a definitive judgment. As for the King, he was "negative" about German military prospects as late as 21 May.[66] In spite of his earlier predictions about "walled nations," Mussolini himself now showed an instinctive grasp of the revolutionary nature of German methods which his generals lacked. But he still had to reckon with their opinions. He was also doubtless as mindful as Ciano that a mistake in timing could be fatal. Until the German attack in the West, some on the Allied side still desired an enemy they could "defeat heavily and swiftly," as a purported British naval intelligence summary (that the Italian Navy intercepted and Mussolini read) put it.[67] The document was probably bogus, part of an elaborate British disinformation scheme designed to influence the Italian leadership, but in this case it accurately represented Allied intentions. Chamberlain had asked Reynaud on 27 April for French bases from which an RAF bomber force might pound Italy's industrial centers. The British Joint Planning Committee viewed the virtually defenseless Genoa–Turin–Milan triangle with lip-smacking anticipation. In early May they judged that "the Italian" was "not renowned for endurance under conditions of strain and direct attack," and apocalyptically predicted that air action against Italy might "at best . . . mean the end of Fascism and the collapse of Italy." At worst, air bombardment would "probably fatally weaken Italian offensive operations against Egypt, Tunis, and in the Balkans owing to the need for them to recall air forces for the defence of the home country."[68] The planners overstated the effects of air attack and underestimated the resilience of the Italian home front. But Italy was clearly vulnerable, and the persistent overestimates of French strength by Italian air intelligence presumably made the situation seem even worse than it was.

Mussolini also had to solve a delicate internal problem before he could move. He must convert the monarchy, for Italy could not go to war without a high command. That function remained a constitutional prerogative of the King, notwithstanding Mussolini's announced intent of leading the armed forces in person. Badoglio had repeatedly raised the thorny question of war leadership from early April on. In mid-April, Soddu had sought to prepare Mussolini's assumption of command in person, à la Hitler, with Badoglio serving (like Keitel) as executive assistant. Cavagnari, for once more Mussolinian than Mussolini, insisted that each service chief be free to conduct his own war under the Duce's guidance. This solution would have maximized Cavagnari's own power, and removed any danger of Army interference in the *arcana* of naval warfare. But Soddu and Mussolini brushed Cavagnari aside; Badoglio would have a direct role as part of "the high command hierarchy." This was not enough for Badoglio himself, and on 3 May he once more insisted that a purely advisory position was unacceptable to a "commander of the status of a Badoglio (to use the expression You have had the kindness to use in my regard)."[69] Badoglio's letter and the action in France and Flanders prompted Mussolini to take the initiative. As was characteristic of his dealings with the monarchy, his method was indirect. He apparently commissioned Soddu to sound out the King and Badoglio. Soddu acted with both imagination and duplicity, balancing delicately between Duce, Badoglio, and King. To General Puntoni, the King's first aide-de-camp, Soddu argued that political and military coordination in a modern "totalitarian" war required a "single military and political command" that only Mussolini could exercise. To sweeten the pill, Soddu suggested presciently that it was perhaps not politic to saddle the Crown with such grave responsibility. The monarchy should preserve the capacity to "save the Nation in case the Regime were to become shaky or actually threaten to crumble." He added that alongside Mussolini would be a chief of general staff, who, in Soddu's eyes, "could not be other than Badoglio." Soddu apparently sought to gain the monarchy as an ally for Badoglio, and reassure the King that the conduct of the war, though delegated to Mussolini, would be under professional supervision. Finally, Soddu urged haste, and suggested ominously that if the King did not delegate command to Mussolini of his own accord, the dictator might confront them all with a *fait accompli*. Soddu apologized to Puntoni for not having approached the sovereign directly, excusing himself disingenuously by explaining that "his every movement was watched";

he had not "wanted his presence at the Quirinal to be misinterpreted at Palazzo Venezia."[70]

Before seeing Puntoni, Soddu had already informed Badoglio of Mussolini's intentions. According to the account he gave the marshal, Soddu had insisted to Mussolini that Badoglio have a command function. The marshal would sign all orders to the Armed Forces – an arrangement Soddu had made palatable to Mussolini with a suggestion as prescient as that about limiting the monarchy's liabilities in case of defeat. "In case things went badly," Mussolini could "torpedo" Badoglio in order to retain his own prestige intact.[71]

The King got wind of what was afoot. Characteristically obstinate over points of form, Victor Emmanuel ultimately conceded the substance. On 1 June he agreed to delegate to Mussolini command of the armed forces *in combat,* but not command of the armed forces as a whole. In practice, this nebulous and unworkable distinction remained inoperative, but the King also attempted to preserve his prerogatives in another way. On the first day of war, 11 June, he gave Mussolini command not with a legally binding royal decree, but by simple proclamation. The King had only half surrendered, and his memory was long. In his parting interview with Mussolini in July 1943, minutes before the dictator's arrest, Victor Emmanuel III bitterly recalled rumors that the Duce, in 1940, had threatened to "boot [the King] in the butt" unless he delegated command.[72] That Mussolini did not do just that in May 1940 is a measure of his dependence on the monarchy – a fetter he hoped war and victory would sever.

During this maneuvering, the military situation had been changing with unprecedented rapidity. On 16 May Ciano still judged reports of German breakthrough exaggerated, and an optimistic Loraine report of Allied resistance momentarily swayed Mussolini. But a day later German triumph was clear. Ciano did his best to maintain a measure of private skepticism, even while "moderates" like Grandi fawningly embraced intervention, claiming " 'that we have to admit that we have gotten it all wrong,' and must prepare ourselves for new eras." In public, Ciano too began to "speak of the German victories as if they were a triumph of his own policy."[73] Evidently at Mussolini's request, he addressed a great rally in Milan's Piazza del Duomo on 19 May. On the way, Ciano passed through Cremona and demonstrated publicly a newfound solidarity with Farinacci, who according to his own later account had organized the occasion to quash rumors that he himself would soon replace Ciano as foreign minister. To the Milan crowd Ciano hailed the glorious past of Milanese Fascism, and "the spirit of dedication, the spirit of faith, in which the Italian people is preparing to meet the new tasks to which it may be called." He did not forget to hint at Italy's "aspirations." At Mussolini's request, Ciano described the dictator as "our sole Chief in peace and war" – a warning to the King not to insist too long on his high command prerogatives. The crowd reacted with "very moderate warmth," despite frenetic agitation by Party activists. Ciano returned with the impression that Milan "viewed [Italy's] entry into the war, even under present conditions, as an unwelcome necessity."[74]

From Ciano's point of view, the most important task was now to secure some sort of advance agreement with the Germans on dividing the booty. Italy's intervention in World War I and the fateful ambiguities of the 1915 Treaty of London were much on his mind. He therefore proposed to meet Ribbentrop at some point after the first of June and engage in an exercise in the "new geography."[75] Nothing came of the idea, probably because Italy's bargaining position as a nonbelligerent facing a victorious ally was as yet too weak, and also because French collapse in early June came far more quickly than expected.

In one sector Ciano could take action: his private fief in Albania, ruled by his satrap, Lieutenant-General of the King Francesco Jacomoni di San Savino. As early as 30 April Ciano had spoken lightheartedly to his minister in Athens, Emanuele Grazzi, of a landing on Corfù, and had appalled him by inquiring after Albanians disposed to "remove" the Anglophile King of Greece. By 17 May, Ciano had already decided to visit Tirana for four days beginning on the 22nd. Mackensen had the impression that Ciano intended "not only to inspire Italian military and civilian authorities, but also – and perhaps primarily – to . . . make contact personally with Albanians whose employment seems useful at some point for the accomplishment of certain tasks."[76]

The nature of these tasks emerges only in part from Ciano's diary, which mentions the "warm reception everywhere" of the Albanian crowds, and records with satisfaction that "the Albanians are enthusiastically launched on the road to intervention; they want Kossovo and Ciamuria. It is easy for us to increase our popularity by making ourselves exponents of Albanian nationalism."[77] Ciano did not confine himself to raising the temperature publicly. On the evening of 23 May he summoned General Carlo Geloso, chief of the Army's Albanian Command. After inquiring about the comparative strengths of Italian and Greek forces along the border, Ciano enlarged on the political situation:

he considered probable the entry of Italy into the war in a few weeks: two or three, he subsequently specified.

He added that on the basis of the political situation he considered it probable that for now we would not operate against Yugoslavia except in the event of an internal collapse of that state which required a rapid reaction. Instead, he spoke explicitly of a large-scale operation against Greece, which is becoming a genuine aero-naval base for the Allies, a state of affairs that must be avoided.

Geloso replied that he would need at least ten or eleven divisions, of which two must be motorized and one armored; he also requested instructions from his superiors in Rome.[78] Something he said, or information from Jacomoni, appears to have convinced Ciano that the general lacked enthusiasm; in the next days the foreign minister promoted Geloso's removal in favor of General Sebastiano Visconti Prasca, who was commanding a corps on the French border after a tour of duty as military attaché in Paris. While in Albania, Ciano also seems to have conferred with Nebil Dino, secretary of the Tirana *Fascio,* and given orders to recruit irregulars from both sides of the Greek border to create disorders in Ciamuria. For the moment, the Albanians were to limit their expressed aspirations to Greek territory. Albanian claims against Yugoslavia would have to wait.[79]

Despite the emphatic nature of Ciano's remarks to Geloso, neither Mussolini nor his military advisers planned to attack Greece at this point. The idea was as much the creation of Ciano's ambition as the Albanian coup had been: a move within the general framework of Mussolini's aims, but displaying the combination of ingenuity and fecklessness characteristic of Ciano. When Geloso's report of his interview with the foreign minister finally reached Badoglio on 7 June, the marshal's chief assistant commented that it was "interesting how everybody gives directions and orders without realizing that war is no joking matter."[80]

Nor did Mussolini so consider it. A further Hitler message had arrived on 18 May, announcing breakthrough: "the miracle of the Marne of 1914 [would] not repeat itself!" Mussolini's reply was warm, and promised "important news in the next days," but went no farther. He was still "weighing the possibilities," as Bottai noted after a conversation that same day. By the time Ciano had returned from Albania on 25 May, however, Mussolini had taken the final decision. A stream of reports had been arriving from Alfieri, who had with much pomp taken up his station in Berlin. The ambassador emphasized the confidence of the Germans and the shattering successes of tanks and *Luftwaffe.* Ernst von Weizsäcker, Ribbentrop's chief subordinate, as well as Goebbels and Göring, pressed for Italian action, and for staff talks. The Göring message, which urged Italian intervention as soon as Allied forces in Flanders capitulated and the Germans turned toward Paris, made a deep impression in Rome, although Göring probably spoke without consultation with Hitler. On the evening of 25 May Mackensen arrived with yet another message from the Führer, this one proclaiming that the Allies in the low countries were doomed. Hitler estimated he had encircled sixty divisions, and claimed British leadership was "miserable" and French reserve divisions rotten. Mussolini received the news in the highest of spirits, and promised to answer immediately with "important news." Earlier in the day, the Navy ministry had sent a warning order to Italian merchant captains to scuttle their ships, in case of war, if capture by blockading forces seemed imminent. On the afternoon of 26 May, after a tumultuous Party youth ceremony at which placards demanding *"guerra"* had emerged from the serried ranks, Mussolini told Mackensen that "the time had come." He would strike "in the next days." He could not bear to wait longer. He was "the most impatient of all Italians."[81]

The skin of the bear, I. Other Italians were also becoming impatient.[82] This was a new development. Reaction to the German coup in Scandinavia had been limited, and, despite Ciano's patronizing remarks about the *"popolo,"* not entirely favorable. In Milan, reported one police informant, "no excessive enthusiasm" for Italian intervention reigned.[83] The public was "in the majority anti-German," even though an undercurrent in the cafés, "especially in the center of town, . . . support[ed] the Germans."[84] Some "view[ed] with a jaundiced eye the continuously arrogant behavior . . . of England."[85] But the general view, in the words of an informant who had mingled with the crowd at the Milan trade fair in mid-April, was "may God save Italy from a war for which no one sees the necessity."[86]

The German attack in the West on 10 May did not in itself change this attitude. In Turin, "the great majority of the population did not have words enough to condemn" the German assault on the low countries. "Every section of the population without any distinction whatsoever between social classes" shared this "indignation."[87] Two days later, "commentators, in the majority, lament[ed] the fate of these two small nations [Holland and Belgium]." Nevertheless, "some" now considered Italian action inevitable: "We cannot wait until the Germans have won before intervening."[88] In Padua, many now felt the moment had come: "Now or never (*ora o mai più*) for our territorial aspirations."[89] In Milan, by 12 May, a shift in opinion was perceptible. "Some" now recognized that Italy's "rights and interests," and "the future of the *Impero*," required war.[90] The next day, another informant reported that "public opinion in general and the various specific groups (*i vari ambienti*) [were] gradually recognizing the just cause defended by the new Germany and [were] converting themselves to it" – although fear that a victorious Germany could "turn its appetites toward Italy" (a recurrent theme in reports from the North in general and Milan in particular) accompanied this feeling.[91] Rome seems to have lagged slightly. On 12 May "the state of mind of the majority of the Roman population still [clung] to views contrary to . . . intervention because it [was] impossible to understand the motives that supposedly compel us to go to war."[92] Some "old Fascists" of the World War I generation even displayed hatred for the Germans, and talked of volunteering to fight alongside the French.[93]

In the North, expressions of dissent rapidly diminished. By 14 May, an informant reported from Milan that "no one deludes himself any more about the chances that Italy can succeed in remaining outside the war to the end." It was a "question of choosing the opportune moment, and this the Duce, in whom there remains an unlimited confidence, must see to."[94] In Genoa, by 16 May, the population was reportedly moving toward support of the Germans: "even known anti-Fascists are reflecting, and have begun to lose much of their hope."[95] At Pisa, the public "commented for the most part on the military successes of Germany with admiration and enthusiasm, and not without words of indignation against England and France."[96] In Milan, informants reported on the same date "a certain evolution in public opinion

. . . which although remaining distrustful of the Germans and only in part agreeing with the official line . . . is on the other hand resigning itself to present necessities."[97] In the movie houses, Hitler's appearance on newsreels now met with applause, despite the dislike of Germans "felt by a strong majority" of the people of Lombardy.[98] But on 17 May one report to Mussolini himself emphasized that the situation in Milan was still far from satisfactory:

—a fairly large mass, composed especially of elements of the middle classes, makes no mystery of being against war.
—a minority, composed of young students and of the most ardent Fascists, supports our intervention and loses no opportunity to organize demonstrations.
It is in any case certain that the great majority of the Milanese have no love at all for Germany. As far as the recent demonstrations are concerned, it is interesting that the population did not participate.[99]

But even to outsiders, things were rapidly changing. Ambassador Phillips, whose reporting was sober and accurate on points subject to corroboration, remarked that the Party's poster campaign was "undoubtedly stimulating widespread anti-British sentiment." Berlin concluded by 17 May that "certain hitherto retarding elements have reversed themselves under the effects of the German advance," and General Franz Halder of the German army staff dryly noted that "internal resistance to war in Italy is melting . . . Mussolini has a free hand."[100]

In Rome, opinion swung into line. On 21 May, a report noted that all but a minority considered Italy "could no longer remain an inert spectator of the events that are rapidly unfolding, but must be an important factor in the formation of the New Europe that shall soon be redeemed from the slavery of Franco-British hegemony."[101] According to another report, "the people are for war because they are counting on its taking a rapid course and on an immediate, victorious peace."[102] Ciano, upon his return from Albania, received "hearty welcomes" at the railroad stations along his way to Rome: "The people want to know what will be done, and I even hear many voices demand war. Until a few days ago, that did not happen."[103]

In these days, Mussolini showed to Ciano and Anfuso the transcript of a routinely intercepted telephone conversation between a prominent journalist and Gaetano Polverelli, an early newspaper associate of Mussolini's who was now a high official in the Ministry of Popular Culture. Both the conversation and Mussolini's reaction are instructive. Polverelli's caller began: "Gaetano, have you seen how the Germans are gobbling up everything? What's left for us? What are we waiting for? All these years we've been talking about Nice, and now it's going to end up in the hands of the Germans." Polverelli was reassuring: "You're right, but I don't think there is cause for alarm. I expect Our Friend has thought of everything. It would be strange if he had not. It isn't a case of fighting a war, but of not being absent."

To Ciano, whose "defeatism" he still felt the need to combat, the "Friend" was sarcastic:

[they] evidently see further than I do . . . but this same thing is what thousands of Italians are saying every day. . . . I have to content not only P. [the caller] and Polverelli, who may well be carried away by professional zeal, but less well known Italians, who are asking themselves what I am doing behind this balcony . . . if I absent myself, as Polverelli says, in a moment like this. I have often asked myself if the Italians want their country to become great. Sometimes, I have my doubts, but in my better moments I believe that they desire it. . . . we will enter the war at Germany's side because the Italian people would never pardon me for having lost a chance like this.[104]

These words, directed at Ciano, hardly do justice to Mussolini's own motives; he had, after all, been working for nine months to create a situation in which Italy could fight to best advantage. But his remarks are an accurate comment on Italian public opinion. To dismiss the wave of bellicosity that swept Italy in late May as merely "the dogmas of the new conformism, repeated by millions of mouths, and collected, at the end of the artificial circuit, by the informers of the police" is too charitable, as is the parallel thesis that the public was prey to "a sort of collective hysteria, an excitement similar to that created by a sporting event."[105]

Visions of a Mediterranean triumph, cheaply bought, seduced the educated classes. The diary of Michele Lanza, second secretary of the Berlin Embassy, is symptomatic. Despite a virulent upper-class distaste for the plebeian leaders of the regime and dark misgivings about the future, Lanza nevertheless wrote on 1 June 1940 lines that suggest some continuity in breadth of aspirations, if not in taste for risk and internal revolutionary motivation, between the older traditions of Italian diplomacy and Mussolini's expansionism:

There is no doubt that the guiding idea of our foreign policy as a "Great Power" (and the initial error was probably that of considering ourselves – and insisting that we be considered – one, after the accomplishment of unity) has been to achieve hegemony [predominio] in the Mediterranean, an idea that, for a strange combination of reasons, has been in great part realized in the last years. It would have been necessary to stop for at least a century before proceeding further. But a fundamentally mistaken foreign policy, conducted by factious and susceptible dilettantes whom we have not found the moral courage to oppose, has placed us unexpectedly, at the moment of a tremendous conflict, right in the path of Great Britain. . . .

It is now a fight to the death. Either we win and become in reality the principal Mediterranean power, a great Empire, which, in any case, we do not have sufficient strength and aptitude to control and exploit. Or we lose, and in that sorry case the British will not pardon us the danger they will have run . . ., and will reduce us from the status of a great power to that of a secondary, more or less "protected" state.[106]

In the same vein, a postwar semiofficial military author has written with a delightful lack of self-consciousness that Mussolini entered the war "in order to resolve the great problems of our national life," but imprudently did so without the "quasi-certainty" of Axis victory. Mussolini "wanted to cut corners (*bruciare le tappe*) and obtain in the course of a generation what was, if at all, realizable by several generations."[107]

By late May, imaginations in Roman political and business circles were "galloping," according to the writer of the private intelligence service of the head of the Stefani news agency:

Paris and London are supposed to capitulate immediately! [But] one should not take possession of the bear's skin without having killed him first. Could a second miracle of the Marne occur in France? In general, miracles do not repeat themselves . . . in any case, opinion is general *that it will be the British Empire above all that pays.* . . . To Italy would fall *Tunisia, Corsica, Malta, the two Somalias* [French and British] and the *Sudan.* . . .

A few days later, the same writer had himself begun to divide up the bear's skin: "Balbo and the Victory [the Duke of Aosta] are the two figures upon whom the gaze of the Italians will concentrate during the next weeks. They are to realize the conjunction (without a break) of our Empire from Tripoli to Addis Ababa and beyond, toward Kenya."[108]

The major industrialists also adapted to the new climate, although they were far from conspicuously bellicose. As late as mid-March, Giovanni Agnelli of FIAT reported to his shareholders that Italy had remained out of the war "thanks to the realistic and far-seeing policy of Mussolini." Alberto Pirelli published in early May a survey of the economic effects of the European war that emphasized, between the lines, Italy's inability to fight the war of attrition Pirelli considered under way. Only with the "triumphal German advance" of May did Pirelli come to the realization, enshrined in the preface to the second volume of his study, published in June, that "the crushing superiority of the armies of the Reich" had "overturned the [Allied] attempt at a long war of endurance that deliberately counted on the blockade and on the exhaustion of stockpiles."[109]

The wider public's views on war aims are not easily discernible, but by the end of May enthusiasm, particularly among the young, ran high: "In the spirit of the masses of the university students there exists only one burning desire: to fight for the greatness of Italy, for the historical and geographical aspirations, for the independence of the *Impero.*"[110] From Milan, an informant reported on 4 June conclusions based on soundings that included people who were "scarcely adherents" of the regime and the Axis. The public now believed that the war,

although fearsome, is necessary for us too, that the friendship with Germany is not a danger and an evil for us Italians, but a good, and [is] the only chance for Italy to assure its interests and its territorial demands. This is the talk of the day, and while most people painted in dark colors the situation in Milan with respect to the Italo-German friendship, and of our intervention in war, today most agree that the decision of the Duce will find Milan ready to do everything commanded.[111]

From Florence, a regional police inspector reported to Bocchini on 9 June that

The doubters have fallen silent, and the anti-Fascists are ultracautious. . . . the expectation of a swift, easy, and bloodless war against a France bled white and an England disorganized and with a decimated fleet, is rapidly maturing.[112]

The Italian public was ready to partake of the spoils.

The end of appeasement. The great German victories that produced such a dramatic rise in temperature in Italy did not fail to have effects elsewhere. Even before the cataclysmic morning of 10 May, British and French policy toward Italy was deliquescent. After refusing at the end of April to commit itself to war in the event Italy attacked Yugoslavia, the War Cabinet decided on 6 May to consider loosening contraband control in the Mediterranean with a view to soothing Mussolini.[113] The following day the revolt of the Conservative back-benches against Chamberlain's conduct of the war came to a head. The German attack in the West finished the job. The "old, decayed serving men"[114] of Chamberlain's set relinquished control to Winston Spencer Churchill, who proclaimed on 13 May that he had nothing to offer but "blood, toil, tears and sweat," and that his policy was "to wage war, by sea, land, and air, with all our might" in order to secure "victory at all costs . . . victory, however long and hard the road may be." Privately, he attempted to stiffen the pusillanimous and anti-Semitic United States Ambassador, Joseph P. Kennedy: Great Britain would "never give up as long as he remain[ed] a power in public life even if England [were] burnt to the ground."[115]

British attempts to appease Italy, or at least "to leave to Mussolini, as to the Italians themselves, sole and entire onus of any decision he may make," proceeded as before. From Rome, Loraine advised "Fabian tactics." By 14 May, Halifax had thought better of declaring war in the event of Italian attack on Yugoslavia. The next day, in Cabinet, he suggested to the new prime minister the "dignified and noble" letter to Mussolini that Churchill dispatched on 16 May.[116] Halifax and his advisers also arranged a meeting on the evening of 15 May between Bastianini and the foreign secretary's assiduously conciliatory and increasingly defeatist parliamentary private secretary, R. A. Butler.[117] Butler promised Bastianini that the British Government intended to "eliminate all inconveniences lamented by [Italy]." Loraine made a similar communication in Rome. Bastianini in turn made effusive promises of good behavior: "He thought that [Britain] underestimated the sense of honour of the Fascist State. They were not a pack of jackals waiting to join in the hunt when their possible quarry was suffering a reverse."[118] Ciano urged a "truly radical and definitive" solution: the total abolition of control on Italy's Mediterranean shipping. The British did not promise so much. They did, however, release all merchandise accumulated in Italian ports under the "hold-back guarantee" system, and on 21 May dispatched an emissary to Rome with full negotiating powers.[119]

At this point, more serious issues than contraband control raised their heads. French military collapse was obvious, and political collapse was not far behind. By 17 May, Ambassador Guariglia reported that some in the French Cabinet hoped to assuage Italy's Mediterranean aspirations with concessions that included their ally's position at Gibraltar. Guariglia's contacts suggested pathetically that France's continued existence as a factor in the European balance of power was in Italy's interest. Reynaud himself offered on 18 May to open talks on Italy's "situation in the Mediterranean," and appealed to the United States ambassador for a further message from Roosevelt to Mussolini. Daladier, now foreign minister under Reynaud, painted for the British ambassador "lurid pictures of what war with Italy would mean to France at this moment." He was thinking over "immediate concessions." The prospect of having "2,000 Italians bombing and attacking all vital spots within reach" made Daladier quail. He did not agree with the British ambassador's correct view that Mussolini "could not be bought off."[120]

In London, despite equal skepticism about the efficacy of even the most tempting offer, the War Cabinet reluctantly joined the French appeal for a Roosevelt message conveying Allied willingness to make concessions to Italy at war's end. But notwithstanding some outside pressure for immediate concessions, the majority of the Churchill Cabinet was by this point primarily concerned to avoid French accusations that British intransigence stood in the way of successfully bribing Mussolini. Such accusations might serve as ammunition against Britain in the increasingly probable event that the German advance impelled France to seek a separate peace.

In some quarters the habit of appeasement nevertheless died hard. Unofficial hints from a subordinate of Bastianini's that "a great many influential people in Italy . . . desired to see a peaceful solution of the Mediterranean problem" gave Halifax an opening. Although Churchill lacked enthusiasm, the foreign secretary on the evening of 25 May offered Bastianini immediate negotiations on all political issues between Britain and Italy. Halifax did not even bother to consult the French, whose acquiescence he took for granted.[121] The next morning, Reynaud flew to London, herald of French collapse. The battle was lost, Pétain and Weygand on the verge of pressing for armistice, hope of United States aid vain. For the French, nothing remained but recourse to a massive bribe to the Italians in the hope that they would yet abstain – and perhaps even condescend to mediate between *Grossdeutschland* and the defeated West.[122]

German interest in Italian entry into the war inevitably declined. At the Wilhelmstrasse, in the best Bismarckian tradition, State Secretary Ernst von Weizsäcker envisaged "pushing I[taly] against Fr[ance]," then "richly rewarding I[taly] in order to perpetuate the [Italian] conflict with Fr[ance]." Party circles, inebriated with ideological fellow feeling and propaganda about Italian might, urged Mussolini to "go for the throat" of the Allies. The German army staff was profoundly indifferent. By 21 May, the Upper Rhine attack seemed more than feasible – *"ohne Italien."* The German navy now saw Italian participation as "thoroughly undesirable," a viewpoint in sharp contrast with its intermittent attempts in the previous months at persuading Cavagnari to resupply German U-boats and otherwise assist Germany in ways that would embroil Italy with the West. The naval staff now concluded that Italy could help Germany most by remaining neutral and serving as a transshipment point for imports.[123]

Hitler had been interested enough in Italian help at the outset to promise Mussolini a steady flow of information during the offensive in order to help the Duce choose the moment to act. But as German armor tore great gaps in the French front and drove headlong for the Channel coast, the importance of Italian aid notably diminished. Even more important, Hitler began to discern in the middle distance the possibility that adversity might yet bring England to see reason – and acknowledge his supremacy on the continent. On 17 May, despite what General Halder of the army staff contemptuously described as the Führer's "incomprehensible anxiety" over the southern flank of the German breakthrough, Hitler predicted to the staff officers of General Gerd von Rundstedt's Army Group A that "England, once destructively beaten in north France," would be ready to come to terms "on the basis of [its] power at sea against the power [of Germany] on the Continent." Hitler had no desire to destroy the British: "England was just as necessary on earth as the Catholic Church" – hardly a very comforting note given the Führer's religious views, but a token of his longstanding admiration of the British role as white *Ordnungsmacht* east and south of Suez. National Socialist Germany was not yet ready to step into *those* shoes. Hitler predicted peace within six weeks by Anglo-German "gentleman's agreement." Three days later, as Guderian's armor reached the Channel, Hitler was "beside himself with joy." From the French he proposed to extract "the return of German territory and other possessions stolen in the last 400 years." To the British, he was still exceedingly magnanimous. They could have "a separate peace at any time after the return of the [German] colonies."[124]

Hitler's early enthusiasm for Italian *Waffenbrüderschaft* did not survive the breakthrough. On 18 May Reich Foreign Minister Ribbentrop announced to the newly arrived Ambassador Alfieri that the Führer was "very satisfied with Italy's attitude." The remark was scarcely a ringing invitation. Alfieri received the distinct impression that "at least for now," Hitler was not interested in Italian action. In the ensuing days the Italian ambassador reported bellicose promptings from Göring, Goebbels, and even from the conservative and not overly Italophile Weizsäcker, but Hitler himself held back.[125]

The probable cause of his reticence emerges from a remark of 21 May to the German army chief of staff, General Franz Halder, by his foreign service liaison officer, Hasso von Etzdorf: "In general, a slight contradiction has begun to develop between us and Italy. For Italy the chief enemy has become England; for us the chief enemy is France. We seek contact with England on the basis of a division of the world."[126] These lapidary phrases indeed characterized Hitler's policy, with the proviso that he insisted, then and later, that the British confess openly that they had lost the war, concede in advance

German mastery over the continent, and implicitly accept a junior partnership in Hitler's enterprise. Nor, as Hitler's remark about the return of Wilhelmine Germany's colonies suggests, was the "division of the world" to restrict the Reich to the continent. Any such agreement, from Hitler's point of view, could only represent a temporary expedient, until Greater Germany had destroyed the Soviet Union and was free to replace Britain as the bulwark of the "white race" in Asia and the champion of Europe in the final struggle for world mastery with the United States. To produce contact with Britain on his terms, which implicitly required the removal of Churchill as prime minister, Hitler relied not on diplomacy but on the unfolding of German power in France, and later on psychological warfare with the backing of aerial bombardment and invasion threat.[127] In this framework, Italian pressure on Britain in the Mediterranean might have a place, even while Italian intervention complicated the task of reaching agreement. Hence Hitler's ambiguity about Italian assistance, and his unwillingness simply to overrule the Italian bid to enter the war. That course was clearly open, although at the sacrifice of the personal relationship with Mussolini that Hitler still, if decreasingly, prized.

While Hitler and his subordinates contemplated their good fortune, the Allies deliberated, enveloped in impending doom. The Roosevelt appeal to Mussolini that French and British had solicited met with the same reception as its predecessor. Ciano replied that negotiations "would not be in the spirit of Fascism." To François-Poncet, who on 27 May made far-reaching offers of territory in North Africa, Ciano was similarly adamant. It was "too late." He confirmed to Loraine that Mussolini now refused to continue contraband control negotiations. If France "came forward with an offer tomorrow to cede Tunis, Algeria, and Morocco, Mussolini would decline to discuss it." Loraine was dignified, and utterly firm: "war would be met with war"; "if Mussolini chose the sword he would be met with [the] sword."[128]

In London, a similar spirit at last prevailed. In the meetings of the War Cabinet on 26, 27, and 28 May, Churchill carried with him the overwhelming majority of his colleagues in rejecting Reynaud's shrill calls for concessions to Italy. The qualified opposition of Halifax and Chamberlain was ineffectual, despite Halifax's private grumbling that Churchill was talking "the most frightful rot," and tended to work himself up "into a passion of emotion when he ought to make his brain think and reason." It was not a moment for the unimaginative common sense of reasonable, conciliatory, and excessively decent men like Halifax. Churchill refused to risk British morale by entering with the French upon the "slippery slope" of negotiations, or by making appeals Mussolini "would certainly regard with contempt"; "nations which went down fighting rose again, but those which surrendered tamely were finished."[129]

The day of the climactic War Cabinet meeting, Churchill asked the chiefs of staff what measures they had taken "to attack Italian forces in Abyssinia . . . and generally to disturb that country" if Italy intervened. If France were still Britain's ally after Italy declared war, it was important "that at the outset collision should take place both with the Italian Navy and Air Force, in order that we can see what their quality really is, and whether it has changed at all since the last war." Unless Italian fighting ability was high, Churchill refused to contemplate a "purely defensive strategy" in the Mediterranean: "Risks must be run at this juncture in all theaters." Churchill assumed — and his assumptions had the force of an order — that the Admiralty had a plan for the Mediterranean "in the event of France becoming neutral." In the ensuing weeks he devoted himself to ensuring that it had such a plan; when Halifax brought rumors of a forthcoming Italian ultimatum to the West, Churchill prepared to answer it with immediate air attack on Italy.[130] Appeasement, even in the Mediterranean, was dead. The Entente Cordiale was in fragments; the French were about to go their way.[131] Of the Scylla and Charybdis Mussolini now faced — an Anglo-German "division of the world" at the expense of Italy's aspirations, or the weight of Great Britain's wrath — the latter was to prove the more dangerous.

2. Mussolini unleashed

"The stuff of which the Italian people is made is sound." While Fascist activists and university students attempted to recreate the enthusiasm of 1915's "radiant May," the Germans looked forward to a swift victorious peace, and the Western alliance collapsed, Mussolini moved to implement his decision to intervene. On 26 May he informed Ciano that Italy would enter the war in mid-June. But on 28 May news of the unconditional capitulation of Belgium prompted him to move the date forward. Mussolini summoned Badoglio and the service chiefs to Palazzo Venezia at 11 a.m. on 29 May. He had already assured himself of Badoglio's support; in his outburst to Ciano and Anfuso, the Duce had contemptuously remarked that Badoglio was "more or less satisfied," although "like all marshals," he "evidently [didn't] like the word war."[132]

At the meeting, Mussolini announced that "any day after the fifth of next month [was] good to enter the war."[133] The situation did "not permit further delay, because otherwise we will incur greater risks [by staying out] than those produced by a premature intervention." American help for the Allies, if it arrived at all, would be too late. French resistance on the remaining river lines of northern France would presumably prove weak, particularly if Italy entered the war.

After these premises, Mussolini confirmed his directives of 31 March, which he explicitly linked, in threadbare self-justification, to his predictions from the spring of 1939 of an exclusively naval and air war: "On the land front we cannot do anything spectacular; we will remain on the defensive." There remained a chance of action in the Balkans, which Mussolini mentioned in a sybilline phrase that led to a certain confusion, at any rate for the Air Force: "one can foresee something on the eastern front: the Yugoslav contingency." But this was purely a contingency. The principal effort of the

talian Armed Forces would be against British bases and naval forces in the
Mediterranean. Mussolini did not go into detail, presumably to avoid a discussion that might place his decision to intervene in doubt. In any case, he
had been carefully monitoring German air and U-boat successes against the
Allies,[134] and probably did not share his subordinates' gloom about Italian
prospects.

The Army was another matter. On 25 May or shortly thereafter, Graziani
had submitted a long memorandum, listing in detail the deficiencies of
Italy's ground forces, and concluding that the Army was incapable of offensive action, even against the Yugoslavs, without an ironclad guarantee that
the French would not move in the western Alps.[135] However, he had ended
his tale of woe on a hopeful note: "The Army would at first maintain a
defensive attitude, in the most favorable conditions to oppose a French offensive, or would be in the position – as soon as the general military situation
and its own increasing efficiency would permit – to undertake itself an action
in the West or East, or to send forces to the German front."[136] Mussolini
was to hold Graziani to these promises. At the meeting, Mussolini referred
to Graziani's memorandum, and adjudged the situation "not ideal, but satisfactory." Waiting would not improve anything, and would give the Germans "the impression that we were arriving when it was all over and the risk
was minimal" – an important consideration "at the moment of the final
peace settlement." As for civilian morale, the public had come far since early
May. "Now, two feelings agitate the Italian people: first, the fear of arriving
too late in a situation that devalues our intervention; the second, a certain
desire for emulation – to jump from aircraft, fire at tanks, and so on." That
pleased Mussolini. It demonstrated "that the stuff of which the Italian people
is made is sound."

No one contradicted Mussolini, or showed surprise when he announced
that he was now taking command of the armed forces pending arrival of the
King's written delegation of authority. Mussolini was triumphant. He had
"realized his true dream," Ciano commented, to become *"condottiere* of the
nation at war." The next morning, 30 May, Mussolini presented Ciano with
a message for Hitler announcing that Italy would enter the war on 5 June.
Mussolini asked Hitler to advise him if this date conflicted with German
plans. A few more days' delay might be arranged, but "the Italian people
was now impatient. . . ." Mussolini also confirmed that he regarded it "necessary not to extend the conflict to the Balkan and Danubian basin, from
which Italy too must draw raw materials no longer coming in from beyond
Gibraltar." He intended to make a declaration in this sense at an appropriate
moment to "exercise a calming influence on those peoples."[137]

Hitler met Ambassador Alfieri on the morning of 31 May at Bad Godes-
berg and received the letter with "warmth." Ribbentrop had been more
noncommittal, and had earlier greeted Mussolini's communication by
remarking that it was all "very interesting." He had noted with particular
attention Mussolini's reference to the Balkans; some German high command

and diplomatic authorities had feared an Italian foray against Yugoslavia earlier in the month, even after they received word of Ciano's assurances to the Yugoslavs.[138]

A curious episode followed Mussolini's announcement of the date. Hitler although Mussolini's message had "deeply moved" him, requested a postponement of Italian intervention for a few additional days. The *Luftwaffe* was about to launch a massive attack on the airfields around Paris, where the remnant of the French air force had concentrated. Italian action on 5 June might result in French redeployment before the German blow fell.[139] Mussolini, though perhaps suspecting ulterior motives, agreed. Delay would permit shipment of further equipment and one of Italy's armored divisions to Libya. He therefore replied that his "program" was as follows: "Monday, 10 June, declaration of war and speech to the Italian people, and on the morning of 11 June, commencement of hostilities." The declaration of war was an idea of Ciano's. Mussolini had wanted to dispense with "that formality," but Ciano was characteristically preoccupied with saving appearances, particularly in view of the attitude of the United States to "such recondite legal questions."[140]

Before Ciano could dispatch Mussolini's message, the Germans changed their minds. The *Luftwaffe* apparently succeeded in readying its strike earlier than Hitler had anticipated on 31 May. On the evening of 2 June, Ribbentrop telephoned Mackensen that 5 June was entirely suitable. But Mussolini now desired to hold to 10 June, a date "for which even press communiqués and so on had now been prepared down to the last detail," as he told Mackensen upon receiving word of Hitler's sudden reversal. Delay would permit the reinforcement of Libya, would work upon the already shaken nerves of the Allies, and would further raise the impatience of the Italian people, whom Mussolini described as troubled by fear of arriving "too late."[141]

This last remark, and Mussolini's intention of issuing a formal declaration of war, produced scorn and anger at Führer headquarters. For the first time, Hitler openly derided his ally. He raged in front of his army adjutant, Lieutenant Colonel Engel, and General Wilhelm Keitel of the *Wehrmacht* high command, who punctuated Hitler's outburst with "humorous interjections":

I would never have considered the Duce to be so primitive. I have often wondered recently about his political naïveté. The entire letter is proof that in political matters I must be even more cautious than hitherto with the Italians. . . . Apparently Mussolini imagines this foray for booty as a stroll in *passo romano*. He will be amazed. The French have less respect for the Italians than for us. In general, rather bad form [*an sich eine blamable Angelegenheit*]: first they are too cowardly to come in and now they are in a hurry to get their share of the booty. Declarations of war are the sign of a hypocritical political attitude, which attempts to give the appearance of chivalrous behavior. They only became fashionable with increase of civilization. In the ancient world, there were no declarations of war, but surprise attacks and invasions [*da wurde überfallen und marschiert!*] That is the correct, the healthy method. I myself will never sign a declaration of war, but rather act.

No hint of the Führer's contempt for his allies reached the Italian leadership – although Hitler did not interrupt his supervision of preparations for the imminent second phase of the battle of France in order to receive Alfieri.[142]

Phony war or real one? While Hitler fumed, Badoglio and his colleagues had been putting into effect – after a fashion – the decisions of 29 May. On the morning of the 30th, Badoglio had called together the service chiefs to coordinate last-minute preparations. Badoglio explained that Mussolini's remarks about Yugoslavia were "a sort of warning order to be ready for actions that may become possible in the future." At the moment, the principal concern was the western frontier. Graziani then briefed his colleagues on the Army's deployment plan. It provided for an army group of twenty-five divisions, under the nominal command of Crown Prince Umberto, to face France. Roughly twenty-one divisions remained in reserve in the Po Valley, and a covering deployment of five divisions secured the Yugoslav border.[143] Graziani's briefing was obviously necessary; it soon emerged that Pricolo, as the result of Mussolini's remark about Yugoslavia, had set in motion his deployment on the understanding that action against Italy's eastern neighbor was imminent. Badoglio reiterated that "for now" action against Yugoslavia was not under discussion. Pricolo had made a mistake.[144]

To his credit, the Air Force chief did attempt to argue that *some* attempt to seize the initiative was necessary: "Our Army is on the defensive. The Navy doesn't have any definite objective. . . . The Air Force can and should take some offensive action." He proposed to bombard French bases in Corsica. But Badoglio refused in the name of Mussolini, who, as the marshal had announced earlier in the meeting, did not now "intend to act offensively" against France in the air. By a process of elimination, the Italian war effort had narrowed to an offensive by Cavagnari's submarines, of which three-quarters would be on station at the outset of hostilities. During Pricolo's complaints about the passivity of Italian strategy, Cavagnari had announced vaguely that "the directives" – whether his own or Mussolini's he did not specify – were "to remain on the defensive to the left and right," and to "hold the Sicily Channel." This passive conception was Cavagnari's own, rather than Mussolini's or even Badoglio's. Cavagnari's 29 May operation order listed in devastating detail the steps the Allies were likely to take, perfunctorily recommended that the fleet seize every occasion to meet the enemy with parity or superiority of forces, and commended to his subordinates the only objective the Italian Navy consistently pursued throughout the war, protection of Italian communications with Sardinia, Sicily, Libya, and Albania, and defense of the Italian coastline.[145]

These directives paid lip service to Mussolini's order to strike at the British, but Cavagnari had no intention of risking ships. Nor did he perceive that if strategic surprise was difficult, tactical surprise might well have accompanied a bombardment or landing on Malta or a raid on Gibraltar or Alexandria. But such operations required planning, a willingness to run risks, and close coordination with the other services – measures Cavagnari rejected. His deputy, Admiral Odoardo Somigli, was so sheepish about the Navy's passivity that he misled the German naval attaché, who concluded on 1 June that the Navy intended "the strongest possible commitment of fleet and Air Force at the outset against the British Suez position."[146] The Navy was to spend the summer avoiding just that mission.

Badoglio and others also raised difficulties in the ensuing days. The situation in Libya, where Balbo reported British armored forces concentrated on his eastern border, was worrying – so worrying that Graziani judged an attack imminent: "[T]hey will attempt to gain an immediate success, in order to save [their] prestige which is everywhere shaken."[147] Badoglio was still obsessed with the alleged numerical preponderance of the French, and feared an offensive from Tunisia. As late as 10 June, SIM estimated French strength in Tunisia at eight infantry divisions plus native cavalry. In actuality, two of the six infantry divisions in Tunisia had begun shipment to France on 21 May, and from 7 June on, the French faced Balbo with four infantry divisions and a motley collection of fortress troops and reserve cavalry. Balbo shared Badoglio's misapprehension, and complained to one of Rintelen's subordinates that Rome had left him "in the lurch" in an "almost hopeless" situation.[148] On 1 June Balbo flew to Italy to plead his case with Badoglio and Mussolini. Badoglio offered air reinforcements extracted from a reluctant Pricolo, and delay until more equipment arrived. Badoglio insisted forcefully to Mussolini that the French would fight on, despite German predictions of victory in six or seven weeks. He was convinced, despite all the evidence, that Italy had "time to intervene without cutting the figure of carrion crows [*senza fare la figura di corvi*]." An immediate move might achieve some success with submarines, but Balbo would face defeat, and that would be "counterproductive." Badoglio demanded that Italy procrastinate "at all costs" until at least the end of June.[149] Mussolini made no comment. Badoglio, as he was prone to, came away with the mistaken impression that the dictator agreed, while Mussolini actually held to 10 June as his goal.

Badoglio ultimately cooperated, and on 5 June, after further discussions with Mussolini, called in the service chiefs for a final conference. Badoglio's colleagues appeared "calm and serene, or perhaps only resigned." Graziani posed as "rough soldier." Soddu and Cavagnari were largely silent, with "an occasional superhuman smile."[150] Pricolo was modest and unassuming. Badoglio announced that Mussolini's purpose in declaring war was merely to transform Italy from a *de facto* quasi-belligerent into a *de jure* belligerent.[151] Mussolini intended to "reserve the Armed Forces, and especially the Army and the Air Force, for future events." On 4 June Mussolini had allegedly told Badoglio he was inventing nothing new. He would do "the same as the Germans and the French, who were opposite each other for six months without doing anything."[152] Italy would fight a phony war against France.

As for Britain, Badoglio directed Pricolo to prepare bombardments of Malta and Alexandria, and mentioned that Ettore Muti, reverting to a role for which he was more suited than that of secretary of the Party, proposed to lead a raid on Gibraltar using a staging airfield in Spain. Graziani raised the question of a Malta landing, but encountered Cavagnari's decided opposition. The coast was unsuitable, and "bristling with weapons of all kinds." Cavagnari did not deign to explain his views, but he and his staff justified their inaction two weeks later in a memorandum that asserted that Malta was not a "decisive objective"; the threat it offered to Italian communications was "of secondary importance."[153] The subsequent course of the war was hardly to justify such confidence. As Badoglio remarked during the 5 June conference, "one should never think that the enemy is stupid."

Despite these words of warning, Badoglio was satisfied that, under the circumstances, he and his colleagues had done everything possible. He commended to them "that calm and serenity that should distinguish general staffs," and announced that a directive governing organization and powers of the *Comando Supremo* would shortly be forthcoming.[154] Mussolini "was most serene, and the people tranquil." It fell to Graziani to close this last peacetime meeting of the service chiefs with a remark that flew in the face of western military wisdom from Clausewitz to the apocryphal Murphy, whose First Law decrees that anything that can go wrong, will. "When the cannon sounds," Graziani predicted with apparent bravado, "everything will fall into place automatically." It was a fitting epitaph for the Italian general staff tradition, and for the Italian war of 1940.

Mussolini's intent in entering the war in so unspectacular a manner held no mysteries for Badoglio, whose assistant, General Quirino Armellini, noted in his diary that the dictator evidently proposed "to declare war, in order not to fight it, and then sit at the peace table as a belligerent in order to claim his share of the booty." In his memoirs, Badoglio reported that Mussolini had justified intervention with the cynical remark that he needed "a few thousand dead" to secure a seat at the imminent peace conference. The entire maneuver, Armellini noted wonderingly, must be "a colossal bluff . . . played out coolly, with the mentality of a poker player."[155] The Italian ambassador in Paris, Guariglia, apologetically explained Italian policy, about which he was in the dark, in similar terms in his parting interview with Daladier.[156] A corollary to this strategy was the plan Badoglio, in briefing his colleagues on 5 June, ascribed to Mussolini: the Duce "did not want to burn all our bridges toward France, in order to stay on their good side."

Historians have generally accepted the Badoglio interpretation of the decision to enter the war, and have argued that Mussolini intended to "leave the road open to a subsequent rapprochement with France, in order to counterbalance, at least in part, the absolute continental supremacy" the Greater German Reich had gained through its victories. According to Giorgio Rochat, Mussolini did not even "desire the complete defeat of Britain, which would place Europe at Germany's mercy, but [rather] a peace that would not totally overthrow the European balance." Italy entered the war "without counting on its armed forces." Mussolini, as Denis Mack Smith has elegantly summed up, proposed "to declare war, not to make it."[157]

The phony-war theory does not do justice to the evidence. Ciano's diary, Mussolini's remarks to Ciano and Anfuso at the end of May, the 29 May service chiefs' conference, and Mussolini's actions in the early stages of the fighting make clear that despite his initial instructions to the services, he sought a genuine, if short war. His promises to his generals of a seat at the peace conference were a tactical expedient to overcome their last feeble objections and stimulate the timid rapacity of Casa Savoia. As Mussolini complained several months later, the generals didn't want to make war. They "always expect that everything will resolve itself – in their formula – 'on the political level.' " He added scornfully that *he* would deal with politics – the generals' job was to fight.[158] In June 1940, Mussolini did not bluff the West, or the Germans, or even Italian opinion. He bluffed his military, who discovered too late, that Mussolini, and the situation into which he had flung them, demanded far more than a "stroll in *passo romano*."

As for Mussolini's alleged desire for rapprochement with France, it was a figment of Badoglio's ever-active political imagination, which contrasted sharply with the self-satisfied traditionalism with which he approached his profession. That the French themselves had suggested that such a rapprochement was in Italy's interests could scarcely have commended it to Mussolini. His own conquests, not ties with decadent and defeated France, would secure Italy's independence in the new Europe emerging from Hitler's victories. Fear of Germany did provoke Mussolini to express on 8 June the hope that French resistance on Somme and Aisne would wear the Germans down and prevent them from reaching the end of the war "excessively fresh and strong."[159] This fear, however, was merely a further spur to his own forward policy, not inspiration for Franco-Italian diplomatic *combinazioni*.

Phony war against France was a temporary expedient to pacify Badoglio. It did not emerge clearly at the 29 May conference, although Mussolini had ordered Italian forces to defend by land and concentrate on the British at sea. He had on 30 May, after a private talk with Badoglio, ruled out air raids on France, presumably because of the purported superiority of the French air force. But it took Badoglio's 1 June plea for a month's delay, and French promises not to attack first – which Badoglio encouraged and relayed to Mussolini on 4 June – before the dictator ordered through Badoglio a total ban on offensive action against France.[160] The decision came as a surprise to Ciano, who until 5 June assumed that Mussolini "intended to unleash from the outset the air attack [in which Ciano planned to participate] against France as well." Mussolini's adherence to the Badoglio line was grudging; the dictator confided to Ciano that if air attacks on southern France could "finish the job" before the impending German drive on Paris, they might be worth the attempt.[161] In the event, the phony war survived Italy's entry into the conflict by less than twenty-four hours.

Militarily, it of course made sense to "reserve the armed forces, and especially the Army and Air Force, for future events," as Badoglio rendered Mussolini's intentions at the 5 June conference. The principal Italian effort against Great Britain would place sufficient strain upon Italy's meager resources. Italian action against France might also provoke spasmodic air retaliation, endangering the vulnerable port and industrial facilities of northwest Italy, a result damaging to the regime's prestige and in no way helpful to the effort against Britain. Finally, if the French fought on for a month or so, as Badoglio expected, it was vital that they not use their presumed if fictitious preponderance to strike at Libya from Tunisia. The rules of engagement Badoglio promulgated on 7 June reflected these concerns. On land and in the air, Italy would take no offensive action whatsoever against France. At sea, Italian forces were to attack French and British if they were encountered together, but to spare French forces alone, unless the French struck first or Italian failure to act would place *Regia Marina* units at a tactical disadvantage. In accordance with tradition, Badoglio nevertheless urged the Navy's submarines to take any "good anonymous shot" they could get, even at French forces.[162]

Italy's strategy on the eve of war was a compromise between Mussolini's warlike intent and Badoglio's retarding influence. That influence was limited, however. From "circles around Mussolini" Mackensen received word by 8 June that Italy intended to "remain passive toward France until the separate peace, then turn against England as fiercely as possible with an offensive against Egypt and the English fleet at Alexandria." Badoglio's assistant Armellini, less hidebound than his master, felt by 9 June that French collapse would free Italy to strike at the British Middle East position with prospects of success.[163] Mussolini would have a fair chance, a chance Cavagnari could not easily refuse, to measure his fleet against the Royal Navy. On land, Balbo could at last execute his long-touted offensive against Egypt. The British might be tenacious defenders, but Mussolini had Hitler's word that their leadership was "miserable." Above all, they were few in number: the British Middle East command had a mere 36,000 British and Commonwealth troops in Egypt, and many units lacked men and equipment.[164] A swift Italian drive on Suez, with naval support, might carry all before it.

The last days before 10 June ran out swiftly and uneventfully, at least in Rome. Badoglio consoled himself with the thought that a swift peace "could not be ruled out." The remaining powers in Italy also accommodated themselves to the new situation. When Ciano brought the King the declaration of war for signature on 1 June, the monarch was merely "resigned." But within a few days Victor Emmanuel was "preparing to be a soldier and nothing but a soldier." The *Osservatore Romano* struggle apparently convinced the Pope that further action would be both useless and dangerous. To a Yugoslav Catholic notable, Pius XII complained that he "no longer had any influence over Mussolini" and that the clergy was "infiltrated with Fascist doctrines."

The Pope did not have far to look to apportion blame for this latter state of affairs. Five months earlier, he himself had praised "the enlightened action of the Regime and its Chief" to a high Fascist dignitary, and had contemptuously dismissed the liberal state Fascism had destroyed as "the Masonic period."[165] Nor did war impel the Church to disassociate itself in any significant way from the regime; only defeat could do that. For the moment, *mare nostro* might yet become *mare cattolico*. As for the industrialists, they were more conscious than most of Italy's dependence on its German ally. They now turned rather timidly to securing a share of the booty, and above all to preserving their existence in the face of Greater Germany's crushing economic superiority.[166]

Ciano, once Mussolini had selected the date for intervention, had tried to counter "with all methods" the military's pressure for delay, as he had once intrigued for neutrality. Fear of arriving "too late" had seized him as well, although Loraine gave him pause by pointing out that Britain "had not got the habit of being beaten in war." Ciano arranged for himself the command of a bomber squadron at Pisa, and by 2 June, as he informed Mackensen, he was "burning to be on board his machine." He intended to be a "soldier-minister" rather than a "minister-soldier" while his faithful *chef de cabinet,* Filippo Anfuso, dealt with business at Palazzo Chigi. In the last days, Ciano was frank with the Allied and United States ambassadors. Ambiguity now served no purpose. On 7 June, he informed Phillips that Italy would enter the war "in a few days," and on the 9th told François-Poncet that "the die was cast." French and British Embassy staffs would be leaving on the 11th or 12th. Ciano arranged to receive the French and British ambassadors on the afternoon of 10 June to hand them the declaration of war, but was solicitous enough to schedule their visits early, so that they might return to their embassies before the massive organized crowd assembled beneath Mussolini's balcony to hear his long-awaited "decisions of historic importance."[167]

On the eve, Mussolini was "utterly calm." When Mackensen arrived bearing yet another Führer situation report, Mussolini announced himself to be "in a good position by sea and air." In response to Hitler's favorable reception of a suggestion in Mussolini's 2 June letter for token Italian participation on the German front with some regiments of *Bersaglieri,* he now offered the entire "Po" Army, which he described as "an outstanding, superlatively equipped instrument, organized down to the last detail under his personal supervision." He was willing to commit it wherever Hitler desired – "and here he even let fall the word England." Had Badoglio heard these words, he might have revised his view that Mussolini had entered the war merely to sit at the peace table. This was too absurd to be bluff. With Italy's declaration of war imminent, with what he described to Mackensen as "his higher duties as Supreme Commander"[168] swelling his pride, Mussolini had wholly surrendered to fantasy, and had even abandoned temporarily his lack of enthusiasm for ground cooperation with the Germans.

The formalities on 10 June went quickly. Ciano, resplendent in uniform as a major of the *Regia Aeronautica,* presented the declaration of war to the Allied ambassadors in turn. Hostilities would begin at midnight. The day before, François-Poncet had broken down and wept while discussing French collapse with Ciano, and had demonstratively proclaimed himself "an honest admirer of the Führer and of *Generalfeldmarschall* Göring."[169] Now, he was once more relatively dignified. The Germans, François-Poncet told Ciano, "were hard masters," and he advised Ciano not to get himself killed. Loraine was "laconic and imperturbable," but as Ciano showed him to the door, the two exchanged a long and cordial handshake.[170] At about 6 p.m., Mussolini spoke from the central balcony of Palazzo Venezia to the assembled throng. Italy took the field "against the plutocratic and reactionary democracies of the West" to resolve the problem of its maritime frontiers. The "titanic struggle" about to begin was "but one phase in the logical development of our Revolution." It was the struggle of "young and prolific nations against the sterile and declining ones." It was the struggle between "two centuries, and two ideas." As he had planned, Mussolini included reassurances for the small nations. Italy did not intend to drag Switzerland, Yugoslavia, Greece, Turkey, or Egypt into the conflict. But this assurance had a menacing proviso. Italian restraint toward these small neutral countries depended "on them, and only on them." Concluding to what his press described as "deafening acclamations," the Duce exhorted the Italian people to "hasten to arms, and demonstrate [its] tenacity, [its] courage, and [its] valor."[171]

The skin of the bear, II. Ciano departed for war, smoothly asking Mackensen to convey "warmest and most heartfelt greetings" to Ribbentrop, "on the eve of the day in which the treaty bearing both their signatures came into effect in its full force." The King, along with Puntoni and other aides, repaired to a headquarters in the vicinity of the French frontier. Mussolini, Badoglio, and the service staffs remained in Rome. The first days of the Italian war were relatively uneventful. The *Regia Aeronautica* bombed Malta without effect at dawn on 11 June. That night, the RAF struck back at industrial targets in Milan and Turin, killing fourteen and wounding thirty civilians. Mussolini was "especially angry" over this first attack on Italian cities. In retaliation, Badoglio authorized air strikes against southern France. The next morning, Mussolini appealed once again to Hitler for antiaircraft batteries, and offered a motorized division in exchange.[172] Worse followed. The commander-in-chief of the French navy, Admiral François Darlan, whose political ambitions had not yet affected his fighting spirit, ordered the heavy cruiser squadron at Toulon to bombard Genoa, as the Allies had planned in April. The raid did little damage to military-industrial targets, but the French force paraded up and down the Italian coast with impunity, despite fire from coastal batteries and an attack by a gallant but superannuated Italian torpedo boat.[173] Cavagnari's fleet was at its war station at Taranto, and the Air Force was apparently not aware that it must take primary responsibility for defense of Italy's northwestern coasts.[174] Someone had blundered.

Mussolini reacted with further bombardments of air bases in Corsica and southern France, and small offensive actions by Army Group West in the Alps. On 16 June, the "rapid evolution of the general situation" (the Germans had just reached Dijon) led Graziani to order a major operation. The overwhelming French defensive strength that Graziani and SIM had erroneously assumed now seemed less impressive. But preparation would take ten days, unless further German progress produced utter French collapse. In that case, the Italians would attack, ready or not.

On the morning of 17 June, Reynaud fell from power, and the new French premier, Marshal Pétain, appealed to Hitler for an armistice. Mussolini ordered his commanders to "maintain pressure all along the front." The Germans must not arrive at Nice first. But in mid-afternoon, Alfieri telephoned to say that Hitler, before replying to the French appeal, desired to meet Mussolini at Munich or the Brenner. This proof of his ally's solidarity, and perhaps fear of stiffening French resolve, caused Mussolini to order operations in the Alps suspended, although preparations for the large-scale offensive were to continue at speed. Apparently in high spirits, he telegraphed the King that "things have gone as was easily predictable. I leave at 2100 hours for Munich, invited by the Führer to confer about surrender terms."[175]

But when Ciano, summoned from Pisa, arrived in Rome to accompany Mussolini, he found him "discontented"; "this unexpected breaking out of peace disturbs him." It might deprive the Italian people of the chance to demonstrate its valor. Worse, if the British as well were to begin negotiations before Italy had seized Egypt, a speedy Anglo-German compromise might sacrifice Italian claims. Later, in the train speeding northward, Ciano and Mussolini discussed terms for the French. Mussolini was "radical," and wanted to occupy France totally. He also "aspired" to the French fleet. But Hitler had won the war, "without the active military cooperation of Italy," and Hitler would have the last word. Mussolini's "reflections on the Italian people and . . . armed forces" were "extremely bitter."

As the train continued toward Munich on the morning of 18 June, Ciano and his assistants drafted Italy's demands on France, demands that accorded fully with the vision intoxicating the Italian public and the political elite. The French army in all theaters would demobilize, and turn over all crew-served weapons. Italy would occupy France to the Rhône (with bridgeheads at Lyon, Valence, and Avignon) along with Corsica, Tunisia, and Djibouti. At its discretion, Italy could occupy other French territories, metropolitan, colonial, or mandated, that might be of use in the war against Great Britain. French communications facilities would be open to Italian use at any time. Italy could occupy the naval bases of Algiers, Mers-el-Kébir, and Casablanca. The French would neutralize Beirut. Italy would immediately receive the French fleet and air force, and all rolling stock in the occupation areas. The French would carry out no demolitions. Finally, France would denounce its alliance with Great Britain and expel all British forces from its territories. Ciano submitted the document to Mussolini, who approved it during a stop at the Brenner.[176]

The Munich meetings included a two-hour private conversation between the dictators, a simultaneous Ribbentrop–Ciano talk, and a general conference at the end that included Keitel and Roatta.[177] The Hitler–Mussolini talk was cordial, even effusive, the Ribbentrop–Ciano conversation rather less so. Hitler proposed, to Mussolini's relief, to settle the French question "forever," and he and Ribbentrop greeted Italian claims to Nice, Corsica, Tunis, and Djibouti favorably. Hitler was also willing to countenance an Italian armistice occupation zone stretching to the Rhône. He himself proposed to occupy the entire French Atlantic coast, with its bases against England. Hitler also raged at the Swiss, those "renegade Germans," while Mussolini took note. However, German acquiescence to Italy's aspirations had definite limits. Ribbentrop evaded a Ciano bid for Algeria, and pushed forward Spain's claims to Morocco – a transparent cloak for the longstanding German interest in Morocco to which Ribbentrop referred in passing. As for Britain, Ribbentrop and Hitler appeared smitten with a sudden incongruous pacifism. Ribbentrop alleged that he was already seeking contact with London through Sweden.[178] If the British wanted to continue the war, war they could have. Germany, however, sought to assuage humanity's need for peace and "harmonious coexistence." Ribbentrop brushed aside Ciano's claims to Egypt and the Sudan with the remark that they "depended on the future development of the conflict" – a conflict Germany now sought to end as rapidly and bloodlessly as possible. The Germans feared that if war continued on the periphery, the United States would eventually intervene. Germany, Mussolini concluded, was like "a bold and lucky gambler . . . . [who] has become somewhat nervous and proposes to convey his abundant winnings rapidly home."

In the course of the conversations, both Hitler and Ribbentrop repeatedly emphasized the need to avoid the flight of the French government or fleet to North Africa. The French fleet held the naval strategic balance between British and the Axis; neutralization or scuttling was probably the best solution, since the French were unlikely to surrender it tamely. Mussolini eventually came to similar conclusions, and recognized the disastrous strategic impact of a French fleet fighting on against Italy in British service. Fear of that very contingency had considerable effect on his actions in the next days.

Finally, the Germans secured Italian agreement on negotiating procedures for the armistice. A French delegation would receive conditions at German headquarters. No agreement negotiated between France and Germany would take effect until the French had also come to terms with Italy. Ciano pressed unsuccessfully for a "parallel" or joint negotiation, but Hitler assured him tactfully that "Italy would scarcely want to negotiate at the same place as that at which the Franco-German armistice negotiations took place."[179] The Führer did not explain that he planned to return to the site of Germany's humiliation in 1918, Compiègne. He assured the Italians that his commitment to keep fighting until France conceded Italy a satisfactory armistice protected their interests. If the French refused, force would decide, and Italy would occupy "a large portion" of southern France. Roatta made clear that Italian preparations were under way.

Afterward, Mussolini was "notably embarrassed." The sensation "that his own role was of secondary importance" was infinitely painful. Ciano considered that Mussolini – in sharp contrast to the Germans, he might have added – "fears that the hour of peace is approaching and sees his life's unrealized dream, glory on the battlefield, vanishing once again."[180]

Order, counterorder. Upon return to Rome on 19 June, Mussolini ordered immediate resumption of the small offensive actions set in motion before his stop order of 17 June. At Munich, Roatta had already arranged with Keitel for a German advance toward Chambéry and Grenoble to take the northern sector of the French Alpine defenses in the rear. Graziani consequently pressed Badoglio to launch the full-scale offensive under preparation since 17 June, to exploit the demoralization of the French that the German thrust would presumably create. The attack would be ready by 23 June. Badoglio approved the operational plan, but characteristically added that its implementation depended on "the development of the political situation."[181] His reluctance was apparent.

Mussolini thereupon lost patience. He summoned Badoglio, Graziani, and Pricolo to Palazzo Venezia in the late afternoon of 20 June.[182] Mussolini claimed, probably disingenuously, that the Germans had already presented the French with armistice terms (unknown to the Italian generals, the French delegation had not even arrived at Compiègne). The French air force was now out of action, and the Army of the Alps was withdrawing westward. Mussolini pointed out that further delay would permit the Germans to reach Marseille first. He demanded that the attack begin "*at dawn tomorrow, Friday, 21 June 1940.*" Badoglio objected that Keitel and Roatta had agreed that the Italian action develop "in correlation" with that of the Germans. Mussolini insisted once more that the attack must begin next morning. Graziani, whom Badoglio asked for an opinion, suggested an operation limited to the extreme northern sector of the front, where the German advance would aid it. The Italian center and left would then attack after success in the North.

Mussolini cut Graziani off: it was "necessary to act simultaneously along all axes of advance." The attack would begin at 0300. The situation "imposed action because it would be a grave blow to our prestige to receive territory from the hands of our ally, without having occupied it." In any event the operation would be "a favorable occasion to show how our troops fight." Stubbornly, Badoglio asked whether this was a direct order; he had clearly not given up his delaying action. Mussolini confirmed the order.

Pricolo objected that at 0300 his pilots could not see to fly. Mussolini consented to delay until 0330. Graziani, always ready with the last word, assured Mussolini sycophantically that "the morale of the troops was of the highest" and that they "yearned" to cross the French border. At seven that evening, army staff transmitted to Army Group West the order to launch an "all-out attack" all along the front, from Mont Blanc to the sea.[183]

But all was not yet settled. Ciano interceded with Mussolini after the meeting. Ciano found it "very inglorious indeed to throw oneself on a defeated army." More practical considerations also moved him: "The armistice is at the gates, and if our Army fails to break through at the first blow, we would close the campaign with a resounding defeat." The transcript of a telephone call between Roatta in Rome and General Pietro Pintor, commanding the sector nearest the coast, also weakened Mussolini's resolve. Pintor declared himself "absolutely unprepared" to attack the next day.[184] Even more disquieting was news from the political front. In the course of 20 June, Rome received alarming rumors that the French government was preparing to transfer to North Africa and continue the war.[185] Mussolini conceived a fear that Italian attack could "disturb the Franco-German negotiations." The French perhaps contributed to Mussolini's indecision by requesting that Italy cease operations so that France might negotiate without the appearance of duress. Shortly before 8 p.m., Mussolini countermanded the attack order. Before the army staff could transmit this latest change to the field, however, word came from the attaché in Berlin, General Efisio Marras, that the Germans still intended to drive south from Lyon. Reassured, Mussolini once again confirmed the attack. However, probably in view of Pintor's complaints, he now confined the all-out effort to the northernmost sector of the front, as Badoglio and Graziani had originally recommended.[186]

Mussolini had at last overruled his generals in direct confrontation, as he was to do increasingly in the course of the summer. But his troops made little impression on the French. Casualties in the units engaged were sometimes heavy, and cases of frostbite numerous, for the weather was persistently hostile. In North Africa, far to the south, the war got off to a similarly depressing start. The armored cars of the 11th Hussars, advance guard of the British 7th Armored Division, harassed Balbo's isolated garrisons on the Libyan border from 11 June on. Balbo had intended to forestall British raids by seizing at the outset the Egyptian border settlement of Sollum, where the limestone plateau of the interior descended precipitously to the sea and formed an easily defensible position. But Badoglio's veto on offensive action had handed the initiative to the British. By the night of 16–17 June, the situation was alarming. A British force reportedly including over 300 armored cars – more than the British had in the entire theater – overran two companies of Libyan colonial troops, fourteen tanks, and an artillery battery. The Italian drivers, "alarmed by the fire of the armored cars, abandoned the field." A part of the Libyan troops "dispersed," as Balbo delicately put it in his report. Between Tobruk and Bardia, far in the Italian rear, British raiders ambushed and gutted a convoy of thirty trucks. An Italian general was missing and presumed captured – the first of many.[187]

In Rome, Mussolini admitted in his triumphant announcement to the King of the impending Duce–Führer conference at Munich that affairs in Libya were not going "all that brilliantly." Nevertheless, the French armistice appeal of 17 June revived Italian offensive spirit. After a series of messages full of gloom, Balbo suddenly announced that "given the French situation" he was concentrating most of his artillery on the Egyptian border, and was preparing "an offensive column that will presumably be ready to move on the 25th."[188] The end of the French threat from Tunisia opened the road to Alexandria.

The next day Balbo reported success. Italian air strikes had compelled the British to disperse, and conduct a guerrilla war with armored cars. He intended to attack as soon as possible, "given the radically altered political situation." Mussolini, on his return from Munich, had Badoglio remove the restriction on offensive action into Egypt. Balbo replied with another request for the promised antitank guns and other equipment, and a proposal for a foray into Tunisia "with motorcycle troops and cavalry" to expropriate French army equipment. In a letter to Badoglio on 20 June, Balbo pointed out that his tanks had only machine guns. The British armored cars "riddle them with rounds which merrily perforate the[ir] armor." War under these conditions, he concluded dramatically, had the character of a contest "of meat against iron." He requested fifty German tanks and fifty armored cars to spearhead the drive into Egypt, "the only [front] in the world where the British can be attacked directly, at a vital point – the Suez Canal – and our certain, shattering success (if we had a few armored fighting vehicles) would have a moral and material effect of the first importance."[189]

The promises for the future were by this point not enough to calm Mussolini. General Lastrucci, the general missing since the attack on the Tobruk-Bardia convoy, had turned up prisoner. Mussolini fumed to Ciano, and blamed defeat on the Italians, who had been "an anvil for sixteen centuries, and could not, in a few years, become a hammer." His raw material was inadequate; "Even Michelangelo needed marble to make his statues; if he had only had clay, he would have been no more than a potter." When Badoglio relayed Balbo's request for German armor, Mussolini refused. He would tolerate no German interference in his theater. He did agree, however, to send to North Africa the "Po" Army's entire complement of seventy M11/39 medium tanks – the only ones available in the entire Army. Balbo assured Badoglio that he and his commanders would "do wonders" with the tanks.[190] Wonders were indeed what Mussolini was shortly to demand.

Armistice but no peace. On the political front, further disappointment was in store. In the early evening of 21 June Alfieri communicated to Rome the

German draft armistice, which Ciano had requested pressingly the day before in order to assure the "coordination" of Italian and German demands.[191] The conditions, Ciano thought, were

moderate [ones], that prove Hitler's intention is to arrive swiftly at an agreement. Under these conditions, Mussolini does not feel able to advance claims to occupy territory; that could provoke the breaking off of the negotiations and produce a real crack in our relations with Berlin. Therefore he will limit himself to requesting the demilitarization of a frontier strip 50 kilometers wide, and reserve our requests for the moment of the peace [negotiations]. Mussolini is very humiliated by the fact that our troops have not made a step forward. Even today, they were unable to pass, and stopped in front of the first French strong point that resisted.

Mussolini had earlier made it clear to the Germans that he did not want to see the French armistice delegation before 23 June, presumably to give Graziani time to break through in the Alps. He now reversed himself. He wanted the French negotiators "as soon as possible." The next morning, as the Italian Army attacked all along the front, Mussolini informed Hitler he had decided to renounce occupation of the left bank of the Rhône, Corsica, Tunis, and Djibouti. He desired to "ease the acceptance of the armistice by the French." Hitler replied drily that "whatever you may decide, France has been informed that the [Franco-German] armistice will only come into force" when Italy and France had come to an agreement. Hitler obviously did not find his ally's tergiversations impressive.[192]

Mussolini's reasons for reducing his immediate demands upon the French have intrigued both participants and historians.[193] Roatta thought that Mussolini, having failed to break the French front in the Alps, was intent on demonstrating his sportsmanship [signorilità] by not claiming more than he had conquered.[194] More plausibly, Faldella has suggested Mussolini feared he would be unable to impose more far-reaching conditions in face-to-face confrontation with a French armistice delegation emboldened by the absence of the Germans from the negotiations.[195] In his memoirs, Alfieri advanced the already mentioned hypothesis that Mussolini desired to spare the French in order to maintain some semblance of a continental balance of power.[196] This explanation has enjoyed wide popularity.[197] Finally, one former diplomat has suggested that Mussolini was so confident of imminent victory that he expected to secure his war aims against both France and Britain shortly, regardless of the armistice conditions.[198]

Few of these suggestions hold up when tested against the evidence. Mussolini's humiliation over the results of the first day's attack in the Alps and over the situation in Libya did contribute to his decision to reduce his demands, and helped prompt his request, also expressed on the evening of 21 June, to see the French delegates as soon as possible. But Mussolini maintained his decision, and communicated it to Hitler the next day, even after hopes of military success had revived. The corps of Gambara, Mussolini's favorite, might yet break through to Nice.[199] Even after the actions of 22 June proved unsuccessful, Mussolini did not give up hope. Roatta distinguished himself proposing to the Germans that several battalions of picked Italian troops air-land at Lyon and points south to participate in the occupation of southern France. Graziani was still prodding his subordinates "to insist upon the advance with the greatest energy and activity along the entire front" scarcely twelve hours before the armistice finally took effect in the early hours of 25 June.[200] Mussolini continued the war, even while abandoning his occupation claims. As a demonstration of *signorilità,* and still more as an attempt to maintain France as a factor in the balance of power, his performance at this point – and, as will emerge, throughout summer, fall, and winter of 1940 – leaves something to be desired.

The suggestion that Mussolini expected a swift peace, and was therefore willing to postpone gratification temporarily is more plausible. Ciano's version of Mussolini's motives lends some support to this view, although Mussolini made no prediction to Ciano of when he expected peace. To cheer up the generals, who were doubtless low in spirits and restive over the Alpine fiasco, Mussolini remarked on the evening of 22 June that "once France was eliminated, England would . . . give in." "With little effort we shall have much," he assured them. But these comforting words, like his earlier promises to Badoglio of a phony war, were a deliberate appeal to his generals' congenital opportunism. From Mussolini's point of view, England must not give in before Italy had secured mastery of the Mediterranean by force. On the morning of 23 June, before the French delegates arrived, Mussolini added to the new Italian armistice conditions the stipulation that the French neutralize their Mediterranean bases "in order to permit [Italy] full freedom of maneuver in the war against Great Britain."[201]

Actually, the principal thrust of Ciano's diary remarks and Mussolini's own account to Hitler quite adequately explain the decision, if one considers them in the context of the Italian strategic situation. The Army's failure to break through in the Alps and consequent French outrage at Italian demands might well have produced a breaking off of negotiations and a decision by the French government, navy, or North African authorities to fight on. Reports that the French were preparing to adopt precisely that course so alarmed Mussolini on the evening of 21 June, at the time of his decision to reduce his claims, that he briefly suggested to Berlin urgent Axis pressure on the Spaniards to attack French Morocco.[202]

Continued French belligerence in the Mediterranean would produce a veritable chasm between Italy and Germany. Even more important, it would place Italy in an extremely dangerous situation. The French fleet, as Mussolini himself had pointed out at the end of the Munich meeting, would fight on in British service, with unforeseeable consequences. On land, Balbo would face a two front war. The converse was also true. With the French eliminated, the Italian Navy in the Mediterranean and Balbo's desert forces had – at least theoretically – an excellent chance of dealing with the British. Beside such a prospect, the immediate satisfaction of Italian aspirations against France paled.

After "humiliation" in the Alps, Mussolini predictably disassociated himself from the armistice signing, which took place "almost clandestinely." Ciano and Badoglio met the French delegation at Villa Incisa outside Rome on the afternoon of 23 June. Like his German counterpart, Keitel, Badoglio insisted on conducting the negotiations personally. He was acquainted with some members of the French delegation, and treated them with exquisite though embarrassed courtesy. The negotiations – for unlike Compiègne, genuine negotiations took place – were swift. The Italians yielded in the face of French reluctance to surrender what remained of their air force, or the Italian anti-Fascist emigrés. Otherwise, except for the occupation zone, the document closely resembled its German model; the French fleet would concentrate in French ports under Italo-German supervision. Shortly after 7 p.m. on the evening of 24 June, Badoglio and the French signed. Hostilities officially ceased at 0135 hours the next morning. Upon receiving the armistice from Badoglio and colleagues, Mussolini remarked that it was "more a political than a military armistice after only fifteen days of war – but it gives us a good document in hand."[203] His unhappiness was obvious.

Nor was Mussolini alone, although other Italians had different reasons for chagrin than he. As Ciano noted on 25 June, the armistice conditions were not yet public, but already rumors were circulating, "creating a noteworthy sense of unease." People had believed in "immediate occupations at no expense," and expected that "all the territories not conquered by arms" would pass to Italy automatically. As Ciano accurately predicted, disappointment was destined to increase.[204] Italy's war had begun badly.

Mussolini had nevertheless intervened, as he had promised Hitler at the Brenner in March, for Italy's "honor and interests" – above all the latter, as he interpreted them. The German victories had overcome the objections of King, generals, and admirals, and had stirred in the public that fear of arriving "too late" that Mussolini hoped was eagerness "to jump from aircraft, fire at tanks, and so on." He now launched Italy in pursuit of vast Mediterranean and Middle Eastern ambitions, in the shadow of Germany's war with Britain far to the north and in competition with Hitler's interest in a temporary compromise that would leave him free to turn and rend the Soviet Union.

CHAPTER 4

June–September 1940: Duce strategy in the shadow of Sea Lion

Se quel guerriero
Io fossi! Se il mio sogno
Si avverasse! . . . Un esercito di prodi
Da me guidato . . . E la vittoria – e il plauso
Di Menfi tutta! – E a te, mia dolce Aïda,
Tornar di lauri cinto. . .

(*Aïda*, I,i)

1. *War, not peace*

On to Suez. The war against France was over. The war against Great Britain, as the *Comando Supremo*'s 25 June bulletin announced dramatically, continued, and would continue until victory. The day of the French armistice, Ciano remarked encouragingly to Mackensen that "he scarcely believed that London would see reason in time – as was desirable in the interest of England itself as well as that of European civilization . . . the Führer, who had offered the British chances enough in the past, would then doubtless act with lightning-like speed, nor would Italy hold back."[1] The Italian military leadership would have agreed. On 25 June, Badoglio assured Balbo in Libya that the promised equipment was coming. The seventy medium tanks from the "Po" Army would enable Balbo to "dominate the situation." The British, Badoglio judged, lacked "drive."[2]

That afternoon, Badoglio met the service chiefs to discuss the radically new strategic situation. He rambled inconclusively in a manner that suggested inability to formulate a coherent war plan even now that French collapse made action seem feasible even to him. In essence, however, he approved Cavagnari's reluctance to attack Malta, a question of "limited importance" best left to the Air Force. Italy's main effort against Egypt, which Badoglio now revived without a trace of embarrassment, would have to wait until the French North African colonies acknowledged Pétain's authority. Then, after he had "bolt[ed] the doors" defensively, Balbo could move. Badoglio belatedly directed Roatta to study the operational and logistical difficulties involved in a drive on Alexandria across 500 kilometers of desert:

It is possible that if the Egyptian [internal] situation were to become serious for Great Britain, it would be appropriate for us to make a vigorous foray [*una puntata decisa*] that would serve to give the Duce that [necessary] element of substantiation for our claims toward Egypt [*che servirebbe a dare al DUCE quell' elemento di consistenza per le pretese verso l'Egitto*].[3]

Badoglio was still holding open the possibility of bluff, of getting "much with little effort." But Mussolini was not counting on internal collapse of the British Middle East position, or interested in "elements of substantiation" for claims against Egypt. He wanted to conquer it.

On 26 June Badoglio again contacted Balbo. News from General Marras in Berlin that the German staff was talking of "immense preparations to invade England" the following week had apparently galvanized Mussolini. "Time seems to be getting shorter and shorter," Badoglio informed Balbo, "and we may be compelled to attack toward the East as soon as possible unless we want to remain with empty hands at the conclusion of peace." Balbo was to "put wings to everybody's feet." Mussolini was "quivering," Badoglio explained, and would probably not long delay in giving the signal to move.[4]

Mussolini did not confine his activism to the Mediterranean theater. On 26 June he also dispatched an urgent message to Hitler pressing for Italian participation in the invasion of Britain, a matter he had apparently already raised at Munich. The offer was more than a propagandistic attempt "merely to demonstrate his share in victory"[5]; it was a desperate expedient to deny Hitler a purely bilateral settlement with Britain. This anxiety in Rome, and the sudden decisions that each new report of the progress of Operation Sea Lion (as the Germans soon christened their invasion) were permanent features of Italian planning throughout the summer. News from the North made action seem urgent, but above all gave Mussolini leverage to move his generals.

Badoglio's reading of Mussolini's intentions in North Africa proved correct. By 28 June the French colonies had fallen into line. Balbo now had only the Egyptian front, and the marshal directed him to concentrate all vehicles there and "do everything to be ready by 15 July." As the official history comments, Balbo never acknowledged the message. The naval anti-aircraft defenses of Tobruk failed to recognize the distinctive silhouette of the S.79 tri-motor, and shot Balbo and his suite down in flames on the evening of 28 June as they were attempting to land on their way to hunt British armored cars. But this "extremely sorrowful event," as Badoglio described it to Balbo's chief of staff, was not to disturb "the rhythm of preparation" for the attack on Egypt.[6]

Mussolini himself was unmoved; his chief concern was to find a suitable replacement. Graziani, the regime's chief colonial fighting soldier, was the obvious choice. Badoglio not unjustly considered his colleague misplaced as Army chief of staff, for Graziani "lacked adequate training and had no familiarity whatsoever with the problems of such an important staff."[7] Badoglio probably considered it politic to thus remove a rival from Rome and prox-

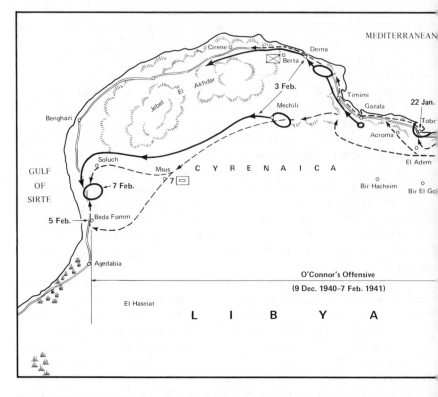

Map 2. Advance and defeat in North Africa. *Source:* United States Military Academy, *A Military History of World War II: Atlas* (West Point, New York, 1956), map 74.

imity to the Duce, but despite later Graziani accusations, his chief motivation was apparently to put his colleague's qualities as a troop leader to best use. Graziani later lamented that Badoglio and Mussolini, at this point absent in northern Italy touring the Alpine front, had hustled him off to Libya without a face-to-face briefing on his mission. At the time, however, he merely noted in his diary the receipt of "verbal directives" by telephone from both Mussolini and Badoglio. On 30 June he flew to Benghazi to take up his command.[8] Formally, he remained chief of staff, but Roatta took over in name as well as in fact the day-to-day running of the Army staff in Rome.

As Graziani landed in Libya, the situation gave even well-informed and skeptical observers cause for optimism. Badoglio's assistant Armellini now noted enthusiastically that the Navy, although the British at Gibraltar and Alexandria combined still outnumbered it in battleships, was nevertheless "well on the way toward supremacy." In North Africa, concentration against Egypt would soon produce "a powerful mass of troops." Roatta and his subordinates had drafted the offensive study Badoglio had requested on 25 June, and had concluded – in a document that has not found its way into the official histories or the memoirs of the participants – that

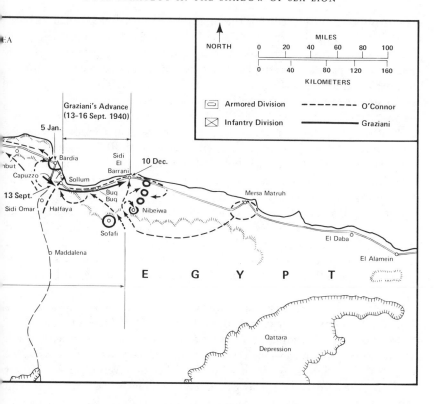

currently, given the present situation, and with the arrival in port of the material presently being readied or awaiting embarkation for Libya, *our land forces in North Africa are sufficiently strong for the initiation in the near future of a decisive offensive with, as objective, the Anglo-Egyptian forces presently in Egypt.*

The Army staff correctly judged that the British had three divisions, of which one was armored. Italian forces had parity in weapons, and numerical superiority.[9] Mussolini and even Badoglio were equally enthusiastic. Mussolini spent the days after the French armistice in a growing state of exultation. He returned to Rome on 2 July from the Western Alps "enthusiastic about what he had seen," and announced to Ciano that the Italian Army had broken through the "Alpine Maginot Line." The march on Alexandria was a *"fait accompli."* Even Badoglio now judged that the removal of France made an Italian offensive "easy and foolproof."[10]

On the diplomatic front, Ciano was again active. Before 10 June he had failed to secure the desired German guarantees for Italy's aspirations. He now intended to stake Italian claims before the Germans could defeat or compromise with Britain, or ease, to Italy's disadvantage, the armistice conditions imposed on France. For the moment convinced of German victory, Ciano felt it politic to patch up his relations with Ribbentrop and Hitler.[11]

Ciano's war aims program was lengthy and explicit. In deference to both German and Spanish interests, he abandoned the claims advanced at Munich to Algeria and Morocco. But France to the River Var, Corsica, Tunisia (with border rectifications toward Algeria), Djibouti, and an extension of Libya to the south remained. From Britain, Italy would take Malta, British Somaliland, Perim, and Socotra. Aden would go to Yemen; Cyprus to Greece, possibly in exchange for Ciamuria. Egypt was to be "fully independent with exclusive treaty of alliance with Italy." The Sudan would become the Italo-Egyptian Sudan. The Mandates (Syria, Lebanon, Palestine) would blossom into "independent states, allied to Italy." Finally, Ciano proposed the vivisection of Switzerland along the central chain of the Alps, leaving Italy the Valais, the Ticino, and the Grisons. As Mussolini, in the tone "of a demigod rendering judgment," announced to his entourage during his alpine tour, "the New Europe . . . could not have more than four or five large states; the small ones [would] have no further raison d'être and [would] have to disappear."[12]

But events, both military and diplomatic, seemed to endanger Mussolini's program. Churchill's defiant and piratical attack on the French fleet at Mers-el-Kébir on 3 July eliminated a potential threat to Britain's control of the Atlantic, upon which continued resistance to Germany depended. Given the naval balance of forces, the incapacity of the Pétain government – whatever its feelings toward Britain – to guarantee that France's fleet would remain outside German control, and Britain's own desperate situation, the action was a strategic necessity. But it might well have led France into the Axis camp as a belligerent had the Germans been more receptive. Following the attack, Hitler did indeed suspend the armistice clauses requiring French naval demobilization. The Italians, who had made no attempt to catch the British at a disadvantage on 3 July, had to follow suit.[13]

These developments perturbed Mussolini. Hitler had mentioned at Munich that he planned to reclaim Alsace-Lorraine, and had seized most of France as an occupation zone. The Führer's final aspirations there were as far-reaching as Mussolini's, and included much of northeastern France and a vassal state ("Burgundy") extending southward under the gentle viceroyalty of Heinrich Himmler. But now and later Mussolini was unable to see that Hitler had not the slightest intention of allowing France a place in the New Order. In the aftermath of Mers-el-Kébir, Mussolini immediately feared that France was "attempting to slide surreptitiously into the anti-British camp," in order to "defraud" Italy of its booty.[14] Other Italian leaders, however, saw advantages. French reprisal air raids on Gibraltar encouraged Roatta to suggest enlisting French ground forces against the British in Egypt. The idea was not entirely fantastic: independently, the French themselves seriously contemplated a joint Italo-French naval operation to free the French squadron the British had immobilized at Alexandria.[15] Mussolini was unconvinced, and would not listen to French offers of air bases in Algeria. He feared "placing himself in the condition of then – at the peace – not being able to advance territorial requests."[16] French "nonbelligerence" on the Axis side was an intolerable threat, a threat Mussolini instructed Ciano to parry energetically in the forthcoming Berlin talks.[17] These were hardly the acts of a man who sought to balance German preponderance with Franco-Italian rapprochement.

Even more menacing than French cooperation loomed the danger that peace would once again "break out" prematurely. Vatican peace soundings on 28 June at once encountered Mussolini's decided hostility. In Berlin, Alfieri, who wanted a peace of sorts, insisted to the American chargé that Britain should come to terms before total annihilation ensued. When Alfieri informed Rome of the interested reaction of the U.S. Department of State, Mussolini authorized release of the information to Hitler. This was no peace move. Simultaneously, he ordered Alfieri to ascertain Hitler's reaction to the despised papal *démarche*. Mussolini merely intended to smoke out whatever peace contacts might have already taken place without his knowledge; Italy had to secure a seat at any Anglo-German negotiations "for the division of the world."[18]

Greece, Switzerland, Yugoslavia. Meanwhile Mussolini planned extension of the war to other powers besides Britain. The choleric governor of the Dode-canese, Cesare Maria De Vecchi di Val Cismon, "Quadrumvir" of the Fascist Revolution, had begun as early as 18 June to bombard Rome with reports of foul doings in the Aegean. Suda Bay on Crete was host to "one aircraft carrier, four cruisers, three destroyers."[19] While Ciano and Mussolini were away at Munich, Anfuso browbeat the Greek minister in Rome, and directed Grazzi to protest in Athens. The Greeks denied the charges "in the most categorical manner," but did not appease the Quadrumvir. On 26 June, he reported that "the Englishman, following his custom, has taken refuge in the Greek waters of Amorgos, which he considers his own." Three to four "enemy" destroyers had established a base at Milos, and, "as usual in the Greek Islands [the British] are the bosses."[20]

Upon his return from the Alps, Mussolini was "furious" and decided "if this music should continue, to pass to action." Ciano also tried his hand at intimidating the Greek minister, and cabled Grazzi that he had talked "in a manner such as to leave no doubts about our intentions should Greece continue to act as an accomplice of the British." The Greek dictator Metaxas replied anxiously that he had done nothing to deserve such accusations; he was determined to defend Greek neutrality against any power that might attempt to violate it. He also offered full facilities to the Italians to send observers to the Greek Islands to see for themselves. From Athens, Grazzi courageously contradicted Ciano and insisted that the Greeks were telling the truth, as did the naval attaché, Captain Sebastiano Morin. De Vecchi, however, persisted. The British ships were still at Milos, "mixed in with the

Greeks." "Diplomatic affirmations" that the destroyers were Greek, not British, were "not, I say again, not, credible." Mussolini took a similar line, and directed Ciano to inform Hitler during the Berlin talks that Italy intended to occupy the Ionian islands. He also began to contemplate once more the land attack on Greece through Albania first conceived in the spring of 1939, but now furnished with a new pretext. The action would follow if the bulk of the British Mediterranean Fleet "should base itself on the Greek islands."[21] Both plans were vaguely connected with Italy's offensive strategy against Britain's Middle Eastern position, but they were above all intended as acts of imperial aggrandizement and vengeance, and as salutary lessons to others in Italy's sphere.

But Greece, though a source of irritation, was as yet relatively unimportant. Ciano apparently pressed for early action, but Mussolini was preoccupied with the larger "parallel war" against Britain. Even in the Balkans, he had bigger game in mind. In May, he had abandoned his intention of attacking Yugoslavia in order to enter the war "through the front door." French collapse now left him with a large unemployed army in the Po Valley. Graziani needed equipment, not more troops. The Germans showed little interest in Italian aid against the British homeland, even before Hitler's formal rejection in a letter of 13 July.[22] Mussolini's appetite for Yugoslavia could therefore revive, in concomitance with a similar interest in Switzerland. Even before Italy had entered the war, Graziani had directed General Mario Vercellino, the commander of the "Po" Army, to prepare to cut the Ticino salient "in the eventuality that Swiss neutrality is violated by others." Hitler's pique at the Swiss at Munich further inspired Mussolini. A remark of the German minister in Berne to his Italian colleague that Berlin thought Mussolini "hostile" to partition ("only for this reason it cannot be done") may also have whetted the dictatorial appetite. On 7 July, Soddu, Mussolini's military factotum, confided to Roatta that "Germany intended to invade Switzerland." Roatta thereupon prepared to move the necessary troops, and briefed Vercellino on his mission on 21 July. But the expected German action did not materialize, and Mussolini's other projects took priority.[23]

Hitler himself involuntarily helped resuscitate the Yugoslav plan. By 1 July, when he had a long and important talk with Alfieri, Hitler had fully recovered from the attack of pacifism suffered in June. He did his best to emphasize his ruthlessness, perhaps on the principle that much of what he told the Italians would find its way to London and counterpoint the appeal to the British public over the head of Churchill that he hinted he was considering. The coming assault on Britain would be "very bloody," and would include "absolute air warfare" against the civilian population. Actually, Hitler did not even order his staffs to begin planning Operation Sea Lion, the cross-Channel invasion, until the next day, and did not order actual preparations until 16 July. Hitler also mentioned with relish to Alfieri the extraordinary collection of documents of the French and Allied commands that the

German army had found abandoned in a railway wagon at La Charité-sur-Saône. Certain Balkan countries, above all Yugoslavia, "appeared in a most interesting light." Alfieri reported that Hitler had excitedly pointed out Yugoslavia on the map, denounced its "equivocal and hostile" policy toward Rome, and insisted that "at the opportune moment, Italy [would] have to settle, to clarify many things. . . ."[24]

The effect of Alfieri's report was immediate. Soddu informed Roatta on the afternoon of 3 July that Mussolini considered this "the favorable moment to act against Yugoslavia." Hitler would give Italy " 'carte blanche' for the development of operations through Carinthia and Styria as well [as across the Yugoslav border]." The invasion would tentatively take place in August. Badoglio and Roatta began to make the necessary arrangements. Five divisions would remain on the French border. The rest were to move East "as silently as possible" to the Parma–Padua area. The Air Force was to ready fields along the Yugoslav frontier "to receive, at the opportune moment, the mass of aircraft." Mussolini directed his son-in-law to seek Berlin's approval.[25]

The Germans received Ciano on 7 July with unexpected warmth. Hitler was "extremely kind, almost solicitous" during the two-hour conversation at the Reich Chancellery.[26] He emphasized his determination to continue the war, although he also implied he would soon mount a "skillful appeal . . . to isolate the British government further." He also insisted that despite British aggression at Oran and elsewhere, the "eternal France" remained an implacable enemy of the Axis. Ciano exploited this welcome opening to press for an immediate and draconian peace treaty to secure Italy's claims on France – a goal both he and Mussolini pursued pertinaciously throughout summer and fall. Hitler parried successfully with the argument that a humiliating settlement might encourage the British to move in French Equatorial Africa or Morocco, and would require Germany to relinquish the French Atlantic coastline where it now occupied bases vital against Britain.

Ciano drew back, and contented himself with stressing Mussolini's eagerness to help strike the final blow against Britain. He also repeated Mussolini's offer of troops and aircraft to aid a cross-Channel invasion. The attack on Egypt would begin, Ciano claimed with excessive optimism, between 20 and 30 July. In the meantime a major naval battle was possible. Finally, Ciano sought Hitler's approval for Italian moves against Greece and Yugoslavia. Greece "awaited with impatience the moment in which England would violate her," and while waiting was helping the British sink Italian submarines. Italy proposed to preempt the British by occupying Corfù and other Greek islands. As for Yugoslavia, a "typical Versailles creation of anti-Italian bent," Mussolini had decided to "liquidate" it in roughly a month.

Hitler was for the moment noncommittal about the Greek plan, but reacted with decision to Mussolini and Ciano's bid to destroy Yugoslavia. Under current conditions the risks were too great. If Italy attacked Yugoslavia, Hungary would fall upon Rumania, and the Russians would seize the long-coveted Turkish straits. While the Yugoslav problem was Italy's to solve "when the appropriate hour struck," action now would be dangerous except if a general Balkan war had already broken out. Ciano reluctantly concurred, and implied that Mussolini would also agree. But Ciano also did his best to avoid damping his master's enthusiasm. In reporting to Mussolini, Ciano weakened Hitler's warnings about Yugoslavia; it would present "a very simple problem" once "the English question was liquidated, *or at least on the way to an easy liquidation*" – a call for Italian self-control considerably less blunt than that ascribed to Hitler in the German minute. Ciano also claimed Hitler's approval for an Italian deployment, "to be able to act with the greatest speed as soon as a suitable opportunity presented itself." As for Greece, Ciano affirmed without embarrassment that Hitler was "decidedly favorable [*nettamente favorevole*] to an action to forestall any . . . British move [on the islands]."

Ciano clearly exaggerated German enthusiasm. Privately, Hitler was not averse to landings on Crete and Cyprus, islands from which the *Regia Aeronautica* might conceivably drive the British fleet from the eastern Mediterranean.[27] Despite Italian protestations, however, an attack on Corfù and its neighbors clearly served little purpose in the war against Britain. Hitler had undeniably refrained from laying down the law to Ciano over Greece, in contrast to his remarks on Yugoslavia. Hitler had evidently not realized, as he did later in the summer, that any disruption in southeastern Europe, even a limited Italian action against Greek islands, might produce British or Russian threats to the Rumanian oilfields. He was also not yet aware of the full extent of his ally's irresponsibility where Greece was concerned – that realization came only in August.

Exorcising the specter of peace. Even discounting his embellishment of Hitler's remarks, Ciano had secured a great deal – if Germany could deliver. Mussolini was "satisfied with the results." German support for Italy's war aims implied the war would continue until Italy achieved those aims: an Anglo-German "division of the world" at Italy's expense was now a shade less likely. Ciano had emphasized to Hitler and Ribbentrop that Mussolini was "decisively favorable to the continuation of the war and against any compromise solution." Ciano also greeted with indifference suggestions by Alfieri that he raise the subject of peace with Hitler.[28]

Mussolini's long-time confidential agent in Berlin, the mysterious Giuseppe Renzetti, drove the point home by spreading the word in German official circles "that the day they gave in [to peace feelers Germany had allegedly received from British industrialists], they would place England in the position of a nation that has not lost the war, and Germany would then, after a few years, find itself constrained to begin the war again."[29]

Soon after Ciano's return, Mussolini had further cause for alarm. On 13 July Hitler responded belatedly and negatively to his fellow dictator's urgent offer of troops for the invasion of England. Italian participation would complicate the already daunting logistical and command problems the operation posed. Instead, he exhorted Mussolini to concentrate on Egypt.[30] Mussolini's reaction to this rebuff is unknown, but it is unlikely that he took it kindly. Despite the welcome confirmation that invasion was not imminent (Hitler had stressed the need for long and exacting preparation), the letter ominously suggested that Germany merely sought to make Britain "ready for peace." Mussolini may well have interpreted this remark as another sign that Anglo-German negotiations without Italy impended.

Such a reaction would help to explain the apparent Italian spoiling maneuver that followed. Hitler had hinted to Alfieri (on 1 July) and confided to Ciano (on 7 July) that he contemplated a last "skillful appeal to the English people" in order to "isolate further" the British government (whose assault on the French fleet Hitler obviously – and correctly – interpreted as an act of defiance against Germany). News of the forthcoming speech leaked out after Ciano's return to Rome. The German leadership suspected Ciano in person of deliberately divulging word of possible compromise and of the speech through his own press and through American journalists. "Responsible quarters" in Dr. Joseph Goebbels' Ministry for Popular Enlightenment and Propaganda bubbled over with righteous indignation, which they vented under the seal of secrecy in briefing the representatives of the German press on 17 July:

It has now been established that Count Ciano, after his reception by the Führer, gave information on these high political doings to [Virginio] Gayda [Editor of *Il Giornale d'Italia,* and Mussolini's chief foreign policy mouthpiece] and to some American journalists, in order that [the information] be exploited for news purposes. The Americans jumped on it and without knowing the German version told the story with an English slant. Gayda himself wrote a long article, which hinted at the secret in a manner transparent to the well informed. A mighty indignation reigns in Berlin over the behavior of Ciano and Gayda. Damage has been done first of all in terms of news management, because the German press, due to higher directives, was not able to take a stand on these extremely important questions, and was upstaged by the Italian press. Far greater damage has been done in the political arena, because now the counterarguments of Churchill are being circulated to all conceivable parts of the world, without Germany being able to say anything on the matter at this point.[31]

The Gayda story appeared on 15 July and predicted triumphantly that "in a very few days" Great Britain would be "invited to render its final accounting," and would have to choose either "submission to the rejuvenating and healing forces of Europe, or an extraordinarily long and severe war. . . ."[32] American reports, particularly one by John T. Whitaker of the *Chicago Daily News,* indeed "told the story with an English slant." Whitaker explained that "with their usual skill in propaganda," Berlin and Rome had "exploited the general desire for peace and the feeling of many people that England continues the war unnecessarily, now that France is defeated." Whitaker's story, along with a similar one from the Associated Press correspondent, cited "diplomatic circles" as a source, and predicted that Ciano would go to Berlin in the next days for further discussions. Small wonder that the Germans, apparently including Ribbentrop (who according to the Propaganda Ministry spokesman protested directly to Rome) interpreted the stories as attempts to attenuate the impact of Hitler's forthcoming appeal, and to strengthen Churchill and the diehards. While no direct evidence links Ciano or Mussolini to the American reports, the Gayda leader was semiofficial, and was presumably the product of Mussolini's aversion to a Hitler appeal, an aversion the Duce displayed privately to Ciano.[33]

The latter journeyed to Berlin on 18 July, after the Germans informed him at the very last moment that Hitler would speak the next day. The speech, to a *Reichstag* session at the Kroll Opera House, was lengthy, self-congratulatory, and full of praise for Germany's military leaders, eleven of whom received promotion to field marshal on the spot. At the end, Hitler made the barest mention of peace – Germany, confident of victory, addressed to England a last "appeal to reason." He gave no details, perhaps out of anger over Churchill's fiery radio speech of 14 July, which had predicted a British offensive in 1942 and implied that British efforts would lift "the dark curse of Hitler . . . from our age." Hitler's feeble offer nevertheless impressed Ciano as "sincere," and caused consternation in Rome. Despite Ciano's telegraphic assurances that the Germans expected the war to continue, Mussolini greeted his returning son-in-law with dismay. The speech had been "too skillful," and he *"fear[ed]"* that the British might find in it a handle to open negotiations." Ciano concluded that "now, more than ever, he wants war."[34]

Mussolini need not have worried. The "appeal to reason" did not appeal to the British; in any case, Roosevelt's renomination for a third term the day before Hitler's offer was a decisive assurance of increasing United States support. London had nevertheless observed skeptically an unofficial German "peace reconnaissance" through various go-betweens in the preceding weeks. The most conspicuous of these had been Dr. Carl Burckhardt, former League of Nations high commissioner for Danzig, who had insisted, probably at the prompting of Weizsäcker of the foreign office, that "there were some 'local demands' of Italy he [Hitler] was bound to support, but in general he wanted 'a white peace like Sadowa.' " The "appeal to reason" itself received an uncompromising public answer in a 22 July speech by Halifax, the very man the Germans not without reason considered the chief Cabinet voice for compromise. Hitler was predictably wrathful, and ordered no further feelers to London: "If the English want their downfall, they can have it."[35]

The Halifax speech was not Britain's last word. When King Gustav V of Sweden approached both British and Germans in early August with an offer to mediate, Churchill's draft reply defiantly proclaimed that the British government would "rather all perish in the common ruin than fail or falter in their duty." Halifax's final version, although less flamboyant, nevertheless put forward Churchill's magnificently impudent demand that Hitler offer proposals to right "the wrongs that Germany has inflicted upon other nations."[36] Churchill more or less simultaneously blocked a possible channel the British ambassador in Washington, Lord Lothian, had opened to the German chargé d'affaires there.[37] A further German approach in early September, as the *Luftwaffe* shifted its aim to London and the climax of the battle of Britain approached, produced similar results. A Berlin lawyer in the service of the *Sicherheitsdienst* of the SS, Dr. Ludwig Weissauer, contacted the British minister in Stockholm. Weissauer claimed to act for the Führer in person — a claim not intrinsically improbable, despite Hitler's earlier wrath — and presented one more "last chance offer" which if refused might lead to "the loss to Britain of Egypt, the Middle East, and ultimately India." The world would "be divided into two economic spheres, one continental, organized by Germany, the other maritime and colonial, organized by the British Empire." The offer included "political independence of European countries now occupied by Germany, . . . including 'a Polish State' but excluding Czechoslovakia"; Germany would possibly receive "some compensation elsewhere." Weissauer was as cavalier about Italian desiderata as Burckhardt's Berlin contacts had been in July: "Questions concerning the Mediterranean, Egypt, and French, Belgian and Dutch colonies" were "open to discussion." The War Cabinet considered the offer coldly and returned an answer similar to that given the king of Sweden.[38]

Rome was naturally not privy to these activities, but feared precisely this sort of German neglect of its interests. Halifax's harsh public reply to the "appeal to reason" temporarily reassured Ciano, who by 28 July expected the German final attack on Britain to begin momentarily. But a week or so later both the Japanese ambassador and "a highly secret Soviet source" reported Anglo-German negotiations were underway through the king of Sweden. Alarmed, Ciano instructed Alfieri in Berlin to determine, "with the utmost caution and secrecy," the facts of the matter.[39]

Alfieri's soundings, which he conducted with an ineptitude that aroused the despair of his subordinates, proved reassuring. Mention of rumors that wide strata in Britain favored peace prompted Ribbentrop to exclaim in evident irritation that "Churchill [was] crazy, and the English imbeciles." Ribbentrop insisted the German offensive would soon begin, and would be "violent, with swift success," even though flight of the London government to Canada might complicate the "final phase of the war." Peace was clearly not at hand. But Rome could not resist a further spoiling maneuver. The British minister at the Vatican, D'Arcy Osborne, received word that the Italian press authorities had "instructed journalists not to deny widespread rumors" that he was conveying to London "peace proposals communicated through the Pope."[40] After this final nervous twitch, the Italian leadership subsided, and devoted itself to waging war — or in the case of the high command, to avoiding Mussolini's pressure to wage it.

2. The Mediterranean and Africa

The reluctant admirals. The impending fleet action that Ciano had announced to Hitler took place on 9 July in the angle between Sicily and Calabria. Ciano, touring the battlefields of France and Belgium as Ribbentrop's guest, got through by telephone to Admiral Cavagnari in Rome around midnight. Ciano perhaps expected a victory, for his face immediately darkened. The British had hit the *Cesare,* and the Air Force "had supposedly not done its job." Nevertheless, according to the admiral, one could say that "things had gone well."[41]

Upon his return to Rome, Ciano discovered otherwise. Navy and Air Force were bickering. Cavagnari "maintained that air action had been completely lacking in the first phase of the battle." Once the *Regia Aeronautica* had finally arrived, it had directed its bombs at the Italian fleet as well as at the enemy. From the Air Force side, "brilliant reports" abounded – reports Ciano, with no illusions about his own service's efficiency, greeted with appropriate skepticism. Nevertheless, Mussolini convinced himself that "in three days he had annihilated 50 percent of British naval power in the Mediterranean."[42] He appeared to have vindicated a triumphant assertion in 1938 that the Italian battle fleet, thanks to "the temper of [its] men, and the orders they will receive," would not remain meekly inactive within defended anchorages. The Italian press and radio suggested that:

For the first time since the fifteenth century Italy had re-asserted the principle of her supremacy in the Mediterranean. This supremacy would call for further efforts of heroism, of will-power and devotion, but in principle it was already claimed and historically sanctioned by blood and victory. The words *mare nostrum* were no longer mere words of hopeless rhetoric.[43]

Mussolini's rejoicing and the clamor of the agencies of the Ministry for Popular Culture were premature.

The battle off Calabria resulted from the encounter of the Italian fleet, under the tactical command of Admiral Inigo Campioni, with Admiral Andrew Cunningham's Mediterranean Fleet from Alexandria. Both were covering convoys: the British, two from Malta; the Italians, one to Benghazi in order to deliver the M.11/39 tanks and other equipment to Graziani. Cunningham's forces consisted of one relatively modernized battleship, the *Warspite,* and two ancient and practically unimproved ones, *Malaya* and *Royal Sovereign.* The aircraft carrier *Eagle,* with seventeen Swordfish and two biplane fighters, provided a meager air reconnaissance and strike capability. Campioni had *Cesare* and *Cavour,* sixteen cruisers, crushing superiority in light forces, and, at least in theory, the cooperation of most of the *Regia Aeronautica.* Naval intelligence had also received and decrypted the entire British operation order on 4–5 July, and Rome thus knew the planned courses and positions of the British forces.[44]

Campioni nevertheless labored under severe disadvantages. Rome was closer to him than London to Cunningham, and Italian tradition did not place the same emphasis on initiative or show the same respect for the judgment of the "man on the spot" as the British. Cavagnari issued firm instructions.[45] Campioni was to display the utmost prudence. The fleet would remain close to Italian bases. It might "possibly" strike at the British Gibraltar squadron or the Mediterranean Fleet from Alexandria if it encountered either separately. Above all, it was to delay contact as long as possible so that the Air Force could do its work. Despite the pleas of the captains and divisional commander of the new battleships still undergoing trials, Cavagnari refused to allow *Littorio* and *Vittorio Veneto* to join the fleet for the action. His primary aim was to minimize risk. But as the British navy had discovered in analyzing its own unsatisfying performance at Jutland, prudence is more a domestic virtue than a military one.

From Cunningham's point of view, the action was in retrospect "most unsatisfactory."[46] He failed to destroy the Italian fleet. Campioni's superiority in speed meant that only *Warspite* got within range of *Cesare* and *Cavour*. Fifteen minutes of contact at a range of thirteen miles produced a hit at the base of *Cavour*'s after funnel that put part of her power plant out of action. Campioni thereupon retired in disorder toward Messina under cover of a thick smokescreen, while the *Regia Aeronautica* belatedly arrived in force to compound the confusion. The air crews were inadequately trained for action against ships, poorly briefed, and had no radio contact with the fleet. They bombed both Campioni's and Cunningham's forces impartially until dusk.[47]

Admiral Weichold of the German liaison staff in Rome judged that Cavagnari and his subordinates had missed major opportunities. The Italian fleet had superiority in speed. Cavagnari and Campioni possessed "outstanding knowledge of the situation and of enemy intentions," a battleground in the vicinity of their own bases, and the two practically moonless nights of 8/9 and 9/10 July to fling their numerous torpedo craft at the British. The German admiral prophetically summed the situation up for Berlin on 10 July: the Italian Navy had *apparently missed its decisive hour.*"[48] Weichold had no cause to retract that judgment.

The repercussions of the action on the morale of the Italian naval high command were disastrous. In his memoirs, Cunningham chivalrously advanced the supposition that "it was too much to expect the Italians to stake everything on a stand-up fight." "Never again," he added, "did they willingly face up to the fire of British battleships, though on several subsequent occasions they were in a position to give battle with great preponderance in force."[49] Cavagnari had earlier been reluctant to face risks, and had argued that Britain, which unlike Italy could replace lost ships, could take more chances than the *Regia Marina*. The same argument has formed the mainstay of the postwar official historians' defense of Italian strategy.[50] In 1940, however, it was not a strategic judgment but an expression of the naval leadership's inferiority complex. British battleships in the shipyards could not affect the issue in the Mediterranean, especially with England itself in mortal peril. Had Cunningham lost *Warspite,* the Royal Navy might well have evacuated the eastern Mediterranean – a course for which an influential party at the Admiralty had pressed after French collapse.[51]

After the battle off Calabria Cavagnari shifted from passive resistance to active complaint. An innocuous set of "strategic directives" that Mussolini and Badoglio issued on 11 July seemed to single out the Navy in recommending "decision and audacity." Cavagnari protested at what he evidently took as a deliberate affront. The *Comando Supremo* apologetically withdrew the document, then reissued it with appropriate emendations.[52] Nor did Cavagnari repeat the experiment conducted off Calabria. In the next months only his light forces succeeded in finding the British. The results were depressing. On 19 July, during a sweep north of Crete, one Italian light cruiser went down after a fight with a theoretically inferior British and Australian force. This time, even Mussolini gained the impression that the Navy had conducted the action in a "not very brilliant manner."[53]

The submarine force, Mussolini's pride, also failed to live up to his expectations. By the end of July, the Italians felt compelled to report to their German allies the loss of thirteen boats. The Navy had made a belated discovery. The clarity of the Mediterranean waters permitted British aircraft to detect submarines as deep as 70 meters beneath the surface. The German naval staff in Berlin was mildly surprised at this confession. With a show of conscious virtue its war diarist noted that the Germans had "long since, and repeatedly, both through the Italian naval attaché . . . and through the German attaché in Rome, informed the Italian navy of the considerable improvements in modern anti-submarine defense and of the difficulties which [German] U-boats [had had] to contend with throughout." Berlin would have been still more surprised had they known that British aircraft and surface vessels had caught Italian submarines on the surface in daylight "time and again." The British recognized that Italian crews were capable of "great individual gallantry," but swiftly conceived a low opinion of their adversaries' training, skill, and initiative.[54]

There remained only the miracle weapons: aerial torpedoes and the manned, steerable torpedolike devices a group of diving enthusiasts attached to the submarine flotilla at La Spezia had developed – not always with encouragement from above – since 1935. Torpedo aircraft were of course an Air Force responsibility. In August, pressure from Mussolini led Pricolo to commit a hastily formed unit, partly manned by cadres from the aerial torpedo school, to an ill-prepared and predictably unsuccessful attack on Alexandria. Similarly, the first attempts to penetrate Alexandria harbor with the *"maiali"* ("hogs," as their crews named the manned torpedoes in homage to their appearance and handling qualities) ended in disaster. Swordfish aircraft from Egypt caught the carrier submarine *Iride* at the unprotected Libyan anchorage Cavagnari had chosen, and sent it to the bottom.[55]

Despite these disappointments, the Italians soon received a second favorable opportunity for a fleet action. By the end of August, *Littorio* and *Vittorio Veneto* were ready at last. Simultaneously, the British launched a major operation from both ends of the Mediterranean to pass a convoy through to Malta and convey an additional carrier and battleship to Cunningham. Campioni's fleet, now with four battleships and superiority of force, sortied at dawn on 31 August with orders to turn back to Taranto at 1900 hours, around dusk, should contact not occur. Cavagnari kept the fleet on a tight rein. At 1430 hours he ordered Campioni to reverse course at 1600 unless already in combat. Campioni complied. The Italian forward elements turned back around 1730, about thirty minutes before they would have made contact with the British (had not Cunningham, unknown to Rome, turned south earlier in the afternoon to close for the night on the Malta convoy he was protecting).[56]

Cavagnari apparently left no explanation for his order, nor have the Italian official historians sought to provide one. At the time, the naval staff claimed to the Germans that contact before sunset "was no longer possible."[57] But Cavagnari could scarcely have made such a calculation at 1430 from the information then available to him about British movements. An air reconnaissance report sent at 1205 placed the British on a course converging with Campioni's. Cavagnari presumably ordered Campioni to reverse course in order to prevent the fleets from meeting before dusk.

A rationale beyond the dictates of simple pusillanimity probably motivated Cavagnari's decision. The Italian naval leadership apparently expected that the cross-Channel invasion threat would compel the British to evacuate the eastern Mediterranean to concentrate for the defense of the home island.[58] To challenge Cunningham on his way west would hardly be profitable, if Italy were about to gain Mediterranean supremacy by default. Nevertheless, the Navy's failure to close with the British on 31 August apparently enraged the Duce, who now gave Cavagnari a direct order to engage without fail at the next opportunity.[59] But neither Cavagnari nor his alter ego, Admiral Odoardo Somigli, had any intention of giving in. Mussolini might send the fleet to sea when the British were in the vicinity; he could hardly compel it to meet the enemy without personally invading the naval war room and assuming tactical control. Mussolini probably never considered such a course, for he was even less conversant with naval affairs than land warfare. Nor was Cavagnari's outright removal currently practical. The admiral had yet to give indisputable proof of incompetence, and the difficulties of selecting a suitable replacement presumably acted as a brake. No assurance existed that a new man, chosen of necessity from the restricted circle of senior naval officers, would prove any more forceful or expert than the incumbent.

Cavagnari and Somigli were not the only restraining influence on Mussolini. In mid-September, the Navy's theory of the "fleet in being" gained an illustrious convert. Though Badoglio had earlier shared Mussolini's impatience, he now swung around to the prudent course, presumably yielding to pressure from Cavagnari and the gradually dawning realization that the war was likely to last into the winter. On 16 September Badoglio forwarded to Cavagnari a *Comando Supremo* directive that, as the postwar official history puts it, "approved the course of action hitherto followed by the Navy."[60] Inexplicably, and perhaps a trifle disingenuously, Badoglio concluded that the results of the first two months of naval warfare were on the whole more favorable to Italy than to Britain. "Who would have any interest in changing this state of affairs?" he asked – and answered himself: "Obviously the stronger navy, that is, the English." The Italian Navy, on the other hand, would be well advised to maintain the present situation. "To conceive of a naval battle as an end in itself" was "absurd," Badoglio wrote in one of his many attempts to dampen Mussolini's warlike enthusiasm.

With the surrender of Badoglio to the Navy view, the last possibility of swift Italian success at sea vanished. The Navy consolidated its victory by insisting that "since every other objective appears secondary in comparison with that of assuring the troops deployed on the Egyptian frontier the capacity for a decisive breakthrough, all the energies of the armed forces must converge towards the accomplishment of that goal."[61] To the Army, possibly with German aid, Cavagnari thankfully left the task of asserting Italian supremacy in the Mediterranean.

The distant viceroy. While Cavagnari was refusing to risk his ships, and Marshal Rodolfo Graziani, as will emerge, was deploying all his ingenuity to persuade Rome that land attack on Egypt was unfeasible, the commander of the most distant and apparently desperate of Italian theaters insisted on taking the offensive. The young Amedeo II of Savoia-Aosta, Duke of Aosta, Viceroy of Ethiopia,[62] had succeeded Graziani in 1937–8 after the latter's failure to suppress the endemic "rebellion" in the newly conquered *Impero.* The duke initially made little progress, but by the spring of 1940 had achieved limited success through a combination of force and conciliation, although Mussolini, in March, called for ruthless use of mustard gas to crush resistance for good before Italy went to war against the West.[63]

The *Impero* was scarcely ready to face external enemies. In June 1940 it possessed supplies sufficient for about eight months of war.[64] With the British firmly established in Egypt, only an occasional long-range transport aircraft slipping surreptitiously across the Sudan linked Rome with Addis Ababa. Amedeo had several courses: to await the decision of the war elsewhere; to seize the initiative and maintain Italian prestige through limited attacks on the neighboring British and French colonies; and, finally, to stake the *Impero*'s meager resources on a major offensive north through the Sudan to Egypt, in coordination with Graziani's advance. Badoglio himself had in desperation entertained the last plan in the late fall of 1935, when British intervention in the Ethiopian conflict had seemed imminent. The Italian leadership in East Africa had continued to nurse it as a long-term project, in accordance with Mussolini's goal of using the *Impero*'s manpower against Britain's imperial position. In response to a Badoglio request in September

1939 for studies of attacks on Djibouti and British Somaliland, Amedeo had again suggested the more ambitious northward offensive. But Badoglio, as with Balbo's contemporaneous proposals for a march on Alexandria, had rejected the viceroy's concept of operations out of hand.[65] Nor did an offensive from East Africa figure in Italian planning in the spring of 1940. Mussolini's 31 March directives mentioned attacks on Djibouti, and on Kassala on the Sudanese border, but did not include the British Somaliland operation, much less the drive on Egypt. Amedeo's gloom during his early April visit to Rome had reinforced this tendency. At the beginning of June, Mussolini and Badoglio ordered Amedeo to adopt a strict defensive. The mission of the *Impero* was merely to endure.[66]

Nevertheless, as the French were negotiating the armistice at Villa Incisa on 23 June, Amedeo requested permission to advance on Kassala, an important communications center across the Sudanese border. Mussolini was evidently as yet unenthusiastic, and Badoglio asked Amedeo to consider whether he could hold Kassala as well as take it; a setback would be harmful. Amedeo replied that the seizure of Kassala would deprive the British of their main line of advance against Eritrea, provide an indispensable jumping-off point for "longer-range offensive actions," and maintain Italian morale and "prestige among the populations."[67] The viceroy, despite his cautious language, may well have now hoped for an all-or-nothing offensive toward Egypt.

In the event, the only offensive operations Amedeo carried out were the actions against Kassala and other Sudanese border posts, similar probes into Kenya, and the invasion of British Somaliland. The Kassala action received Mussolini's sanction on 1 July. Within two days, perhaps as a result of Alfieri's report of Hitler's remarks on the forthcoming invasion of Britain, Mussolini was impatiently requesting word of when the operation would begin. Amedeo's forces, with the support of an air force that crushingly outnumbered the RAF in the area, occupied the town on the following day.[68]

Amedeo did not press further, for difficulties in another part of his extensive theater led to the diversion of Italian efforts in an entirely different direction. The French armistice raised the question of Djibouti. To neutralize or secure it was vital, for its excellent port facilities and railroad were unique in the region. A British landing force from Aden, across the straits of Bab-el-Mandeb, could advance down the railway to Addis Ababa, or north to Eritrea. To forestall any such development Amedeo set up a commission to supervise the demilitarization and neutralization of Djibouti as provided in the Franco-Italian armistice. But the French theater commander, General Paul Legentilhomme, refused at first to recognize the armistice, and countered Italian demands with all the obstructionist arts for which his nation's officialdom is justly famous. The Italian commission did not pass the Djibouti border for some weeks.[69]

The Italians could not attack Djibouti directly. Militarily, such an undertaking was not without difficulty,[70] and Legentilhomme might call for British help. Worse still, direct Italian action against the French on the Red Sea might produce dramatic repercussions in Tunisia, for the attitude of the French colonial empire as a whole toward the armistice was as yet far from clear. Finally, an Italian attack on French forces could not fail to bring down on Mussolini the displeasure of his German ally. On the other hand, the Italians could, and did, strike at what they took to be the chief cause of Legentilhomme's intransigence: the encouragement he received from his neighbors in British Somaliland.

That sunbaked and dusty colony was no great prize. It had few resources, fewer roads, and no deep-water port. Its conquest, unlike that of Kassala, led nowhere. Nevertheless the operation did not, as one postwar commentator has suggested, result solely from an atavistic ambition of Badoglio to "bring home to the peace table anything available."[71] Rather, Amedeo himself urged it as a method of bringing Djibouti under control; once Somaliland was "cleared of Englishmen," direct contact between French and British would be impossible. Badoglio concurred, and by 19 July the operation had received the Duce's authorization and blessing. But the confused situation in Djibouti, which had originally impelled the Italians to plan the operation, now illogically compelled temporary postponement. Legentilhomme's Vichyite successor, General Maxime Germain, arrived at Asmara in Eritrea on 14 July and attempted, at first without success, to enter Djibouti and impose his authority. Legentilhomme, who also faced an outbreak of defeatism among his colonial administrators and the French population, lost his nerve. By 22 July, Germain could assure the head of the Italian armistice commission that Legentilhomme would not raise the standard of revolt against Vichy, and was withdrawing French units stationed in British Somaliland as part of the joint Anglo-French effort.[72] On 25 July, entrusted by message from Vichy with full civil and military powers, Germain entered the town of Djibouti and took control, to the intense relief of both the Italians and the local French business community. Legentilhomme departed ingloriously for British Somaliland and Aden in time to avoid the firing squad that Badoglio, with casual vindictiveness, had ordered Amedeo to prepare should the general fall into Italian hands.[73]

Germain's success finally cleared the way for the attack on Somaliland. The operation had now acquired a momentum of its own; no one appears to have asked why it was still necessary now that Vichy had reined Djibouti in. On 27 July three columns of Italian troops, under the command of General Guglielmo Nasi, began their march through the bush towards Berbera, the capital of British Somaliland. Badoglio cheered them on with radioed exhortations.[74] Nasi's troops enjoyed a superiority of perhaps five to one, and command of the air. By 15 August, Nasi had forced the main British blocking position south of Berbera. The British commander withdrew to the coast, and Nasi's pursuit was far too slow to impede British embarkation. By 19 August this "small but at the time vexatious military episode," as

Churchill later described it, was over. Mussolini, who had followed the action anxiously through Amedeo's infrequent and often vague situation reports, was well pleased, and praised his viceroy in fulsome terms.[75]

Even while the operation was getting under way, Badoglio and Amedeo began to consider wider prospects. On 2 August, as Nasi's columns crossed the British border, the viceroy proposed to Rome a further limited operation in the Sudan to secure a buffer zone that would insulate dissident tribes within Ethiopia from British agents. The coming of war had produced no immediate increase in guerrilla activity, but the arrival of the ex-Emperor, Haile Selassie, at Khartoum under British patronage presaged nothing good.[76] In the ensuing days, Amedeo expanded his proposals. The buffer zones, once seized, would free his forces from worries about their rear and allow an advance on Atbara and thence down the Nile to Khartoum. But before beginning to redeploy his troops for the action, the viceroy asked a question which was also the subject of much interest in Rome: How much longer was the war likely to last? If a considerable prolongation was probable, and if additional supplies, particularly of automobile, truck, and aircraft tires were not available, the viceroy felt that "one must renounce any action not indispensable" and "conserve one's forces as long as possible."[77]

Badoglio replied with his first and last attempt at a coordinated strategy for Italian forces in the Middle East. Back in mid-July, Badoglio and Mussolini had unsuccessfully urged on Graziani a diversionary attack on Egyptian border strongpoints to prevent the RAF from shifting aircraft south against Amedeo's then-forthcoming move on Somaliland. Now, in mid-August, Badoglio belatedly attempted to fit activities in the Western Desert and the Sudan into a grand design for the conquest of Egypt. A currently expected movement by Graziani, Badoglio informed Amedeo, would be limited in scope, but would serve to seize bases of departure "for a further offensive of considerably greater range" that would produce "tangible results." Graziani would have a "decisive superiority of forces," his logistical preparations would presumably be complete, and the desert heat would have subsided considerably, facilitating movement. Egypt itself, Badoglio continued, was "anything but hostile," despite the rule of a government "imposed by England"; an Italian advance might provoke disturbances in the British rear. Badoglio therefore ordered preparations to repulse a possible British incursion from Kenya, to seize the buffer zone in the Sudan, and, last and most importantly, to prepare for the offensive toward Egypt. He also disclosed the reason for his optimism: Germany had passed to the offensive in the air over southern England. The German plan was apparently to cause the fall of the Churchill government and produce peace negotiations – a prospect Badoglio, unlike Mussolini, regarded with anything but horror. If Churchill hung on, Germany intended to "pass to a totalitarian offensive" and land on the island. In that case, the Germans foresaw six weeks of combat, which, the marshal added, "would take us to the end of September – early October, the period in which we ourselves will give the new blow" by attacking Egypt.[78] But

Badoglio's euphoric mood did not last. By 26 August, his predictions of German triumph in the far north were far more cautious: "Let us hope that the war ends by October, but let us accustom ourselves to the idea that it will last longer." He now conceded to Amedeo that it was "natural that the execution of any plan be subordinated to one's resources," and let fall the grandiose vision of a coordinated offensive against Egypt.[79]

If German delays in dealing with the British, and Graziani's reluctance to move against Egypt cooled Badoglio's enthusiasm, the difficulties that Nasi's troops had encountered in Somaliland despite crushing numerical superiority gave pause to Amedeo and his advisers in Addis Ababa. Italian casualties had been over two thousand dead, as the theater chief of staff, General Claudio Trezzani, reported at the end of August in a confidential letter to Badoglio written, as Trezzani emphasized, from one Piedmontese to another.[80] The "extremely aggressive spirit of the [native] troops" and "the admirable spirit of self-sacrifice of the Italian [junior] leaders, to whom no one ever had to say '*en avant les épaulettes*' " were partly responsible. But the excessive casualties also resulted from other, less commendable causes – in particular, from "the utter technical and professional incompetence [*la grandissima incapacità tecnico-professionale*]"[81] of those same junior leaders. Trezzani's comments illustrate the effects of Pariani's personnel and training policies, and illuminate subsequent events on all Italian fronts:

As long as it is a question of risking one's skin, [the junior leaders] are admirable; when, instead, they have to open their eyes, think, decide in cold blood, they are hopeless.[82] In terms of reconnaissance, security, movement to contact, preparatory fire, coordinated movement and so on, they are practically illiterate. . . .

The relative absence of British prisoners, Trezzani continued, resulted from errors at a higher level:

The coastal column on which we had counted a great deal to close the escape route at Berbera and catch them in the trap, ground to a halt, to a large extent out of bad luck. Some swore that the trail was excellent; in reality, it was good only in some areas and extremely poor in others. But much also depended on the men. We had placed at the head of the two echelons officers whom we knew to be hostile to one another, hoping that this would put wings on their feet. On the contrary, it appears that both of them concentrated essentially on preventing the other from getting there.

This was a curious style of military leadership, although not without precedent in past Piedmontese campaigns. Trezzani nevertheless remained confident of ultimate success. But by the first week in September, Amedeo himself had lost heart. Badoglio's current caution in repeating German predictions of an early end to the war had struck home. The maintenance of the political and territorial integrity of the *Impero* now took absolute priority. Until he received 100 replacement aircraft, 10,000 tires, and 10,000 tons of gasoline, Amedeo insisted he would be "utterly unable to move except to defend himself" – and even defense, without resupply, would become "in time ever more difficult and uncertain."[83] The warning proved a self-fulfilling prophecy. As the weeks passed, as September slid into October and the war continued, guerrilla activity and RAF harassment of Amedeo's forces increased. British concentrations along the borders grew ominously. The *Impero,* after its brief and costly effort in Somaliland, waited for the Germans or Graziani to prevail in the north, or for the British to strike from the Sudan and Kenya.

The dilatory marshal: July. As the Army staff appreciation had suggested, the difficulties facing an Italian thrust into Egypt were imposing, but far from insoluble. Graziani had 167,000 men, divided into two groups: 5th Army, facing Tunisia, and 10th Army on the Egyptian border. Initially, Graziani's forces had 339 L.3 light tanks and 8,500 motor vehicles (excluding motorcycles). In the course of July, the seventy M.11/39 medium tanks promised Balbo arrived, along with a further 500 wheeled vehicles. In the air, Graziani had over 300 fighters and bombers. Unfortunately, the medium tanks were balky and ill designed, the L.3 light tanks almost useless, only seven armored cars were available, and many of the trucks were unsuitable for off-road travel. Despite long experience in Libya, the *Regia Aeronautica* had inexplicably failed to provide much of Graziani's fighter force with the sand filters without which no aircraft engine could function for long in the desert. Finally, Hitler maintained his refusal to furnish the Italians materiel, and even placed French booty off-limits at the end of July.[84]

Nevertheless, the British position was not enviable. Their combat forces in Egypt amounted to a mere 36,000 men. A further 27,500 were more or less permanently occupied preventing Arabs from massacring Jews in Palestine. Moreover, the refusal to declare war on Italy of that persistent Italophile, King Farouk, as well as the potential danger from the large Italian community and from the mercurial and potentially hostile Egyptian population kept a major proportion of British forces in Egypt tied down to static defense and internal security. The large Egyptian forces the British had armed and trained under their security treaty with Egypt were unusable in the field, and an outright danger in the event of British reverses. Churchill's theater commander, General Archibald Wavell, could release for the desert only the 7th Armored Division, the 4th Indian Division, and some Australian and New Zealand troops. All were extremely short of equipment. 7th Armored had only 65 of its intended 200 cruiser tanks – and some of the 65 were without proper armament. The 4th Indian Division was short a brigade and much of its artillery. The Australians and New Zealanders were even less well provided for. In the air, the RAF in Egypt had only one modern fighter, a Hurricane, and a varied assortment of obsolete and obsolescent fighters, bombers, and flying boats.[85]

In defeat, Graziani, his numerous apologists, and the Italian official historians have depicted a miserably equipped Italian force, pushed forward for momentary political gain in defiance of the sound military advice of the

Army's leadership. Mussolini allegedly compelled Balbo and Graziani to fight a contest of "meat against iron," of "flea against elephant" in the face of an enemy "furnished with all the equipment modern technology could provide."[86] In reality, the opposing forces were relatively evenly matched throughout summer and early fall. Graziani's greatest deficiency was not equipment but ingenuity and will. He lacked the imagination to perceive that his army's lavish rations of *pasta,* canned tomatoes, Parmesan cheese, and mineral water and choice wines for the officers imposed an unacceptable logistical burden in the desert; British generals survived well enough on bully beef, tea, and an occasional dram of whiskey.[87] Above all, Graziani did not perceive that most of his troops were superfluous. Had he ruthlessly stripped all his remaining units of transport, he could have secured enough vehicles by mid-August to motorize fully two divisions and a brigade task force of Libyan troops. Graziani and his principal subordinates considered the idea, then dropped it. Even modest attempts to create a 10th Army mobile force built around a medium-tank battalion met with his disapproval.[88] Such steps would fly in the face of the Army's most cherished dogma: that strength lay in numbers.

The small, agile, and fully motorized force that Graziani refused to create, committed in August and boldly handled, might well have driven the British at least as far as their railhead at Mersa Matruh, and perhaps even farther – although the marshal was not the man to lead such an expedition, as he amply proved in the following months. Nor did the Army's general level of leadership, tactical training, and staff work suggest it was equal to such a task. The junior officers, as in other theaters, were inadequately trained, and in some cases even lacked aggressiveness. Nevertheless, the conventional picture of an Army sacrificed at Mussolini's insistence in pursuit of an entirely chimerical and purely political vision is untenable. Mussolini had the word of both Badoglio and the Army staff that the invasion of Egypt was *militarily* feasible. Small wonder that he subsequently insisted that his subordinates deliver.

Mussolini's pressure on .Graziani for an immediate attack indeed varied throughout the summer as a function of the imminence – as viewed from Rome – of "peace breaking out" through Anglo-German compromise or Sea Lion's success. But fear of appearing at the peace table with empty hands or of exclusion from the negotiations was no more than a spur to an action Mussolini envisaged as a fit culmination to his parallel war. The fall of Egypt would administer the *coup de grâce* to Great Britain, and permit the creation of an *Impero* from Tunisia to the Persian Gulf, from Palestine to Kenya. Fear of arriving "too late" was above all a convenient goad for his military subordinates. Graziani could ignore Mussolini's correct strategic judgment that delay worked in favor of the British – but the marshal could not challenge an order to move allegedly given for reasons of high policy. *La politica* was Mussolini's exclusive province.

Initially, Graziani seemed ready enough to advance. Hitler's 1 July prediction to Alfieri that the *Luftwaffe* would be ready to attack England within ten to fifteen days probably inspired Mussolini's message to Graziani on 3 July that it was "a vital interest for Italy that [he] be ready to launch the offensive by day 15 [July] in order to be in synchronization with the German action."[89] Graziani thereupon ordered preparation of a local attack on the border town of Sollum, and pursuit if the enemy gave way. General Mario Berti, 10th Army's commander, made no objection to Graziani's face. But once back at his command post, he protested that logistical preparations would require twenty-two days. Graziani confirmed the original timetable, and sharply reminded Berti that the general conduct of the campaign was Graziani's own sphere.[90]

Graziani soon found that his own superiors had other ideas. A series of contradictory suggestions emanated from Rome throughout July. Hitler's 13 July letter made clear invasion of England was not imminent; Mussolini and Badoglio immediately directed Graziani prepare by the end of the month a far-reaching Egyptian offensive, not the local attack on Sollum. Badoglio was buoyant, and confided to the Germans that "the un-neutral behavior of the Greeks would be revenged after success in Egypt" – an order of business he consistently sought to impose on Mussolini's all-devouring aggressiveness. The latter quality soon prompted the dictator to revive the Sollum operation, now as a preliminary to the march on Alexandria. On 19 July Mussolini added that the Sollum attack would also prevent the RAF from contesting Amedeo's drive on Berbera, and ordered Graziani to move no later than 22 July.[91] Graziani protested, demanding more time and the right to do things his own way. Mussolini acquiesced, approved Graziani's actions as the latter described them in a lengthy memorandum of 23 July, and expressed certainly "that after being for some weeks the anvil it will soon be possible to become the hammer – which, gripped by your firm hands, will give the enemy the decisive blows." Badoglio followed up by repeating that Mussolini left Graziani "completely free" to do what he wanted.[92]

Graziani took these last words at face value. On 23 July he reported to Rome that the entire conception of an attack on Egypt was dubious, given the terrain and the summer heat, and proposed delay until the end of October.[93] Clearly he was anything but obsessed with making a triumphal entry into Alexandria. His unpublished diary for the summer of 1940 records "escapades" to the gubernatorial seaside bungalow at Apollonia and to his villa at Tripoli, lengthy and effusive Fascist Party and Party Youth ceremonies, elaborate luncheons for local dignitaries, and close attention to such unmilitary details as the reestablishment of the governor's box at the Benghazi theater.[94]

Mussolini, himself not above seeking at his seaside retreat at Riccione a brief respite from the burning Roman summer, summoned Graziani at the beginning of August to give an account of himself.[95] New and insistent reports of an imminent invasion of Britain, and the persistent nightmare of a compromise peace presumably increased Mussolini's sense of urgency.[96]

The dictator also expressed his disquiet to Ciano in a tirade against "the Italians" – a recurrent theme whenever the Duce encountered difficulties. When thwarted in his territorial war aims Mussolini tended to fall back impotently, in conversation with his son-in-law, on his internal and "meta-physical" goals: the destruction of the monarchy, Church and bourgeoisie and the remolding of the Italian character. After receiving Graziani's request for delay, he raged against "the demographic decadence, the tendency to alcoholism, and the lack of attention to detail [*pressapochismo*] which distinguishes [Italy] in every sector." He promised "a tremendous speech entitled 'The Secret Running Sores of Italy' " to "confront the nation violently with its own image," and he recalled with relish that he had ordered the reforestation of the Apennines in order to render the Italian climate "more rigorous" and produce "a more thorough selection and the improvement of the race."[97]

These private fulminations produced no action beyond the recall of Graziani to Rome. The Duce entrusted himself to the beneficent influence of *lo stellone*, to the hope that the armed forces would muddle through somehow, that everything would yet "fall into place automatically." No fundamental reform was possible, for in moments of confidence, Mussolini preferred to ignore incompetence and corruption among his subordinates; in times of depression, he was prone to immobility and a fatalism comparable to that of his northern colleague in the later stages of the war. "Nations receive the destiny that they themselves have created," Mussolini had said in the fall of 1939. Were Italy to fail the supreme test, it would richly deserve the fate awaiting it. Even setbacks might help "improve" the "race." As Ciano told Bottai in early July, Mussolini simply refused to confront squarely the problem of military and administrative inefficiency: "He lives this war in a state of metaphysical exaltation. It is as though his aim is to harden the Italians through travail and sacrifice."[98]

These latter activities were precisely what most Italians were at pains to avoid. The momentary enthusiasm with which a large proportion of the population had entered the war did not last. The British air raids of the first week (until French collapse closed the staging bases in southern France) generated what one police informant described as "a genuine sense of panic." Reports reached Britain from Yugoslav sources that the inhabitants of Trieste had repaired to the shelters during an air raid only to find the crews of the city's antiaircraft guns already in possession (the troops remained under cover until the "all clear").[99] The steadily increasing economic pressure on the poorer classes, a phenomenon on which many observers of the Italian scene commented, did not help morale either. Wartime trade regulations also caused grumbling among the shopkeepers and other pillars of the *petite bourgeoisie* and of the regime.[100]

But, as one observer remarked in mid-July, "hope in a swift end to the war" still damped down economic discontent. The public, in the words of a police informant, was "now accustomed to thunderous swift victories, [and] impatient to hear sudden, striking deeds in every communiqué." German successes, the police superintendent of Modena reported to Rome, had "spread the conviction that the match would soon, to all intents and purposes, be closed, since everyone awaited daily the news of a landing in England." But the Germans could not oblige, and the British would not give in. The failure of Hitler's "appeal to reason" led some Italians to suspect the "war with England presents no small difficulties and can therefore last longer than hoped."[101]

The British themselves drove the point home pitilessly in mid-August. As Göring's air armadas savaged southern England, RAF Bomber Command struck back not only at Berlin, but also (a prodigious navigational feat) at Milan. The raids appalled the public: "many conjectures are made, since northern Italy, at least after the fall of France, felt itself safe enough." Anti-German sentiment continued strong, particularly in the North, and as early as mid-July financial magnates and industrialists, including Pirelli, began to complain to the authorities that the tightening German control of the European economy was a major threat to Italy's interests, and their own. "Fear of the coming German hegemony, strengthened by the motives of envy and jealousy" were the themes upon which "the opposition" in Italy played, according to a depressing *Dienststelle Ribbentrop* report Hitler saw in late July. The informant emphasized that high Vatican circles were convinced that "Italy [could] not hold up under a major shock — either militarily, or economically, or in terms of morale." He also warned that "scarcely thirty percent of the population still [stood] behind the Fascist system."[102]

The regime did its best. The press tirelessly whetted public appetite for the fruits of impending British collapse. Mussolini himself attempted to give the war on the home front the character of business as usual.[103] He refused to speed preparations for his attack on Yugoslavia by requisitioning civilian vehicles or disrupting the train schedules that catered to the annual August exodus to sea and mountain of Italy's city dwellers. His bureaucracy scarcely deviated from its placid peacetime routine; the Ministry of War had by September 1940 returned to the time-honored Roman custom of shutting for the day at 2 p.m. In the fall, Mussolini ordered a massive demobilization of the Army units in Italy to alleviate an agricultural labor shortage.[104] But such measures, far from encouraging "sacrifice," further promoted the attitudes Lanza of the Berlin Embassy observed during a brief visit to Milan in mid-September:

everyone thinks only of eating, enjoying themselves, making money, and relaying witticisms about the great and powerful. Anyone who gets killed is a jerk — and will shortly be a traitor [*Chi ci lascia la pelle è un fesso (fra poco sarà un traditore)*]. He who supplies the troops with cardboard shoes is considered, in the end, a sort of hero.[105]

Mussolini clearly had his work cut out for him, if he ever came to realize the extent to which his regime encouraged such tendencies.

The dilatory marshal: August–September. Despite his wrath at his fellow countrymen, the conference to which Mussolini invited Graziani ended on 5 August – typically enough – without clear-cut results. Graziani delivered to Mussolini and Badoglio a second long memorandum enumerating all the reasons why he should wait until October, and claimed misleadingly that action against Egypt "had always been considered unfeasible, except in an exceptionally favorable circumstance, by both the General Staff and the Army Staff." Defeat in the desert was "always *total* [*totalitaria*] *and irremediable.*" Badoglio contested Graziani's version of the previous views of the staffs, and added that his own earlier opposition had resulted solely from the French threat, now happily removed. The marshals and Mussolini eventually agreed upon a plan: General Pietro Maletti's Libyan mobile force would push north from Siwa Oasis to outflank the British on the border, while Berti's 10th Army would attack north of the Sollum escarpment and proceed, if possible, as far as Sidi el Barrani. Graziani was in one sense successful; he emerged from the meeting without pinning himself down to a definite starting date. This vital point seems to have escaped Mussolini, who gained the impression that action was imminent, as did Badoglio, who informed Rintelen two days later that the offensive would begin "toward the fifteenth."[106]

But Graziani had not said his last word. Poor flying weather detained him in Rome, and he seized the occasion to lobby Ciano:

[Graziani] describes the attack on Egypt as a very difficult enterprise indeed [*un'impresa molto seria*] for which the preparation is far from being perfect. Above all, he attacks Badoglio, who is not putting a brake on the Duce's aggressive ardor, which "for a man who knows Africa, can only mean that he has gone soft, or, even worse, is in bad faith."

Having thus done his best to undermine Badoglio, Graziani repeated his prediction of a "total disaster" if the attack proceeded. As Graziani had doubtless intended, Ciano passed the conversation on to Mussolini, who was "much pained," and concluded that the problem was psychological. Graziani was too loaded down with honors and emoluments to take risks: "One should not confide command positions to those who do not have at least one rank to conquer"; Graziani had too many to lose.[107] But Mussolini once more avoided calling Graziani to account, perhaps in the expectation that he would proceed as ordered, though with some additional delay. In the ensuing days, Greece and Yugoslavia, temporarily more pressing, occupied his attention. Finally, news from the north appeared to lessen temporarily the urgency of Italian action. Ribbentrop's spleen against the British ("Churchill is crazy, and the English imbeciles") led Alfieri to judge that Anglo-German talks were not in progress. On the military front, Mussolini had word by 10 August of further delays in German plans for the cross-Channel attack.[108]

In the course of the following week, however, evidence again mounted that the Germans were determined to crush Britain shortly. By 18 August Mussolini had once more reversed his attitude, and had concluded, as Ciano put it, "that at the end of next month we shall have both victory and peace." He consequently drafted a long and vehement telegram urging Graziani to move immediately.[109] The message was one of the few orders to Graziani that summer that Mussolini wrote personally, and it reflects the dictator's preoccupations far more accurately than the directives relayed through the stolid Badoglio. Like later historians, the marshal tended to interpret Mussolini's orders, however megalomaniacal, as bluff, as a cloak thrown for reasons of prestige over more limited, more "political" projects of the sort that had led Italy's leaders to commit the nation to war in 1866 and 1915.

A careful reading of Mussolini's directive shows that his use of the political motive was purely tactical. It was an appeal to Graziani's own finely tuned opportunism, but, warming to his subject, Mussolini could not restrain himself from expressing the far-reaching nature of his aims. He began with the political motive: the invasion of Great Britain was decided, and would take place "within a week or a month." Irrespective of the date, Graziani must attack upon the day "the first platoon of [German] soldiers" touched English soil. Mussolini momentarily softened the blow by insisting that he "did not fix territorial objectives – it is not a question of shooting for Alexandria or even Sollum." He was merely asking Graziani to attack "the British forces to [his] front," and he assumed "full personal responsibility" for the decision. But he continued in a less conciliatory vein: Graziani had "indisputable superiority of troops, equipment, and morale." Additional air power was available, and five "ships of the line" stood ready in support; Mussolini did not mention his difficulties with Cavagnari. The dictator summed up:

After twelve months of waiting and preparation it is time to attack the forces that defend Egypt. I have no doubt of the definitive outcome of the battle. Once the enemy is beaten, the greater or lesser extent of his defeat will give guidance for further action. Marshal Graziani, as I told you at our last encounter, time is working against us. The loss of Egypt will be the *coup de grâce* for Great Britain, while that rich country [Egypt] – necessary for our communications with Ethiopia – is the great prize that Italy awaits and which – I am certain – you will give it.

These rousing words had a dramatic, if momentary, effect. When he received them, Graziani had just sent off to Rome the minutes of a new commanders' conference at Benghazi. He and his subordinates, in solemn conclave, had declared themselves "unanimously and decisively contrary to any possibility of offensive action," and Graziani assumed the "dolorous task" of requesting new and more appropriate orders or an inspection (presumably by Mussolini or Badoglio) to judge the situation on the spot. He also offered to resign, should it seem "useful."[110]

Graziani maintained this bold front only briefly. Mussolini's new directive left to Graziani the choice of objectives and allowed him to revert to the earlier limited action against Sollum. He could therefore justify the operation to his subordinates, and dispatched an immediate and firmly worded warning order to Berti. Graziani's original recalcitrant letter and the minutes of the commanders' conference caused "a bit of discussion" in Rome, as Roatta tactfully reported to Graziani. But, Roatta continued, "everyone considered that your telegram answered affirmatively the intentions of the Duce, and cancelled out, automatically, what was said in your report."[111]

If Graziani temporarily fell into line, his principal subordinate did not. Berti greeted the warning order with an answer Graziani charitably described to Badoglio as "involuted and indeterminate." The 10th Army commander confessed – the remark gives the measure of his competence – that after more than two months of war the capabilities of the supply service were "unknown." He did not indicate when he would be ready to move. Graziani already suffered from "doubts" about Berti, and replied with directives that left the commander of 10th Army in no doubt about his superior's expectations. The initial objective would be the Sollum escarpment, but Graziani now insisted that Berti strike out for Sidi el Barrani, eighty kilometers further east, if opportunity offered. Temporarily entering into the spirit of the operation, Graziani noted in his diary that with the order to Berti he had "broken the barrier that prevent[ed] him from moving forward without restraints." But not all restraints had fallen; further Berti resistance apparently compelled Graziani to fly to Tobruk himself to give detailed orders to 10th Army.[112]

Meanwhile, in Rome, fear of an Anglo-German compromise was again growing. A 20 August Halifax speech gave Ciano the unpleasant if erroneous impression that "the possibility of a deal with Germany is not excluded." "Can this explain the delay in the [German] attack?" the Italian foreign minister asked himself with misgiving. Alfieri reported disquietingly on 23 August that German air attacks on Britain might merely be an attempt "to create . . . a growing wave of panic, to produce strong currents favorable to a friendly compromise with Germany, and to reinforce those already existing." Hitler, Alfieri reported correctly, was still "not at all convinced of the necessity of the final struggle; even today, persuaded more than ever of the enormous difficulties of the postwar period that would follow the collapse of the British Empire, he was supposed to be cultivating the plan of a vigorous military offensive, limited to the air, as the auxiliary of a last peace offensive, attempted *in extremis*."[113]

Despite these threatening stirrings, Mussolini took the plunge in Egypt a few days later in an upsurge of impatience and ebullient self-confidence, rather than in fear. On 27 August he announced to Ciano that the attack would begin in early September, whatever happened to the invasion. Mussolini had word that Keitel ostensibly concurred in his own view that the fall of Cairo would be "more important than the fall of London." Badoglio therefore passed on Mussolini's decision to Graziani: the attack must commence between 8 and 10 September. Badoglio added the obligatory political rationale ("if there is an agreement between the Germans and the English, we will be out of any discussions if we do not have at least one battle against the

English"), but Mussolini had other concerns. He wanted Egypt, and while spurring Graziani onward, congratulated himself on 1 September that the war might well continue "beyond the current month and perhaps beyond the winter, since that [gave] Italy the chance to make greater sacrifices and to better affirm [its] rights."[114]

In North Africa, Graziani's temporary enthusiasm had evaporated. On 31 August the RAF thoroughly and repeatedly bombed his headquarters at Tobruk. Graziani took to his shelter, and remained there for more than two and a half hours, characteristically blaming the precision of the attack on espionage and betrayal. He then returned by night to Cirene, further in the rear, where the deep tombs of the ancient Greek colonists offered superior air raid protection. He counted the "crucial day of 31 August" as "one of the most dangerous in his life." In his wars against Austrians, Libyans, and Ethiopians he had never faced air attack. He was clearly unnerved.[115]

Graziani recovered partially in the ensuing days, and resumed his prevarication, demanding more time and equipment. An exchange of letters with Badoglio brought a warning that Mussolini would soon override all restraints and personally order action. Badoglio also complained that Graziani had failed to make known in good time the difficulties he now alleged. Graziani seethed; Badoglio's conduct, he wrote, was "even more bestial and ambiguous than usual. Not knowing how to stand up to the pressure of the Duce, and knowing that he has not sent the necessary equipment, he pushes me to attack, in order to have a high-level scapegoat [un responsabile espiatorio]." Badoglio's letter was "an unsurpassable monument of mendacity and moral cowardice." Graziani meditated a forlorn hope flight to Rome, then rebutted Badoglio's charge in a furious telegram, while privately heaping vituperation on his superiors, who were "either traitors, or utterly lacking in a sense of responsibility."[116] Imprecations did not ward off Rome's final word, which came on the afternoon of 7 September: "Duce orders that operation in question begin Monday 9 September. Acknowledge." Mussolini had finally lost what little patience he possessed. If Graziani's immobility continued, he declared to the Council of Ministers on 7 September, he would sack him. Mussolini also vented his annoyance with Cavagnari's Fabian tactics. A renewed conviction that Sea Lion was imminent added to Mussolini's vehemence.[117]

Graziani finally turned to face the British, while confiding hysterical resentment and misgivings to his diary for future self-justification:

And thus is accomplished what may well be recorded as a crime of historic proportions – against the commission of which I have fought with all my strength as long as I have been able. It is against the most elementary logic [and] prudence – it can only be justified by some hidden political rationale [una occulta ragione politica], and may God provide that it is indeed thus and that everything goes well. . . . For whatever evil may occur, I, before God and my soldiers, am not responsible.

Rodolfo Graziani, Benghazi, 7/9/1940, 1625 hours.[118]

On 9 September Berti's divisions belatedly began their movement to contact.

Graziani's difficulties were not over. General Maletti, that "old wolf of the desert," as Graziani described him in his memoirs, neglected to take with him the local Arab guides provided, and got his brigade group lost and almost out of water while still within Italian territory. Graziani had to call in the Air Force to find Maletti and set him on the right track. The delay, and Maletti's excessive consumption of fuel in soft sand led Graziani to give up his original intention of turning the enemy's desert flank and enveloping the British border forces. Maletti therefore came under Berti's direct command, and moved off at dawn on 13 September in 10th Army's frontal assault on Sollum and Halfaya.[119]

The movement was lethargic and tactically inept. The intricate formations of Berti's leading divisions resembled, to one British observer, nothing so much as "a birthday party in the Long Valley at Aldershot." Some units panicked under fire, and, according to one irreproachably Fascist eyewitness (Alessandro Melchiorri, a high Party leader) some junior officers deserted their troops under fire. The intrepid commander of Berti's lead elements, General Annibale "Electric Beard" Bergonzoli, who was responsible for what little élan the advance possessed, on at least one occasion drove artillery lieutenants out of hiding and back to their guns with blows.[120] Under Graziani's constant prodding Berti finally managed to occupy Sidi el Barrani by 16 September, while the British withdrew unscathed.

In Rome, Mussolini inevitably expected more than that bleak desert outpost. He looked forward to the rapid conquest of the British main position at Mersa Matruh, whence Italian bombers with fighter escorts could in theory drive the British fleet from Alexandria. Ciano, although skeptical as usual, noted the ebullience of the chief of military intelligence, General Giacomo Carboni, "who had never engaged in facile optimism." Carboni now considered progress as far as Mersa Matruh "easy," and the seizure of Alexandria "possible." Ciano therefore dispatched to Graziani the former minister in Cairo, Quinto Mazzolini, as political adviser and presumably as future Italian high commissioner for Egypt.[121]

Although enraged at Berti, who in Ciano's words "because of his slowness is supposed to have made us lose our booty," Mussolini was "radiant." He had gambled against the advice of his military and had won. He telegraphed his satisfaction to Graziani, and exhorted relentless pursuit. Graziani snapped out of his earlier paranoid depression, and penned a grandiloquent dispatch about the enemy's precipitate retreat after the loss "of more than half his armor." Even Mussolini found immodest or inadvisable Graziani's concluding claim that the British would soon "learn to recognize the valor of the Italian soldier," for the dictator had it deleted from the version of the dispatch that immediately appeared under banner headlines. Actually, Graziani had no intention of soon proceeding beyond Sidi el Barrani. In a message to Badoglio on 17 September, he refused to specify how long a halt further logistical preparations would require.[122] The hopes British retreat had aroused in Mussolini were obviously destined to disappointment.

3. "Ruhe auf dem Balkan"

Greece or Yugoslavia? While prodding Graziani forward, Mussolini had proceeded with his Balkan projects. If Britain succumbed by the end of the summer, disposing of German objections, the operation could go forward. Roatta produced in early July a *"studio"* that concluded action was feasible, especially if Italian troops could outflank the main Yugoslav defenses with an attack through Austria as well as a direct thrust across the Julian Alps. He requested an immediate decision on redeploying the bulk of the army in the Po Valley from west to east, and staff talks with the Germans and Hungarians. Thirty-nine divisions would concentrate in the eastern half of the Po Valley by 27 August. Final movement to the jump-off positions in Austria and on the Italo-Yugoslav border would require another fourteen to thirty days, depending on whether civilian rail traffic continued or lapsed in favor of troop movement.[123]

From the beginning, Badoglio procrastinated. He was convinced that Yugoslavia would "keep good and quiet" and that Germany "did not want complications in that direction." A *Comando Supremo* memorandum of 12 July noted that shortages of tanks and antitank guns made it "convenient to act against Yugoslavia only after our problems in North Africa have been liquidated." Badoglio replied to Roatta with a request for a more general study which would also deal with "enemy forces and the politico-military situation," in order to "be able to present to the Duce the complete picture" – of Italian weakness. Roatta nevertheless went ahead in briefing the army's artillery, engineer, and air cooperation specialists on the Yugoslav problem, and ordered that they begin work.[124] On 16 July, Soddu conveyed to Roatta the suggestion that troop movement should begin. Evidently Badoglio had failed to dissuade Mussolini. On 20 July a *Comando Supremo* directive approved the Army staff's proposed deployment: two armies attacking frontally across the Julian Alps, and one striking south from Austria deep into the rear of the main Yugoslav defenses. Roatta confided to Graziani the impression "that it is not really expected that we will act; but, in any case, we are preparing seriously." Perhaps to avoid alarming Graziani with the possibility of a vast new Balkan front diverting resources from North Africa, Roatta did not disclose the full extent of that seriousness.[125]

Despite reassurances to Graziani, Roatta pressed ahead with alacrity; this was clearly an operation in which he believed. On 22 July he took the first step toward securing the indispensable cooperation of the Germans by casually remarking to General Enno von Rintelen, the military attaché, that intervention in the Balkans could become necessary "in the course of the war." This might take the form of a joint Italo-German operation, or a purely Italian one that would nevertheless pass across German territory. In order to speed planning for the latter case, Roatta requested German documentation on Yugoslav border fortifications facing Austria, a request Rintelen immediately relayed to Berlin. Roatta followed up by briefing Crown Prince Umberto (the nominal operational commander, as for the attack on France), his major subordinates, and their chiefs of staff. Meanwhile, the Italian press intensified its attack on Yugoslavia, causing serious worry in Belgrade. At the end of July, Roatta ordered the preparatory movement of the troops to the eastern part of the Po Valley completed by the end of August. But problems inevitably arose. Despite Roatta's repeated pleas, Mussolini refused to permit further requisitions of trucks from the civilian economy. The units designated for the Yugoslav operation therefore failed to receive anything like the already exiguous quotas of vehicles theoretically assigned them. Roatta estimated that the shortages amounted to some 9,000 trucks.[126]

Badoglio still felt no sense of urgency. As late as early August he considered that the concentration against Yugoslavia was "exclusively for purposes of intimidation, and no more." Mussolini had other ideas. If Hitler objected to an Italian move against Yugoslavia because of the danger of a further Russian advance in the Balkans, Mussolini intended to head the Russians off with his own version of the Molotov–Ribbentrop Pact. In mid-July military intelligence intercepts disclosed Yugoslav attempts to secure Soviet protection against the Axis, and may have suggested to Mussolini that the road to Zagreb and Belgrade lay through Moscow.[127] Upon his return from the seaside on 4 August he urged Ciano to contact the Russians, and he returned to the subject with enthusiasm two days later. He intended to attack in mid-September. Ciano was therefore to "keep the Croats heated up," and to reach rapidly an Italo-Russian agreement "of a 'sensational' character," complete with a Ciano flight to Moscow – à la Ribbentrop – for the signing.[128]

Before taking the matter up with the Russians, however, Ciano consulted Mackensen. Ciano gave the German ambassador a full account of various Russian hints that closer ties were desirable. Although Ciano was not willing to promise Constantinople to the Soviets, as the Germans, if pushed to the wall, had been prepared to do in August 1939 to secure their nonaggression pact, Ciano was ready to encourage the Russians to demand the demilitarization of the Dardanelles. Most of Turkey would presumably fall within the Soviet sphere, while Moscow would recognize as an exclusive Italian preserve all areas bordering upon the Mediterranean, as well as that sea itself, thus delivering Italy's hapless eastern neighbor up to Mussolini.[129]

Unaware of Mussolini's instructions to Ciano, Badoglio imprudently had a directive drafted for Roatta that began with an almost plaintive "it is not our intention to take the initiative in the East, and we must not disturb the peace in that sector." On 8 August Mussolini overruled Badoglio. That evening, the *Comando Supremo* promulgated an entirely different directive. From the end of August on, Umberto's forces were to hold ready to launch the

Yugoslav operation within fifteen days, and the "Po" Army would prepare to attack from Austria within a month of notification. The Germans (not yet consulted) would provide 5,000 trucks – with drivers. Finally, the *Comando Supremo* directive authorized Roatta to go beyond his earlier tentative contacts, and hold formal staff talks with Berlin on the details of German cooperation. Under the illusion that the German political authorities had already agreed, Roatta called Rintelen to his office and passed on the Italian requests. Mussolini did not even await the German reply. On 11 August, he simply ordered Badoglio to be "ready to the East" on 20 September.[130]

On the same day, Mussolini determined to solve the Greek question, in abeyance since July. The process of decision had begun soon after Ciano's Berlin visit. Inflammatory reports from Rhodes continued to bombard Rome. On 12 July De Vecchi's aircraft attacked the *British Union,* a tanker attached to the Mediterranean fleet, in waters off Crete. Apparently in the course of the action, they also bombed and strafed a Greek buoy tender and a destroyer sent to its aid, but without causing damage or casualties. The Greeks replied with a strong protest. De Vecchi denied that his S.79s had attacked any Greek vessel, and suggested that the whole affair was proof of "the Greek attitude of lying [and serving as] accomplice to our enemy." "And," he continued, "to your fine diplomats who whine about me (who has had to amuse himself with the Greeks here for four years) I can answer that in French 'Greek' means 'swindler.' "[131]

Badoglio ordered De Vecchi to leave Greeks strictly alone,[132] but military preparations of a sort were already under consideration in Rome. On 16 July, Roatta called in General Geloso, whose Albanian expertise fitted him for the task, and entrusted him with the preparation of an up-to-date *studio* of operations from Albania against Greece and Yugoslavia.[133] At this early date, presumably all Roatta had in mind was to ensure that if Mussolini called for these operations, they would take place under the auspices of the Army staff rather than those of the Ministry of Foreign Affairs. In the same period, presumably on orders from Mussolini, the Navy apparently prepared a plan of its own for the occupation of the Ionian Islands.[134]

De Vecchi's reports continued. British merchant ships ranged the Aegean "without or under false colors." The "usual pullulations in Greek anchorages" persisted, and informants confirmed "the presence of enemy agents on Crete who are controlling [Greek] ground installations." On 24 July, De Vecchi complained that the Aegean was full of "cargo ships, especially tankers that are English, and cover themselves with Greek flags, hiding themselves in the Greek anchorages where one has no idea what all that fuel is for unless it is to refuel enemy warships." De Vecchi's informants, whom he claimed were "less equivocal and decrepit than those of the naval attaché in Athens," reported the presence in the Greek Islands and in Cretan anchorages of various British destroyers.[135] Whatever the merits of his intelligence agents, De Vecchi's pilots were clearly trigger-happy. On 30 July one of his flying boats bombed a Greek destroyer anchored at Naupaktos in the Gulf of

Map 3. Italy and Greece. *Source:* I.S.O. Playfair, *The Mediterranean and Middle East,* I (London, 1954), pp. 222–3.

Corinth, and two days later an Italian aircraft attacked a Greek customs boat near Aegina, almost within sight of Athens.[136]

Despite the Quadrumvir's activities, Ciano actually maintained his equanimity until early August, perhaps as a result of Hitler's lack of enthusiasm for an Italian foray. While not above bullying the Greek minister and forcing the removal of the Greek consul-general in Trieste for being "incurably anti-Italian," Ciano was averse to "alarming Greece at the moment" by reinforc-

ing the Albanian Command or taking other hostile actions. The Italian press therefore duly celebrated the anniversary of Metaxas's dictatorial regime on 4 August, much to the general's surprise and pleasure.[137]

What happened next remains one of the most confused episodes of an already confused and eventful period. Ciano apparently took Mussolini's renewed interest in an invasion of Yugoslavia as incitement to move on Greece as well. Ciano may also have felt he had a personal score to settle. Metaxas imprudently replied to Ciano's peremptory demand for the dismissal of the Greek consul-general with a message of sympathy and support for his beleaguered diplomats. In a cipher the Italians routinely read, the Greek dictator remarked on Ciano's "brutal and boorish manner." Ciano later expressed to Mackensen considerable resentment over the insult.[138] Another, weightier consideration probably influenced Ciano. Graziani's deep pessimism during his visit to Rome in early August presumably reinforced Ciano's latent skepticism about Italy's prospects in the larger "parallel war" against Britain. If Egypt were unattainable, territorial guarantees (to use a favorite phrase of the period) were obviously necessary elsewhere – and what would be more suitable and easy than the enlargement of Ciano's own "Grand Duchy" in Albania?

On 6 August, in the same conversation with Mackensen in which he sought Berlin's views on Russia, Ciano "repeatedly spoke . . . with great sharpness about the un-neutral attitude of Turkey and Greece." He much preferred "to strike [at the Greeks] accordingly," but regrettably the *Comando Supremo* "considered that the present moment was not suitable." In the next few days Ciano evidently resolved to manipulate Mussolini into overruling Badoglio. To increase the pressure on Athens, one of the minister's chief subordinates, Zenone Benini, spoke in intimidating tones to the Greek minister in Rome on 7 August. On 10 August Ciano raised with Mussolini the question of "difficulties arisen at the Greco-Albanian border." As Ciano noted demurely for the record, "it was inappropriate to dramatize the situation, but the Greek attitude is extremely treacherous [*infido*]." The "difficulties" were clearly ones that Ciano and his satrap in Tirana, Jacomoni, had summoned up for the occasion. In June, unknown assailants had decapitated an obscure Albanian bandit and sheep-stealer, Daut Hodja, at his residence at Konispoli in southern Albania. Hodja had perhaps served at various times as an Italian agent engaged in stirring up trouble across the border in Ciamuria. Nevertheless, he had doubtless made numerous enemies in the course of a long and checkered career, and the Italian authorities had merely intimated to the Greeks in late July that they would soon make a routine request for the extradition of the culprits, who had fled to Greece.[139]

In his interview with Mussolini on 10 August, Ciano seems to have made use of a memorandum prepared by Jacomoni that represented Hodja as an Albanian freedom-fighter whom Greek agents had treacherously assassinated. Ciano doubtless did not find Mussolini's reaction disappointing. Mussolini proposed "a forceful gesture, since he [had] an unpaid account since 1923, and the Greeks deluded themselves if they [thought] he had wiped the slate clean." The next day he "again spoke of the Greek question," wanted particulars on the ethnic situation in Ciamuria, and prepared a Stefani communiqué to "begin to agitate the problem." He also ordered Ciano to summon Jacomoni and Visconti Prasca, and talked of a "surprise attack on Greece toward the end of September." Ciano on the other hand thought it better to move more quickly: it was dangerous to give the Greeks time to prepare.[140]

That evening, the Stefani news agency released Mussolini's bulletin, which purported to be a story from the Fascist Party newspaper in Tirana, *Tomori:* Greek agents had assassinated a certain Daut Hodja, Albanian patriot, and exhibited his head across the border to intimidate the "proud unredeemed populations" of Ciamuria. Nor was this the only example of the Greek "policy of oppression" – and Mussolini proceeded to fabricate others. The Albanian-Italian press blossomed with banner headlines about bleeding Ciamuria. At the foreign press briefing in Rome on 12 August the representatives of the Ministry of Popular Culture announced that the assassination had "created an enormous impression" in Italy, a claim that was only true in the sense that attentive observers of Italian policy realized something new was afoot.[141]

Mussolini and Ciano did more than issue communiqués. Ciano met with Jacomoni and Visconti Prasca on the evening of 11 August, and informed them that Mussolini, "for political reasons," had decided to occupy Ciamuria. The next morning Ciano accompanied Visconti Prasca and Jacomoni to Mussolini, who "fixed the political and military lines of action against Greece."[142] Ciano noted complacently:

If Ciamuria and Corfù are given up without a shot fired, we will not ask for more. If, instead, resistance is offered, we will go all the way [spingeremo l'azione a fondo]. Jacomoni and Visconti Prasca consider the action feasible and even easy, but on condition that we act quickly. The Duce, however, remains of the opinion, *for reasons of a general military nature* [emphasis supplied], to postpone the action until towards the end of September.

According to Visconti Prasca's postwar account, Mussolini, after a general briefing on the Albanian internal situation and on irredentist sentiment, asked the general if the troops already in Albania were sufficient to carry out a "sudden occupation of Epirus." Visconti Prasca replied that "a large-scale *coup de main*" would probably succeed. But given that the bulk of Visconti Prasca's troops were currently deployed defensively against Yugoslavia, the necessary movements would require fifteen days. If redeployment took longer, surprise would disappear, and the operation would turn into a major campaign necessitating large additional forces.[143]

The day after the conference with Mussolini, Visconti Prasca stopped by Roatta's office to request the equivalent of three more divisions. Roatta had already gotten wind of the project from Soddu, and suspected Visconti Prasca of deliberately circumventing the Army staff; he was apparently somewhat cold to the head of the Albanian Command (who later accused Roatta of deliberately sabotaging the Greek operation). Visconti Prasca reported that "the first phase of the action from Albania would consist only of a threat; the second phase, of the occupation of the part of Epirus claimed by Albania." That the "threat" would eliminate surprise and make the second phase impractical without overwhelming force does not seem to have troubled either general. Badoglio, too, went along, and on 14 August ordered Roatta to prepare three divisions for shipment.[144]

But Roatta had other problems besides Greece. Badoglio, who called him in shortly afterwards, gave him new instructions from Mussolini on Yugoslavia. The Germans would themselves attack from Austria. Only if they did not desire to participate would Italy operate from the north. In that case, troop movement would have to begin in a few days. Badoglio confirmed that "political agreements" on the subject already existed between Rome and Berlin – an assumption soon proved false. He also directed Roatta to arrange Hungarian cooperation. Visconti Prasca's request for more troops for Greece prompted a complacent remark from Badoglio that "many armchair strategists" occupied themselves with "possible future operations." But as he had told Mussolini, "when other more important questions" had been settled, Italy would be able to "obtain whatever [it wanted] from Greece, without employing even one soldier." Therefore, Badoglio concluded, "no change for Albania."[145]

To compound the confusion, Soddu called Roatta in the early afternoon of 13 August and informed him that Badoglio "had not been brought up to date by the Duce on the Albanian question." Mussolini had decided on action, as Visconti Prasca had suggested, and would inform Badoglio of his plans. Later, Roatta had a "clarificatory talk" with Soddu; things were "not exactly the way Visconti Prasca reported them":

The idea of the Duce is that Yugoslavia will stay put under the threat of an effective deployment of ours (not to mention the Germans and Hungarians) on its borders. In that situation, we can act against Greece. Therefore, the action against Greece does not exclude that – potential or actual – against Yugoslavia.

Orders would come down on the matter. Soddu also promised that Visconti Prasca's channel jumping would cease; Mussolini would give "appropriate orders" to Badoglio on Albania. Meanwhile, Ciano seems to have again called Visconti Prasca in and ordered him directly and presumably in Mussolini's name to prepare to attack in fifteen days, starting from 14 August.[146]

What was going on? One can only theorize. Three ruling conceptions – all mutually exclusive in practice – are discernible. First came the Ciano and Visconti Prasca project of an immediate surprise attack on Epirus and Corfù before the Greeks could mobilize. Second was the program both Mussolini and Ciano on occasion supported of intimidating the Greeks into concessions by propaganda and threat, in the manner, presumably, of the Soviet absorption of Bessarabia in June. Finally came Mussolini's own view. Without totally excluding an immediate surprise attack, and while placing considerable faith in intimidation, Mussolini seems to have preferred to wait until the end of September, when "reasons of a general military nature" – the collapse of Great Britain – would presumably permit a simultaneous Italian attack on Greece and Yugoslavia. Obviously, the propaganda buildup required for intimidation conflicted with the military need for surprise. But no one in the Italian leadership fully comprehended at the time that elementary truth. Even Ciano, who had earlier feared allowing the Greeks time to prepare, was by 13 August confident that if they refused to cede Ciamuria and Corfù the Italian Army would rapidly crush all resistance.

The Germans intervene. The Germans, however, had their own views about both Greece and Yugoslavia. Berlin referred Roatta's 22 July request for information on Yugoslav border fortifications to Hitler in person, and the Führer ordered the German files on the subject sent to him for perusal. He was apparently not yet greatly alarmed, for he took no decision.[147] But Roatta's request of 9 August for actual German military cooperation and Rome's sudden interest in Greece inevitably brought matters to a head.

Initially, however, Ciano was successful in allaying German fears about Greece. On the morning of 12 August, as Daut Hodja's murder hit the headlines, he predicted to Mackensen that the Italian press would react "rather violently to this new atrocity added to the unsettled Greek account." However, that did not mean, Ciano continued, "that anything was *'imminent'* or *'décidé.'* " In Berlin, the German foreign office smoothed the waters by informing the press confidentially that the Stefani communiqué was merely "a very friendly Italian warning to Greece. . . . no weighty foreign policy actions are to be expected *for the moment.*" Greece would have to "fall into line with Italy."[148]

The Germans in any case saw some use for the Italian campaign. Berlin's representative in Athens, Prince Viktor zu Erbach-Schönberg, exploited Ciano's threats to prod Metaxas to seek German protection. The Greek dictator parried. In Berlin, Weizsäcker was equally unsuccessful; despite an attempt to sound menacing, he left the Greek minister with the impression that the Germans "did not wish complications," and found their ignorance of Italian policy embarrassing. That embarrassment was fully evident on the morning of 14 August, when Ribbentrop asked Alfieri what Rome intended. Alfieri inevitably had even less information than Ribbentrop, and wired Rome for instructions.[149] Even before Alfieri's report arrived, Ciano attempted to reassure the Germans. On the evening of 13 August he remarked to Otto von Bismarck,[150] councillor of the German embassy, that Italy "hoped, with sufficient diplomatic pressure on Greece, to be able to push through its demands." A longstanding Mackensen informant and other sources gave the impression that one should expect no "immediate consequences" from the Daut Hodja affair.[151]

But at this juncture an incident occurred that upset both German and Italian calculations. At 0830 on the morning of 15 August a submarine torpedoed an obsolete Greek cruiser, the *Helli,* as she lay in the harbor at Tinos, bedecked with flags as part of a local religious festival. The explosion and subsequent fire killed one Greek sailor and wounded twenty-nine. Several minutes later, two further torpedoes aimed at merchant shipping within the harbor exploded harmlessly against the mole. Fragments from these last weapons recovered later were unmistakably Italian.[152]

Ciano, for once mystified, ascribed the incident to "De Vecchi's lack of restraint," and privately deplored the consequences; he proposed to "carry the polemic onto the diplomatic plane" by sending the Greeks a note on the border question. The Navy denied to Admiral Weichold, the German liaison officer, that it had any news on the subject from its boats; Italian forces had no orders to attack Greek warships. The naval high command war diary recorded laconically that an "unknown submarine" was responsible, and the official historians preserved a coy silence as late as 1972.[153]

Fortunately, De Vecchi's posthumous memoirs disclosed the secret in 1960. Continuing British traffic in the Aegean goaded Cavagnari and Mussolini on 14 August to order a submarine based on Rhodes to attack neutral merchant shipping clandestinely. The operation was to last five days, from 20 to 25 August, and was similar to the Navy's "unknown submarine" exploits in the Spanish war. De Vecchi had taken up the idea with characteristic enthusiasm. On his own initiative he sent the submarine *Delfino* out immediately, on the evening of 14 August, after apparently ordering its commander, Lieutenant Giuseppe Aicardi, to sink everything in sight in the vicinity of Tinos and Sira. Aicardi, according to his patrol report, sunk the *Helli* in order to prevent it from attacking him after he dispatched the merchant shipping in Tinos harbor. De Vecchi had apparently left him with the impression that war with Greece was inevitable and imminent.[154] But war was not as imminent as all that; Ciano soon swallowed his embarrassment, and drafted a relatively restrained note to the Greeks, demanding a "rapid, decisive and complete" solution to the Ciamuriote question. He ordered Alfieri to tell Ribbentrop that Italian plans against Greece were purely a precaution against British landings. Further developments that could even "assume a conciliatory character" might take place in early September.[155]

Ciano did not have long to wait for the reply. Hitler's staff had briefed him on 14 or 15 August on Roatta's request for the staff talks for the Yugoslav operation. He now reached his decision, a decision in which the *Helli* incident, by suggesting the full extent of his ally's trigger-happy irresponsibility, probably played a part. He wanted "peace and quiet on the German southern border," lest upheaval give the British a foothold there. Staff talks were "superfluous," and the Italians would receive no information on Yugoslav border fortifications. The *Wehrmacht* high command informed Rintelen that Ribbentrop had made "no promises relative to Yugoslavia"; the German attaché was to tell Roatta that no military talks were possible "before the political side was cleared up."[156]

Ribbentrop undertook the latter task, the more so since two other matters remained unresolved: Ciano's request for German views on closer Italian relations with the Soviet Union, and the Greek question, on which the Reich foreign minister had as yet received no reply to his inquiry. Ribbentrop summoned Alfieri on the morning of 16 August, and swiftly disposed of the Ciano–Molotov pact: any agreement that increased Russian interest in the Dardanelles was dangerous. Ribbentrop also reiterated Hitler's aversion to action against Yugoslavia that would distract from the "life or death struggle" against England. The Serbs were in any case "no mean soldiers." Alfieri raised the Greek question himself, as Ciano had instructed, remarking perhaps a shade imprudently that "the German answer had already emerged" rom Ribbentrop's remarks about Yugoslavia. Ribbentrop readily agreed, ₃nd noted Ciano's assurances that plans against Greece were purely precau‑ ionary. Germany was not averse to mere precautions, but Ribbentrop made ·lear that Italian action against either Greece or Yugoslavia might bring ₃ussian intervention elsewhere in the Balkans and destroy "the status quo ₃hich we have a paramount interest [*sommo interesse*] in maintaining."[157] The ₃erman warning could not have been clearer. Ciano summed it up in a much ₃uoted diary entry:[158]

₃lfieri has had an interesting conversation with Ribbentrop. The result is: 1.) that ₃e German government does not desire too marked a rapprochement between us ₃nd the Russians; 2.) that we must put aside any project of an attack on Yugoslavia; ₃.) that even a possible [*eventuale*] action against Greece is not at all well thought of ₃n Berlin. It is a thoroughgoing "halt" all along the line.

Ciano consigned his threatening note to his filing cabinet, rather than to ₃he Greeks, while Mussolini dictated a suitably meek reply to Berlin, assur‑ ₃ng good behavior. The war against Britain took priority over all else. The ₃roposed Italo-German staff talks, Mussolini revealed, "were only to explore ₃ontingencies, in order to be prepared for all possibilities." On Greece, Italy ₃ould take the dispute "onto the diplomatic plane," and would take no ₃ilitary steps other than reinforcing the Albanian garrison, a move Ciano ₃nsisted to Mackensen was not a prelude to attack. But despite these profuse ₃ssurances, Ciano also ordered the press clamor against Greece continued.[159] ₃he Greek question remained open, temporarily.

The Yugoslav operation was clearly beyond help. While Ribbentrop took ₃he matter up with Alfieri, Rintelen conveyed the German refusal to Bado‑ ₃lio. Without German cooperation, as Badoglio remarked to Roatta on 18 ₃ugust, an attack on Yugoslavia would have to be "exclusively frontal." It ₃ould be "hard, cost a lot, would only with difficulty lead to decisive results, ₃nd therefore might lead the Serbs to conclude that they had resisted to good ₃urpose." Mussolini seemed to agree that "Germany did not desire 'an ₃dventure' in the Balkans before the affair with England (on which delays ₃xist and doubts persist) is resolved." Badoglio directed Roatta to continue ₃he time-consuming deployment on the heavy artillery in forward positions ₃n the Yugoslav border as a precaution "in case the Yugoslavs should commit ₃ome folly." The bulk of the divisions designated for the operation would, ₃owever, remain in the eastern part of the Po Valley rather than deploying ₃or the attack by 20 September (as Mussolini had ordered on 11 August). On ₃o August, Badoglio confirmed these instructions. Later the same day, after ₃ conference with Mussolini, Badoglio informed the service chiefs that the ₃mportance of the Yugoslav affair had "lapsed." To Mussolini, "20 Septem‑ ₃er or 20 October [was] all the same."[160] For the moment, the matter ₃ested.

The fate of the Greek operation was more involved, and the German veto ₃id not affect Italian planning as decisively as in the Yugoslav case. On the military side, the operation led to a major tug-of-war between Mussolini and Badoglio. On 17 August, the day Ribbentrop's remarks to Alfieri reached Rome, Mussolini succumbed temporarily to Badoglio's pressure (although Soddu later complained to Roatta that the marshal had deliberately disregarded "executive orders" from Mussolini on Greece). Badoglio reported to Armellini that "against Greece, nothing will be done," and ordered Roatta to hold the reinforcements planned for Albania. Even if that deployment took place, only one of the three divisions planned would now go, and it would have a defensive mission. Not for the last time, Badoglio explained to Roatta that Italy could resolve the Greek and Yugoslav questions at the conclusion of peace, "without striking a blow." With Mussolini's tacit approval, Badoglio roundly rebuked Visconti Prasca, who had cabled excitedly from Tirana that "the orders of the foreign minister" required that "the military preparation at the Greek frontier must be completed within fifteen days." But Badoglio was not fully confident that Mussolini had subsided; he ordered Roatta to draft directives for the Albanian Command in case an operation was necessary after all.[161]

Badoglio's rebuke to Visconti Prasca was timely, for Jacomoni had been feverishly preparing Albanian guerrilla bands to spread terror and despondency behind Greek lines, while Visconti Prasca hurried his troops southward to be ready by the end of the month. Jacomoni also proposed a mock attack by his Albanian desperadoes on an Italian border post, a stratagem reminiscent of Himmler's bogus Polish raid on the Gleiwitz radio station in August 1939.[162] Back in Rome, Mussolini had by now conceived the expectation that British collapse would give him "victory and peace" by the end of the next month. In the same 20 August conference with Badoglio in which he gave up the Yugoslav operation, he nevertheless insisted on Greece. Badoglio therefore once more directed Roatta to "stand by" to send the three divisions to Visconti, and "to study the possible lines of action." But Badoglio still doubted the Germans would permit Mussolini to act. He did approve the request of Jacomoni and Visconti Prasca for weapons for their Albanian guerrillas, but remained jealous of his prerogatives and determined to prevent rash acts. Roatta and Soddu were to tell Visconti Prasca and Jacomoni decisively that "no one [was] to move for actions across the border without orders from the General Staff."[163]

The Germans now made their weight felt again, this time to more effect. The Duce's placatory message of 17 August apparently failed to reassure – at least with respect to Greece. *Wehrmacht* high command intelligence sources, and the Greek military attaché (at Metaxas's orders) brought word of "threatening troop concentrations on the Greco-Albanian border."[164] Apparently after consultation with his master, Ribbentrop summoned Alfieri once more on the afternoon of 19 August, on the rather transparent pretext that Hitler had heard of Mussolini's desire for a dining car similar to that of the Führer's special train and had decided to present one to his friend and ally. After this likely story, Ribbentrop passed on to his principal purpose, to caution Rome against even diplomatic pressure on Greece. Should the Greeks refuse Italian demands, war might result, with British and Russian intervention. Ribbentrop therefore urged Rome to be tolerant. To ensure that the message got through, the *Wehrmacht* high command ordered Rintelen to drive it home in yet another visit to Badoglio. Berlin clearly thought the Italians were deaf. Badoglio agreed "totally and emphatically," with Rintelen, and promised to "use his influence" to avoid Balkan complications of any sort.[165]

The Germans also sought to tranquilize – and intimidate – the Greeks. In Athens, Erbach continued his discreet pressure on Metaxas's government, while the latter unsuccessfully sought assurances of military assistance from Britain. The Greek request caught the British on the horns of the dilemma that was to impale them throughout the winter and spring of the following year: assistance to Greece beyond that which the Mediterranean Fleet could provide was incompatible with Britain's major strategic aim in the Mediterranean and the Near East: the elimination of Italy from North Africa and Ethiopia as a prelude to driving Germany's ally to the wall. London thought it essential that Greece fight rather than give in, but could offer nothing more than funereal assurances of political support at the peace table, "whatever the immediate outcome."[166] Metaxas also sought reinsurance by sending his minister in Berlin to see Ribbentrop, to the latter's intense embarrassment. Concerned "not to queer the Italians' pitch," Ribbentrop lectured the Greeks against mobilizing, "for the Czech crisis had begun with [a mobilization] and had led to the total annihilation of Czechoslovakia." But Rome's continued silence convinced Metaxas that the Germans had intervened to cool Mussolini, despite their threatening words. For the moment, only an occasional random salvo from the Italian press testified to Mussolini's continued interest.[167]

North Africa takes priority. Long before Ribbentrop's performance, German insistence that the Italians leave Greece alone had finally taken effect in Rome. Mussolini, following Alfieri's conversation with Ribbentrop on the 19th and Rintelen's visit to Badoglio on the 21st, promulgated a new set of directives for the Italian armed forces, giving unquestioned primacy to the attack on Egypt, and endorsing Badoglio's view that Greece and Yugoslavia would offer no resistance after British defeat. Ciano also curtailed his Albanian preparations, while instructing Jacomoni to keep the affair "alight." Badoglio hastened to capitalize upon his master's changed mood. On 22 August, after the usual morning conference with Mussolini, Badoglio summoned the service chiefs. The shipment of equipment to Graziani took highest priority. The deployment against Yugoslavia for 20 October would consist only of artillery and some covering troops. As for Greece, the deployment planned for 1 September (Mussolini's "executive orders" to Badoglio of a few days before) shifted to 1 October. Furthermore, Badoglio and Roatta did not prepare to ship the necessary reinforcing divisions to Albania; they presumably hoped Mussolini would simply forget. The Army staff informed the Navy that transport of the three divisions was "for now to be only planned"; execution depended on "further explicit orders," and the movement was "not seen as imminent."[168]

The Navy therefore derequisitioned the ships it had laboriously assembled, and dissolved the organizations formed to supervise embarkation at Bari and Brindisi. Roatta also stamped down hard on Visconti Prasca, who had "taken off in fourth gear" by transferring the "Centauro" armored division to the Valona area in Southern Albania "for maneuvers." That movement, and various other redeployments of Visconti's forces to advanced positions in Southern Albania had evidently been the cause of Metaxas's alarm. Roatta sharply ordered Visconti Prasca to cease, and followed up with a letter passing on the happy news of the new readiness date (1 October), set "by order of the Duce." The three divisions would not embark until further notice; Visconti Prasca would receive further information and operational directives "in good time."[169]

But passive resistance had its limits. Mussolini had, after all, ordered a deployment by 1 October. When Roatta reported to Badoglio that the operational directives for Visconti were ready, and pointed out that readiness by the date set required that shipment of the three divisions begin by 1 September, Badoglio felt compelled to consult Mussolini. The result was predictable. Mussolini ordered the movement begun immediately. Roatta's staff had in the meantime drafted directives for an eight-division operation to seize Epirus down to the line of the Arta River. A landing force from southern Italy would simultaneously occupy Corfù, a variant Roatta himself had added in order to forestall the "rapid British intervention" there that he foresaw an Italian advance limited to continental Greece would trigger.[170] The Roatta plan was remarkable for its boldness. It did not presuppose the simultaneous Bulgarian offensive against Thrace that Mussolini, in the actual event, sought to secure. It also assumed that the Greeks would deploy only three of their fifteen peacetime divisions against the Italian thrust; the need to overawe the Bulgarians in the northeast and the difficulties of movement across the Pindus Mountains to Epirus would presumably enable Visconti Prasca's troops to pull off their coup. The Army staff ascribed to the Greeks its own obsession with being safe everywhere, and its own inability to concentrate force at the decisive point. Even Badoglio had no qualms about the operation's tactical feasibility. His only recorded comment was that "[t]he action will be preceded and accompanied by a notable mass of aircraft – all else is secondary." The *Regia Aeronautica,* raining death and destruction from on high, would disperse the Greeks as it had the Ethiopian tribal levies.[171]

Movement of the three divisions to reinforce Visconti Prasca proved an intractable problem. A British submarine had penetrated the mine barrier at the mouth of the Adriatic and had sunk an unescorted ship on the Durazzo–Bari run on 16 August. Troop transports therefore had to cross in convoy, with inevitable delays. Even more important, Mussolini's orders that North Africa take priority created a shortage of shipping for other purposes, and made it impossible to complete the unloading of the three divisions in Albania before the end of September.[172] The readiness date of Visconti Prasca's deployment therefore shifted once more, from 1 October to 20 October, and its realization became steadily more problematical as August drew to an end. Roatta informed Visconti Prasca on 31 August that the three divisions would be on shore by 10 October, but cautioned him emphatically that "this reinforcement *does not* mean that your excellency is without further question [*senz'altro*] to take up an offensive deployment on the Greek frontier for 20 October next, but is designed solely to put you in a position to be able to do so when and if such an order is given [*quando ne venisse dato l'ordine*]."[173] A few days later, on 4 September, Roatta forwarded to Visconti the Army staff "Contingency 'G' " directive and authorized him to begin a skeleton deployment, to be completed "at the last moment" to avoid alarming the Greeks or disclosing Italian operational intentions. But Roatta emphasized that the "operations . . . are for now only to be *studied;* they will take place only as a result of explicit orders from this staff." The Army staff also compiled directives for operations from Albania against Yugoslavia, and for a defensive posture on both fronts, and likewise sent them forward to Visconti Prasca. From Roatta's point of view, an attack on Greece was at this point far from inevitable.[174] Nevertheless, Mussolini's self-denial was only temporary. He had pursued the idea of an attack on Greece since 12 August, despite Badoglio's foot-dragging, and the German veto. Mussolini still wanted his forces ready to deal with the Greeks even without German success against Britain, or German approval.

4. The long summer ends

A plethora of "progetti." For the moment, however, Badoglio was more or less in control, and did not hide from Rintelen his satisfaction over Berlin's veto of the Greek and Yugoslav projects.[175] Mussolini concentrated on kicking the reluctant Graziani into action. Once a direct order had accomplished that task on 7 September, other worries besides Greece occupied the Italian leadership and Mussolini himself. Difficulties with France had dragged on through the summer. At the time of the crisis over Djibouti in July, Mussolini had told Badoglio he intended to be patient until about 20 August. If the French had not complied with the armistice by that date, he intended to clamp down. By late July, Mussolini's entourage and the Foreign Ministry were considering the occupation of further areas in France, and the colonial authorities "work[ed] and intrigue[d] prodigiously" to train administrators for the colonies France was to lose. By early August, even Badoglio had discarded his long-standing francophilia. The French, he told Rintelen, were cheating on the armistice; they refused to demobilize in North Africa. Unless they did so soon, strong measures would be necessary.[176] Roatta was even more vocal, and took the lead in urging action on his superiors; it was time to "act with the mentality *of victors.*" On 22 August he proposed preparations for action in France and North Africa "in the face of the deceitful French attitude."[177] At the end of August, reports from the various Italian Armistice Commissions supervising French disarmament indicated that the French were increasingly adopting a tone of "conspicuous arrogance." Roatta ordered on his own authority a staff study of the occupation of France to the Rhône. The successful Gaullist revolt in the French central African colony of Chad was apparently the final blow. It seemed to threaten the eventual defection of all French North Africa, with consequent "serious embarrassment" in Libya and the Mediterranean. On 30 August Badoglio formally ordered Roatta to prepare studies of operations against the French in Tunisia, in Corsica, and on the mainland.[178]

Removal of the French threat in June had freed Mussolini and Badoglio for the Egyptian venture, and for thoughts of Yugoslavia and Greece. The reappearance of that threat at the end of August as a result of Vichy prevarications and Gaullist buccaneering therefore seriously complicated Rome's planning. When Roatta returned on 9 September from one of his periodic inspections of the Yugoslav frontier deployment, he found "still no decision, even a general one, on the *many* operational plans that are boiling in the pot." Yugoslavia, France to the Rhône, Corsica, Tunisia, Greece with Corfù, and the occupation of the islands in front of Zara on the Dalmatian Coast as part of the Yugoslav operation all demanded attention simultaneously. But as Roatta noted for Graziani's benefit, "given our scarcity of equipment, these projects in general exclude one another with a degree of self-evidence which I hope will not escape the higher authorities." On 10 September it emerged that Mussolini indeed had a preference. Mysteriously, he was suddenly "raving [*furente*] against Yugoslavia." Contingency "E" therefore once more became "preeminent," and Mussolini's thoughts again turned to a "Ciano–Molotov Pact" to forestall possible Soviet objections to an Italian foray against Yugoslavia.[179] On 10 September Mussolini also disapproved plans to give Jacomoni's desperadoes parachute training. Badoglio directed Armellini and Pricolo to drop the matter: "Greece is on the wane."[180]

The origin of this sudden Yugoslav inspiration is unclear. In the succeeding days, Mussolini informed his generals that he expected an internal upheaval [*"un rivolgimento"*] in Yugoslavia "in the near future." Actually, the situation there, and especially in Croatia, was relatively quiet. The Yugoslav government seems to have been occupied with what the foreign minister, Cincar-Marković, described to the Italian representative in Belgrade as the task of cleansing the nation of "the masons and Jews who contaminate all [its] politics," and seeking in conspicuous Germanophilia reinsurance against Italian claims. It was "obvious," Prince Regent Paul declared to the German minister, that Yugoslavia must "opt for Germany"; Italy, on the other hand, inspired only "mistrust."[181]

Rumors of Yugoslav contacts with Germany, and of German agents in Croatia, may indeed have led to Mussolini's "furor," perhaps in conjunction with a diplomatic report from Belgrade that repeatedly emphasized Prince

Paul's ambiguous nature and policy. But in these same days Mussolini was also once more fully convinced that the great air battles in progress over southern England would end in British defeat.[182] His prediction of internal disorders in Yugoslavia may well have reflected nothing more than a judgment that British collapse would inflame the Croats and sap the will of the Yugoslavs to resist, and a need to present the operation in a militarily plausible light to his generals. Whatever Mussolini's reasons for reviving the Yugoslav project, Badoglio, despite skepticism, could hardly object to its new form, which was fully in accordance with his own view of the relationship between war and policy. One would obviously have to be ready "to profit from possible internal turmoil" in Italy's eastern neighbor.[183] The Germans could not then object — and it was supremely important to arrive before they did.

On 11 September Badoglio briefed Mussolini on the multiplicity of *studi* and *progetti,* and pressed for a decision on priorities. The result was a slight clarification. Mussolini "suspended" action against France to the Rhône as incompatible with the Yugoslav operation. The French would receive just retribution "once peace was concluded." Yugoslavia now received the highest priority, although "more in the form of an occupation than of an offensive," as Badoglio put it. The operation was now to be ready to launch by 20 October, the date set in late August for the skeleton deployment on that border. For Greece, the transport of the three divisions, just begun, would continue until completion at the end of September. Unlike the Yugoslav operation, Mussolini set no date for the actual deployment. Badoglio, who confided to Roatta on 10 September that he was "patiently dismantling" the Greek operation, had evidently made progress. On other fronts, units in Sardinia were to make ready to move on Corsica; the Italian leadership suffered at this point from chimerical fears of an Anglo-Gaullist landing there. Tunisia had lowest priority, for that operation required massive reinforcement of Fifth Army in Tripolitania, which Balbo and Graziani had stripped of equipment to support the drive on Egypt. No such reinforcement could begin until the end of the transport of the three divisions to Albania released additional shipping.[184] Egypt remained the preeminent Italian theater.

The fate of Sea Lion. While Mussolini and the Italian military leadership grappled with their bewildering multiplicity of plans and with Graziani's dilatory advance, the whole shape of the war was changing. Despite massive preparations for the invasion of Britain, Hitler was less and less convinced of either the advisability or the necessity of a landing.[185] The German army and navy struggled between themselves over the operational plan. The navy could not hope to protect more than a narrow beachhead. The army wanted as wide a front as possible to disperse British reserves and swiftly bring Germany's crushing ground superiority to bear. Whatever the width of the front, invasion required German air superiority over southern England. That task *Reichsmarschall* Hermann Göring failed to accomplish. The problem was one of military psychology, not operational planning. A childlike faith in indiscriminate bombing possessed the leaders of the *Luftwaffe*. It was "in the air that England can be compelled to yield," as Göring put it – and in the air alone.[186] The German air force therefore lifted its increasingly successful attacks on the RAF bases in the immediate invasion area, and on 7 September turned its full weight on London. The shift from support of Sea Lion to "absolute" air warfare condemned Germany to an uncertain continuation of the struggle and changed the entire context within which Mussolini had been operating far to the south.

Hitler's reasons for permitting Göring to embark upon his own "parallel war" are unclear.[187] Possibly the ebullient self-confidence of the "thick one" was still persuasive, although *Luftwaffe* failure to block British evacuation at Dunkirk should have warned Hitler that Göring was not fully conscious of his service's limitations, or his own. The tactical difficulties of Sea Lion – for the *Wehrmacht* was not well versed in amphibious war – presumably made Göring's siren song attractive. Hitler may also have feared that full-scale invasion and total British defeat might bring the United States into the war, an outcome less likely if air action could force the British to terms. In any case, by 6 September Hitler was already "of the firm conviction that the forcing of England to its knees can be achieved even without a landing." A failed landing would destroy the myth of German invincibility, with incalculable consequences. Sea Lion could not proceed without certainty of success.[188] That certainty the *Luftwaffe* could not provide. On 15 September, in the climactic battle over London, Göring's pilots failed to break the RAF, despite perfect weather. As an Atlantic low closed in, Hitler put Sea Lion off "indefinitely" on 17 September. In this limbo the operation remained until its final cancellation in February 1942.[189]

While Hitler's interest in Sea Lion waned, his receptiveness to other proposals for dealing with Britain grew. The ever-increasing threat of United States intervention may have played a role in the gradual decline of the invasion project. Contrary to German hopes, Roosevelt's concern with reelection in November 1940 did not paralyze United States policy. In early September the president ceded to Britain fifty obsolete destroyers by executive order, circumventing a still piously isolationist Congress. This belated response to Churchill's plea for vessels with which to keep the sea lanes open until the escorts laid down in British yards were ready in early 1941 was a most unneutral act. It marked the beginning of United States "nonbelligerence" at Britain's side. It still required the shock of Pearl Harbor and Hitler's unwise declaration of war to thrust the United States into the European war in December 1941. But to Hitler and his advisers the situation in September 1940 must have looked increasingly gloomy; Britain's hope in America was evidently not entirely misplaced.[190]

Germany clearly needed a strategy designed to destroy Britain or force compromise before the United States could intervene. At the briefing of 6 September at which he noted Hitler's "firm conviction" that a landing might not prove necessary, the head of the German navy, Admiral Erich Raeder, attempted to provide such a strategy. He insisted on "the decisive significance of German and Italian operations in the Mediterranean area in the direction 'Gibraltar–Suez Canal.' " Raeder's "Mediterranean strategy" was not new. At the end of June, General Alfred Jodl, perhaps the closest of all Hitler's military advisers, had drafted a long memorandum on dealing with England "if political methods do not lead to the objective"; he had proposed the "activation" of the Italians to attack the Suez Canal, and of the Spaniards to seize Gibraltar.[191] Hitler had indeed pressed Jodl's recipe on Alfieri and Ciano in early July. But the Germans were never overly sanguine. After a briefing from Rintelen, Halder unflatteringly concluded that "Italy's economic dependence and lack of organizational ability [*Gestaltungskraft*] hinder a decisive Italian effort." Germany would have to attack Gibraltar unassisted while German armored units crossed to North Africa to "strike decisively at the British in the Mediterranean, drive them from Asia [Minor], help the Italians construct their Mediterranean Empire, and with the help of Russia reinforce the Reich we have created in Western and Northern Europe."[192]

Despite the encouragement of his generals, however, Hitler was far from enchanted with the idea of a German "war on the periphery." From the point of view of his own war aims – the seizure of *Lebensraum* in the east as the basis of German "world mastery"– the Mediterranean strategy and even Sea Lion were undesirable expedients which the inexplicable refusal of the British to accept his domination of continental Europe had forced upon him. At the end of July, after the unhelpful British reply to his "appeal to reason," he had ordered the "intellectual preparation" of a lightning campaign against the Soviet Union. In Hitler's view, such a campaign would remove Britain's last hope of a "continental mercenary [*Festlandsdegen*]," free the Japanese from Soviet pressure, and paralyze the United States through increased Japanese activity in the Pacific: "*When hope in Russia falls away, America too falls away*, for an immense revaluation of *Japan* in East Asia follows. . . ."[193]

The German army staff concluded by the end of July that a fall campaign against the Soviet Union was impossible, although Hitler and his military advisers were agreed that the German army would cut through the Soviets like a hot knife through butter.[194] A "diversionary maneuver" or "stop-gap action," in Hitler's words, therefore became necessary to see Germany through the winter should the invasion of Britain prove unfeasible.[195] But unlike Admiral Raeder, who considered the Mediterranean theater "decisive," Hitler did not favor a major German effort in the South. This was not solely the result of ideological preoccupations with blood and soil in the East. The Mediterranean was a strategic dead-end. As Andreas Hillgruber has convincingly argued, no defeat in the Middle East or Mediterranean could have driven Britain from the war so long as it could count on Roosevelt's support. Every month that Britain continued made the military intervention of the United States more likely. British unreasonableness ultimately raised the unpleasant prospect of a beleaguered Germany, exposed to Soviet encroachments from North Cape to the Dardanelles, dependent on Stalin for oil and other vital materials, and defending a far-flung perimeter against the vastly superior sea power and the growing air and ground strength of an Anglo-American coalition. The destruction of the Soviet Union was the only way Germany could maintain its momentum, secure the hegemonic position won in May and June of 1940, and prepare with some chance of success for the ultimate contest for world mastery with the United States.[196]

In the face of such far-flung perspectives, the Mediterranean was indeed of modest importance. In any event, practical difficulties stood in the way of German intervention there. Hitler had repeatedly recognized the Mediterranean as Mussolini's sphere. At this point he could scarcely invade it even to promote increased Axis efficiency and "help the Italians construct their Mediterranean Empire." Germany must nurture the prestige of the "one man" who appeared to guarantee Italian loyalty to the alliance. The utmost tact was necessary, and even if Mussolini were to agree to German help the Germans would have to tread lightly. Above all, serious as the political problem was, the purely military difficulties of supplying a German army in North Africa across a sea Germany did not control, through convoys organized and protected by an ally whose military leadership the Germans did not trust, were distinctly thought-provoking.[197]

Nevertheless, Hitler "agreed wholeheartedly," in Raeder's too hopeful words, with the admiral's proposals of 6 September, and ordered the *Wehrmacht* high command to begin planning. Subordinates had already begun to sound out the Italians. By 14 September, even before Sea Lion's indefinite postponement, Hitler had decided to prepare a panzer corps for Libya. He also expressed interest in urging the Spaniards into the war. Franco had offered in June to join in the division of the spoils, but as with Japan, Hitler had left the offer unanswered in the expectation of compromise with Britain. In any case, the Spanish price was high: Franco demanded much of French North Africa and vast quantities of food, fuel, and military equipment. Only at the end of July, after England had obviously failed to respond to his "appeal to reason," had Hitler's interest in Spain and Gibraltar revived. But his military subordinates took an even gloomier view of Spanish capabilities than they did of Italy's. Admiral Wilhelm Canaris, chief of military intelligence, returned in late August from preliminary discussions with Franco and other Spanish leaders with the view that "the consequences of an alliance with this unpredictable nation are not foreseeable." Hitler, despite doubts of his own, nevertheless wooed Franco with determination from mid-September on.[198]

A necessary accompaniment to the "Mediterranean strategy" and, for that matter, even for Sea Lion, was some means for keeping the United States quiescent during fall and winter, until Germany could defeat England, bring it to "reason," or cut the Gordian knot through the destruction of the Soviet Union. The obvious remedy was to accept the Japanese offer and conclude an alliance that would take that nation to war with the United States should

Roosevelt enter the European conflict. In theory, the Japanese threat would immobilize the United States, at least temporarily. Such an agreement would also be a fitting cap to the ambitious triangular structure Ribbentrop had begun with the Anti-Comintern Pact of 1936–7, but which had suffered almost total eclipse following German "betrayal" of Japan through the Molotov–Ribbentrop Pact. Ribbentrop's secret emissary, Ambassador Heinrich Stahmer, arrived in Tokyo on 7 September. By sacrificing clarity and binding force he cut through all Japanese attempts at delay and secured a demonstrative but substantially empty agreement by 27 September. Meanwhile, in order to brief the Italians on the Japanese negotiations and Hitler's increasing interest in Spain, and impose a renewed German veto on Italian discussions with the Soviet Union, Ribbentrop telephoned Ciano on 13 September and invited himself to Rome.[199]

The view from Rome. The Italians as yet had only fragmentary information on German intentions or on the changing situation as Hitler and his advisers perceived it. Sea Lion's progress had kept Mussolini, Ciano, and the Italian military on tenterhooks. The massive German air offensive had relieved Mussolini of the doubts about German ability to invade Britain that Ciano had brought back from a visit to Berchtesgaden at the end of August, during Axis attempts to impose a solution on the eternal Hungarian-Rumanian dispute. By mid-September Mussolini once more believed the landing was imminent, but also expected a war conveniently prolonged enough beyond the landing to permit Italy to achieve its various aspirations. Ciano, on the other hand, contemplated with foreboding the consequences of a lengthened war, even while he hoped that Mussolini's instinct proved correct "this time as well." Ciano's talk with Hitler had led him to doubt Germany would attempt Sea Lion, although the Führer, suiting his words to his audience, had successfully if untruthfully convinced Ciano of German determination to fight to the bitter end rather than seek a compromise peace. As the climax of the air battles over London approached, Ciano suspended judgment: "Perhaps we shall get the truth out of Ribbentrop," he noted on 14 September.[200]

Badoglio similarly clung to the hope in the Duce's lucky star: On 9 September Rintelen recorded that the marshal "still hope[d] very strongly for a rapid end to the war through the successes of the German *Luftwaffe* and an early landing in England." Rintelen had in the meantime apparently received orders to stress the difficulties of the cross-Channel enterprise, and he noted that "a certain agitation" accompanied Badoglio's insistence that prolongation of the war would place the Duke of Aosta in East Africa "in a very difficult situation." Badoglio was also less buoyant than in the past about prospects in Egypt. Lack of transport would prevent Graziani from achieving more than "tactical successes" in the coming offensive.[201]

Even while they expected or merely hoped for the landing in England, the Italian leaders were dimly aware that the Germans had designs in the Mediterranean, should the war continue into the winter. When General Marras, the Berlin military attaché, approached Jodl of the *Wehrmacht* high command on 3 September with one more plea for German or captured equipment for the Italian forces, Jodl instead suggested shipment of "one or two" panzer divisions to North Africa to put the winter months to good use and "liquidate the situation in the Mediterranean." The German units could begin work after the Italians had completed the first phase of their offensive; it would be at least six weeks before outloading of the divisions from southern Italian ports could begin. Marras reported the conversation to Rome, pointed out that the proposals had "above all a political aspect," and suggested that one might conveniently decline by alleging logistical difficulties. The suggestion found favor. Badoglio did ask Graziani for an opinion, but without particular urgency. The latter, intent on Sidi el Barrani, took his time about replying. When he did, on 26 September, it was to deny that his supply system could cope with the additional burden the "undoubtedly useful" German force would impose.[202] But the Germans pressed further; Rintelen returned from consultations in Berlin with orders to sound out Badoglio directly. The marshal parried, in the same conversation of 9 September in which he betrayed agitation about the prolongation of the war. Sea transport to Libya was allegedly not sufficiently secure to permit shipment of German armor — an excuse both Rintelen and the German naval attaché found implausible. Only Roatta looked upon the proposal with favor, but his voice carried little weight.[203] Mussolini and Badoglio were determined to keep the Germans out of Italy's war.

Rome was also aware of increasing German interest in another sensitive area: the Balkans. Alfieri reported in late August his judgment that Germany had ulterior motives in vetoing operations against Greece: Marras had gained the impression that the Germans feared above all else an independent Italian action before Germany was ready "to bring all its strength to bear in order to give a more or less definitive shape to that region."[204] In the Italian view, however, the Germans were not entirely content to put the Balkans on ice in the meantime. Economically, Germany was expanding ever more voraciously into an area in which, since the Anschluss, it had been the major trading power. The Italian minister of corporations, Renato Ricci, reported ominously to Mussolini in early September on the "gigantic" new Danube port facilities under construction in Vienna. The new port would render that city a "formidable fulcrum of German economic penetration."[205] German economic preponderance in the "New Europe" indeed threatened more than Italian interests in the Balkans; it appeared to endanger the very existence of Italian industry. At the urging of Alberto Pirelli and of other business magnates, Ciano, his subordinates, and Minister of Exchange and Currency Riccardi attempted throughout summer and fall of 1940 to press on Berlin Italian claims to joint leadership of the coming German economic *"Grossraum."* But the Germans coldly evaded all commitments, although they were willing to correct their press's "one-sided" treatment of Europe's economic future. A Riccardi pilgrimage to Berlin in mid-October predictably failed to secure Italy's interests.[206]

Politically, the unstable Balkan situation finally drew the Germans into direct intervention to protect their oil supply. As early as 26 August, as he prepared to entrust to Ribbentrop and Ciano the thorny task of arbitrating the Rumanian-Hungarian dispute, Hitler ordered two panzer divisions to the southeastern corner of occupied Poland to stand by for a move on the Rumanian oilfields. Heavy Soviet concentrations in Bessarabia threatened intervention should war break out between Hungary and the Rumanians. To counter this menace, Hitler decided to guarantee what remained of Rumania after the arbitration.[207] On 30 August, he ordered preparations to send a "strong military mission" to Rumania to back the guarantee and protect the oilfields. Hitler's decision to compel the cession of most of Transylvania to Hungary produced serious disturbances in Bucharest, which ended on 5 September with the abdication of King Carol. The charismatic chief of the Rumanian army, General Ion Antonescu, proceeded to form a new and decidedly pro-German regime. The general obligingly resurrected an earlier request of King Carol's for a military mission to modernize the Rumanian army and protect the country against further territorial mutilation. On 15 September the German army's intelligence chief arrived in Bucharest to make the necessary arrangements.[208]

Ciano, in the meantime, had attempted to safeguard Italian influence in Rumania by seconding German initiatives, while the minister of popular culture urged on his editors the line that the German and Italian guarantee of Rumania resulting from the arbitration showed Italy's Balkan influence extended to the very borders of the Soviet Union. Ciano even pressed slightly ahead of his allies, and advised Antonescu to break diplomatic relations with Britain. But the general was leery, for he feared British air reprisals against his all-important oil. So, for that matter, did the Germans.[209] Worse, from Ciano's point of view, was to come. On 15 September, the Italian military attaché in Bucharest reported that the sending of the German military mission to Rumania was "probable" and that a German general was expected in Bucharest shortly. By 18 September, the Italian leadership had learned that the Germans were preparing to send ground units totaling about 12,000 men to the Ploesti area in a few weeks.[210] On the eve of Ribbentrop's visit, the view from Rome thus presented certain ominous features.

Nevertheless, it was not yet entirely clear that the Germans had failed decisively in the north, or that the strategic situation was rapidly changing to the disadvantage of Germany and still more to that of its ally.[211] To Mussolini the future seemed increasingly favorable. He had conjured away the danger of a negotiated peace: Germans and British were locked in mortal combat, and Germany was committed to support Italy's Mediterranean goals. Italy, with the advance into Egypt, was about to carve out those goals by force of arms. In three months of war, Mussolini had conquered British Somaliland, for what it was worth. He had overcome Graziani's fierce reluctance to join battle, and in the process worked off much of his long-standing diffidence in the face of professional military advice. The King had not dared interfere with the conduct of the war. Now, even if the Navy still held back and the Germans failed in the north, the way to an independent and decisive Italian victory at Suez was open. In the next month, Mussolini's self-confidence was to culminate in further demands on Graziani, and in the decision to attack Greece.

CHAPTER 5

The attack on Greece

This is an action I have meditated on for many months, [since] before
our entry into the war, and even before the outbreak of the war itself.

Mussolini, 15 October 1940

1. *Alexandria or Athens?*

Facing the "new situation." Ribbentrop did not come to his conferences with
Ciano and Mussolini on 19, 20, and 22 September bearing the "truth" about
Sea Lion's indefinite postponement. He did convey a Hitler letter proposing
a Führer–Duce meeting at the Brenner or in North Italy. Hitler conceded
difficulties over England, and gave no assurance that the war would end
soon.[1] Ribbentrop himself was more optimistic, and gloated that London
would "soon lie in rubble and ashes." Even the skeptical Ciano noted without cavil Ribbentrop's assurances that the landing was "ready and possible."
As important to the Italian leaders, however, was Ribbentrop's fierce insistence that Hitler would fight rather than negotiate; Berlin had rejected the
mediation efforts of the king of Sweden.

Ribbentrop also produced for Italian approval a number of expedients to
see the Axis through the winter, should war continue. First was of course
the Japanese pact, which Ribbentrop and Hitler hoped would deter or render
ineffectual United States intervention. Hitler and Ribbentrop also proposed
to hasten Spanish belligerence, despite Franco's exorbitant demands for
French North African territory, and for food, fuel, and materiel. Mussolini
was not conspicuously enthusiastic about bringing Spain in; a German operation against Gibraltar would merely replace one guardian of Italy's prison
gate with another. To Ribbentrop, Mussolini suggested that if the war were
likely to continue, the Axis should reserve the Spanish card for "the right
moment." Also in prospect for the winter, according to Ribbentrop, was a
diplomatic attempt to turn Russia toward the Persian Gulf and India. Concurrently, Ribbentrop maintained Berlin's veto over Italo-Soviet bargaining,
which might encourage a Russian advance in the Balkans. He also reiterated
German aversion to an Italian foray against Greece or Yugoslavia. Mussolini

agreed that the war against Britain took precedence, while nevertheless denouncing Greece as a Mediterranean Norway. Once Italy had conquered Egypt, the British fleet might seek shelter in Greek harbors, necessitating action. Ciano, who was given to distorting the diplomatic record to further his own purposes, recorded a less categorical statement of Mussolini's priorities: "It [was] therefore also necessary to proceed to the liquidation of Greece; all the more so because when our ground forces have progressed further into Egypt, the English fleet will . . . seek refuge in Greek ports." But even in Ciano's version, Mussolini agreed with Ribbentrop that the principal objective was to defeat England.

Ciano evidently still hoped to influence Mussolini to attack Greece; the Ciano version of Mussolini's remarks would also help refute eventual German complaints of nonconsultation. Mussolini indeed appears to have concluded from Ribbentrop's remarks that Germany conceded him a "free hand . . . in Greece and Yugoslavia," as the dictator reported to Victor Emmanuel III.[2] But Mussolini's actions in the ensuing weeks demonstrate that he interpreted this free hand as one more generic assurance of noninterference in the Italian sphere, rather than a lifting of the German August veto on immediate attack.[3]

Almost as an afterthought, Ribbentrop privately informed Ciano that Rumania had requested a military mission, and Germany planned to send one to stiffen the Rumanians and protect the oilfields. The Italians thus received their first official notice of the German step that had perturbed them throughout the previous week. Ribbentrop's failure to inform the Italian leaders earlier, to ask them for their views or invite their participation as an ally and a fellow guarantor of Rumania, understandably rankled. Ciano, tactfully or guilefully, made no immediate protest.

Finally, the talks touched on North Africa. Mussolini claimed that progress was "thoroughly satisfactory," and alleged that Graziani had completed preparations for the second phase of the attack, which would cover the 120 kilometers to Mersa Matruh. Graziani would come to Rome in the next days to talk over details. The third and final phase would traverse a further 300 kilometers, and conclude with the conquest of Alexandria. Ribbentrop inquired after the probable date the campaign would end; Mussolini answered "somewhat hesitatingly" that he hoped to wind up operations by the end of October. After the occupation of Mersa Matruh, Italian air action against Alexandria would force the British fleet to withdraw from the eastern Mediterranean and perhaps compel them to break out past Gibraltar, since the Suez Canal was too dangerous a passage under air attack. Mussolini emphasized that strong British resistance was likely, "for the loss of [Egypt] would possibly result in the collapse of the entire Empire."

Mussolini's claim of readiness for the next phase in Egypt was of course untrue. Graziani had announced to Badoglio on 17 September a period of "standstill of which [he could] not specify the limits," and complained of the continuing failure of promised equipment to arrive, of the effect of the "unusual" climatic conditions even on his native troops, of the thoroughness with which the British had sabotaged all sources of water in the area they had evacuated, and of the alarming deterioration of the dirt track over which his sole supply line ran. Badoglio had reassured him that there was "no impatience" in Rome.[4] Momentarily, Badoglio was correct. Mussolini thought it wise to wait for ten days or so until the significance of the new developments the Germans had announced became clear. The morning after the first conference with Ribbentrop, Mussolini summoned Graziani to Rome for 29 September to brief him on "the new political situation" and examine with him "the program of action." By then, it would perhaps be clearer whether the Germans were going to land in Britain, whether and when Spain would enter the war, and what effect Spanish belligerence would have on the French — upon whose forbearance in Tunisia Graziani's capacity to attack Egypt theoretically depended. Extensive French naval movements to parry the impending Anglo-Gaullist descent on Dakar had aroused the undisguised alarm of Badoglio, Ciano, and presumably of Mussolini as well.[5]

Despite the uncertainty of the situation and Graziani's renewed procrastination, however, Mussolini drew comfort from the prolongation of the war into the winter. As he told Badoglio on 22 September, a rapid end would be "catastrophic [*un fallimento*]." Mussolini seems to have hoped to induce Graziani, once the latter arrived in Rome, to resume the offensive in early October; at least that was the date Mussolini indicated to Mackensen toward the end of the Ribbentrop visit.[6] But Mussolini did not confide his intention to Badoglio, who expected that the next phase of the North African campaign would begin late in the coming month. On 25 September, after conferring with Mussolini, Badoglio addressed the service chiefs.[7] Yugoslavia and Greece, Badoglio assured his colleagues, were questions for solution "at the peace table, without regard for the views of those involved."[8] The deployment against Yugoslavia would continue, but "very much in depth." Action was improbable except in the event of an internal upheaval, which now "was not considered imminent." Mussolini had evidently changed his mind on that score since mid-September; Ribbentrop's renewed warning and the decline of the fortunes of Sea Lion made it temporarily impolitic to pursue Yugoslavia. The three divisions that would arrive in Albania by the end of September, Badoglio continued, would give Italy roughly nine divisions there, enough to "keep Greece in its place."

In the Mediterranean, the situation was "obscure and chaotic indeed." The affair at Dakar, where action had begun on 23 September and was still in progress, raised the possibility of the complete defection of French North Africa. Mussolini also feared that a joint German-Spanish attack on Gibraltar could lead to a British attempt to occupy some other Mediterranean base, such as Corsica or Bizerte.[9] On this point, Badoglio announced he had reassured Mussolini. The Army staff had already made plans to occupy Corsica; for Bizerte, the marshal ordered Roatta to prepare a *studio* of an amphibious landing from Sicily.

The general situation was more hopeful. Despite continuing German assurances that Sea Lion was still possible until mid-October, Badoglio was now convinced that the operation would not take place. If, as seemed likely, the war lasted into the winter, its "baricenter" would shift to the Mediterranean. The German and Italian staffs would have to meet in order to decide the methods and goals of joint action. Badoglio envisaged, as did the Germans, an attack on Gibraltar and a further advance into Egypt to Mersa Matruh or beyond in order to bombard Alexandria harbor and drive the British fleet from both eastern and western Mediterranean. "We," Badoglio predicted, would then "dominate" the Mediterranean and "nothing . . . could stop us." But Badoglio opposed fiercely any German armored help in Africa. Roatta had allegedly concluded that shipment of even one of the two *Panzerdivisionen* Berlin had offered would require three months.[10] Badoglio himself insisted that "we have an abundance of men, and . . . in Africa these men are superior to German troops." If he had to negotiate with the Germans, he would insist on equipment alone. Only in the air would he request complete German units, and in the air, Italy would not be a suppliant. The stiffness of RAF resistance over southern England had evidently caught the Germans unawares, for at the beginning of August they had belatedly taken up Mussolini's June and July offers of aid against the British Isles. Some 200 *Regia Aeronautica* fighters and bombers, sorely needed in the Mediterranean and North Africa, departed for Belgian air bases in late September.[11] Badoglio closed the meeting with the promise that although the Germans "were not people with whom one [could] deal easily," he would press his point of view upon them forcefully.

Here was a strategic vision even more parochial than that of Admiral Raeder, who, while predicting that a concentrated effort in the Mediterranean would be "decisive," at least pressed for such a solution in order to deal with Britain before the United States could enter the war. In Badoglio's version of the "Mediterranean strategy" any such consideration was absent. The Italian military leaders could see no further than the "parallel war" design of the spring, now rapidly losing its relevance as United States assistance to Great Britain rendered a clear-cut German and Italian victory steadily less likely. Nor did Badoglio's interest in Italo-German staff talks stem from a desire for genuine coordination. In the event, Badoglio used his proposed conference with Keitel, held in November, to confirm temporarily the exclusion of the Germans from the Mediterranean theater, even while Italy's own war there collapsed ignominiously.

The service chiefs' conference of 25 September marked the end of the first phase of Mussolini's war against Britain. Although he had not yet dismissed Sea Lion entirely from his calculations, it was no longer at the center of Italian strategy. Mussolini evidently felt considerable *Schadenfreude* at his ally's failure to lay the recalcitrant Britons low. Italy now had an entire winter to improve on Germany's performance by striking the decisive blow against the British Middle East position. As one Italian historian has pointed out, Mussolini might now reasonably envisage his own emergence as the "sole 'victor' of the Axis."[12] Hence Mussolini's delight at the war's prolongation, which was anything but "another desperate attempt to sound impressive" to his entourage.[13] Some of that entourage, and the regime's journalistic and business milieux, shared Mussolini's hopes. The private intelligence service of the chief of the Stefani news agency noted in early October that "[w]e want to reach Suez with our own forces alone; perhaps we will win the war and not the Germans."[14]

The campaign in Egypt had highest priority and for the moment eclipsed all else. Preparations against Yugoslavia lapsed, to the unfeigned regret of Roatta, who remarked in a letter to Graziani that ". . . it disappointed everyone, at the center and at the periphery, that we gave up Contingency East, an affair that had truly been well and thoroughly prepared."[15] The major consequence of dismantling that operation was that Mussolini could carry out a partial demobilization of the home army, a step he had apparently contemplated as early as July but had rescinded in view of the massive requirements of the Yugoslav project. The needs of the civilian economy were now all the more pressing, particularly the demands of agriculture, which had to make up for cut-off overseas food imports. Increasing shortages compelled the government to introduce rationing of cooking oil and fats on 1 October, the first step of its kind, and one that had inevitable repercussions on home-front morale.[16] Mussolini also presumably intended that demobilization strengthen in the public mind the reassuring sensation of "business as usual" – a principle Hitler also acted on until disaster at Stalingrad compelled sterner measures.

The demobilization Mussolini now carried out was immeasurably more drastic than that planned in July. Of the 1,100,000 men under arms in Italy, 600,000 would return home. Only the year classes of 1917 through 1920 would remain with the colors. Not until the class of 1921 reported for training in the spring would the home Army's strength begin to rise again toward the million mark. The effect on the Army's structure and effectiveness was dramatic. Demobilization by classes rather than by units disorganized the entire Army. The plan also required dissolution of the remaining army group command (established to control the Yugoslav operation), two field army commands, and a host of lesser units. The basic directive that Soddu promulgated on 2 October "in accordance with higher decisions" ordered demobilization begun on 10 October, and gave Roatta discretion to maintain enough home Army divisions at war strength to accomplish the remaining contingency missions, now reduced essentially to a number of small operations against France, and the Corfù landing. The remaining divisions would descend to something approaching minimum peacetime strength or – as a subordinate of Roatta later put it – would shrink to "larvae" with about 3,000 officers and men apiece.[17]

Mussolini apparently acted without direct consultation with Badoglio, but Soddu did clear the demobilization measures with the marshal, who heartily approved. Demobilization ruled out any speedy revival of the Yugo-slav operation – Badoglio, for one, did not regret its passing – and would presumably inhibit sudden Mussolinian urges to open new fronts that winter. Badoglio's only observation was sage but ineffectual: it was inadvisable to "preserve too many skeletal major units." He therefore proposed that the Army add a number of line divisions to the headquarters and service units being deactivated.[18]

Roatta and Soddu did not see fit to follow Badoglio's advice, although the Army's massive shortages of equipment made it expedient to discard the overblown Pariani-Soddu seventy-three-division framework and concentrate trained manpower and arms in a smaller number of solid formations.[19] Perhaps they feared admitting to Mussolini that Italy could not support anything approaching seventy-three divisions. Perhaps they dreaded the wrath of their fellow generals, whom drastic reductions would put out of work. Most probably they were still prisoners of the Army's faith in numbers. In this same period Roatta did take a stand on one issue: Mussolini's recently announced intention of abolishing the Italian Army's cavalry.[20]

Whatever his motives, Roatta declined to reduce the number of the home Army's divisions, apparently in expectation that the spring call-up of the class of 1921 would permit the "notable augmentation" of the units temporarily reduced to peacetime strength. In this course he received Graziani's support during the latter's visit to Rome, of which more later, even though Graziani was probably acting against his own best interests as commander in North Africa. Roatta did record a mild protest: in a letter that went out over Graziani's signature, he warned Soddu that *"no misunderstandings* of any sort whatsoever should exist over the unavoidable consequences" of the measure. Demobilization would render the home Army largely unusable during the winter. It would waste utterly the training accomplished and the unit cohesion laboriously achieved in the summer. Remobilization would be impossible for several months; an emergency call-up would require ponderous administrative preparation. Badoglio meekly agreed to Roatta's arrangements, and merely noted that "what matters now is that there be manpower for the sowing – no complications are in sight."[21]

Whether Badoglio had the Greek operation in mind is not clear, although demobilization, at least in theory, did not greatly impair the Army's capacity to mount "Contingency 'G' " or the Corfù landing that went with it (even though the "Bari" division, earmarked for the landing, was as late as 15 October scheduled to descend to 70–80 percent of war strength). Roatta assured Rintelen on 3 October that "if an intervention in Greece were to become necessary," the forces currently in Albania would suffice.[22] But for the moment Mussolini's relegation of the Greek question, like the Yugoslav one, to the peace table remained in effect. Badoglio and Roatta stamped down on Visconti Prasca, who had begun to shift one of his three newly arrived divisions to an advanced position on the Greek border in contravention of Roatta's orders of late August and early September, and in flagrant disregard for verbal directives Badoglio had personally given Visconti Prasca during a visit of the latter's to Rome.[23] With Badoglio's approval, Roatta informed Albanian Command on 2 October that "in this phase" it was "not (I say again, not) a question of deploying offensively at the Greek border, but simply of maintaining one's self a few days' marches away from it in view of a possible (I say again, possible) deployment to be assumed only on order of this Staff."[24] Badoglio followed up with a stern directive to the Army staff that permitted Roatta to continue and keep up to date *studi* for "Contingency 'G,' " but warned that "for the moment any such action is postponed." "For clarity," as one of the marshal's assistants put it, Badoglio provided a copy of the directive to Ciano's secretariat, while Roatta ordered Visconti on 4 October to stop distribution to subordinate units of the Albanian Command operations plan implementing the "Contingency 'G' " directive.[25]

Badoglio and Roatta were fully capable of minor obstructionism, as over the shipment of the three divisions to Albania. But it is most unlikely that they would have had the temerity to issue such orders (and to have informed Ciano into the bargain) without Mussolini's backing. Nor, at this point, does Mussolini seem to have been concealing his true intentions from his generals. He no longer had much reason to do so. Throughout the summer, he had shown progressively less compunction about commissioning *studi* and *progetti,* ordering deployments, setting deadlines, and taking upon himself the heavy responsibility of driving his military subordinates into action. It is also unlikely that Mussolini's consignment of Balkan questions to the peace table, which Badoglio replayed to his colleagues at the 25 September conference, was a mere ruse to camouflage the machinations of Ciano's minions in Albania and present the high command with a *fait accompli.* As will emerge, when Mussolini finally decided to deal with Greece in mid-October, his first step was to summon Badoglio and issue orders to the three services through normal channels. Up to that point, the Greek project was in abeyance.[26]

Spain, France . . . or Greece? While the Italians nervously contemplated the possibility of German intrusion into their sphere, Hitler had begun to rethink the premises of Germany's emerging Mediterranean strategy. Vichy resistance to the inept Anglo-Gaullist attack on Dakar,[27] coupled with Franco's continued reticence, brought about a gradual tactical reversal in Hitler's attitude. France now seemed to offer greater potential advantage as an ally than Spain.[28] On 26 September, Raeder again pressed his version of the Mediterranean strategy on Hitler as an antidote to invasion of the Soviet Union the next spring, a project of which the admiral had just heard and to which he objected as a diversion of resources from *his* war against Britain. That power, he warned, sought always to "throttle the weaker" of its enemies, and the Italians were the preordained and unsuspecting victims. As yet they had even refused German help. This could not continue: "the Mediterranean must therefore be cleaned out *in the winter.*" As on 6 September, Hitler agreed "fundamentally" with Raeder's proposals.[29]

But it was Hitler himself who would have to deal with the practical political problems over which Raeder had glided effortlessly. Hitler proposed an unprecedented step: he would consult present and prospective allies in person – first Mussolini, "possibly" Franco, and even Pétain – in order to decide "whether collaboration with France or Spain offered the greater advantage." France probably constituted the best bargain: "Spain asked much but offered little." The question was a thorny one. If he were indeed to "yoke France to [the German] wagon," he would have trouble not only with Spain but with Mussolini as well. As Hitler summarized the problem only too authoritatively, the solution of the North African conflicts between France, Italy, and Spain was "only possible through a grandiose fraud."[30]

It was to the accompaniment of such considerations on Hitler's part that Ciano arrived in Berlin on 27 September for the ceremonial signing of the Tripartite Pact with Germany and Japan. The pact itself was no more than a façade, a circumstance of which the Palazzo Chigi was well aware.[31] Spain was the chief topic of Ciano's Berlin conversations. Hitler made clear that Franco's exorbitant demands, and the likelihood that Spanish claims in North Africa would drive the French there over to the British and Gaullists, had soured him on the project. He therefore wanted to see Mussolini immediately at the Brenner to talk the Spanish question over. Ciano accepted. Hitler had other news of great interest. Ciano noted: "[n]o landing. No destruction of England in the near future. From Hitler's words there now emerges concern with a long war." With Ciano and his party, the Germans were of an "impeccable kindness." Ciano's journalistic mouthpiece, Giovanni Ansaldo, who habitually accompanied his master on these diplomatic journeys, remarked with justifiable cynicism that German solicitude was "proportionate to the need they have for us."[32]

This observation of Ansaldo's was perhaps indirectly connected to Ciano's parting shot before entraining for Rome. In conversation with Weizsäcker of the German foreign office, Ciano spoke "rather strong words about the Greeks." Despite Weizsäcker's objection "that the Greek matter had been described in the discussions [presumably those just concluded] as not exactly pressing," Ciano insisted that "something must happen in order to deprive the British fleet, should it flee from Egypt, of the bolt-hole of the Greek islands." Weizsäcker, by his own account, rejected this thought, which Mussolini had raised briefly with Ribbentrop in Rome.[33]

These remarks were not the first evidence of Ciano's continued interest in Greece after Ribbentrop's 19 September warning. On the 24th, the Italian foreign minister had told the papal nunzio, the philo-Fascist and antisemitic Cardinal Francesco Borgongini-Duca,[34] that the Church would soon be able to apply in Macedonia and Greece, under the aegis of the Fascist state, the same propaganda as in Albania: "We intend to occupy all of it, because [the Greeks] are people whom we can in no way trust, and they are maintaining an absolutely disgusting attitude. . . ." When Borgongini-Duca asked the date of the action, Ciano replied, "Soon [*prossimamente*], but not immediately [*subito*]."[35] Ciano was more reassuring to foreign diplomats: Italy would "take no action at present, but await a general postwar settlement of [the] region's problems." But he refrained from giving any such assurance to the Greeks directly, and persisted in describing Greece as the only "dark spot in the Balkans" to those he presumably hoped would repeat his words in Athens. On 3 October, before departing with Mussolini for the Brenner, Ciano attempted to enlist the support of the King. He showed himself "impatient to give a lesson to Greece because of its ambigious — as he puts it — conduct." He also had other objects in view: he spoke of a "possible [*eventuale*]" partition of Switzerland.[36]

What exactly was Ciano up to? The coincidence of his renewed agitation with the growing realization that the Germans would probably not win the war before winter is suggestive. The heavy atmosphere in the German capital had much impressed Ciano, although he did not feel the situation as yet justified "the pessimism of some circles, who begin to evoke the memory of the previous war and fear the worst." Ciano was also in agreement with the sophisticated arguments of that seasoned diplomat, Michele Lanza of the Berlin Embassy: loyalty was a "beautiful thing" — for the lower orders. For "those who govern," there could be only one loyalty, "that to the national interest of one's own country." If an alliance endangered the nation, it was "an unavoidable duty to detach oneself from [that alliance] at all costs."[37] Loyalty toward the German alliance Ciano had helped bring about was hardly his dominant emotion. He was also increasingly skeptical about Italian military prospects in the Mediterranean. Given these premises, Ciano's pressure for an attack on Greece was not entirely illogical, nor did it derive solely from personal ambition for the enlargement of his Albanian "Grand Duchy." In his conversation with Weizsäcker, Ciano had remarked that Italy must "soon seize securities [*Sicherungen schaffen*] in Greece." Later in the month, shortly before the meeting at Palazzo Venezia that settled the final shape of the operation, Ciano similarly insisted to Jacomoni that the affair had nothing to do with Albanian claims on Greece; rather, Italy needed "bargaining counters." According to a longstanding high-level confidential informant of Mackensen's, Ciano expected that the international situation would soon worsen. Russia, as a consequence of Roosevelt's probable reelection, would presumably move away from the Axis toward the Anglo-American coalition. The Turks, whom Russian pressure on their northern borders currently immobilized, would then presumably be free to aid Greece against Italian attack. The present was probably "the last favorable moment." Much later, after German power had flattened Greece and Yugoslavia in the spring of 1941, Ciano even broached to Mussolini himself the desirability of a compromise peace, "now that we have secured our booty," and in conversation with the former ambassador to London, Giuseppe Bastianini, again referred to Greece as a bargaining counter.[38]

One vital element of Ciano's calculations escaped Mackensen: the anti-German one. Ciano's Albanian satrap Jacomoni reported on 24 September that he was continuing to "keep alight the torch of Ciamuria." However, some Albanians allegedly feared that Italy would not act swiftly enough to forestall German Balkan conquests, which Jacomoni linked to the alleged pro-Greek intrigues of the German consul-general in Tirana, Eberhard von Pannwitz.[39] Jacomoni carefully attuned his warning to Ciano's long-held preoccupation with blocking German penetration of Italy's Balkan preserve, and it doubtless struck a responsive chord at Palazzo Chigi. In his 1941 conversation with Bastianini, Ciano defended his role in memorable and thoroughly unrepentant terms: ". . . despite everything, he claimed as his initiatives, [taken] in order to prevent Germany from reaching the Mediterranean, the seizure of Albania, the creation of the kingdom of Croatia [in 1941][40] and the action in Greece." If Ciano had been enthusiastic to break that small nation from May to August 1940, he was doubly so in the fall. Despite – and indeed because of – German disapproval, it was time to think of the future, to stake out Italy's spheres of interest, to secure "guarantees." Ciano, unlike his father-in-law, had a healthy respect for the capabilities of the United States. He probably expected, and perhaps now secretly hoped, that U.S. entry into the war would put an end to German pretensions, and would produce stalemate. In that event, the more Italy had in hand, the stronger its position.

Egypt delayed. Mussolini had other concerns. Graziani arrived as ordered on 29 September. He had attempted to prepare the ground by demanding more time to construct a metalled road and an aqueduct (Graziani took himself seriously as a new Roman) from the Libyan border to the new Italian forward base at Sidi el Barrani. Mussolini's reaction has not survived, but by 28 September Badoglio's entourage was aware that Mussolini intended that the advance into Egypt resume between 10 and 15 October.[41]

According to Graziani's account of his visit to Rome, written in early December,[42] he and Badoglio conferred before meeting with Mussolini. Badoglio allegedly asserted, of his own accord, that need for massive logistical build-up precluded attack on Mersa Matruh before mid-December. Graziani had cautiously concurred: "one could perhaps remain within these limits." The two marshals had then proceeded to Palazzo Venezia. In Mussolini's antechamber, Badoglio, with the help of Mussolini's chamberlain, outmaneuvered Graziani (and Soddu, who was hanging about close to the seat of power) and slipped in for a brief private conference with Mussolini. The fuming Graziani finally received permission to enter:

The Duce did not have the expression which I had seen so many times upon meeting him. He was rather dour [*piuttosto ermetico*] and not very expansive. He had me take a seat and asked me, "First of all, how's your health?" "Excellent, Duce, as you see," I replied. "That is already a lot," he remarked. I had the impression he was disquieted on this point. (Perhaps some one had once again made insinuations about my physical condition?)

The Duce briefly questioned me about the situation. I gave him all the necessary facts, maintaining myself within the limits of reality and of the absolute truth without either pessimism or optimism. I showed him some maps which he had not seen, and which he retained.

Then he added: ". . . the month of July has given us British Somaliland – September, Sidi Barrani – October can give us Mersa Matruh. Mersa Matruh will permit us to move forward our aviation, which then can begin bombarding Alexandria escorted by fighters – Mersa Matruh itself is nothing but a name, but what is important is that the country and the world should know that we are advancing. In any case, I never set territorial objectives.

Following these directives you will be able to resume the march toward the middle of October."

At this point Marshal Badoglio jumped up and said: "That's impossible – he won't be able to make that deadline."

However, he did not insist on December, as he had in our [previous] conversation.

The Duce turned to me and asked: "And what do you think?" I answered that I would be able to be more precise once I had returned to my headquarters and examined all the elements of the problem.

The Duce remained silent [*ermetico*], but he was evidently not satisfied. . . .

Despite Badoglio's outburst, which apparently attracted Mussolini's wrath, neither marshal displayed much moral courage. No final decision resulted, although Badoglio gained the impression that he had carried the day.[43]

Mussolini's primary purpose in pressing the attack was strategic. Mersa Matruh appeared to be the key to Egypt. If the Italians could base fighters on its landing ground, the *Regia Aeronautica*'s numerical preponderance might at last drive Cunningham's fleet from Egyptian harbors. The destruction of British command of the sea would permit Italian naval support for Graziani's advance. Incidentally, it would also allow "solution" of the Greek problem, possibly without fighting, even before the end of the larger war, which Mussolini now probably expected in the spring of 1941. To move Graziani, Mussolini emphasized his habitual pretext. He repeated the claim he had made in August: he "never set territorial objectives." What was important was prestige: "that the country and the world should know that we are advancing." Like the desire for easy pickings and the fear of missing great opportunities upon which Mussolini had played in seducing his military and people into war, the maintenance of prestige was a need that Badoglio, Graziani, and every other member of the Fascist elite could feel in their bones. Indeed, Mussolini later played on this theme in attempting to convince that stern guardian of martial virtue, Marshal Emilio De Bono, that the Greek fiasco had been necessary. "The Army," Mussolini told De Bono in November, "had need of *glory*."[44]

In October, a further success would have been indubitably useful in Mussolini's unequal prestige struggle with his former junior partner, Hitler, who had conquered Europe from North Cape to Biarritz while Italy had secured half of Menton, British Somaliland, and the unpromising and waterless real estate around Sidi el Barrani. The Italian internal situation was also probably beginning to cause mild concern. The public's summer disappointment and anxiety over the absence of swift victory was turning to disgruntlement and foreboding. Rationing of cooking oil and fats on 1 October came as a "thunderbolt from a blue sky"; everyone had expected it, but not so soon. The introduction on the same day of mandatory whole wheat bread, after a mere three and a half months of war, contrasted menacingly with Italy's performance in World War I: white bread had survived until 1917. Some cities, such as Genoa, contained obdurate pockets of *"pietismo"* toward France and Britain.[45] But Mussolini was not primarily after prestige, or a momentary distraction for the home front. He wanted more permanent assets. The sense of urgency he was attempting to communicate to his generals was the result of a growing realization that the currently favorable strategic situation in North Africa would not last.

Despite the inconclusive result of the 29 September conference, Ciano noted that Mussolini was for the moment convinced that he had had his way. He was "in good humor and delighted that Italy could secure in Egypt a success that would give it that glory it had sought in vain for three centuries." Such historic aspirations obviously required rather more than a token advance without territorial objectives. It required the conquest of Egypt. It also required the resumption of the advance, and on this point, Mussolini complained, he was rather irritated with Badoglio. In Mussolini's view, Badoglio had apparently "assumed the role of retarder of Graziani's march." Graziani's caution in reserving his reply until safely returned to the bomb-proof tombs at Cirene had diverted Mussolini's anger to Badoglio. By 5 October Mussolini had apparently resolved to replace Badoglio in the spring – apparently with Graziani![46]

That worthy was unwilling to contradict Mussolini face-to-face over the date on which the offensive was to resume, but he as usual had no compunction about conveying his views through intermediaries. Immediately after the 29 September meeting, Graziani encountered Ciano in the anteroom at Palazzo Venezia. Graziani proposed, "in a tone and manner loud enough so that Badoglio could hear," to drop by the Ministry of Foreign Affairs. To Ciano, whom Mussolini had empowered to ascertain "what he really thought," Graziani insisted that he needed much more time – "at least all of November." Graziani foresaw lengthy British resistance at Mersa Matruh, and would not move without thorough logistical preparation. Prophetically, in his own case at least, he once more affirmed that retreat in the desert meant rout.[47]

Ambiguities at the Brenner. With the date the offensive would resume still unsettled, Badoglio still resisting, Graziani still in Rome because of poor flying weather, and Mussolini "very much taken" with the idea of expeditious attack, Ciano and his father-in-law set out on the evening of 3 October for the Brenner to review the "new situation" with Hitler. Mussolini was in an uncommonly good humor. For once Hitler was, if not at a loss, at least unable to escape admitting a setback.[48]

In his opening monologue, Hitler implied strongly that Sea Lion was dead. Night bombing of British cities continued, and he had hopes of yet breaking the islanders' morale. The Axis might also induce the Russians to become "active" against India, and thus create the Rome–Berlin–Tokyo–Moscow bloc that had long been an obsession of Ribbentrop's.[49] But Hitler was skeptical, and his private inclination emerged from his remark that "even in the worst case, the Russians would present no problem for Germany." Coalition plans against Britain had not diverted his thoughts from the single daring stroke that would solve all his strategic difficulties: a lightning spring campaign against Russia.

Hitler's hint made no impression on the Italians, who were unaware of the full magnitude of his aspirations and the basic framework of his strategy. Ciano, indeed, noted the increase in what he interpreted as German "anti-Bolshevism,"[50] but did not recognize that these expressions of hostility to the Soviet Union had little to do with that nation's brand of political theology, or derive primarily from the ursine Soviet reaction to the Axis guarantee of Rumania in September. They were rather a consequence of the German failure to bring Great Britain to "reason." Ciano had never read *Mein Kampf;* it was, after all, heavy going. Indeed, he was unable the following summer to perceive a "persuasive and evident reason" for the German assault on the Soviet Union.[51] But although the Italians drew no conclusions from Hitler's vaguely menacing remarks about Russia, omission of the customary homily on the dangers of Soviet Balkan aspirations, dangers the Germans had invoked all summer to temper Italian ambitions, may have struck Ciano and Mussolini as a significant lessening of German hostility to Italian action in the southeast.

As expected, the principal issue at the Brenner was the choice between Spain and France. Hitler announced his plan to bring them "into line together." He was even willing to sound out both Franco and the French in person. However, he was careful to emphasize for the Italians his deep underlying hostility to France, from which he proposed ultimately to extract Alsace-Lorraine, "strategic borders" in the west, Agadir or Casablanca, and a contribution to a future German *Mittelafrika.*[52] At the end of his monologue, Hitler added an offer of armored units, Stuka aircraft, and minelaying aircraft for the attack on Egypt. Mussolini greeted Hitler's remarks with polite agreement on grand strategy, but made clear that his acquiescence to a Franco-German-Italo-Spanish alliance had a price: immediate and full satisfaction of Italy's "modest" claims: Nice, Corsica, Tunis, and Djibouti. French collaboration with the Axis must not prejudice Italian aspirations. Hitler parried with his usual arguments, but some embarrassment. As for Spain, Mussolini maintained as he had two weeks earlier to Ribbentrop that the Axis should wait. Finally, Mussolini announced that he did not need

German aid in Africa until the third phase of the offensive, and final march on Alexandria. Even at that point, he only wanted trucks, tanks, and Stukas; he made no mention of the German units Hitler had offered. Mussolini announced that the second phase of the attack, the drive on Mersa Matruh, would begin between 10 and 15 October, and would conclude within the month. The Italians would then be able to bomb Alexandria. His generals, Mussolini confessed, had told him that it was "incautious" to move now. He had nevertheless given Graziani the "strict order" to begin the attack. Mussolini of course had done nothing of the sort – yet. As for the final stage of the conquest, Mussolini expected to begin it in mid-November. He was firmly convinced of victory. British defeat would have "immense repercussions" in India and the Middle East.

Despite the absence of any trace in the documents, one cannot exclude the possibility that the Balkans, and Greece in particular, figured in the Brenner discussions. Circumstantial evidence points in that direction. In particular, a remark of Ciano's two weeks later to Mackensen that Hitler had conceded "full freedom of action" on Greece appears to support the contention that the Germans had given Italy a "green light" at the Brenner.[53] The strategic directives Mussolini promulgated immediately upon his return to Italy did indeed revive the Greek operation, and Mussolini later implied strongly in a letter to Hitler that the matter, as well as others that do not figure in the Brenner minutes, had "been the subject of our meeting" there.[54] Roatta's correspondence with Graziani provides more direct evidence. In the week after the meeting, Roatta learned from Soddu that Greece, as well as Yugoslavia and Rumania, had indeed apparently figured in the discussions:

Greece: Germany gives Italy carte blanche.
Yugoslavia: For now, we do nothing; at the conclusion of peace, Germany supposedly will reserve for itself certain zones (Maribor, Celje, etc.), placing the rest at Italy's disposal.
Rumania: We are, in some manner, to accompany the German mission by sending a regiment (Soddu is thinking of the 3rd Grenadiers).[55]

Soddu's remarks scarcely elucidate the terms of the discussion, which may indeed have been unclear to the participants. The absence of any mention of Greece, Yugoslavia, or Rumania in the minutes of the principal conversation, at which Ciano and Ribbentrop were present, suggests that Führer and Duce had dealt with them in a private tête-à-tête.[56] Mussolini's sketchy grasp of spoken German had apparently led to misunderstandings between the two dictators in the past, and, as General Halder later noted, the Brenner conversations indeed gave rise to "a plethora of ambiguities in the [foreign] offices on either side."[57]

On Greece, Hitler in all probability gave Mussolini the usual generic assurances about Italy's Mediterranean rights. He may also have failed to restate as emphatically as had Ribbentrop in Rome the need to postpone action until after victory in the wider war. Perhaps Hitler's inability to offer definite hope of soon defeating Britain led him to soften in some manner his August veto, or, more probably, qualify it by once more expressing agreement with a preventive strike. According to reports reaching the German naval high command in late October, Hitler had given Italy "a free hand in Greece . . . in the event that a military action . . . became necessary in order to block a British initiative." Mussolini later invoked precisely that pretext in his letter to Hitler announcing the attack.[58]

But Hitler did not actually encourage the Italians to occupy Greece as part of the developing German Mediterranean strategy, as one author has suggested.[59] As will emerge, as late as 24 October Hitler proposed to draw Greece into the Axis fold by consent rather than force. Nor did the Italians' total disregard for Hitler's pet idea of a descent on Crete suggest that the Germans inspired the attack on Greece in any direct sense, or even that they tacitly approved it in the expectation of a strategic payoff in the war against Britain. Ciano's record of the Brenner conference even contains a remark of Hitler's which reads remarkably like previous German warnings against immediate attack: the war was all but won, but the Axis still had to avoid "any action that might be of less than absolute utility in the struggle . . ."[60] In the end such cautions did not weigh heavily against Hitler's assurances that Greece was and would remain part of Italy's sphere.

As for Rumania, it is significant that Hitler later felt a certain remorse over Germany's action there, which he set in motion unilaterally a week after the Brenner. Contrary to Soddu's account of what had passed between the dictators, Italy received no invitation to participate. Perhaps Hitler had had second thoughts. He was to remark later in the month that secrecy was of the utmost importance in dealing with his allies: ". . . every second Italian was either a traitor or a spy."[61] He may have had qualms about furnishing Ciano, in particular, with too detailed an account of his plans until *Luftwaffe* fighters and *Flak* were safely in position around the oil wells, where both Germans and Rumanians awaited British incursions with not entirely unjustifiable trepidation.[62] Finally, Mussolini had perhaps simply misunderstood a torrential Führer monologue. Whatever the truth, Hitler's failure to live up to his apparent assurances on Rumania had momentous consequences.

The two pillars. In the wake of the Brenner meeting, Mussolini formulated his plans for the coming months. During a lengthy conversation with Ciano on the return voyage, he announced that he would dismiss the "inept and corrupt" Ettore Muti from the secretaryship of the Party, presumably in order to prepare the home front for the winter. He intended also to "push Graziani to put forward the date of the offensive."[63]

Mussolini returned not to Rome but to his Berchtesgaden in the hills above Forlì, the villa at Rocca delle Caminate. There he produced a "Note on the Further Development of Operations in Egypt," and dispatched it to Badoglio in Rome by air courier.[64] Mussolini evidently did not yet want to confront his generals in person. The "Note" conceded that the seizure of Sidi el Barrani was an "indisputably brilliant tactical success," but only a further advance to Mersa Matruh would produce strategic success. Graziani must move between 10 and 15 October. He had a "clear superiority – at the present moment – in artillery, tanks, airplanes," and in morale. The only problem was water, but in October less was necessary than during the summer. The desert temperatures were now tolerable for acclimated Italian troops, while still unbearable for "people of the north."

Mussolini attempted to encourage Graziani further by claiming that the British would "not defend Mersa Matruh except in the measure strictly necessary to slow down our advance and disengage their formations." Mussolini may actually have believed this; his comments at the Brenner suggest that he expected the British to make their principal stand at the delta. He was in fact wrong; under the guns of their navy, the British intended to hold Mersa Matruh, the terminus of the vital railroad from Alexandria which the *Regia Aeronautica* had been unable to cut. An Italian advance would have exposed Graziani's forces to a long-prepared British counterattack, with potentially disastrous results. Nevertheless, the argument for the attack was strategically unimpeachable. As Mussolini had insisted throughout the summer, and again repeated, "the attacker must not waste time." It was true, he conceded, that postponement until November would permit further reinforcement, but it was "equally true that the British were reinforcing at an equal and perhaps greater rate." Mussolini concluded by announcing that "once arrived at Mersa Matruh, we shall see which of the pillars of the English Mediterranean defense should be brought down: whether the Egyptian or the Greek one." As Armellini noted in his diary, the Greek enterprise had reappeared, now apparently "no longer attuned to the satisfaction of Albanian irredentist claims, but to the elimination of a support of Britain. No longer, therefore, Ciamuria, but all the way to Salonika and the Greek naval bases."[65]

Actually, Armellini's analysis was not quite correct. The Greek project had passed through a number of distinct phases. In July, the Duce had (under the spur of De Vecchi's tirades) envisaged a sort of Mediterranean version of Hitler's preemptive action in Scandinavia. In mid-August, he adopted the Ciano–Jacomoni–Visconti Prasca proposals for a *coup de main* in Epirus, but planned to launch the operation after Germany's invasion of Britain. With invasion dead and buried, the Greek plan inevitably reacquired an anti-British justification – both for the consumption of the generals, and, eventually, of the Germans. But its principal purpose remained throughout that of adding Greece to what Jacomoni orotundly described as "the framework of the Empire of Rome."[66]

For the moment, despite Mussolini's renewed interest, the operation still remained in abeyance. After the Brenner, in the course of a Mussolini visit to the northern armies, Soddu suggested to Roatta that Germany's concession of carte blanche in Greece made additional reinforcements necessary for Albania. Roatta therefore secured Mussolini's approval for the alerting of two alpine divisions. But Mussolini evidently did not consider the matter of immediate importance. Roatta did not find it yet necessary to exempt the two divisions from the partial demobilization now beginning. On 12 October Roatta even reached an agreement on indefinite postponement with Visconti Prasca, who was in Rome to discuss administrative matters. "Being uncertain about what tomorrow held," Roatta noted for Graziani's benefit, "after phoning Excellency Soddu, we established that the troops located on the Greek border were to assume 'winter quarters' more or less where they are, doing the necessary [construction] work on the spot."[67]

For the moment, Egypt still remained the priority Italian theater and Mussolini's major concern. Badoglio informed Graziani, who had replied ambiguously to Badoglio's September request for an opinion on German help, that Mussolini considered "our present equipment sufficient." The dictator declined the German offer "for the imminent second phase." Graziani, before taking flight for Cirene, replied that, as he had mentioned "in the conversations on the subject," there were certain necessary conditions before he could attack with hope of success. It was "impossible for [him] to guarantee the resumption of the action for the date set (10–15 October)." If he left Rome on 6 October, he could only be back at his headquarters on the 8th and it would take him a few days more before he could have a clear picture of the possibilities. It was "superfluous" to mention, he assured Badoglio, that he would do his utmost to make the date of the attack conform as closely as possible with Mussolini's instructions.[68]

Berlin, Bucharest . . . and Rome. For the moment, Mussolini remained oblivious to these renewed difficulties on the Graziani front. After a rest at Rocca delle Caminate, he inspected Army units in the Po Valley and on the eastern border, with a cloud of generals and *gerarchi* great and small in attendance. In Berlin and Bucharest the chain of events that was to culminate in Mussolini's decision to attack Greece was in motion. On 19 September, after the return of his army intelligence chief from talks with Antonescu, Hitler informed Keitel that – unsurprisingly – he had decided to respond favorably to the Rumanian request for a military mission. Troops amounting to about one division would enter Rumania "as quickly as possible." Problems remained. The Germans had to approach the Hungarians for transit rights, and did not secure agreement until 30 September.[69] By 2 October a further difficulty had developed. From Bucharest, *United Press* carried a report that German ground and *Luftwaffe* troops were expected. This untimely disclosure placed both Germans and Rumanians in a dilemma.

Weizsäcker contacted Ribbentrop, who was on his way to the Brenner, and suggested some sort of joint German-Rumanian communiqué, franker disclosure of German plans to Rome, and consideration of what line to take should Italy, as the other guarantor of Rumania, ask to participate in the occupation. Weizsäcker added that Moscow would also need a "prior and pacifying explanation" of the action, or "disadvantageous repercussions" might ensue.[70] But Ribbentrop failed to take his chief subordinate's warning to heart. He later told Weizsäcker that he did not "feel himself guilty" of having failed to inform the Italians adequately of the move into Rumania. Ribbentrop's protestation of innocence is mildly surprising; on 24 September he had ordered Weizsäcker's deputy Woermann to avoid discussion of Rumania with Alfieri's temporary replacement, Guelfo Zamboni. Even before he received that directive, Woermann had misleadingly told the Italian diplomat that Berlin had not yet decided to send troops.[71] Ribbentrop, who did not return to the subject at the Brenner, evidently desired to prevent the Italians from learning more than he himself had doled out to Ciano in Rome. The only apparent response to Weizsäcker's plea was a telephone call to the foreign office press section in Berlin from its chief, Paul Carl Schmidt,[72] who was on Ribbentrop's train. Schmidt directed that the German press hold publication until the first foreign papers reported the actual sending of troops.[73]

Perhaps the Brenner meeting distracted Ribbentrop, for he failed to take any immediate steps to inform Germany's allies and friends of the impending move. His omission was indeed to have "disadvantageous repercussions." On 7 October, *United Press* carried a report from Bucharest that 15,000 German motorized troops had arrived in the preceding twenty-four hours. The report was wrong; the German advance party had not even left Berlin. But the news had immediate effects in Rome. A dispatch of the Italian minister in Bucharest, Pellegrino Ghigi, arrived on 8 October, found its way to Mussolini, and presumably drove the point home. The arrival of German "instruction" units was imminent, and would complete, "rapidly and totally," the task of "establishing German hegemony" in Rumania. Even at this late date Antonescu and his closest advisers were still "outspokenly desirous" of greater Italian activity in Rumania, "alongside and in agreement with Germany." But the Rumanians, Ghigi reported, did not seem "capable . . . of taking independent initiatives of any great importance."[74]

The hour was obviously late. From the Yugoslav border, where he was inspecting troops, Mussolini telephoned Ciano in Rome. He ordered a démarche in Bucharest to prompt a Rumanian request for an Italian "military mission" alongside the German one. Ciano noted that Mussolini was "furious that only the German troops are present in the oilfields." Evidently Mussolini believed the *United Press* report, and assumed the *Wehrmacht* was already on the spot. Hitler had clearly not followed up on his apparent assurances at the Brenner.

Ghigi's cautions that Antonescu dared not cross the Germans had little effect. At Mussolini's order, Ciano entrusted his representative in Bucharest with the hottest of all diplomatic hot potatoes – a step to be executed at Ghigi's own discretion. Ciano directed him to judge whether Antonescu was willing to request an Italian contingent alongside the Germans in the oilfields. The request must appear "as a natural desire of Rumania, even, and above all, in the eyes of the German government."[75] The Germans had acted behind Italy's back; two could play that game.

While awaiting results, Mussolini attempted to limit damage on the propaganda front. On 8 October the Italian press received orders not to mention
the sending of German troops to Rumania. The next day, the Ministry of
Popular Culture prepared, with Mussolini's authorization, and, in all probability, at his direct order, a press release for launching by a fictitious
"Roman Information Agency" as soon as the Germans officially announced
their action. The release stressed the strategic usefulness to Italy of the German move to secure the oilfields against British sabotage. The measure met
with "comprehension and solidarity" in Rome. The Ministry of Popular Culture apparently attached considerable importance to the prompt appearance
of the release alongside the very first German wire service reports of the troop
movement. In the small hours of 13 October, the ministry duty officer peremptorily stopped the presses at the principal Rome daily, *Il Messaggero,* until
the editors, who had begun their press run without the release, could correct
the omission.[76]

Meanwhile, the uproar in the foreign press that the second *United Press*
dispatch from Bucharest produced finally awakened Ribbentrop to the need
to placate Italians and Russians. Berlin instructed Mackensen to explain that
the Rumanian military mission question had now "entered an active stage."
Antonescu had invoked the Vienna guarantee to request help against "aerial
sabotage attempts," presumably by the British. Ribbentrop's subordinates
dispatched a similar but less specific message to Moscow, where Molotov
received the British sabotage story with scornful laughter.[77]

Ciano was more restrained. When Bismarck, acting for Mackensen, presented him with Ribbentrop's message on 10 October, Ciano received it
"without comment." Bismarck nevertheless gained the correct impression
that the communication touched a "sore spot." Mackensen later reported
that although externally the Italians were doing everything possible "to save
face with elegance," his secret informant close to the Palazzo Chigi reported
that Ciano and advisers felt the German move had taken place "outside the
common framework of Axis policy."[78]

Decision. The matter came to a head on 12 October, when Mussolini returned
from reviewing troops and Fascist youth organizations in the north. Much
unpleasant information awaited him. First, Badoglio presented Graziani's
Parthian shot – the refusal, in reply to Mussolini's "Note," to guarantee
resumption of the offensive by 10 to 15 October.[79] Second, Mussolini probably received in the course of the same day a transcript of a telephone conversation of 8 October between Ribbentrop's special press representative in
Rome, Leithe-Jaspar of the *Dienststelle Ribbentrop,* and Braun von Stumm of
the foreign office in Berlin. Tactlessly, considering that he was speaking on
a tapped line, Stumm insisted that even if the Italians wanted to publish a
reply to foreign press reports of the arrival of German troops in Rumania,
"they were not to" – the German press had received orders to remain silent.
Such arrogance was hardly likely to soothe Mussolini.[80] In addition, Ger-

man units actually began arriving in Bucharest at noon on the same day, 12 October, reportedly to cheers and cries of *"Heil!"* from the population. Mussolini was presumably aware of the event by early evening. Finally, and probably decisively, Ghigi reported that he considered it unlikely that Antonescu would dare ask for Italian units without "prior agreement between [Italy] and Germany."[81]

By the end of the day, Mussolini was beside himself. In an often and justly quoted passage, Ciano recorded his father-in-law's wrath:

above all, he is incensed about the German occupation of Rumania. He says that this has profoundly and dangerously shaken Italian public opinion, for no one expected this result from the Vienna arbitration [and the resulting guarantee]. "Hitler always faces me with *faits accomplis*. This time I will pay him back in his own coin. He will discover from the newspapers that I have occupied Greece. In this way the equilibrium will be reestablished."

Ciano asked if Mussolini had converted Badoglio. Mussolini replied that he had not, "yet," but would "hand in his resignation as an Italian if anybody [made] difficulties about fighting the Greeks." Ciano was ecstatic: "At last, the Duce seems to have decided to act." Personally, he was convinced that the operation would be "useful and easy."[82]

The immediate motives that finally impelled Mussolini to act at this point are clear. His irritation with Graziani undoubtedly contributed to his mood, and impelled him to do *something*. But it was not decisive. Not until 16 October did Mussolini receive Graziani's definitive judgment that he would not be ready for another couple of months.[83] And, as will emerge, as late as the 15th Mussolini proposed to launch the Greek attack as part of a simultaneous two-pronged offensive in which Graziani's forces would also play their part. The Greek thrust would further undermine British prestige and Britain's hold on the eastern Mediterranean. But its fundamental purpose was the obvious and long-harbored one of adding Greece to Italy's booty.

The German descent on Rumania threatened that goal, and was gratuitously humiliating into the bargain. Despite Ribbentrop's remarks to Ciano on 19 September about the impending German move, and Hitler's apparent willingness at the Brenner to concede Italian participation, Mussolini had learned of the actual occupation primarily "from the newspapers." The force of his reaction suggests that he felt personally betrayed.[84] The Germans had gone ahead brusquely and unilaterally in a situation in which they were at least formally in partnership with Italy. Although Hitler and Ribbentrop had avoided the extremes of secrecy of the days before the March 1939 Prague coup, this was not enough. Germany and Italy were now, after all, allies in war.[85]

The German action also threatened a marked loss of domestic prestige. General Armellini summed it up: "Hitler is occupying Rumania; Mussolini cannot remain at parade rest." Hitler's action seemed the final step in the establishment of German hegemony in the Balkans. Since the Anschluss, and not merely in Rumania, the Germans had proceeded through the stages of "economic penetration," "political influence," and "military control," as Ghigi had described their progress in one of his reports.[86] The exclusive Balkan hunting preserve of the Fascist state that Mussolini had attempted to safeguard since the 1920s no longer existed. Without swift and unilateral action to safeguard its interests, Italy could expect nothing more than crumbs from the German table.

But although it jolted Mussolini into action and imparted to the operation a defensive character against Germany distinct from the more purely aggressive schemes of July and August, or of the spring and summer of 1939, the German occupation of Rumania was the occasion rather than the fundamental cause of Mussolini's decision. His constant preoccupation throughout the summer with both Yugoslavia and Greece, the abandonment of the Yugoslav project only because it required German help, and his revival of the Greek action after the Brenner meeting make clear that an attack on that unfortunate country was only a matter of time. Without the Rumanian affair, Mussolini might well have postponed action – until spring.

2. Mussolini takes command

Palazzo Venezia. On the morning of 13 October Mussolini broke the news to his military subordinates. Badoglio received orders to prepare the services to attack Greece from 26 October on. The date was the consequence of the Navy's requirement, established in September, for twelve days to assemble shipping for Corfù. Badoglio, apparently without immediate objection, issued a warning order to the services.[87] The ponderous machinery of the three staffs began to turn – slowly.

As always, decision and command were easier than implementation. Nagging details remained. First and foremost was the indeterminate nature of the operation itself. Badoglio's order merely set in motion the "Contingency 'G' " plan to seize Epirus down to the Arta River, leaving the rest of Greece untouched.[88] In the "new situation," now that Britain was no longer on the verge of destruction, and was reinforcing Egypt, an attack limited to Epirus would have as its foreseeable consequence a British occupation of Greek naval and air bases. Therefore, a far more extensive action than the Army plan provided was apparently necessary. In any case, an action that went "all the way" – as Mussolini had planned even in August in the case of resistance – was more appropriate to his style, his ambition to include Greece in his Mediterranean empire, and his immediate objective of answering the German occupation of Rumania.

At 11 a.m. on 14 October Mussolini conferred with Badoglio and Roatta.[89] He informed them that "the operation against Greece will not limit itself to Ciamuria, but will take in the whole country, which in the long run may prove a nuisance." Mussolini would write to Hitler on the subject but, Roatta noted, "of the actual beginning of the operation he [would] give notice only at the last moment." Mussolini also planned to ask King Boris of Bulgaria to "descend to the sea" in Thrace when the Italians attacked. Roatta briefed Mussolini on the difficulties of extending the attack toward Salonika and Athens; that would require a further ten divisions and three months for deployment. Italy would also have to abandon the Corsica and Bizerte operations, or reduce the scope of demobilization. Mussolini apparently approved the latter alternative.

Badoglio then raised the delicate question of who was to command the imposing force of twenty divisions. The day before, Badoglio and Roatta, at the latter's prompting, had agreed to urge replacement of Visconti Prasca with some more senior commander. Visconti was later to charge that this project, of which he naturally got wind, was a plot Roatta had hatched in order to prevent him from receiving the automatic promotion to full general that command of an army of twenty divisions entailed. Perhaps Visconti Prasca was at least partly right.[90] But Roatta was on firm ground, given the rigid seniority system of the *Regio Esercito*. And, as Badoglio conceded, excellent military reasons existed for superseding Visconti Prasca, who had served under Badoglio during preparations for the Ethiopian venture, but "had never commanded anything."[91] The marshal's mistrust of Visconti's fitness for independent command soon proved all too well founded.

Mussolini evaded Badoglio's suggestion. He agreed to establish an army command under some unspecified senior general (Geloso, Ambrosio of Second Army, and Mario Vercellino of the "Po" Army were the candidates mentioned). Visconti Prasca would have a corps along with Gambara and General Enrico Francisci of the Fascist Militia, like Roatta a veteran of Guadalajara. Badoglio and Roatta presumably included the last two candidates in order to make supplanting Visconti Prasca palatable to Mussolini and Ciano. Mussolini did not, however, give up his insistence on immediate attack. Toward the close of the meeting, Roatta asked him "what was to be done in the meantime in Albania," given the warning order of the previous day specifying that the eight-division "Contingency 'G' " operation be ready to launch on 26 October. Mussolini replied – without directly confronting the issues Badoglio and Roatta had raised – that preparations were to continue, that Visconti Prasca was to remain in command for the moment, and that Gambara was to join him in some unspecified capacity. The meeting thus ended almost as inconclusively as the Mussolini–Badoglio–Graziani conference of 29 September, with one essential difference: Mussolini had set an unambiguous deadline, and had confirmed it.

Nevertheless, Mussolini's repeated insistence on 26 October did not convince Badoglio, who immediately afterward remarked to Roatta that the Greek operation would not begin before the conquest of Mersa Matruh. Even Soddu was skeptical. Mussolini's military advisers had evidently not yet understood that, in contrast to the period before 12 October, the dictator had at last set himself a course of action, and was determined to carry it out whatever difficulties the "experts" might raise.[92]

If Badoglio, Roatta, and Soddu were still oblivious to the firmness of Mussolini's intentions on 14 October, they had cause to revise their opinions the next morning. At 11 a.m. the Duce held a conference at Palazzo Venezia for all directly concerned with the Greek operation: Ciano, Jacomoni, Visconti Prasca, Badoglio, and Roatta. The last, who did not hear of the meeting until the last moment, arrived late. Roatta was surprised to learn what was afoot: *"I immediately realize[d]* [he wrote Graziani], *that yesterday's situation has changed and that it is a question of initiating operations on the 26th, with the objective of the total occupation of Greece."*[93]

That was indeed the case; Mussolini began the conference in a manner that made clear he would brook no argument:[94]

The purpose of this meeting is to define the general characteristics of the action I have decided to undertake against Greece.

This action, in its first phase, will have objectives of a naval and territorial character.

The territorial objectives are those that will secure for us all of the southern Albanian coast, those in other words which the occupation of the Ionian Islands, Zante, Kephallynia, and Corfù, and the conquest of Salonika will give us. When we reach those objectives, we shall have improved our position in the Mediterranean against England.

In a second phase, or simultaneously with these actions, the total occupation of Greece, to put it out of the war, *and to ensure that in all circumstances it will remain in our politico-economic sphere.*

Having thus defined the question, I have also established the date, which in my view cannot be postponed even by an hour: that is, the twenty-sixth of this month.

This is an action I have meditated on for many months, [since] before our entry into the war, and even before the outbreak of the war itself.

Turks and Yugoslavs, Mussolini added, would not move, and he was working to enlist King Boris as "a pawn in our game." Mussolini then asked Jacomoni for his views, which the latter expressed with characteristic ambiguity. The Albanians were "impatient and full of enthusiasm." However, the Durazzo bottleneck and the Albanian roads were causing supply problems. The Greeks were likely to fight, particularly if the Italian action were "prudent and limited," rather than "swift, resolute, and massive." Jacomoni also suggested that the Greeks might receive British aid. Here Mussolini interrupted to insist that no such aid would come. Jacomoni persisted, briefly: a partial Italian occupation of Greece would leave air bases for the British from which they could strike at southern Italy and Albania. Mussolini thereupon changed the subject, and asked about Greek public opinion. Jacomoni fell back into line; the population "appeared very profoundly depressed." Ciano added that a "sharp cleavage" divided the common people from the "plutocratic" ruling class responsible for the nation's "anglophile spirit." The lower orders were "indifferent to all events, including . . . our invasion." Ciano's assessment contrasted dramatically with the reports Grazzi continued to forward from Athens.[95]

On the military side, Visconti Prasca was no less optimistic: his troops would swiftly execute "a series of envelopments." He had prepared the operation "down to the smallest details"; it was as perfect as "humanly possible." The general did express reservations over the feasibility of the Salonika drive because of the approaching rainy season. But Mussolini insisted: the British must not land there, as they had in the previous World War. Mussolini then solicited from his assistants a staged border incident to give "the appearance of irresistible necessity [*fatalità*]" to the operation. A "bit of smoke" would mask the aggression and provide "a justification of a metaphysical character." Jacomoni, Visconti Prasca, and Ciano volunteered the services of their Albanian irregulars. Mussolini set the date for 24 October, two days before the main attack; the resulting incidents convinced no one, despite the wounding of two unfortunate *Carabinieri*. [96]

After Mussolini had ordered Visconti Prasca not to "preoccupy himself excessively with losses," and Visconti alleged that he had ordered his battalions to attack relentlessly, "even against a division," Badoglio finally spoke up. He agreed with Mussolini that British land help to Greece was unlikely, although air support was possible. However, a simultaneous attack on Mersa Matruh would keep the British occupied. Graziani, Badoglio claimed, could be ready by 26 October. The remark evidently aroused Mussolini's enthusiasm:

I would prefer Graziani's attack to take place a few days in advance. The fact of the conquest of Mersa Matruh will render even more difficult the possibility of . . . [British] help [to the Greeks], especially in view of the probability that we shall not stop. Once the Egyptian pivot is lost, *the British Empire would be in a state of defeat even if London could still hold out.*

Mussolini was still looking forward to a triumphal entry into Alexandria in the near future. Graziani's preliminary objections had not affected his optimism, nor induced him, as some have suggested, to withdraw tacitly from the war against Britain in favor of a war more attuned to Italy's limited capabilities, a Balkan *"Sonderkrieg"* against Greece. [97] Mussolini wanted both Alexandria and Athens. But a subtle change in his priorities had occurred. The Egyptian offensive was now, at least provisionally, subordinate to the Greek one. Mussolini's most urgent immediate purpose was to counter the German move into Rumania. To this end, Graziani's attack took on the role of a diversion, a thrust that would keep the RAF occupied while Visconti Prasca crushed the Greeks.

Badoglio nevertheless had qualms. He conceded that tactically "the operation for Epirus planned by Visconti Prasca is fine [*va bene*]." "Given security on our left flank" (by the Bulgarians), Badoglio considered that "the enemy forces should not present much difficulty." But he had his doubts about the strategic soundness of the action. To stop in Epirus "did not correspond to the situation." "I do not exaggerate," he proceeded, "in saying that we must occupy Crete and the Morea as well if we want to occupy Greece." The occupation of the whole of Greece would still require twenty divisions and three months. Roatta spoke up, but not to support Badoglio. As he later confessed, he had concluded that further objections "would not have served to avert the war Mussolini wanted."[98] Without insisting on the need for more time, Roatta observed that "in order not to stop with Epirus, we would have to intensify the shipment of troops [to Albania]." It was important not to "give the impression that we are out of breath and cannot proceed further." Roatta therefore proposed to "study immediately the problem of the total occupation of Greece."

Mussolini, without contradiction, thereupon predicted that the "liquidation of Epirus" would be finished by 10–15 November, leaving a full month for the transport and deployment of the second-phase troops. Visconti Prasca spoke up with an objection that was hard to counter. The Albanian ports were so poorly equipped that more troops could only disembark with any speed when captured Greek harbors were available. If Durazzo remained the principal Italian base for the Salonika drive, each single division would require a month for shipment and deployment. Mussolini, as with Jacomoni's tactful doubts, changed the subject: "To clarify the conceptions we are dealing with," he wanted to know "how the march on Athens after the occupation of Epirus was viewed."

From this point on, even the feeble opposition of Badoglio and the doubts of Jacomoni subsided. Visconti Prasca did not see any great difficulty in marching on Athens. No more than "five or six divisions" would be necessary. Badoglio apparently agreed; Athens was more urgent than Salonika, where he did not expect a British landing. Roatta concurred, although to confuse the Greeks he insisted that two divisions exert "pressure" toward Salonika. Mussolini concluded that "ideas were becoming more definite: operation in Epirus – Salonika – observation of that which might result from Bulgarian intervention, which I consider probable." Naturally, Mussolini "agreed fully" on the occupation of Athens.

Now that Mussolini had secured unanimity, the problem of how to get to Athens remained. Visconti Prasca asserted that the capital was 250 kilometers from Epirus, over "high, jagged, and denuded hills," with a "mediocre" road network. But the general added comfortingly that the valleys ran east to west – in the direction of Athens. Roatta observed that this was "only true up to a point": a 2,000-meter-high mountain range (the Pindus) stood in the way. But Visconti Prasca was confident: there were "a large number of mule tracks." He had traveled the route many times. Mussolini evidently assumed that Visconti Prasca's assurances closed the matter, and pressed on to the question of reinforcements for the second phase. Visconti Prasca now had a solution to that problem as well. The three additional mountain divisions he wanted could land "in a single night" at the Epirote port of Arta, once his troops had taken it. No one challenged this inspired improvisation. The Navy, like the Air Force, had no representative at the conference, presumably because Mussolini hoped to avoid a united front of the service chiefs and Badoglio. Roatta, who must have realized from long experience with troop movements that an Arta landing was anything but simple, was presumably too cowed to object. The meeting, which had lasted about an hour and a half, closed with Mussolini's summing up: "offensive in Epirus; observation and pressure on Salonika, and, in a second phase, march on Athens."

"At all costs." The meeting of 15 October is perhaps the best single illustration of Mussolini's military dilettantism, of the incompetence of his generals, and of the subservience to which he had, although with difficulty, now reduced them. Mussolini himself had no clear idea of the technical limitations of his military instrument. He was convinced, rightly enough, that it could and should be able to function more effectively than it had up to this point. He found the thought of "anyone [making] difficulties about fighting the Greeks" humiliating and enraging. But he did not pause to reflect that Albania, far from being a "bulwark" dominating the Balkans, was as yet unsuited to supporting more than the small forces that Visconti Prasca had already deployed there. The regime had built new roads, but they were too few, and many existed as yet only on paper.[99] The bottlenecks at Durazzo and Valona remained almost insuperable obstacles to the landing and support of large forces.

Mussolini's action in forcing the operation on his military leaders was hardly illogical in terms of his own premises and goals. He had, he felt, been right in the past – in Ethiopia and Spain. His entry into the war still appeared a shrewd and well-timed stroke. He had been justified, so far, in dismissing the "usual difficulties of the experts" in Egypt. The Greek operation would presumably take a similar course. Moreover, Mussolini's victory over the experts had been an easy one. He had taken care not to consult the service chiefs as a group, and had succeeded in dividing and overriding Badoglio and Roatta. Badoglio had feebly insisted on twenty divisions and three months, only to succumb to Mussolini's "two-phase" plan, which seemed to solve the problem. Even Visconti Prasca had doubts about the logistical underpinnings of that seductive project. In the end, however, no one had dissented.

In the aftermath of the conference, Badoglio ineffectually attempted to wriggle off the hook.[100] In this endeavor the Navy, apparently piqued at its exclusion from the decision making, helped. On the afternoon of 15 October, Cavagnari's deputy Somigli told Roatta that the operation was "inopportune." Italy was about to occupy continental Greece "slowly, *by land and on foot.*" As soon as Italian troops crossed the border, the British would commence the occupation "which we are attacking Greece in order to avoid." The action would create further difficulties in supplying Libya and the Dodecanese, and would put British air bases within range of the fleet at Taranto. But neither Somigli nor Cavagnari dared say anything of the sort to Mussolini. The Navy also doubted the vital point of the Mussolini–Visconti Prasca "two-phase" plan, the Arta landing. Harbor depth was apparently inadequate. A shortage of shipping lengthened from "a single night" to an entire month the disembarkation of the three mountain divisions Visconti Prasca had effortlessly conjured up at Palazzo Venezia. Badoglio seconded the Navy's complaints about the strategic inadvisability of the whole affair. He had now discovered that Visconti Prasca's claim of 2 : 1 superiority in Epirus was simply untrue: the Italians had a slight edge over the Greeks only before Greek general mobilization. But the next day, Badoglio failed to press the point home to Mussolini at the usual daily audience. Mussolini parried with the reassuring news that he had written to King Boris.

That afternoon, the situation, in Badoglio's eyes, changed. Cavagnari delivered a memorandum insisting that landings in the Gulf of Arta were definitely unfeasible. This new and highly significant fact allowed Badoglio to call a meeting of the service chiefs for the next morning, 17 October. At the conference, Cavagnari briefed his colleagues. The only suitable spot was the open beach north of Preveza, and unloading Visconti Prasca's three reinforcing divisions there would require three months. Roatta recommended abandoning the idea in favor of transporting the divisions directly to Albania and attacking only when they were on the spot. Badoglio predictably agreed, and proposed that "in view of the fact that there had emerged an entirely new and different element from that which General Visconti had maintained (the impossibility of a landing in the Gulf of Arta), and that (a fact of lesser importance) the numerical relationship between the opposing forces in Epirus is also different from that mentioned earlier," he would ask Mussolini for an audience for himself and the service chiefs the next morning, in order to decide "what was to be done." Badoglio added that Mussolini had planned that the attack on Mersa Matruh should precede or at least begin simultaneously with the Greek operation. This, too, was now apparently impossible. A memorandum of Graziani's announcing that he could not move for at least two more months had just reached the *Comando Supremo*.[101]

To prepare the ground for his remonstrance to Mussolini, Badoglio visited Ciano and spoke "with great seriousness" and a certain element of bluff. The three service chiefs had "unanimously pronounced themselves" against the Greek action (a claim Roatta's account of that morning's meeting hardly bears out). Badoglio asserted that "present forces would not be adequate" and that the Navy considered a landing impractical. He warned that the prolongation of the war meant "the exhaustion of our slim resources." Politically, Ciano insisted, the moment was ideal: Greece was isolated. Military affairs were Badoglio's province, Ciano noted disingenuously: "Badoglio will have to tell Mussolini without reticence what he has told me."[102] Ciano had done his best to set the operation rolling; he now sanctimoniously invoked his civilian status as an excuse for taking no action on Badoglio's feeble protests. Badoglio soon received worse news. On the afternoon of 17 October, Cavagnari sent the latest word on the Arta question. The Greeks had dredged a new access channel, permitting deep-draft ships to use the harbor. As Badoglio contemptuously remarked to Roatta, the original memorandum Cavagnari had read to the service chiefs "was not worth a cigar butt."

Later commentators, such as Faldella, have described Badoglio's proposal as an attempt to confront Mussolini with the concerted opposition of the service chiefs to the operation on strategic grounds.[103] But that interpretation credits Badoglio and colleagues with more courage and prescient opposition to the Greek action than they showed at their 17 October meeting. According to Armellini, Cavagnari had at least raised one strategic issue, the possibility that British aircraft might use Greek bases to drive the fleet from Taranto. But the admiral failed to push the point.[104] Badoglio was not prepared to address such potentially explosive issues with Mussolini, who had already disregarded similar objections on 15 October. Badoglio hoped rather to smother the Greek operation, from which he and his associates feared inconvenience rather than disaster, under a plethora of technical difficulties. Simultaneously, he apparently hoped to influence Mussolini indirectly through the allegedly unanimous and collegial manner in which Roatta, Cavagnari, and Pricolo had supposedly "pronounced" against action.

Cavagnari's reversal on the Arta landing thus removed Badoglio's foremost technical argument, and left him helpless when Soddu and Mussolini took the offensive the next day. Soddu had accompanied Mussolini on a tour of the steelworks at Terni, in central Italy, on 17 October, and had spent much of the day in conference with Mussolini in the latter's special train. Back in Rome by evening, Soddu learned from Roatta what was afoot, and immediately laid down the law: ". . . it has already been decided that the operation will begin on the 26th." Soddu contacted Badoglio's assistant Armellini and advised him to find a way to avoid convening the service chiefs. The next morning, both Soddu and Ciano were up and about at an uncharacteristically early hour to head Badoglio off. The sources do not make clear the exact sequence of events, but Badoglio apparently threatened resignation to Soddu. Mussolini, whom Ciano apprised of Badoglio's recalcitrance, thereupon had "a violent explosion of rage," and called Badoglio's bluff. At 0920 hours, Armellini called Roatta: the service chiefs' meeting with Mussolini would not take place.[105]

In a tirade to Ciano, Mussolini proclaimed that he would personally go to Greece "to witness the incredible shame of Italians who are afraid of the Greeks." He intended "to march at all costs." If Badoglio indeed offered his resignation, the dictator would accept it on the spot. But as Ciano noted, Badoglio failed to offer his resignation when he called on Mussolini at the normally appointed hour of 11 a.m. Badoglio did not even voice the objections made to Ciano the day before. All Badoglio secured was a two-day postponement. He proposed to send Visconti a further division, and to straighten out the logistical impasse that was already developing.[106]

Badoglio and Mussolini also discussed Graziani's latest memorandum. Mussolini had earlier in the morning already been in an "appalling humor over the Graziani affair." He was now "rabid," and momentarily despondent about the whole Egyptian enterprise. Badoglio told Roatta later in the day that Mussolini "would probably no longer give the order to proceed on Mersa Matruh, where we would be in an even worse position than at Sidi Barrani." On 18 October, Mussolini had Badoglio convey Graziani a stinging reprimand, and an order, soon countermanded, to do as he liked.[107]

Visions of victory. Military preparations for the attack on Greece now went forward rapidly and chaotically. Pricolo informed Roatta on 18 October that the Durazzo bottleneck would apparently prevent the additional air units transferring to Albania from receiving bombs, equipment, and ground crews before 3 or 4 November. Remarkably, in view of Badoglio's enthusiasm for massive bombardment, the Air Force planned to provide only sixty bombers and forty-five fighters in close support. Pricolo sought first to destroy the enemy's air force, then the Greek navy and its bases, and finally, and decidedly last, to attack troop concentrations and defensive positions. He also hoped to oppose a British landing on Crete, which he considered likely.[108]

On the ground, the Army staff scrambled to ready units to reinforce Visconti Prasca. Immediately after the 15 October conference, Roatta secured from Soddu a provisional suspension of demobilization for the classes of 1915 and 1916. But Soddu insisted on sending the class of 1914 home on schedule, although Mussolini had on 14 October approved in principle Roatta's proposal to cancel demobilization of units destined for Albania and for support of the plans against France. Roatta ordered the readying for shipment by 31 October of two infantry divisions, two alpine divisions, and a motorized division. The next day, Badoglio ordered that Roatta exploit the two-day delay secured from Mussolini to supply Visconti Prasca with an additional infantry division. The Albanian Command could then move the "Piemonte" division, in reserve on the left flank near Korçë, south to back up the Epirus thrust. But the infantry divisions Roatta had ordered readied in Italy were at half strength following the release of the older classes. Roatta therefore proposed the substitution of the motorized division, which came from the "Po" Army and was therefore closer to war strength; Visconti Prasca had just asked for a division of that type to land at Arta and exploit his coming breakthrough. But Arta was not currently available, and Durazzo, far from the front, had the only harbor installations capable of unloading vehicles. A shipping shortage further complicated the problem. The motorized division would therefore probably require fifteen days or more to cross and unload, and would not be ready for use before mid- or late November even though its greater mobility once landed would render its arrival on the actual battlefield as swift as that of a regular infantry division. The Air Force's transport requirements and the need to ship mountain artillery and antiaircraft batteries to Visconti Prasca also made immediate decision on priorities essential. Badoglio decreed that the Air Force should take precedence, the artillery and antiaircraft guns come next, and the motorized division follow. A mountain infantry division, which by then would be up to strength, would go last of all.[109]

Roatta informed Visconti Prasca on 19 October that the motorized division would probably not complete unloading in Albania before mid-November. That worthy made no objection. Later he attempted to obfuscate his own heavy responsibilities with a barrage of accusations that Rome, and particularly Roatta, had first plotted his replacement and then failed to reinforce him because of the chaotic condition of the home Army, of which Visconti Prasca had received no warning.[110] Despite Visconti Prasca's ex post facto fulminations, the port bottleneck was the principal obstacle to timely reinforcement; indeed, it rendered difficult the support of the units already in place. Civilian traffic added to the confusion, especially at Durazzo. The weather also proved uncooperative, particularly toward the end of the month. Shortly after the attack began the Navy regretfully estimated that the low capacity of Valona and Durazzo, even in the absence of unfavorable weather and enemy action, would delay until mid-December the unloading of the three divisions by then destined for Albania.[111]

A major strategic difficulty also developed, although the Italian military leadership failed to appreciate its seriousness. Mussolini had dispatched his promised letter to King Boris of Bulgaria on 18 October. It apprised that sly and experienced Balkan monarch of Italy's decision to begin "the settling of accounts with Greece" by the end of the month, and offered Bulgaria a "historic opportunity" to participate, in pursuit of its goal of an outlet to the Aegean in Thrace. Boris declined with exquisite politeness. Hostile neighbors and Bulgaria's military weakness precluded action.[112] The refusal had no effect on Italian military planning. The "Contingency 'G' " plan merely presupposed Bulgaria's benevolent neutrality, and Badoglio and Roatta continued to assume that the mere threat of Bulgarian action would root the bulk of the Greek army to the spot in Thrace while Visconti Prasca's forces excised Epirus. They mistakenly ascribed to the Greeks their own obsession with being strong everywhere.

One detail did trouble Roatta and Badoglio as the deadline approached. From about 20 October on, the realization dawned in Rome that the Greeks were mobilizing, and that they had concentrated four divisions in Macedonia, opposite Visconti Prasca's left flank at Korçë. By 24 October, Badoglio's staff was aware that 220,000 men in eight divisions would face the Italian forces once Greek mobilization was complete. Only six divisions, it now appeared, would remain facing Bulgaria. The Greeks would have a further four divisions in reserve, and 300,000 men left over! The only Italian advantage was that until the Greeks completed their mobilization, Visconti Prasca would have a slight numerical edge (150,000 men against 120,000 men) in Epirus.[113]

Roatta had already concluded by 21 October that the situation on Visconti Prasca's left flank was ominous. He succeeded in securing diversion of the "Piemonte" division from the task of backing up the thrust in Epirus to that of reinforcing the Korçë sector. He also suggested to Visconti Prasca that the remaining division on the Yugoslav border, the "Venezia," move south for the same purpose as soon as Yugoslavia confirmed neutrality.[114] But neither Rome nor Tirana took more urgent steps. Mussolini remained adamant. A steady, drenching, torrential downpour began in Albania on 26 October, washing out roads and bridges, and turning the terrain over which Visconti Prasca was to advance into a sea of mud. Roatta's operations chief, General Francesco Rossi, cabled from Tirana to suggest that Rome give the Albanian Command discretion to set the attack date. The Navy seconded the proposal, presumably because of heavy seas, which subsequently caused the abandonment of the Corfù landing. Badoglio took the issue to Mussolini, who predictably if imprudently decreed that the date of 28 October remained "immovable."[115] Mussolini presumably had in mind the success his prodding of Graziani in August and September had brought. In any case, he had to act before a new German veto could stop him, and by 26 October, as will emerge, Hitler was on his way south.

Later, the generals claimed they had only acquiesced because of the prospect of Bulgarian assistance, and above all because Mussolini, Ciano, and Jacomoni had assured them that Greek political collapse would reduce the operation to an occupation against token resistance.[116] Ciano had indeed given substance to this claim with his 15 October remark about the alleged gulf between the anglophile, plutocratic Greek ruling class and the brutish masses, indifferent to everything, including Italian invasion. Mussolini lent further plausibility to the generals' claims in a harangue to a service chiefs' meeting in November, after the initial Italian defeat. He insisted he had been deceived. Jacomoni, particularly, had promised an uprising in Ciamuria, and upon this premise, Mussolini insisted, the operation had rested. But in October neither Mussolini, nor Ciano, nor Jacomoni expected "politics" to carry the burden. To Mussolini such an idea would have been uncongenial in any case: witness his instructions to Visconti to pay no attention to losses. Mussolini explained to Ciano on 23 October that the first blows had to be "very heavy." He hoped that "everything [would] fall to pieces at the first shock," and exhorted Visconti Prasca on the eve of action to attack "with the greatest possible decisiveness and violence." Mussolini demanded a *Blitzkrieg,* not a *Blumenkrieg.*[117]

Ciano, through Jacomoni, did attempt to apply to Greece the same systematic buying up of political opponents that had proved so successful in Albania in 1939. Jacomoni's creature, the Albanian Fascist magnate Nebil Dino, reported from Athens that he had had "interesting conversations." Not trusting Grazzi, Ciano sent that troublesome but occasionally useful ornament of the regime, Curzio Suckert Malaparte, to the Greek capital. Malaparte was to report on conditions there and to tell Grazzi that the minister "could write as he liked," but Ciano was "going to make war on Greece just the same." When Bastianini stopped in to see Ciano in late October and expressed doubts about the action, Ciano assured him that it would be a

"military promenade." Pressed, he attempted to imply that bribery had prepared the way. But Bastianini's account suggests strongly that Ciano was
relying on the military to carry the operation through. Privately, like Mussolini, Ciano was bellicose. When Pricolo briefed him on the plan of attack
on 24 October, Ciano pronounced it "good, because energetic and decisive."
Like Mussolini, he felt "a hard blow at the outset" might "make everything
crumble in a few hours." Jacomoni was apparently the source of Ciano's
conception, although predictions of military victory did not prevent Jacomoni from requesting additional funds to supplement the five million lire
already appropriated for "political" purposes.[118]

Ciano showed no enthusiasm whatsoever for a diplomatic solution. His
ultimatum for delivery to the Greeks was mere window dressing. Ciano
ordered Grazzi to present it to Metaxas a scant three hours before the invasion
began, too late for negotiation. In the document itself, the Italian government demanded the right to occupy "certain strategic points." But Ciano
was so little interested in a bloodless outcome that he failed to inform Grazzi
what strategic points Rome had in mind, although Grazzi had just reported
that the Greeks were now worried enough to consider joining "an anti-
British combination that would include all the Mediterranean powers." The
Greek foreign ministry was indeed desperate. Its chief, probably acting on
his own initiative, told Erbach but not Grazzi that Greece would "show
understanding" toward an Axis demand for bases, an attitude that foreshad-
owed tentative Greek attempts to seek reinsurance with Germany even after
the Italians had attacked.[119]

In any case, whatever political expectations the Italian leadership may
have harbored played no major role in planning. The military's surrender to
Mussolini was a consequence of pusillanimity, of Mussolini's adroit maneuvering, and of his increasing determination to have his way. It also derived
from the generals' firm conviction that the operation, although strategically
inopportune, was eminently feasible tactically. Badoglio and the rest
assumed throughout that the Greeks would fight – halfheartedly and incom-
petently. SIM's latest assessment of the Greek army was more than mildly
scornful. The great majority of Greek unit commanders, "although well
equipped intellectually," did not seem fully up to maintaining "that cohesion of will and spirit which is necessary to face the struggle." The quality
of the noncommissioned officers was "not very high," and the troops were
"difficult to command," for they mirrored "the characteristics of the Greek
people, [characteristics] that are for the most part negative from the military
point of view: impatience with discipline, small desire to work, easily roused
to enthusiasm but equally easily inclined to despondency."[120] Such comi-
cally unselfconscious chauvinism goes far to explain Badoglio's offhanded
approval of the Epirus operation at Palazzo Venezia. Even the King, who
should have known better, predicted as late as 5 November that "at the first
hard blow" the Greek army would "begin to crumble, and no one [would]
succeed in stopping it."[121]

Roatta did toy with the prospect that an "exceptionally favorable situation (serious Greek internal collapse and consequent abolition of resistance worthy of note)" might telescope the Epirus phase into the march on Athens, and eliminate the need for an intervening buildup. But this delightful possibility was not a precondition for the Epirus attack. Roatta explicitly assured Badoglio and the service chiefs on 17 October that the "conquest of Epirus with currently available forces" was possible, although he added that a long wait would ensue before the reinforcements needed for the second phase arrived.[122]

Nor did Badoglio himself show any interest in a political solution. When Roatta, having "heard talk" of an Italian ultimatum to Greece, prepared on his own initiative a staff study "for the possibility that Greece will declare itself in agreement with the Axis," Badoglio offhandedly dismissed it: "Fine — I'll read it when the collapse comes."[123] Badoglio also rejected out of hand a suggestion from Roatta that the consul on Corfù should inform the Greek local authorities that the landing force had orders only to fire if fired on. "This is war — and nothing else," was Badoglio's lapidary response — a significant contrast with his reluctance to fire on the French in June.[124] Badoglio wrote with evident relish to De Vecchi on 22 October about beginning "the punitive expedition against Greece," and ordered him to torpedo "everything that flies the Greek flag" after midnight on the 27th. On 24 October, at the last service chiefs' meeting before the attack, the marshal even spoke of "launching" a division in the direction of Salonika, in addition to the Epirus thrust.[125] He shared the King's expectation that a crushing Italian blow would throw the Greeks back in disorder and ruin. Italy was, after all, a great power — and some British authorities, who should have known better, also expected the Greeks to "crumple up."[126] A month later, after the consequences were more than clear, Soddu provided a fair summary of the attitude of the Italian leadership on the eve of the operation:

The war against Greece was begun in the conviction, common to all, that the enemy was devoid of serious military qualities: this atmosphere of "military promenade" resulted in disorientation as soon as we realized that the enemy, sufficiently well organized and enjoying numerical superiority, was reacting in a manner that had not been foreseen.[127]

Declaration of independence. The diplomatic preparations for the campaign were less involved than the military ones. Neither Mussolini nor Ciano believed that the Turks would aid their Greek allies; the Balkan Pact merely obligated Turkey to intervene if Bulgaria also attacked Greece. As for Yugoslavia, Ciano was confident. He benevolently informed Belgrade that Italy planned "precautionary measures" against Greece, but was in no way hostile to Yugoslavia. The Yugoslav minister for foreign affairs, Alexander Cincar-Marković, responded with "great satisfaction," and obsequiously paid tribute to "the magnanimity so far shown by Italy." Ciano also proposed to "smooth the waters" in Moscow by conferring with the Soviet ambassador immediately after the attack had begun. Mussolini approved; the démarche could obviously do no harm. To Ciano, the gesture meant more: he noted that it might "perhaps prepare the terrain for the future."[128] He presumably had in mind a renewal of the Russo-Italian contacts Germany had vetoed.

The major diplomatic problem was Germany, and this problem only Mussolini could solve. After announcing to his ministers on 19 October that action was "imminent," although without specifying its direction,[129] Mussolini retired to Rocca delle Caminate to compose the letter to Hitler he had mentioned to Roatta and Badoglio on 14 October. The letter was the cleverest the Duce had written since his long communication to the Führer in January. Mussolini began by announcing that he had thought long and hard over "some of the problems that were the object of our examination" at the Brenner, and had reached certain conclusions he felt bound to impart.[130] French collaboration with the Axis was unthinkable. The French were secretly pro-British, and were in touch with London through Lisbon. If they joined the Axis, they would attempt to monopolize credit for victory over Britain, and would "be capable of presenting us with the bill." Mussolini once more demanded an immediate peace treaty to secure Italy's "modest" claims. He then passed on to what he termed the "English positions on the continent," which he listed at length, although with a certain geographical license: Portugal, Yugoslavia, Greece, Turkey, Egypt, Switzerland. He was certain that Hitler would agree on the need to "unhinge" them, if the war continued. The Yugoslav state, "as it is now," was unacceptable, although Mussolini did not intend to move in that direction now. For Greece, however, he had decided to "end the delays, and that right soon."[131] Greece was a cornerstone of British naval strategy. It had "an English king, an English political class, and an immature people trained to hate Italy." Since May, Greece had placed its naval and air bases "at the disposal of Great Britain"; in the last several days, British officers had allegedly "taken possession of all the airfields in Greece." Mussolini summed up: "Greece is in the Mediterranean what Norway was in the North Sea, and must not escape the same fate."

As for Egypt, Mussolini emphasized that the "resumption of operations [was] subordinated to a heavy task of logistical preparation" similar to that which Sea Lion had required. Mussolini nevertheless hoped to conduct operations on the Greek and Egyptian fronts simultaneously; he had evidently recovered from his earlier despondency about the North African situation. After the conquest of Mersa Matruh, he would have to "examine" with Hitler the question of assistance in the form of German "armored equipment." Finally, after a parting shot at the Swiss ("with its incomprehensibly hostile attitude Switzerland is posing the question of its own existence"),[132] Mussolini again insisted that Spanish nonbelligerence was currently more convenient than Spanish intervention. The Axis should only play the Spanish card if the war were to drag on through all of 1941, or if the United States became an open belligerent. Mussolini closed by once more implying that all of the questions just raised had been "the subject of our meeting at the Brenner."

The letter was a *tour de force*. In it, Mussolini had attacked all of the foundations of the German Mediterranean strategy that Hitler had attempted to lay at the Brenner. Mussolini refused to admit France to the continental coalition, and, on top of this, demanded his pound of flesh immediately. On Greece, Mussolini proposed to act on the basis of a series of flimsy excuses about Greco-British collusion. To block possible objections, he had invoked the example of German preemptive action in Norway and Hitler's consistent approval of similar Italian operations in the Mediterranean, an approval Hitler had presumably reaffirmed at the Brenner. As for Egypt, Mussolini now refused point-blank to permit German ground units in North Africa, although Hitler may not have caught this last barb, due to an error in the German translation of the letter.[133] Mussolini's remarks about the necessity of thorough logistical preparation, similar to that for Sea Lion, must have nevertheless sounded ominous. Finally, Mussolini's hostility to immediate Spanish entry into the war appeared to rule out the Gibraltar operation. To Hitler, the document could only have read as a total rejection of German help in the Mediterranean, and as an uncompromising assertion of Italian freedom of action. Italy would do it itself.

After composing his letter, Mussolini returned to Rome on 22 October. Ciano noted that Mussolini's reticence in the letter about the actual date of the operation was, naturally enough, deliberate: "He fears that a halt order will once again arrive." "Many signs," Ciano continued, suggested "that in Berlin they are not enthusiastic about a move of ours on Athens." Ciano, presumably at Mussolini's instructions, forwarded the letter to Berlin by courier on 23 October. It did not arrive there until the next evening, and Hitler had long since departed for the west in order to convert French and Spaniards.[134]

Berlin: warning, but no decision. Ciano was quite correct about the lack of enthusiasm an Italian move against Greece aroused in Berlin. But Hitler took a considerably more hesitant and ambiguous line than in August. The Germans needed Italian cooperation in order to "clean out the Mediterranean" that winter. As Hitler lamented to Field Marshal von Brauchitsch of the German army high command on 10 October, "Italy [was] limited in its effectiveness as an ally by the passivity of the generals and the internal resistance of Ciano."[135] Under these circumstances, Hitler had to squeeze maximum advantage from his personal rapport with Mussolini. The latter's annoying pressure at the Brenner for an immediate draconian peace with France presumably warned Hitler that he must handle his ally even more carefully than hitherto.

The news (vague at first, and then increasingly detailed and precise) that Italy was preparing to attack Greece therefore did not lead to results even remotely comparable to the repeated warnings to Rome that Ribbentrop and the *Wehrmacht* high command had fired off in August. First of the warnings was a Mackensen report of 16 October that relayed complaints from Ciano and Mussolini about the German consul-general in Tirana, who had in September indiscreetly predicted to his Greek colleague that Germany would not permit an Italian attack. In his protest, Ciano remarked to Mackensen not once, but twice that Italy was "on the eve of a conflict" with Greece. Mackensen downplayed the importance of the remark, and concluded two days later that "[u]nless . . . the Greek theme was dealt with in a new light at the Brenner conversation," Mussolini would hold his hand until after British defeat.[136]

This information was too vague to cause alarm at Hitler's mountain retreat at Berchtesgaden, the *Berghof,* despite knowledge there that the Greek theme had indeed appeared in a new light at the Brenner. But on 19 October Mackensen soon relayed more definite, if confusing, warnings. Military sources close to the Italian Ministry of War were predicting a synchronized offensive against Greece and Egypt on 23 October. In Greece the objectives were Athens and Salonika, but not Crete or the Peloponnesus. Ciano, Mackensen reported, had confidently predicted that the Turks would not join an Italo-Greek conflict, and had remarked that "Italy had full freedom of action with respect to Greece, as indeed the Führer had conceded to the Duce."

As with his remark about "the eve of a conflict," Ciano was perhaps attempting to undermine in advance future German complaints of nonconsultation. But he obviously did not intend to give the game away, and in the event his studied vagueness was successful. Mackensen informed Berlin that Ciano's words were "very noteworthy" when seen in connection with talk in military circles about an impending operation. But he did not yet predict an attack on Greece, presumably because he had no evidence that Mussolini himself, "whose voice in the matter [was] the only decisive one," had come around to Ciano's point of view.[137]

Berlin did not immediately respond, although reports about imminent Italian action continued. The *Luftwaffe* liaison officer in Rome, General Max von Pohl, reported on 18 October that a lieutenant colonel on Pricolo's staff had told him Italy intended to attack Epirus on the 25th or 26th, and reach Athens "within seven days."[138] But not all the reports reaching the German foreign office and *Wehrmacht* high command were ominous. On 23 October, General von Rintelen talked with Roatta, who was reassuring. The claims that Italy intended to attack Greece shortly were mere "rumor," and a landing on Crete "had never been considered," since it would involve the unacceptable risk of a full-scale fleet action.[139] The next day, Badoglio was similarly evasive: Italy had information that the British intended to occupy Greek territory. On the Italian side, "all preparations had been made, in order to intervene as soon as the first Englishman set foot on Greek soil." Badoglio promised dutifully to inform the German attaché when and if that occurred. Almost simultaneously, Mackensen reported that General von Pohl emphatically judged that Italy would strike "in the coming days." This news fitted in with a whole series of "thoroughly reliable reports." But neither the Italian government nor the Italian military authorities had said anything to Mackensen or his attachés about the matter, and Mackensen ventured no definitive judgment of his own.[140] On the day Mussolini's letter arrived in Berlin, the Germans still had no clear picture of what impended.

Appropriately enough, the German reaction to these reports was ambiguous and confused. Ambassador Karl Ritter, the Wilhelmstrasse's political troubleshooter, was in charge at the foreign office on 18 and 19 October while Ribbentrop prepared to depart with Hitler for the long excursion through occupied France to meet Laval, Franco, and Pétain. Later, in the course of the "search for the guilty ones" who had purportedly failed to inform Hitler of Rome's Greek plans, Ritter summarized the events of those days in a memorandum.[141] On the 18th, he had apparently received a 17 October telegram from Pohl which has not survived, but which probably contained the first definite word of what was afoot. Ritter prepared a telegram for Rome, directing Mackensen to approach Ciano and put a stop to it. On the 19th, Ribbentrop, who in the meantime had seen the draft telegram, telephoned Ritter from south Germany and told him that "we could not hold back the Italian government with such an emphatic démarche."[142] Ribbentrop was willing to consider a "friendly inquiry," and gave Ritter permission to draft and send one.

Before Ritter could do this, Mackensen's telegrams arrived, reporting the rumors in Italian war ministry circles, the second talk with Ciano, and Pohl's prediction. Ritter therefore telephoned Ribbentrop, who had not yet received the second of Mackensen's telegrams; Ritter read it to him. When the ambassador reached Ciano's remark about the "full freedom of action" Hitler had purportedly conceded, Ribbentrop broke off and ordered the "friendly inquiry" stopped. The matter now had to go before the Führer. An hour and a half later, Baron Gustav von Steengracht, Ribbentrop's *chef de cabinet,* called Ritter to announce that "the Führer had decided that no question should be directed to Rome."

Weizsäcker, who talked with Ribbentrop on 20 October, immediately before the departure for the west, responded the next day to Mackensen's suggestion that the German move on Bucharest had touched an Italian "sore spot." Ribbentrop, the state secretary wrote, did not feel guilty of having misled the Italians. But Weizsäcker also made it clear that the "most authoritative quarters" in Germany were fundamentally in agreement with both Mackensen and Weizsäcker: it was necessary to "handle our other Axis-end gently." Weizsäcker emphasized that "for the moment we are not sending you any directive, and have not even given you the task of asking officially if there is anything in the story, and if so, what."[143] This last phrase revealed a certain skepticism about the reports from Rome, even in the well-informed and not overly Italophile Weizsäcker. Further evidence suggests that similar skepticism still prevailed in the "most authoritative quarters" as well, and that Hitler's failure to act on the reports was as much due to a lack of confidence in their veracity as to a desire to "handle [his] other Axis-end gently" in the interests of organizing the continental coalition. Word reaching Field Marshal von Brauchitsch and General Halder at the army staff as late as 24 October suggests Hitler was annoyed at the Italians, but not seriously alarmed: "Apparently Ciano [was] once again active in order to set in motion the occupation of Corfù and of the Greek islands to the south."[144] Hitler considered such a move "absurd," and intended to write to Mussolini. The Führer also "repeatedly refer[red] to the fact that the . . . war in the eastern Mediterranean [would] lead to a swift victory if one occupie[d] Crete" by air assault. But although he requested that the *Luftwaffe* explore the requirements for such an operation (along with an air landing in the Canary Islands and air support for the attack on Gibraltar), he did not think it immediately necessary. Brauchitsch, substituting wish for fact, erroneously reported that Hungary, Bulgaria, Slovakia, and Spain had joined the Tripartite Pact, which Hitler now planned to press into service as the framework of his continental coalition. (Actually, Hitler was as yet merely considering inviting them to join; the procession of satellite leaders to Berchtesgaden did not begin until late November.)[145] Yugoslavia, still according to Brauchitsch, was about to join, and Greece was "possible." This massive demonstration of European solidarity against Great Britain would serve as a suitable "countermeasure, in case Roosevelt is [re-]elected."

An Italian parallel war in the Balkans thus had no place in Hitler's designs at this point. As late as 24 October, while realizing that something was afoot in Rome, and of a need to counter the "activity" of Ciano, Hitler did not believe that Mussolini would act. The evident military absurdity of the Italian plan as Mackensen and Pohl reported it, and the omission of Crete, perhaps contributed to this lack of urgency. Nor did Hitler's chief military advisers take the matter seriously until after receiving news of the contents of Mussolini's 19 October letter. The war diary of the *Wehrmacht* high command suggests Roatta and Badoglio's denials prevailed over Pohl's judgment that the Italians were about to move. Until the evening of 25 October, when Keitel telephoned from Hitler's entourage in France with news that Mussolini's letter had disclosed "offensive intentions against Greece," the *Wehrmacht* high command found Badoglio's assurances "convincing." Even the foreign office was as late as the 25th "not yet convinced" that the Italians intended to attack.[146]

To the Florence station. The memoirs of former members of Hitler's and Ribbentrop's entourages contain dramatic tales of how the Führer was "beside himself" when he received warning of the Greek affair during his journey in the west, and of how he "hastened to the scene of the crime" to restrain Mussolini. But hindsight and Hitler's subsequent vociferous denials of responsibility for his ally's actions have almost certainly colored the accounts, which in addition are contradictory on details of time and place.[147]

The chain of events that took Hitler to his meeting with Mussolini in

Florence on the morning of 28 October is difficult to reconstruct with any certainty, but it nevertheless holds the key to Hitler's intentions. After a preliminary conversation with Pierre Laval, now Pétain's deputy prime minister, and a difficult encounter at Hendaye with the refractory Franco, Hitler and Ribbentrop spent the evening of 24 October in their special trains at Montoire-sur-Loire, near Tours. There Hitler met with Pétain, inconclusively, but to the immediate satisfaction of both parties.[148] Pétain left Montoire at 7:45 p.m.,[149] and Ribbentrop telephoned Ciano in Rome to report.

As Weizsäcker had written Mackensen, Ribbentrop was now at last conscious of the need to keep the Italians fully informed in order to allay mistrust. Ribbentrop was "in general optimistic" about the results of the Franco-German discussions. Ciano was less pleased: he did not attempt to hide his "distrust and suspicion," and was determined to prevent damage to Italian interests from "the insertion of France into the Axis." Ribbentrop proposed that Hitler visit northern Italy in the near future to report on the negotiations. Ciano apparently gained the impression that Ribbentrop had in mind a meeting on 3 or 4 November.[150]

Even before setting out on his pilgrimage across France, Hitler had apparently intended to visit Mussolini at the end in order to agree on a course of action.[151] Ribbentrop's proposal, although new to the Italians, thus represented no radical change in German policy. Even Ciano, at least at first, associated Hitler's desire for a meeting with the negotiations with France rather than with the Greek affair. No new decision supervened in the next hours. Ribbentrop composed a lengthy telegram for Ciano and Mussolini, setting forth some of the details of the Franco and Pétain talks, and announcing that Hitler intended to write Mussolini directly and hoped to visit him "soon" in northern Italy. Ribbentrop's reference to a letter fits with Brauchitsch's news that Hitler intended to write Mussolini about the absurdity of Ciano's Greek plans. But Hitler was obviously not seriously alarmed yet. He approved Ribbentrop's message to Ciano during the evening of 24 October, and Ribbentrop's aides dispatched it from Montoire at 0400 on the 25th, an hour before the trains set off on the long way home to Berlin through occupied Belgium.[152]

But in the course of the night new information had arrived. First, probably, came Mackensen's account of Pohl's certainty that the Italians were about to attack. Berlin received this at 1940 hours on the 24th, and almost certainly repeated it to Ribbentrop's train by teleprinter. Next came Rintelen's account of Badoglio's "convincing" reassurances, which the foreign office received at 2345, but which may well have reached Hitler through *Wehrmacht* channels earlier. On top of these reports, Berlin dispatched Mussolini's letter, suitably translated, to the trains by teleprinter at 0120 hours on the 25th.[153] Nevertheless, Ribbentrop's telegram of the night before, with its proposal of a meeting soon, but not immediately, went out at 0400. Hitler probably did not read Mussolini's letter until later in the morning. His entourage may have hesitated to awaken him with it. Perhaps, as was his custom, he also needed time to meditate on it before action. In any case, not until early the afternoon of 25 October did Hitler announce a change in plan. At 1230, Mackensen delivered Ribbentrop's telegram on the French discussions to Ciano, who thanked the German ambassador warmly. Shortly thereafter, in Berlin, the foreign office fed another alarming message into the teletype link to Ribbentrop. Mackensen now reported that a "totally reliable source" revealed that Ciano's assistant Anfuso had told friends the previous afternoon that the "action" against Greece would begin "this weekend," in other words, either the very next morning (Saturday, 26 October) or at the latest the following day (Sunday, 27 October). Ciano was to depart "at once" for Tirana.[154]

This report, transmitted from Berlin at 1340 on 25 October, was apparently the final blow. While the principal contemporary sources on Hitler's motives both give Mussolini's "fiery letter" about France as the sole cause of Hitler's decision to hasten south to Florence,[155] chronology suggests that the Mackensen telegram, and hence the Greek affair, was also involved. Coming on top of the "offensive intentions" disclosed in Mussolini's letter, and his attack on Hitler's French policy and of the entire German Mediterranean strategy, it presumably convinced Hitler that a consultation was now urgently necessary.

Hitler and Ribbentrop did not, however, act on Anfuso's remark about "this weekend." When Ribbentrop telephoned Ciano once more, shortly before 3 p.m. on the 25th, it was to propose a meeting at Florence for the beginning of the next week. The date agreed, after Ciano had consulted Mussolini, was Monday, 28 October.[156] Hitler was now at last alarmed. But the information at his disposal was still contradictory enough to preclude an all-out attempt to stop the attack, despite his fear that an Italian campaign in Greece would produce a long-drawn-out and inconvenient Balkan conflict.[157] Roatta's denial to Rintelen that anything was underway apparently impressed Hitler; he and Ribbentrop repeated it with relish in the ensuing months in order to embarrass the Italians.[158] Too swift and decisive a German démarche might also prove embarrassing if Anfuso's version of the operation's timing proved untrue and Mussolini's letter merely meant that he planned to deal with Greece in the course, say, of the next several weeks.

In any case, the practical difficulties of meeting with Mussolini before Monday without either offending the Italians or giving the appearance of undignified haste were insuperable. At the slow speeds Hitler's special train employed (presumably for security reasons), he could not have arrived in Florence before the small hours of 27 October.[159] Nor would an aerial descent on the Eternal City in the manner of the opening sequence of *Triumph of the Will* have been good form. A private message to Mussolini was now equally out of the question. If Mussolini were about to attack Greece, Roatta and Badoglio had lied, coldly and deliberately, to Rintelen. Mussolini himself had in any case lashed out in his letter at Hitler's French and Spanish policies, had rejected German interference in the Mediterranean, and had announced his decision to end *"any* delay" over Greece.[160] A renewed German veto would cause irreparable harm to the Axis. Mussolini's prestige and the personal understanding between the two dictators was at stake. Only a face-to-face talk would do, and if the talk came too late, so much the worse.

As he rolled south, Hitler may have consoled himself with the thought that German indulgence over the Greek escapade, should Mussolini actually launch it, might produce renewed Italian agreement on France. In addition, Hitler may, unlike Ribbentrop, have felt guilty of treating the Italians roughly over Rumania. The well-informed foreign office liaison officer to the German army high command, Hasso von Etzdorf, noted on 28 October that "the Führer does not desire to hold [Mussolini] back any more [on Greece], with reference to Germany's action in Rumania." Etzdorf's version probably exaggerated Hitler's acquiescence to the Italian attack, and above all represented the interpretation of Weizsäcker, Etzdorf's chief contact.[161] But it does appear that Hitler was concerned at having acted brusquely over Rumania. Perhaps failure to invite Italian participation weighed on his conscience. As the meeting at Florence approached, Hitler still hoped to prevent the Greek undertaking, if both Roatta's and Anfuso's remarks proved false, or inject strategic sense into it by delaying Mussolini until a German force was ready to descend on Crete, the key to the eastern Mediterranean. Above all, however, he was determined to prevent a crisis within the Axis.

Hitler achieved only the latter aim. On 27 October, as the trains waited in Munich before departing for the Brenner, Rintelen belatedly attempted to redeem himself with the announcement that the attack was "as good as certain" the next morning. General Jodl, in Berlin, concurred. The final word came from Rome in the small hours. Mackensen telegraphed that Ciano had called him at 9 p.m. and announced that Grazzi would deliver an ultimatum to the Greeks "in the course of the night." Significantly, Ciano added that military operations would begin at 0600 "whatever happens" – an unmistakable warning to the Germans not to interfere, and an expression of the Italian leadership's determination to inflict on the Greeks a shattering defeat in the field before permitting surrender.[162]

The news seems to have reached the trains somewhere north of Florence, at about 8 a.m. on 28 October.[163] Hitler's army adjutant, Lieutenant Colonel Engel, recorded the German dictator's resulting outburst:

Führer enraged, when he hears of Italy's attack on Greece. Furiously reproaches German liaison staffs and attachés, who do nothing but attend diplomatic functions and are no spies. He remarks that this fact has ruined many a project of his. His judgment of the situation is that the Duce is perturbed over his – that is, Germany's – economic influence in the Balkans, and he [Hitler] doubts that the Italians will be capable of forcing Greece to its knees, for the Greeks, all things considered, are no mean soldiers. The Führer says word for word "this is revenge for Norway and France." But he, the Führer, could not have acted other than in secrecy, for every second Italian was either a traitor or a spy. Hard words for Rintelen, who has allowed himself to be tricked. The only advantage is that the British will now be forced to fight there as well. Führer demands immediate contact with Mackensen and wants to speak to Mussolini. Is very worried that the Italian action can drag the entire Balkans in, and give the British a welcome occasion to set up air bases there.[164]

After this lapse, Hitler controlled himself "remarkably well." By 11 a.m., when he arrived in Florence, he was composed. On the station platform, Mussolini greeted him with panache: "Early this morning, in the dawn twilight, victorious Italian troops crossed the Greco-Albanian border." Hitler, his interpreter noted, was a good loser.[165]

The Führer smoothly began discussions at the Palazzo Vecchio with the announcement that he had come to Florence to apprise Mussolini of his conversations with Laval, Franco, and Pétain, "and to speak with him about the Greek question." But Hitler did not in fact mention Greece again except to offer two German divisions for the "protection" of Crete against the British. Ciano was doubtless exultant, and he recorded Hitler's words with a characteristic twist of his own: the Führer allegedly remarked that he had come to Florence not only to report on his recent diplomatic endeavors, but also "to offer full German solidarity in the action begun by Italy against Greece."[166] Although Ciano did not know it, that grudging solidarity would soon be very necessary indeed. Mussolini had overreached himself. His attempt to add Greece to his booty, to strike at Suez from the north as well as the Western Desert, and to demonstrate his independence from his over-mighty ally was soon to turn to disaster so irretrievable that only German rescue could save him and the regime.

CHAPTER 6

To the *Berghof:* Italy's end as a great power

We, as Italians, have lost the war.
The Axis will have to win it.
Marshal Emilio De Bono, 16 December 1940

1. Defeat

Talk in Florence and "Blitzkrieg" in Albania. The discussions were most satisfactory to the Italians. Ciano had feared that the Germans would come bearing "a cup of rue for our claims against France." Soddu, perhaps reflecting Mussolini's fears, had despairingly told Roatta on 26 October that "Hitler will arrive in Florence in order to communicate the conditions of peace with France, *already concluded.*"[1] Mussolini may have expected that Hitler's assurances on France would prove no more valid than those over Rumania.

Nothing of the sort happened. Hitler spoke soothingly of the "modest demands" of Italy and Germany, which the French, having expected worse, would surely accept. He insisted that he would never conclude peace with France without total satisfaction of Italian claims. Mussolini in return disparagingly conceded that the French could provide "passive cooperation" with the Axis. But he also pressed once more, in vain, for an immediate treaty. On Spain, Hitler temporarily conceded defeat. Franco was not true Führer material, and despite promises, had been "very vague" about when he would enter the war. Hitler and Mussolini nevertheless agreed to press for a meeting of all three dictators at which the Axis would announce with fanfare Spain's accession to Tripartite Pact and Pact of Steel, and its entry into the war. Hitler was cautious about the Soviets: he was just as mistrustful of Stalin "as Stalin was of him." But to the Italians' great surprise and interest Hitler announced that Molotov would come to Berlin shortly for negotiations. One might perhaps yet steer the Russians south toward India, although Hitler feared – and would not tolerate – Russian designs on the Dardanelles or Finland. As at the Brenner, Hitler also noted that the guarantee of Soviet immobility was the combat-readiness of the German armed forces. The Italians, as usual, failed to appreciate the full significance of the remark.[2]

While the dictators and their foreign ministers discussed high politics in the Palazzo Vecchio in Florence, Visconti Prasca's divisions pressed forward under the torrential Albanian rains. They made best progress along the coast, where by 9 November reconnaissance forces had penetrated some sixty kilometers into Greece. But in the center, tenaciously held field fortifications and expertly employed artillery stopped Visconti Prasca's principal thrust at the crossroads of Kalibaki, north of Janina. Much of Greek artillery was French, and superior to anything the Italians were able to bring up across the boglike mule tracks and mountain torrents of Ciamuria. Greek superiority in fire support lasted until quite late in the campaign, and was one source of the disastrous showing the Italians made. East of Kalibaki, the alpine division "Julia" struck out across the mountains toward the pass of Metsovon to cut Greek lateral communications with Kalibaki and Janina. Within a week, local counterattacks on the division's flanks compelled it to withdraw toward its starting point. On the extreme left of the Italian line around Korçë the situation deteriorated even more rapidly, as the Greek concentration at Florina moved forward to take the pressure off the weaker Greek front in Epirus.

Nevertheless, Badoglio and his subordinates seem to have remained optimistic during the early days of the invasion. Badoglio assured Rintelen on 30 October that an "insuperable mountain barrier" covered the Italian left. An *Italian* attack in that area was nevertheless feasible if the Greeks concentrated their forces solely against the Epirus thrust. But the Greeks proved uncooperative. Simultaneously, weather triggered Cavagnari's characteristic caution. On 29 October his subordinate Somigli informed Roatta that heavy seas and high winds made the Corfù landing impossible, although some on the Naval staff thought otherwise and grumbled to the Germans. Still, the Corfù plan was not yet quite dead. When Mussolini descended on Apulia on 10 October to direct the advance into Greece in person, Cavagnari followed. Perhaps to restore his sagging credit, the admiral ordered the landing rescheduled for 2 November. Then Soddu conveyed to Mussolini the first of several impassioned Visconti Prasca pleas for reinforcements. Fulminating at Army staff and *Comando Supremo,* whom Visconti Prasca held responsible for his own impending defeat, Mussolini directed the cancelation of the Corfù assault and the diversion of the landing force (the "Bari" division) to Valona. Mussolini also pressed for more energetic air action. He believed "that 500-bomber raids against Athens and Salonika [could] produce enemy political collapse." When Pricolo pointed out the difficulties and risks that lay ahead, Mussolini reportedly replied, "You forget that I am conducting a lightning war like the Germans in Poland." Albania, unlike North Africa, was evidently close enough for Mussolini to feel confident that he could impart to operations "that rapid rhythm," as he wrote encouragingly to Visconti Prasca on 31 October, "that events, more than doctrine, peremptorily impose."[3]

Mussolini was by now furious at his military subordinates. At Florence, he had told Hitler that he could trust none of them: "My soldiers are brave fellows, but I can't have any confidence in my officers." Badoglio's subterranean maneuvering against the Greek enterprise had violently irritated Mussolini, who had also vented his displeasure in a 26 October letter once again spurring Graziani forward. Ciano too was disgruntled. He had indeed gone to Tirana to supervise operations on the spot. There he recorded the ever more frequent complaints from Visconti Prasca and Jacomoni of the alleged "ill will" of the *Comando Supremo*. Under the influence of his Albanian subordinates, Ciano noted that "Badoglio was convinced that the Greek question would be resolved at the peace table and acted on that basis; the result has been a preparation far less efficient than we might have been justified in expecting." Mackensen's high-level informant, in a report that also accurately rendered the gist of Mussolini's letter to Graziani, disclosed on 1 November that both Mussolini and Ciano were already inclined to blame Badoglio for having delayed the operation until the rains had come.[4]

Ciano nevertheless remained blithely optimistic. On 1 November the weather temporarily cleared, and he flew over Salonika on a "bombing mission with all the trimmings" that produced some 500 casualties, mostly women and children. Once back in Rome, he gleefully told Mackensen that the advance was making good progress despite the weather. Once Preveza and Arta fell, Visconti Prasca would attack from Korçë toward Salonika "in a couple of weeks," and cut off Greek forces in Thrace.[5] Ciano's optimism presumably derived from a report of Visconti Prasca's to Jacomoni of 31 October praising the "irresistible élan" of the troops and proclaiming that the operation proceeded "at an accelerated rhythm." Visconti Prasca also reported high morale among the Albanian blackshirts – the very troops who were in reality beginning to desert to the enemy in droves. One of the wounded heroes had purportedly announced in pidgin-Italian, "We all die, so that DUCE pass." Doubtless inspired, Ciano left Rome on 2 November for pheasant shooting and political discussion in the Sudetenland with Ribbentrop.[6]

Simultaneously, the situation in the Korçë area presaged disaster. Visconti Prasca called for Air Force "mass action" to relieve the Greek pressure. By 3 November, Badoglio had realized that the situation was "very delicate." It was now clear that Bulgarian neutrality posed no threat to the Greeks; the Turks had hinted that they would strike if King Boris moved. The Greeks could therefore concentrate practically all of their army against Italy, and a large portion of it against the vulnerable Italian left flank. Roatta insisted to Badoglio that if Visconti Prasca did not break through in Epirus "in a few days," and if Greek pressure around Korçë continued, it would become "necessary to have the courage to take up a defensive stance in Epirus as well and prepare a powerful counterblow (that is, a return to the original project; to begin the action with twenty divisions)." Badoglio agreed. But Visconti Prasca remained blissfully unaware of impending doom. When Badoglio almost plaintively warned him, speaking as his "old superior," Visconti replied that the situation around Korçë was "not disquieting . . . and ever more favorable."[7]

Halt in Epirus and judgment at Taranto. By 3 November Mussolini was well aware that Greek resistance was "greater than anticipated." But he had a remedy: an amphibious landing to take the enemy in the rear and crack open the Epirus front. Warships would land a regiment of Bersaglieri at Preveza under the guns of the fleet.[8] Unlike many of Mussolini's military inspirations, this proposal was not entirely harebrained, given experienced troops, a minimum of cooperation between the three services, and surprise. The Germans had carried off far more difficult coups in Norway against defenses considerably stronger than those on the Greek coast, and the Italians would have had an advantage conspicuously denied to Hitler and Raeder: local naval superiority. Aggressively employed, Cavagnari's fleet would have had no difficulty covering the landing force and keeping it supplied; even after Taranto, the British were unable to interdict traffic between Italy and Albania effectively.[9]

But Mussolini's subordinates greeted the proposal with immediate, categorical, and unanimous disapproval. Impending failure emboldened the service chiefs to speak with the collegial voice so conspicuously silent before the operation began. At a meeting on 3 November Roatta announced that the Army opposed the Preveza project, which would take an inordinate amount of time. Roatta also did not think the diversion would shake the Greeks unless Visconti Prasca was about to break through in any case, and then it would be superfluous. Although Roatta was more conscious than anyone else that the principal impediment to bringing the full weight of the Italian Army to bear was the low capacity of Durazzo and Valona, the Preveza landing inexplicably did not strike him as a convenient way of securing another port.[10]

On 4 November, in an atmosphere of impending crisis, Mussolini met Badoglio and the service chiefs at Palazzo Venezia, and belatedly conceded that "in order to defeat Greece at least twenty divisions are necessary." Asked how long such a deployment would take, Roatta predictably quoted the figure of two and a half months, and appealed to Mussolini to allow the service staffs to do the job their own way. Mussolini thereupon reproached him: in twenty days the Army staff had not sent "a single battalion." Presumably Mussolini was drawing upon Visconti Prasca's recriminations to Ciano. Actually, as Roatta emphasized, the "Bari" division, numerous smaller units, and considerable amounts of equipment had arrived or were crossing to Albania. Mussolini retreated, and reassured his subordinates: ". . . no one is in less of a hurry than I am." A second winter at war was "preoccupying," but "indispensable." When peace came, Italy would "have more sacrifices and thus more rights." Italy was certain of conquering Greece in the long run; there was "no point in being in a hurry."[11] Mussolini had fallen back on his customary last-ditch rationale: if "lightning warfare" was impossible, "sacrifice" would have to assure Italy's expansion.

Although he did not mention it to the service chiefs, Mussolini had already decided on a remedy, albeit a dubious one, for the deteriorating situation in Albania. He dispatched Soddu to take over the army group command that the sending of ten more divisions would necessitate, and relegated Visconti Prasca to one of the two field armies to form under Soddu. The latter had expertly parried Badoglio and Roatta efforts to replace Visconti Prasca with a more senior general, and had secured Visconti's agreement to his own supersession with promises that they would both come out of the campaign as marshals.[12] But the chaos Soddu found in Albania apparently came as a shock to that consummate intriguer, and he immediately resolved to jettison Visconti Prasca. Mussolini had in any case already made up his mind; by 5 November Roatta had word from "on high" that Visconti Prasca's days in Albania were numbered. The Greeks had now counterattacked at Korçë, and Visconti Prasca's troops had given way: "on the eighth day of operations, the other side has the initiative," noted Ciano. But Mussolini and Ciano were not yet aware that disaster was imminent. On the evening of 6 October Ciano predicted, not for the last time, that the Italian forces around Korçë would be able to hold the Greeks.[13]

Ciano was wrong. On 8 November, Soddu's first direct report to Mussolini arrived. Soddu described stiff resistance in Epirus, the Greek counterattack at Korçë, and the utter disorganization of Visconti's command. Italian forces must "take up a posture from which to throw back any enemy initiative, while awaiting the reinforcements that would permit us to resume action as soon as possible."[14] In other words, Italy must abandon the offensive. Mussolini conferred with Badoglio and Roatta, then reluctantly ordered the advance suspended. Privately, Mussolini vented his irritation at Badoglio for being "very lugubrious" and for again asking for four months in which to prepare the "total offensive" that would finish the Greeks.[15]

On 10 November, Mussolini and his military leaders at last had it out.[16] In a Palazzo Venezia meeting with the service chiefs, Mussolini saddled Visconti Prasca and Jacomoni with the blame for the fact that "things [had] not gone as one might have thought." But he was now confident that, "fortunately," the Greek Army's "dynamism" was "already exhausted or in the process of being exhausted." Soddu had revealed himself "the man of the situation," and would reorganize the chaotic Albanian command structure. The only problem now was when and how Italy could resume the offensive. Mussolini thereupon read the chiefs a "Note for the General Staff" in which he announced Soddu's elevation to army group commander, the raising of the forces in Albania to seventeen divisions as rapidly as possible, and the resumption of the offensive along the coast without fail by 5 December, "in order to prevent Great Britain from giving effective support to Greece, and above all for reasons of prestige."[17] The Italian Army must not long labor "under the morale problem of not having been able to break through the Greek defensive system." This was a rationale familiar to all.

Mussolini also proposed to bomb Greece proper to "demonstrate to the Greek population that the assistance of the British air force is insufficient or nonexistent," and to "disorganize the civil life of Greece, sowing panic everywhere." Mussolini explained with obvious relish the significance of this last order:

Therefore you must choose – square kilometer by square kilometer – [the parts of] Greece to bomb. . . . All urban centers of over 10,000 population must be destroyed and razed to the ground. This is a direct order. . . . It will be the second time that this has happened – the first time, Rome saw to it.

Finally, Mussolini surveyed the strategic situation, which "could not be more favorable." Yugoslavia was immobilized. Bulgaria was allegedly "a thorn in the side of the Greeks." Russia was drawing closer to Italy's German ally. Britain, although not "on its knees," would concentrate on defending the British Isles and Egypt. Mussolini closed with the ringing assertion that he could not tolerate "that the conviction that we are incapable of defeating the Greeks should be spread abroad in the world."

Badoglio took the floor, and at last stood up to Mussolini. Characteristically, his motives were personal rather than military. Now that defeat had come, he was willing to take considerable risks to disassociate himself and Roatta from the entire affair. He may even have hoped to escape from his own heavy responsibility for the increasingly compromised military situation by provoking Mussolini to dismiss him arbitrarily. Whatever his purpose, Badoglio's oration was a masterful pastiche of truth, half-truth, and fiction, couched in a manner scarcely calculated to spare the dictator's dignity:

Permit me, Duce, to tell you something about what happened before the preparations we are now making.

I have reread the entire [Comando Supremo] diary: on 14 October you called us together here – Roatta and me – and asked us how many troops were required to attack Greece. Roatta, on the basis of the studies made by the Army staff, declared that twenty divisions were necessary. It was therefore a question of sending a further ten divisions, and we also discussed the sending of an army group command and an additional army command.

On 15 October you called us together once more, here. Also present were Count Ciano, General Soddu, Governor General Jacomoni, and General Visconti Prasca.

As a result of the briefings given by Count Ciano, Governor General Jacomoni, and General Visconti Prasca, YOU took the decision to attack on 26 October, a date that – as is known – was subsequently shifted to 28 October.

We attempted to do everything that could be done in that space of time in the best way possible.

I have made these remarks in order to demonstrate that neither the Comando Supremo nor the Regio Esercito staff had anything to do with this affair, which was carried out in a manner that totally contradicts our whole system, which is founded on the principle of first preparing oneself well, and then taking risks.[18]

Badoglio proposed to confer with Roatta and Cavagnari and examine the transport problem, after which he would inform Mussolini of "the exact amount of time" needed before resuming the offensive.

Mussolini, as Badoglio told Armellini after the meeting, momentarily "swallowed it," and gave Badoglio a free hand. But within days the dictator was once more pressing for an early December offensive. Badoglio simply ignored this pressure, and allowed four months for the buildup. Not forgetting that the Greeks might in the intervening period reinforce their positions, he ordered Roatta to consider sending corps- and army-level siege artillery to Albania.[19] The assumption at the basis of both Mussolini's and Badoglio's projects was the same: the Greeks could only defend, not counterattack. That assumption proved as illusory as its predecessors.

On 14 November General Alexandros Papagos, chief of staff of the Greek army, passed over to a general counteroffensive. His troops now markedly outnumbered the Italians. They were also better trained, better led, and considerably more determined. Germany's ostentatious refusal to break relations emboldened the Greek leadership to press their advantage, as did a British landing on Crete and the arrival in Athens of a small RAF fighter and light-bomber force. Metaxas and his military were confident; the Greek dictator hoped from the beginning to "chase [the] Italians out of Albania."[20] In London, Churchill had at first pressed for immediate aid to Greece beyond the small air contingent General Sir Archibald Wavell, the commander-in-chief, Middle East, was willing to send. But when the secretary for war, Anthony Eden, returned from a long mission to Cairo and briefed Churchill on Wavell's plans for a major blow against Graziani, the prime minister relented.[21] For the moment, he was content to follow with benevolent interest the unexpected progress of his Greek allies, who after the fall of Korçë publicly proclaimed that they fought "for the liberation of Albania." Metaxas was gambling that his troops could drive the Italians into the sea before spring and German help for Italy came. A decisive Greek victory might induce Yugoslavia and Turkey to join a common front; at the very least, it would ensure that Greece and Britain could concentrate without distractions against the Germans when the latter attacked.[22]

On the Italian side, Soddu had by now achieved his ambition of superseding Visconti Prasca. Mussolini had ordered the latter demoted to corps commander, then returned to Italy on 13 November. Soddu was less divorced from reality than his predecessor, but no more able to master events or the Greeks. Once the *Regio Esercito* ceased to advance, the Greeks no longer had to fear for their flanks, and the vast frontages (only eight divisions to cover 140 kilometers) permitted easy infiltration into the Italian rear. As the Greek advance gained momentum, Soddu reported that "no miracle solutions existed" – surely the understatement of the month. By 15 November he was already considering a withdrawal on the Korçë flank in order to shorten the Italian front, which a hodgepodge of battalions from different divisions, thrown in as they arrived on the scene, held thinly. On 16 November the defenders of Ersekë, the vital connecting link between the newly constituted 9th and 11th Armies, made a precipitate and – to Soddu – "incomprehensible" withdrawal. The front wavered, and on 18 November Soddu gave his subordinates discretion to conduct the withdrawals that were in any case under way: "from this moment, resistance on present positions has the purpose of permitting the evacuation of equipment and artillery." From Rome Badoglio praised his subordinate's moral courage in ordering retreat: "It is a question of hanging on, then we shall prevail. *Bravo* Soddu." Mussolini was not so enthusiastic. He attempted on 21 November to brake Soddu's retrograde progress with a protest against the evacuation of Korçë, but the movement was already under way.[23]

Even hanging on to the new positions proved difficult. The troops had by now been fighting for three weeks in abominable weather at the end of a long and chaotic supply line. The units lacked horses and above all mules, the only practical means of moving ammunition, food, and wounded in the mountains. Further back, on the roads, the Army was desperately short of trucks. The weather, a British surface attack on a convoy on 12 November, and the Valona–Durazzo port bottleneck did the rest. Since trucks could only land at the Durazzo docks, units destined for the Epirus front and therefore sent to Valona often deployed without their artillery or supply services, with predictable results. Nor was the Tirana air shuttle, which absorbed all of Italy's transport aircraft and left East Africa almost cut off, a remedy. It ferried troops, but no heavy equipment. Soddu and his army lived from hand to mouth, and their first withdrawal was by no means their last.

While the Greeks readied their counteroffensive, the British struck at the Italian fleet at Taranto on the night of 11/12 November with Swordfish torpedo bombers from the carrier *Illustrious*. By morning, *Littorio, Duilio,* and *Cavour* rested on the harbor bottom. Admiral Cunningham and his subordinates had been preparing operation "Judgement," as they not inappropriately dubbed it, since August. The idea was not new. It had occurred to Cunningham's predecessor, Admiral Sir Dudley Pound, as early as 1938, and Cunningham had included it in the spring of 1939 in a summary of proposed actions against Italy in the event of war.[24] Cunningham had originally scheduled the operation for 21 October, the anniversary of Trafalgar, but technical difficulties compelled postponement until mid-November, when the moon was again right. The British thus conceived and almost carried out the operation independently of events in Greece.[25] It was the fruit of the aggressive leadership of Cunningham and of the increasing pressure from Churchill upon his Middle East commanders to punish the weaker of Britain's enemies. Nevertheless, from a strategic point of view the British timed the attack extraordinarily well. It eliminated at one stroke even local predominance of the Italian Navy in the central Mediterranean, and guaranteed, if Cavagnari's attitude were not guarantee enough, that the *Regia Marina* would not interfere with British aid to Greece.

Despite complaints to Roatta and Badoglio about the dangerous consequences that war against Greece would have for the fleet at Taranto, Cavagnari and Somigli had taken no special precautions. Not only did the battleship squadron remain there but – as Cunningham had anticipated in planning "Judgement" – it failed to sortie to meet the British as they advanced into the central Mediterranean from Alexandria and Gibraltar to cover the launching of the Swordfish. Antiaircraft defenses at Taranto remained inadequate, and neither local naval command nor Navy staff in Rome took steps to remedy, even by improvisation, a shortage of torpedo netting. Coordination of defensive fires and searchlights around the anchorage remained slipshod.[26] As Ciano not unjustly noted:

When Badoglio came to see me at Palazzo Chigi the last time [on 17 October], he said that if we attacked Greece we would immediately have to move the fleet, which would no longer be safe. And why has this not been done, two weeks after the beginning of operations, and with a full moon?[27]

The Taranto sinkings were hardly decisive in the long run. Only *Cavour* suffered irreparable damage, and Campioni did sortie from Naples, the new fleet base, in order to challenge the British Gibraltar force on 16–17 November. But here again the fleet broke off and retreated whence it came too rapidly for the British to follow. Inaccurate air reconnaissance reports had convinced Admiral Campioni that the Gibraltar force had three battleships to his two. The British also failed to exploit Taranto fully in order to strike decisively at Italy proper or at Graziani's maritime supply line. Only the 9 February battleship bombardment of Genoa gave the Italians a foretaste of things to come.[28]

But Taranto was indeed a judgment. The German naval staff war diarist viewed the proceedings with a characteristic mixture of *Schadenfreude* and alarm:

A black day for the Italian Navy!. . . . the English success must be spoken of as the greatest naval victory of the war. . . . The smartly executed attack of British torpedo aircraft . . . presents the Italian leadership with a bitter final accounting for the minimal activity displayed up to now by the weapon that at the beginning of the war was considered their sharpest: the fleet![29]

Mussolini and Cavagnari had lost Italy's war at sea.

Ruler across the knuckles. Even before Taranto and the Albanian débâcle, Hitler had begun to contemplate the unwelcome necessity of shoring up his Italian ally, or at least of limiting the damage Italian action had caused. By 1 November he had lost "all inclination for close military cooperation with Italy." The Italians must indeed "do it alone." Even diplomatic assistance such as breaking German relations with Greece was "out of the question."[30] On 3 November, Hitler met with General Wilhelm von Thoma, an armor expert who had just returned from an exploratory visit to Africa with the grudging cooperation of the Italians – Badoglio had privately expressed the grim hope that once Thoma had seen the lunar desolation of the desert land-scape, the Germans would cease importuning to send troops there. Thoma was indeed extremely pessimistic about terrain, climate, Italian logistical capabilities, and above all Italian leadership. Hitler promptly "wrote off" the Libyan project.[31]

The next day, Hitler presided over a major conference of his military advisers at the Reich Chancellery. He was "visibly depressed," and his army adjutant, Gerhard Engel, had the impression, not for the first or last time, that "at the moment, he doesn't know what to do next."[32] Hitler did not expect the Italians to attack Mersa Matruh before the end of December. After that, lengthy logistical preparations for a further thrust, and the infernal heat of the African summer, would supervene. German aid would thus be a waste before the fall of 1941. In addition, the Italians insisted that Tripoli, the only fully efficient port in Libya, did not have the capacity to support a German expeditionary force in addition to Graziani's troops. Hitler would have to plead with Vichy for Tunisian ports. Finally, Hitler sharply criti-cized Italian military leadership, in which he now had "small confidence." It was "operationally dubious to send German troops into action across a sea we do not command, with an ally who does not commit his forces to the utmost in order to hold that sea open." But he had to take some action to retain Axis initiative in the increasingly dangerous situation that Italy's Greek foray and continuing North African procrastination had summoned up. In contrast to his doubtfulness at the Florence meeting, Hitler now determined to "force the entry of Spain into the war." The assault on the Rock would be a purely German enterprise designed to drive the British from the western Mediterranean.[33]

When he turned to the situation in Greece, Hitler's full alarm over the potential effect of Italian irresponsibility was evident. From the beginning of the war he had feared sabotage or direct attack, whether ground or air, Russian or British, on the all-important and exceedingly vulnerable Ruma-nian oilfields. This fear had produced the move into Rumania that had unleashed Mussolini's attack on Greece; now the attack on Greece, which apparently opened Greek bases to the British, further intensified Hitler's anx-iety. Although considerable *Luftwaffe* forces were now in position in Rumania, they were theoretically not enough to prevent British aircraft from turning the oilfields into a heap of smoking ruins. By 4 November Hitler had word that the British were trying to establish air bases both around Salonika and on the Aegean island of Lemnos. He therefore directed Halder and Brauchitsch to prepare a ground attack on Greek Thrace[34] and Mace-donia. It might be useful to support the Italians, should their Albanian offensive continue to flounder. But Hitler's primary purpose was to protect the Rumanian oilfields and secure his southern flank should he attack the Soviet Union the following spring.[35] The warning order to the German army did not entirely signify that Hitler had given up hope of luring Greece into his camp. His obstinate refusal to go beyond nonbelligerence toward Greece throughout the winter of 1940–1, and extensive secret contacts between Berlin and Athens, suggest that Hitler was eager to avoid a Balkan operation. The most Metaxas was willing to concede, however, was the assurance that Greece would not permit "the British to attack German interests from Greek soil."[36] In the end, Greek insistence on driving the Italians into the sea, the increasingly acute need to maintain Mussolini's prestige, and intensifying Greek cooperation with Britain all conspired to push Germany to act once the snow melted on the Balkan mountains.

Nevertheless, Mussolini's declaration of independence did induce Hitler to abandon "war on the periphery" as a potential solution to Germany's strategic problems. Pique, genuine and well-founded misgivings, and finally the Italian military fiascos of the next weeks converted the assault on Gibraltar and the land attack on Greece into no more than support operations to prevent Italian collapse.[37] Hitler was more than ever inclined to seek victory not in the Mediterranean but in the Ukraine. The directive for the German armed forces that resulted from the 4 November conference noted that "political discussions with the purpose of clarifying the attitude of Russia for the coming period" had begun, but ordered that "whatever the result these discussions may have, all preparations for the East ordered orally up to now" must continue. These words were an ominous prelude to Molotov's visit to Berlin on 12 and 13 November, which Hitler considered a test of Soviet intentions. The visit proved decisive. If Stalin's 21 October reply to Ribbentrop's invitation had presaged no fundamental Soviet concessions, Molotov's crude exposition of his master's goals came as something of a shock even to Hitler. Soviet ambitions extended from the vital nickel deposits of Petsamo in North Finland to the Danish Narrows and the Dardanelles. German attempts to steer the Soviets southward toward India did not interest the heirs of Tsar Alexander. Muscovite enthusiasm for staking out spheres of influence "according to standards that would last for centuries" was limited; Molotov returned again and again to the embarrassing questions of Finland, Rumania, and Bulgaria. By the end, despite virtual failure, Hitler was "genuinely relieved": "M[olotov] had let the cat out of the bag." The Führer immediately ordered the construction "in the greatest haste" of three major eastern field headquarters from which to direct the coming campaign. On 5 December, after an unencouraging Soviet reply to the proposals made to Molotov, Hitler passed judgment: "The decision over European hegemony [will] come in war against Russia."[38]

But when Hitler received Ciano at the *Berghof* on 18 November, nominally to discuss the Spanish question, no word about "the East" passed the Führer's lips. The atmosphere was at first "heavy." Hitler was "pessimistic and consider[ed] the situation very much compromised by what ha[d] happened in the Balkans." His criticisms of Italy's activities were "open, rapid-fire, and unanswerable."[39] Hitler had cordially detested Ciano since the scene at Salzburg in August 1939, was fully aware of Ciano's role in instigating the Greek operation, and had no intention of letting him down lightly. Hitler blamed on Italy the danger to the oilfields, Bulgarian hesitations about entering the Tripartite Pact, increased Russian interest in the Balkans, and Turkish skittishness. To ward off the "psychological consequences" of Italian failure, Germany would have to take Gibraltar. If the British established themselves in force in continental Greece, Germany would invade that country through Bulgaria in the spring.

As Hitler pointed out, the attitude of Bulgaria depended partly upon that of Yugoslavia. He therefore asked Ciano point-blank what Italy was ready to give in order to neutralize the latter state, and suggested a guarantee of Yugoslavia's present borders as well as the tempting prize of Salonika. To sweeten the arrangement for Italy, he proposed demilitarization of Yugoslavia's Adriatic coast, making that sea an Italian lake in law as well as in fact. Ciano, who "had little comment on the Führer's remarks and had merely attempted to ascribe the failure against Greece to a tactical error of the Italian command," appeared most impressed with the proposal.

Such projects were not entirely new to either Germans or Italians. Prince Regent Paul and his associates had approached the German high command in early November through the Yugoslav military attaché in Berlin. The attaché had emphasized Yugoslavia's continued interest in an old Serb aspiration, an Aegean outlet at Salonika. An important Yugoslav journalist acting for Minister President Dragiša Cvetkovitch made analogous remarks to a German colleague close to the foreign office. The German minister reported similar stirrings from Belgrade: the Serbs preferred to despoil their Balkan Pact allies themselves, rather than see Italy or Bulgaria despoil them with unfortunate strategic consequences for Yugoslavia.[40]

Prince Paul's court minister and chief confidential adviser, Milan Antić, made even more definite overtures to the Italians. Antić's emissary, a Serb lawyer named Vladislav Stakić, met Ciano in the greatest secrecy in Rome on 11 November, and announced Yugoslav willingness to forget past misunderstandings, which included two accidental Italian air raids in early November on the Macedonian border town of Bitolj.[41] The Yugoslavs evidently saw Greek humiliation of Italy as a unique occasion to reinsure themselves with the Axis, and particularly the Italians, at the lowest possible cost. Stakić had proposed "very extensive guarantees," including the demilitarization of the Adriatic – the entire Adriatic, not merely the Yugoslav side. Ciano noted that "even alliance is spoken of." By Stakić's account, Ciano himself raised that issue, and insisted vehemently that Yugoslavia had nothing to fear from Italy, whose aspirations lay south of Albania. Ciano offered to transform the 1937 Pact, still nominally in effect, into an alliance not against Britain, for he knew Prince Paul's sentiments, but – for instance – against the Soviet Union, and "perhaps," as he replied to an enthusiastic interjection of Stakić's, against Germany. Ciano was happy to discard his Croat friends and return to his 1937 line. A firm Italo-Yugoslav alliance, he now felt, would be far better than "taking home with us a nervous and untrustworthy group such as the Croats."[42] Mussolini himself had encourʌged Ciano's talks with Stakić, although not out of love for his eastern neigh-bors.

At Berchtesgaden, Ciano mentioned the Stakić feeler, and proposed to pursue it while keeping Hitler informed. If genuine negotiations resulted, Ciano disingenuously promised that he would invite the participation of Germany. At the end of the conversation, Hitler again turned to the Medi-terranean. Neither he nor Ciano mentioned Taranto, but it was obviously in their thoughts. Italy must take Mersa Matruh as soon as possible so that German long-range bombers could mine the Suez Canal and annihilate the British fleet. A German army would then descend from Rumania to the Aegean in early spring to throw the British out of Greece. That would be all. Hitler consigned the final attack on Egypt to the fall of 1941, by which time, although he of course did not mention it, the destruction of the Soviet Union would have opened the road to the Middle East from north as well as west.

Ciano seemed to the Germans to be "generally relieved by the prospect of being able to liquidate the Greek undertaking successfully in the manner proposed." Mussolini, apprised of Hitler's Yugoslav proposal, accepted without qualifications. In return, Hitler provided Ciano with a letter to Mussolini — sealed, naturally, lest Ciano peruse it before his master. The letter reiterated Hitler's unhappiness that Mussolini had not consulted him before going ahead in Greece, and proposed the same remedies for the result-ing disaster that Hitler had pressed on Ciano. Despite Hitler's "heartfelt greetings" and expressions of "loyal comradeship," the letter's purport was unmistakable. "He has given me the ruler across the knuckles," Mussolini remarked to Ciano after meditating on it. In his reply, Mussolini agreed to Hitler's proposals, with the sole reservation that Yugoslavia should not swoop upon Salonika before Italy had delivered "a first blow" against Greece. Prematurely, Mussolini insisted that he had "had his black week," but now the worst was over.[43]

Badoglio goes. For Marshal Pietro Badoglio at least, the worst was indeed over. He had not limited his ex post facto defiance of Mussolini to the 10 November service chiefs' meeting. Word rapidly spread from circles around the *Comando Supremo* that Badoglio had openly disapproved of the Greek operation from the beginning. Farinacci was probably the first to bring these rumors to Mussolini's attention, although the ever-vigilant police may have preceded him. On 9 November the Ras of Cremona wrote Mussolini a bril-liantly polemical letter, which he followed up or delivered in person three days later.[44] Farinacci fulminated against "the military chiefs, and above all Badoglio, [who] go about claiming that the enterprise was decided against their will." "If we were in Russia," Farinacci added with a touch of envy, "these gentlemen would already have ceased to pontificate!" The question required an "extremely careful political evaluation." Was it possible in the present situation to "get rid of Badoglio and his entourage?" Farinacci did not hesitate: ". . . considering public opinion calmly in all its aspects, I am convinced that great advantages could be gained by a forceful gesture," especially if "after a decision of yours that struck deep, we could advance swiftly and victoriously in Greece and Africa." After rehearsing Badoglio's iniquities, from his share in responsibility for Caporetto to his current role in thwarting Mussolini's offensive ardor, Farinacci demanded a ruthless purge: "My dear Duce, I consider that in your interest, in the interest of Fascism, and above all in that of Italy, it is an absolute necessity to liquidate a certain kind of past with the liquidation of those military leaders who no longer enjoy the confidence not only of the nation, but even of the Army." Presumably as a measure of his sincerity, Farinacci ended by offering to serve in that most distant and desperate of Italian theaters, East Africa, as Mussolini's envoy and confidential agent.

On top of Badoglio's words at the service chiefs' conference, Farinacci's letter and his presumably impassioned face-to-face advocacy impelled Mussolini to consider dismissing Badoglio not in the spring, but immediately. By 13 November Mussolini had begun "to distrust Badoglio profoundly," and ordered Ciano to "increase surveillance to the maximum" for the forthcoming conference between Badoglio and Keitel at Innsbruck, now scheduled after many delays for 15 November. Ciano seems to have taken these remarks as a cue, and have joined forces at this point with Farinacci to destroy Badoglio. Farinacci hoped to renovate the military under Party auspices, Ciano hoped to save his own political skin by sacrificing Badoglio. At a ceremonial luncheon on 15 November, Farinacci "assaulted" Mussolini, and attempted with Ciano's assistance to persuade De Bono, as a member of the old guard, to "stick with them" against Badoglio rather than playing his usual role as the military's spokesman within the Party. Farinacci, never a subtle negotiator, made clear to De Bono the consequences of refusal: "If you don't join us we'll knife you too." Muti's replacement as secretary of the Party, Adelchi Serena, had made similar if less direct overtures to De Bono the previous day. Farinacci followed up by forwarding to Mussolini an anonymous memorandum, purportedly from a senior officer, which roundly denounced the Army's current organization, the ineptitude of preparations for the Greek action, and the Navy's negligence at Taranto.[45] Farinacci presumably hoped to persuade Mussolini that a purge of the high command would meet with acquiescence or even favor in the military.

But Badoglio himself made Farinacci's case with indiscretions at Innsbruck. The Badoglio–Keitel conference was without significance for the conduct of the war; neither marshal had any real power. Badoglio, whose francophilia had turned in the course of the summer to a rancid mixture of resentment and mistrust, conveyed Italy's continued suspicion of Franco-German rapprochement, while simultaneously asking for German help in restraining eventual Yugoslav attempts to exploit Italy's embarrassment in Greece. Such topics were of minor significance beside Badoglio's revelations about the origins of the Greek operation. He cavalierly shrugged off respon-

sibility for the fiasco, which was due to "a question outside his own baili-
wick." Mussolini and Ciano had allegedly expected Bulgarian "influence" to
tie the Greeks up in Thrace, and had bet on "revolution" in Epirus; the
Germans naïvely concluded that Badoglio had taken a firm line against the
operation. Not to be outdone, Keitel misleadingly confided that had he
known in time, he would have descended on Rome by air to advise against
the attack.[46]

Mussolini learned of Badoglio's words almost immediately. In his letter
reporting the 18 November talks with Hitler at the *Berghof,* Ciano disclosed
that Mackensen had informed him "very confidentially" of Badoglio's
remarks to Keitel. Mussolini was "naturally beside himself," and even the
King judged that Badoglio "was not conducting himself very loyally."[47] On
21 November, Mussolini announced to Ciano the imminence of a change of
the guard "in the military sector." Meanwhile, Badoglio was not content
with just one *faux pas;* he next confided in Alessandro Pavolini, minister of
popular culture and close associate of Ciano's:

There is no doubt that Jacomoni and Visconti Prasca have heavy responsibilities in
the Albanian affair. But the greatest blame must be placed elsewhere – and it is all
in the Duce's command. It is a command he is unable to exercise. Let him leave it
to us, and when things don't go well, let him strike down those responsible.

Badoglio presumably intended either to provoke Mussolini to dismiss him
before the military situation deteriorated further, or to capitalize upon the
Greek disaster in order to achieve undisputed control of Italian strategy. The
result was "fulminating." Mussolini denounced Badoglio to Ciano as an
"enemy of the Regime" and a traitor, remarks Ciano presumably relayed to
Farinacci.[48]

On 23 November the Party chieftain struck, apparently without directly
consulting Mussolini, who was engaged in a leisurely perusal of the Army
list in search of a suitable successor for Badoglio. Farinacci's Cremona newspaper, *Regime Fascista,* accused the *Comando Supremo* of a "certain lack of
foresight and of proper timing" in mounting the Greek operation. An open
secret in the regime's inner circle now became public property, prematurely
and dangerously. Badoglio took immediate umbrage. To remain in office he
had swallowed much, but public attacks on his personal prestige were intolerable. "In crude words" he denied responsibility for the Greek disaster and
demanded a full and explicit retraction by Farinacci. Failing this he threatened to resign immediately. As even Armellini, Badoglio's "devoted creature," noted, this was "indeed a bit late."[49]

A Farinacci retraction was scarcely likely. Ciano was certain his ally would
"plant high explosive under his own newspaper presses rather than agree."
Mussolini was determined to "get rid" of Badoglio, although he continued
to proceed slowly, "because that is his nature in cases of this sort and because
he wants to let things take their natural course." Caution notwithstanding,
Mussolini called upon the King on the morning of 25 November, told the

tale of Badoglio at Innsbruck, and confided his intention of having it out one way or the other, that same day. The King made no move to save Badoglio. Cavagnari also tottered. Mussolini had consulted the retired Grand Admiral of World War I, Paolo Thaon di Revel, who had "expressed himsel in terms not overly flattering" about Cavagnari and Somigli, whom he held responsible for Taranto.[50]

With Badoglio, Mussolini was initially conciliatory. The press, he claimed disingenuously, was irresponsible (". . . one of the sectors of Italian life he had not yet been able to organize . . ."). But he nevertheless made clear that he would tolerate no more dissidence. He reproached Badoglio for the leaks about the marshal's alleged opposition to the Greek war. This rebuke finally impelled Badoglio to go. After meditating overnight, he sent Mussolini his letter of resignation. Now it was Mussolini's turn to hesitate, perhaps because Farinacci's attack had "not produced a good impression" on political opinion; the dictator proposed to think the matter over for twenty-four hours.[51]

The next day, 27 November, Mussolini unexpectedly greeted Badoglio warmly. He tried half-heartedly to persuade Badoglio to stay on, and simultaneously explored the chances of a retraction. Farinacci answered by proclaiming in the lobby of the Chamber of *Fasci* and Corporations that he would go into enforced exile on the Lipari Islands rather than take back a word. In a vehement letter to Mussolini on 28 November he defended his conduct and countered suggestions that his attack on Badoglio had proved a political disaster:

If one of us, in a moment of such gravity, had committed even the least of the deeds done by the Marquis of Caporetto, he would be at this moment – and justly – at [the prison island of] Lampedusa. Can you imagine the fate that would have been reserved for Farinacci if he had gone to Germany to accuse the Duce?

I ask you to pardon me if I have caused you all this trouble, but I have a clear conscience. When they unjustifiedly wanted to pin responsibility for the failure in Greece upon the political leadership, and people in Italy were already beginning to talk – albeit prudently – I felt the need, o my Duce, to take up a position that has completely changed the public attitude.

I have no office to defend, nor do I ask for ministerial posts or lavish perquisites. [All] I ask is that you be faithful to the Revolution, to Fascism, to the Regime and [all] I seek is to be the mastiff at your heels.

Whether he reserved his teeth for the regime's enemies, or for Mussolini should the latter show insufficient faithfulness to the revolution, Farinacci did not disclose. Not for nothing did Mussolini both hate and fear him.[52]

No way out existed. Badoglio had to go, despite the damage his resignation might do to public confidence. The problem of the succession remained, and the circle of suitable candidates was small. Only the superannuated De Bono and the surviving marshals of World War I outranked Graziani, as was theoretically desirable in a chief of the *Comando Supremo*. Other possibilities were Alfredo Guzzoni, currently without a command, Pietro Pintor, head of

he Italian armistice commission dealing with the French, and Pietro Gaz-
era, a former minister of war now serving as one of Amedeo d'Aosta's prin-
ipal subordinates in East Africa.

Guzzoni had commanded the invasion of Albania in 1939, and despite
Ciano's acid description of his "little dyed wig and hyper-inflated pot-belly,"
was reasonably competent. But his talents appeared more suited to replacing
oddu as undersecretary of war and deputy chief of the *Comando Supremo,*
ositions to which Mussolini appointed him on 29 November. Gazzera was
n Farinacci's partisan description a "creature of Badoglio," and in any case
was indispensable in Ethiopia. Mussolini judged Pintor "too slow and doc-
rinaire," perhaps as a result of the general's reluctance to attack in the Alps
n June. Farinacci was even less complimentary: "Pintor *is* Badoglio – only
worse."[53]

Mussolini did toy with the idea of assuming the position himself, in the
manner of Hitler's dismissal of Blomberg. But by 30 November, when he
denounced Badoglio roundly in the Council of Ministers, he had made up
his mind. That afternoon he summoned General Ugo Cavallero, and after a
hort conversation in which Cavallero demonstrated both familiarity with
nd qualified optimism about the situation in Albania, informed him that
he Badoglio crisis was "irremediable." Cavallero himself would be the suc-
essor. No direct evidence links Farinacci or Ciano with Cavallero's unex-
ected appointment, but informed opinion took their involvement for
granted. "The Farinaccians win," noted De Bono enviously.[54] Cavallero was
ndeed an associate of Farinacci. The general's ties to Palazzo Chigi, where
he had served as military adviser and as the Italian representative in the Pact
f Steel military liaison committee, were also close. He was the father-in-law
f Jacomoni, in whose elevation to the nobility he had had a hand.[55] Never-
heless, Ciano apparently did not press actively for the appointment, and
displayed no marked enthusiasm for Cavallero in his diary. Both that source
nd the postwar testimony of a high propaganda official in daily contact with
Ciano suggest that the foreign minister proposed Gazzera to Mussolini, with
Cavallero as deputy chief.[56] Ciano resigned himself quickly, however, to
Mussolini's choice. He sounded out Guzzoni on the latter's relationship with
Cavallero, and announced to the Germans that he himself was "very con-
ented" with the appointment.[57] Subsequently, of course, Ciano came to
egard the general as a dangerous competitor for Mussolini's favor, and, as
he prospect of defeat became clearer in 1941 and 1942, as a possible aspirant
o the honor of playing the Italian Pétain vis-à-vis the Allies.[58]

Despite the political circus surrounding the supersession of Badoglio, Cava-
lero was a logical choice.[59] He had unusual military expertise and long
ervice as a senior industrial manager. This combination of talents was
unique in the armed forces; along with Cavallero's consummate sycophancy,
t was to keep him in office until January 1943. He was also monumentally
unpopular in the military establishment, a quality that made him initially
far more dependent on Mussolini than either Gazzera or Pintor would have

been. Cavallero had resigned as undersecretary of war after a violent quarrel with Badoglio in 1928, and his reputation had suffered permanent damage in 1933, when it emerged that the giant Ansaldo steel and shipbuilding combine that he then managed had delivered mild steel to the Navy in place of armorplate. His fellow generals thenceforth paraded professional and financial jealousy as moral outrage, although Cavallero was apparently personally blameless.

It was now Badoglio's turn to have second thoughts: the selection of an old enemy as his successor goaded him to return to Rome and solicit royal intervention. But despite the willingness of the minister of the royal household, Count Acquarone, to cabal on Badoglio's behalf with De Bono and Armellini, the King was unhelpful. Cavallero, Victor Emmanuel remarked, was "undoubtedly a man of great value from a professional point of view." Badoglio, who appeared at the Quirinal on 3 December with a "green" face, was "physically destroyed . . . and mentally intorpidated," an opinion Acquarone relayed to Mussolini. Serena had already briefed the leaders of Party and Militia: Badoglio, "the man of Caporetto," would shortly *"be thrown out* — more or less — . . . *in disgrace."*[60] All across Italy, a massive Party attack on Badoglio's prestige "in order to defend the Duce," as Serena put it later, was beginning.[61] On 4 December, although the political repercussions of the step still preoccupied him, and although he was anxious to conciliate Badoglio, who now announced that he was disposed to retract his resignation, Mussolini released the marshal from office.[62]

More or less simultaneously, De Vecchi and Cavagnari departed under an even greater cloud than Badoglio. Now that war with Greece had actually come, De Vecchi was less eager than in the summer, and for good reason. The Aegean was now indeed a British lake. "In this situation," noted Ciano on 15 November, "Comrade De Vecchi thinks it appropriate to hand in his resignation . . . even though he was one of the most active — indeed, the most active, of those who excited Mussolini to make war on Greece." Now that "the time for the rats to go on deck [to abandon ship] seems to have come, he wants to be the first to disembark." This devastating judgment presumably stemmed from a desire to share out responsibility for the Greek fiasco, and was almost certainly unjust. De Vecchi was in many ways grotesque, but no coward. His resignation was the consequence of a recrudescence of his running conflict with the military bureaucracy in Rome over authority and supplies. Already in August De Vecchi had attempted to resign after exchanging insulting letters with Badoglio, whom Mussolini had pacified by remarking that there was no reasoning with lunatics. In November, De Vecchi may have had a political motive as well. De Bono had apparently written a letter to his fellow Quadrumvir that hinted at joint action in the political crisis De Bono saw approaching. The need to be in Rome in case Mussolini were to falter presumably reinforced De Vecchi's desire to leave Rhodes. But the consequences of his resignation must have sorely disappointed him. Mussolini refused his offer to serve elsewhere, an offer De Vecchi characteristically accompanied with megalomaniacal demands for "many gold stripes on his cuffs." The moment that Mussolini had anticipated with relish since 1938, in which De Vecchi would make "such a great and definitive pratfall that he would feel himself demolished in his own esteem, even more than in that of others" had come.[63]

Cavagnari's going on 7 December produced more stir than that of De Vecchi. The crews at the naval base at Messina burst into cheers while their embarrassed but equally pleased officers attempted to quiet them. At Taranto satisfaction was general as well.[64] Cavagnari defended himself in his reply to Mussolini's letter of dismissal with the claim that "the Italian Navy, prepared during many years of tenacious work, has up to now stood up to and continues to stand up to the pressure of almost the whole fleet of the strongest naval power in the world."[65] He or his subordinates also spread the story that he had resigned by choice rather than serve with Cavallero, and rumors circulated that before the British attack Mussolini had personally decreed the concentration of the battle fleet at Taranto — in order to pass it in review.[66] Such tactics were both discreditable and futile. The hulk of the *Cavour,* emerging grimly from the waters of Taranto harbor, was sufficient monument to Cavagnari's tenure of office. Whether his successor, Admiral Arturo Riccardi, and Mussolini's other new military subordinates could do better remained to be seen.

2. Disaster

A truce through Hitler? While the military change of the guard ran its course, Italy's position in Albania continued to dissolve. Even before the beginning of the withdrawal, the *Regio Esercito* was in difficulty. It faced the short-term claims of the Albanian theater, the requirements of the long-term offensive buildup, the insatiable demands of North Africa, and readiness for the occupation of Corsica and southern France, a readiness Mussolini insisted on maintaining. Roatta reminded his superiors on 13 November of his October warning of the consequences of demobilization, and began to agitate for a reversal. Mussolini agreed at first only to partial remobilization, using men not previously called up from the classes of 1910 through 1915. Roatta refused to accept this concession, and insisted on gradual but complete reconstitution of the Army. On 21 November Badoglio took the matter to Mussolini once more, and persuaded him. On 23 November, the day after the retreat from Korçë, he decreed total remobilization.[67]

The decision inevitably had little immediate impact. The Greeks continued to advance, though Soddu had initially expected withdrawal to ease the pressure, and even Roatta had judged that the enemy, "although emboldened," was now in logistical difficulties. Soddu demanded "a new spirit" from his subordinates. He lamented the absence of Italian counterattacks. He deplored the constant requests for air support against "small infiltrations" that units were perfectly capable of dealing with themselves. Too many divisions, he complained, had lost machine guns, mortars, and artillery. He insisted on "severe and above all immediate" measures against those who abandoned weapons or positions. He requested, symptomatically, that commanders visit their troops; some battalions had never seen their divisional commander. Finally, without a trace of embarrassment, he reminded his subordinates that "it [was] not enough to give orders: one must personally check up on their execution."[68]

An officer corps that needed reminding of these truths was in sorry shape indeed. Nor did Soddu's exhortations have any noticeable effect; simultaneously, the commander of 11th Army, General Carlo Geloso, announced that his retreat had carried him beyond the planned line of resistance. Greek pressure continued unabated, and the troops "were for the most part tired." Why the Greeks were not equally tired Geloso did not explain. Soddu in reply urged him to consider what would happen if he did not make a stand at some point, and implored him to rethink the matter "with that faith that animates us, and above all taking into account the political and morale factors inevitably linked to the decision now being made."[69]

In 9th Army's sector on the left, abandonment of Korçë had not solved Soddu's problems. At the end of November the Greeks renewed their pressure there as well. Soddu commanded his subordinates to require "if necessary, even the supreme sacrifice" by the defenders, a demand that revealed the extent to which the philosophy of the "easy war" had replaced the routine acceptance of death without which no army can function. Mussolini told the Council of Ministers on 30 November that the situation was "grave," and "could even become dramatic," but it was not until the morning of 4 December that the latter adjective became fully appropriate. Soddu temporarily lost his head. The Greeks had broken through and taken Pogradec, a town north of Korçë vital to the Italian defense. Soddu telephoned his former deputy at the War Ministry, General Antonio Sorice, that he judged further military action "impossible." Only a "political intervention" could save the situation, an idea that apparently originated with Vercellino, the despairing commander of 9th Army.[70]

The news temporarily shattered Mussolini: "There is nothing to be done. It is absurd and grotesque, but that's the way it is. We must ask for a truce through Hitler." Ciano was aghast: "The Greeks would demand, as a first condition, the personal guarantee of the Führer that nothing more would be done against them." To his diary Ciano insisted with his usual bravado that he would put a bullet through his head before telephoning Ribbentrop on such an errand. By his own account, which probably exaggerated his role, Ciano persuaded Mussolini that the Greeks could not attack forever: "Time will give us victory, but if we give in it is the end." The loss of Albania would indeed have been the end for Ciano's career. In any case, whether at Ciano's insistence, or on advice from Guzzoni (who despite his appearance was cool-headed in a crisis) or of his own accord, Mussolini ordered Soddu to stand. The enemy could not keep it up: "behind him he has no war industry and can only count on supplies from Great Britain." As well as this sound judgment, Mussolini also passed on the fruit of his despair, a plan he and Ciano had concocted for a retreat to two separate redoubts, one at Valona and another in northern Albania around Tirana and Durazzo. This was indeed a recipe for total disaster. As Armellini noted, the new perimeters would be longer than the line Soddu was struggling to hold.[71] It was also unlikely that Soddu's troops would arrive on the new lines in any condition to stand.

The only solution was to defend in place, and Mussolini overcame his despondency long enough to dispatch Cavallero to Albania with a mandate to stiffen Soddu or relieve him. In private, Mussolini lamented: "Every man commits in the course of his life a fatal error, and I committed one when I believed General Visconti Prasca; but how could one avoid it if the man appeared so sure of himself and all the elements [of the situation] gave the greatest assurance?" Mussolini voiced once more a perennial complaint that he was to repeat ever more vehemently in the days to come. The "human material" he had to work with was "worthless." He would have to found a racial "warrior aristocracy" from the Po Valley for which the masses would merely manufacture weapons. He renewed his promise of a "third wave," that after victory "would plough under those men and institutions that have in these hours revealed their true nature."[72]

Fortunately, Cavallero reported by the evening of 5 December that Soddu proposed to maintain a continuous front. The retreat to the Valona and Tirana redoubts was only an "extreme hypothesis." The weather, which had aided the Greeks in their initial defense, now did the same for the Italians, particularly around Pogradec. By 7 December Cavallero could report the immediate crisis over. Italy would not lose Albania in the near future. Nevertheless, Soddu's days in command were numbered, even though it emerged that by "political intervention" he had probably meant a diplomatic action to secure German or Bulgarian help, rather than a request for a truce.[73] The Greeks continued their advance, but with diminished striking power.

Desert débâcle. Disaster in North Africa followed swiftly upon crisis in Albania. Mussolini's mid-October despondency over the Egyptian offensive had not lasted. In the euphoria that the approaching "punitive expedition" against Greece had engendered, Mussolini had on 26 October once more dispatched a letter spurring Graziani onward. The long halt at Sidi el Barrani, Mussolini maintained, had helped only the enemy. Continued delay in order to complete aqueduct and road would enable the British to render a renewal of the Italian offensive "practically impossible," while the RAF was "literally flattening" Graziani's rear — à propos of which Mussolini uncharitably remarked that Graziani's command post at Cirene was too far from the front. Mussolini concluded with his now traditional political motif: "I repeat that at the peace table we shall take home with us only what we conquer militarily." Sidi el Barrani was in itself no prize. Graziani could either attack or resign.[74]

Graziani replied with a long self-justificatory letter, and duly offered his resignation. If he stayed on, he insisted on the "full and absolute confidence of the Chief." This unexpectedly firm reply took Mussolini aback. He had intended to push Graziani forward, not relieve him of command when no suitable replacement existed. Graziani had called Mussolini's bluff, and the latter on 1 November ordered him to "consider the matter closed" and to once more enjoy "full confidence."[75] Mussolini also announced less welcome news: the Greek front now took priority. Graziani was to mount diversionary attacks while continuing to prepare to take Mersa Matruh. Mussolini had also communicated slightly earlier through Badoglio that he did not now envisage further operations beyond that point. In reply to a long and ambiguous Graziani disquisition on the advantages and disadvantages of a *Panzerdivision* for Libya, Badoglio once more made it clear that Mussolini had no intention of accepting German troop offers. A Badoglio strategic directive of 7 November, which reiterated Mussolini's insistence upon the primacy of the Greek front, did not provide any comfort.[76]

Graziani indeed had cause for complaint. No one had consulted him about the attack on Greece. In January 1941, his persecution complex fully aroused, Graziani claimed to Mussolini in person that the Roman authorities had mounted the affair conspiratorially behind his back, circumventing him as Army chief of staff and slighting his interests as North African commander.[77] In his memoirs, Graziani accused Roatta of falsely ascribing to him approval of the "Contingency 'G' " plan in September, and claimed that his former deputy had only told him about the Yugoslav operation on 1 October.[78] Actually, Graziani had kept abreast of the planning of both Greek and Yugoslav operations throughout the summer through Roatta's reports, and had approved the Greek plan by radio message on 26 September.[79] Mussolini's "two pillars" memorandum of 5 October had apprised him of Mussolini's renewed interest in Greece. But he did hear of the actual attack virtually "from the newspapers." Badoglio's message informing him of the launching date left the *Comando Supremo* on 22 October but did not reach Cirene until 1 November. A follow-up message dispatched when Graziani did not acknowledge the original arrived the day of the attack.[80]

Apart from this grievance, Graziani remained short of trucks and armored vehicles. Supplying the advanced forces around Sidi el Barrani was already a very considerable task, and Graziani's subordinates lacked the spare parts and trained mechanics to maintain the vehicles they did have. Almost 2,000 of the 5,140 army vehicles in Cyrenaica on 10 November were down for maintenance. Graziani had received 956 vehicles from Italy in the summer and fall, and a further 664 trucks were either in transit or awaiting shipment within the month.[81] His complaints of inadequate support were thus not entirely justified, particularly in view of the Tripoli port bottleneck, which like its Albanian counterpart prevented any dramatic increase in the supplies and equipment shipped. Still, Mussolini did order an M-13/40 medium tank battalion destined for Graziani diverted to Albania in late October, and the campaign there swiftly proved a bottomless pit into which ever greater volumes of equipment from the skeleton units in Italy and the exiguous monthly production of the war industries disappeared. Graziani's principal problem was that he refused to make the best of what he had by concentrating his vehicles in a small mobile force. After the discussions in late October with General von Thoma, he had belatedly contemplated forming an armored division from units in North Africa and motorized reinforcements from Italy, but the project remained on paper.[82]

Graziani was at least ostensibly preparing to renew the advance at some unspecified point in late December. Under his supervision, Berti had grouped the forward units of 10th Army (1st and 2nd Libyan Division, "3 January" Blackshirt Division, Maletti's brigade group, and the "Cirene" and "Catanzaro" Divisions) in a series of temporary strongpoints in a semicircle around Sidi el Barrani. The strongpoints were too far apart to be mutually supporting, and Berti attempted to cover the ten to thirty kilometer gaps between them with motorized patrols. Graziani was not happy, but not alive to the situation's full danger. His insistence on advancing with overwhelming superiority in manpower so intensified his logistical difficulties and absorbed his available vehicles that a more elastic deployment was impossible.

Graziani did not expect any serious British challenge. In late November he did urge on 10th Army some action to close the most conspicuous gap in the ring of strongpoints – the very gap through which British armored forces were shortly to pour.[83] But despite increasingly ominous intelligence reports of British reinforcement of Egypt and offensive intentions, Graziani remained confident of getting his own blow in first. Berti even went on leave to Italy to seek treatment for piles and visit his sick and aged mother, and returned to Libya a full five days after the British had begun the destruction of his command.

In the last days before the catastrophe, Graziani received numerous warnings. As early as 2 December radio intercepts suggested British mechanized units were moving west in force. Air reconnaissance confirmed that the enemy was unusually active. But Graziani's intelligence staff and that of 10th Army came to the remarkable conclusion that the movements were either defensive preparations against forthcoming Italian attack, demonstrations to cover the sending of British troops to Greece, or a routine relief of forward troops.[84]

Not until the night of 8/9 December did the crescendo of British air bombardment, naval gunfire, and patrol activity at last awaken Graziani.[85] Then, in the early morning of 9 December, tanks of the British 7th Royal Tank Regiment broke into Maletti's perimeter at Nibeiwa from the west, after destroying a number of Italian medium tanks parked outside with their crews scurrying about in various stages of undress.[86] Three hours later, Maletti was dead and his troops either casualties, prisoners, or dispersed. 7th Armored Division meanwhile rolled through the thirty kilometer gap between Maletti and the "Cirene" division strongpoints to the south, and attacked the "Catanzaro" division far in the Italian rear. In the three days that followed, the 7th Armored and 4th Indian Divisions, the only two major British units committed, destroyed the two Libyan Divisions, the "Cirene," the "3 January" blackshirts, and most of the "Catanzaro" Division before pressing westward toward Libya.

While what remained of 10th Army desperately attempted to form a defensive line on the frontier, Graziani bombarded Rome with recriminatory rhetoric. By 12 December he was insisting hysterically that all of Cyrenaica was in danger:

I consider it my duty, rather than sacrificing my useless person on the spot, to go to Tripoli, if I succeed in getting there, to keep flying on that citadel at least the banner of Italy, while awaiting that the mother country put me in condition to continue to fight. From myself down to the last private, we have the deepest conviction that we have made every possible effort to resist, after those efforts I made to make Rome understand the true conditions in this theater of operations, and the equipment needed to deal adequately with them without having to put the troops out front with rifles and with very few antitank guns to fight the battle of flea against elephant. Let this be said as my last will and testament, and in order that everyone assume in the light of history the responsibility for what is today occurring here.[87]

The possibility that Graziani had totally lost his head rather daunted Mussolini, who now faced the second loss of nerve of a theater commander in a week. He replied steadyingly that he counted on Graziani "as always, and more." The enemy must have his own problems, and enough artillery was available between Bardia and Tobruk to break the British attack.[88] This did not placate Graziani, who replied with the famous telegram "from man to man" of 14 December:

Your affirmations of greatest trust in me may move me but cannot make me forget that this confidence should have been conceded, in full, beforehand, when I was attempting to convince you with all my strength in order to make you understand the truth. You have not listened to me. You have not permitted me to address myself to you directly any longer. . . . You have continued to listen to those who are either deliberately tricking or betraying you. I have been described as having become incompetent, inept, and preoccupied only with safeguarding my point of departure. I know everything: facts and names. At this moment of supreme responsibility in the face of history and of the *Patria* it is now wretched, but utterly legitimate and necessary that I should talk to you as man to man. You did not give me the recognition due me upon my return from Ethiopia. You then called me to the post of chief of staff of the Army without giving me the chance of exercising my authority freely; instead all those close to you sniped at me: at me, who alone had the courage never to tell you untruths. Then you sent me here without even giving me the chance to talk with you. You have forgotten that if the Ethiopian victory was possible it was because you permitted me to communicate freely with you, jumping all the *canaille* who would have wanted to prevent me. Now, Duce, there is only one arbiter, destiny, to whose superior powers I cannot oppose anything except my own mortal ones which I will continue to use to animate myself and all others up to the last moment. I am suffering the consequences of a state of affairs created not by my blindness or by my will, but by those of all those who have miserably betrayed you, and with you, Italy.[89]

This operatic outburst was embarrassing. How could a dictator tolerate such nonsense? Guzzoni feared for the Duce's authority, and immediately had Armellini destroy all trace of the message, although Mussolini later made no attempt to hide the fact that Graziani had sent him an "insolent" telegram. Guzzoni also restrained Mussolini's first impulse to fire Graziani. The next day, the dictator replied longsufferingly that the past was past, "and what counts is the future and the saving of Cyrenaica." But he did not forget. In 1942, as Rommel advanced on El Alamein and Axis victory in North Africa appeared momentarily within reach at last, Mussolini ordered a secret enquiry into Graziani's conduct in 1940–1 with a view to breaking him.[90]

Fortunately for Graziani's disorganized forces, the British did have their difficulties. After rolling up the border defenses and enveloping the Libyan strongpoint of Bardia by 14 December, they stopped. Replacing the 4th Indian Division, dispatched to East Africa immediately after its successful assault upon Graziani's forward troops, and opening the port of Sollum to supply a further advance took up the latter half of December. Both Armellini and the German staffs in Berlin thought at the time that the Italians should have used this respite to break contact and withdraw,[91] perhaps to a stronger position in the hills of Cyrenaica such as the Derna–Berta–Mechili line. The British would then have had to lengthen their supply lines further and mount a systematic assault in terrain less favorable to tanks than the desert. A concentration of all available Italian mobile and armored forces around Mechili might with *Luftwaffe* support have held for some time British attempts to turn the position's flank. Alternately, Graziani might have abandoned the border positions and Bardia and have attempted to hold in force the stronger fortifications at Tobruk. He did neither. From the beginning he proposed to hold everything: the border, Bardia, Tobruk, and ultimately Derna–Berta–Mechili. Successive defensive positions would ostensibly slow the British and possibly even stop them.[92] In reality, the plan was a recipe for the piecemeal sacrifice of what remained of 10th Army. But Mussolini was only too happy to approve it.[93] He was not the man to press his generals to retreat, and he was presumably mightily relieved that Graziani did not intend to carry out his 12 December threat to retire in panic to the Tripoli citadel.

On 3 January the Australian 6th Infantry Division opened the assault on the foremost of Graziani's bastions, Bardia. The position fell not to masses of armor – despite claims to that effect in the Italian official histories – but to a conventional infantry assault that breached Italian minefields and wire against minimal opposition.[94] Only twenty-three tanks accompanied the Australians, who fanned out on foot inside the Italian defenses. By 5 January the battle was over. The British captured the water plant and harbor facilities intact, took 40,000 prisoners, and secured 400 guns and 13 medium and 117 light tanks, many of them in working order. Mussolini was vexed. Clearly this latest defeat was not entirely a case of flea against elephant. As Eden quipped to Churchill, never had "so much been surrendered by so many to so few."[95]

Tobruk came next. The Australians closed on its outer defenses by 7 January, while 7th Armored Division screened the western approaches against interference from Graziani's remaining forces on the Derna escarpment to the west. Continuing logistical difficulties did not prevent the British field commander, General Richard O'Connor, from resuming the attack. On 21 January the Australians again led the way with eighteen medium tanks in support. Italian resistance "varied from the negligible to the very stubborn," and some Italian defensive strongpoints suffered 50 percent casualties. But the defense was utterly uncoordinated. Once again Australian battalions received the surrender of Italian divisions; by 22 January, when resistance ceased, O'Connor's troops had captured another 25,000 prisoners, 258 artillery pieces, and 87 tanks, at a cost of 400 Australian and British casualties.[96]

Graziani reacted swiftly. He now proposed to withdraw from Derna and the Berta–Mechili line toward Benghazi; a newly formed armored brigade was incapable of protecting his desert flank. Since he had failed to fill out the brigade with all available tanks, it could scarcely be otherwise. Even now Graziani did not dispense with histrionics: in one message to Rome he described himself as the "captain commanding a ship about to go down."[97] He did not propose to go down with it. On 31 January he ordered the tattered remnants of 10th Army to evacuate Cyrenaica, then flew to Tripoli leaving his chief of staff, the faithful General Tellera, to conduct the retreat.

Graziani's order came too late. O'Connor learned of the withdrawal through signals intelligence and air reconnaissance, and launched 7th Armored Division across the desert south of Graziani's forces. By the morning of 5 February a few British infantry companies and a small but steadily increasing force of armored cars and tanks lay unexpectedly across 10th Army's escape route at Beda Fomm. Tellera's troops attempted with considerable bravery and much disorganization to break out in a series of piecemeal attacks. The British held. By 7 February 10th Army had ceased to exist. In two months of fighting O'Connor had taken 115,000 prisoners. The way to Tripoli and to the total elimination of Italian dominion in North Africa lay open, if the British chose to take it. Neither Graziani nor the four remaining Italian divisions in Tripolitania were likely to stop them. In an abject message to Rome, Graziani pleaded nervous exhaustion and begged Mussolini to relieve him of command.[98] On 11 February Graziani flew back to Italy. The next day Erwin Rommel, newly promoted to *Generalleutnant* and enjoying Hitler's fullest confidence, landed at Castel Benito, south of Tripoli. The Italian war in Africa was over.

Albanian stalemate. Albania offered no consolation. The Greeks, after mid-December, concentrated their efforts on the center and right of Soddu's line, hoping to take Valona and deprive the Italians of one of their two ports. Metaxas held to his strategy of driving the invaders from Albania before Germany could interfere. Geloso of 11th Army did his best, but his troops slowly continued losing ground. On the coast, the "infiltration of a few Greek patrols" routed the "Siena" division in mid-December, and inland the Greeks forced the left wing of 11th Army back upon Klisura. Even as Cavallero pronounced the "period of crisis almost overcome" with the arrival of fresh divisions from Italy, the Greeks pressed on with a bewildering succession of attacks and sudden infiltrations to set up blocking positions in the Italian rear. Mussolini refused to accept the situation. He bedeviled Cavallero with peremptory demands for an active defense, for counterattacks major and minor, for the resumption of the offensive. His constant pressure expressed itself in contradictory orders and sudden decisions of dubious merit, and accentuated the already pronounced tendency of both Soddu and Cavallero to consider the "most important strategy to be that not toward the Greeks, but toward Palazzo Venezia." Not that the experts would have mastered the situation more rapidly if left to themselves — Soddu, at least, was clearly unable to cope, and the disparity between Cavallero's frequent assertions that the worst was over and the continuing retrogression of the front induced Mussolini by late December to regret having appointed him.[99] Without fear of Mussolini as well as of the Greeks, the generals might have withdrawn even faster and farther than they did.

During his first weeks as head of the *Comando Supremo,* Cavallero proposed a major offensive on the Italian left to recapture the initiative and retake Korçë at some point in early February. The Greeks did not cooperate. Their drive on Valona required immediate attention, and Mussolini insisted that 11th Army along the coast, not 9th inland, should launch the first major Italian counteroffensive, to gain time for the arrival of further reinforcements from Italy. Simultaneously, Mussolini made Cavallero "personally responsible" that 11th Army hold Tepeleni and Klisura, where the Greeks were attempting to drive a wedge between the two Italian armies to compel their separate withdrawals on Valona and Durazzo.[100]

On 29 December Mussolini called Soddu home "for consultations." The general never returned, and in mid-January resigned from the service, ostensibly for reasons of health. Mussolini had not forgiven his former associate's panic of 4 December, and the bad relations between Soddu and Cavallero that were the inevitable consequence of their presence in Albania together without a clear-cut division of responsibility further hastened Soddu's removal. The last straw, according to Ciano, was the revelation that even in Albania Soddu was allowing his artistic inclinations free reign: he passed his evenings composing soundtrack music for films.[101] Soddu's comfortable philosophy ("a fine plate of *pasta* . . . and a little music") had proved his undoing.

Cavallero assumed command of the Albanian theater while retaining the *Comando Supremo* post. He immediately took up Mussolini's project of a counteroffensive along the coast.[102] But the Greeks refused to yield the initiative. By the evening of 1 January their attack on the Italian center, through Klisura toward Berat, had made enough progress so that Cavallero had to divert carefully hoarded reserves to plug the gap. The counteroffensive receded ever further in the future. To save Klisura, Cavallero and Geloso launched a newly arrived division, the "Wolves of Tuscany," into an ill-prepared local counterattack. The ensuing débâcle is a convenient illustration of why the Italian Army failed, time and time again, to do more than slow the Greek advance.[103]

Under the command of General Ottavio Bollea, a former aide of Badoglio, the division disembarked in the first days of January and proceeded by forced marches to the area south of Berat. Recently reconstituted after partial demobilization, it arrived without mules or motor transport, organic artillery, a full complement of headquarters and service troops, and communications equipment. Many of the troops were practically untrained. It consisted of only two regiments, each of three infantry battalions.

On the morning of 9 January the division went into action after an exhausting twenty-four hour approach march in rain and snow across the disorganized rear areas of the demoralized units already in line. The purpose of the attack was to relieve fierce Greek pressure on the "Julia" alpine division, now reaching the end of its resources after two and a half months of uninterrupted combat. The "Wolves" arrived on their start line during the night, and had no chance to reconnoiter the terrain to their front. The division's chief of staff accidentally sent back to Berat a truck containing the only available topographical maps of the area. He also failed to coordinate adequately with the artillery of the "Julia," his only source of fire support.

Bollea and his chief of staff lost control at an early stage; they allowed their two regiments to become entangled on a single mule track during movement to contact. Although the "Wolves" were attacking downhill and faced only four battalions of Greeks, they rapidly lost an entire battalion of their own to encirclement. On 11 January, after two days of fighting, the division was back on its start line in considerable confusion. From that point the situation deteriorated rapidly. The Greeks sensed weakness, and pressed forward. In the ensuing four days the "Wolves" ceased to exist as an organized force. On the evening of 16 January the corps commander, General Camillo Mercalli, finally succeeded in locating Bollea, who had abandoned his troops and in a state of nervous prostration was warming himself by a fire in a rear area Albanian hamlet. The division was down to about 160 officers and men; over 4,000 were dead, wounded, or missing.

Responsibilities are fairly clear – and widely distributed. The higher commands from Cavallero downward were clearly at fault in not allowing the division a breathing space before the attack, but the condition of the "Julia" presumably made delay seem inadvisable. Bollea himself was incompetent, and, it later emerged, ill as well. His chief of staff's negligence over the maps was fully in accordance with *Regio Esercito* tradition, but nevertheless inexcusable. The two regimental commanders had lost control of their troops. By the end, one was a prisoner with his entire staff; the other succeeded in rounding up some 300 men and fighting his way back to Italian lines on 17 January. As for the troops, they had in many cases simply not fought – but given the conditions, the manifest ineptitude of their leaders, and their own lack of training, one can scarcely blame them.

Instructively, Bollea continued in service despite Mussolini's extreme displeasure over the fiasco. Guzzoni mounted an investigation, but Cavallero resisted doggedly and brought it to nothing. Geloso of 11th Army was critical of his subordinate's performance but tended to excuse it on grounds of illness. Cavallero himself ultimately decreed that Bollea, "after a suitable rest period, could still be usefully employed commanding a major unit, as long as he is not in a condition of serious disability." This indulgent toleration of incompetence was perhaps partly a result of a recognition on Cavallero's part that the "Wolves" had not had time to prepare their attack. He later reminded Geloso that units going into action should have a chance to reconnoiter, receive guides and liaison officers from neighboring units, and enjoy adequate logistical support.[104] But Cavallero's action was above all a manifestation of the tendency of the military caste to close ranks in order to protect members from the consequences of failure.

The collapse of the "Wolves" sealed the fate of Klisura. Mussolini reacted violently to its fall, which he had given Cavallero stern orders to prevent, and demanded to know what steps Cavallero had taken against those responsible. Mussolini also summoned his major commanders in Albania to a conference in Apulia on 14 January. At the meeting, he attempted with indifferent success to infuse spirit into Cavallero, Geloso, and Vercellino, then returned to Rome "dark-faced and pessimistic." In the ensuing days he bombarded Cavallero and Cavallero's staff with demands to "do something about this passivity." There was only one way: "attack, attack!"[105] He had been saying little else for three weeks. Finally, on 23 January, Cavallero mounted a counterattack that secured a momentary breathing spell. Mussolini was elated, and ordered that if the Greeks "showed any sign of crisis" Cavallero was to drive home his attack ruthlessly. Predictably, the Greeks held, succeeded in partially reconquering the terrain lost, and retained the initiative.[106] In mid-February, before Cavallero was ready to launch his counteroffensive, they resumed their drive on Valona. The attack centered on the vital road junction of Tepeleni, west of Klisura. It failed, and on 22 February Cavallero ecstatically announced that he had finally stopped the enemy. In response to Mussolini's all too predictable demand for an Italian offensive, Cavallero proposed a plan he had already outlined to Geloso.[107] The objective Cavallero chose was Klisura. If it fell, he and Mussolini hoped that Greek morale would crumble at last.

Much was at stake, and Mussolini himself made the journey to Albania in early March to watch his troops break through. The Germans were massing in Rumania, and on 28 February they began throwing bridges across the Danube into Bulgaria. Italy must make some dent in the Greek front before the *Wehrmacht* descended on Thrace. Mussolini emphasized to Geloso that the Germans would otherwise claim all the credit; the "military honor of the nation, which . . . is the only honor the nation has" was at stake.

But the twelve divisions Cavallero had assembled for the battle made not the slightest impression on the Greeks. As Cavallero explained after the fact, it was impossible to penetrate well-organized mountain defenses without "troops who know how to employ infiltration tactics and are strongly provided with officers." The Italian Army had no such troops. As Geloso had admitted earlier to Mussolini, even the relatively few officers he did have often had only sketchy training.[108] After a round of visits to the units, Mussolini returned to Rome to await the German thrust that would end the war with Greece he had begun.

Rout on the home front. Catastrophe in the Mediterranean and North Africa and inglorious stalemate in Albania shook the regime to its foundations. The war suddenly and unexpectedly changed from promenade in *passo romano* to a desperate undertaking that might already be lost. The public had initially greeted the attack on Greece with a certain favor,[109] although without the extremes of enthusiasm of the students who demonstrated in the streets of a number of major Italian cities on 29 October.[110] Initial expectations ran high, "given Italy's rank as a great power."[111] But by the end of the first week in November the public had begun to sense disaster. British air raids on Naples in retaliation for the Italian bombing of Greek cities drove the point home. Taranto and the Greek counteroffensive produced an ever more rapid decline in morale, a decline the regime's press did nothing to allay. It displayed a "stupefying fecklessness," as one police informant put it, in publicizing insignificant Italian actions with banner headlines while simultaneously printing in small type *Comando Supremo* communiqués which of necessity admitted Soddu's steady retreat into Albania.[112] Even Mussolini's belated conversion to what he described as "hav[ing] the courage not to hide the truth from the country" had little effect – except a breach of security when a communiqué accidentally disclosed withdrawal from Korçë while Soddu's troops were still in the town.[113]

Mussolini committed his personal prestige to the struggle. Even before Taranto he was aware that "the internal situation [had] worsened and that there was need for his word." On 18 November, anniversary of the 1935 League of Nations sanctions against Italy, he addressed the provincial leaders of the Party, summoned to Rome for the purpose. He blamed the British for the war, implied Italy's entry into it had produced France's collapse, and without embarrassment suggested that British propaganda held the world record for mendacity. The present conflict was a latter-day Punic War that would end with "the annihilation of the modern Carthage, England." As for the Greeks, their hatred of Italy was "inexplicable." Without reference to his own responsibilities, Mussolini now admitted that the "harsh mountains and muddy valleys of Epirus [did] not lend themselves to 'lightning warfare,' contrary to the claims of the incorrigible practitioners of map-pin strategy." The high point of the speech was Mussolini's promise that Italy would "rupture the kidneys" of Greece just as it had those of the Ethiopians. Whether it took two months or twelve mattered little. The war, Mussolini insisted with more truth than he knew, had just begun. He closed with an exhortation to "liberate the nation from its residual petit-bourgeois dead wood" of anglophiles, defeatists, and practitioners of "a certain pacifism of an intellectualloid and one-worlder bent."[114] In remarks not for publication, he also gave the Party discretion to deal with such dubious characters with its own time-honored methods.

The Greek tide continued to rise. By early December, the coincidence of the increasingly desperate Albanian situation, the introduction of a draconian rationing system for food as well as oil and fats,[115] the relief of Badoglio, and the British assault on Graziani, produced the regime's most serious crisis since the murder of Giacomo Matteotti in 1924 – a parallel the minister of popular culture did not shrink from drawing for his journalists.[116] The crisis was first of all the consequence of suddenly disappointed expectation, expectation the press had imprudently nourished. The police superintendent of Forlì described the public reaction tellingly in a report to Rome in late December:

The successful beginning of warlike activities on our fronts had here as well induced the majority of the townspeople to judge with excessive frivolity the prosecution of military operations, and therefore the recent painful episodes in Greece and on the Egyptian front have surprised public opinion all the more forcefully, in view of the strength of the illusion of an easy war.[117]

Increasing economic difficulties compounded the problem. Out of fear that available food stocks would not last until the next harvest, the regime imposed rationing of pasta, rice, and flour on 1 December at the drastically low level of two kilograms of each per person per month. Since a workingman normally consumed 400 grams of pasta per day, and the diet of the poorer segments of the population, particularly in the South, consisted almost exclusively of bread and pasta, the amount was patently inadequate.[118] More or less simultaneously, the distribution network for staple foods and heating fuel partially broke down. Some provinces, particularly rural ones, maintained adequate supplies. Others, above all the large urban areas and parts of the South, suffered shortages of everything from pasta to charcoal. Long lines in front of shops frequently threatened to and sometimes did degenerate into brawls and small-scale demonstrations against the authorities.[119]

In addition, prices rose inexorably, despite an ineffectual freeze imposed in July. The Milan cost of living index, according to the police superintendent there, rose from 474.31 in July to 499.53 in late December.[120] The regime had last conceded a general salary increase in March 1940. The constant upward creeping of prices of staples, and the rapid proliferation of semilegal devices such as "price supplements" and surcharges for the "reservation" of scarce goods, along with the development of an outright black market, inevitably struck the least affluent hardest. In the North, the conditions of the urban workers became increasingly difficult, and in some cases almost desperate. The police superintendent of Venice reported that the families of the unskilled labor force at the vast mainland industrial complex of Porto Marghera

barely make ends meet, in absolutely miserable conditions, rounding out their budgets with the meager proceeds of work by the women, and, in the end, with various expedients not excluding the more or less concealed prostitution of young girls. When such expedients are not available, conditions become absolutely unbearable.[121]

The situation in the South was doubtless far worse, although long-standing acclimation appears to have dulled the sensibilities of the authorities there.

Parallel to the crisis in public morale, a fierce struggle developed within the regime. Ciano, nouveau riche defender of bourgeois impropriety and perquisites, fought for his own survival. Farinacci, proponent of an anti-bourgeois, anticlerical, racialist "third wave" of Fascism at home, and of unreserved cooperation with Germany abroad, fought to purge the military. Between these two unlikely political "friends" reigned an uneasy entente, as in May 1940.[122] With Ciano and Farinacci stood Starace, who now reasserted himself after dismissal as secretary of the Party in October 1939. As Fascist Militia chief of staff, Starace had a finger in military as well as civilian concerns, and by mid-December, "swollen with self-importance," he was taking part under Cavallero's patronage in some meetings of the service chiefs.[123] A lesser light, and former satellite of Starace's, Adelchi Serena, had replaced Muti as Party secretary at the end of October. Muti, as well as displeasing Ciano by showing an unexpected degree of independence and a lively appetite for personal profit, had also demonstrated a complete lack of aptitude for converting the disorganized and bloated Party machinery into the instrument needed to mobilize and control the home front.[124] Serena was little improvement: the first of a series of wartime stopgap solutions in the Party leadership, he was "bound hand and foot" to Ciano, as the foreign minister boasted in early November.[125]

In the background, but still in a sense allied to Ciano, stood the ambiguous figure of Guido Buffarini-Guidi, undersecretary at the Ministry of the Interior.[126] But Buffarini was not the only power at that all-important ministry, and Ciano also entertained extremely close relations with Buffarini's rival, the chief of police, Arturo Bocchini. After Bocchini's sudden death on 19 November, his successor, the jovial and supremely devious Neapolitan, Carmine Senise, continued Bocchini's custom of reporting in person to Ciano on the internal situation. Other members of the loose grouping around Ciano and Farinacci were Riccardi and Ricci, ministers respectively of exchange and currency and of corporations. Last but not least was Pavolini of the Ministry of Popular Culture, who depending on taste was a "close friend" or a "creature" of Ciano's.[127] In the military sector, Cavallero at first complemented the dominance of the "Ciano–Farinacci axis" in the political one.

In the ambiguous middle of the political spectrum stood the self-appointed moderate Fascists, above all Bottai and Grandi. Unlike the Ciano–Farinacci group, the moderates were a category rather than a loose-knit clique. Bottai apparently attempted in mid-December to persuade Mussolini to make a direct and personal appeal to the public's patriotism. The suggestion was an implicit criticism of the attempt the Party was making to enforce enthusiasm with knobkerries and castor oil. Bottai's cautions echoed similar remarks of his friend Ciano, who was too politically astute not to recognize that Farinacci and Serena were in danger of doing more harm than good. But Bottai, although a potential candidate as a moderate, activist, but intellectually discerning secretary of the Party, was ultimately no less hostile to Badoglio than the rest. Despite a show of solidarity with the marshal early in the crisis, Bottai had taken by January to commenting approvingly on the caging of "the tiger, Badoglio."[128]

Grandi, who did not share Bottai's ties with Ciano, was the most important moderate. As a former foreign minister, he was implicitly a rival and potential successor to the latter. In the fall of 1940 rumors flew that he had urged his subordinates at the Ministry of Justice to speed up their work on the recodification of Italy's laws, since he, Grandi, "did not have much more time to lose in his current position."[129] In late October he had decided to make "honorable amends" for the ostentatious anglophilia of his London days. On an official visit to his German counterparts he asked especially for an audience with Hitler.[130] At the interview on 25 November, Grandi sycophantically emphasized his "joy and pride" in at last meeting the Führer of the great movement he had for so long admired from afar. He dismissed his long years as London society's favorite Fascist as a painful period endured as a "paratrooper in enemy territory." The Germans did not take to him, although Grandi let it be known he had found the personality of the Führer particularly impressive.[131]

Once back in Rome, Grandi became "extraordinarily active," while still doing his best to avoid alienating Ciano and Farinacci prematurely. Lurid rumors of Ciano's disgrace and Grandi's appointment as minister of foreign affairs began to circulate.[132] Grandi had replaced Ciano "so to speak, for a morning," then Countess Edda Ciano had rescued her husband in a dramatic scene with her father, Mussolini. Ciano was off to Moscow, Berlin, or Rio de Janeiro as ambassador.[133] So insistent were the rumors that Ciano made a special point of telling Mackensen on 12 December that they were unfounded, although Grandi unwittingly remained the "man of the England-clique." Presumably at Ciano's bidding, Anfuso added that Grandi was in fact consciously intriguing, and was canvassing support for his candidacy among his friends and hangers-on in the Fascist Chamber, of which he was president.[134] But beyond such activities Grandi dared not go. When Farinacci challenged him in early January to "come forth from [his] reserve" and associate himself with Ciano, Farinacci, and the regime in a public display of solidarity, Grandi was "displeased and terrorized" – a measure of his unwillingness to take risks.[135]

Less cautious than Grandi and the other moderates, at least verbally, was an ill-assorted but predominantly military-monarchical opposition. The Army, as an institution, resented Farinacci's attack on Badoglio, and resented still more the concerted campaign on the theme of Badoglio's alleged "treason" which Farinacci, Serena, and Starace mounted through press, Party and Fascist Militia in early December. General Ambrosio of 2nd Army drafted but did not send a fiery letter to Badoglio dismissing the newspaper article of "the exstationmaster Farinacci" as a "vulgar mystification of the facts." Ambrosio exhorted Badoglio to "sweep away the aspirants to the Napoleonic succession" and seize power, as Ambrosio, Badoglio, and the King were to do in July 1943.[136] Even the segments of the Army with least cause to love the higher staffs in general or Badoglio in particular were unanimous in their indignation. Feeling ran so high in early December that the Party, fearing military "demonstrations," organized preventive counter-demonstrations of its own. Starace appears to have ordered local militia commands to prepare a sort of coup d'état, an occupation of the territorial army corps headquarters, in case of need. But the Army never went beyond grumbling. A "discipline based on apathy and don't-give-a-damn-ism," as Guzzoni described it to De Bono, reigned.[137]

The retired or semiretired Marshals De Bono and Enrico Caviglia, the discredited but still vociferous De Vecchi, and an assortment of allies and hangers-on from the military and even the Party did constitute a sort of dissident sect. De Bono had lost his job as commander of Army Group South when that unnecessary bureaucracy had vanished after the French armistice. But despite his seventy-four years the Marshal retained an aide-de-camp and a map room in Rome through which he kept abreast of the rapidly deteriorating military situation. Judging from his diary, much of De Bono's wrath at the Party, Farinacci, and Ciano was a consequence of the belief that they had blocked his own candidacy as Badoglio's successor and had attempted to remove him from the scene with an offer of De Vecchi's post in the Dodecanese. De Bono preferred to remain in Rome as the center of a sort of politico-military salon: "all sorts of people, military and civilians [alike] come here to commiserate and say their piece." Even Fascists of the old guard such as Francesco Giunta aligned themselves with De Bono; Giunta recognized the "extramilitary responsibilities" in the Greek affair. De Bono also maintained contacts with Badoglio both in person and through Armellini.[138]

The intentions of this circle were a curious mixture. Caviglia attempted unsuccessfully to induce De Bono to join him in a complaint to Mussolini against the Party's divisive tactics. The regime's insistence that the war was a "Fascist war," the Party's attack on the very bourgeoisie that furnished the officers of the armed forces, and the overweening arrogance of local Party functionaries were sapping the enthusiasm and morale of even the most patriotic Italians. De Bono found Caviglia's language too strong: "it isn't the moment; outside they would think we were plotting."[139] But De Bono was not averse to daydreaming about plots. Armellini too had reached the point of latent revolt against the regime, and noted frequently in his diary the many others "who see it as I do."[140] By mid-January, De Bono had evolved a seductive and appropriately operatic vision of a military coup. All one would have to do would be to "have 'boots and saddles' sounded, mount up, put oneself at the head of the Genoa Cavalry Regiment, and, waving a flag, cross Rome toward Piazza Venezia crying out 'Long live the King!' " Badoglio, in bitter retirement, entertained visions of power and vengeance, although he did not propose to share the risks of storming Palazzo Venezia. As Armellini commented, "all are fed up, but nobody dares move." De Bono himself best summarized his own situation and that of many others: "I, too, am a broken-down slave [un servaccio]; but on the other hand what purpose would the revolt of one individual serve?"[141] By mid-March De Bono was fulsomely attempting reconciliation with Farinacci, "always [his] friend of the Matteotti era." De Bono confessed himself pained at rumors that Ciano felt De Bono "was not conducting himself toward him [Ciano] as [he] should."[142]

The one individual whose revolt would have mattered was of course the King. But Victor Emmanuel made no move, not because he was "sluggish and irresolute," as De Bono unkindly put it, but out of choice. The King had approved Cavallero's appointment, even when his aide Puntoni suggested that it would prove unwelcome to the Army. The most the King did was to point out the unpopularity of Ciano, Cavagnari, and Somigli, and advise Mussolini in mid-December to restrain Serena and Farinacci. Beyond that he would not go. His habitual constitutional scruples perhaps played some part, but his healthy fear of the Germans was probably more important. Both ideology and strategy would dictate immediate, merciless *Wehrmacht* counteraction against a military-monarchical overthrow of the Fascist regime. The King was in any case confident that Mussolini would "know how to get out of this one, too."[143]

As for the other powers in Italy, the Vatican and the industrialists, they remained similarly silent. After its disastrous peace efforts in the spring and the battle over the *Osservatore Romano,* the Vatican shrunk from further ruffling Mussolini's susceptibilities. Apart from an occasional dignified protest against anticlerical asides in *Regime Fascista,* and discreet efforts to improve Italy's relations with France and Yugoslavia (but not Greece, despite or because of Ciano's remarks in late September), the Church kept silent and offered its tacit support to the Italian war effort.[144] The man "Providence

[had] placed in Our Path" still had some claim upon Church loyalties; a repetition of the ambiguous Vatican role in World War I was unthinkable. As Mussolini later remarked to Heinrich Himmler, the Pope would not make things too difficult for the regime; he was, at bottom, an Italian at heart. Besides, the Church's religious mission still seemed to have some points of contact with Mussolini's expansionism, as that mission later led the Church into tacit support for the National Socialist "crusade against Bolshevism" in 1941.[145] As for the industrialists, they were too busy profiting from the dramatic wartime increase in demand for manufactured goods, and too closely associated with the regime, to seek to detach themselves at this point. By early 1941 the leadership of FIAT appears to have placed its hopes in German victory even while fearing German economic domination. Others, such as Count Volpi, whose relations with Ciano apparently underwent a sudden and dramatic improvement in this period, believed that "a negotiated compromise peace [was] essential if all belligerents [were] not to go down in common ruin and disaster." All voted with their check books by investing massively in real estate, a form of wealth that would presumably survive even defeat.[146]

Despite the absence of an organized internal challenge, Mussolini was unable with his own resources to recapture the confidence of the public, although Pavolini did his best in mid-December to make the press more believable and inspire in the public a "realistic evaluation of the war."[147] The Party's offensive on the home front was at least as damaging as economic privation to Italian morale and to the support the regime enjoyed. The public interpreted the campaign against Badoglio, not entirely incorrectly, as an attempt to make him a scapegoat for the sins of the political leadership. His dismissal produced surprise, "disorientation," "anxiety and perplexity," and "a notable and ill-concealed state of unease."[148] In Badoglio's native region around Asti in Piedmont, opinion was so markedly in his favor that the local police superintendent reported to Rome that overt propaganda against him would lead to "serious incidents." Some quarters recognized that Badoglio was far from blameless, and his frivolous behavior in going hunting during the first week of the Greek operation aroused hostile comment.[149] But on the whole the Party's clumsy attacks, particularly after Serena directed the local organizations all over Italy to take them up, gave Badoglio's reputation new luster. De Bono put it succinctly in mid-December: "Badoglio had no friends; now he has a whole lot of them."[150] Farinacci's continued sniping throughout early December in *Regime Fascista* intensified this effect,[151] for Farinacci's anticlericalism, radicalism, and outspoken enthusiasm for the German connection did not make him popular.

The police superintendent of Verona summed up mercilessly the consequences of the campaign at the local level: Party propaganda and "certain measures aimed at establishing a vigilant network to strike at possible manifestations of defeatism, [measures] frequently both poorly understood and worse executed, distorted on occasion through a deficient sense of political responsibility, of good taste, [and] of proportion (they even went so far as to make some attempts to burn Badoglio in effigy and to encourage servicemen to spy on their officers) [had] produced a painful impression and a feeling of irritation in the public. . . ."[152] In Brescia the Fascists ran out of castor oil, an important additive for aviation gasoline in addition to its other uses, and had fallen back upon dosing their victims with "nauseating mixtures of unspeakable mineral oils" which confined those "purged" to bed for several days. Such tactics, the police superintendent there noted guardedly, "increased the number of the enemies of the regime."[153]

In mid-December, Mussolini recognized that further attacks on Badoglio were dangerous. The regime could not suddenly denounce its highest military figure of fifteen years' standing without raising embarrassing questions about its own judgment. Further, as Roatta pointed out to Guzzoni, the Party's campaign was damaging the morale of the Army, "which [asked] no more than to obey with its customary fidelity."[154] Guzzoni appears to have earned Farinacci's undying enmity in this period, perhaps for making that same point to Mussolini.[155] The dictator permitted Badoglio to call on him on 9 December, and allowed the radio, although not the press, to mention that the conversation had been "cordial." The news momentarily placated public opinion.[156] But by 13 December the British Broadcasting Corporation's very effective Italian programs had begun to exploit to the full Farinacci's articles and the Party's activities as evidence of a major civil-military crisis within the regime.[157] Mussolini therefore ordered Farinacci and the rest of the press to drop the subject completely. Pavolini pointed out to his editors that "attacks on categories or groups of citizens who are not doing their duty" had been necessary. But it was impolitic to "insist further," since "abroad, these things can be taken as evidence of an alleged split in the Italian people." The "unity" of the population behind the regime was the proper note to strike. Ciano's influence apparently secured the rehabilitation of the term *"Patria,"* and Pavolini pointed out its advantages to his editors as a word "which in difficult times touches the deep and secret well-springs of the race." Mussolini apparently ordered both Pavolini and Serena to make these same points by telephone to Farinacci on 13 December, and the next day ordered the prefect of Cremona to confiscate the press run of *Regime Fascista* on the pretext that a letter it had published went too far. Farinacci was furious, but impotent.[158]

Mussolini also did his best to defend Ciano from the almost universal hatred that now surrounded him – if Badoglio was the regime's scapegoat, Ciano was the public's. Despite private complaints that Ciano had given him "incorrect information" over Greece, Mussolini had no intention of replacing his son-in-law, or even the egregious Jacomoni, whose survival the public ascribed to an alleged relationship between his wife and Ciano.[159] Their removal, Mussolini presumably judged, would emphasize his own responsibilities for the current crisis. He had, after all, permitted Ciano to preen himself as the regime's heir apparent since 1936 and before. Ciano's consignment to oblivion would be a sign of weakness that would neither impress opponents nor reconcile critics. Finally, who could replace him? Grandi was impossible. Mussolini had discarded him once already for "going to bed" with the West. Despite Grandi's groveling protestations of loyalty to regime, Duce, and German alliance, his appointment would mean only one thing to the outside world: Italy sought compromise peace with Britain. That signal Mussolini had no intention of sending. Mussolini therefore stuck by his son-in-law. In mid-December, at the height of the Grandi rumors, and to the outrage of De Bono and others, the press carried conspicuously a florid address to Ciano from a national convention of Fascist veterans' organizations. "For your information, Count Ciano has nothing to reproach himself for," Mussolini thundered to a visitor who had the temerity to suggest a change of the guard at the Ministry of Foreign Affairs.[160]

Strong measures were nevertheless necessary. Some internal enemies of the regime resorted to psychological warfare: rumors of a devastating British defeat in Libya, with the capture of 175,000 prisoners and 900 tanks, spread rapidly throughout Rome and the peninsula on 17 December. A further drop in morale inevitably resulted when the news turned out to be fantasy.[161] On 23 December, Churchill thundered over the BBC his justly famous address to the Italian nation. British armies were "tearing and [would] tear [their] African empire to shreds and tatters. . . ." Conveniently, responsibility for this regrettable outcome rested on one man. One man, "and one man alone [had] ranged the Italian people in deadly struggle against the British Empire . . . . one man who, against the Crown and Royal Family of Italy, against the Pope and all the authority of the Vatican and of the Roman Catholic Church, against the wishes of the Italian people, who had no lust for this war, [had] arrayed the trustees and inheritors of ancient Rome at the side of the ferocious pagan barbarians."[162] The invitation to the Italian establishment to jump ship was obvious, and – in the long term – effective. For the present, it was more important that Mussolini's initial confidence that the public would not consider the North Africa disaster "also the fault of the political leaders" proved unfounded. In this respect Farinacci showed better judgment than his master. The lord of Cremona was privately sarcastic about Mussolini's decision in late December to publish a Graziani report on the desert catastrophe that emphasized, excessively, the disparity between the Italian infantry divisions and British armored and motorized units.[163] While this explanation perhaps helped preserve faith in the valor of the Italian fighting man, it also raised the question of what had happened to the billions of lire spent on armaments. The truth, which was that the regime's military experts had spent the money preparing for World War I, was too simple to find credence. The public preferred to draw the conclusion, dangerous to the regime, that the recently enriched and conspicuously consuming *gerarchi* of the inner circle had eaten up the defense budget.[164]

The police and the mail censorship authorities began to come across increasing numbers of leaflets and chain letters holding the regime responsible for defeat. An ingenious inhabitant of the North Italian city of Brescia drafted and circulated a letter that purported to be Badoglio's reply to *Regime Fascista*'s attacks. It was a stinging and politically clever rebuke to "Mr. Farinacci, Solicitor," who had presumed to judge the professional competence of Badoglio and of the Italian general staff corps, and it was soon in wide circulation all over Italy. On stylistic grounds alone the letter was clearly not Badoglio's, although some historians have accepted it as genuine; in any case, the Milan police ran the author to ground in mid-February.[165] Notwithstanding these evidences of dissent, the police remained confident that the regime did not yet face any significant organized underground opposition.[166] But the situation was increasingly dangerous.

In mid-January Mussolini at last took drastic action to restore morale with a novel experiment in government. Almost without warning, he mobilized his ministers, high Party officials, and members of the Chamber of *Fasci* and Corporations under forty-five years of age, and sent them to the Albanian front. The only prominent exception was Giuseppe Tassinari, minister of agriculture, responsible for ensuring that Italy's grain supplies lasted the winter. Otherwise, Mussolini himself, with assistance of the permanent bureaucracy, planned to run the Italian state single-handed.[167]

The temporary change of the guard fulfilled a number of functions. It removed from view the most conspicuous objects of the public's wrath, Ciano above all. It might recapture the atmosphere of the brave days of the Ethiopian venture, when high figures in the regime had served as junior officers, symbolizing the unity between leaders and led that characterized that most popular of all Italian wars. Finally, even if the measure failed to rekindle popular enthusiasm, the fact that eminent *gerarchi* were suffering along with the troops on the jagged and sleet-swept mountains of Albania would perhaps assuage the public's thirst for retribution. One or two – particularly Grandi and Bottai – might die a glorious death. If ever the tree of faith needed watering with the blood of martyrs – and potential rivals – now was that time.[168]

The *gerarchi* understandably did not see things with Mussolini's sovereign detachment. Ciano was aggrieved, even furious. Bottai and others irately thronged the antechamber at Palazzo Venezia, denouncing the action as "an authentic coup d'état of the Duce in order to free himself from Fascism and rely on other political tendencies for support."[169] That it was not, for what other organized "political tendencies" existed? What Mussolini achieved was the alienation, in some cases permanent, of many of the highest representatives of what passed for Fascism's governing elite. Bottai already felt out of place inside the regime that he had long attempted unsuccessfully to liberalize and moderate.[170] Ciano had lost the robust faith in his father-in-law's leadership that his diary gives witness to in the late 1930s. By February 1941, his friends were spreading abroad his protestations of blamelessness for current disasters, protestations that implicitly accused Mussolini.[171] In his diary, Ciano increasingly showed the skepticism and critical detachment that turned in 1943, under the pressure of his own dismissal as foreign minister and of Italy's defeat, to active disloyalty. As for Grandi, his mobilization came as a shock. He was one of the last to receive notice, and had blithely assumed that Mussolini's failure to have him called up had "political significance" as a sign that his long-awaited elevation to the Ministry of Foreign Affairs was near. The disappointment of "going back, at forty-five, to tramping the snow" as an *Alpino* was therefore all the more galling, as Ciano noted gloatingly in his diary.[172]

Correctly sensing that his subordinates resented their "forced voluntarization," Mussolini "stiffened in his decision and [became] brusque in manner." At Ciano's parting audience on 25 January, the Duce discharged his wrath, making "certain observations that he could without question have dispensed with." A suggestion that Ciano leave his bomber squadron at Bari to lead the Italian delegation to the state funeral of Count Csáky, his Hungarian counterpart, sent Mussolini into a towering rage. To Ciano's ill-concealed surprise and disappointment, Mussolini also refused to allow his son-in-law to join him at Bordighera in early February for the abortive meeting arranged at Hitler's request with the still obstinate Franco.[173]

Mussolini emphasized his displeasure with a stern directive to Cavallero. The *gerarchi* were not to receive special treatment at the front: "no servants or suitcases."[174] With the exception of Ciano, who in a manner typical of all air forces passed his ground time in the best hotel in Bari, the great and powerful of the regime suffered in mud, rain, and snow, calling down curses upon Mussolini. Grandi perhaps exaggerated after the war when he declared that he "had made contact with [his] friends, and jotted down, there in the trenches of Greece [Albania] the plan of the resolution [for the Grand Council of Fascism] that later marked the end of Mussolini."[175] For the moment the dissident *gerarchi* could only grumble. But Grandi was probably right in implying that Mussolini's decision to send the ornaments of the regime to the front generated a deep-seated rancor, which reinforced political calculation and provided much of the motive power behind the vote at the Grand Council of Fascism of 24/25 July 1943 that felled the regime.

Mussolini's inspiration found no more favor with the public than with the *gerarchi*. Initially, hopes rose that the wholesale shipment of ministers to Albania was a prelude "to their substitution with elements that would inspire confidence." But when no announcement appeared of a change of the guard, and above all of Ciano's replacement, public opinion became "skeptical and indifferent" to this "purely temporary and propagandistic measure," which among its other disadvantages seemed to decapitate a number of vital ministries at a critical moment.[176] The population remained in a state of "distrustful passivity," and under the "peaceful surface of public order, there ferment[ed] an unsatiated spirit of opposition and discontent that demand[ed], in the name of the best of Italian nationalism, fundamental reforms of the administrative and governmental structure to assure the

Fatherland its dignity and its political and economic independence."[177] A "widespread state of prostration and distrust . . . in all strata of the population now infect[ed] those same Fascists who at one time were the most convinced and faithful."[178] In the North, in particular, the public increasingly demanded an accounting for the lives sacrificed as the result of "vanity and incompetence," and expressed "open, violent, resolute hostility against the Roman ruling circles that [had] brought the Italian people to this humiliating situation before the entire world." Local pride, particularly in Italy's economic capital, Milan, fueled this sentiment: Rome was a "synonym for intrigue and corruption."[179]

The Party's inept attempts to eradicate defeatism with castor oil and *manganello,* the Fascist club, added to the regime's enemies. Mussolini's faith in such methods was apparent in a dangerously naïve analysis of the internal situation he confided to De Bono in late January: ". . . forty million citizens are annoyed with the privations; . . . two million [are] internal enemies; but . . . the two million Fascists keep everything in line."[180] Senise of the police seems to have made some effort in late February to persuade Mussolini that a Party plan for a "thrashing week" was inopportune.[181] In Milan, at any rate, the police intervened to restrain "some sporadic episodes of violent actions by Fascists against individuals considered defeatists, or grumblers, or not in line with the necessities of the moment."[182] The uselessness of the Party was now fully apparent even to the servants of the regime. In the words of the police superintendent of Palermo, words that drew from Senise an unusual tribute ("Here is a man who has the courage to tell the truth"), the Party had done "nothing truly substantial in this delicate moment. . . ." It had failed to create a new ideological consciousness even among the young. Its activities were instead confined "to the persecution of small episodes of presumed anti-Fascism, episodes that on investigation amount to no more than a humble and timorous letting off of steam by those who find the present situation humiliating."[183] As the police superintendent of Venice, one of the least Fascist of Italy's major cities, had explained in December, ordinary coercion could not generate enthusiasm: "police measures, even if applied on a large scale, to a social group [the middle classes] that maintains a formal obsequiousness, are not suitable instruments for modifying a jealously conserved psychological position."[184]

The new blows that Graziani's collapse in Cyrenaica and British naval bombardment of Genoa on 8 February dealt to morale finally prompted Mussolini to give a lengthy speech, broadcast throughout Italy, on 23 February. His insistence that Great Britain could not win the war, despite its victories, temporarily reassured much of the public, although De Bono noted sarcastically that "only *Balilla* [Fascist Youth] and morons [could] take it seriously."[185] But few failed to perceive that promises of final victory rested not upon Italian strength, but upon that of Italy's ally, to whom Mussolini perforce paid fulsome tribute. The war had once more become an Anglo-

German duel. The public, with a "hope that humiliates," waited for Germany to "save even Italy," while simultaneously dreading the arrogance of the victorious Teutons.[186]

The brilliant German spring campaign in the Balkans and Rommel's unexpected success in driving the British almost out of Cyrenaica in April 1941 dispelled the immediate crisis in Italian morale, but did not restore public confidence in the regime. In mid-April, as Field Marshal Wilhelm List's armor rolled south toward Thermopylae and Athens, a police informant in Milan reported without compunction that

> many, many pessimists see Italy as a protectorate of Germany, and conclude that if we needed three wars, the loss of the *Impero,* the serious losses of the Navy, the sacrifice of our raw materials and gold reserves, the closing of all [foreign] markets, and the forfeiture of a conspicuous part of the merchant marine in order to achieve the loss of our own political, economic, and military independence, there is certainly nothing to be proud about in the policies followed and the results achieved up to now.[187]

Mussolini's attempt to crush resistance at home through triumph abroad had led to disaster in both theaters.

3. *Consequences*

Between Germany and Britain. "Failure has had the healthy effect of once more compressing Italian claims to within the natural boundaries of Italian capabilities," Hitler remarked matter-of-factly to his generals on 5 December.[188] He was not entirely correct: Italian claims still extended from Corsica to Aden. But Italy's bid to seize them by force had failed catastrophically. Despite the blow to his pride, Mussolini had no choice. He sought German help, even though the price of that help was the abandonment of an independent Italian strategy. The "parallel war" became a subsidiary part of the larger German war, the Mediterranean a secondary theater, and Italy a German satellite with no more than a consultative role in determining strategy even in *mare nostro.* Italy ceased to be a great power even in name.

Mussolini made the first limited appeals for aid in mid-November. At Innsbruck, Badoglio asked Keitel for a contingent of German transport aircraft to speed the airlift to Albania. Hitler agreed, and by mid-December fifty Junkers 52s were shuttling from Foggia in southern Italy to Tirana.[189] Marras followed up in Berlin with a request for 3,000 trucks to shore up Soddu's strained supply system. To make them instantly available, they would drive to Albania through Yugoslavia; presumably at Mussolini's insistence, 600 of the trucks would be Italian, "to avoid giving an impression of utter penury." The Germans reluctantly accepted, subject to Yugoslav approval.[190] But the Yugoslavs, despite their intrigues with both Ciano and Germans, proved unexpectedly averse to joining the Tripartite Pact. In an interview with Hitler at the *Berghof* on 28 November, Cincar-Marković refused to commit himself to the Axis, despite Hitler's personal offer of Salonika, of territorial guarantees for Yugoslavia – by implication against Italy – and an exhortation to make the most of his nation's advantageous position before spring came and "the iron dice rolled." In early December the Yugoslavs refused both a German request for truck transit and a separate and doubtless highly embarrassed Italian plea.[191]

German help in the Mediterranean did not depend upon Yugoslavia, and Hitler moved swiftly to implement the proposals of his 20 November letter. Göring's chief assistant, Field Marshal Erhard Milch, descended on Rome on 5 December to arrange the operation of fighters, *Stukas,* and Ju 88 medium bombers from Sicily and Southern Italy against the British fleet. But help in the air was not enough. In the wake of Soddu's panic on 4 December, Mussolini did more than dispatch Cavallero to Albania. At Ciano's suggestion, he called on Alfieri, who had been recuperating at Capri from a lengthy illness, and sent him to Berlin in the greatest haste with an urgent appeal to Hitler for "any kind of help, so long as it comes quickly."[192] German propaganda and troop movements must convince the Greeks that a descent through Bulgaria into Thrace was imminent. Otherwise the Italian front might collapse.

Ribbentrop, although probably more courteous than available Italian accounts suggest, was almost sarcastic. No one would believe a German threat, given the Balkan winter and the still far from complete German concentration in Rumania. When Alfieri asked that the Germans compel Bulgaria to mobilize, Ribbentrop was equally discouraging. Alfieri asked after the Yugoslavs. Ribbentrop in reply emphasized the hostility to Italy they had shown throughout the current negotiations, although he was careful not to reveal the concessions his master had made to that hostility. Finally, in desperation, Alfieri asked for materiel and direct German military assistance, but could not produce precise requests: Ciano and Mussolini had neglected to consult with their military subordinates to draw up a shopping list. Alfieri was off to a humiliating start.[193]

His ensuing interview with Hitler on 8 December was slightly more successful. The latest news from Rome was good. Cavallero was hopeful that the front would hold. Alfieri nevertheless repeated his request for German or Bulgarian bluff, or Yugoslav accession to the Tripartite Pact. Hitler expressed "deepest sympathy," but pointed out that the situation was the consequence of Italy's failure to keep Germany informed. When Rintelen had inquired in October about plans for Greece, Roatta had denied anything was afoot. No easy remedy now existed. The Italians would simply have to hold until German intervention in March. Hitler characteristically diagnosed the problem as one of willpower. It was imperative to restore order at the front, "even with barbaric methods such as shooting generals and colonels who gave up their posts, and decimating units." The situation required a man of "iron nerves and barbaric resolve." Evidently fearing that Mussolini had no such man available, Hitler proposed an immediate meeting of the two dictators, and the next day ordered Rintelen to descend on Albania to "exert military influence" on the Italian command. Hitler had no intention of standing idle while his ally collapsed or the British secured bases from which to strike at Rumania or Italy. In consonance with his 4 November decision, he had recently remarked yet again that German intervention in Libya was "disposed of."[194] The Balkans were another matter.

But negotiation might preclude intervention. The total Italian dependence Alfieri's pleas revealed, and an unofficial suggestion of the Greek minister in Berlin that Athens would favorably consider a *status quo ante* peace, seem to have prompted Hitler to authorize his military intelligence chief, Admiral Wilhelm Canaris, to approach Metaxas in mid-December through the Greek minister in Madrid. Canaris's alluring offer would have permitted the Greeks to keep their conquests, but it elicited no response.[195] Metaxas, who himself at about the same point made overtures through the German military attaché in Athens, ultimately held to what his British allies described as a "robust attitude."[196] Greek opinion demanded ruthless prosecution of the "holy war" against the Italian invaders. Metaxas, as a German agent put it, "would not have remained chief of the government longer than six hours, and would probably have been a dead man" had he accepted Ciano's original ultimatum. Greek victories in Albania scarcely engendered willingness to make peace, nor did Metaxas himself, in the end, trust the German guarantee upon which a settlement would inevitably rest. He still hoped he could resist Germany with British help after he drove the Italians into the sea, or that Germany would move east in the spring to seek conquests not in the Balkans, but in the broad fields of the Ukraine.[197]

But only the removal of the British from the Balkans could free Hitler for the latter pursuit – and here as elsewhere he ultimately put his trust in force. He was increasingly inclined to rescue the Italians, lest continued defeat threaten both Axis alliance and Fascist regime. On 13 December he promulgated the directive for operation "Marita." Up to twenty-four German divisions would assemble gradually in Rumania. When the weather permitted, perhaps as early as March, this massive force would roll south through Bulgaria to "take possession of the north coast of the Aegean and – should this be necessary – of the entire Greek mainland." The operation was no end in itself. The majority of units committed were to withdraw swiftly toward *"other employment."* The meaning of that cryptic phrase emerged less than a week later, on 18 December, when Hitler issued in the greatest secrecy the most momentous order of his career: Contingency *Barbarossa.* "The German *Wehrmacht,"* the directive began, "must be prepared to crush Soviet Russia in a swift campaign even before the end of the war against England."[198] This *"Weltblitzkrieg"* would render vain increasing United States aid to Britain, free Japan to tie up the Americans in the Pacific, and open the road for German armor into the Middle East through Turkey and the Caucasus.[199] Once Greater Germany secured the immense resources of European Russia,

Central Asia, and the Middle East, no coalition could defeat it, and world mastery would be within its grasp.

Such grandiose calculations were far from the minds of Hitler's Roman allies. Mussolini declined Hitler's invitation to an immediate meeting, although he did not exclude one later in the month. The recent upheaval in the high command and the Albanian situation allegedly required Mussolini's presence in Italy. Actually, Albania was not yet threatening enough to overcome his "fear of appearing a poor relation in need of help." Mussolini had soon recovered from his 4 December panic, and had once more resolved to defeat Greece with Italian arms alone. On 8 December, Ciano ordered Alfieri to take back the earlier appeals for help. This reply presumably piqued Hitler, but he had to agree, while nevertheless emphasizing that a Führer–Duce conference was imperative. The Germans had to make do with pointing out to all who would listen that Italian retreat was "an ephemeral phenomenon, in other words a military episode" that was "utterly without consequences for the outcome of the war."[200]

Neither Germans nor Italians could so easily dismiss the British North African offensive, for it converted Italy's military situation from the merely critical to the catastrophic. O'Connor's attack was the stroke that rendered Italy's dependence upon Germany almost total. Against the Greeks, defense was feasible; in North Africa, once Graziani had failed to extricate 10th Army from encirclement at Sidi el Barrani and Bardia, only German help could in the long run prevent the British from reaching Tripoli.

Rome's first reaction was an over-hasty order to Marras to "buy up instantly all available tanks and artillery pieces, whatever the price." More followed. On 16 December Mussolini met with his ministers as he had in August 1939, to draw up a list of the raw materials Italy would require to continue war production through the following year. Ciano dispatched the list to Alfieri the next day with orders to appeal directly to Hitler. At Mussolini's orders, Cavallero also summarized all of Italy's requirements for Rintelen on 19 December. Mussolini swallowed his pride and now, for the first time, sought German ground troops for an Italian theater. The "parallel war" was over – only a German armored division, which Cavallero now requested, could save Tripolitania for Italy. Italy also needed complete equipment for ten divisions organized in five army corps, a staggering figure Roatta had chosen on the basis of losses in North Africa and Greece.[201]

The next day, Cavallero once more left for Albania, while Guzzoni and Roatta descended to details. Guzzoni emphasized to Rintelen that Italy needed help badly and immediately, and once more requested a German threat to Greece through Rumania. In Libya, Italy would welcome not merely one, but two German armored divisions. Since Italian industry could not replace in time the equipment already lost, German materiel was equally necessary; Italian production of medium tanks amounted to only forty-seven a month. The weight of the war, Guzzoni insisted, was "now upon Italy which finds itself in a difficult situation due to the vulnerability, besides the peninsula itself, of the theaters between which it must distribute its forces: the *Impero,* Libya, Dodecanese, Albania."[202] Roatta followed with a breathtaking list of requirements: equipment for thirty divisional and twenty corps artillery battalions, 8,000 trucks, 750 ambulances and maintenance vehicles, 1,600 small antiaircraft cannon, 900 88-mm guns (complete with searchlights, rangefinders, and sights), 800 medium tanks, 300 armored cars, 675 antitank guns, 9,000 mules, 300 long- and medium-range radio sets, 20,000 rolls of concertina wire, 500,000 engineer stakes, 10,000,000 sandbags, and various minor items. Roatta confessed that the Italian leadership had until now not grasped the true seriousness of the war. The refusal of the German offer of armored units in September had been "very foolish."[203]

Hitler received Alfieri's requests for raw materials on 19 December. After his experts had worked their way through them, the German Foreign Office invited an Italian military-economic delegation to Berlin. Hitler also renewed his request, which he repeated once more on 23 December, for an immediate meeting with Mussolini and the latter's military advisers.[204] Much to their surprise, the Italian armaments delegation met on 30 December with what General Marras described as "much understanding, frankness, cordiality, and results considerably greater than on any earlier occasion." The Germans still insisted their own production was barely sufficient for the *Wehrmacht.* They refused to supply German tanks, armored cars, or field artillery, but now belatedly offered a wide selection of captured French and Czech weapons, with ammunition. They also did their best to satisfy Italian raw material requests, although urgent *Wehrmacht* needs later led to a shortening of the promised ration of gasoline and naval fuel oil.[205]

Keitel and Jodl, who led the German negotiations, nevertheless exacted a strategic price for their forthcomingness. Italy must hold in Albania and Libya at all costs until Germany could strike through Bulgaria in early March. To Albania, following up a suggestion Marras had made on 28 December, the Germans were willing to commit an alpine division. For Libya, Jodl suggested an armored corps might be more appropriate than the reinforced brigade blocking force (*"Sperrverband"*) that the German high command had envisaged sending in the immediate aftermath of the Sidi el Barrani disaster. No German cordiality could hide the fact, as Lanza of the Berlin Embassy pessimistically noted, that the Italians had "now definitively passed under the control of the German general staff." The next day Mussolini sent on to Cavallero in Albania confirmation of that bitter state of affairs: the Germans "posited as condition for their intervention that the present line be maintained at all costs."[206]

While the Italian delegation negotiated, the first echelon of German divisions intended for descent on Greece in the spring began to roll through Hungary to concentration areas in Rumania. This tangible sign of impending help unleashed a last flurry of Italian misgivings about the devastating blow a German swoop on Salonika would deal Italy's prestige. General Marras forwarded from Berlin a long and despairing report concluding that the Germans wanted Salonika and the Balkans for themselves. The Greeks would present little resistance to the massive German advance, while fighting to the end on the Italian front; Germany would reach Athens first. Marras therefore urgently recommended "timely politico-military agreements" to coordinate German and Italian actions – and implicitly, to secure a greater share of the proceeds. Alfieri seconded these recommendations.[207]

These reports, the sudden and contemporaneous collapse of Bardia's defenses, and a further invitation from Hitler, at last moved Mussolini to agree to a pilgrimage to the *Berghof*. He also renewed through Guzzoni pleas for German armor for Libya.[208] But Mussolini was still not resigned to impotence in the Balkans. On 10 January, while protesting to Mackensen his pleasure over the forthcoming meeting, set for the 19th, he forwarded Marras's report of German designs in Greece to Cavallero with the remark that "we must precede the Germans in the task of annihilating Greek resistance." At the 14 January meeting with Mussolini in Apulia, Cavallero pointed out some of the difficulties involved, and took up Marras's suggestion that Italy hasten to coordinate its Albanian activities with Germany's descent to the Aegean before it was too late. Italy, in Cavallero's "most humble opinion," must "decisively, at once, and without possibility of ambiguous interpretation place its effort on the plane of the Axis." Rome must press Berlin to demonstrate that "Greece was fighting simultaneously against Italy and Germany." The continuing refusal of Italy's ally to declare war on Greece, and possible Greek acquiescence in a German but not Italian occupation in the spring would cause "incalculable damage" to Italy's prestige. This danger Mussolini might ward off at the forthcoming Berchtesgaden meeting.[209]

Roatta reinforced Cavallero's arguments a few days later. Continuing logistical difficulties prevented any really serious Italian offensive in Albania for many months. Roatta suggested as a consolation that if one considered the Axis as a whole, the Italians had fulfilled the essential function of tying down and wearing out practically all of the Greek Army, thus opening the way for German success. He also proposed, much as he had in June for the attack on France, that Italy send a contingent to participate in the German thrust. Marras reported from Berlin that Hitler was "very sensitive to considerations of prestige," and might even agree to halt the German advance at Salonika while the Italians dealt with the principal Greek resistance and occupied the remainder of the country. But the collapse of the "Wolves of Tuscany" and the continuing Greek advance evidently depressed Mussolini so much that he lacked the effrontery to raise such demands. As the appointed day approached, he was ever more conscious that he would be visiting Berchtesgaden "in an obvious condition of inferiority."[210]

Hitler was well aware of Mussolini's susceptibilities, and was as determined as he had been throughout the summer and fall to spare his ally's personal prestige. Unfortunately, that prestige was at risk whether Germany intervened or abstained. Therefore Hitler's strategic imperative that "Italy must hold to the Axis and not collapse" took priority.[211] The possibility that the opposite might occur was by now a subject of general speculation in diplomatic circles.[212] As early as October the British had apparently put out a vague peace feeler through Switzerland to the Vatican, perhaps to indicate that they still considered Mussolini a valid negotiating partner.[213] By mid-December the Foreign Office had begun to meditate seriously on the terms to offer if O'Connor's "sweeping victory over the Wops," in the unlovely words of Sir Alexander Cadogan of the Foreign Office, compelled the Italians to "crawl" to Britain. The chiefs of staff had considered that prospect even before the desert offensive. Once Graziani's forward units disintegrated they proceeded with Churchill's approval to plan landings in Sicily and Sardinia for the event of Italian collapse. The only dark spot on the horizon was the Balkans. The Greek drive on Valona, to which Churchill attached the highest importance, was apparently slowing. Worse, German buildup in Rumania presaged a spring offensive against which Greece would be helpless. Greek collapse might lead to a further German advance through Turkey toward the Persian Gulf and Egypt. Mussolini's prediction in one of his periodic efforts to cheer up Graziani that the threat to Greece would distract the British from finishing off North Africa was proving correct.[214]

In mid-January Wavell visited Athens and pressed on the Greeks a mechanized force for Salonika as well as the bombers the British already proposed to locate there. Metaxas refused: landing of British ground troops or air units capable of striking Rumania would bring certain German retribution. London therefore provisionally authorized Wavell and O'Connor to press on to Benghazi instead, rather than divert further resources to Greece.[215] Almost by default, the defeat of Italy before German aid could save Mussolini remained Britain's strategic aim in the Mediterranean.

The British also continued to probe diplomatically, although details are obscure. In late December, the British minister in Sofia met with the apostolic delegate to Bulgaria and discussed – at whose initiative is unclear – the question of "a just and honorable peace." The two diplomats' reports of the conversation diverge markedly, but the upshot was that the apostolic delegate conveyed to his masters in Rome an ostensibly British request for Vatican mediation in the Anglo-Italian conflict. Of necessity the Vatican refused to transmit the request to Palazzo Chigi.[216] One needed little imagination to predict Mussolini's reaction to what he would certainly regard as treasonous interference.

The Vatican refusal, which the apostolic delegate relayed on 1 February, probably did not daunt the British. The fall of Bardia and Tobruk seems to have raised London's sights, for the British intimated that they no longer considered Mussolini a suitable negotiating partner. Perhaps more than military victory lay behind this stiffening of London's attitude. Contacts through Lisbon, where the Italian ambassador had hinted in mid-January that Italy "would be very willing to listen" to British suggestions, may well have led to a rebuff. Whom did London have in mind as a partner: Grandi, or the monarchy? Loraine, for one, had as early as late November advised Halifax that the enthronement of Amedeo D'Aosta was "the last chance of having a friendly and reasonably liberal non-Fascist Italy"[217] – a highly ironic remark in view of the Aosta family reputation as Fascist candidate for the throne if the incumbent were to waver in his support for the regime.

Italy thus returned to its position as bone of contention between the two principal antagonists, with the difference that both parties now considered it a mere object of their own policies rather than a great power capable of independent action. For the moment, the regime survived. In 1941 Hitler still held the advantage in power, and could bolster Mussolini faster than the British could destroy him. Nevertheless, as Hitler explained to his military assistants in a series of *Berghof* conferences on the Italian problem on 8 and 9 January, subtlety was essential. A combined Italo-German high command for the Mediterranean theater, as the impulsive naval operations chief, Admiral Kurt Fricke, proposed, would not do. It would give the Italians license to pry into German planning, with the "great danger that the Italian Royal House [would] relay [the] information to England." Italian generals and political leaders were not all that "reliable and loyal to the Axis," although Hitler did not expect overt hostility from Ciano for the moment. Even the decisive exercise of German "influence" on Italian military activities through the liaison staffs in Rome, as Mackensen, Rintelen, and Ribbentrop proposed, was "difficult because of the well-known mentality of the Italians." Nor was it likely "on personal and material grounds," that they could successfully follow German advice. It was supremely important that Germany make no outright demands, for "with too extensive demands the danger [existed] that even Mussolini might jump ship." Hitler would not sanction any measures that might "offend or harm the Duce and thus lead to the loss of the strongest binding link of the Axis, the mutual trust of the respective chiefs of state." The only politically practical way to exert the necessary control was to tie offers of German units to Italian acceptance of conditions governing their employment, on a case by case basis: German mastery on the installment plan. Hitler proposed the immediate commitment of a motorized blocking force to hold what remained of Libya, and the transport of a corps of alpine, motorized, and armored troops to Albania.[218] He himself would secure Mussolini's agreement at the forthcoming conference.

Berchtesgaden and after. The long-awaited meeting at the *Berghof*, which Mussolini attempted to keep secret even if he could postpone it no longer, was the first installment. Since Cavallero was fully occupied "both in spirit and in person" in Albania,[219] Guzzoni made the journey, along with Ciano. The conversations fell naturally into separate political and military discussions. On the 19th, Ciano and Ribbentrop surveyed the political situation, and Ribbentrop again cautioned the Italians against rapprochement with Russia, despite renewed and insistent overtures from Molotov in December.[220] Simultaneously, the two dictators conferred privately, and Mussolini confided to Hitler his internal difficulties: "the unreliable but [as yet] inoperative attitude of the King, . . . [and] the Badoglio affair." A general discussion between dictators and foreign ministers then covered the time-honored French and Spanish problems, which Pétain's sudden dismissal in early December of his collaborationist deputy, Pierre Laval, had compounded.[221] Hitler was also "extremely anti-Russian, . . . and not very precise about what he intend[ed] to do in future against Great Britain." Invasion was clearly impractical, although the threat still had its uses. Ciano and Mussolini were still unaware that Hitler proposed to cope with Britain by seeking the decision over European hegemony in war against Russia.

The military conversations were more important than the political ones. While foreign ministers and dictators talked, Guzzoni briefed Keitel and Jodl.[222] In Albania, the low capacity of the ports still prevented rapid buildup. Preparations for a major Italian offensive in the direction of Korçë and Kastoria would require another two months. Italian forces were nevertheless prepared "to march earlier, not to give battle, but to exploit the collapse that could occur in Greece even before the actual entry into action of the Germans." Some illusions evidently died hard. On the question of German alpine troops for Albania, Guzzoni made it clear that the port bottleneck made shipping and supplying more than one German division impossible without seriously cutting into the Italian buildup. Since Hitler insisted, unbeknownst to the Italians, on sending an entire corps to render German participation decisive rather than symbolic, Guzzoni's reservations led to a marked cooling of German interest, and effectively killed the plan. Mussolini had in any case regarded the idea of German units in Albania as intolerably humiliating from the beginning, and was not displeased at its passing.[223] In discussing North Africa, Guzzoni conspicuously failed to make clear the full seriousness of the situation (Tobruk fell four days later). Keitel and Jodl provided information on the composition and transport requirements of the *Sperrverband,* whose commander, General Hans von Funck, was already reconnoitering in Libya. Guzzoni also emphasized the hopeless plight of East Africa. Concentric British assault from the Sudan and Kenya was imminent, and "no possibility of influencing operations there except to a minimal degree" existed. The Germans had no suggestions.

The climax of the *Berghof* meeting came next day, 20 January. Hitler, with a "singular mastery" that impressed both Ciano and Guzzoni,[224] delivered for Mussolini, the foreign ministers, and the generals a two-hour monologue on the military situation and German plans. The descent through Bulgaria would begin in March. Overt German moves toward Greece might produce raids on the Rumanian oilfields and large-scale British troop landings. Therefore the crossing into Bulgaria must take place immediately before the actual attack. For the same reason, and probably also in reaction to Guzzoni's remarks the previous day, Hitler now appeared willing to give up the idea of intervention in Albania. On Gibraltar, he wanted one more try; Mussolini had agreed in the political discussions to invite Franco to Italy and again seek to convince the reluctant Caudillo to enter the war. As for North Africa, Hitler remarked that "the judging of the situation there was essentially the business of the Italian military." It was "immeasurably important" that they hang on. He had evidently not found Guzzoni's relatively cheerful exposition to Keitel and Jodl altogether convincing. If Tripoli fell, Hitler continued, the Axis would lose its remaining chance, along with the Gibraltar operation, of clearing up the ambiguous position in French North Africa. Hitler proposed to send the *Sperrverband* as soon as possible. The Italians agreed.[225] The destruction of much of 10th Army had had one beneficial effect: the consequent decrease in supply requirements and port congestion now facilitated the commitment of German forces.

Mussolini's pilgrimate to the *Berghof* was as important for its psychological effects as for its immediate practical results. He had departed for Germany "dark-faced and nervous," and returned "mildly intoxicated, as after every conference with Hitler." De Bono, who saw him soon after his return, commented that "the man is so serene that he seems mad."[226] Mussolini was to need all the serenity he could muster, for in the ensuing weeks the final catastrophe in Cyrenaica unfolded, and consolidated German control over the Italian war effort. The fall of Tobruk immediately followed the Duce–Führer meeting, and in the next ten days Graziani's defense collapsed. Rintelen argued that it was pointless to send German forces if Graziani merely proposed to await the British in a "fortified camp around the town of Tripoli." Funck, back from Libya, made the same case in person on 1 February, and Hitler ordered transport of the *Sperrverband* held until the Italians gave assurances that it would arrive in time, and have room to operate successfully. He refused to jeopardize German prestige by committing troops to a forlorn hope, and ordered Rintelen to find out from the Italian high command what orders they had given Graziani, and how long he thought he could continue to hold part of Cyrenaica.[227] Before the answer came, however, Hitler had made up his mind, even while O'Connor's forward units raced to cut off the remnants of 10th Army at Beda Fomm.

Hitler explained to his generals on 3 February that the loss of North Africa was militarily bearable. But the "strong psychological repercussions" in Italy would not be: "England could then put a pistol to Italy's breast and force it to choose between concluding peace and retaining its extra-European possessions, or exposing itself to the harshest air bombardment, after the loss of Libya." By eliminating Italy's foothold in North Africa, the British would also free considerable forces for mischief elsewhere. Germany must therefore hold Libya. After some discussion, Hitler ordered the *Luftwaffe* air corps now operating from Sicily and southern Italy against the British fleet to mount strikes to slow the enemy advance. The Führer also adopted Funck's conclusion that the *Sperrverband* was no longer adequate. A *Panzerdivision* would have to back it up. Brauchitsch suggested the augmentation of the *Sperrver-*

band with a tank regiment, and the diversion of an armored division from the Greek operation to Libya along with a corps staff to direct operations. Hitler agreed. The trains again rolled south.[228]

With the commitment of its troops in Italian theaters, Germany acquired the right to stipulate the conditions of their employment. Hitler demanded that the Italians place what few mobile forces they still possessed under the command of General Erwin Rommel, whom he chose on 5 February to command German forces in Africa. In a cleverly drafted letter, Hitler gently explained to Mussolini that the narrow bridgehead around Tripoli was neither defensible in the air nor suppliable by sea. Only forward defense in the Great Sirte desert stood any chance of success. Hitler was too skillful a psychologist to voice the threat his offer implicitly held over the Italians' heads, but his subordinates were not so restrained in private. In the crude words of Jodl, the *Wehrmacht* high command would "not send a single man to North Africa, and if some small German special purpose forces were already in action there, it would . . . withdraw them" should Italy fail to accept the German conditions.[229]

Mussolini made no difficulties. He may well have rejoiced that Hitler's request coincided with his own long-standing inclination to yield as little ground as possible. Rintelen and his superiors in Berlin made clear to Rome by 4 February that Germany would only send ground troops if Italy planned a forward defense; the next day Mussolini personally ordered Graziani to fight "as far forward as possible." Unfortunately the dictator did not presume to spell out the location of the main line of resistance, and Graziani predictably exploited ambiguity, and proposed siting his main position at Homs, a mere sixty miles east of Tripoli. This plan would concede to the British the port of Misurata and the all-important water sources of the settled and irrigated area around it.[230]

Even before Graziani's proposal reached Rome, however, Mussolini had received Rintelen on the morning of 9 February and yielded to the German attaché's insistence that the Italians must not allow the British to cross the Sirte wastes. Guzzoni therefore demanded that Graziani's successor, General Italo Gariboldi, deploy east of Misurata. Rommel, in his first reconnaissance, drove the point home to Roatta, who had flown to Tripoli to see for himself. On 13 February the German mission told Roatta bluntly that if Graziani's successor insisted on merely defending the Homs line, "they would once more submit the decision to the Führer," with the unspoken premise that the latter might order the German buildup halted.[231] Germany's war in Africa was under way. Only East Africa was outside German reach; despite dogged Italian resistance in the best World War I manner at Keren gorge, the gateway to Eritrea, the British eliminated effective opposition in the *Impero* by mid-May.

In the Mediterranean, the *Luftwaffe* punished the British fleet. But air action alone was not enough. In mid-February, Raeder met Riccardi at Merano in the South Tyrol and pressed him to take risks: only a fleet action could reestablish the situation. Riccardi parried; his oil supplies and air reconnaissance were allegedly inadequate. Then he gave in wearily. But as Hitler had foreseen in January, German advice alone was insufficient. Raeder's pressure and a British cryptographic coup that compromised the operation order produced disaster off Cape Matapan on 28 March. The Navy lost three heavy cruisers, and the *Vittorio Veneto* barely escaped.[232] The defeat, immediately before Germany's victorious progress down through the Balkans to Crete, further emphasized Italy's new satellite status. Raeder had driven the point home by sternly warning Riccardi off when the latter intimated that Mussolini contemplated a landing on Corsica.[233] The Germans did not intend to suffer another 28 October.[234]

Matapan, like Taranto, was hardly crippling in material terms. By summer the Italian fleet was again equal to the British in battleship strength. By December 1941 it was superior, thanks to the extraordinary skill and bravery of the Italian frogmen who penetrated Alexandria harbor with steerable torpedoes and sank the battleships *Valiant* and *Queen Elizabeth*. Along with the loss of the *Barham* to a German submarine the month before, and Japan's entry into the war, sinking the *Prince of Wales* and *Repulse* off Malaya, the Italian exploit compelled the Mediterranean Fleet to operate entirely without battleships for much of 1942. But memories of Taranto and Matapan deterred the Italian leadership from ruthlessly pursuing their weakened enemy, and by midsummer oil shortage immobilized the fleet's heavy units and ended the small remaining chance of a temporary Mediterranean victory for the Axis.

In the Balkans, as elsewhere, the war once more became an Anglo-German duel. The death of Metaxas at the end of January and the increasing magnitude of the German threat led to a Greek change of heart. After extraordinarily confused and confusing negotiations with Eden and Sir John Dill, chief of the imperial general staff, Metaxas's successors accepted a British expeditionary force.[235] Churchill abandoned the opportunity to drive Italy from North Africa before Rommel's forces were ready.[236] But so long as the Italians continued to hold the bulk of the Greek army in Albania and the Yugoslavs and Turks remained immobile, no outside chance existed of even temporarily blocking a German advance to the Aegean.

Hitler for his part tactfully refrained from exerting direct control in the Balkans over his prostrate ally. Although Mussolini's Albanian March offensive was premature from Germany's standpoint, Hitler refused to dictate postponement. He would magnanimously if contemptuously permit his allies to "burn their nose,"[237] but his subordinates were not averse to speculating on a compromise solution under German patronage. The political effects of the German army's Danube crossing at the end of February and the subsequent German concentration in Bulgaria raised naïve hopes in the *Wehrmacht* high command, even though the Greeks had refused in mid-

February the latest of a series of German offers to mediate, and continued to resist the notion of negotiations with the despised Italians.[238] When Marras reported these stirrings to Rome in late February, Guzzoni appealed despairingly to the Germans to declare their intentions. Through both Marras and Rintelen, Guzzoni announced that "Italy intended to defeat Greece before the possibility [of a compromise peace] came up." The German foreign office also probed the Italian attitude toward a political settlement, and elicited the ill-tempered reply that such projects "did not interest" Italy.[239] New reports from Marras of *Wehrmacht* high command hopes that German concentration in Bulgaria could still gain "a great political success, avoiding, if possible, a new conflict" provoked a frantic telephone call from Guzzoni. It was "inadmissible," the general shouted to Marras and to the ubiquitous wiretappers of Göring's "Research Office," that "the Germans should attempt to enter Greece peacefully, while our men fight and die." But Berlin, beyond communicating good wishes and German intentions of acting against Greece in early April, was unhelpful. German "last chance" offers to Greece continued.[240]

Nevertheless, German freedom of action was limited, even before any residual possibility of compromise ended with the large-scale landing of British ground troops at the Piraeus on 7 March. To lure the Bulgarians into the Tripartite Pact, Hitler had assured them their long-coveted outlet on the Aegean in Greek Thrace. As Weizsäcker recognized, this promise made a peaceful solution impossible so long as Greece refused to give up territory. In any case, only the smashing of Greek resistance by force would serve what had become Germany's principal aim in the Mediterranean theater: the shoring up of Italian morale and Mussolini's all-important prestige. As Hitler remarked in exasperation in early February, he could not really avoid intervening militarily in Greece, for if he did not, "the Italians would fall away."[241]

German aid in the Balkans had its price even beyond the humiliation implicit in having to accept it. Despite his best efforts, Mussolini had to acknowledge German hegemony even over Yugoslavia. In the course of February, the Duce himself held two meetings with Stakić and elaborated on Ciano's earlier suggestion of an Italo-Yugoslav alliance.[242] Mussolini hoped that such an agreement, with its threat of a Yugoslav descent on Salonika, would shock the Greeks into surrender before the Germans moved south.[243] It would also offer him a chance to persuade Hitler that Yugoslav adherence to the Tripartite Pact, and thus direct subordination to Germany, was superfluous. But the Germans saw through this game. At the end of February, while Rome contemplated with fury the prospect of a German deal with Greece, Ribbentrop insisted on a "unified approach" in the Yugoslav question. Mussolini weakly conceded to Germany the conduct of future Axis negotiations with that country.[244] When Prince Paul's accession to the Tripartite Pact on 25 March provoked a Serb military coup that in turn triggered Hitler's instantaneous and drastic reaction, Mussolini followed bewildered in his ally's wake in the invasion of Yugoslavia and Greece. Italy's own war was over. Nothing remained but to follow where Hitler led, until German war culminated in German victory or engulfed Fascist regime and Italy itself in ruin.[245]

Conclusion
The meaning of Fascist Italy's last war

> The political genius of the Duce is beyond dispute. Anyone who
> doubts it has only to look at the depth of the abyss into which he has
> thrown Italy.
>
> Galeazzo Ciano, to his jailors, 1943/44

Ciano, as he faced execution in the winter of 1943–4 for voting against his
father-in-law at the Grand Council meeting that provoked the regime's fall,
saw a truth of sorts. The very magnitude of Mussolini's aspirations had
brought disaster. "One man," Ciano wrote in his farewell letter to the King
in December 1943, "one man alone, Mussolini, through unscrupulous personal ambitions, 'out of thirst for military glory' (to use his own actual
words) ha[d] deliberately led the nation into the bottomless pit."[1]

While Mussolini had far more help than Ciano's reiteration of Churchill's
shrewd propaganda implied, and "thirst for military glory" scarcely did the
dictator's motivations justice, Ciano was clearly right in proclaiming Mussolini's preeminent responsibility for what had occurred. Mussolini had a
genuine foreign policy program: the creation of an Italian *spazio vitale* in the
Mediterranean and Middle East. Success would have raised Italy at last to
the status of a true great power, a goal Mussolini shared with the Italian
establishment, although the latter, like the generals and admirals, lacked his
taste for risk. Internally, expansion would consolidate Fascist power, eliminate all competing authorities and unwelcome restraints, and mold the Italians into a people "worthy" of the imperial mission Mussolini claimed for
them.

Italy's catastrophic defeat in its "parallel war" and the ultimate destruction of *Grossdeutschland* in the wider conflict fortunately deprived Mussolini
of the opportunity to implement his program. Nevertheless, his attempts to
realize it between 1939 and 1941 were remarkably consistent and tenacious.
His frequent changes of mood, which Ciano assiduously chronicled, in no
way obscure the thrust of his policy throughout nonbelligerence. Diplomatically, Mussolini refused all commitments, such as leadership of a neutral
bloc, that might inhibit entry into war. Economically, he did his best to
reduce Italian dependence on and trade with the Allies to the lowest level
compatible with procurement of the raw materials indispensable for his

armament programs. Domestically, he struggled to prepare Italian opinion for the sacrifices those programs, and eventual entry into the war at Germany's side, demanded. After the failure of Hitler's "peace offer" of October 1939, Mussolini's hopes of a temporary truce in the campaign against the "demo-plutocracies" rapidly declined. His only wavering resulted from fears of a formal Russo-German alliance and of German encroachment in the South Tyrol. But his National Socialist allies were profuse in assurances on the first point, and eventually moved to avoid friction over the second.

In the spring of 1940, as Hitler's determination to attack in the West became unequivocally apparent, Mussolini abandoned attempts to restrain his ally, attempts that derived from awareness that the Italian armed forces were not yet capable of making a decisive contribution to Axis victory. After the Brenner meeting in March, he imposed upon his subordinates plans for a naval and air war that was a direct descendant of the visions of a Mediterranean conflict he had entertained from 1935 on. Italy's war would be "parallel" to that of Germany north of the Alps. But the persistent overestimates of Allied strength and the "supine acceptance of the situation of the moment" of Mussolini's military advisers prevented any immediate move, or effective offensive planning. The military rightly assumed that until 1943 at least Italy would be unequal to an offensive against British and French combined, even if the Germans distracted the Allies in the north. They also lacked the imagination to foresee French defeat. Only the German victories in the West unleashed Mussolini to carry King and generals into war with promises that they need not fight and assurances that political considerations must override professional qualms. By the end of May, Italian public opinion as well had swung from fear of "a war for which no one sees the necessity," as a police informant put it in April, to fear of arriving "too late" at the division of the spoils. Mussolini swiftly exploited the latter emotion.

Despite his assurances to Badoglio, Mussolini envisaged a war – short, but genuine enough – to assert Italy's supremacy in the Mediterranean by force of arms. With the French armistice, he could concentrate on the British in the Mediterranean and Middle East. But the defensive mentality prevalent before French collapse and the resulting lack of preparation proved insuperable obstacles. Hope of a swift naval decision dissipated as early as 9 July, when Cavagnari's ships, despite parity of force and proximity to their own bases, retired in confusion from a brief encounter with Cunningham's Mediterranean Fleet. Subsequently, Mussolini proved unable to compel his admirals to seek decisive action. On land, Graziani revealed himself an unparalleled virtuoso of procrastination. Finally, in early September, a succession of direct orders from Palazzo Venezia drove the marshal forward to Sidi el Barrani. The Italian desert offensive was not, in the usual interpretation, the product of "purely political motives, in the expectation of an imminent peace,"[2] but yet another Mussolinian attempt to compel the generals to fight by alleging political motivations they could not readily challenge.

Throughout the summer, as Mussolini struggled with Graziani, the possibility of a subsidiary foray into the Balkans intrigued the Italian leadership. Mussolini proposed to attack Yugoslavia, and, at Ciano's urging, Greece, during or after decisive action in the desert. Once Italy had invaded Egypt, and Germany landed in Britain, the Balkan fruit would be ripe for picking – a situation Mussolini consistently expected to materialize at the end of September. The Germans, better informed than Mussolini about the prospects of cross-Channel invasion, were also less inclined than in the spring to tolerate Italian adventures in the southeast, especially because their ally's contribution to the common war effort had so far been negligible. Consequently, in mid-August, despite expressed willingness to permit Italy to "solve" the Yugoslav "problem" after the elimination of Great Britain, Hitler and Ribbentrop insisted that Mussolini postpone his wars in southeastern Europe until after final victory, which implicitly was not in sight. Mussolini and Ciano acquiesced in bad grace, but continued to prepare for the Greek operation. Unlike the Yugoslav one, it seemed feasible without German cooperation or logistical support.

Late September and early October brought reluctant German admission that invasion of Britain was impractical for the moment – an admission Mussolini greeted with a relief that paralleled the fear with which he had regarded German interest throughout the summer in compromise peace with Britain. He himself now saw a chance to succeed where Hitler had failed, and to emerge from the Egyptian campaign as the "sole 'victor' of the Axis."[3] Both before and after the Brenner conference with Hitler on 4 October, Mussolini pressed Graziani to advance further. Then, under the sting of the German occupation of Rumania, in which Mussolini apparently thought Hitler had invited Italian participation, then broken his word, the Duce ordered the Greek operation into motion in mid-October. The march on Athens would be a blow against Britain of the kind "meditated" since the spring of 1939 and before, a foray to add Greece to Italy's booty, and a demonstration of Italy's independent status within the Axis.

Badoglio and his associates had been dubious of the Greek project throughout the summer, although the Italian Army evinced a discreet enthusiasm for attack on Yugoslavia. In October, however, Mussolini's military subordinates fell into line as they had in May, and as Graziani had in September – with the difference that no one seems to have entertained serious doubts about the ability of the exiguous Italian forces in Albania to drive the enemy from Epirus. Later, of course, the generals excused their acquiescence in the project, and their miserable performance, with tales that Mussolini and Ciano had promised them a stroll in *passo romano.*

The fiasco in the Albanian mountains that followed was the greatest blow to the regime's prestige since Guadalajara, and the greatest shock to its internal stability since the Matteotti crisis of 1924. Army and Party clashed over responsibility, while disaster at Taranto and in North Africa rendered Italy's war irretrievably lost. Defeat ended Italy's aspiration to great power status, and produced an Anglo-German struggle over the nation's allegiance reminiscent of the days of nonbelligerence. Hitler won for the moment, with swift commitment of the *Luftwaffe* and Rommel to the Mediterranean theater, and with the massive buildup in Rumania for the spring drive to the Aegean. Germany now directed the war even in Italy's theater, and Italian collapse convinced Hitler, who had always harbored doubts about Italian fitness for junior partnership in the racially organized New Order, that after victory in Russia he need not "have further regard for Italy." His allies were "merely eaters, not fighters."[4] Rommel would move on Alexandria and *Wehrmacht* thrusts through Turkey and Transcaucasia would seize the Middle East, while the vast resources of the Soviet Union placed world mastery within German grasp.[5]

Internally, defeat was the beginning of the end for the Fascist regime. The German successes in the Balkans and North Africa in April and May 1941 stabilized the military situation, and checked the dissolution of Mussolini's power that had become perceptible during the hard winter. But the internal crisis had led many in the Italian Army to toy with the idea of a coup, and had, above all, created the disaffection within Mussolini's own party that provoked his dismissal in July 1943. Grandi intrigued in Rome and caballed with the disgruntled *gerarchi* in Albania. Ciano, whose self-esteem Mussolini's "observations" on his performance had bruised, grew ever more insistent on distinguishing his responsibilities from those of his father-in-law.[6] Not even Farinacci could restrain an occasional outburst at what he perceived as Mussolini's ineptitude.[7] As for the establishment and the wider public, they increasingly deserted the regime in the name of the very Italian nationalism that had caused them to support it. Defeat, not war, created the gulf between the "nation" and that "one man alone" from whom Churchill coldly and deliberately sought to separate the Italian people.

The wider significance of Italy's war inevitably extends beyond the history of the regime it ended. In 1939 and 1940 Mussolini demonstrated that his goals were not so different from those of Hitler as many historians have assumed. His tenacity suggests that to compare him to his German ally is not merely, as Renzo De Felice has suggested, a "mechanical application of characteristics, of tendencies, typical of National Socialist [foreign policy]" to the explanation of an entirely different phenomenon.[8] Mussolini sought to turn the world — at least that part of it within reach — upside down. Externally, Italy would rule a vast empire; internally, he would remake "the Italians" into a cruel and domineering master race under his own unchallenged control.

Like Hitler's quest for *Lebensraum*, Mussolini's expansionism and his decision to go to war in 1940 proceeded above all from the dictator's own vision, not from internal social or political pressures. Mussolini did not choose empire to preserve the social order at home. That ploy, known as "social imperialism," has recently enjoyed wide and unmerited popularity as an explanation for foreign policies as diverse as those of the United States, Wilhelmine Germany, Victorian Britain, and Hitler's Führer state.[9] Mussolini's expansionism, like that of his German ally, was the precise opposite of "social imperialism." He did not seek preservation of the Italian social order through external adventures to distract the lower orders from demanding a larger share of the national wealth. Rather, he quite consciously risked and generated internal disaffection by the pursuit of conquests that demanded sacrifice, but would ultimately confer on him the power and prestige to remake society at home.

This is not to say that short-term internal considerations had no role in Mussolini's decision to enter the war. He had to weigh the effects of abstention on what Carlo Gambino has described as the "enormous Party . . . whose only element of cohesion was . . . imperial and warlike rhetoric."[10] The cult of the Duce might carry Party and regime through. Nevertheless, abstention, if not, in Gambino's words, "a greater risk than war," might prove dangerous internally while Hitler's run of luck lasted – and Mussolini expected it to last. The enthusiasm for an "easy war" which the German victories engendered in much of the public by late May 1940 presumably reinforced whatever fears Mussolini may have entertained for the regime's stability if he prolonged nonbelligerence further. But these pressures were largely of Mussolini's creation: he had nurtured the PNF on "imperial and warlike rhetoric" because he sought empire, and he had struggled in vain for years to prepare the day when the Italian public would rise to its feet and demand war. Fear of domestic political repercussions no more compelled Mussolini to go to war in 1940 than the threat of economic collapse without fresh infusions of booty, a threat breakneck rearmament had created, forced Hitler to launch in 1939 what he knew might become a world war.[11]

Yet a vital distinction between the two regimes exists, a distinction that makes attempts to explain them as manifestations of that elusive generic phenomenon, fascism (small "f"), seem heavy-handed.[12] Hitler sought world mastery. His hierarchically organized, pseudoscientifically planned, and technologically secured racial utopia would have brought history in the conventional sense to a halt. As Klaus Hildebrand has convincingly argued, Hitler's expansionist program summed up territorially and revolutionized in internal and social terms the traditional aims of post-Bismarckian Germany. Mussolini was not quite so ambitious, although he too aspired to destroy the social order at home through conquest abroad. He started from a less secure position than did Hitler, and commanded a nation with neither resources nor traditions for a bid for global supremacy. Mussolini merely sought an Italian nationalist utopia, not biological World Revolution.[13] Nevertheless, the defeat that doomed him, his regime, and Italy's great power aspirations cannot cancel out the magnitude of his purpose.

Appendixes

1. The diaries of Count Galeazzo Ciano

This book makes considerable use of Ciano's diaries, particularly the wartime ones. Some examination of their reliability is therefore in order.

Most scholars, including the late Mario Toscano, have accepted the genuineness and reliability of the diaries.[1] But caution is necessary. According to some accounts of those who knew him, Ciano devoted considerable time after his removal as foreign minister in February 1943 to rewriting.[2] Suspicions of this sort receive support from the serious anachronism (the reference in the 12 December 1940 entry to Rommel, who had no connection with the Italians until February 1941) that Andreas Hillgruber first pointed out. The discrepancy has recently led David Irving, for one, to dismiss the diaries as totally unreliable.[3]

However, the Rommel anachronism is not necessarily evidence that the diaries are a fabrication, or even that the text is thoroughly corrupt. Examination of Allen Dulles's films of the original agendas (NARS Microcopy T-586, roll 25)[4] suggests that very little editing took place. Ciano crossed out one long passage (25 October 1939) and two short ones (5 December 1940, 8 July 1942). He also removed the pages for 13–18 April 1940, 27 January–23 April 1941, 24 July–21 September 1941, 18–23 August 1942, 12–21 September 1942, and 1–2 February 1943 (apparently because he made no entries for those days). Above all, he tore out the page for 27/28 October 1940, and rewrote the entries for 26, 27, and 28 October on the remaining pages. Presumably the original entry for 28 October was simply too embarrassing to leave in.

But this evidence of limited tampering actually speaks in favor of the authenticity of what remains. Had Ciano edited the diaries extensively in 1943, then recopied them into fresh agendas, he would presumably have been more careful to cover his tracks. The Rommel anachronism (a slip of the pen for *Roma*) was probably the result of a delayed entry, made several months after the event from notes kept separately. The internal evidence of the diaries themselves is decisive. Had Ciano worked them over thoroughly, he would not have left in remarks so excruciatingly embarrassing in retrospect as his 12 October 1940 judgment on the Greek enterprise: "In truth, I think the operation will be useful and easy." He would instead have retouched the text to give himself a more statesmanlike pose, rather than the mercurial, feckless, and often refreshingly cynical personality that actually emerges. Further, had he tampered with the diaries extensively, they would almost certainly fail to dovetail, as they do with almost incredible precision, with the Italian and German diplomatic correspondence. While Ciano undoubtedly embellished his own activities in setting them down on paper, the diaries remain the single most important source on Fascist Italy at war.

2. Military expenditure: Italy and the powers compared

Popular wisdom rightly distinguishes between lies, damn lies, and (worst of all) statistics. The figures below are in many cases rough approximations. The reader should therefore resist the impression of certainty that numbers inevitably but often spuriously convey. The figures given for the military and state expenditures of Italy, France, and Britain are official or derived from official figures; those for Germany private estimates; national income and Gross National Product totals by their nature consist in part of educated guesses. Differences in internal price structure, international currency complications, different budgetary practices in each of the four nations and the fact that the Italian figures (except national income) are by fiscal rather than calendar year, detract from the rigor of the comparison. Nevertheless, the aggregate figures for the entire 1935–8 period do provide a relative measure of national effort. 1935, the year of Ethiopia and the first year of serious rearmament (or failure to rearm) is a convenient starting point. 1938, the "last normal year," is the last year for which French national income or German state expenditure are readily available. Aggregate figures for 1935–9 suggest that Italy retained a diminishing edge (in terms of effort, not absolute figures or results) over Britain.

Table A2.1. Italian service expenditures, 1935/6–1939/40

Year	Army	%	Navy	%	Air Force	%	Other procurement	%	Total military	%
1935/6	7,093	58.2	2,850	23.4	2,241	18.4	—	—	12,184	100
1936/7	9,050	56.2	3,423	21.3	3,628	22.5	—	—	16,101	100
1937/8	5,794	45.7	2,970	23.4	3,923	30.9	—	—	12,687	100
1938/9	6,685	44.5	3,429	22.8	4,296	28.6	602	4.0	15,012	100
1939/40	14,869	52.8	5,206	18.5	6,964	24.8	1,102	3.9	28,141	100

Source: Italy, Ministero del Tesoro, Ragioneria Generale dello Stato, *Il bilancio dello Stato negli esercizi finanziari dal 1930–31 al 1941–42* (Rome, 1951), pp. 257, 407, and Francesco A. Répaci, "Le spese delle guerre condotte dall'Italia nell' ultimo quarantacinquennio," *Rivista di Politica Economica* (April 1960), tables 2, 4.

Table A2.2. Italy and the powers compared

Year	Military expenditure	State expenditure	National income	Military as % of State	Military as % of National income	Military in million $[a]
ITALY (million lire)						
1935/6	12,184[b]	35,100[b]	(1935) 101,157[c]	34.7	12.0	999
1936/7	16,101	43,600	(1936) 107,367	36.9	15.0	1,175
1937/8	12,687	41,400	(1937) 127,839	30.6	10.0	672
1938/9	15,012	42,300	(1938) 137,877	35.5	10.9	796
Aggregate:						
1935/6–1938/9	55,984	162,400	(1935–8) 474,240	34.5	11.8	3,649
1939/40	28,141	62,400	(1939) 152,641	45.1	18.4	—
Aggregate:						
1935/6–1939/40	84,125	224,800	(1935–9) 626,881	37.4	13.4	—
FRANCE (million Fr.)						
1935	12,657[d]	49,868[d]	221,000[d]	25.4	5.7	835
1936	14,848	55,789	255,000	26.6	5.8	906
1937	21,235	68,164	304,000	31.2	7.0	859
1938	28,976	82,345	340,000	35.2	8.5	840

BRITAIN (million £)

Aggregate:						
1935–8	77,716	256,166	1,120,000	30.3	6.9	3,440
1939	92,726	150,116	—	61.8	—	—
Aggregate:						
1935–9	170,442	406,282	—	42.0	—	—
1935	137.1[e]	841.8[e]	4,100[f]	16.3	3.3	671
1936	186.0	902.2	4,400	20.6	4.2	924
1937	256.4	979.0	4,600	26.2	5.6	1,265
1938	397.5	1,033.0	4,800	38.5	8.3	1,944
Aggregate:						
1935–8	977.0	3,756.0	17,900	26.0	5.5	4,804
1939	719.0	1,490.0	5,000	48.3	14.4	—
Aggregate:						
1935–9	1,696.0	5,246.0	22,900	32.3	7.4	—

GERMANY (million RM)

			GNP		% of GNP	
1935	6,000[f]	14,100[f]	74,000[f]	42.6	8.1	2,415
1936	10,800	17,300	83,000	62.4	13.0	4,352
1937	11,700	21,400	93,000	54.7	12.6	4,704
1938	17,200	32,900	105,000	52.3	16.4	6,908

Table A2.2. Italy and the powers compared (cont.)

Year	Military expenditure	State expenditure	GNP (million RM)	Military as % of State	Military as % of GNP	Military in million $[a]
GERMANY (million RM)						
Aggregate:						
1935–8	45,700	85,700	355,000	53.3	12.9	18,379
1939	30,000+	—	130,000	—	23.0+	—
Aggregate:						
1935–9	75,700	—	485,000	—	15.6+	—

[a] Sullivan, "A Thirst for Glory," Appendix. The exchange rates used are the average rate for each year according to the Federal Reserve Board.

[b] Italy, Ministero del Tesoro, Ragioneria Generale dello Stato, *Il bilancio dello Stato negli esercizi finanziari dal 1930–31 al 1941–42* (Rome, 1951), pp. 257, 407, and Francesco A. Répaci, "Le spese delle guerre condotte dall'Italia nell' ultimo quarantacinquennio," *Rivista di Politica Economica* (April 1960), tables 2, 4.

[c] Rosario Romeo, *Breve storia della grande industria in Italia* (Bologna, 4th rev. ed., 1972), p. 412.

[d] Robert Frankenstein, "À propos des aspects financiers du réarmement français," *Revue d'histoire de la deuxième guerre mondiale,* No. 102 (1976), p. 3; Alfred Sauvy, *Histoire économique de la France entre les deux guerres,* II (Paris, 1967), pp. 576–9.

[e] Robert Paul Shay, Jr., *British Rearmament in the Thirties* (Princeton, N.J., 1977), p. 297 (figures rounded off).

[f] Berenice Carroll, *Design for Total War* (The Hague, 1968), pp. 184, 187. Gross national product is slightly larger than national income. Carroll's figures for British national income are almost certainly too low: Alan Milward, *The German Economy at War* (London, 1965), p. 7, gives £5,242 million for 1938. However, the Carroll figures cover the 1935–7 period, which Milward's do not.

Abbreviations

AA	Auswärtiges Amt (German foreign office).
ACS	Archivio Centrale dello Stato (Rome) (followed by further abbreviations, or, for private papers, the name of the individual).
ADAP	*Akten zur deutschen auswärtigen Politik 1918–1945* (Baden-Baden, Frankfurt a.M., 1950–) (followed by series, volume, and document number).
ADM	Admiralty files (PRO).
ADSS	*Actes et documents du Saint-Siège rélatifs à la seconde guerre mondiale.* (Vatican City, 1967–) (followed by volume and document number).
AOI	Africa Orientale Italiana (Italian East Africa).
AS	Africa Settentrionale (North Africa).
AUSE	Archivio dell'Ufficio Storico dell'Esercito, Rome (Italian Army Archives).
AUSMM	Archivio dell'Ufficio Storico della Marina Militare, Rome (Italian Navy Archives).
BA	Bundesarchiv, Koblenz.
BAMA	Bundesarchiv-Militärarchiv, Freiburg im Breisgau.
CAB	Cabinet (PRO).
CID	Committee of Imperial Defence.
CSD XVII	Commissione Suprema di Difesa, "Verbali della XVII Sessione" (NARS T-586/461).
DBFP	*Documents on British Foreign Policy* (London, 1947–) (followed by series, volume, and document number).
DDF	*Documents diplomatiques français 1932–1939* (Paris, 1963–) (followed by series, volume, and document number).
DDI	*I documenti diplomatici italiani* (Rome, 1952–) (followed by series, volume, and document number).

DGPS/ DAGR Direzione Generale Pubblica Sicurezza, Divisione Affari Generali e Riservati (ACS,MI) (directorate-general of public security, division of general and confidential affairs).

DGPS/DPP Direzione Generale Pubblica Sicurezza, Divisione Polizia Politica (ACS,MI) (directorate-general of public security, political police division).

DGPS/SCP Direzione Generale Pubblica Sicurezza, Segreteria del Capo della Polizia) (ACS,MI) (directorate-general of public security, secretariat of the chief of police).

DIMK *Diplomáciai iratok magyarország külpolitikájához 1936–1945* (Budapest, 1962–) (followed by volume and document number).

FRUS *Foreign Relations of the United States. Diplomatic Papers* (Washington, D.C.) (followed by year and volume number).

GFM German foreign ministry microfilms (NARS T-120) (followed by serial and frame numbers).

GNR German naval records (Washington, London, Freiburg im Breisgau) (followed by file PG number).

Graziani diary Graziani diary, 20.6–7.9.1940, ACS, Graziani, bundle 70, "Appendice."

GWB Greek White Book (Royal Ministry for Foreign Affairs, *Italy's Aggression Against Greece* [Athens, 1940]; followed by document number).

IWM Imperial War Museum, London.

KTB Kriegstagebuch (war diary).

KTB/OKW *Kriegstagebuch des Oberkommandos der Wehrmacht (Wehrmachtführungsstab)* v. I (*1 August 1940–31 Dezember 1941*), ed. Hans-Adolf Jacobsen (Frankfurt a. M., 1965).

KTB 1/SKL Kriegstagebuch der Seekriegsleitung, 1. Abteilung (GNR) (war diary, operations section, German naval high command).

MAG Ministero dell'Aeronautica, Gabinetto (ACS) (Air Ministry, cabinet of the minister).

MCP Ministero della Cultura Popolare, Gabinetto (ACS) (Ministry of Popular Culture, cabinet of the minister).

MI Ministero dell'Interno (ACS) (Ministry of the Interior).

MMG Ministero della Marina, Gabinetto (ACS) (Navy Ministry, cabinet of the minister).

OKH Oberkommando des Heeres (German army high command).

OKL Oberkommando der Luftwaffe (German air force high command).

OKM Oberkommando der Marine (German naval high command).

NARS National Archives and Records Service, Washington, D.C. (usually followed by microcopy, roll, and frame numbers).

OO Benito Mussolini, *Opera Omnia,* eds. Edoardo and Duilio Susmel (Florence, 1951–63) (followed by volume number).

PA	Politisches Archiv des Auswärtigen Amts, Bonn (German foreign ministry archives).
PAC	Ministero della Real Casa, Primo Aiutante di Campo (ACS) (first aide-de-camp to the King).
PC	Presidenza del Consiglio (ACS) (Prime Minister's secretariat) (followed by year and file number).
PNF/SPP	Partito Nazionale Fascista, "Situazione politica ed economica delle Provincie" (ACS) (Party public opinion files, by province).
PRO	Public Record Office, London.
Roatta letters	Diary-letters from Roatta to Graziani, July 1940–January 1941, ACS, Graziani, bundle 42 (reference by entry date).
"Segnala-zioni"	Private political intelligence reports to the head of the Stefani news agency (ACS, Agenzia Stefani/Manlio Morgagni, bundle 9).
SD	Sicherheitsdienst der SS (SS Security Service: the intelligence arm of the SS).
SIM	Servizio Informazioni Militari (Italian Army intelligence).
SPD/CO	Segreteria Particolare del Duce, Carteggio Ordinario (ACS) (Mussolini's papers, ordinary correspondence).
SPD/CR	Segreteria Particolare del Duce, Carteggio Riservato (ACS) (Mussolini's papers, confidential correspondence).
State	United States Department of State, decimal files (NARS).
USE	Stato Maggiore Esercito, Ufficio Storico (Italian Army historical office).
USMM	Ufficio Storico della Marina Militare (Italian Navy historical office).

All dates in the Notes follow the European system: day, month, year.

Notes

All dates in the Notes follow the European system: day, month, year.

INTRODUCTION

1 Franz Halder, *Kriegstagebuch* (Stuttgart, 1962–4) [henceforth "Halder"], II, p. 212.

2 See particularly the works of Luigi Salvatorelli (with the notable exception of his *Corso di storia per i licei*, III [Milan, 1935]). For Croce, Denis Mack Smith, "Benedetto Croce: History and Politics," *Journal of Contemporary History* 8:1 (1973).

3 See De Felice's four massive volumes, *Mussolini il rivoluzionario, 1883–1920; Mussolini il fascista*, I, *La conquista del potere, 1921–1925; Mussolini il fascista*, II, *L'organizzazione dello Stato fascista, 1925–1929; Mussolini il duce*, I, *Gli anni del consenso, 1929–1936* (Turin, 1965–74) (henceforth De Felice, *Mussolini*, I,II,III,IV), and his *Storia degli ebrei italiani sotto il fascismo* (Turin, 3rd rev. ed., 1972). For the quotations above, *idem, Mussolini* IV, p. 24 and his "Alcune osservazioni sulla politica estera Mussoliniana," in *idem*, ed., *L'Italia fra tedeschi e alleati* (Bologna, 1973), p. 73.

4 For the quotations, Salvemini, *Preludio alla seconda guerra mondiale* (Milan, 1967), p. 29; Denis Mack.Smith, "Mussolini, Artist in Propaganda. The Downfall of Fascism," *History Today*, 9 (1959) (also *idem, Mussolini's Roman Empire*, New York, 1976); Donald C. Watt, "The Rome-Berlin Axis, 1936–1940: Myth and Reality," *The Review of Politics*, 22 (1960), p. 524. For the full variety of interpretations of the regime's foreign policy, see Jens Petersen's brilliant "La politica estera del fascismo come problema storiografico," in De Felice, ed., *L'Italia fra tedeschi e alleati*.

5 For descriptions and critique of most such approaches, De Felice, *The Interpretations of Fascism* (Cambridge, Mass., 1977). Henry A. Turner, Jr. has rightly emphasized the paramount importance of ultimate goals in any analysis of Fascism or National Socialism: "Fascism and Modernization," *World Politics*, 24:4 (1972).

6 Thucydides, V, 90.

7 See the subtle, penetrating, but fundamentally rigid treatments of Palmiro Togliatti, *Lezioni sul fascismo* (Rome, 1970 [1935]) and Ernesto Ragionieri, *Sto-*

ria d'Italia, IV, *Dall'unità a oggi* (Turin, 1976). Enzo Santarelli's excellent *Storia del fascismo* (Rome, 1967) is less orthodox.

CHAPTER I
"THERE HAS BEEN MUCH BLUFF"

1 Watt, "The Rome-Berlin Axis," p. 524.
2 Alberto Aquarone, *L'organizzazione dello stato totalitario* (Turin, 1965), pp. 303–9. For similar views, modified in later volumes in a more laudatory direction, De Felice, *Mussolini,* II, 460–70.
3 See Meir Michaelis, *Mussolini and the Jews* (Oxford, 1978).
4 Giorgio Rochat, "La repressione della resistenza araba in Cirenaica (1930–31)," *Il Movimento di Liberazione in Italia,* No. 110 (1973); Rodolfo Graziani, *Pace romana in Libia* (Milan, 1937).
5 Mussolini to Badoglio, 30.12.1934, in Rochat, *Militari e politici nella preparazione della campagna d'Etiopia* (Milan, 1971), pp. 376–9.
6 ACS, Graziani, bundle 60, "Direttive per l'azione politico-militare" (for which I am indebted to Brian R. Sullivan) and ACS, Graziani, bundle 33. See also Rochat, "L'attentato a Graziani e la repressione italiana in Etiopia nel 1936–37," *Italia Contemporanea,* No. 118 (1975).
7 Benedetto Croce, in Mack Smith, *Italy, a Modern History* (Ann Arbor, 1959), p. 455.
8 Galeazzo Ciano, *Diario 1937–1943* (Milan, 1980) ed. De Felice (henceforth Ciano), entries for 22.2.1939, 17.7.1941 (for the diaries' reliability, see Appendix 1); Ugo Cavallero, *Comando Supremo. Diario 1940–43 del Capo di S.M.G.* (Bologna, 1948), pp. 297–9; Teodoro Sala, "1939–1943. Jugoslavia 'neutrale,' Jugoslavia occupata," *Italia Contemporanea,* No. 138 (1980).
9 Hans-Günther Seraphim, ed., *Das politische Tagebuch Alfred Rosenbergs 1934/35 und 1939/40* (Munich, 1964), p. 28; H. R. Trevor-Roper, ed., *Hitler's Secret Conversations, 1941–1944* (New York, 1953), Nos. 132, 268; also Carmine Senise, *Quando ero Capo della Polizia (1940–1943)* (Rome, 1946), p. 93.
10 Alessandro Lessona, *Memorie* (Florence, 1958), p. 333.
11 See the remarks of two major police figures: Guido Leto, *OVRA. Fascismo-Antifascismo* (Bologna, 1952), p. 145; Senise, *Polizia,* pp. 93–4.
12 For Roosevelt, William F. Langer and Everett S. Gleason, *The Challenge to Isolation, 1937–1940* (New York, 1952), p. 7; for Hitler, Edward N. Peterson, *The Limits of Hitler's Power* (Princeton, N.J., 1969), pp. 14–15.
13 Hans Mommsen, *Beamtentum im Dritten Reich* (Stuttgart, 1966), p. 98, n. 26; *idem,* "Ausnahmezustand als Herrschaftstechnik des NS-Regimes," in Manfred Funke, ed., *Hitler, Deutschland, und die Mächte* (Düsseldorf, 1976); for contrary views, Otto Dietrich, *12 Jahre mit Hitler* (Munich, 1955), pp. 132–3; Karl Dietrich Bracher, "Tradition und Revolution im Nationalsozialismus," in Funke, ed., *Hitler;* Klaus Hildebrand, "Le forze motrici di politica interna agenti sulla politica estera nazionalsozialista," *Storia Contemporanea,* 5:2 (1974).
14 Watt, "The Rome-Berlin Axis," p. 527.
15 *Designs in Diplomacy* (Baltimore, 1971), pp. 412–13. See also Ciano's 1940 warning to the Vatican ("We read everything, and Mussolini, too, reads everything"), ADSS, I,274.
16 See Alan Cassels, *Mussolini's Early Diplomacy* (Princeton, N.J., 1970), ch. 4.

17 Eden to Waterlow, No. 439, 6.12.1937, minuted "copy to Rome," PRO FO 371/21148, R 8129. For the reaction, Ciano, 23.12.1937.

18 Ciano, 1.11.1937.

19 Mackensen to AA, 12.3.1941, PA, Deutsche Botschaft Rom, Geheimakten, item 508/40.

20 Ciano, 11.1.1939; also DDF,2,VII,283.

21 See ACS SPD/CR, bundle 68, folder "Guadalajara," file "Commenti della stampa estera sulla battaglia," which contains clippings and embassy press reports, most marked in Mussolini's colored pencil.

22 Fulvio D'Amoja, *La politica estera dell'Impero* (Padua, 1967), p. 185.

23 Ciano, 7.11.1937; 15.3, 16.3, 20.3.1939.

24 Aquarone, *L'organizzazione*, p. 307 and n. 2.

25 *Ibid.;* Lessona, *Memorie*, p. 186.

26 Trevor-Roper, *Secret Conversations*, Nos. 98, 208.

27 *OO*, XXIV, p. 235.

28 Lessona, *Un ministro di Mussolini racconta* (Milan, 1973), p. 171; *idem, Memorie,* pp. 325–6.

29 Ciano, 2.5.1939; also Gerhard Engel, *Heeresadjutant bei Hitler 1938–1943* (Stuttgart, 1974), p. 98.

30 Quirino Armellini, *Diario di Guerra. Nove mesi al Comando Supremo* (Milan, 1946), p. 48.

31 See Dietrich von Delhaes-Guenther, "Die Bevölkerungspolitik des Faschismus," *Quellen und Forschungen aus italienischen Archiven und Bibliotheken,* 59 (1979), and Ercole Sori, "Emigrazione all'estero e migrazioni interne in Italia tra le due guerre," *Quaderni storici,* 10:2/3 (1975).

32 Giuseppe Bottai, *Vent'anni e un giorno (24 luglio 1943)* (Milan, 1949), p. 191; P. Sylos Labini, *Saggio sulle classi sociali* (Bari, 1974), pp. 125–9, 188, and Gordon A. Craig, *Germany 1866–1945* (New York, 1978), p. 187.

33 See Joseph La Palombara, "Italy: Fragmentation, Isolation, Alienation," pp. 282–329 in Lucian W. Pye, Sidney Verba, eds., *Political Culture and Political Development* (Princeton, N.J., 1965).

34 Ester Fano Damascelli, "La 'restaurazione antifascista liberista.' Ristagno e sviluppo economico durante il fascismo," *Il Movimento di Liberazione in Italia,* 23:104 (1971), and the special issue of *Quaderni Storici,* 10:2/3 (1975). For Mussolini's rural-demographic fixation, see Piero Melograni, *Gli industriali e Mussolini* (Milan, 1972), pp. 193–207, and Delhaes-Guenther, "Bevölkerungspolitik des Faschismus."

35 Himmler minute, 11.10.1942, *Vierteljahrshefte für Zeitgeschichte,* 4:4 (1956), pp. 423–6.

36 Mussolini, in Ciano, 3.6.1939.

37 Aquarone, *L'organizzazione,* pp. 160–3; De Felice, "Mussolini e Vittorio Emanuele III Primi Marescialli dell'Impero," in Università dei Studi di Messina, *Scritti in onore di Vittorio de Caprariis* (Rome, n.d.); for Mussolini's views, Ciano, 4.1, 18.6.1938; 27.3.1939.

38 Ciano, 27.3.1939; 18.6, 4.11.1938.

39 See DDF,2,VII,424.

40 Ernst Rudolf Huber, *Verfassungsrecht des Grossdeutschen Reiches* (Hamburg, 1939), p. 230; for Huber on that "so-called total state," Italy, pp. 234–5.

41 For the events of July 1943, see F. W. Deakin, *The Brutal Friendship. Mussolini, Hitler, and the Fall of Italian Fascism* (New York, rev. ed., 1966).

42 See Trevor-Roper, *Secret Conversations*, No. 132.

43 DDI,9,III,536.

44 Ryan (Durazzo) to Halifax, No. 46, 18.4.1939, PRO FO 371/23717, R 3219.

45 See Charles F. Delzell, "Pius XII, Italy and the Outbreak of War," *Journal of Contemporary History*, 2:4 (1967).

46 Such as Ernesto Rossi, *Padroni del vapore e fascismo* (Bari, 1966); but see the dispassionate demolition by Melograni, *Gli industriali e Mussolini*.

47 Ettore Conti, *Dal taccuino di un borghese* (Milan, 1946), pp. 544, 625.

48 See Pietro Grifone, *Il capitale finanziario in Italia* (Turin, 2nd ed., 1971), and Ernesto Cianca, *Nascita dello Stato imprenditore in Italia* (Milan, 1977).

49 Valerio Castronovo, *Giovanni Agnelli* (Turin, 1971), pp. 560–9.

50 Conti, *Dal taccuino di un borghese*, p. 655.

51 Roland Sarti, *Fascism and the Industrial Leadership in Italy*, (Berkeley, Los Angeles, 1971), p. 127, and Cardinal Eugenio Pacelli in DDF,2,VII,216.

52 Richard A. Webster, *Industrial Imperialism in Italy, 1908–1915* (Berkeley, Los Angeles, 1975); see, however, R. J. B. Bosworth, *Italy, the Least of the Great Powers* (London and New York, 1979). In the words of Giampiero Carocci, in Italy "the only great force whole-heartedly interested in imperialism was the state" (*La politica estera dell'Italia fascista (1925–1928)* [Bari, 1969], p. 13).

53 Conti, *Dal taccuino di un borghese*, p. 549.

54 Wolfgang Schieder, "Der Strukturwandel der faschistischen Partei Italiens in der Phase der Herrschaftsstabilisierung," p. 90, in Schieder, ed., *Faschismus als soziale Bewegung. Deutschland und Italien im Vergleich* (Hamburg, 1976); also Aquarone, *L'organizzazione*, pp. 175–88; Antonio Gambino, *Storia del PNF* (Milan, 1962), chs. 5, 6; Adrian Lyttelton, *The Seizure of Power. Fascism in Italy 1919–1929* (New York, 1973), pp. 299–307.

55 See De Felice, *Mussolini*, III, pp. 359–61, who suggests unconvincingly that this strategy was an alternative to, rather than a concomitant of, imperial expansion.

56 Mussolini, "Viatico al Duca d'Aosta, Viceré d'Etiopia," 18.11.1937, ACS, SPD/CR, Carte della cassetta di zinco, autografi vari, box 8, folder XV; Ciano, 8.1.1938; and *OO*, XXIX, p. 190.

57 Ciano, 13.11.1937.

58 For Spain, John F. Coverdale, *Italian Intervention in the Spanish Civil War* (Princeton, N.J., 1975), pp. 266–71; for the racial campaign, De Felice, *Storia degli ebrei italiani*, pp. 371–92; on war, Aquarone, "Public Opinion in Italy Before the Outbreak of World War II," pp. 209–20 in Roland Sarti, ed., *The Ax Within. Italian Fascism in Action* (New York, 1974).

59 Pieri, "La stratégie italienne sur l'échiquier Méditerranéen," p. 62, in *La guerre en Méditerranée 1939–1945* (Paris 1971).

60 "Mussolini e le forze armate," *Il Movimento di Liberazione in Italia*, No. 95 (1969), p. 12.

61 "L'esercito e il fascismo," in Guido Quazza, ed., *Fascismo e società italiana* (Milan, 1973), p. 119.

62 *Ibid.*, pp. 111–112; Rochat, *Militari e politici*, pp. 225–31; full text, Francesco Rossi, *Mussolini e lo stato maggiore* (Rome, 1951), pp. 24–5.

63 Rochat, "L'esercito e il fascismo," pp. 112–13.

64 Rochat, *L'esercito italiano da Vittorio Veneto a Mussolini* (Bari, 1967), pp. 571–5, 593–4; *idem*, "L'esercito e il fascismo," pp. 105–7; see the excellent *Breve storia dell'esercito italiano dal 1861 al 1943* (Milan 1978) by Rochat and Giulio Massobrio for the most recent restatement of Rochat's overall view.

65 ADAP,C,IV,485; Pompeo Aloisi, *Journal* (*25 juillet 1932–14 juin 1936*) (Paris, 1957), pp. 346, 348–9, 362, 369, 372, 374.

66 For the cruiser raid, Emilia Chiavarelli, *L'opera della marina italiana nella guerra italo-etiopica* (Milan, 1969), pp. 93–4; for the blockships and secret weapons, AUSMM, bundle "Mezzi d'assalto. Documentazione varia 1935–40"; also USMM, *I mezzi d'assalto* (Rome, 1972), ch. 1.

67 Aloisi, *Journal*, p. 249. Two recent Italian studies (Chiavarelli, *L'opera della marina*, and Rosaria Quartararo, "La crisi mediterranea del 1935–36," *Storia Contemporanea* 6:4 [1975]) have overemphasized British unpreparedness and argued or implied that Italian victory was likely. Such conclusions rest on assumptions about the effectiveness of Italian aircraft, submarines, and naval leadership that proved false in 1940. For a more balanced view, see Arthur Marder, "The Royal Navy and the Ethiopian Crisis of 1935–36" *American Historical Review* 75:5 (1970).

68 See Appendix 2, Table A2.2.

69 See Pariani circular, 80350, 6.12.1938, NARS T-821/107/000076–81.

70 For the 1866 disasters, Mack Smith, "The King and the War of 1866," in his *Cavour, Victor Emmanuel and the Risorgimento* (London, 1971); for Adua, Roberto Battaglia, *La prima guerra d'Africa* (Turin, 1958); for Caporetto, Alberto Monticone, *La battaglia di Caporetto* (Rome, 1955).

71 Olindo Malagodi, *Conversazioni della guerra 1914–1919* (Milan, Naples, 1960), I, p. 200.

72 Piero Pieri, in Giorgio Bocca, *Storia d'Italia nella guerra fascista* (Bari, 1969), p. 105; Rochat, *L'esercito italiano*, p. 3.

73 On Badoglio, Piero Pieri, Giorgio Rochat, *Pietro Badoglio* (Turin, 1974); and Giovanni De Luna, *Badoglio. Un militare al potere* (Milan, 1974).

74 For Badoglio's powers, Lucio Ceva, *La condotta italiana della guerra. Cavallero e il Comando Supremo 1941/1942* (Milan, 1975), pp. 129–34.

75 See Rochat, *Badoglio*, chs. 12–16; Rochat, *Militari e politici;* DDI,7,X,174.

76 The details are obscure, but see Armellini, *Diario*, p. 8; Navy memorandum, n.d. (but February 1937) in ACS, MMG, 1940, bundle 213; and Brian R. Sullivan, "A Thirst for Glory: Mussolini, the Italian Military, and the Fascist Regime, 1922–1940" (dissertation, Columbia University, 1981), ch. 7.

77 For this conception, see Leslie Hore-Belisha, *The Private Papers of Hore-Belisha,* R. J. Minney, ed. (London, 1960), p. 115; Mussolini's "Relazione per il Gran Consiglio," NARS T-586/405/000045-46; DDI,8,XII,59; Mussolini's remarks to the February 1940 Supreme Defense Commission (Chapter 2.2); DDI,9,III,669.

78 See Appendix 2, Table A2.1.

79 Emilio Faldella, *L'Italia e la seconda guerra mondiale* (Bologna, 1960), p. 87.

80 Navy Staff memorandum D.G. 10/A2, December 1938, apparently quoting Army terms of reference (Mariano Gabriele, *Operazione C 3: Malta* [Rome, 1965], p. 297) (emphasis in original).

81 Ciano, 14.2.1938; see also Ceva, "Appunti per una storia dello Stato Maggiore

generale fino alla vigilia della 'non-belligeranza,' " *Storia Contemporanea* 10:2 (1979), pp. 237–9.

82 See Pariani's remarks in Rintelen to OKH, Nr. 146/38 g. K., 13.5.1938, NARS T-78/365/6326837–42.

83 Cavagnari to Badoglio, 18.11.1937, AUSMM, bundle 2688; Badoglio to Valle, Cavagnari, Pariani, 30.11.1938, ACS, MAG, 1938, bundle 72, folder 11 III 5.

84 Gabriele, *Operazione C 3*, pp. 295–300; USMM, *L'organizzazione della marina durante il conflitto*, 1, (Rome, 1972), pp. 316–20.

85 Mussolini to Sirianni, 15.8.1927, ACS,SPD/CR, Carte della cassetta di zinco, autografi vari, box 4, folder V,C.

86 Sirianni to Mussolini, 26.9.1932, AUSMM, bundle 2611, folder 4.

87 USMM, *L'organizzazione*, graph between pp. 272 and 273.

88 *Ibid.*, p. 79; Fortunato Minniti, "Il problema degli armamenti nella preparazione militare italiana dal 1935 al 1943," *Storia Contemporanea*, 9:11 (1978), pp. 42–3.

89 Cavagnari to Mussolini, 24.10.1935, AUSMM, bundle 2684, folder "Sanzioni."

90 Unsigned, undated memorandum, probably by Cavagnari, with Mussolini's V (*visto*, "seen") in ACS, MMG, bundle 195. Internal evidence places the document in late 1935; an unsigned memorandum (25 June 1936) in the same file mentions a program submitted to Mussolini the previous December.

91 Ufficio Piani memorandum, 13.1.1936, p. 23, ACS, *ibid.*

92 See Cavagnari's correspondence on raw material allocation from this period with the head of the General Commissariat for War Production, General Dallolio: AUSMM, bundle 2684, folder "Sanzioni."

93 Unsigned memorandum, July 1936, ACS, MMG, bundle 195.

94 Unsigned memorandum, 27.1.1937, ACS, MMG, bundle 221.

95 Unsigned memorandum, 26.8.1937, *ibid.*; minutes of meetings between Mussolini, Cavagnari, and the finance minister, 3.12.1937, ACS, MMG, bundle 701; Ciano, 4.12.1937.

96 Rintelen to Reichswehrministerium, 17.6.1937, NARS T-78/364/6325967.

97 Cavagnari to Badoglio, 18.11.1937, AUSMM, bundle 2688.

98 See USMM, *L'organizzazione*, pp. 72, 81–2.

99 Löwisch to OKM, No. G.1564, 16.8.1939, GNR PG 33745.

100 See particularly the war diary of the German Naval Liaison Staff in Rome, 30.8.1940, GNR PG 45948.

101 Cavagnari memorandum for Mussolini, April 1940, USMM, *L'organizzazione*, pp. 351–2. For a cautious defense of Cavagnari, Gerhard Schreiber, *Revisionismus und Weltmachtstreben* (Stuttgart, 1978), pp. 266–71.

102 Weichold to OKM, 1.9.1940, GNR PG 45951.

103 Report of Generalleutnant Ludwig, 13.11.1928, in Petersen, *Hitler-Mussolini* (Tübingen, 1973), pp. 22–23.

104 Figures: Minniti, "Il problema degli armamenti," pp. 28-35; M. M. Postan, *British War Production* (London, 1952), p. 15.

105 Giuseppe Santoro, *L'aeronautica italiana nella seconda guerra mondiale* (Rome, 1957), 1, p. 14.

106 See the laments of Valle's successor, General Francesco Pricolo, to the Air Force

commander in North Africa (Pricolo to Porro, 17.7 and 21.7.1940, ACS, MAG, bundle "A.S. – 1940. Ispezione Gen. Pricolo – Relazioni," folder "Corr. con il Generale Porro").

107 William Green, *Famous Bombers of the Second World War* (Garden City, N.Y., 1959), p. 17; Francesco Pricolo, *La Regia Aeronautica nella seconda guerra mondiale* (Milan, 1971), p. 104.

108 F. Filippi, "Appunti per una storia del motore aeronautico in Italia," *Atti e rassegna della società degli ingegneri e degli architetti di Torino* (October 1965), pp. 326–8.

109 Nr. 293/39 g.Kdos., "Werturteil über die ital. Fliegertruppe u. Flakartillerie," GNR PG 32937.

110 Porro to Pricolo, 19.6.1940, 28.7.1940, 3.10.1940; Pricolo to Porro, 1.8.1940; ACS, MAG, bundle "A.S. – 1940. Ispezione Gen. Pricolo – Relazioni," folder "Corr. con il Generale Porro."

111 Douhet, *Il dominio dell'aria* (preface by Balbo) (Milan, 1932); also Claudio G. Segrè, "Douhet in Italy: Prophet Without Honor?," *Aerospace Historian* (June 1979). The RAF developed delusions analogous to Douhet's: see Williamson Murray, "British and German Air Doctrine Between the Wars," *Air University Review* (March–April 1980).

112 Valle to Badoglio, 12.1.1935, in Rochat, *Militari e politici*, pp. 379–81.

113 Pricolo, *La Regia Aeronautica*, pp. 140–2; Santoro, *L'aeronautica italiana*, I, p. 21. For Mecozzi, see his "I quattro compiti delle ali armate," *Rivista Aeronautica*, 13:9,10,11 (1937).

114 Pricolo to Mussolini, 16.4.1941, SPD/CR, 278/R, Valle, Gen. Giuseppe, folder 2.

115 Ceva, "Un intervento di Badoglio e il mancato rinnovo delle artiglierie italiane," *Il Risorgimento*, 28:2 (1976), pp. 125–6; Minniti, "Il problema degli armamenti," pp. 11–12.

116 Quoted in Canevari, *Retroscena della disfatta*, p. 253.

117 Ceva, "Un intervento di Badoglio," pp. 118–24, 127–8; Minniti, "Il problema degli armamenti," pp. 15–20; *idem*, "Due anni di attività del 'Fabbriguerra' per la produzione bellica (1939–1941)," *Storia Contemporanea*, 6:4 (1975), pp. 851–2, 858–61.

118 Badoglio to Mussolini, October 1926, p. 12, ACS, Badoglio, box 2, folder 4/4.

119 Ministero della Guerra, *Norme per l'impiego delle grandi unità* (n.p., 1928), p. 3.

120 See Rintelen to Reichswehrministerium, 11.6.1937, NARS T-78/364/6325963–66.

121 Minniti, "Il problema degli armamenti," pp. 20–2; USE, *L'esercito italiano tra la 1ª e la 2ª guerra mondiale* (Rome, 1954), p. 270.

122 Mario Caracciolo di Feroleto, *E poi? La tragedia dell'esercito italiano* (Rome, 1946), pp. 63–4. On the earlier lack of urgency in tank development and motorization in general, see Castronovo, *Agnelli*, pp. 582–5.

123 Roatta to Graziani, 22.10.1940, ACS Graziani, bundle 42; Comando Supremo internal memorandum, 21.7.1940, NARS T-821/130/000898.

124 Luigi Federzoni, *L'Italia di ieri per la storia di domani* (Milan, 1967), p. 189.

125 According to Canevari, who claims authorship: *Retroscena della disfatta*, p. 234.

126 Rintelen to Reichswehrministerium, 12.3.1937, 18.6.1937, NARS T-

78/364/6326154–59, 6325963–66; Pariani to Farinacci, 22.6.1937, ACS, ACS, SPD/CR, bundle 41.

27 For the "Po" Army's teething troubles, see (in chronological order), NARS T-821/374/000924, 000183–84, 000908–12, 000873–76, 000880, 000899–902, 000957–58.

28 Also to occupy Carinthia in case of war with Germany – but planning for that contingency did not continue: War Ministry memorandum, 9172, 30.12.1938, NARS T-821/107/000179–80.

29 Ciano, 24.8.1939; Enno von Rintelen, *Mussolini als Bundesgenosse* (Tübingen, 1951), p. 66.

30 Rintelen to OKH, 20/38 geh., 14.7.1938, NARS T-78/365/6326712–14; ADAP,D,VI, Appendix I,V; Rintelen to OKH, 50/39 g. Kdos., 3.3.1939, GNR PG 45170.

31 USE, *L'esercito italiano*, p. 124 n. 1.

32 Minutes, USE, *L'esercito italiano*, pp. 240–59; for Mussolini's opposition, Lessona, *Memorie*, pp. 325–7, and *idem, Un ministro di Mussolini racconta*, pp. 171–2.

33 Rintelen to Reichswehrministerium, 26.2.1937, NARS T-78/364/6326213; Coverdale, *Spanish Civil War*, pp. 219, 258.

134 See Coverdale, *Spanish Civil War*, pp. 181–6.

135 During training season, from May through August (February through June in Libya), the Army rose to 320,000 men (Pariani memorandum for Mussolini, 14.1.1939, pp. 50–8 in Ceva, "Un intervento di Badoglio").

136 Pariani circular, 80350, 6.12.1938, NARS T-821/107/000076–81; Caracciolo, *E poi?*, p. 43; Faldella, *L'Italia*, p. 114.

137 See Ciano, 8.4.1939, Bottai, *Vent' anni*, p. 126, and Pariani's after-action circular to his commanders, 28430, 9.4.1939, NARS T-821/107/000073.

138 Faldella, *L'Italia*, p. 115; Cavallero, *Comando Supremo*, pp. 332–3.

139 Victor Emmanuel III to Mussolini, 11.6.1937, ACS, SPD/CR, bundle 68, folder "Guadalajara," 3.

140 On 10 June 1940 the Army had approximately 53,000 officers under arms, but only 40,000 NCOs and specialists (USE, *L'esercito italiano*, p. 331).

141 The economic policies of Fascist Italy are as yet imperfectly explored, but see Felice Guarneri, *Battaglie economiche tra le due grandi guerre*, 2 vols. (Milan, 1953); Carlo Favagrossa, *Perché perdemmo la guerra. Mussolini e la produzione bellica* (Milan, 1946); Shepard B. Clough, *The Economic History of Modern Italy* (New York 1964); the special issue of *Quaderni Storici*, 10:2/3 (1975); and nn. 48 and 51 above.

142 Santoro, *L'aeronautica italiana*, I, pp. 15, 39.

143 Ciano, 6.2.1938; also DDF,2,VII,165.

144 Regular budget military expenditure: 43,190,000,000; colonies, 7,815,000,000; "exceptional" expenditures (Ethiopia, Spain, Albania, additional military spending, etc.) 76,500,000,000 total: 127,500,000,000 lire on war and empire (Francesco A. Répaci, *La finanza pubblica italiana nel secolo 1861–1960* [Bologna, 1962], pp. 145, 168, 331, 354).

145 Favagrossa, *Perché perdemmo la guerra*, pp. 77–8.

146 For Army and Air Force fuel stocks, ADAP,D,VIII,236; for Italian internal estimates, USE, *L'esercito italiano*, and Air Force staff memorandum, 1.12.1939, NARS T-821/144/000683.

147 Figures: for Italy from Ministero delle Corporazioni, "Relazione alla Commissione Suprema di Difesa (Sessione febbraio 1940 – XVIII), Sviluppo dei piani autarchici," p. 16, ACS, MMG, bundle 88; for Germany and Great Britain, David S. Landes, *The Unbound Prometheus* (Cambridge, 1972), p. 459.

148 On the Supreme Defense Commission and the General Commissariat for War Production, Minniti, "Aspetti organizzativi del controllo sulla produzione bellica in Italia (1923–1943)," *Clio* (Oct.–Dec. 1977), pp. 305–40; on war industry, Favagrossa, *Perché perdemmo la guerra*, pp. 32–43; for the comparison with the USSR, Francesco Rossi, *La ricostruzione dell'esercito* (Rome, 1947), pp. 129–30.

149 Ferrari to Mussolini, 31.1.1928, Canevari, *Retroscena della disfatta*, pp. 419–26.

150 Bottai, *Vent'anni*, pp. 122, 127; Ciano, 29.4.1939.

151 Ceva, "Altre notizie sulle conversazioni militari italo-tedesche alla vigilia della seconda guerra mondiale," *Il Risorgimento*, 30:3 (1978), p. 177; Ciano, 29.4.1939. For Air Force internal figures (930 combat-ready line aircraft), table, 31.12.1938, ACS, MAG, 1939, bundle 31, folder 3 V 31; see also ch. 2, n. 59.

152 Ciano, 23.8, 26.8.1939, and De Bono on "the madness of attacking, proposed by that criminal [delinquente] Pariani" (De Bono diaries, notebook 43, 3.9.1939, ACS).

153 Ciano, 6.2.1938; 12.2.1940.

154 See Federico Chabod, *Storia della politica estera italiana dal 1870 al 1896* (Bari, paperback edition, 1971), pp. 179, 328. Chabod's defense of Mazzini (". . . the nation in Mazzini is always indissolubly linked with humanity . . . and liberty, which together constituted its two limits") is unconvincing. Nationalism is by its nature an assertion of the inferiority – and consequent expendability – of outsiders. The road from Mazzini to Graziani proved short.

155 For Mazzini, *OO*, XXIX, p. 316, and Bottai, *Vent'anni*, p. 158; for Crispi, *OO*, XXVIII, p. 231.

156 See Bosworth, *Italy, the Least of the Great Powers*; De Felice, *Mussolini*, I; Christopher Seton-Watson, *Italy from Liberalism to Fascism, 1870–1925* (London, 1967), pp. 413–50.

157 See Giorgio Rumi, *Alle origini della politica estera fascista (1919–1923)* (Bari, 1968).

158 See the list in Cassels, *Mussolini's Early Diplomacy*, p. 394, n. 12.

159 For Ethiopia: Petersen, "La politica estera fascista," pp. 50–1; Turkey: DDI,7,III,604; Corfù, Germans, Magyars, Croats: Cassels, *Mussolini's Early Diplomacy*, chs. 4, 6, and Carocci, *La politica estera dell'Italia fascista*, chs. 7, 17; Yugoslavia and Alexander's murder: Faldella, *L'Italia*, p. 16, and Esmonde M. Robertson, *Mussolini as Empire Builder. Europe and Africa 1932–36* (New York, 1977), pp. 23–8, 85 (but on Alexander see also De Felice, *Mussolini*, IV, pp. 514–17); Albania: G. Zamboni, *Mussolinis Expansionspolitik auf dem Balkan* (Hamburg, 1970) and Bottai, *Vent'anni*, p. 107.

160 De Felice, *Mussolini*, IV, pp. 393, 519–33.

161 Petersen, "La politica estera fascista," pp. 50–5.

162 Roberto Cantalupo, *Fu la Spagna* (Verona, 1948), p. 42.

163 See Marder, "The Royal Navy and the Ethiopian Crisis," particularly p. 1339.

164 Grandi to Mussolini, 30.1.1934, ACS, Grandi, folder 8; Renzetti memorandum, 16.10.1934, ACS, MCP, bundle 165, folder 20.

165 Aloisi, *Journal,* p. 382; in July 1936 Mussolini approved the proposal of his minister of colonies, Lessona, for the raising of a 500,000 man black army (Mussolini to Lessona, 12.7.1936, ACS, MAG, 1938, bundle 93, folder 12/III/1/1). For more on the project, which the slow progress of "pacification" impeded, see ACS, Graziani, bundle 40A.

166 00, XXVIII, pp. 69–70; for Italo-German relations in this period, see Petersen's very thorough *Hitler-Mussolini.*

167 ADAP,D,I,2.

168 De Felice, "Alcune osservazioni sulla politica estera Mussoliniana," p. 65. De Felice's suggestion that Mussolini pursued Grandi's policy, though with diminishing room for maneuver, until early 1940 is not persuasive. Even less so is the attempt of Harry Cliadakis, "Neutrality and War in Italian Policy, 1939–1940," *Journal of Contemporary History* 9:3 (1974) to extend the date to October 1940.

169 Ciano, 6.11.1937.

170 R. Campbell (Belgrade) to Eden, No. 121, 8.11.1937, PRO FO 371/20436, R 6616.

171 Yugoslav minute, 25.3.1937, in Jacob B. Hoptner, *Yugoslavia in Crisis, 1934–1941* (New York, 1964), p. 83; Ciano, 5.12.1937.

172 Ciano, 25.8.1937, 28.4, 30.4, 10.5.1938; Ciano memorandum, 2.5.1938, in Ciano, *L'Europa verso la catastrofe* (Verona, 1948), pp. 305–16.

173 Ciano to Grandi, 16.2.1938, *L'Europa,* pp. 245–6; D'Amoja, *La politica estera dell'Impero,* p. 110.

174 For the April agreements, D. C. Watt, "Gli accordi mediterranei anglo-italiani del 16 Aprile 1938," *Rivista di Studi Politici Internazionali,* 26:1 (1959); for Spain, Coverdale, *Spanish Civil War,* pp. 345–71.

175 Badoglio to Cavagnari, 3698, 27.4.1938, ACS, MMG, bundle 68, folder 12, and Ciano, 21.4–24.4.1938; for more on the Brenner fortifications, see chapter 2, n. 78.

176 Axel Kuhn, *Hitlers aussenpolitisches Programm* (Stuttgart, 1970), pp. 72–3; for the 1938 dinner speech, Max Domarus, *Hitler: Reden und Proklamationen 1932–1945,* I (Munich, 1965), pp. 860–1.

177 Ciano, 5.5.1938.

178 Perth to Halifax, No. 785, 24.8.1938, PRO FO 371/22439, R 7253; also DDF,2,VIII,194, 217, 260, 261, 315, 323, 332, 339, 369.

179 00, XXIX, pp. 100, 101.

180 See Gerhard L. Weinberg, *The Foreign Policy of Hitler's Germany. Starting World War II, 1937–1939* (Chicago, 1980), p. 340; Ernst von Weizsäcker, *Die Weizsäcker-Papiere 1933–1945,* ed. Leonidas E. Hill (Frankfurt a. M., 1974), p. 128.

181 See the remark of Kánya, the Hungarian foreign minister, in *Weizsäcker-Papiere,* p. 137, and Mussolini to Victor Emmanuel III, 3.9.1938, ACS, SPD/CR, Carte della cassetta di zinco, autografi vari, box 5.

182 Ciano, 25–27.9.1938; Pariani, Valle, Cavagnari to first aide-de-camp (of the King), 27.9, 30.9.1938; Navy operations order, 29.9.1938; Cavagnari to first aide-de-camp, 16.10.1938, all in ACS, PAC, Sezione Speciale, bundle 64,

folder "Misure precauzionali FF.AA." The Navy archive refused me access to its Munich crisis files.

183 Ciano, 28.9.1938; DBFP,3,II,1186, 1231, III,345.

184 Schacht's testimony at Nürnberg, in Christopher Thorne, *The Approach of War 1938–39* (London, 1967), p. 84; Filippo Anfuso, *Dal Palazzo Venezia al Lago di Garda* (Bologna, 1957), pp. 84–6.

185 Ciano, 14.10.1938.

186 For this episode, see Ciano, 18–20.11.1938; ADAP,D,IV,128, 129.

187 Ciano, 5, 7, 8, 14.11.1938; Ciano to Grandi, 14.11.1938, *L'Europa,* pp. 383–5; Raffaele Guariglia, *Ricordi 1922–1945* (Naples, 1949), pp. 353–66.

188 Ciano, 30.11.1938; see also De Bono diaries, 2.12.1938, notebook 43, ACS.

189 Ciano, 2.2.1939.

190 Mussolini, "Relazione per il Gran Consiglio," undated but 4.2.1939, NARS T-586/405/000039–46; undated minute by General Vittorio Ambrosio (accompanying correspondence establishes he saw Mussolini on 27 January) NARS T-821/145/000211–12; minutes of service chiefs' meeting, in Ceva, "Appunti per una storia dello Stato Maggiore generale," p. 242.

191 Ciano, 19.2.1939; ADAP,D,VI,52; Jerzy W. Borejsza, "L'Italia e la guerra tedesco-polacca del 1939," *Storia Contemporanea* 9:4 (1978), p. 616.

192 ADAP,D,VI, Appendix, III,V; Italian record in Toscano, "Le conversazioni militari italo-tedesche alla vigilia della seconda guerra mondiale," *Rivista Storica Italiana,* 64:3 (1950).

193 All from Mussolini, "Relazione per il Gran Consiglio," NARS T-586/405/000039–46. For earlier Mussolini remarks about the geopolitical parameters of independence, see Canevari, *La guerra italiana* (Rome, 1948–9), I, p. 211 (1926–7), and Romeo Bernotti, *Cinquant'anni nella Marina militare* (Milan, 1971), p. 232 (1935).

194 See Ciano, 15.3–8.4.1939, passim; ADAP,D,VI, particularly 15, 37, 45, 55; and unsigned note for Ciano in Mussolini's hand (mentioned in Ciano, 16.3.1939) NARS T-586/25/0043–44.

195 Mussolini, in Bottai, *Vent'anni,* pp. 126–7.

196 Grandi to Mussolini, 7.4.1939, NARS T-586/449/026903–07.

197 See ADAP,D,VI,256, 303; *Allianz Hitler-Horthy-Mussolini* (Budapest, 1966), 55, 57; Ciano 12.5.1939; also Bottai, *Vent'anni,* pp. 126–7.

198 Ciano, 6–7.5, 13.5.1939. For the negotiations, Toscano, *The Origins of the Pact of Steel* (Baltimore, 1967); on Mussolini's irritation over foreign slurs on the loyalty of the Milanese, see, in corroboration of Toscano, Mackensen to AA, No. 191, 12.5.1939, PA, Büro des Staatssekretärs, Italien, Bd. 1.

199 For Mussolini's thinking, see his memorandum for Hitler of 30.5.1939 (DDI,8,XII,59) which General Cavallero delivered in early June.

200 ADAP,D,VI,433.

201 Ciano, 26.5.1939.

202 Ciano, and ADAP,D,VII,43, 47.

203 Ciano, 15.8, 18.8.1939; Badoglio to Pariani, Cavagnari, Valle, 4625, 16.8.1939, in Faldella, *L'Italia,* pp. 132–3; see also the "Po" Army plans for a descent on Croatia, April–July 1939, NARS T-821/108/000695ff., and, for the outcome, DDI,9,XIII,162, 186, and Badoglio to Mussolini, 31.8.1939, Faldella, *L'Italia,* p. 134.

204 Ciano, 22.8.1939.

205 Ciano, 24.8.1939; DDI,8,XIII, pp. 400–1; also Mario Luciolli (pseud. Donosti), *Mussolini e l'Europa. La politica estera fascista* (Rome, 1945), pp. 212–13, and Aquarone, "Public Opinion in Italy."

206 Ciano, 25.8–1.9.1939; DDI,8,XIII,250, 293, 298; for a detailed account, Ferdinand Siebert, *Italiens Weg in den Zweiten Weltkrieg* (Frankfurt a. M., 1962).

207 Ciano, 4.9.1939; Badoglio to Mussolini, 31.8.1939, in Faldella, *L'Italia,* p. 134.

CHAPTER 2
BELLICOSE NONBELLIGERENT

1 DDI,9,XIII,529, 563, and Appendix I, p. 409; for the speeches, Giuseppe Gorla, *L'Italia nella seconda guerra mondiale* (Milan, 1959), p. 8.

2 Bottai, *Vent'anni,* pp. 135–6; Guarneri, *Battaglie economiche,* II, p. 499; Ciano, 1.9.1939.

3 For the expression, Alexander Cadogan, *The Diaries of Sir Alexander Cadogan 1938–1945* (London, 1971), p. 171.

4 COS 939 (Revise), July 1939, PRO CAB 53/51; CID 368th Meeting, 24.7.1939, pp. 4–5 (emphasis in original), PRO CAB 2/9; Williamson Murray, "The Role of Italy in British Strategy 1938–1939," *RUSI Journal,* 124:3 (1979), pp. 43–9.

5 For fuel stocks, p. 47 above; for London's information, Industrial Intelligence Center, ICF/464, 16.1.1939, PRO FO 371/23842; Ministry of Economic Warfare, I.646/2, 8.5.1940, PRO CAB 21/980; and the wistful FO memorandum, 28.7.1940, PRO FO 371/24952, R 7456.

6 But see the defense of Chamberlain's Italian policy in D. C. Watt, "Britain, France, and the Italian Problem," *Les relations franco-britanniques de 1935 à 1939* (Paris, 1975), particularly pp. 293–4.

7 C-in-C Mediterranean to Admiralty, 88, 15.5.1939, PRO ADM 1/9946.

8 Meeting of the War Cabinet, PRO CAB 65.

9 Brantes note, 2.8.1939, PRO CAB 53/53.

10 François Bédarida, *La stratégie secrète de la drôle de guerre* (Paris, 1979), pp. 81–2; DDI,9,I,77, 212.

11 Paul Otto Schmitt, *Statist auf diplomatischer Bühne* (Bonn, 1949), p. 453.

12 Halder, I, pp. 86, 90; ADAP,D,VIII,384; also 224.

13 Michael Salewski, *Die deutsche Seekriegsleitung 1933–1945,* I (Frankfurt a. M., 1970), pp. 128, 152–5, 224–34; Schreiber, *Weltmachtstreben,* particularly p. 204; Halder, I, p. 3; DDI,9,I,170, 308; *Weizsäcker-Papiere,* p. 186.

14 Bottai, *Vent'anni,* p. 137; ADSS,I,191; Ciano, 6.9.1939.

15 On Ciano, see above all Giordano Bruno Guerri's exhaustive and entertaining *Galeazzo Ciano. Una vita 1903–1944* (Milan, 1978).

16 *The Ciano Diaries, 1939–1943* (Garden City, N.Y., 1946), p. xxxi.

17 See the biased but fascinating Dienststelle Ribbentrop informant report on the Ciano family and Italian internal politics, GFM 803/274869–913.

18 See Felix Gilbert, "Ciano and His Ambassadors," Gordon A. Craig and Felix Gilbert, eds., *The Diplomats, 1919–1939* (Princeton, 1953).

19 On the position of Balbo, Grandi, and the other "moderates," see Farinacci to Mussolini, 5.2.1940, NARS T-586/462/033930–32, and Ciano, 28.11,

8.12.1939, 19.1, 14.2, 23.3.1940; for the ambiguity of the "party of business," Castronovo, *Agnelli,* pp. 578–92, Guariglia, *Ricordi,* pp. 442–3, and Enzo Santarelli, *Storia del fascismo* (Rome, 1973), III, pp. 186–91. For Balbo, Loraine to Halifax, 20.1.1940, PRO FO 371/24949, R 1507; Caracciolo, *E poi?,* pp. 42, 51–5; USE, *In Africa Settentrionale. La preparazione al conflitto. L'avanzata su Sidi el Barrani* (Rome, 1955), pp. 47–50, and Aquarone, "Nello Quilici e il suo 'diario di guerra,' " *Storia Contemporanea,* 6:2 (1975), pp. 332–4.

20 See the remarkable memorandum of the anti-Fascist exile Max Salvadori on conversations with Bastianini in London, 30.1.1940, PRO FO 371/24938, R 1497.

21 Farinacci to Mussolini, 13.9.1939, NARS T-586/117/031590–602.

22 Ciano, 15.9, 7.11.1939, 19.1.1940, Bottai, *Vent'anni,* p. 152; ADAP,D,VII, 507; Mackensen to AA, No. 596, 29.9.1939, GFM 583/242211; Phillips to Hull, No. 27, 15.1.1940, NARS, State, 740.0011 European War 1939/1481.

23 Ciano, 5.9.1939.

24 Loraine to Halifax, 13.9.1939, PRO FO 371/23820, R 7951; Loraine to Halifax, No. 1026, 10.10.1939, PRO FO 371/23821, R 8868; Loraine to Halifax, 4.12.1939, PRO FO 800/319.

25 Ciano, 5.9, 15.9.1939.

26 Siebert, *Italiens Weg in den Zweiten Weltkrieg,* pp. 349–50, 382–3; Ciano, 4.9, 5.9.1939; DDI,8,XIII,590; DDI,9,I,45, 161, 196, 198, 217, 218, 243, 504; ADAP,D,VII,553; ADAP,D,VIII,16.

27 Ciano, 9.9.1939.

28 Ciano, 8.9.1939; Ministry of Popular Culture minute of telephone conversation with Goebbels, 9.9.1929, ACS, MCP, bundle 160, folder 14; ADAP,D,VIII,38.

29 Press instruction, 19.9.1939, and "Rapporto del Ministro Alfieri," 20.9.1939, ACS, Agenzia Stefani/Manlio Morgagni, bundle 5; Ciano, 19.9.1939.

30 *OO,* XXIX, pp. 311–13. In the original typescript (ACS, SPD/CR, Carte della cassetta di zinco, autografi vari, box 9, folder XVII, A) the sentence quoted begins "When I. . . ," with the "and if" added in Mussolini's hand, probably after the speech and at Ciano's suggestion (see Ciano, 23.9.1939).

31 Bottai, *Vent'anni,* p. 145; Ciano, 4, 6, 10, 11, 13.10.1939; ADAP,D,VIII,205; Alfieri to prefects, 6.10.1939, ACS, MCP, bundle 1, folder 2.

32 Ciano, 26.9, 27.9, 30.9.1939; "Rapporto dei direttori dei giornali presso S.E. il Ministro Dino Alfieri," 29.9.1939, ACS, Agenzia Stefani/Manlio Morgagni, bundle 5; Bottai, *Vent'anni,* p. 144.

33 *OO,* XXIX, pp. 315–17.

34 ADAP,D,VIII,176, pp. 148–9; DDI,9,I,552, p. 336; Ciano, 3.10.1939.

35 Ciano, 15.9, 24.9.1939; Bottai, *Vent'anni,* p. 142; DDI,9,I,394; some possible antecedents in DDI,9,I,58, 76, 89, 138, 170, 186. See also Frank Marzari, "Projects for an Italian-led Balkan Bloc of Neutrals, September-December 1939," *Historical Journal,* 13:4 (1970).

36 ADAP,D,VIII,128, 145; Ciano, 29.9.1939; DDI,9,I,505, 523.

37 DDI,9,I,446, 535, 542; see also the extraordinary German informant report, 16.11.1939, GFM 1571/380217–18, which quotes Italian telegrams (DDI,9,II,189, 197); ADAP,D,VIII,176, pp. 148–9.

38 DDI,9,I,583, 650, 836; on the Rumanian role, Marzari, "Balkan Bloc."
39 ADAP,D,VIII,266 (see also 231). For British and French interest, see meetings of the War Cabinet, 14.9, 6, 10, 19, 26, 28.10, 1.11, 3.11.1939, PRO CAB 65; Halifax to Loraine, No. 117 Saving, 20.11.1939; Loraine to Halifax, No. 1078, 26.11.1939, PRO FO 371/23755, R 9084, R 9380; DDI,9,I,714; DDI,9,II,282. Contrary to the assumption common in the literature (most recently Alfredo Breccia, *Jugoslavia 1939–1941. Diplomazia della neutralità* [Milan, 1978], pp. 208ff.), the British government did not take an early lead in urging on the small powers a bloc under Italian patronage. For more detail, see Knox, "1940, Italy's 'Parallel War,' Part I. From Non-Belligerence to the Collapse of France" (diss., Yale University, 1976), pp. 103–16.
40 Marzari, "Balkan Bloc," p. 774.
41 DDI,9,I,60, 65, 96, 166; GWB,45, 47; Emanuele Grazzi, *Il principio della fine* (Rome, 1945), pp. 65–8; Ciano, 12.9.1939; ADAP,D,VIII,96.
42 ADAP,D,VIII,96; Mackensen to AA, No. 556, 23.9.1939, GFM 1848/421079; see also Ciano, 19.9.1939, and Mackensen to AA, No. 433, 6.9.1939, GFM 583/242186.
43 Azienda Minerali Metallici Italiani, "Appunto per il Duce," "Miniere di nichelio di Lokris (Grecia)," 4.3.1939, ACS, PC, 1937–39, 3/1–10/707/2.
44 Grazzi, *Il principio della fine*, pp. 79–80.
45 See John Koliopoulos, *Greece and the British Connection, 1939–1941* (Oxford, 1977), pp. 115–20; Knox, "Italy's 'Parallel War,' " pp. 120–3.
46 Ciano, 12.10.1939.
47 Lane to Hull, Nos. 282, 287, 21.9, 22.9.1939, NARS, State, 740.0011 European War 1939/483, 521; Minutes of Pariani-Graziani-Ambrosio meeting, 29.9.1939, NARS T-821/107/000161-63.
48 Intelligence digests, 9.10, 15.10, 29.10.1940, ACS, MMG, bundle 73, folder 9; Campbell to Cadogan, 1.1.1940; French Embassy (London) memorandum, 4.1.1940; Rapp to Halifax, No. 14, 17.1.1940, PRO FO 371/24884, R 323, R405; Campbell to Halifax, No. 48, 10.2.1940, *ibid.*/25036, R 2139; minute by Shone, 26.2.1940, *ibid.*/24886, R 2881; ADAP,D,VIII,395. For full treatment of Ciano and the Croats in this period (but no evidence about the Communists) see Breccia, *Jugoslavia*, pp. 232–46.
49 See chapter 1, n.85; DDI,8,XII,59, point 4; Ciano, 8.1.1939.
50 *Allianz Hitler-Horthy-Mussolini,* 79.
51 Ironically, Bombelles was a double agent for the Yugoslavs (Ciano, 10.5.1940, and Wilhelm Höttl, *The Secret Front* [London, 1953], p. 132).
52 DDI,9,III,194.
53 DDI,9,III,58; Ciano, 22.1.1940; Bottai, *Vent'anni,* pp. 157–8; Graziani to Army Group E, 2nd, 6th, 8th Armies, 1800, 20.2.1940; Navy memorandum on operations against Yugoslavia, February 1940, NARS T-821/109/000361-62, 126/000995-1030; Breccia, *Jugoslavia*, pp. 145–6.
54 Löwisch to OKM, OKW, No. G.1659, 9.9.1939, GNR PG 45170, and USE, *La preparazione,* pp. 60–1.
55 Guarneri, *Battaglie economiche,* II, p. 434; Valle to Mussolini, 16.10.1939, ACS, MAG, 1939, bundle 9, folder 2 I 40; Favagrossa to Pariani, Cavagnari, Valle, 1849, 1923, 24.9, 26.10.1939, ACS, MAG, 1939, bundle 30, folder 3 V 18.
56 De Bono diaries, 3.9.1939, notebook 43, ACS; Bottai, *Vent'anni,* p. 140; DDI,9,I,249.

57 Ciano, 10.9.1939; De Bono diaries, September–October 1939, passim, notebook 43, ACS; Farinacci to Mussolini, 13.9.1939, NARS T-586/117/031590.

58 Ciano, 18.9.1939; USE, *L'esercito italiano*, pp. 137–8.

59 Ciano, 18.9.1939; ADAP,D,VII,432; Valle to Badoglio, 25.8.1939, NARS T-821/144/000530-31; Pricolo, *La Regia Aeronautica*, pp. 84, 125–31; Santoro, *L'aeronautica italiana*, I, pp. 31–6 ("modern" types: S.79, B.R. 20, Cant. Z.506 and 1007, C.R. 42, G.50, M.C.200). The Regia Aeronautica had a total of 5,344 aircraft on its property books on 31 October 1939, but Valle controlled the criteria measuring readiness – criteria still in the process of definition at the end of September 1939 (see correspondence in ACS, MAG, 1939, bundle 12, folder 2 I 94). On paper Valle could produce almost any number of "combat-ready" aircraft desired. A postwar military investigation unconvincingly cleared him (see Valle, *Uomini nei cieli* [Rome, n.d.], pp. 243ff).

60 Ciano, 24.9.1939; De Bono diaries, 11.9.1939, notebook 43, ACS.

61 *Ibid.*, 7.10.1939; memorandum forwarded with Farinacci to Mussolini, 14.10.1939, NARS T-586/117/031603-25 (memorandum alone in Ceva, "Un intervento di Badoglio," pp. 159–86); Ciano, 24.9, 19.10.1939; Bottai, *Vent'anni*, pp. 145–6.

62 Ciano, 19.10, 30.10.1939. Of the major figures, only Ciano, Bottai (National Education), Grandi (Justice), Teruzzi ("Italian Africa"), Thaon di Revel (Finance), and Cavagnari remained (*OO*, XXIX, pp. 527–8).

63 Federzoni, *L'Italia di ieri*, p. 191; Löwisch to OKM, No. G.2209, 3.11.1939, GNR PG 48836; Charles to Halifax, 6.11.1939, PRO FO 371/23798, R 9765; Giacomo Carboni, *Memorie segrete* (Florence, 1955), p. 61; Armellini, *Diario*, pp. 29, 82, 100; Ciano, 30.11.1939.

64 Ciano, 27.10.1939; for Valle's recommendation of Pricolo, Valle to Mussolini, 1.1.1938, NARS T-586/456/029989/A-90/A, and transcript of Valle-Pricolo telephone conversation, 30.10.1939, ACS, SPD/CR, 278/R, "Valle, Gen. Giuseppe," folder 1; ADAP,D,VIII,406.

65 DDI,9,II, Appendix VII.

66 Unsigned memorandum, "Argomenti per il rapporto," 14.11.1939, ACS, MCP, bundle 75.

67 *OO*, XXIX, p. 327; police reports, 16, 19, 21.11.1939, ACS, Ministero dell'Africa Italiana, bundle 2.

68 *OO*, XXIX, pp. 329–31.

69 Ciano, 25, 26.10.1939.

70 Toscano, *Origins of the Pact of Steel*, pp. 106, 187, 291 (n. 191), 311; Italian minute, 23.6.1939, in De Felice, *Il problema dell'Alto Adige* (Bologna, 1973), pp. 102–7; DDI,8,XII,334.

71 DDI,8,XII,281, 388; DDI,9,I,287, 486, 581; DDI,9,II,601–08; ADAP,D,VIII,231, 244, p. 214 n. 3; Bohle to Landesgruppe Italien, No. 519, 9.9.1939, GFM 2130/465580; Bocchini to Himmler (probably passed to Hitler), 18.9.1939; telephone transcript, Himmler to Dollmann, 25.9.1939, NARS T-175/53/2556947-48, 2556956.

72 ADAP,D,VIII,244; also DDI,9,I,798.

73 Ciano, 9.11, 11.11, 21.11.1939; De Felice, *Il problema dell'Alto Adige*, pp. 51–4; ADAP,D,VIII,386 n. 6; DDI,9,I,160.

74 Ciano, 20-21.11.1939; ADAP,D,VIII,382; DDI,9,II,270; for the Czech situ-

ation, see DDI,9,II,16, 17, 18, 24, 254, 264, 266, 284, and Vojtech Mastny, *The Czechs Under Nazi Rule* (New York, 1971), pp. 105–22.

75 "Wir haben Freunde die uns betrügen": DDI,9,II,240; Ciano, 26.11.1939, and Mackensen to AA, No. 862, 26.11.1939, GFM 1571/380225-26.

76 Unsigned note, 24.11.1939, ACS, SPD/CO, 1ᵃ Serie, bundle 259; *Il Messaggero* (Rome), 11.12.1939; Graziani to Monti, Bolzano and Treviso corps commanders, 14600, 15.12.1939, NARS T-821/41/000408-10; Army Staff memorandum, 20.10.1942, *ibid.*, 500/000675-78 (emphasis in original).

77 Bottai *Vent'anni*, p. 127; Pariani to XIV Army Corps (Treviso), 13092, 31.10.1939, NARS T-821/41/000404-05.

78 As Siebert, *Italiens Weg in den Zweiten Weltkrieg*, p. 391, seems to suggest. The fortification of the German frontier remained a priority task throughout the spring and much of the summer of 1940 despite Italy's intervention at Germany's side. On 11 May, long after Mussolini's decision in principle to enter the war that year, and two days before his decision to act before the end of the month, he confirmed that work in the north should go forward as planned, while at the same time suspending that opposite Yugoslavia (Soddu to Roatta, 120189, 24.5.1940, NARS T-821/19/000261). In early July, the Army Staff proposed and Badoglio and Mussolini approved the suspension of construction opposite France, and the continuing of that on the German border, "concentrating [on it] indeed, funds and materials" (Roatta to Soddu, 3805, 7.7.1940, *ibid.*/000866ff). On 10 July 1940 Mussolini directed Monti to complete all three lines of fortifications on the German border by the end of 1941, while discreetly avoiding "too much show" (Roatta to Graziani, 153, 14.7.1940, ACS, Graziani, bundle 42). A Soddu directive of 19 July therefore suspended floodlit night work, which had proceeded through the winter (Soddu to Roatta, 132226, 19.7.1940, NARS T-821/19/000259). Only at the end of July did the work slow drastically, and then only because, according to Soddu, "Hitler had apparently asked the Duce why they were still working on [the German] border"; no trace of any such embarrassing question appears in the diplomatic correspondence. Monti's organization dissolved in early August 1940, but even then work did not cease entirely, and the Army still planned completion within four years (Roatta to Graziani, 205, 27.8.1940, ACS, Graziani, bundle 42; Roatta, Soddu and Monti correspondence, NARS T-821/45/000198, 000203, 000224-30, and Cavallero, *Comando Supremo*, p. 307). See also Army Staff memorandum in n. 76 above: "reasons of political opportuneness" produced the drastic slowdown in August 1940.

79 See Ciano, 9.5, 27.1.1940.

80 Ciano, 28.11, 2.12, 3.12.1939; ADAP,D,VIII,410; Halder, I, p. 142.

81 Ciano, 7.12.1939; Bottai, *Vent'anni*, pp. 147–50; also DDI,8,XIII, appendixes I and II.

82 Bottai, *Vent'anni*, pp. 150–1; Giacomo Acerbo, *Fra due plotoni d'esecuzione* (Bologna, 1968), pp. 422–3; Graziani note, 13.12.1940, in Rossi, *Mussolini*, p. 153; USE, *L'esercito italiano*, pp. 142–3; Ciano, 9.12.1939.

83 Ciano, 16.12, 21.12.1939 (text, Ciano, pp. 701–23); Bottai, *Vent'anni*, p. 154.

84 Ciano, 23.12.1939; Mackensen to AA, 23.12.1939, No. 1071, GFM 1848/421111-13.

85 Ciano, 27.12.1939, 3.1, 5.1, 6.1.1940; Mackensen to AA, 24.12.1939, GFM

1571/380254–55; Mackensen minute, 26.12.1939, GFM 2281/480567–68; Weizsäcker to Ziemke, No. 11, 23.12.1939, GFM 1848/421110.

86 Ciano, 26.12.1939; also DDI,9,II,705, and Vicomte Jacques Davignon, *Berlin, 1936–1940* (Paris and Brussels, 1951), pp. 170–93.

87 Hans-Adolf Jacobsen, *Fall "Gelb"* (Wiesbaden, 1957), pp. 89–99; Telford Taylor, *The March of Conquest* (New York, 1958), pp. 60–3; Halder, I, p. 152; Ernst von Weizsäcker, *The Memoirs of Ernst von Weizsäcker* (London, 1951), p. 222; also ADAP,D,VIII,533, 557.

88 ADAP,D,VIII,211, and Toscano, *Designs in Diplomacy*, pp. 61–4; Bottai, *Vent'anni*, p. 140; Ciano, 16.10.1939.

89 DDI,9,I,761, 772, 792, 807; DDI,9,II,114; *Kommunistische Internationale*, November 1939, p. 1008; Ciano, 7.11.1939; Gayda, "Il falso e il vero," *Il Giornale d'Italia*, 8.11.1939.

90 ACS, DGPS/DAGR, Cat. C1, Conflitto Germano-Polacco, bundle 1; prefect telegrams in ACS, PC, 1937–39, 15/2/8691, "Conflitto Russia-Finlandia"; Weber to AA, Nr. 21, 5.12.1939, PA, Staatsekretär, Italien, Bd. 2.

91 ADAP,D,VIII,410; Ciano, 4.12, 9.12.1939; DDI,9,II,290, 450, 538.

92 Ciano, 28.12.1930; DDI,9,II,684, 741; Loraine to Halifax, No. 1293, 29.12.1939, PRO FO 371/23814, R 12223; ADAP,D,VIII,494; Toscano, *Designs in Diplomacy*, pp. 137–8; Siebert, *Italiens Weg in den Zweiten Weltkrieg*, pp. 383–4.

93 See Ciano, 18.12, 21.12, 27.12, 28.12.1939; Enrico Caviglia, *Diario* (Rome, 1952), p. 215; Osborne to Halifax, No. 244, 22.12.1939, PRO FO 371/23791, R 12126.

94 Osborne to Halifax, No. 25 Saving, 25.12.1939, PRO FO 371/23791, R 12217; Farinacci to Mussolini, 25.1.1940, NARS T-586/489/049071; Plessen to AA, No. 6, 2.1.1940, PA, Staatsekretär, Italien, Bd. 2.

95 ADAP,D,VIII,432, 435, 439, 440, 444, 519; DDI,9,II,570, 579, 582, 588, 602, 603, 633, 682, 727, III,105; GFM 119/119246, 1571/380244–47, 380259–61, 380283, 2131/466574–82, 2134/476447.

96 Ciano, 2.1.1940; Ciano to Pricolo, 32B/60011, 30.1.1940, and Pricolo, "Appunto per il Duce," 148, 7.2.1940, ACS, MAG, 1940, bundle 170, folder 9 V 34–35; Welles report, 26.2.1940, FRUS, 1940, I, pp. 25–6.

97 DDI,9,II,674; Ciano, 23.12.1939.

98 Meeting of the War Cabinet, 15.12.1939, PRO CAB 65; Bédarida, *Stratégie secrète*, pp. 202–13, 227, 230–1, 532–3; Cadogan, *Diaries*, p. 240.

99 Nichols minute, 26.12.1939, PRO FO 371/23758, R 12073.

100 FO Memorandum, 12.1.1940, PRO FO 371/24884, R 720.

101 English text of Stalin's reply to Ribbentrop's greetings on Stalin's sixtieth birthday, *The New York Times*, 25.12.1939, p. 12; for the Italian reaction, Ciano, 28.12.1939; DDI,9,II,717.

102 For the phrase (Ciano's) see FO memorandum, n. 100 above; Ciano, 26.12.1939; Ciano minute, 30.12.1939, *L'Europa*, p. 500; DDI,9,III,40,44.

103 DDI,9,11,705 (remark by Tippelskirch, Halder's G-2).

104 See Llewellyn Woodward, *British Foreign Policy in the Second World War*, I, (London, 1970), p. 30, and PRO FO 371/24949, R 1103; DDI,9,III,40.

105 This, and what follows, from DDI,9,III,33; see also the draft with Mussolini's corrections in ACS, SPD/CR, Carte della Valigia, box 1, folder 14. For the translation Hitler read, ADAP,D,VIII,504.

106 This information presumably came from Himmler, during his 20 December visit. Mussolini was fully aware of German treatment of the non-Jewish Polish population (Ciano, 4.12.1939; DDI,9,II, Appendix VIII); his "full approval" of Hitler's Jewish policy therefore has a certain macabre significance.

107 Ciano, 5.1.1940. Siebert, *Italiens Weg in den Zweiten Weltkrieg,* p. 395, makes the unintentionally humorous assertion that the letter was "a courageous and wise appeal, the formulations of which ring almost prophetically across the intervening years and disclose a Mussolini who in certain moments was the more realistic and far-seeing of the two dictators." For Siebert's earlier view of Hitler's place in history, see his editorial comments in *Deutschenspiegel. Ein Lesebuch,* introduction by Giuseppe Bottai (Florence, 1943), p. 555–6.

108 DDI,9,III,50; "Glaubt nicht an meinen Sieg!" (Halder, I, p. 154); Elizabeth Wiskemann, *The Rome-Berlin Axis* (London, 2nd rev. ed., 1966), pp. 225–6; Siebert, *Italiens Weg in den Zweiten Weltkrieg,* pp. 394–7, and De Felice, "Sulla politica estera mussoliniana," pp. 72–3, who reads the document as an example of Dino Grandi's "policy of the decisive weight."

109 See André, "La politica estera del governo fascista durante la seconda guerra mondiale," in De Felice, ed., *L'Italia fra tedeschi e alleati,* pp. 118–19.

110 Ciano, 9.1.1940; DDI,9,II,470; III,2,9,165; ADAP,D,VIII,535; for Mussolini on the United States ("land of negri and Jews"), Ciano, 6.9.1937; also William Phillips, *Ventures in Diplomacy* (Boston, 1950), p. 229.

111 DDI,9,III,40; for more Mussolini bellicosity, Ciano, 31.12.1940.

112 ADAP,D,VIII,518; DDI,9,III,78, 95, 126, 137, 141.

113 ADAP,D,VIII,527; Ciano, 10.1.1940.

114 Ciano, 5.9.1940; for detailed treatment of Italy's economic relations with the belligerents, Knox, "Italy's 'Parallel War,' " pp. 175–204.

115 See ADAP,D,IV,451.

116 Giovanni Host Venturi, Minister of Communications, in Mackensen to AA, No. 140, 18.1.1940, GFM 1571/380287.

117 See W. N. Medlicott, *The Economic Blockade,* I (London, 1952), pp. 1–138.

118 ADAP,D,VIII,33,394,464; Wiehl minute, 4.11.1939, GFM 2131/466270–73.

119 See table, GFM 1848/421093.

120 ADAP,D,VIII,277.

121 DDI,9,I,328; correspondence in ACS, MAG, 1940, bundle 152, folder 9 V 5/2–1; Guarneri, *Battaglie economiche,* II, pp. 430–40.

122 See particularly meetings of the War Cabinet, 19–21.11.1939, PRO CAB 65; Ciano, 24.11, 6.12.1939; ADAP,D,VIII,389, 398; DDI,9,II,368; and the numerous documents on the coal crisis in ADAP,D,VIII, DDI,9,II, and GFM 1848.

123 Halifax memorandum, W.P. (G.)(39)131, 4.12.1939, PRO FO 371/23806, R 11101; meeting of the War Cabinet, 6.12.1939, PRO CAB 65.

124 Halifax to Loraine, No. 712, 7.12.1939; Loraine to Halifax, No. 1087 ARFAR, 7.12.1939, PRO FO 371/23838, R 11075, R 9856; Loraine to Halifax, Nos. 1246, 1250, 17.12, 18.12.1939, PRO FO 371/23807, R 11827, R 11828.

125 Correspondence in ACS, MAG, 1939, bundle 75, folder 9 V 6/4.1; DDI,9,III,300.

126 ADAP,D,VIII,410; DDI,9,II,438, 699, 744, 763; Ciano, 3, 10, 20, 23,

28, 29.12.1939; Loraine to Halifax, Nos. 1267, 1268, 1276, 22.12, 24.12.1939, PRO FO 371/23828, R 11941, R 11970, R 11990; FO minute, 28.12.1939, *ibid.*, R 12214.

127 See Ciano, 14.1, 16.1.1940; ADAP,D,VIII,509, 542, 593; DDI,9,III, 130.

128 Medlicott, *Blockade*, I, pp. 297–9; Ciano, 14, 15, 18.1.1940; DDI,9,III,146; Mackensen to AA, No. 140, 18.1.1940, GFM 1571/380287.

129 Meeting of the War Cabinet, 29.1.1940, PRO CAB 65; see also departmental papers, W.P.(G.)(40)20, 21, 26, 27, PRO CAB 67/4. Chamberlain's remark does not bear out the judgment of Siebert and Martin (*Italiens Weg in den Zweiten Weltkrieg*, p. 405; *Friedensinitiativen*, pp. 130–1) that the British intended their proposal as "economic blackmail." The War Cabinet naïvely saw the scheme as an attempt to "appease" the Italians and avoid the friction the inevitable stoppage of German seaborne coal would otherwise entail. Nor do the available records justify Martin's hint that the British may have "consciously" intended to "drive Italy into Germany's arms." Chamberlain had already demonstrated that he lacked the resolution for that course.

130 See Loraine to Halifax, No. 41, 10.1.1940; PRO FO 371/24937, R 571; Loraine to Halifax, Secret, 22.1.1940, PRO FO 371/24949, R 1507; two Loraine letters of 22.1.1940, *ibid.;* Loraine to Halifax, No. 24 Saving, 30.1.1940, *ibid.*, R 1595; Loraine to Halifax, Nos. 86, 26 Saving, 27 Saving, 2.2.1940, *ibid.*, R 1743, R 1744; meetings of the War Cabinet, 31.1, 2.2, 7.2.1940, PRO CAB 65.

131 DDI,9,III,30. Sale of trainers to France continued, and deliveries ultimately amounted to 6 Ca 313s, 49 FN. 305s (a single-engined monoplane) and 100 Ca 164s (a single-engined biplane) (ACS, MAG, 1940, bundle 148, folder 9 III 1.1).

132 Ciano, 7.2, 8.2.1940; Halder, I, p. 193.

133 Ciano, 7.2, 8.2.1940; Medlicott, *Blockade*, I, pp. 300–1; Woodward, *British Foreign Policy*, I, pp. 147–8; meeting of the War Cabinet, 10.2.1940, PRO CAB 65.

134 Meeting of the War Cabinet, 10.2.1940, PRO CAB 65.

135 Meetings of the War Cabinet, 12, 14, 15, 16, 17.2.1940, PRO CAB 65.

136 Ciano, 18.2.1940; DDI,9,III,344, 359; meetings of the War Cabinet, 20, 22, 23.2.1940, PRO CAB 65.

137 All from Ciano, 16.2.1940.

138 See Ciano, 20.2–22.2.1940; DDI,9,III,131, 151, 159, Appendix II, 1; ADAP,D,VIII,581, 589, 592, 623, 627, 634.

139 For the quotations, Medlicott, *Blockade*, I, p. 301, n. 1; Bottai, *Vent'anni*, p. 159.

140 Favagrossa memorandum, 11.12.1939, in Favagrossa, *Perché perdemmo la guerra*, pp. 247ff; Ciano, 10.1, 11.1.1940.

141 See Ciano, 16.1.1940; speech draft, with Mussolini's corrections, ACS, SPD/CR, Carte della cassetta di zinco, box 9, folder XVIII, B; Osborne to Halifax, No. 3 Saving, 23.1.1940, PRO FO 371/24938, R 1409; and the "Segnalazioni" of the private intelligence service of Manlio Morgagni, head of the Stefani official news agency (ACS, Agenzia Stefani/Manlio Morgagni, bundle 9) under the date 24.1.1940 (henceforth "Segnalazioni," with date).

142 Ciano, 29.1, 1.2.1940.

143 All from Ciano, 20.1, 23.1.1940, Bottai, *Vent'anni,* pp. 156–8; see also Ciano, 28.1.1940.

144 Bottai, *Vent'anni,* p. 158.

145 For what follows, Commissione Suprema di Difesa, "Verbali della XVII Sessione (8–14 febbraio 1940 – XVIII)" (henceforth CSD XVII, with page number), NARS, T-586/461; for the departmental reports on the various agenda topics, ACS, MMG, bundle 88.

146 All from CSD XVII, pp. 48, 38, 40, 33, 25–6, 101, 49; German steel production was 22.5 million tons in 1939.

147 See his remarks to the Hungarian military attaché, DIMK,IV,531.

148 Mussolini, in CSD XVII, p. 24.

149 War Ministry and Air Force Ministry reports, "I combustibili liquidi nel quadro economico e militare," February 1940, ACS, MMG, bundle 88, and CSD XVII, pp. 58, 63, 64.

150 CSD XIII, p. 63. The figure seems excessive.

151 *Ibid.,* pp. 63–70.

152 Ciano, 11.2.1940.

153 CSD XVII, pp. 74–81; Ciano, 12.2.1940.

154 All from CSD XVII, pp. 128–35, p. 68; see also Ciano, 14.2.1940; Bottai, *Vent'anni,* p. 158.

155 Unsigned memorandum, "Rapporto ai giornalisti del 22 febbraio 1940 XVII ore 19," ACS, MCP, bundle 75; Ciano, 25.2.1940.

156 Fred L. Israel, ed., *The War Diary of Breckinridge Long* (Lincoln, Nebraska, 1966), p. 64.

157 Ciano, 26.2–29.2.1940; Welles report, FRUS, I, 1940, pp. 21–33; DDI,9,III,394, 395.

158 Phillips to Hull, No. 1781, 1.3.1940, NARS, State, 865.00/1886; DDI,9,III,437.

159 Ciano, 1.3.1940.

160 Ciano, 2.3, 3.3.1940; DDI,9,III,436; ADAP,D,VIII,652; meeting of the War Cabinet, 4.3.1940, PRO CAB 65.

161 Ciano, 4.3–9.3.1940; Bottai, *Vent'anni,* pp. 159–61; meetings of the War Cabinet, 6.3–9.3.1940, PRO CAB 65; DDI,9,III,459, 475, 476, 489, 505.

162 Ciano, 7.3.1940.

163 *Ibid.,* 8.1.1940; Mackensen to AA, No. 58, 12.1.1940, GFM 1848/421121.

164 Ribbentrop to Mackensen, No. 254, 7.3.1940, GFM 4459/EO86889.

165 For Hitler's motives, ADAP,D,VIII,663, pp. 672–3; also *ibid.,* 667, 670.

166 Ciano, 4, 8, 9.3.1940; DDI,9,III,391, 511.

167 Ciano, 10.3.1940; Dino Alfieri, *Due dittatori di fronte* (Milan, 1948), p. 42.

168 This and what follows from ADAP,D,VIII,665; see also DDI,9,III,512.

169 See for example Siebert, *Italiens Weg in den Zweiten Weltkrieg,* pp. 417–18.

170 ADAP,D,VIII,663; DDI,9,III,492.

171 For what follows, ADAP,D,VIII,669; DDI,9,III,524.

172 The last two *Littorios* were not scheduled to be combat-ready before 1942; the figure of 120 submarines was exaggerated. Possibly Ribbentrop's interpreter misunderstood Mussolini; four battleships (*Littorio, Vittorio Veneto,* and the modernized *Doria* and *Duilio*) were due to join the fleet that summer.

173 ADAP,D,VIII,669, p. 711 n. 12; Graeff note for Mackensen, 13.3.1940, GFM 4459/EO86895–97; DDI,9,III, Appendix II, 2.

174 Ciano, 11.3, 13.3.1940; meeting of the War Cabinet, 11.3.1940, PRO CAB 65; DDI,9,III,537; Noble minute on Loraine to Halifax, No. 228, 1.3.1940, PRO FO 371/24961, R 3314; also Loraine to Halifax, No. 238, 1.3.1940, *ibid.*, R 3435.

175 Ciano, 14.3.1940; "Segnalazioni," 14.3.1940; Welles report, FRUS, I, 1940, pp. 92–6; see also Guerri, *Ciano*, pp. 463–4, 475–6.

176 All from Ciano, 12.3, 13.3.1940.

177 Welles report, FRUS, 1940, I, pp. 96–106; Ciano, 16.3.1940; DDI,9,III,470.

178 Hero of a celebrated sixteenth-century comic novel by the Bolognese writer Giulio Cesare Croce.

179 All from Ciano, 16.2, 17.2.1940

CHAPTER 3
"THE MOST IMPATIENT OF ALL ITALIANS"

1 See Ciano, 18.3.1940; Bottai, *Vent'anni*, p. 162; for what follows, ADAP,D,IX,1. Quotation on preceding page: Anfuso, *Dal Palazzo Venezia*, p. 130.

2 Ciano, 19.3, 20.3.1940; Loraine to Halifax, No. 252, 19.3.1940; Communication by M. Cambon, 20.3.1940, PRO FO 371/24936, R 3563, 24937, R 3795; Welles report, FRUS, 1940, I, pp. 110–13.

3 ADSS,I,272.

4 DDI,9,III,604, 636; Ciano, 27.3.1940.

5 Ciano, 5.4, 7.4.1940, and Dingli minutes in Quartararo, "Il 'canale' segreto di Chamberlain," *Storia Contemporanea*, 7:4 (1976), pp. 704–9.

6 Intelligence digest, 28.3.1940, ACS, MMG, bundle 201, folder "Italia – notizie pervenute da S.E. il Capo di Stato Maggiore Generale."

7 Ciano, 23.3.1940; Rochat, "Mussolini, chef de guerre," *Revue d'histoire de la deuxième guerre mondiale*, No. 100 (1975), p. 52.

8 DDI,9,III,689.

9 Ciano, 2.4, 11.4.1940; DDI,9,III,716; DDI,9,IV,642, p. 495.

10 For Amedeo's visit to Rome, see Ciano, 6.4.1940; Carlo De Biase, *L'Impero di "faccetta nera"* (Milan, 1966), pp. 150–4; and Sullivan, "A Thirst for Glory," ch. 5.

11 All from minutes, 9.4.1940, in Faldella, *L'Italia*, pp. 728–34. The minutes belie Faldella's statement (p. 147) that the service chiefs believed Mussolini still intended Italian intervention for 1942–3; in that case, prophecies of doom would have been superfluous.

12 Ciano, 9.4.1940; ADAP,D,IX,68; DDI,9,III,116.

13 Mackensen to AA, No. 652, 9.4.1940, GFM 582/241992; ADAP,D,IX,69: Ciano, 9.4.1940.

14 "Rapporto ai direttori dei giornali provinciali," 10.4.1940, ACS, MCP, bundle 75; *OO*, XXIX, p. 375.

15 Ciano, 10.4.1940; Campbell to Halifax, No. 120 DIPP, 15.4.1940, PRO FO 371/24939, R 4752; ADAP,D,IX,84.

16 DDI,9,IV,37; ADAP,D,IX,92.

17 Italian translation of radiogram from commander-in-chief, armed forces, Belgrade, to subordinate commands, N. 2157, 12.4.1940, forwarded by Admiral

Parona to Sebastiani, 13.4.1940," *visto* by Mussolini, ACS, MMG, bundle 107, folder 15.

18 Mackensen to AA, No. 714, 16.4.1940, PA, Büro des Staatsekretärs, Italien, Bd. 2; Charles to Halifax, No. 368, 13.4.1940, Osborne to Halifax, Nos. 39 DIPP, 40 DIPP, 14.4, 15.4.1940, PRO FO 371/24939, R 4571, R 4742, R 4765; Charles to Halifax, Nos. 375 DIPP, 390 DIPP, 15.4, 17.4.1940, PRO FO 371/24940, R 4907.

19 Meetings of the War Cabinet, 14, 17, 18, 27, 30.4.1940, PRO CAB 65; Bédarida, *Stratégie secrète*, pp. 444–54, 472, 491–2, 503–5, 511–16, 518; report by chiefs of Staff Committee, 21.4.1940, WP(40)134; Halifax memorandum, WP(40)141, PRO FO 371/24942, R 5438, R 5581; DDI,9,IV,269, 311.

20 Ciano, 11.4.1940; the fleet actually amounted to 730,000 tons.

21 Badoglio to Mussolini, 5298, 11.4.1940, in Faldella, *L'Italia*, pp. 150–51.

22 Badoglio to Mussolini, 5306, 13.4.1940, *ibid.*, pp. 152–3.

23 Cavagnari memorandum, USMM, *L'organizzazione*, pp. 351–2.

24 Faldella, *L'Italia*, p. 149 (Faldella finds the phenomenon "inexplicable"); Domenico Cavagnari, "La marina nella vigilia e nel primo periodo del conflitto," *Nuova Antologia*, 357 (August 1947), p. 379.

25 For the quotation, diary of General Alfred Jodl (OKW) (henceforth Jodl), 19.4.1940, International Military Tribunal, *Trial of the Major War Criminals* (Nuremberg, 1947–9), XXVIII. For German post-Brenner planning, Jodl, 22.3, 26.3, 27.3.1940; Halder, I, pp. 233–7; Jacobsen, *Fall "Gelb."* pp. 128–30.

26 Rintelen, Plessen to AA, No. 584, 27.3.1940, GFM 582/241986 (seen by Hitler on 30 March, according to the records of Walter Hewel, Ribbentrop's liaison man to Hitler's headquarters: GFM 1924H/431540–41); Rintelen to OKH, G. Kdos. 33/40, 27.3.1940, and Löwisch to OKM, B. Nr. Gkdos. 1028/40, 30.3.1940, GNR PG 45177; Jodl, 26.3.1940.

27 Rintelen memorandum in USE, *La preparazione*, pp. 166–8; Rintelen to OKH, No. 45/40 g. Kdos., 17.4.1940, IWM AL 1007; for German planning, Halder, I, pp. 242–9; Jodl, 5.4, 6.4.1940; ADAP,D,IX,46.

28 Graziani memorandum, USE, *La preparazione*, pp. 168–70. The document disposes of Graziani's vivid and detailed memoir account (*Ho difeso la patria*, Milan, 1947, pp. 202ff), which accuses Badoglio of having pressured an unwilling but vacillating Mussolini into dropping the German proposal, against Graziani's advice.

29 Badoglio to Mussolini, 5318 S., 15.4.1940, in USE, *La preparazione*, pp. 170–1.

30 Badoglio memorandum, undated, in Faldella, *L'Italia*, p. 751; Rintelen, Mackensen to AA/OKH, No. 716, 15.4.1940, GFM 1571/380306; Rintelen to OKH, No. 45/40 g. Kdos., 17.4.1940, IWM AL 1007; Jacobsen, *Fall "Gelb,"* p. 130.

31 Phillips to Hull, No. 265, 16.4.1940, NARS, State, 740.0011 European War 1939/2255; KTB 1/SKL,A,8, 16.4.1940, GNR PG 32028; "Rapporto ai giornalisti del 15 aprile 1940 XVIII," ACS, MCP, bundle 75; Charles to Halifax, No. 329, 18.4.1940, PRO FO 371/24950, R 5162.

32 Ciano, 20.4.1940; ADAP,D,IX,138; DDI,9,V,130.

33 Ciano, 20.4, 21.4.1940; *OO*, XXIX, p. 378.

34 *OO*, XXIX, pp. 378–81; Gorla, *L'Italia nella seconda guerra mondiale*, p. 80;

Mackensen to AA, Nr. 1159, 1159II, 24.4.1940, GFM 2281/481305–09; Phillips to Hull, No. 1876, 7.5.1940, NARS, State, 740.0011 European War 1939/3291; PRO FO 371/24942, R 5670; "Discorso non officiale del 21 aprile 1940," in ACS, MI, DGPS/DPP, bundle 225, "Discorsi del Duce."

35 Ciano, 22.4.1940.

36 Ciano, 22.4, 23.4.1940; Charles to Halifax, No. 417, 22.4.1940, PRO FO 371/24941, R 5188; Bédarida, *Stratégie secrète,* pp. 445, 453.

37 Ciano, 24, 26, 28.4, 1.5.1940; DDI,9,IV,166, 189, 219, 227, 232, 262, 263; ADAP,D,IX,185; Hull to Phillips, 29.4.1940, Phillips to Hull, 1.5.1940, FRUS, 1940, II, pp. 691–95. Mussolini's claim of nonintervention in the Western hemisphere was not quite frank. One of his long-term projects was to use the Italian community in Brazil and massive aircraft sales to the Brazilian air force to penetrate the country and "shake the entire South American democratic system" (Ciano, 9.11.1937).

38 Ciano, 25.4.1940; Gorla, *L'Italia nella seconda guerra mondiale,* p. 80; KTB 1/SKL,A,8, 24.5.1940, GNR PG 32028.

39 Quoted in Charles to Halifax, No. 352, 27.4.1940, PRO FO 371/24943, R 5717. For another Grandi effusion, see his "Appunto per il Duce," 9.8.1940, NARS T-586/449/026895.

40 Michele Lanza (pseud. Leonardo Simoni), *Berlino, Ambasciata d'Italia (1939–1943)* (Rome 1946), p. 84; Ciano, 24.4, 26.4.1940; *Weizsäcker-Papiere,* pp. 202–3; David Irving, *Hitler's War* (New York, 1977), p. 125 note; ADAP,D,IX,165; Mackensen to AA, No. 765, 25.4.1940, GFM 582/242002.

41 Ciano, 1.5, 3.5.1940; Bottai, *Vent'anni,* p. 171.

42 DDI,9,IV,228; Ciano, 3.5.1940.

43 ADAP,D,164, 165; DDI,9,IV,190. In the light of Hitler's message, it is unlikely that when he expressed on 26 April the desire to "keep the Balkans quiet by all methods" (ADAP,D,IX, pp. 194–5) he was referring to the danger of Italian attack on Yugoslavia, as Martin van Creveld, *Hitler's Strategy, 1940–1941. The Balkan Clue* (Cambridge, 1973), p. 10, has suggested. Hitler's 26 April remark referred rather to direct threats to his Rumanian oil supply. After the German victories in the West, which sharply if temporarily reduced Hitler's readiness to run risks, the Germans admonished the Italians to leave Yugoslavia and Greece alone to avoid touching off a Hungarian-Rumanian war with possible Soviet intervention. But in April Hitler felt need enough of Italian help to be as willing as in the previous August to countenance a Mussolinian foray against Yugoslavia and/or Greece, if that were the price of Italian backing.

44 Ciano, 3.5.1940. See also the claim of Graziani, *Ho difeso la patria,* p. 191, that "toward the end of April" Mussolini suddenly requested a "studio" of an operation against Yugoslavia on an "urgent" basis.

45 Badoglio, in minutes, 6.5.1940, Faldella, *L'Italia,* pp. 735–8.

46 Badoglio to Mussolini, 15.4.1940, USE, *La preparazione,* p. 171; Badoglio figures from minutes, 6.5.1940, in Faldella, *L'Italia,* p. 735.

47 André Truchet, *L'Armistice de 1940 et l'Afrique du Nord* (Paris, 1955), pp. 105, 369–71.

48 USE, *L'esercito italiano,* appendix 81; Badoglio, in minutes, 6.5.1940; Faldella, *L'Italia,* p. 746; Henri Azeau, *La guerre franco-italienne* (Paris, 1967), p. 63; for more on intelligence failure, Carlo De Risio, *Generali, servizi segreti e fascismo* (Milan, 1978), ch. 1.

49 For Carboni and the Germans, see Carboni to Soddu (German translation), 22.4.1940, NARS T-821/347/000847–48; for error after intervention, compare Truchet, *L'Armistice*, pp. 369–71 (four infantry divisions in Tunisia, 25.6.1940) with order of battle map attached to Army Staff memorandum, 30.6.1940, NARS T-821/127/000677 (seven divisions).

50 Balbo to Mussolini, 11.5.1940, USE, *La preparazione*, pp. 172–4.

51 Soddu memorandum, 13.5.1940, *ibid.*, pp. 74–6.

52 Favagrossa to Mussolini, 13.5.1940, *ibid.*, pp. 176–80.

53 See Rintelen to OKH, No. 45/40 g. Kdos. 17.4.1940; also Bürkner (OKW/Ausland) to OKH, No. 63/40 geh. Kdos. Chefs., 23.5.1940, IWM AL 1007.

54 Figures from Santoro, *L'aeronautica italiana*, I, pp. 33–6, 88–9, II, 146 ("modern" types: S.79, B.R.20, Cant. Z.506 and 1007, C.R.42, G.50, M.C.200); USE, *L'esercito italiano*, pp. 306, 149–50, and, for readiness, Comando Supremo note, 31.5.1940, NARS T-821/130/000079.

55 ADAP,D,IX,212, 232; DDI,9,IV,353.

56 Ciano, 10.5.1940; Loraine to Halifax, No. 491 DIPP, 10.5.1940, PRO FO 371/24943, R 5152; DDI,9,IV,335.

57 Ciano, 11.5.1940; also Partito Nazionale Fascista, "Appunto per il Duce," 11.5.1940, ACS, MCP, bundle 11, folder 154; Phillips to Hull, Nos. 333, 336, 11.5, 12.5.1940, NARS, State, 740.0011 European War 1939/2832, 2857; Mackensen to AA, No. 871, 12.5.1940, GFM 1571/380318–20.

58 "Rapporto ai giornalisti dell'11 maggio 1940 XVIII," ACS, MCP, bundle 75.

59 Mackensen to AA, No. 874, 13.5.1940, GFM 582/242010; ADAP,D,IX,725; Mackensen to AA, No. 883, 15.5.1940, GFM 1571/380321. On Oriani, see the drumfire of anti-Vatican editorials in *Regime Fascista* throughout May; *OO*, XXIX, pp. 299–300n; De Felice, *Mussolini*, I, pp. 186–7, n. 1. For the *Osservatore Romano* crisis, Ciano, 16.5.1940, and Anthony Rhodes, *The Vatican in the Age of the Dictators, 1922–1945* (London, 1973), pp. 245–6.

60 Centuries of Papal rule had given the Romagna, Mussolini's own region, a long-standing and vehement anticlerical tradition.

61 Mackensen to AA, No. 894, 16.5.1940, GFM 230/152209.

62 See Mussolini's remarks to Anfuso and Ciano at the end of May, and the interpretation of Anfuso, *Dal Palazzo Venezia*, pp. 130–1, 133.

63 For a similar phrase, coupled incongruously with the traditional interpretation of Mussolini as opportunist, see David D. Roberts, *The Syndicalist Tradition and Italian Fascism* (Manchester, 1979), pp. 185, 326.

64 Ciano, 14.5.1940; ADAP,D,IX,239, 242; Phillips to Hull, No. 340, 13.5.1940, NARS, State, 740.0011 European War 1939/2916.

65 Roosevelt to Mussolini, 14.5.1940, FRUS, 1940, I, pp. 704–5; DDI,9,IV,415, 445, 487; Ciano, 15.5, 16.5.1940; ADAP,D,IX,255.

66 Ciano, 9.5, 10.5, 18.5, 21.5.1940.

67 British Royal Navy decrypt, 6.5.1940, forwarded to Sebastiani by Admiral Parona, 7.5.1940, *visto* by Mussolini, ACS, MMG, bundle 105, folder 15. The words quoted are underlined, probably by Mussolini.

68 Bédarida, *Stratégie secrète*, pp. 512–13, 518; J.P.(40)147, 6.5.1940, PRO CAB 21/1427.

69 Soddu to Cavagnari, 20.4.1940, and undated naval staff memoranda and drafts attached, ACS, MMG, bundle 213; Faldella, *L'Italia*, p. 122.

70 All from Paolo Puntoni, *Parla Vittorio Emanuele III* (Milan, 1958), pp. 11–12.

71 Remarks of Badoglio to Armellini, *Diario,* p. 2.

72 Faldella, *L'Italia,* p. 123; Puntoni, *Parla Vittorio Emanuele,* p. 144.

73 Ciano, 16.5, 17.5, 20.5.1940, and De Bono diaries, 20.5.1940, notebook 44, ACS. De Bono commented: "What cheek!" ("bella faccia di bronzo!!")

74 Farinacci to Grandi, 2.1.1941, NARS T-586/449/026999; speech text: ACS, MCP, bundle 114, folder 112; Ciano, 19.5.1940; Gorla, *L'Italia nella seconda guerra mondiale,* p. 82.

75 Ciano, 21.5.1940; Bottai, *Vent'anni,* p. 175.

76 Grazzi, *Il principio della fine,* pp. 98–100; Mackensen to AA, No. 902, 17.5.1940, GFM 4459/E086937; Etzdorf note, 21.5.1940, GFM 1247/337401.

77 Ciano 22.5, 23.5.1940.

78 Geloso to Soddu, 10, 25.5.1940, NARS T-821/127/000171–72.

79 Memorandum of telephone conversation between Soddu and Sebastiani [Mussolini's secretary], 27.5.1940, NARS T-586/1091/067876; Sebastiano Visconti Prasca, *Io ho aggredito la Grecia* (Milan, 1946), p. 2; Francesco Jacomoni, *La politica dell'Italia in Albania* (Bologna, 1965), p. 226.

80 Handwritten note with Armellini's initials, 7.6.1940, on 6 June memorandum of Badoglio's office summarizing Geloso's report, NARS T-821/127/000169.

81 ADAP,D,IX,272, 276, 317, 320; DDI,9,IV,488, 493, 497, 516, 530, 553, 568, 584; Bottai, *Vent'anni,* p. 147; Ciano, 26.5.1940; Anfuso, *Dal Palazzo Venezia,* p. 129; Mackensen to AA, No. 981, 26.5.1940, GFM B14/B001896.

82 The analysis that follows derives from extensive reading of the police informant public opinion reports in the files of the Ministero dell'Interno, Direzione Generale Pubblica Sicurezza, Divisione Polizia Politica, and of the "Situazione politica ed economica delle Provincie" files of the Partito Nazionale Fascista (ACS). The results are impressionistic – but given the nature of the material, it is hard to see how else to use it. I have endeavored to select representative samples with as much detachment as possible. For corroboration, see Leto, *Ovra,* pp. 211–13, and Melograni's ground-breaking *Rapporti segreti della polizia fascista 1938/1940* (Milan, 1978); I saw both works only after writing this section.

83 Informant report, 16.4.1940, Milan, marked *Partito* ("[send it to the] Party") in Mussolini's hand, ACS, PNF/SPP, bundle 6.

84 Informant report, 11.4.1940, Milan, *ibid.*

85 Informant report, 10.4.1940, Milan, marked *Partito* in Mussolini's hand, ACS, PNF/SPP, bundle 6.

86 Informant report, 21.4.1940, Milan, *ibid.*

87 Informant report, 10.5.1940, Turin, *ibid.,* bundle 25. See also informant report, 12.5.1940, Milan, *ibid.,* bundle 6.

88 Informant report, 12.5.1940, Turin, marked *Partito* in Mussolini's hand, underlining in original (probably by Mussolini), *ibid.,* bundle 25.

89 Informant report, 11.5.1940, Padua, *ibid.,* bundle 11.

90 Informant report, 12.5.1940, Milan, *ibid.,* bundle 6.

91 Informant report, 13.5.1940, Milan, *ibid.*

92 Unsigned "Promemoria per il Duce. Notizie varie della capitale," 12.5.1940, *ibid.,* bundle 19.

93 Informant report, 13.5.1940, Rome, marked *Partito* in Mussolini's hand; passage quoted is underlined heavily (*ibid.*).

94 Informant report, "Situazione internazionale," 14.5.1940, Milan, *ibid.*, bundle 6.
95 Informant report, 16.5.1940, Genoa, *ibid.*, bundle 1.
96 Informant report, 16.5.1940, Pisa, *ibid.*, bundle 14.
97 Informant report, 16.5.1940, Milan, *ibid.*, bundle 6.
98 Informant report, 16.5.1940, Milan, *ibid.*
99 Unsigned "Promemoria per il Duce," 17.5.1940, *ibid.*
100 Etzdorf note, 17.5.1940, GFM 1247/337396; Halder, I, p. 308; Phillips to Hull, No. 378, 18.5.1940, NARS, State, 740.0011 European War 1939/3133.
101 "Notizia fiduciaria," 21.5.1940, Rome, ACS, MI, DPP, bundle 217; see also another "notizia fiduciaria," 19.5.1940, *ibid.:* "Many people are almost afraid of arriving in the war too late."
102 Informant report, 21.5.1940, Rome, *ibid.*
103 Ciano, 25.5.1940; also Bottai, *Vent'anni*, p. 174.
104 Anfuso, *Dal Palazzo Venezia*, pp. 125–6.
105 Bocca, *Storia d'Italia nella guerra fascista*, p. 163. U. Alfassio Grimaldi and Gherardo Bozzetti, *Dieci giugno 1940. Il giorno della follia* (Bari, 1974), pp. 42-55, also neglect the sudden enthusiasm for a swift and profitable war that swept large segments of the public in May and June 1940. The authors' concentration on providing "comfort for an entire nation" and "vindication for its honor" (p. 55) is perhaps responsible.
106 Lanza, *Berlino*, pp. 120–1. Such lines inevitably summon up an overwhelming sense of déjà vu in anyone conversant with the history of Prussia-Germany. See Ludwig Dehio, *Germany and World Politics in the Twentieth Century* (New York, 1967) and Fritz Fischer, *Germany's Aims in the First World War* (New York, 1967). For an account of the politics of Liberal Italy that stresses some continuities with later Fascist expansionism, see Bosworth, *Italy, the Least of the Great Powers.*
107 Rossi, *Mussolini*, p. 45.
108 "Segnalazioni," 23.5, 29.5.1940.
109 Castronovo, *Agnelli*, p. 592. Castronovo's analysis of the unreality and unrealism of FIAT policy in 1939–40 is suggestive of the attitudes of the major industrialists as a group, although no serious study on that subject exists. For Pirelli, see his *Economia e guerra*, 2 v. (Milan, 1940) (quotations from II, p. 7).
110 Informant report, 27.5.1940, Pisa, ACS, PNF/SPP, bundle 14.
111 Informant report, 4.6.1940, Milan, *ibid.*, bundle 6.
112 Direttore Generale di P.S. di Zona, Florence, to Bocchini, 9.6.1940, MI, DGPS/DAGR 1920/1923–45, Cat. A5G, bundle 20.
113 Meeting of the War Cabinet, 6.5.1940, PRO CAB 65.
114 Cromwell's phrase, quoted by Leo Amery in the debate of 7 May.
115 Kennedy to Hull, 15.5.1940, FRUS, 1940, III, pp. 29–30; for Kennedy's 1938 remark that he "understood [Germany's] Jewish policy completely," ADAP,D,I,457; for his defeatism, Kennedy to Hull, 24.5.1940, FRUS, 1940, III, pp. 31–2; Kennedy to Hull, 16.5, 21.5.1940, Nos. 1237, 1400, NARS, State, 740.0011 European War 1939/3005 1/10, 3018 4/10.
116 Loraine to Halifax, No. 513 DIPP, 13.5.1940, PRO FO 371/24944, R 5995; meetings of the War Cabinet, 14.5, 15.5.1940, PRO CAB 65; DDI,9,VI,445.

117 Unsigned minute, 15.5.1940, PRO FO 371/24943, R 5946. For Butler's views, DDI,9,II,218, IV,61; Cadogan, *Diaries,* p. 275; Woodward, *British Foreign Policy,* I, p. 204 n. 1, and Quartararo, "Il 'canale' segreto di Chamberlain," particularly p. 701.

118 DDI,9,IV,432, 434; meetings of the War Cabinet, 15.5, 16.5.1940, PRO CAB 65; Butler minute, 16.5.1940, PRO FO 371/24943, R 5946.

119 DDI,9,IV,451, 474, 475, 498; meeting of the War Cabinet, 19.5.1940, PRO CAB 65.

120 DDI,9,IV,465, 471, 485; Bullitt to Hull, Nos. 760, 767, 20.5.1940, NARS, State, 740.0011 European War 1939/3174, 2855 1/28; Campbell to Halifax, Nos. 241, 262 DIPP, 21.5, 23.5.1940, PRO FO 371/24959, R 6168.

121 Meeting of the War Cabinet, 25.5.1940, PRO CAB 65; DDI,9,IV,589, and Halifax to Loraine, No. 413, in meeting of the War Cabinet, 26.5.1940, Confidential Annex, PRO CAB 65.

122 See Woodward, *British Foreign Policy,* I, pp. 198–9; meeting of the War Cabinet, 26.5.1940, Confidential Annex, PRO CAB 65.

123 Etzdorf note, 27.5.1940, GFM 1247/337409; DDI,9,IV,516, 553; Halder, I, p. 307; KTB I/SKL,A,9, 18.5.1940, GNR PG 32029; for Italo-German naval relations during nonbelligerence, see Salewski, *Seekriegsleitung,* I, pp. 152–5, 224–34, and Schreiber, *Weltmachtstreben,* pp. 201–17, 231–9.

124 Halder, I, p. 302; postwar testimony of Generals Sodernstern and Blumentritt, in Walter Ansel, *Hitler Confronts England* (Durham, N.C., 1960), p. 71; Jodl, 20.5.1940.

125 DDI,9,IV,491, 516, 553.

126 Halder, I, p. 308.

127 On all this, see Martin, *Friedensinitiativen,* pp. 243–4; Klaus Hildebrand, *The Foreign Policy of the Third Reich* (Berkeley, Los Angeles, 1973), pp. 91–104; Andreas Hillgruber, *Hitlers Strategie. Politik und Kriegführung 1940–1941* (Frankfurt a. M., 1965), pp. 144ff.

128 DDI,9,IV,609, 696; Phillips to Hull, 27.5.1940, FRUS, 1940, II, pp. 712–13; Ciano, 27.5.1940; Loraine to Halifax, Nos. 714, 721, 28.5.1940, PRO FO 371/24947, R 6331.

129 Woodward, *British Foreign Policy,* I, pp. 202–4; meetings of the War Cabinet, 27.5, 28.5.1940, Confidential Annexes, PRO CAB 65; Stuart J. Woolf, "Inghilterra, Francia e Italia; settembre 1939-giugno 1940," *Rivista di Storia Contemporanea,* 3:4 (1972), pp. 490–4.

130 Churchill minute, 28.5.1940, Churchill, *Their Finest Hour* (New York, paperback ed., 1962), p. 109; meeting of the War Cabinet, 4.6.1940, PRO CAB 65. Five years later, as the puppet republic of Salò collapsed about his ears, Mussolini claimed to several associates that Churchill had urged him to go to war in 1940 (in secret correspondence Mussolini allegedly possessed, but which only Duilio Susmel, the dictator's faithful chronicler, has ever admitted seeing, although only after promising not to divulge its location or contents). Churchill's purpose, according to one baroque version, was to place Mussolini at Hitler's side "to act . . . as moderator and conciliator at the decisive moment" of a negotiated peace (Lessona, *Memorie,* p. 376).

For more on this theory, see Mack Smith, *Mussolini's Roman Empire,* pp. 220, 283, and Howard McGaw Smyth, *Secrets of the Fascist Era* (Carbondale, 1975), pp. 214–21. Both Susmel and Smyth misinterpret a 1943 German foreign office analysis of captured Palazzo Chigi files, a report Smyth admits is the only documentary evidence of Churchill letters to Mussolini after the published one of 16 May 1940. The actual text of the German report (Hencke memorandum, 20.11.1943, GFM 131/71169–74; printed in translation in Deakin, *The Brutal Friendship*, pp. 507–10) merely establishes that the Germans learned of Churchill's "letters" from "public explanations given by the British Prime Minister" – a statement that contradicts Susmel's claim, which Smyth endorses, that it was the *Italian* foreign ministry files the Germans were examining that contained the evidence of further Churchill letters. Actually, Churchill read his 16 May letter and Mussolini's 18 May reply over the air during his 23 December 1940 broadcast to Italy (see chapter 6.2). That is how the Germans knew of it; the reference to "letters" (plural) in the German report is in all likelihood a slip of the typewriter. For summaries of four purported backchannel Churchill letters to Mussolini from a much earlier period (December 1939–January 1940) see Franco Bandini, *Vita e morte segreta di Mussolini* (Milan, 1978), pp. 99–104; the contents are banal.

131 Other last-minute French appeals to Rome also met with contemptuous rejection: Ciano 31.5, 1.6.1940; DDI,9,IV,644, 652, 657, 659, 661, 772, 748, and Bullitt to Hull, 3.6.1940, FRUS, 1940, II, p. 716.

132 For the demonstrations, see the prefect and police telegrams in "Dimostrazioni ostili alla Francia e all'Inghilterra e per l'intervento dell'Italia nel conflitto," ACS, PC 1937–39, 15/2/8182/17; Ciano, 26.5.1940; Anfuso, *Dal Palazzo Venezia*, p. 128; also Badoglio, *L'Italia nella seconda guerra mondiale* (Verona, 1946), p. 37.

133 For what follows, DDI,9,IV,642.

134 See DDI,9,IV,Appendix I.

135 Graziani to Mussolini, 11, 25.5.1940, NARS T-821/130/000089–98; printed in part in USE, *La preparazione*, pp. 181–4, and Rossi, *Mussolini*, pp. 161–4, both of which omit without benefit of punctuation the concluding sections of the memorandum, which outlined the proposed deployment and made clear that Graziani's full listing of his forces' deficiencies was – characteristically – purely for the record.

136 *Ibid.*, 000097–98. Graziani had evidently not altogether ruled out the upper Rhine plan. But despite later hints from Alfieri and the Germans, and Graziani's own requests for guidance in this regard, Mussolini did not clear Roatta to visit Berlin, although he had purportedly agreed in principle to the visit (ADAP,D,IX,323; Rintelen to OKH, g. Kdos., No. 55/40, 66/40 g. Kdos. 17.5, 28.5.1940, IWM AL 1007).

137 Ciano, 30.5.1940; DDI,9,IV,646, ADAP,D,IX,356.

138 DDI,9,IV,679; Lanza, *Berlino*, p. 118; for Ciano's assurances, Mackensen to AA, No. 894, 16.5.1940, GFM 230/152209; ADAP,D,IX,341; for the earlier alarm, Halder, I, pp. 305–6, ADAP,D,IX,328; for Hitler's own less urgent view, and the similar judgment of the German navy, Halder, I, p. 316, and KTB 1/SKL,A,9, 22.5.1940, GNR PG 32029. For a different interpretation, which ignores Mussolini's 13 May remark to Ciano, see Creveld, *Hitler's Strategy*, pp. 9–10.

139 ADAP,D,IX,357, DDI,9,IV,680. Creveld, *Hitler's Strategy*, pp. 10–11, suggests that Mussolini's "ostensibly conciliatory letter" of 30 May "alarmed" Hit-

ler, who allegedly feared Italian action against Yugoslavia. According to Creveld, Hitler's reply "recommended" that Mussolini make a public statement of his desire to keep the Danube basin and the Balkans out of the conflict. Further, the Führer's alleged reason for requesting Mussolini to postpone his entry into the war (the need to prevent the French air force from redeploying), was merely a "ridiculous pretext" which the Germans dropped "with almost indecent haste" once Mussolini had "made up his mind to comply" with German desires in the Balkans. Ehrengard Schramm-von Thadden, *Griechenland und die Grossmächte in Zweiten Weltkrieg* (Wiesbaden, 1955), p. 45, advances a similar if less detailed version. Actually, Mussolini himself had suggested both the statement to the Balkan neutrals and the possibility that Hitler might for military reasons request delay in Italy's intervention (DDI,9,IV,646). On the German side, the air attack was genuine (see Halder I, pp. 329, 333) although the destruction of most *Luftwaffe* records makes it impossible to determine its originally scheduled date.

140 DDI,9,IV,706; ADAP,D,IX,366, 373; Ciano, 30.5.1940.

141 ADAP,D,IX,370, 371.

142 Engel, *Heeresadjutant bei Hitler*, pp. 81–2; DDI,9,IV,726, 729.

143 Minutes, 30.5.1940, Faldella, *L'Italia*, pp. 739–42; Roatta to Badoglio, 12, 29.5.1940, NARS T-821/130/000117–21. For the 10 June deployment, which did not differ markedly from Graziani's proposed one, USE, *L'esercito italiano*, pp. 336–9, and map 81.

144 See Santoro, *L'aeronautica italiana*, I, p. 77, which incorrectly places the meeting on 3 June. According to a Badoglio letter of 30 May, Mussolini personally approved the Army's deployment plan (Badoglio to Graziani, 5499, 30.5.1940, NARS T-821/130/000115).

145 Cavagnari directive, 29.5.1940, in USMM, *L'organizzazione*, pp. 353–5. See also his "La marina nella vigilia e nel primo periodo del conflitto," pp. 377–8.

146 KTB 1/SKL,A,10, 4.6.1940, GNR PG 32030.

147 Balbo telegrams, 32923 Segreto, T/1/114, 33033 Segreto, 27.5, 31.5.1940, with handwritten comment by Graziani, all in ACS, Graziani, bundle 41. See also the SIM memorandum for Graziani, 19.5.1940, and the memorandum of the Army Staff operations section, 21.5.1940, *ibid.*

148 Ciano, 29.5.1940; Truchet, *L'Armistice*, pp. 100–6; USE, *L'esercito italiano*, Appendix 88; Hans Heggenreiner, "Deutsch-italienische Zusammenarbeit in Nordafrika," Teil I, "Verbindungsaufnahme mit Marschall Balbo Mai 1940," NARS, German Military Monographs, Ms. D.217, p. 9.

149 Armellini, *Diario*, pp. 14–15; Badoglio to Mussolini, 1.6.1940, USE, *La preparazione*, pp. 190–91.

150 Armellini, *Diario*, p. 20.

151 "Il Duce ha detto che è sua intenzione, con la dichiarazione di guerra, di cambiare lo stato di fatto in stato di diritto."

152 Badoglio, in minutes, 5.6.1940, ACS, Graziani, bundle 51, printed with unacknowledged omissions in Faldella, *L'Italia*, pp. 743–6.

153 Navy Staff memorandum, 18.6.1940, USMM, *L'organizzazione*, pp. 356–60. For the desperate condition of Malta's defenses (five British battalions, a locally raised regiment, and *three* Gloster Gladiator biplane fighters), see Playfair, *Mediterranean*, I, p. 98.

154 For the final arrangement, see Badoglio's directive 5569, 4.6.1940, USE, *La preparazione,* pp. 188–90.

155 Armellini, *Diario,* p. 24, and Badoglio, *L'Italia,* p. 37.

156 Auswertestelle Süd to OKW/Abwehr III, 8.6.1944, summarizing Daladier's minute, NARS T-821/347/000845.

157 Quotations from Gianluca André, *La guerra in Europa, 1939–1941* (Milan, 1964), p. 395; Rochat, "Mussolini, chef de guerre," p. 54; Rochat, *Badoglio,* p. 742; Mack Smith, *Mussolini's Roman Empire,* p. 217. For a treatment of Mussolini's policy toward the Soviets in this period that also stresses the balance-of-power motif, see Toscano, "Italo-Soviet Relations, 1940–41: Failure of an Accord," *Designs in Diplomacy,* pp. 124–252. See also Cliadakis, "Neutrality and War in Italian Policy, 1939–1940," and C. J. Lowe and F. Marzari, *Italian Foreign Policy, 1870–1940* (London, 1975), pp. 369–70.

158 Bottai, *Vent'anni,* p. 192.

159 DDI,9,IV,166, 465; Ciano, 8.6.1940; Armellini, *Diario,* pp. 22–3.

160 Armellini, *Diario,* p. 19; DDI,9,V,728; Badoglio, in minutes, 5.6.1940, Faldella, *L'Italia,* p. 743.

161 Ciano, 5.6.1940; also ADAP,D,XI,350.

162 Badoglio to Graziani, Cavagnari and Pricolo, 28, 7.6.1940, ACS, Graziani, bundle 51. The submarine directive, which confirmed a similar oral order of Badoglio's during the 5 June conference (omitted without benefit of punctuation in the version printed in Faldella, *L'Italia*), does not figure in the Navy's official histories. Santoro, *L'aeronautica italiana,* I, p. 103, prints most of Badoglio's 7 June directive, but omits the sentence in question, though indicating an omission. For the Army's rules of engagement, see also Graziani to Army Group "O" [West], 847, 7.6.1940., USE, *La battaglia delle Alpi occidentali (giugno 1940)* (Rome, 1947), p. 128.

163 KTB Marine Attaché Rom, 8.6.1940, GNR PG 45148; Armellini, *Diario,* p. 24.

164 Playfair, *Mediterranean,* I, p. 93.

165 Puntoni, *Parla Vittorio Emanuele,* pp. 13–14; Ciano, 1.6, 3.6.1940; ADAP,D,IX,366; Lane to Hull, No. 244, 10.6.1940, NARS, State, 740.0011 European War 1939/3650, reporting a conversation with Victor Ruzic, former Yugoslav justice minister; Federzoni to Mussolini, 24.1.1940, NARS T-586/489/049067–70.

166 Martin, *Friedensinitiativen,* p. 388; Castronovo, *Agnelli,* pp. 594ff.

167 ADAP,D,IX,343, 371; Loraine to Halifax, Nos. 855 DIPP, 894 DIPP, 7.6., 9.6.1940, PRO FO 371/24383, C 7179, 24944, R 6079; Ciano, 4.6.1940; Mackensen to AA, Nos. 1049, 1054, 1097, 4.6, 5.6, 9.6.1940, GFM B14/B001945, B001954, and PA, Deutsche Botschaft Rom, Geheimakten, item 330/40, Bd. 43/3; Phillips to Hull, No. 780, 7.6.1940, NARS, State, 740.0011 European War 1939/2855.

168 All from ADAP,D,IX,408.

169 Mackensen to AA, No 1104, 10.6.1940, GFM B14/B002004–05; see also the more charitable diary entry, 11.6.1940.

170 Ciano, 10.6.1940; Mackensen to AA, No. 1107, 11.6.1940, GFM B14/B002017–18.

171 Text, with stage directions, *OO,* XXIX, pp. 404–5.

172 Mackensen to AA, Nos. 1105, 1130, 10.6, 13.6.1940, GFM B14/B002006, B002029–30; Santoro, *L'aeronautica italiana,* 1, p. 103; DDI,9,V,9; ADAP,D,IX,421.

173 See USMM, *Le azioni navali in Mediterraneo dal 10 giugno 1940 al 31 marzo 1941* (Rome, 1970), pp. 83–91.

174 Unsigned naval staff memorandum, "Situazione strategica nel Tirreno," 15.6.1940, ACS, MMG, bundle 195.

175 Ciano, 15–17.6.1940; Graziani to Army Group West, 1601, 1875, 14.5, 16.6.1940; Roatta to Battisti (Army Group West), 17.6.1940; Graziani to Army Groups South and West, 89, 17.6.1940, USE, *Alpi occidentali,* pp. 130–7; ADAP,D,IX,460; Mussolini to Victor Emmanuel III, 17.6.1940, NARS T-586/406/000782–83.

176 DDI,9,V,45. See also Roatta's lengthy report, 18–19.6.1940 in Rossi, *Mussolini,* pp. 168–74.

177 Mussolini to Victor Emmanuel III, 20.6.1940, with enclosed minute ("reconstructed according to memory"), NARS T-586/406/001040; minute alone in *OO,* XXX, pp. 2–5; DDI,9,V,65; ADAP,D,IX,479; Ciano, 18–19.6.1940; Roatta memorandum, 18–19.6.1940, in Rossi, *Mussolini,* pp. 168–74.

178 For what details are available, see Martin, *Friedensinitiativen,* pp. 272–3 and n. 29; for rumors reaching Rome, DDI,9,V,47, 78.

179 According to Schmidt (*Statist auf diplomatischer Bühne,* p. 484), Hitler later remarked to Ribbentrop that he had not wanted to "burden" the Franco-German armistice negotiations with "Franco-Italian animosity." Mussolini, on the other hand, came to the not implausible conclusion that Hitler wanted a private and exclusively German triumph (Ciano, 20.6.1940).

180 Ciano, 18–19.6.1940.

181 Graziani to Army Group West, 93, 19.6.1940, 2050 hrs., USE, *Alpi occidentali,* p. 138; Roatta memorandum, 18–19.6.1940, Rossi, *Mussolini,* pp. 172–3; Graziani to Badoglio, 1, 20.6.1940; Badoglio to Graziani, 474, 20.6.1940, ACS, Graziani, bundle 70, "Appendice."

182 For what follows, minutes, 20.6.1940, NARS T-586/406/000868–70 (emphasis in original).

183 Graziani to Army Group West, 2329, 20.6.1940, USE, *Alpi occidentali,* p. 139.

184 All from Ciano, 20.6.1940; Ciano's approach presumably followed the Palazzo Venezia meeting.

185 ADAP,D,IX,508. Lanza, *Berlino,* p. 133, testifies to similar agitation in the German foreign office; see also DDI,9,V,86, n. 4.

186 DDI,9,V,63; Armellini, *Diario,* p. 34; Marras to Roatta, 971/A/317, 20.6.1940, ACS, Graziani, bundle 51; for the executive order, Graziani to Army Group West, 97, 20.6.1940, 2110 hrs., USE, *Alpi occidentali,* p. 139.

187 Balbo to Badoglio, 16.6.1930, USE, *La preparazione,* p. 200; Balbo to Badoglio, 031, 17.6.1940, ACS, Graziani, bundle 42.

188 Mussolini to Victor Emmanuel III, 17.6.1940, NARS T-586/406/000782–85; Balbo to Badoglio, 01/205.504, 17.6.1940, ACS, Graziani, bundle 42.

189 Balbo to Badoglio, 01/505520, 01/205.594, 01/205.602, 18.6, 20.6.1940, ACS, Graziani, bundle 42.

190 Ciano, 21.6.1940; Badoglio to Balbo, 1/782, 22.6.1940; Balbo to Badoglio, 01/205.692, 23.6.1940, ACS, Graziani, bundle 42.

191 DDI,9,V,75; Weizsäcker minute of talk with Alfieri, St.S. No. 460, 20.6.1940, GFM B14/B002041.

192 Ciano, 21.6.1940; DDI,9,V,83, 91; ADAP,D,IX,507n.3, 525, 526; see also Lanza, *Berlino,* p. 133. As Franca Avantaggiato Puppo, *Gli armistizi francesi del 1940* (Milan, 1963), p. 266 has justly observed, the frequently repeated suggestion (e.g., Pieri, "La stratégie italienne," p. 72) that Hitler induced Mussolini to lower his claims is incorrect.

193 See the list in Puppo, *Gli armistizi francesi,* pp. 267–8.

194 Mario Roatta, *Otto milioni di baionette* (Milan, 1946), pp. 103–4.

195 Faldella, *L'Italia,* p. 186. Fears on this score were well founded: see ADAP,D,IX,522, p. 552.

196 Dino Alfieri, *Due dittatori,* p. 66.

197 See, for instance Puppo, *Gli armistizi francesi,* p. 269; André, *La guerra in Europa,* pp. 405–6; idem, "La politica estera del governo fascista," pp. 121–2; Lowe and Marzari, *Italian Foreign Policy,* pp. 369–70. Marzari proposes the balance-of-power explanation of Mussolini's behavior, and also claims that Mussolini "responded favourably to an appeal from the new French Foreign Minister, Baudoin [*sic*] stressing France's desires for a lasting peace which would serve as foundation for the future collaboration of the two Latin countries." Baudouin actually made such an appeal in mid-May, before his elevation to the Foreign Ministry (DDI,9,IV,465), and another, through the Vatican, on 18 June (DDI,9,V,43). The Italians responded to the first appeal by declaring war, and to the second by renewing the attack in the Alps. For the absence of any significant "contact" with Mussolini, see Baudouin, *Neuf mois au gouvernement* (Paris, 1948), pp. 187, 216.

198 Luciolli, *Mussolini e l'Europa,* p. 233.

199 Ciano, 22.6.1940; Gambara attacked at 10 a.m. (USE, *Alpi occidentali,* p. 77).

200 Graziani to Army Group West, 214/8, 24.6.1940, 1120 hrs., USE, *Alpi occidentali,* p. 175.

201 Armellini, *Diario,* p. 37; DDI,9,V,93.

202 ADAP,D,IX,508.

203 Ciano, 22.6.1940; armistice text: DDI,9,V,95; Puppo, *Gli armistizi francesi,* pp. 269–74; Armellini, *Diario,* p. 42.

204 Ciano, 25.6.1940.

CHAPTER 4
JUNE–SEPTEMBER 1940: DUCE STRATEGY IN THE SHADOW OF SEA LION

1 Mackensen to AA, No. 1199, 24.6.1940, GFM 2281/481392–93.

2 Badoglio to Balbo, 932, 25.6.1940, ACS, Graziani, bundle 42.

3 All from minutes, 25.6.1940, ACS, Graziani, bundle 45.

4 Badoglio to Balbo, 26.9.1940, USE, *La preparazione,* p. 95.

5 Martin, *Friedensinitiativen,* p. 283.

6 Badoglio to Balbo, 979, 28.6.1940, USE, *La preparazione,* p. 96; Badoglio to Tellera, 988, 29.6.1940, ACS, Graziani, bundle 45. The rumor inevitably circulated that Balbo's untimely death was the consequence of Mussolini's fear of over-mighty subordinates. The report of General Tellera, Balbo's chief of staff

(29.6.1940, NARS T-586/468/035768–70) makes clear poor communications and worse fire control were responsible.

7 Badoglio, *L'Italia,* p. 48.
8 Graziani, *Ho difeso la patria,* pp. 225–8; *idem, Africa Settentrionale,* 1940–41 (Rome, n.d.), pp. 44–5; Graziani diary, 29.6.1940, ACS, Graziani, bundle 70, "Appendice" (henceforth Graziani diary).
9 Armellini, *Diario,* p. 45; Army Staff memorandum, "Studio della possibilità di una nostra offensiva contro l'Egitto," 30.6.1940, NARS T-821/109/000341–49 (emphasis in original).
10 Ciano, 2.7.1940.
11 Alfieri, *Due dittatori,* p. 71.
12 DDI,9,V,114; Armellini, *Diario,* p. 47.
13 See P. M. H. Bell, *A Certain Eventuality. Britain and the Fall of France* (n.p., 1974), ch. 7; Eberhard Jäckel, *Frankreich in Hitlers Europa* (Stuttgart, 1966), chs. 1–4; Cavagnari to Badoglio, 494, 4.7.1940, AUSMM, CIAF, bundle 50; Commissione Italiana d'Armistizio con la Francia, "Appunto N°1 . . . ," 4.7.1940, NARS T-586/1347/098976–84.
14 Ciano, 5.7.1940.
15 Robert O. Paxton, *Vichy France* (New York, 1972), pp. 56–7.
16 All from entry of 5.7.1940, Roatta to Graziani, 140, 9.7.1940, ACS, Graziani, bundle 42 (henceforth Roatta letters, by entry date). The letter is the first of a series of diary-letters from Roatta in Rome to Graziani in North Africa – a fundamental and virtually unexploited source on the Italian war of 1940.
17 Ciano, 5.7.1940; ADAP,D,X,193.
18 See Ciano, 28.6.1940; DDI,9,V,142, 161; Heath to Hull, 26.6.1940, FRUS, 1940, III, pp. 38–9; Lothian to Halifax, No. 1204, 2.7.1940, PRO FO 371/24407, C 7578. For a different version of Mussolini's motives, see Alfieri's unsupported and elliptical remark in Weizsäcker minute, StS. No. 500, 29.6.1940, GFM 490/232260; Alfieri, *Due dittatori,* pp. 72–3; and Martin, *Friedensinitiativen,* pp. 281–4.
19 De Vecchi to Badoglio, 84, 18.6.1940, ACS, SPD/CO, Vᵃ Serie (Comando Supremo), bundle 1; the folder cover carries Mussolini's *visto.*
20 DDI,9,V,48, 82, 156; GWB, 79, 82; De Vecchi to Badoglio, 161, 194, 230, 26.6, 29.6, 30.6.1940, ACS, SPD/CO, Vᵃ Serie (Comando Supremo), bundles 2, 3 (folders carry Mussolini's *visto*).
21 Ciano, 3.7, 5.7.1940; GWB, 87–93; DDI,9,V,177, 179; Roatta letters, 7.7.1940; De Vecchi to Badoglio, 234, 4.7.1940, ACS, SPD/CO, Vᵃ Serie (Comando Supremo), bundle 3; Morin to Navy Ministry, 98042, 5.8.1940; De Vecchi to Navy Staff, 22745, 5.7.1940, AUSMM, Scacchiere Egeo – 1940, bundle 1.
22 DDI,9,V,109; according to Roatta letters, 5.7.1940, Mussolini proposed to send 6 regiments of Bersaglieri and 6 of regular infantry, without divisional troops – a force purely symbolic in function. For the German refusal, ADAP,D,X,166.
23 Roatta to Vercellino, 846, 7.6.1940, NARS T-821/112/000725–26; DDI,9,V,53; Roatta letters, 7.7, 9.7, 12.7.1940; for the downgrading and abandonment of the plan, NARS T-821/112/000667–69; Roatta letters, 20.9.1940.
24 ADAP,D,X,73; DDI,9,V,161; for the documents, Germany, Auswärtiges

Amt, *Die Geheimakten des französischen Generalstabes* (*Deutsches Weissbuch Nr. 6*) (Berlin, 1941), and *Dokumente zum Konflikt mit Jugoslawien und Griechenland* (*Deutsches Weissbuch Nr. 7*) (Berlin, 1941).

25 Roatta letters, 3.7.1940; Badoglio to Graziani, Pricolo, 1089, 4.7.1940, NARS T-821/126/000751; Ciano, 5.7.1940.

26 Ciano, 7.7.1940; for the conversation, ADAP,D,X,129, DDI,9,V,200.

27 Halder, II, p. 21.

28 Ciano, 11.7.1940, and the postscript to DDI,9,V,200; also Erich Kordt, *Nicht aus den Akten* (Stuttgart, 1940), p. 393; Alfieri, *Due dittatori*, p. 73.

29 DDI,9,V,201.

30 DDI,9,V,242; ADAP,D,X,166.

31 Anweisung No. 547, 17.7.1940, BA, Sammlung Brammer, Z.Sg. 101.

32 Gayda, "L'ultimo conto," *Il Giornale d'Italia*, 15.7.1940.

33 *Chicago Daily News*, 16.7.1940; also the Associated Press story in (among others) *The Los Angeles Times*, 16.7.1940; Ciano, 22.7.1940.

34 (Hitler speech) Domarus, *Hitler*, pp. 1540–59; Otto Meissner, *Staatssekretär unter Ebert – Hindenburg – Hitler* (Hamburg, 1950), p. 549; (Churchill speech) *The Times* (London), 15.7.1940; DDI,9,V,272; Ciano 19.7, 22.7.1940 (emphasis in original).

35 See Martin, *Friedensinitiativen*, pp. 294–9, 303–4; Makins minute, 16.7.1940; Kelly to Halifax, No. 365, 8.7.1940, PRO FO 371/24407, C 7578; meeting of the War Cabinet, 10.7.1940, PRO CAB 65; ADAP,D,X,220.

36 Draft in Churchill, *Their Finest Hour*, pp. 223–4; final version: meeting of the War Cabinet, 8.8.1940, Confidential Annex, PRO CAB 65.

37 Martin, *Friedensinitiativen*, pp. 318–19; Churchill, *Their Finest Hour*, p. 222.

38 Mallet to Cadogan, No. 1016, 9.9.1940; Halifax to Mallet, no. 737, 11.9.1940, PRO FO 371/24408, C 9598; meeting of the War Cabinet, 11.9.1940, Confidential Annex, PRO CAB 65; Cadogan, *Diaries*, pp. 325–6.

39 Phillips (Rome) to Hull, No. 763, 28.7.1940, NARS, State, 740.0011 European War 1939/4873; DDI9,V,365.

40 DDI,9,V,368, 376; Lanza, *Berlino*, p. 158; Kelly to Halifax, No. 644 (R), 9.8.1940, PRO FO 371/24408, C 8325.

41 All from Lanza, *Berlino*, p. 149.

42 Ciano, 13.7.1940 (see also 16.7.1940).

43 *OO*, XXIX, p. 78; Department of Publicity in Enemy Countries, "Analysis of Italian Propaganda, July 1st–16th 1940," PRO FO 371/24956, R 6863.

44 Mario De Monte, *Uomini ombra* (Rome, 1955), pp. 30–4; also Weichold's report, n. 48 below. USMM, *Le azioni navali*, I, is silent on the subject.

45 Partial text, USMM, *Le azioni navali*, p. 116.

46 Viscount Cunningham of Hyndhope, *A Sailor's Odyssey* (New York, 1951), p. 263.

47 Santoro, *L'Aeronautica italiana*, I, pp. 416ff, and Pricolo, *La Regia Aeronautica*, pp. 249ff.

48 Weichold to OKM, B. No. Gkos. 55/40, 10.7.1940, GNR PG 32211.

49 Cunningham, *A Sailor's Odyssey*, p. 263.

50 Cavagnari to Mussolini, 14.4.1940, USMM, *L'organizzazione*, p. 352, and USMM, *Le azioni navali*, p. 27.

51 Churchill, *Their Finest Hour*, pp. 376–7; Playfair, *Mediterranean*, I, p. 124.

52 Roatta to Graziani, 11.7.1940, ACS, Graziani, bundle 40/B; Roatta letters,

11.7.1940; for the directive, USE, *La preparazione*, pp. 205–6; original in ACS, Graziani, bundle 45.

53 USMM, *Le azioni navali*, ch. 6; Playfair, *Mediterranean*, I, pp. 156–9; Ciano, 22.7.1940.

54 KTB 1/SKL,A,11, 29.7.1940, GNR PG 32031; Playfair, *Mediterranean*, I, p. 163.

55 Santoro, *L'aeronautica italiana*, I, pp. 382–4; USMM, *I mezzi d'assalto*, ch. 2.

56 USMM, *Le azioni navali*, pp. 188–9.

57 KTB 1/SKL,A,12, 31.8.1940, GNR PG 32032.

58 KTB 1/SKL,A,13, 1.9.1940, GNR PG 32033, referring to a Weichold report.

59 Löwisch to OKM, OKW, B. Nr. Gkdos 3140/40, GNR PG 45171; Ciano, 7.9.1940.

60 USMM, *Le azioni navali*, pp. 34–6.

61 Naval staff memorandum, 22.9.1940, ACS, MAG, bundle "A.S. – 1940. Ispezione Generale Pricolo – Relazioni."

62 The Aosta were a collateral branch of the Savoia, descended from Amedeo I, Duke of Aosta, second son of the first King of Italy, Victor Emmanuel II. Emanuele Filiberto, the viceroy's father, had been decidedly more philo-Fascist than Victor Emmanuel III, and had apparently harbored the ambition of supplanting his cousin at the time of the March on Rome.

63 Mussolini to Teruzzi, 16.3.1940, in De Biase, *L'Impero di "faccetta nera"*, pp. 140–1. Amedeo's daily reports for 1938–9 show a steady decline in "rebel" activity (ACS, MAG, "Rapportini di S.E. il Vicerè").

64 USE, *La guerra in Africa Orientale (giugno 1940—novembre 1941)* (Rome, 1971), pp. 32–5.

65 For Italian planning, Badoglio memorandum, 5.11.1935, in Rochat, *Militari e politici*, pp. 481–5; USE, *Africa Orientale*, pp. 20–6; and above all Sullivan, "A Thirst for Glory," ch. 5.

66 Badoglio to Amedeo, 61, 9.6.1940, NARS T-821/137/001085.

67 Amedeo to Badoglio, 54385, 330478, 23.6, 26.6.1940; Badoglio to Amedeo, 1/910, 24.6.1940, NARS T-821/137/000972, 139/001077–79, 137/000963.

68 USE, *Africa Orientale*, pp. 41–66; Badoglio to Amedeo, 1035, 1068, 1.7, 3.7.1940, NARS T-821/137/000914, 000897.

69 Amedeo to Badoglio, 54602, 54760, 26.6, 28.6.1940, *ibid.*, 000953; 000935; also the Gaullist account of the Djibouti events in Edgard de Larminat, *Chroniques irrévérencieuses* (Paris, 1962), pp. 93–113.

70 Larminat, *Chroniques*, pp. 98–100.

71 Canevari, *Retroscena della disfatta*, p. 749.

72 Amedeo to Badoglio, 331030, 331305, and unnumbered, 14.7, 23.7, 2.8.1940, NARS T-821/140/000080–88, 139/000306–09; Mussolini to Amedeo, 1383, 19.7.1940, *ibid.*, 000076; Badoglio to Amedeo, 1407 Op., 20.7.1940, *ibid.*, 000075; Amedeo to Pintor (Armistice Commission, Turin) and Badoglio, 331114, 16.7.1940, *ibid.*, 137/000820–24; Larminat, *Chroniques*, pp. 108–9.

73 Larminat, *Chroniques*, pp. 112–12; Badoglio to Amedeo, 1277/A, 4.8.1940 (copy to Armistice Commission, Turin), NARS T-821/137/000693: "For Gentilhomme [*sic*] and companions, should they fall into your hands, apply to the letter (integralmente) paragraph 14 of the Armistice Convention – Badoglio"

(paragraph 14 prescribed "the treatment reserved for illegal combatants" for French citizens leaving "the national territory in order to participate in any way in hostilities against Italy") (DDI,9,V,95, pp. 79–80).

74 Badoglio to Amedeo, 1748, 7.8.1940, NARS T-821/137/000672: ". . . occorre darci sotto. Su da bravi" (roughly: "up and at 'em").

75 USE, *Africa Orientale,* pp. 47–66; Playfair, *Mediterranean,* I, pp. 171–9; Churchill, *Their Finest Hour,* p. 370; Badoglio (Mussolini) to Amedeo, 2010, 20.8.1940, NARS T-821/137/000568; also Amedeo's equally fulsome reply, *ibid.,* 000567.

76 Amedeo to Badoglio, 2.8.1940, *ibid.,* 139/000306–09; Playfair, *Mediterranean,* I, pp. 182–3; for Haile Selassie's arrival (3 July), Badoglio to Amedeo, 1472, 24.7.1940, NARS T-821/137/000779; Comando Supremo memorandum, 30.7.1940, *ibid.,* 000715.

77 Amedeo to Badoglio, 8.8.1940, *ibid.,* 139/001071–73.

78 All from Badoglio to Amedeo, 1882, 13.8.1940, *ibid.,* 139/000274–76. A short excerpt from this vital document appears in USE, *Africa Orientale,* pp. 67–8, but the official historians have tampered with the section printed, and suppressed the most interesting passages entirely. For Badoglio's information on German plans, Marras to SIM, 1321/A, 7.8.1940, AUSE, Marras file.

79 Badoglio to Amedeo, 2105, 26.8.1940, *ibid.,* 139/000260–262.

80 "Voi che siete un piemontese del Monferrato capirete benissimo un piemontese delle Langhe, che sarei poi io." (Trezzani to Badoglio, 1212, 25.8.1940, NARS T-821/139/000312–316).

81 Marginal note in Armellini's hand: "This is the grave deficiency about which nothing was done when something could have been done."

82 Marginal note in Badoglio's hand: "That's just it!" ("È proprio così!").

83 Amedeo to Badoglio, 2.9.1940, USE, *Africa Orientale,* p. 73.

84 Vehicle figures: USE, *La preparazione,* p. 193; Hitler: KTB/OKW, p. 6.

85 For the British order of battle, Playfair, *Mediterranean,* I, pp. 188–9.

86 USE, *La preparazione,* pp. 91, 107–9; *idem, La prima offensiva britannica in Africa Settentrionale* (Rome, n.d.), pp. 11, 299; Rochat, "Mussolini, chef de guerre," pp. 55–7; Giovanni De Luna, *Benito Mussolini* (Milan, 1978), p. 129.

87 See the description of the booty captured in December: Alan Moorehead, *The Desert War* (London, 1965), pp. 24–6.

88 Minutes, 18.8.1940, USE, *La preparazione,* p. 221; Berti to subordinates, 01/6411, 13.8.1940; Graziani to Berti, 01/207429, 19.8.1940, ACS, Graziani, bundle 42.

89 Badoglio to Graziani, 3.7.1940, USE, *La preparazione,* p. 98.

90 Minutes, 4.7.1940, *ibid.,* pp. 202–5; memorandum listing Berti's objections, 6.7.1940; Graziani to Berti, 01/206.265, 7.7.1940, ACS, Graziani, bundle 45.

91 ADAP,D,X,166; DDI,9,V,242; Löwisch to SKL, 079 19/7 1820, 19.7.1940, GNR PG 33316; Badoglio to Graziani, 14.7, 15.7, 19.7.1940, USE, *La preparazione,* pp. 207–8.

92 Graziani to Badoglio, 23.7.1940, with enclosed memorandum; Badoglio to Graziani, 26.7.1940, USE, *La preparazione,* pp. 209–16; Mussolini to Graziani, 1507, 26.7.1940, ACS, Graziani, bundle 45.

93 Graziani to Badoglio, 03, 29.9.1940, ACS, Graziani, bundle 45, partially

printed in USE, *La preparazione,* pp. 102–3; also Graziani to Badoglio, 01/206850, 29.7.1940, ACS, Graziani, bundle 45.

94 Graziani diary, 30.6-7.9.1940, passim.

95 Ciano, 4.8.1940; Badoglio to Graziani, 1284/A, 4.8.1940, ACS, Graziani, bundle 45.

96 Marras to Soddu, 25.7.1940, AUSE, Marras file; also Roatta to Graziani, 27.7.1940, ACS, Graziani, bundle 40 B.

97 Ciano, 5.8.1940; for a similar tirade (Council of Ministers, 10.8.1940); Bottai, *Vent'anni,* p. 189.

98 Bottai, *Vent'anni,* p. 184.

99 Informant report (Milan), 20.6.1940, ACS, PNF/SPP, bundle 6 (marked *Partito* in Mussolini's hand); also informant report, 12.6.1940, *ibid.;* "Weekly Resumé (No. 44) of the Naval, Military and Air Situation . . . ," WP(40)250, 5.7.1940, PRO CAB 66/9.

100 Phillips to Hull, 715, 12.7.1940, NARS, State, 740.0011 European War 1939/4596; Likus report (Dienststelle Ribbentrop) (seen by Ribbentrop and Hitler), GFM 79/59326–32; Questore, Naples, to Bocchini, 31.7.1940, ACS, MI, DGS/DAGR 1941 (Cat.K1B N.15), bundle 53; Informant report, Milan, 7.7.1940, ACS, PNF/SPP, bundle 6.

101 Likus report, 17.7.1940, GFM 79/59326–32; Questore, Modena, and Questore, Pavia, to Bocchini, 1.8.1940, ACS, MI, DGPS/DAGR 1941 (Cat. K1B N.15), bundle 53.

102 Informant reports, Milan, 25.7, 14.8.1940, ACS, PNF/SPP, bundle 6; also the many reports on the air raids in ACS, MI, DGPS/DPP, bundle 243; Likus report, 17.7.1940, GFM 79/59326–32.

103 See the criticism of Canevari, *Retroscena della disfatta,* pp. 257–9.

104 Soddu to subordinates, 61920, 27.8.1940, ACS,PAC, Sezione Speciale, bundle 67, folder "Circolari Varie 1940"; for the demobilization, see chapter 5.1.

105 Lanza, *Berlino,* p. 168.

106 Graziani memorandum, "Precedenti," 5.8.1940, ACS, Graziani, bundle 45 (emphasis in original); USE, *La preparazione,* p. 104; Graziani, *Africa Settentrionale,* pp. 63–4; Rintelen to OKH, No. 117/40 g.Kdos., 7.8.1940, IWM AL 1007.

107 All from Ciano, 8.8.1940; see also De Bono diaries, 10.8.1940, notebook 44, ACS.

108 DDI,9,V,368, 376; Ciano, 8.8.1940; Marras to SIM, 1321/A, 7.8.1940, AUSE, Marras file; Teucci to Pricolo, 11.8.1940, ACS, MAG, 1940, bundle 63.

109 Ciano, 18.8.1940 (see also 17.8); Mussolini to Graziani, 19.8.1940, USE, *La preparazione,* pp. 105–6.

110 Graziani to Badoglio, 23.8.1940, USE, *La preparazione,* pp. 221–2; for the conference minutes, *ibid.,* 216–21.

111 See Graziani to Mussolini, 6.9.1940 (but not sent), Graziani, *Africa Settentrionale,* pp. 272–5; Graziani to Badoglio, 3031, 20.8.1940, ACS, Graziani, bundle 45; Graziani to Berti, 20.8.1940, USE, *La preparazione,* p. 223; Graziani diary, 20.8.1940; Roatta letters, 22.8.1940.

112 Graziani–Berti–Badoglio correspondence, 21.8–25.8.1940, USE, *La preparazione,* pp. 223–30; Graziani diary, 15.8, 22.8, 25.8, 26.8.1940.

113 Ciano, 22.8.1940; for the speech, *The Times* (London), 21.8.1940;

DDI,9,V,475; for Hitler's views, Wilhelm von Leeb, *Tagebuchaufzeichnungen und Lagebetrachtungen aus zwei Weltkriegen* (Stuttgart, 1976), pp. 251–2.

114 Ciano, 27.8, 1.9.1940; Badoglio to Graziani, 29.8.1940, USE, *La preparazione*, p. 230.

115 Graziani diary, 31.8.1940. Graziani's feeling that he was the victim of savage and unrelenting persecutors (see his papers in ACS, passim, particularly his marginal comments) was a salient feature of his unattractive personality. It is a boon to the historian, for it drove Graziani to assemble his vast and fascinating collection of correspondence, a veritable cross-section of Italian colonial and military policy, in order to assure a steady supply of *pièces justificatives* with which to ward off attack by his numerous real and imagined enemies.

116 Graziani diary, 1.9–7.9.1940; Graziani to Badoglio, 2.9, 5.9, 7.9.1940, USE, *La preparazione*, pp. 231–6; Badoglio to Graziani, 2319, 5.9.1940, ACS, Graziani, bundle 45.

117 Badoglio to Graziani, 7.9.1940, USE, *La preparazione*, p. 236; Ciano, 7.9, 14.9.1940; Armellini, *Diario*, pp. 78, 82.

118 Graziani diary, 7.9.1940 (emphasis in original); quoted partially and inaccurately in Graziani, *Africa Settentrionale*, pp. 72–3.

119 Graziani, *Africa Settentrionale*, pp. 74–82; USE, *La preparazione*, pp. 126–32, 228–45.

120 Churchill, *Their Finest Hour*, p. 401; Melchiorri to Graziani, 22.9.1940, ACS, Graziani, bundle 42.

121 Ciano, 11.9, 14.9.1940; Badoglio to Soddu, 2218/A, 14.9.1940; Ciano to Graziani, 28162, 18.9.1940; Graziani to Ciano, 21.9.1940, ACS, Graziani, bundle 53.

122 Ciano, 16.9.1940; Mussolini to Graziani, 2552, 17.9.1940, ACS, Graziani, bundle 45; Graziani to Badoglio, 17.9, 18.9.1940, USE, *La preparazione*, pp. 143–4, 249–50.

123 Roatta to Badoglio, 145, 10.7.1940, and enclosure, NARS T-821/126/000589–602; unsigned Comando Supremo memorandum, 11.7.1940, *ibid.*, 000581–82.

124 Comando Supremo memorandum, 12.7.1940, NARS T-821/126/000586–88; Roatta letters, 7.7, 12.7.1940; Roatta to Badoglio, 156, 15.7.1940, NARS T-821/126/000784–93; Comando Supremo note by Montezemolo, 12.7.1940, *ibid.*, 000608.

125 Roatta to Badoglio, 154, 15.7.1940, NARS T-821/126/000784–91; Roatta letters, 16.7, 20.7.1940; Roatta to Graziani, 23.7.1940, ACS, Graziani, bundle 40 B.

126 Rintelen to OKH, No.107, 22.7.1940, IWM AL 1007; Roatta letters, 22.7, 24.7, 25.7.1940; Roatta to major commanders, 5200, 27.7.1940, NARS T-821/112/000434–35; Roatta to Badoglio, 12581, 2.8.1940; Soddu to Roatta, 135441, 6.8.1940, NARS T-821/126/000762–67.

127 Marginal note in Badoglio's hand, signed "B," on Comando Supremo memorandum, 3.8.1940, *ibid.*, 000770; Breccia, *Jugoslavia*, pp. 314–19.

128 Ciano, 4.8, 6.8.1940. Proponents of the "balance of power" interpretation of Mussolini's policy (Toscano, *Designs in Diplomacy*, pp. 150, 246 [but qualified, pp. 170–1]; André, *La guerra in Europa*, p. 396; Cliadakis, "Neutrality and War in Italian Policy, 1940–41") have neglected this passage, which suggests that Mussolini's primary aim in seeking rapprochement with the Soviet Union

was to remove a potential obstacle to the destruction of Yugoslavia, not to counterbalance the influence of Italy's over-mighty ally, or (as Cliadakis also suggests) to head off an Anglo-Russian understanding, a danger that did not occur to the Italian leaders until Ambassador Rosso in Moscow brought it up in early September (DDI,9,V,543).

129 ADAP,D,X,10,290.

130 Badoglio to Roatta, [8].8.1940, NARS T-821/126/000781; Comando Supremo memorandum for Mussolini, 8.8.1940 (also not sent), 000777–79; Montezemolo note, 8.8.1940, 000617; Badoglio to Roatta, 1848, 11.8.1940, 000625; Roatta letters, 9.8.1940; ADAP,D,X,343.

131 GWB, 94; De Vecchi to Badoglio, 326, 12.7.1940, ACS, SPD/CO, Vª Serie (Comando Supremo), bundle 4 (folder carries Mussolini's *visto*); Palairet to Cunningham, 12.7.1940, PRO FO 371/24922, R 6771, requesting the ship's removal from Greek waters; MacVeagh (Athens) to Hull, 165, 174, 10.7, 19.7.1940, NARS, State, 740.0011 European War 1939/4563, 4758; Morin to Cavagnari, 02465, 12.7.1940, ACS, MMG, bundle 105; DDI,9,V,232.

132 Badoglio to De Vecchi, 12588, 12.7.1940, AUSMM, Scacchiere Egeo – 1940, bundle 1.

133 Roatta letters, 16.7.1940.

134 Löwisch to SKL, Nr. GKds. 2250/40, 19.7.1940, GNR PG 45098.

135 De Vecchi to Badoglio, 390, 399, 414, 19.7, 24.7.1940, ACS, SPD/CO, Vª Serie (Comando Supremo), bundle 5 (folder carries Mussolini's *visto*).

136 Morin to Cavagnari, 03214, 30.7.1940, AUSMM, Scacchiere Egeo, bundle 1; Morin to Cavagnari, 51529, 2.8.1940, ACS, MMG, bundle 105; GWB, 101, 107.

137 Ciano, 3.8.1940; Mackensen to AA, No. 1479, 8.8.1940, GFM 449/222752; GWB, 104; Roatta letters, 3.8.1940; DDI,9,V,374; Grazzi, *Il principio della fine,* pp. 143–4.

138 Mackensen to AA, No. 1499, 12.8.1940, GFM 449/222757.

139 Mackensen to AA, No. 1458, 6.8.1940, GFM 449/222751; GWB, 109, 110, 115; Ciano, 10.8.1940; Pannwitz to AA, No. 30, GFM B14/B002192.

140 DDI,9,V,386; Ciano, 10.8, 11.8.1940.

141 Grazzi, *Il principio della fine,* pp. 149–51, 155, GWB, 111.

142 Visconti Prasca, *Io ho aggredito la Grecia,* p. 32; Ciano, 12.8.1940.

143 Visconti Prasca, *Io ho aggredito la Grecia,* pp. 32–3.

144 Roatta letters, 13.8.1940; Visconti Prasca memorandum, 13.8.1940, in Rossi, *Mussolini,* p. 84; Visconti Prasca, *Io ho aggredito la Grecia,* pp. 34–6; Badoglio to Roatta, 1889, 14.8.1940, NARS T-821/126/000627.

145 Roatta letters, 13.8.1940; *Allianz Hitler – Horthy – Mussolini,* 89.

146 Roatta letters, 13.8.1940; Comando Supremo memorandum, 16.8.1940, NARS T-821/127/000382.

147 Bürkner (OKW) to Attachéabteilung (OKH), No. 19/40 g.Kdos., 25.7.1940, BAMA, H2/599.

148 Mackensen to AA, No. 1499, 12.8.1940, GFM 449/222757; Anweisung No. 704, 12.8.1940, BA, Sammlung Brammer, Z.Sg. 101.

149 ADAP,D,X,333, 334; Niebelschutz minute, 14.8.1940, PA, Staatssekretär, Aufzeichnungen über Diplomatenbesuche, Bd. 6; DDI,9,V,413.

150 Grandson of the great Bismarck.

151 Mackensen to AA, No. 1515, 14.8.1940, GFM B14/B002170–71.

152 GWB, 120, 129; Palairet to Halifax, No. 685, 17.8.1940, PRO FO 371/24917, R 7109.

153 Ciano, 15.8.1940; Weichold to SKL, 0716, 16.8.1940, GNR PG 34384; Supermarina, Diario Storico, 16.8.1940, AUSMM; USMM, *I sommergibili in Mediterraneo*, I, p. 80 and map 5.

154 See De Vecchi, "Una sconcertante storia del fascismo. Mussolini vero," episode 19, *Tempo*, 15.3.1960, pp. 26–7, and Mario Cervi, *The Hollow Legions. Mussolini's Blunder in Greece, 1940–1941* (Garden City, N.Y., 1971), pp. 30–3.

155 DDI,9,V,420, 429.

156 Halder, II, pp. 63–4; KTB/OKW, pp. 33, 36; Canaris (OKW) to Attachéabteilung (OKH), No. 92/40, 15.8.1940, IWM AL 1007 (see also ADAP,D,X,343 n. 4).

157 ADAP,D,X,353; DDI,9,V,431. Creveld, *Hitler's Strategy*, pp. 19–20, quotes the following exchange: " 'Was he right in assuming that the same [veto] applied to Greece?' [asked Alfieri]. 'Yes, yes, of course,' replied an astonished Ribbentrop, who had obviously not expected this question and was caught with his pants down." According to Creveld, the German veto on Italian action against Greece was thus solely the result of a "blunder" by Alfieri, who had gratuitously assumed that the Germans disapproved of *all* Italian actions in the southeast.

Actually, the dialogue quoted appears nowhere in either German or Italian record, and Ribbentrop himself had originally raised the Greek issue, rather pointedly, three days before. Nor did his reported remark that it was the "paramount interest" of the Axis to maintain the status quo, or German attempts in the ensuing week to drive the point home (see below), testify to any lack of concern about a possible Italian action.

158 Ciano, 17.8.1940.

159 DDI,9,V,435, 445; ADAP,D,X,357, 367.

160 Armellini, *Diario*, pp. 57, 59; Roatta letters, 18.8, 20.8, 22.8.1940; Badoglio to Roatta, 2016, 10.8.1940, NARS T-821/126/000686–87; note in Badoglio's hand, signed "B," on Comando Supremo memorandum, 19.8.1940, "Direttive per Emergenza 'E,' " 000583–85: "These are the directives: put it to bed."

161 Armellini, *Diario*, pp. 57–8; Roatta letters, 18.8, 19.8.1940; Visconti Prasca to Soddu, Roatta, 14420, 16.8.1940; Badoglio to Visconti Prasca, 1944, 16.8.1940, NARS T-821/127/000381, 000370–71.

162 DDI,9,V,442.

163 Ciano, 18.8.1940; Badoglio to Roatta, 2016, 2017, 20.8.1940, NARS T-821/126/000686–87; 127/000141; Armellini, *Diario*, pp. 59–60.

164 KTB/OKW, p. 43 (referring to the previous days).

165 DDI,9,V,451; also 506; Rintelen to OKH, 142/40 g/Kdos., 21.8.1940, IWM AL 1007; KTB/OKW, p. 54; Halder, II, p. 71.

166 Palairet to Halifax, No. 713, 21.8.1940; Halifax to Palairet, No. 553, 24.8.1940, PRO FO 371/24917, R 7238, R 7225; Koliopoulos, *Greece*, pp. 138–41.

167 ADAP,D,X,387, 394; MacVeagh to Hull, 26.8,29.8.1940; Kirk to Hull, 29.8.1940, FRUS, 1940, III, pp. 539–41.

168 Ciano, 22.8.1940; DDI,9,V,467, 484, 469 and note 2; Roatta letters, 22.8.1940; Roatta to Navy Staff, 04258/432, 23.8.1940, NARS T-821/127/000362–63.

169 Roatta to Graziani, 27.8.1940, ACS, Graziani, bundle 40 B; Visconti Prasca to Roatta, 023680, 21.8.1940, NARS T-821/127/000359 (simultaneously, the alpine division "Julia" was moving south from the Yugoslav border by forced marches [DDI,9,V,483]); Roatta to Visconti Prasca, 1618, 1650, 22.8, 23.8.1940, NARS T-821/127/000360–61.

170 Roatta to Badoglio, 1800, 2132, 26.8, 27.8.1940; Badoglio note on Comando Supremo memorandum, 27.8.1940; NARS T-821/127/000351–54, 000372; Roatta to Navy Staff, 3675, 29.8.1940, NARS T-821/127/000349; Roatta letters, 28.8.1940.

171 All from Comando Supremo memorandum, "Direttive per le operazioni in Albania," with Badoglio hand note, 11.9.1940, NARS T-821/127/000197–200. For Badoglio on airpower in Ethiopia, Rochat, *Badoglio,* pp. 656–7.

172 See USMM, *La difesa del traffico con l'Albania, la Grecia, e l'Egeo* (Rome, 1965), p. 15; Badoglio to Roatta, Cavagnari, 2215, 31.8.1940, NARS T-821/127/000345.

173 Roatta to Visconti Prasca, 2020, 31.8.1940, NARS T-821/127/000342–43.

174 Roatta to Visconti Prasca, 2101, 2970, 4.9, 26.9.1940, NARS T-821/127/000195–96, 000192.

175 KTB/OKW, pp. 54, 59.

176 Mackensen to AA, No. 371/40 g., 26.7.1940, GFM 2281/480620–21; "Segnalazioni," 13.7.1940; Rintelen to OKH, 117/40 g.Kdos., 7.8.1940, IWM AL 1007.

177 Roatta letters, 10.8, 22.8.1940 (emphasis in original).

178 *Ibid.,* 29.8, 31.8.1940; Armellini, *Diario,* p. 68; Santoro, *L'aeronautica italiana,* I, p. 125.

179 Roatta letters, 9.9, 10.9.1940; Ciano, 6.9.1940; ADAP,D,XI,42. An outburst of Soviet ill-temper at apparent Italian procrastination (and Italy's participation in the Hungarian-Rumanian arbitration and subsequent anti-Soviet territorial guarantee of Rumania) also impelled Mussolini and Ciano to look again toward Moscow: DDI,9,V,534, 537, 543, and Toscano, *Designs in Diplomacy,* pp. 182–4.

180 Armellini to Santoro, 2423, 10.9.1940; Badoglio note on Benini to Pricolo, 19520/2784, 5.9.1940, NARS T-821/127/000331, 000335.

181 Badoglio to Roatta, Cavagnari, Pricolo, 2458, "Progetti operativi," 12.9.1940, NARS T-821/000639–45, with Badoglio marginal note; Roatta letters, 13.9.1940; DDI,9,V,533; ADAP,D,X,395; Heeren to AA, Nos. 602, 608, 686, 15.8, 17.8, 16.9.1940, GFM 230/152297–99, 152315–16.

182 Breccia, *Jugoslavia,* pp. 337–8, n. 76; Armellini, *Diario,* pp. 78, 83; Ciano, 14.9.1940.

183 Roatta letters, 10.9.1940; Badoglio note on NARS T-821/127/000639.

184 Note in Badoglio's hand for Roatta, undated (but 11.9.1940), NARS T-821/126/000648; Roatta letters, 13.9.1940; Badoglio to Roatta, Cavagnari, Pricolo, 2458, "Progetti operativi," 12.9.1940, NARS T-821/126/000639–45.

185 The literature is considerable, and divergent; see, in general, Hillgruber, *Hit-*

lers Strategie, pp. 166–78, and Hitler's own remarks in Leeb, *Tagebuchauf-zeichnungen*, pp. 251–2 (14.8.1940).

186 See Halder, II, pp. 99–100; Engel, *Heeresadjutant bei Hitler*, p. 87; for similar OKW and Navy views, KTB/OKW, p. 31; KTB 1/SKL,A,13, 10.9.1940, GNR PG 32033.

187 See Hillgruber, *Hitlers Strategie*, pp. 172–3.

188 KTB 1/SKL,A,13, 7.9.1940, GNR PG 32033.

189 KTB/OKW, pp. 70, 76; KTB 1/SKL,A,13, 14.9, 17.9.1940, GNR PG 32033.

190 See Hillgruber, *Hitlers Strategie*, pp. 192–203.

191 KTB 1/SKL,A,13, 6.9.1940, PG 32033; also Raeder minute, 7.9.1940, Gerhard Wagner, ed., *Lagevorträge der Oberbefehlshaber der Kriegsmarine vor Hitler 1939–1945* (Munich, 1972), p. 136; Jodl memorandum, 30.6.1940, International Military Tribunal, *Trial of the Major War Criminals*, XXVIII, pp. 301ff.

192 All from Halder, II, pp. 45–6.

193 *Ibid.*, pp. 47–9 (last quotation, p. 49) (emphasis in original).

194 Hillgruber, *Hitlers Strategie*, pp. 210–11.

195 "Ablenkungsmanöver," Halder, II, p. 47; "Zwischenaktion," Raeder minute, 31.7.1940, Wagner, ed., *Lagevorträge*, p. 128.

196 Hillgruber, *Hitlers Strategie*, pp. 390–2, 344–5, 571–2. For Hitler's expectations of an ultimate titanic struggle with the United States, Hillgruber, "Der Faktor Amerika in Hitlers Strategie 1938–1941," *Aus Politik und Zeitgeschichte*, B.19/66, 11.5.1966; Hildebrand, *Foreign Policy of the Third Reich*, pp. 21–2, 101–2, 106; Meir Michaelis, "World Power Status or World Dominion?" *The Historical Journal*, 15:2 (1972), pp. 331–60, and Jochen Thies, *Architekt der Weltherrschaft. Die "Endziele" Hitlers* (Düsseldorf, 1976), pp. 163–74.

197 See Hitler's later remark: Halder, II, p. 162.

198 KTB 1/SKL,A,13, 6.9.1940, GNR PG 32033; Raeder minute, 7.9.1940, Wagner, ed., *Lagevorträge*, p. 136; KTB/OKW, pp. 68–9; Halder, II, pp. 79, 100; ADAP,D,XI,66, 67, 70; Hillgruber, *Hitlers Strategie*, pp. 137–8, 185; Donald S. Detwiler, *Hitler, Franco und Gibraltar* (Wiesbaden, 1962), chs. 2–4.

199 Theo Sommer, *Deutschland und Japan zwischen den Mächten* (Tübingen, 1962), pp. 394–426; Ciano, 13.9.1940.

200 Ciano, 28.8, 1.9, 14.9.1940; Armellini, *Diario*, p. 83; See also De Bono diaries, 10.9.1940, notebook 44, ACS.

201 Rintelen to OKH, No. 158/40, 11.9.1940, IWM AL 1007.

202 Marras to Badoglio, 3.9.1940; Graziani to Roatta, 25.9.1940, USE, *La prima offensiva britannica*, pp. 26–9; Fleischmann minute, 3.9.1940, IWM AL 1007; KTB/OKW, p. 64; Badoglio to Roatta, 2364, 7.9.1940; Roatta to Graziani, 2427, 10.9.1940, ACS, Graziani, bundle 42.

203 Löwisch to SKL, B. Nr. Gkds. 3111/40, 19.9.1940, GNR PG 45171.

204 DDI,9,V,506; also Lanza, *Berlino*, p. 164.

205 DDI,9,V,557.

206 See DDI,9,V,223, 294, 311, 341, 355, 406, 461, 562; ADAP,D,X,243, 311, 320; XI,115, 173, 177, 181; Clodius minute, 6.8.1940, GFM B14/B002135–36; "Segnalazioni," 18.10, 22.10.1940; Anweisung No. 632, 28.7.1940, BA, Sammlung Brammer, Z.Sg. 101.

207 ADAP,D,X,407 and pp. 453–4; Halder, II, p. 80; Helmut Greiner, *Die oberste*

Wehrmachtführung 1939–1943 (Wiesbaden, 1951), p. 299; in general Hill-gruber, *Hitler, König Carol, und Marschall Antonescu.* (Wiesbaden, 1954), pp. 90–104.

208 KTB/OKW, p. 53; Hillgruber, *Hitler, König Carol, und Marschall Antonescu,* pp. 92–8.

209 Unsigned minute, "Rapporto ai giornalisti," 5.9.1940, ACS, MCP, bundle 75; DDI,9,V,569, 586, 587, 590, 603, 607; Fabricius to AA, No. 1584, 13.9.1940, GFM 271/177016; Weizsäcker minute for Ribbentrop, St.S. No. 703, 14.9.1940, GFM 271/177015.

210 DDI,9,V,590, 603, 607; Roatta letters, 20.9.1940.

211 Roatta, as late as 20 September, merely listed the continuation of the war "through the winter" as a "possibility" (Roatta letters).

CHAPTER 5

THE ATTACK ON GREECE

1 ADAP,D,XI,68; DDI,9,V,602; for the Rome conversations, ADAP,D,XI,73, 79, 83; DDI,9,V,617.

2 Puntoni, *Parla Vittorio Emanuele,* p. 19.

3 Hillgruber, *Hitlers Strategie,* pp. 282–3, suggests that "[t]he decision of Mus-solini to attack Greece was doubtless taken shortly after the visit of Ribbentrop in Rome." Creveld, *Hitler's Strategy,* p. 32, similarly argues that the upshot of the conversations amounted to "tacit German approval" for a move against Greece, a view that Langer and Gleason (*The Undeclared War, 1940–1941* [New York, 1953], p. 105) share. However, the most detailed analysis of the confer-ence (Schramm-von Thadden, *Griechenland,* pp. 88–91) concludes that ". . . Mussolini understood Ribbentrop's words as they were meant by the German side" – as a reaffirmation of August veto.

4 Graziani to Badoglio, 17.9.1940; Badoglio to Graziani, 18.9.1940, USE, *La preparazione,* pp. 143–4.

5 Badoglio to Graziani, 2617, 20.9.1940, ACS, Graziani, bundle 45; Armellini, *Diario,* p. 90; DDI,9,V,612; Badoglio to Goiran (Armistice Commission, Turin), 20.9.1940, AUSMM, CIAF, 1940, bundle 2.

6 Armellini, *Diario,* p. 91; Rintelen to OKH, 0591, 23.9.1940, IWM AL 1007; Löwisch to OKM, B. Nr. Chefs. 16/40, 23.9.1940, GNR PG 45098.

7 Printed in Canevari, *La guerra italiana,* II, pp. 185–7.

8 According to Armellini, this formulation was Mussolini's own: " 'Greece,' says the Duce in a memorandum of his – 'represents a problem that will be resolved at the peace table.' " (*Diario,* pp. 94–5). The document has not surfaced.

9 See Ciano, 24.9.1940; the British were indeed contemplating an amphibious riposte to the loss of Gibraltar – the seizure of the Canary Islands in order to contain German air and U-boat attacks on the north–south convoy routes; they foresaw no further operations in the Western Mediterranean after losing control of the Straits (J.R.M. Butler, *Grand Strategy,* II [London, 1957], pp. 239, 432–3).

10 No such document has surfaced; its conclusion was probably a product of Mar-ras's suggestion that logistical difficulties would provide the best defense against German importunity.

11 For the chequered career of the Corpo Aereo Italiano in Belgium, Santoro,

L'aeronautica italiana, I, ch. 6; for the German initiative, Ciano, 11.8.1940; Ministero dell'Aeronautica, "Appunto per il Duce" [probably by Pricolo], ACS, MAG, 1940, bundle 63; Lanza, *Berlino,* pp. 165–6.

12 De Luna, *Benito Mussolini,* p. 129; *idem,* Badoglio, p. 197.

13 Mack Smith, *Mussolini as Military Leader* (Reading, 1974), p. 29; also *idem, Mussolini's Roman Empire,* p. 231.

14 "Segnalazioni," 7.10.1940 (emphasis in original).

15 Roatta to Graziani, 24.10.1940, ACS, Graziani, bundle 40/B; also Roatta to Badoglio, 292, 19.11.1940, NARS T-821/127/000664–69, and Roatta, *Otto milioni di baionette,* p. 118. For the dismantling, Comando Supremo and Army Staff correspondence, NARS T-821/126/000637, 000652–61.

16 Pieri, "La stratégie italienne," p. 77, mentions pressure from the minister of agriculture (Giuseppe Tassinari) and from the agricultural organizations; for rationing and its repercussions, KTB 1/SKL,A,14, 11.10.1940, GNR PG 32034.

17 Soddu to Roatta, 146522/2-1-10C, 2.10.1940, NARS T-821/127/000609–11; Rossi, *Mussolini,* p. 77.

18 Badoglio note ("sta benissimo . . .") on Soddu memorandum, 1.10.1940; Badoglio to Soddu, 2838, 1.10.1940, NARS T-821/127/000625–27.

19 See Canevari, *Retroscena della disfatta,* pp. 655–8.

20 Roatta letters, 6–10.10.1940.

21 Graziani (autograph signature) to Soddu, 005742, 5.10.1940; Badoglio note on Comando Supremo memorandum attached, NARS T-821/127/000617–23.

22 Roatta to major commands, 006200, 15.10.1940, NARS T-821/354/001001ff; Rintelen report, 181/40 gKdos., 4.10.1940, GNR PG 33316.

23 For Roatta's orders, above, chapter 4.3; for the verbal directive, Badoglio's remark in Canevari, *La guerra italiana,* II, p. 186, and Roatta to Badoglio, 3310, 2.10.1940, NARS T-821/127/000125. Visconti Prasca's memoirs are silent on the subject.

24 Roatta to Visconti Prasca, 3302, 2.10.1940, NARS T-821/127/000126.

25 Badoglio to Roatta (copies to Soddu, Ciano), 2863, 3.10.1940; Comando Supremo note, 2.10.1940, NARS T-821/127/000320–21; Roatta to Visconti Prasca, 4.10.1940, Visconti Prasca, *Io ho aggredito la Grecia,* p. 44.

26 For a different interpretation, which ignores the 25 September service chiefs conference and the Roatta and Badoglio orders of early October, see Creveld, *Hitler's Strategy,* pp. 26–34.

27 See Churchill, *Their Finest Hour,* Book II, ch. 9; Bell, *A Certain Eventuality,* ch. 9; Albert Kammerer, *La passion de la flotte française* (Paris, 1951), pp. 517–23.

28 Halder, II, pp. 109, 114; KTB/OKW, pp. 89, 93.

29 All from Raeder minute, 26.9.1940, Wagner, ed., *Lagevorträge,* p. 143 (emphasis in original).

30 *Ibid.;* KTB/OKW, p. 93; Halder, II, p. 124. Hitler's formula apparently dated from late September (Etzdorf note, 27.9.1940, GFM 1247/337463).

31 Mackensen to AA, No. 2872, 4.10.1940, GFM 2366/489217–19.

32 ADAP,D,XI,124; Ciano, 27–28.9.1940.

33 ADAP,D,XI,135; handwritten addition on Weizsäcker's copy, GFM B14/B002263; Weizsäcker, *Erinnerungen* (Munich, 1950), pp. 302–3; *Weizsäcker-Papiere,* p. 220.

34 See Ciano, 30.7.1938.

35 ADSS,IV,97.

36 Kelly to Halifax, No. 1127, 15.10.1940, PRO FO 371/24891, R 7946 (Ciano to the Yugoslav minister, Rome, 2.10.1940); MacVeagh to Hull, No. 245, 25.9.1940, NARS, State, 740.0011 European War 1939/5731; Puntoni, *Parla Vittorio Emanuele*, p. 21.

37 Ciano, 27–28.9.1940; Lanza, *Berlino*, p. 171.

38 *Weizsäcker-Papiere*, p. 220; Jacomoni, *La politica dell'Italia*, p. 253; ADAP,D,XI,191; Ciano, 6.5.1941; Giuseppe Bastianini, *Uomini, Cose, Fatti* (Milan, 1959), p. 259.

39 DDI,9,V,639.

40 After the Germans destroyed Yugoslavia in April 1941, the Axis promoted the formation of a Croatian regime under Ante Pavelić, whom Ciano produced at the opportune moment from cold storage in Italy.

41 Graziani to Badoglio, 841, 24.9.1940, ACS, Graziani, bundle 42; Armellini, *Diario*, p. 97.

42 Graziani, "Cronistoria degli avvenimenti," 2.12.1940, ACS, Graziani, bundle 45. In his memoirs (*Africa Settentrionale*, pp. 100–2) Graziani printed the document with ex post facto emendations, and billed it as a "diary," which it was not.

43 See Armellini, *Diario*, pp. 98–9, and Badoglio to Amedeo, 1.10.1940 (NARS T-821/139/000137).

44 De Bono diaries, 9.11.1940, notebook 44, ACS (emphasis in original).

45 Informant report, Turin, 7.10.1940, ACS, PNF/SPP, bundle 25; KTB 1/SKL,A,14, 11.10.1940, GNR PG 32034; "Segnalazioni," 1.10.1940; Informant reports, Genoa, 11.7, 10.9.1940 (the latter marked "al Fed[erale]" in Mussolini's hand), ACS, PNF/SPP, bundle 1.

46 Ciano, 30.9, 2.10, 5.10.1940; Roatta to Graziani, 24.10.1940, ACS, Graziani, bundle 40/B.

47 Graziani, "Cronistoria degli avvenimenti," 2.12.1940, ACS, Graziani, bundle 45; Ciano, 2.10.1940.

48 For what follows, see (except where noted) ADAP,D,XI,149; also DDI,9,V,677.

49 For the antecedents, which date from the fall of 1939, Sommer, *Deutschland und Japan*, pp. 296–312; for the continental bloc conception, Hillgruber, *Hitlers Strategie*, pp. 42–3, 178–9, 238–42.

50 Ciano, 4.10.1940.

51 See Ciano, 21.6.1941.

52 For earlier German aspirations of this sort, Fischer, *Germany's Aims in the First World War*, pp. 102–3, 586–91; for German plans in 1940, Gerhard L. Weinberg, "German Colonial Plans and Policies, 1938–1942," in *Geschichte und Gegenwartsbewusstsein. Festschrift für Hans Rothfels* (Gottingen, 1966); Hildebrand, *Vom Reich zum Weltreich* (Munich, 1969); and, from the strategic point of view, Hillgruber, *Hitlers Strategie*, pp. 242–55.

53 See Creveld, *Hitler's Strategy*, pp. 33–9.

54 DDI,9,V,753.

55 Roatta letters, 11.10.1940. The context makes clear that the conversation took place before or during Mussolini's visit to the northern armies (6–10 October). The remainder of Roatta's account of the Brenner discussion tallies with Ciano's minute (DDI,9,V,677).

56 Hitler arrived at the Brenner at 1100 hours and left at 1430. The formal conversation lasted from 1130 to 1350, leaving ample time for a private Führer-Duce discussion (times from Der Sekretär des Führers, "Daten aus alten Notizbüchern (1933–1945)," U.S. Library of Congress, Manuscript Division, Captured German Documents, Item 472 E, and OO, XXX, p. 19n).

57 Halder, II, p. 186; for Mussolini's German, see Petersen, Hitler-Mussolini, pp. 347–8, n. 83, and Guariglia, Ricordi, p. 616.

58 KTB 1/SKL,A,14, 25.10.1940, GNR PG 32034; DDI,9,V,753.

59 Creveld, Hitler's Strategy, pp. 33–9.

60 DDI,9,V,677, p. 656.

61 Engel, Heeresadjutant bei Hitler, p. 88.

62 For Hitler's views on Ciano at this point, see Halder, II, p. 133. For German fears for the oilfields, ADAP,D,XI,151, GFM 182/85387, 85402, 85487–88, 85493, 85504, 85513; and the SD report, "Gegenwärtige Gefahr englischer Bombenangriffe auf das rumänische Ölgebiet," 10.10.1940 (Ribbentrop passed it to OKW), PA, Inland II Geheim, Bd. 422 (Rumänien). For British interest in bombing the oil wells, which for the moment were outside RAF range, see COS (40)13(0), 16.10.1940, PRO CAB 56/80, and meeting of the chiefs of staff, 17.10.1940, PRO CAB 79/7.

63 Ciano, 4.10.1940.

64 See Armellini, Diario, p. 105; USE, La prima offensiva britannica, pp. 30–1; Badoglio's covering letter, ACS, Graziani, bundle 42.

65 Armellini, Diario, p. 106.

66 DDI,9,V,514.

67 All from Roatta letters, 11–13.10.1940.

68 Badoglio to Graziani, 2922, 5.10.1940; Graziani to Badoglio, 40, 5.10.1940, ACS, Graziani, bundle 45.

69 ADAP,D,XI,80, 131.

70 Weizsäcker to Ribbentrop, 3.10.1940, GFM 272/177412–13.

71 ADAP,D,XI,209; Ribbentrop ordered that Zamboni receive no information other than that permissible under his own "eventual directives [erst zu erteilenden Weisungen]," and he requested immediate word if the Italian diplomat returned to the subject (Sonnleithner minute, 24.9.1940, GFM 272/177421; for the later conversation with Zamboni, Woermann minute, 25.9.1940, GFM 272/177422).

72 Better known by his postwar alias of Paul Carell.

73 Unsigned press section memorandum, 3.10.1940, GFM 182/85399. The previous day, the German and Italian press had received the order not to carry any reports on the matter: Anweisung No. 101, 2.10.1940, BA, Sammlung Brammer, Z.Sg. 101; Z.Sg. 102, v. 28, 2.10.1940; Claudio Matteini, Ordini alla Stampa (Rome, 1945), p. 125.

74 DDI,9,V,676 (visto by Mussolini); whether Mussolini saw it before or after his irate telephone call to Ciano is unclear. But it is likely that Mussolini stayed in touch with Rome through teletype links and daily courier runs.

75 Ciano, 8.10.1940; DDI,9,V,694.

76 Matteini, Ordini alla stampa, p. 126; DDI,9,V,699; Appunto by the duty officer [signature illegible], 13.10.1940, ACS, MCP, bundle 11, folder 147.

77 ADAP,D,XI,166, 167, 170.

78 Bismarck to AA, No. 1830, 10.10.1940, GFM 271/146884; ADAP, D,XI,192.

79 Armellini, *Diario*, pp. 110-11; Badoglio to Graziani, 3054, 12.10.1940, 1950 hrs., ACS, Graziani, bundle 45.

80 Telephone transcipt 12276, 8.10.1940, marked in Mussolini's hand *"Micup"* [send it to the Ministry of Popular Culture]; a further annotation suggests that the Ministry received and filed it on 12 October (ACS, MCP, bundle 165, folder 25).

81 Fabricius (Bucharest) to AA, Nr. 1765, 12.10.1940, GFM 1126/322010; DDI,9,V,714.

82 All from Ciano, 12.10.1940.

83 Graziani to Badoglio, Ciano (for Mussolini), 01/1500, 15.10.1940; Badoglio to Graziani, 3198, 18.10.1940, ACS, Graziani, bundle 45; Ciano, 16.10.1940.

84 Hillgruber, *Hitlers Strategie*, pp. 282-4 and nn. 17, 18, argues Mussolini's decision to attack Greece was unrelated to the German move into Rumania. He suggests that Ciano's "often cited and overvalued" diary entry of 12 October is neither "factually nor psychologically convincing" as an explanation of Mussolini's decision, which Hillgruber dates from the September Ribbentrop visit. Actually, the Ciano version is all too convincing, given the dictator's character, Hitler's apparent assurances at the Brenner and later silence, and the news that greeted Mussolini upon his return to Rome on 12 October: Graziani's renewed recalcitrance, the actual and definitive arrival of German troops in Bucharest, and, above all, Ghigi's disappointing reply to the plan to inspire a Rumanian request for Italian troops. Hillgruber also suggests that the text of the Ciano diaries has been "worked over" and is therefore none too reliable (see Appendix 1). The microfilm of the original (NARS T-586/25) reveals no obvious tampering, but the best guarantee of the authenticity of the 12 October entry is Ciano's obvious satisfaction that Mussolini had "finally [*ormai*]" taken the plunge, and the remark — of such unparalleled fatuousness in hindsight — that the operation seemed both "useful and easy."

Creveld, *Hitler's Strategy*, pp. 38 and 202, n. 86, similarly argues that "[t]he claim frequently heard that Mussolini was pushed into his war against Greece by the German occupation of Rumania . . . can, I think, be safely disregarded." But Creveld fails to put anything in its place, and contents himself with the observation that Mussolini, "[p]ossibly losing patience with Graziani," proceeded to order the attack. Presumably, this formula implies a causal connection — and an exclusive one at that — between Graziani's recalcitrance and Mussolini's decision. This interpretation, however, has all the disadvantages of Hillgruber's, and some of its own. Mussolini did not receive Graziani's final and definitive refusal to move until 16 October at the earliest, and on the 15th was still contemplating launching the Mersa Matruh attack before the end of the month (DDI,9,V,728). Thus Mussolini's wrath over Graziani's refusal to guarantee resumption of operations by 15 October is insufficient by itself to explain the decision to strike elsewhere.

85 See Mussolini's remark to Armellini (*Diario*, p. 157).

86 *Ibid.*, p. 111; DDI,9,V,676.

87 Badoglio to Roatta, Cavagnari, Pricolo, 3084, 13.10.1940, and the accompanying documents, NARS T-821/127/000313-17, which include a copy of a

Comando Supremo "Appunto per il Duce" of 18 September on the Navy's requirements; on the memorandum is the note "give the signal for the twelve days. B[adoglio]."

88 See chapter 4.3, and Rossi, Mussolini, pp. 79–83.

89 For the meeting and its aftermath, see (except where noted) Roatta letters, 14.10.1940.

90 Visconti Prasca, Io ho aggredito la Grecia, passim, but particularly pp. 47–9.

91 Badoglio, in Roatta letters, 13.10.1940; for Visconti Prasca's career as Badoglio's assistant during the Ethiopian war buildup, see Rochat, Militari e politici, passim, and Visconti Prasca, Io ho aggredito la Grecia, pp. 10–12.

92 For Mussolini on "expert" advice, see his Brenner remark about his generals (ADAP,D,XI,149, p. 218) and Armellini, Diario, p. 113.

93 Roatta letters, 15.10.1940 (emphasis in original).

94 For what follows, DDI,9,V,728 (emphasis supplied).

95 See particularly DDI,9,V,667, which Ciano forwarded to Badoglio at Mussolini's orders.

96 DDI,9,V,779; Grazzi, Il principio della fine, pp. 236–8.

97 Hillgruber, Hitlers Strategie, pp. 283–4; Hillgruber's interpretation fits Ciano's conception, but not Mussolini's until, perhaps, after 18 October, when Graziani's definitive refusal arrived.

98 Caracciolo, E poi?, p. 62.

99 See Visconti Prasca, Io ho aggredito la Grecia, p. 27.

100 For what follows (except where noted), Roatta letters, 15.10–18.10.1940 (emphasis supplied).

101 Graziani to Badoglio, 01/1500 Op., 15.10.1950, ACS, Graziani, bundle 45; also USE, La prima offensiva britannica, pp. 32–4.

102 Ciano, 17.10.1940.

103 Faldella, L'Italia, p. 283; also Rochat, Badoglio, p. 761.

104 Armellini, Diario, p. 117.

105 Favagrossa, Perché perdemmo la guerra, p. 146; Roatta letters, 17-18.10.1940; Armellini, Diario, p. 117; Ciano, 18.10.1940.

106 Ciano, 18.10.1940; Roatta letters, 18.10.1940; Armellini, Diario, p. 119; Badoglio to Roatta, Cavagnari, Pricolo, 3197, 18.10.1940, NARS T-821/127/000256.

107 Armellini, Diario, p. 119; Badoglio to Graziani, 3196, 3198, 18.10.1940, ACS, Graziani, bundle 45.

108 Pricolo to Roatta, B.01709, 18.10.1940; Comando Supremo, "Appunto per il Duce," 15.10.1940, annex 2; Pricolo to 4th Air Zone and Air Force Command, Albania, 02038, 25.10.1940, NARS T-821/127/000117-18, 000293-94, 000250-54.

109 Roatta letters, 15.10-19.10.1940; Roatta to Badoglio, 10274/D, 18.10.1940; Roatta to major commands, 08420/407, 19.10.1940, NARS T-821/127/000112-115, 000276-79.

110 See anonymous memorandum, n.d. [but 1940–1] in ACS, SPD/CR, bundle 69, folder "Roatta, Generale Mario"; Visconti Prasca, Io ho aggredito la Grecia, pp. 47–9, 81–5.

111 Roatta to Visconti Prasca, 08395/407, 19.10.1940; Visconti Prasca, Io ho aggredito la Grecia, pp. 81–5 (see also Canevari, Retroscena della disfatta, pp.

659–62, 679n); Badoglio to Ciano, 3254, 21.10.1940, NARS T-821/127/000119; Navy staff memorandum, 278, 1.11.1940, AUSMM, Maricotraf, bundle "Trasporti in Albania."

112 DDI,9,V,738, 746.

113 Comando Supremo memorandum, "Grecia. Riepilogo situazione militare al 15. ottobre 1940-XVIII"; Comando Supremo memorandum, 24.10.1940, NARS T-821/127/000221-23, 000246.

114 Roatta letters, 18.10, 24.10.1940; Roatta to Visconti Prasca, 08395/407, 19.10.1940, Visconti Prasca to Roatta, 025008, 21.10.1940, Roatta to Visconti Prasca, 4402, 24.10.1940, NARS T-821/127/000284, 000259-60.

115 Rossi, *Mussolini*, p. 103; Roatta letters, 26.10.1940; Badoglio to Roatta, Cavagnari, Pricolo, 3390, 26.10.1940, NARS T-821/127/000255.

116 See Armellini, *Diario*, pp. 115, 135, 141; Badoglio, in Marras minute, 15.11.1940, Ceva, "L'incontro Keitel-Badoglio del novembre 1940 nelle carte del generale Marras," *Il Risorgimento*, 29:1–2(1977), p. 32; Visconti Prasca in Armellini, *Diario*, p. 227 (in striking contradiction to his postwar account); Puntoni, *Parla Vittorio Emanuele*, p. 26; the postwar remarks of Badoglio (Grazzi, *Il principio della fine*, p. 221; Badoglio, *L'Italia*, pp. 52–4) and Roatta (*Otto milioni di baionette*, p. 127). Similarly, Gianluca André, "L'Italia nella seconda guerra mondiale fino all'intervento degli Stati Uniti nel conflitto," p. 267, in *La politica estera italiana dal 1914 al 1943* (Turin, 1963); *idem, La guerra in Europa*, pp. 668–9; De Luna, *Badoglio*, pp. 200–1.

117 Minutes, 10.11.1940, T-586/406/000873-74; Ciano, 23.10.1940; DDI, 9,V,788.

118 DDI,9,V,755, 764, 778; Grazzi, *Il principio della fine*, pp. 223, 225–7; SD report, 13.11.1940, PA, Inland II Geheim, Bd. 391 (Griechenland); Bastianini, *Uomini, cose, fatti*, pp. 257–8; Ciano, 24.10.1940.

119 DDI,9,V,785, 789; Erbach to AA, No. 514, 24.10.1940, GFM 449/222809.

120 SIM, *Grecia* (a country handbook, produced in October 1940; see Roatta letters, 18.10.1940), NARS T-821/456/000452-54. The head of the SIM since September 1940, General Cesare Amé, inevitably claimed later (in his *Guerra segreta in Italia, 1940–1943* (Rome, 1954), pp. 24–5) that SIM attempted in late October to warn the Italian leadership of the full extent of Greek capabilities. (But see Air Force complaints of intelligence failure, Grote minute, 2.12.1940, GFM 675/258386-87.)

121 Gorla, *L'Italia nella seconda guerra mondiale*, p. 94.

122 Roatta to Visconti Prasca, 4100, 20.10.1940, NARS T-821/127/000299-304; Roatta letters, 17.10.1940.

123 Roatta letters, 27.10.1940; Badoglio note on Armellini covering slip (27.10.1940) to Roatta's memorandum, NARS T-821/127/000238.

124 "No/qui é guerra e basta. B.," note on Comando Supremo memorandum, 19.10.1940, NARS T-821/127/000296; see also Roatta to Badoglio, Cavagnari, Pricolo, 4030, 18.10.1940; Badoglio to Roatta, 3273, 22.10.1940, *ibid.*, 000305, 000297-298.

125 Badoglio to De Vecchi, 22.10.1940, in Ruggero Fanizza, *De Vecchi – Bastico – Campioni. Ultimi governatori dell'Egeo* (Forlì, n.d.), pp. 38–9; Faldella, *L'Italia*, p. 290.

126 Meeting of the chiefs of staff, 21.10.1940, Koliopoulos, *Greece*, p. 142; also Woodward, *British Foreign Policy*, I, p. 512.

127 Soddu to army and corps commanders, Albania, 1155, 27.11.1940, NARS T-821/127/000482–85.

128 DDI,9,V,765, 776; Ciano, 25.10.1940.

129 Ciano, 19.10.1940; Bottai, *Vent'anni*, p. 192.

130 For what follows, DDI,9,V,753; ADAP,D,XI,199.

131 "Per la Grecia io sono deciso a rompere gli indugi e prestissimo."

132 In this connection, Mussolini appears to have enclosed with the letter a report from the Italian minister at Berne describing Swiss rejoicing over British air bombardments of north Italy (Tamaro to Ciano, 18.10.1940, GFM F10/003–04), and a report on alleged Yugoslav guerrilla activities in the Italian and German border areas (fragment, GFM F10/001–02).

133 The German foreign office transmogrified "il concorso dei vostri *mezzi* corazzati" into "die Zusammenarbeit mit Ihren gepanzerten *Verbänden*" (emphasis supplied).

134 Ciano, 22.10.1940; Lanza, *Berlino*, p. 177.

135 Halder, II, p. 133.

136 Mackensen to AA, No. 472/40g, 16.10.1940, and annexes (translations of decrypted telegrams from Greek and Yugoslav representatives in Tirana), GFM 2281/480769–80; ADAP,D,XI,191.

137 Mackensen to AA, No. 1883, 19.10.1940, GFM 449/222805; ADAP,D,XI,191, 194.

138 Löwisch to OKM, Chefsache 18 II Aug., 20.10.1940, GNR PG 45098; Löwisch to OKM, Chefs. 18/40, 19.10.1940, GNR PG 33316; KTB Marine Attaché, 19.10.1940, GNR PG 45148.

139 Rintelen to OKH, OKW, No. 332/40 g. K., 23.10.1940, GNR PG 32211. Despite Roatta's duplicity on the larger issue, his denial that Crete had come up in Italian planning rings true: the justification is pure Cavagnari. Silence on the subject in the available Italian military sources backs Roatta up.

140 Rintelen, Mackensen to AA, SSD HRMA 0825, 24.10.1940, 1930 hrs. (received Berlin, 2345 hrs., 24.10), GFM B14/B002306; ADAP,D,XI,225 (received Berlin, 1940 hrs., 24.10).

141 Halder, II, p. 181; for the narrative, ADAP,D,XI,302.

142 ". . . dass wir der Italienischen Regierung nicht mit einer so betonten Démarche in den Arm fallen könnten . . ."

143 ADAP,D,XI,209.

144 This, and what follows, from Halder, II, p. 148.

145 The Hungarians had originated the idea, which the drafters had not foreseen, of satellite accessions to the pact. After initial coolness, the Germans had taken the matter up from mid-October on in consultation with Rome. Hitler delayed the actual signatures until the Berlin talks with Molotov (12–13 November) made Soviet accession seem unlikely, and removed the danger that the Russians might use the pact to exert influence on the small powers of southeastern Europe (Hillgruber, *Hitlers Strategie,* pp. 336–7).

146 KTB/OKW, p. 129; KTB 1/SKL,A,14, 25.10.1940, PG 32034.

147 See Erich Kordt, *Wahn und Wirklichkeit* (Stuttgart, 1947) pp. 259–60; *idem, Nicht aus den Akten,* p. 408 (Kordt's two versions conflict slightly); Schmidt, *Statist auf diplomatischer Bühne,* p. 505; Creveld, "25 October 1940: A Historical Puzzle," *Journal of Contemporary History,* 6:3 (1971), pp. 87–96, is rightly skeptical of Kordt and Schmidt.

148 On Montoire, see particularly Geoffrey Warner, *Pierre Laval and the Eclipse of France* (New York, 1968), pp. 235–8; also Paxton, *Vichy France*, pp. 74–6; Jäckel, *Frankreich in Hitlers Europa*, ch. 7; Henri Michel, *Vichy, Année 40* (Paris, 1966), pp. 295–335.

149 Führer-Hauptquartier Tagebuch No. 4 (1.8.1940–31.12.1940), BAMA, RW 47/v. 7, III W 3014.

150 Ciano, 24.10.1940; Mackensen to Ribbentrop, No. 1914, 25.10.1940, GFM B14/B002309.

151 See Rintelen, *Mussolini als Bundesgenosse*, p. 109.

152 ADAP,D,XI,228, and n. 1. For the train movements, Führer-Hauptquartier Tagebuch No. 4, BAMA RW 47/v. 7, III W 3014.

153 ADAP,D,XI,225; Rintelen, Mackensen to AA, SSD HRMA 0825, 24.10.1940, B14/B002306; date/time stamp on Italian original of Mussolini's letter, GFM F2/000426.

154 Mackensen to Ribbentrop, No. 1913, 25.10.1940, GFM 449/222811; time of arrival at the trains does not appear on the document, but transmission was apparently instantaneous (see B14/B002311).

155 The sources are Engel, Hitler's army adjutant, as relayed to Halder by Tippelskirch (Halder, II, p. 158), and Hasso von Etzdorf, the well-informed liaison representative of the foreign office to the army high command (Etzdorf note, 28.10.1940, GFM 1247/337515–16).

156 Ciano, 25.10.1940; Ribbentrop to AA, No. 7, 25.10.1940 (arrived Berlin 1508 hrs.), GFM B14/B002308. Creveld, "25 October 1940: A Historical Puzzle," pp. 92–3, argues that Mackensen's report of Anfuso's remarks could not have triggered Hitler's decision to go to meet Mussolini in Florence on 28 October: "Either the Führer regarded this report seriously, or he did not. If he did, he should have advanced the meeting further, or, failing this, sent a direct message; if he did not, why bother at all. To assume that Hitler divided this telegram into a 'serious' and 'non-serious' part, that he was so much affected by it as to change his plans yet failed to notice the urgency of the matter, is scarcely credible." Actually, the possibility Creveld dismisses is all too credible, given the uncertainty under which Hitler was operating. In any case, even if Hitler took both sections of the message seriously, he had no course open that held out hope of stopping the Italians without provoking worse difficulties than would, in all probability, an attack on Greece.

157 Engel, *Heeresadjutant bei Hitler*, p. 88.

158 ADAP,D,XI,497; Ciano minute, 19.1.1941, *L'Europa*, pp. 625–6.

159 For the movements of the trains, see Führer-Hauptquartier Tagebuch No. 4, BAMA, RW 47/v.7, III W 3014, and Der Sekretär des Führers, "Daten aus alten Notizbüchern (1933–1943)," U.S. Library of Congress, Manuscript Division, Captured German Documents, Item 472 E. The need to avoid Vichy France probably dictated the circuitous route.

160 Emphasis supplied. The German translator slightly sharpened the implicitly anti-German tone of the remark: compare ". . . bin ich entschlossen, jedes Zögern zu vermeiden" with ". . . sono deciso di rompere gli indugi e prestissimo."

161 Etzdorf note, 28.10.1940, GFM 1247/337515–16; *Weizsäcker-Papiere*, p. 221.

162 Ritter to Schulze for Ribbentrop (in Munich), No. 104, 27.10.1940, GFM B14/B002317; ADAP,D,XI,242.

163 Schmidt, *Statist auf diplomatischer Bühne*, p. 506.
164 Engel, *Heeresadjutant bei Hitler*, p. 88.
165 Schmidt, *Statist auf diplomatischer Bühne*, p. 506.
166 ADAP,D,XI,246; DDI,9,V,807.

CHAPTER 6
TO THE BERGHOF: ITALY'S END AS A GREAT POWER

1 Ciano, 25.10.1940 (emphasis in original); Roatta letters, 26.10.1940 Armellini, *Diario*, p. 128. Quotation on preceding page: De Bono diaries, notebook 44, ACS.
2 ADAP,D,XI,246; DDI,9,V,807.
3 Rintelen to OKH, OKW, 982, 30.10.1940, IWM AL 1007; Roatta letters, 29.10, 31.10, 1.11.1940; KTB Verbindungsstab beim Admiralstab der Königlichen Italienischen Marine [Admiral Weichold], 4.11.1940, GNR PG 45954; Armellini, *Diario*, pp. 131–3, 145; USMM, *La difesa del traffico*, p. 28; Badoglio to Roatta, Cavagnari, Pricolo, 3524, 1.11.1940, NARS T-821/127/000104; Mussolini to Visconti Prasca, 31.10.1940, Visconti Prasca, *Io ho aggredito la Grecia*, p. 108.
4 Trevor-Roper, ed., *Hitler's Secret Conversations*, No. 148; Ciano, 31.10.1940; Mackensen to AA, 500/40, 1.11.1940 [seen by Hitler], GFM 2281/481735–37.
5 Ciano, 1.11.1940; Consul-General, Salonika, to Palairet, Halifax, 2.11.1940, PRO FO 371/24920, R 8184; Mackensen to AA, No. 1976, 2.11.1940, GFM 449/222875–76.
6 "Noi morire anche tutti, purché il DUCE passi." (Visconti Prasca to Jacomoni, 31.10.1940, and annexes, T-821/127/000549–60; Ciano, 3.11.1940; Ciano minute, 4.11.1940, in Ciano, *L'Europa*, pp. 608–11.)
7 Visconti Prasca–Roatta–Badoglio correspondence, 2.11–4.11.1940, NARS T-821/127/000080–83, 000094–96, 000101–03; Weizsäcker note, 29.10.1940, Fabricius to AA, No. 1921, GFM 265/172444–45; ADAP,D,XI,250; Armellini, *Diario*, p. 138; Roatta letters, 3.11.1940.
8 Mussolini, "Nota per lo Stato Maggiore," 3.11.1940, NARS T-821/129/000785.
9 The Navy held losses to 7 ships and escorts in 3,305 crossings (28.10.1940-30.4.1941) (USMM, *La difesa del traffico*, p. 49).
10 Roatta letters, 3.11.1940; Roatta to Badoglio, 259, 4.11.1940, NARS T-821/127/000078–79.
11 All from Roatta letters, 4.11.1940.
12 *Ibid.;* Armellini, *Diario*, pp. 167, 267–8.
13 Roatta to Badoglio, 264, 6.11.1940, NARS T-821/128/000294–95; Roatta letters, 5.11.1940; Ciano, 6.11.1940.
14 Undated, unsigned "Promemoria per il Duce," with Armellini marginal note, "Presented morning of the 8th," NARS T-821/127/000546–48; internal evidence makes clear Soddu wrote it.
15 Roatta letters, 8.11.1940; Roatta to Visconti Prasca, 5491, 8.11.1940, NARS T-821/127/000077; Ciano, 8.11.1940.
16 What follows, except where indicated, from minutes, 10.11.1940, NARS T-

586/406/000871–90 (emphasis in original) (also in Faldella, *L'Italia,* pp. 760–7).

17 Mussolini, "Nota per lo Stato Maggiore," 9.11.1940, NARS T-821/127/000068–69.

18 Mussolini allegedly struck further pithy Badoglio remarks from the record; see the interpolations in Faldella, *L'Italia,* p. 296.

19 Rintelen to OKH, No. 224/40, 13.11.1940, IWM AL 1007; Badoglio to Roatta, 3728, 10.11.1940, NARS T-821/127/000066–67.

20 Alexander Papagos, *The Battle of Greece, 1940–41* (Athens, 1949), pp. 273ff.; naval attaché, Athens, to Cunningham, 29.10.1940, PRO FO 371/24920, R 8214; also Papagos in military attaché, Athens, to War Office, 26.10.1940, *ibid.,* 24919, R 7915.

21 Churchill, *Their Finest Hour,* pp. 455–63; Creveld, "Prelude to Disaster: the British Decision to Aid Greece, 1940–1941," *Journal of Contemporary History,* 9:3 (1974), p. 68.

22 For Metaxas's views Palairet to Halifax, No. 1219, 27.11.1940, PRO FO 371/24866, R 8620; MacVeagh (Athens) to Hull, 7.12.1940, FRUS, 1940, III, pp. 594–5; SD report, 11.12.1940, PA, Inland II Geheim, Bd. 391 (Griechenland); Woodward, *British Foreign Policy,* I, p. 518.

23 Badoglio–Roatta–Soddu–Mussolini correspondence, 11.11–21.11.1940, NARS T-821/127/000043–46, 000049, 000054–57, 000503–06, 128/000285–88, 209/001153–54; Ciano, 21.11.1940.

24 Cunningham to Admiralty, 88, 15.5.1939, PRO ADM 1/9946.

25 For a different view but no evidence, USMM, *Le azioni navali,* p. 214.

26 For description without explanation, USMM, *Le azioni navali,* pp. 215–20.

27 Ciano, 12.11.1940.

28 Playfair, *Mediterranean,* I, pp. 328–32; USMM, *Le azioni navali,* ch. 12.

29 KTB I/SKL,A,15, 12.11.1940, GNR PG 32035.

30 See Halder II, p. 158 and KTB/OKW, p. 144.

31 Roatta letters, 18.10.1940; Halder, II, p. 162.

32 Engel, *Heeresadjutant bei Hitler,* p. 90; for what follows, Halder, II, pp. 163–5.

33 ADAP,D,XI,323, and KTB/OKW, pp. 150–1, 157.

34 In the original (Halder, II, p. 164) "Turkish-Thrace"; context and other sources (KTB/OKW, p. 150; ADAP,D,XI,323) make clear Halder's pen slipped.

35 Creveld (*Hitler's Strategy,* pp. 57–9) conflates the strategic conceptions of Hitler and Jodl, and argues that Hitler intended the Greek operation as the continuation of an offensive anti-British Mediterranean strategy, a "second-rate substitute" (KTB/OKW, p. 144) for intervention in Libya. This interpretation fails to explain why Hitler was now only interested in those parts of Greece from which the British could strike Rumania, and did not mention Crete, the strategic objective around which his earlier conception had revolved.

36 Canaris minute, 29.11.1940 [conversation with Greek military attaché, Col. Leggeris] GNR PG 33688; also ADAP,D,XI,540, and Schramm-von Thadden, *Griechenland,* pp. 126–7.

37 See particularly Halder, II, p. 212.

38 ADAP,D,XI,211, 323, 325, 326, 328, 329, 404; Hillgruber, *Hitlers Strategie,* pp. 355–6; Engel, *Heeresadjutant bei Hitler,* p. 91; Halder, II, p. 212.

39 Ciano, 18–19.11.1940; for the ensuing account of the talks, ADAP,D,XI,353.

40 ADAP,D,XI,320, 334; Megerle minute of conversation with Danilo Gregorić, 11.11.1940, GFM 881/289582–83; Breccia, *Jugoslavia,* pp. 352ff.

41 Contrary to the assumption of Hoptner, *Yugoslavia in Crisis,* p. 186, and R. L. Knežević, "Prince Paul, Hitler, and Salonika," *International Affairs,* 27 (1951), p. 42, the Bitolj bombing resulted from navigational error. The town looked like the Greek base of Florina, and was roughly the same distance from the frontier and Lake Prespa. See "Segnalazioni," 9.11.1940; Air Force files suggest the Italians apologized unofficially while publicly denying responsibility – although the Albanian air command refused to "confess." (ACS, MAG, 1940, bundle 162, 9 V 14/9.)

42 Ciano, 11.11.1940; Breccia, *Jugoslavia,* pp. 372–6.

43 Ciano to Mussolini, 18.11.1940, Ciano, *L'Europa,* pp. 612–16; Ciano, 22.11.1940; ADAP,D,XI,366, 369, 383; *OO,* XXX, pp. 174–9.

44 Farinacci to Mussolini, 9.11.1940, (*visto* by Mussolini), T-586/117/031626–32. A marginal note of Sebastiani (Mussolini's private secretary) attests to the meeting.

45 Ciano, 13.11, 14.11.1940; De Bono diaries, 18.11.1940, notebook 44, (misdated 18.8), ACS; Armellini, *Diario,* p. 159; Farinacci to Mussolini (initialed "M"), with enclosure, 17.11.1940, NARS T-586/117/031633–41. For a similar, later effort, see Farinacci to Mussolini, 4.12.1940 with enclosure, ACS, Ambasciata Tedesca.

46 OKW memorandum, 25.11.1940, KTB/OKW, p. 980; OKW memorandum, No. 9/40 g.K.Chefs., 20.11.1940, GNR PG 32211; Marras minute, 15.11.1940, in Ceva, "L'incontro Keitel-Badoglio del novembre 1940," pp. 32, 35; KTB 1/SKL,A,15, 18.11.1940, PG 32035.

47 Ciano to Mussolini, 18.11.1940, Ciano, *L'Europa,* p. 616; Puntoni, *Parla Vittorio Emanuele,* p. 25; also the King's scathing assessment of Badoglio, *ibid.,* p. 28.

48 Ciano, 21.11, 22.11.1940.

49 "Zavorra piccolo borghese," *Regime Fascista,* 23.11.1940; Armellini, *Diario,* p. 168; for the description of Armellini, see Puntoni, *Parla Vittorio Emanuele,* p. 27.

50 Ciano, 25.11.1940; Puntoni, *Parla Vittorio Emanuele,* p. 25.

51 Armellini, *Diario,* p. 171; Farinacci to Mussolini, 28.11.1940, NARS T-586/448/026421–22.

52 Armellini, *Diario,* pp. 172–3; Farinacci to Mussolini, 28.11.1940, NARS T-586/448/026421–22; Senise, *Polizia,* p. 103.

53 Ciano, 18–21.1.1941; Rintelen, *Mussolini als Bundesgenosse,* p. 124; Farinacci to Mussolini, 27.11.1940, NARS T-586/117/031642–43 [Gazzera]; Puntoni, *Parla Vittorio Emanuele,* p. 25; Farinacci to Mussolini, 28.11.1940, NARS T-586/448/026421–22 [Pintor].

54 Farinacci to Mussolini, 27.11.1940, NARS T-586/117/031642–43; Ciano, 30.11.1940; Cavallero, *Comando Supremo,* p. 7; De Bono diaries, 2.12, 7.12.1940, notebook 44, ACS; Armellini, *Diario,* pp. 182, 268.

55 See the correspondence in Jacomoni's file, ACS, PC, 1937–39, 1/1.9/35/43.

56 Ciano, 30.11, 23.11.1940, and Celso Luciano, *Rapporto al Duce nel racconto dell'ex Capo-Gabinetto alla Stampa Celso Luciano* (Rome, 1948), p. 15.

57 For the soundings, see Guzzoni's remarks to De Bono (De Bono diaries, note-

book 44, 2.12.1940, ACS); for Ciano on Cavallero, Mackensen to AA, Nos. 2233, 2351, 6.12, 24.12.1940, GFM B14/B002413–14, B002457; ADAP,D,XI,504, 519, 603.

58 See Ciano, 9.7, 28.9.1941, 11.8.1942, and Ceva, *La condotta italiana della guerra*, p. 125.

59 For Cavallero's career, see Ceva, *La condotta italiana della guerra*, pp. 217–19. Contrary to much contemporary opinion, Cavallero was not at this point a protégé of the Germans; they did not welcome the dismissal of Badoglio, whose bogus soldierly frankness had captivated Keitel at Innsbruck (see KTB 1/SKL,A,15, 18.11.1940, GNR PG 32035; OKW memorandum, 25.11.1940, KTB/OKW, p. 980; Rintelen, *Mussolini als Bundesgenosse*, pp. 112–13; Armellini, *Diario*, p. 236.

60 Armellini, *Diario*, pp. 181–5; Puntoni, *Parla Vittorio Emanuele*, pp. 28–30; "Segnalazioni," 5.12.1940 (emphasis in original).

61 Caviglia, *Diario*, p. 310; for the PNF campaign, see the report of a speech by the Federale of Trieste, December 1940, in Ambrosio's papers, NARS T-821/145/000165, and Rochat, *Badoglio*, pp. 767–70.

62 Ciano, 4.12.1940; Armellini, *Diario*, pp. 188–90, for Badoglio's not entirely credible account of the interview; for the decrees (4.12.1940) removing Badoglio from office "at his request" and appointing Cavallero, ACS, PC, 1940,1/2-1/2784, "Capo di Stato Maggiore Generale."

63 Ciano, 15.11, 27.11, 28.11.1940; 10.10.1938; Armellini, *Diario*, pp. 67, 176; Fanizza, *De Vecchi – Bastico – Campioni*, pp. 42–4.

64 Informant report, Messina, 8.12.1940, NARS T-586/1194/090611; Questore, Taranto, to Senise, 23.12.1940, ACS, MI, DGPS/DAGR 1941 (Cat.K1B N.15), bundle 57.

65 Cavagnari to Mussolini, 8.12.1940, ACS, SPD/CR, bundle 22, folder 223/R, "Cavagnari, Domenico," which also contains Mussolini's letter of dismissal (7.12.1940); for the rumors, "Segnalazioni," 5.12.1940.

66 See KTB 1/SKL,A,16, 13.12.1940, GNR PG 32036, quoting Admiral Maraghini, naval liaison chief in Berlin; also Caviglia, *Diario*, p. 310.

67 Sorice–Roatta–Badoglio–Mussolini correspondence, 13.11–26.11.1940, NARS T-821/127/000561, 000594–608, 000640–41, 000664–71; also Roatta to Graziani, 26.11.1940, ACS, Graziani, bundle 40/B; Armellini, *Diario*, pp. 153, 164.

68 Ciano, 23.11.1940; Soddu to Roatta, 311, 23.11.1940, Soddu to army and corps commanders, 1155, 27.11.1940, NARS T-821/127/000489–90, 000482–85; Roatta to Graziani, 26.11.1940, ACS, Graziani, bundle 40/B.

69 Geloso (9th Army) to Soddu, 026698, 27.11.1940; Soddu to Geloso, 28.11.1940, NARS T-821/127/000477–79.

70 Soddu to Vercellino (11th Army), 1413, 30.11.1940, *ibid.*, 000033–34; Ciano, 30.11, 4.12.1940; Soddu to Vercellino, 1.12.1940 (but not sent), NARS T-821/210/000312–13. See also Soddu's despairing report to Roatta, 1648, 4.12.1940, 0700 hrs., NARS T-821/209/001308–12.

71 Ciano, 4.12.1940; Alfieri, *Due dittatori*, pp. 105–6; Mussolini to Soddu, 4.12.1940, in Cavallero, *Comando Supremo*, pp. 14–15; Armellini, *Diario*, p. 195.

72 Ciano, 4.12, 14.12, 24.12.1940, 4.1, 7.1.1941.

73 Cavallero to Mussolini, 5.12.1940, NARS T-821/127/000039; Soddu to Roatta, 2000, 8.12.1940, *ibid.*, 209/000061–62; Ciano, 4.12, 7.12.1940.

74 Mussolini to Graziani, 26.10.1940, USE, *La prima offensiva britannica,* pp. 45–6.

75 Graziani to Mussolini, 29.10.1940, ACS, Graziani, bundle 45; Mussolini to Graziani, 1.11.1940, USE, *La prima offensiva britannica,* p. 46.

76 Graziani to Badoglio, 01/1740, 24.10.1940, Badoglio to Graziani, 3668, 7.11.1940, ACS, Graziani, bundle 45; Badoglio to Graziani, 29.10.1940, USE, *La prima offensiva britannica,* p. 44.

77 Graziani to Mussolini, 6.1.1941 (with ex post facto emendations in Graziani's hand), ACS, Graziani, bundle 45. In printing the document (*Africa Settentrionale,* p. 305), Graziani altered the crucial sentence to imply that he had not heard of the Greek plan before 28 October. The original document merely asserts that he did not receive timely notice of "the commencement of operations on the Greek front."

78 Graziani, *Africa Settentrionale,* p. 102. The entire Roatta passage Graziani quotes from his so-called diary (actually a memorandum written two months after the event) is a fabrication: compare the printed text with "Cronistoria degli avvenimenti," 2.12.1940, ACS, Graziani, bundle 45.

79 Roatta to Graziani, 21.9.1940 (ACS, Graziani, bundle 40/B), which requests Graziani's approval for two "operational directives"; Roatta letters, 20.9.1940, which establishes that one of those directives was that for "Contingency 'G,' " and Graziani to Roatta, 103, 26.9.1940 (ACS, Graziani, bundle 42), which approves the two directives. See also Roatta to service chiefs and major commanders, 3280, 1.10.1940 (NARS T-821/127/000322), announcing the approval of Graziani, then in Rome, for the directives.

80 See the exchange, 22.10–1.11.1940, in ACS, Graziani, bundle 47.

81 Figures (excluding vehicles in Tripolitania), USE, *La prima offensiva britannica,* p. 51.

82 Soddu to Roatta, Badoglio, Graziani, Visconti Prasca, 147779/26.2.166, 21.10.1940, NARS T-821/127/000120; Graziani to Badoglio, 01/1740, 24.10.1940, ACS, Graziani, bundle 45.

83 Tellera to 10th Army, 27.11.1940, USE, *La prima offensiva britannica,* p. 61.

84 See the intelligence summaries in USE, *La prima offensiva britannica,* pp. 64–5; Santoro, *L'aeronautica italiana,* I, pp. 289–90, 347–49; Pricolo to Porro, 11.12.1940, ACS, MAG, "1940. Ispezione Generale Pricolo," folder "Corr. con il Generale Porro"; Armellini, *Diario,* p. 247.

85 Graziani (*Africa Settentrionale,* p. 170) and his apologist Canevari (*Retroscena della disfatta,* p. 594) claimed later that "there was no surprise."

86 Playfair, *Mediterranean,* I, pp. 267–8; Basil H. Liddell Hart, *The Tanks* (New York, 1959), II, p. 45.

87 Graziani to Comando Supremo, 12.12.1940, USE, *La prima offensiva britannica,* pp. 118–19.

88 Mussolini to Graziani, 12.12.1940, *ibid.,* p. 121.

89 Graziani to Mussolini, 14.12.1940, Graziani, *Africa Settentrionale,* p. 147 (original, in Graziani's hand, ACS, bundle 51). For Graziani's role in Ethiopia, Rochat, *Militari e politici,* passim.

90 Gorla, *L'Italia nella seconda guerra mondiale,* p. 119; Armellini, *Diario,* p. 215;

Guzzoni, in *Il processo Graziani,* 111 (Rome, 1950), pp. 1295–6; Ciano, 15.12.1940; Mussolini to Graziani, 162924–162925, 15.12.1940, ACS, Graziani, bundle 45; Graziani, *Africa Settentrionale,* pp. 245ff.

91 Armellini, *Diario,* p. 222 (but incorrectly ascribing the conception to Mussolini, not Graziani); Lanza, *Berlino,* p. 189.

92 See Graziani to Gariboldi (10th Army), 12.12.1940, Graziani, *Africa Settentrionale,* p. 140, and his remark on pp. 144–5 about his "concept of resisting to the last on successive positions."

93 Mussolini to Graziani, 13.12, 15.12.1940, USE, *La prima offensiva britannica,* pp. 121–2, 125; Mussolini to Graziani, 4652, 14.12.1940, ACS, Graziani, bundle 45.

94 Compare USE, *La prima offensiva britannica,* p. 145, with Playfair, *Mediterranean,* I, p. 294, and Gavin Long, *To Benghazi* (Canberra, 1952), ch. 8.

95 Ciano, 5.1.1941; Eden to Churchill, 6.1.1941, Churchill, *The Grand Alliance* (New York, paperback ed., 1962), pp. 12–13.

96 Playfair, *Mediterranean,* I, p. 291; USE, *La prima offensiva britannica,* p. 194; also Long, *To Benghazi,* ch. 9.

97 Graziani to Guzzoni, 25.1.1941, USE, *La prima offensiva britannica,* pp. 342–3.

98 F. H. Hinsley, *et al., British Intelligence in the Second World War,* I (London, 1979), p. 379; Graziani to Mussolini, 8.2.1941, Graziani, *Africa Settentrionale,* pp. 236–7.

99 Mussolini to Cavallero, 4936, 24.12.1940, NARS T-821/127/000019; Ciano, 18.12, 19.12, 23.12, 25.12.1940; Armellini, *Diario,* pp. 236, 240.

100 Cavallero to Soddu, 12.12.1940, NARS T-821/127/000028–29; Ciano, 7.12.1940; Cavallero to Soddu, 99/A, 21.12.1940, NARS T-821/207/000511; Mussolini to Cavallero, 4937, 24.12.1940, *ibid.,* 127/000024–25.

101 Mussolini to Soddu, 5049, 29.12.1940, *ibid.,* 127/000011; Ciano, 30.12.1940.

102 Cavallero to Mussolini, 31.12.1940, NARS T-821/207/000478–79; Cavallero, *Comando Supremo,* p. 43; also Ciano, 31.12.1940.

103 For the account that follows, see the extensive correspondence in the Albanian Command file on the incident, NARS T-821/210/000008off.

104 Ciano, 18.1–21.1.1941; Cavallero to Geloso, 01325, 27.1.1941, NARS T-821/127/000429–30.

105 Ciano, 16.1.1941; Mussolini to Cavallero, 102358, 13.1.1941, *ibid.,* 129/000055; telephone transcript, Mussolini to Col. Bartiromo, 18.1.1941, Cavallero, *Comando Supremo,* pp. 54–5.

106 Cavallero to Mussolini, 02196, 27.1.1941, Mussolini to Cavallero, 5880, 27.1.1941, Cavallero to Geloso, 01485, 31.1.1941, NARS T-821/129/000036–39, 207/000419.

107 Telephone transcript, Cavallero to Mussolini, 22.1.1941, *OO, XXX,* pp. 257–8; Cavallero to Geloso, 02221, 17.2.1941, NARS T-821/207/000389.

108 All from minutes of Mussolini's conversations with Cavallero, Geloso, and Geloso's corps commanders, *OO, XXX,* pp. 62–3, 65, 72.

109 See the informant reports in ACS, MI, DGPS/DPP, bundle 243.

110 Milan, Florence, Ferrara, Cremona, Novara, Reggio Emilia, Sassari: see the reports in ACS, MI, Ufficio Cifra, Telegrammi in Arrivo, 29.10.1940.

111 Questore, La Spezia, to Senise, 23.12.1940, ACS, MI, DGPS/DAGR 1941 (Cat. K1B N.15), bundle 52.

112 Informant report, Milan, 22.11.1940, ACS, MI, DGPS/DPP, bundle 243.

113 Armellini, *Diario,* p. 165; Roatta letters, 23.11.1940.

114 Ciano, 9.11.1940; *OO,* XXX, pp. 30–8.

115 See the frequent references in the reports of the provincial questori to Senise for late December 1940, ACS, DGPS/DAGR 1941 (Cat. K1B N.15), bundles 48–58.

116 "C'è evidentemente una nuova quartarella. . . ." (Unsigned minute, "Rapporto al giornalisti del 11 dicembre 1940 XIX (ore 19:30)," ACS, MCP, bundle 75.)

117 Questore, Forlì, to Senise, 23.12.1940, ACS, MI, DGPS/DAGR 1941 (Cat. K1B N.15), bundle 51; also similar remarks, 22.12–24.12 by the questori of Asti, Alessandria, Cremona, Enna, and Trento, *ibid.,* bundles 48, 51, 57.

118 For the complaints of the southern prefects, see "Segnalazioni," 7.2.1941.

119 See the unsigned draft memorandum on opinion throughout Italy (probably prepared by Senise for Mussolini), 9.1.1941, ACS, MI, DGPS/DAGR 1903–1944 (Cat.R.G.) ("Rapporti con la Germania"), bundle 430, folder 50.

120 100 = 1934 (Questore, Milan, to Senise, 24.12.1940, ACS, MI, DGPS/SCP, Senise, bundle 2).

121 Questore, Venice, to Senise, 22.12.1940, ACS, MI, DGPS/DAGR 1941 (Cat. K1B N.15), bundle 58.

122 Armellini, *Diario,* p. 221; for Starace's renewed influence, see also "Segnalazioni," 15.11.1940.

123 See Farinacci to Graziani, 30.12.1940, ACS, Graziani, bundle 45, which conveys "the solidarity of all gli amici, including Ciano and Starace."

124 See the acid description in Caviglia, *Diario,* p. 310.

125 "legato a fil doppio con me" (ADSS,IV,160). For the description of Serena as "transitorio," "Segnalazioni," 5.11.1940.

126 See Ciano's remark about Buffarini, ADSS,IV,160.

127 Leto, OVRA, p. 233; Armellini, *Diario,* p. 218; Charles to Halifax, 6.11.1939, PRO FO 371/23798, R 9765; "Segnalazioni," 19.10.1940.

128 Bottai, *Vent'anni,* p. 197; Ciano, 12.12.1940; Armellini, *Diario,* pp. 166, 265.

129 SD report, 19.12.1940, GFM 850/248021–23.

130 For Grandi's motives, Lanza, *Berlino,* p. 184; for his "earnest desire" to see Hitler, Mackensen to AA, 1962, 30.10.1940, GFM B14/B002327.

131 ADAP,D,XI,399; Rintelen, *Mussolini als Bundesgenosse,* p. 122; Likus report, 29.11.1940, GFM 43/30536–37.

132 Mackensen to AA, 2282, 12.12.1940, GFM B14/B002435–36; Grandi to Farinacci, 8.12.1940, ACS, Ambasciata Tedesca, folder 1; Armellini, *Diario,* pp. 203, 209, 229; German informant report, 13.12.1940, GFM 881/289444–45; SD reports, 19.12.1940, GFM 850/284021–23; 284030–35.

133 For a less lurid version of Countess Ciano's alleged role, see De Bono's remarks to Armellini (*Diario,* p. 267).

134 ADAP,D,XI,505; Mackensen to AA, No. 2282, 12.12.1940, GFM B14/B002435–36 (both seen by Hitler); Etzdorf note, 17.12.1940, GFM 1247/337557; Armellini, *Diario,* pp. 203, 209; Puntoni, *Parla Vittorio Emanuele,* p. 31.

135 Farinacci to Grandi, 2.1.1941, NARS T-586/449/026999; Ciano, 4.1.1941.
136 Ambrosio to Badoglio, draft (marked *non spedita* in Ambrosio's hand), 27.11.1940, NARS T-821/145/000163–64; Farinacci had worked for the railways.
137 Armellini, *Diario,* pp. 179–80; Rintelen, Mackensen to AA, No. 2275, 12.12.1940, GFM B14/B002420 (source: Roatta); Jo' di Benigno, *Occasioni mancate. Roma in un diario segreto* (Rome, 1945), pp. 40–1; De Bono diaries, 16.12.1940, notebook 44, ACS.
138 De Bono diaries, 28.11, 2.12, 7.12, 18.12.1940, notebook 44, ACS; Armellini, *Diario,* pp. 173, 181–2.
139 Caviglia, *Diario,* pp. 297, 300; De Bono diaries, 7.12.1940, notebook 44, ACS; Armellini, *Diario,* p. 190.
140 Armellini, *Diario,* pp. 151 (Giannini of the Foreign Ministry), p. 174 (De Bono), p. 176 (Lantini, president of the national social insurance agency), p. 191 (Hazon, second-in-command of the Carabinieri), p. 225 (Host-Venturi, Minister of Communications).
141 *Ibid.,* pp. 265–6; Lessona, *Memorie,* pp. 410–12; De Bono diaries, 13.3.1941, notebook 44, ACS.
142 De Bono to Farinacci, 16.3.1941, ACS, Farinacci, box 17, folder 74. De Bono had been chief of police and commandant of the Fascist Militia at the time of the murder, which he had attempted to cover up; for his ties with Farinacci at that point, see De Felice, *Mussolini,* II, p. 680 n. 4.
143 De Bono diaries, 28.11.1940, notebook 44, ACS: Puntoni, *Parla Vittorio Emanuele,* pp. 30–1, 35; Armellini, *Diario,* p. 229.
144 See ADSS,IV,54, 60, 61, 71, 74, 79, 119, 124, 154, 226 (*Regime Fascista,* etc.), 35, 50, 54, 75 (France), 36, 72 (Yugoslavia), 97, 125 (Greece), 152 (Pius XII and the war effort).
145 Himmler minute, 11.10.1942, *Vierteljahrshefte für Zeitgeschichte,* 4:4 (1956), pp. 423–6; Martin, *Friedensinitiativen,* pp. 387–90, 471–3.
146 Castronovo, *Agnelli,* pp. 599–601; for Volpi, Kelly to Eden, No. 397, 17.2.1941, PRO FO 371/26542, C 1587, and ADAP,D,XI,731, p. 1020.
147 Unsigned memorandum, "Rapporto ai giornalisti del 21.12.1940–XIX–ore 19:30," ACS, MCP, bundle 75.
148 Questori, Milan, Pistoia, Florence, Trieste, to Senise, 23.12, 24.12.1940, ACS, MI, DGPS/SCP, Senise, bundle 2, and DGPS/DAGR 1941 (Cat.K1B N.15), bundles 51, 55, 58, which are representative of many others.
149 Questore, Milan, to Senise, 24.12.1940, ACS, MI, DGPS/SCP, Senise, bundle 2.
150 De Bono to Graziani, 20.12.1940, ACS, Graziani, bundle 70, "Appendice."
151 See (among others), Questori, Milan, Mantua, Padua, Verona, to Senise, 23.12, 24.12.1940, ACS, MI, DGPS/DAGR 1941 (Cat.K1B N.15), bundles 53, 54, 58.
152 Questore, Verona, to Senise, 23.12.1940, *ibid.,* bundle 58.
153 Questore, Brescia, to Senise, 24.12.1940, *ibid.,* bundle 49.
154 See Questore, Ferrara, to Senise, 24.12.1940, *ibid.,* bundle 51; Roatta to Graziani, 370, 13.1.1941, ACS, Graziani, bundle 42.
155 Armellini, *Diario,* p. 222; Benigno, *Occasioni mancate,* pp. 67–8.
156 Armellini, *Diario,* p. 203; for public opinion, see among others Questori, Flor-

ence, Ferrara, Parma, to Senise, 23.12, 24.12.1940, ACS, MI, DGPS/DAGR 1941 (Cat.K1B N.15), bundles 51, 54.

157 See particularly "Oltre le cifre," *Regime Fascista*, 12.12.1940.

158 Unsigned memorandum, "Rapporto ai giornalisti del 13 dicembre 1940–XIX (ore 19:30)," ACS, MCP, bundle 75; Ciano, 12.12.1940 ("the Patria, eternal, belonging to all, above individuals, occasions, and factions"); Farinacci to Mussolini, 14.12.1940, NARS T-586/462/033962–64.

159 Ciano, 14.11.1940; also German Embassy agent report, 4.12.1940, GFM 2281/481759; SD report, 19.12.1940, GFM 850/284030–35; unsigned report, February 1941, 881/289373–74.

160 De Bono diaries, 19.12.1940, notebook 44, ACS ("servi, servi, tutti servi!"): Armellini, *Diario*, p. 223; Ugo Ojetti, *I taccuini* (Florence, 1954), pp. 549–50.

161 Ciano, 17.12.1940; Alberto Giannini to Farinacci, 18.12.1940, ACS, Ambasciata Tedesca, folder 1; Gorla, *L'Italia nella seconda guerra mondiale*, p. 113.

162 Churchill, *Their Finest Hour*, pp. 527–8.

163 Armellini, *Diario*, p. 208; Graziani, *Africa Settentrionale*, pp. 169–72; informant report, 20.8.1941, ACS, Ambasciata Tedesca, folder 1, D.

164 See particularly the report of the chief of the Bologna OVRA, Mariano Norcia, to Senise, 18.2.1940, ACS, MI, DGPS/SCP, Senise, bundle 2; Senise (*Polizia*, pp. 80–1) considered Norcia one of his most trusted subordinates.

165 Text and attribution in Mario Cervi, *Storia della guerra di Grecia* (Milan, 1965), pp. 214, 470–2, and Gianfranco Bianchi, 25 *luglio. Crollo di un regime* (Milan, 1963), pp. 234ff; also De Luna, *Badoglio*, pp. 208–9. For the real author's arrest, Questore, Milan, to Senise, 25.2.1941, ACS, MI, DGPS/SCP, Senise, bundle 2.

166 The comprehensive reports of the Questori and OVRA in ACS, MI, DGPS/SCP, Senise, bundle 2, and DGPS/DAGR 1941 (Cat.K1B N.15), bundles 48–58, mention numerous individual episodes of nocturnal graffitti and leaflets, but are unanimous in denying the existence of effective organized opposition. See particularly the remarks of Questore, Turin, to Senise, 23.12.1940, DGPS/DAGR 1941 (Cat.K1B N.15), bundle 57.

167 Ciano, 17.1.1941; Bottai, *Vent'anni*, p. 201; "Segnalazioni," 20.1, 7.2.1941.

168 See Anfuso, *Dal Palazzo Venezia*, pp. 148–9; Guerri, *Giuseppe Bottai. Un fascista critico* (Milan, 1976), p. 202.

169 Ciano, 17.1.1940.

170 See Guerri, *Bottai,* passim.

171 Unsigned agent report, 11.12.1940, GFM 881/289382–85.

172 Ciano, 24.1.1941.

173 *Ibid.*, 25.1, 26.1.1940; Bismarck to AA, No. 170, 27.1.1941, GFM 2281/481051; ADAP,D,XII,31; also Anfuso, *Dal Palazzo Venezia*, p. 153.

174 Cavallero, *Comando Supremo*, p. 56.

175 Grandi, quoted in Deakin, *The Brutal Friendship*, p. 50.

176 OVRA, Savona, to OVRA, Milan, 13.2.1941; OVRA, Bologna (Norcia), to Senise, 11.2.1941, ACS, MI, DGPS/SCP, Senise, bundle 2; ADAP,D,XI,731, p. 1020.

177 Questore, Venice, to Senise, 4.2, 11.2.1941, ACS, MI, DGPS/SCP, Senise, bundle 2.

178 OVRA, Bologna [Norcia], to Senise, 25.2.1941, *ibid.;* on Party discontent, see also De Bono diaries, 28.1.1941, notebook 44, ACS.

179 Informant reports, Milan, 1.2, 3.2.1941, appended to OVRA, Milan, to Senise, 4.2.1941, ACS, MI, DGPS/SCP, Senise, bundle 2.

180 De Bono diaries, 28.1.1941, notebook 44, ACS.

181 "Settimana dello schiaffo": draft "Appunto," 28.2.1941, probably for Mussolini, in ACS, MI, DGPS/SCP, Senise, bundle 2 (also Senise, *Polizia,* pp. 77–8).

182 Questore, Milan, to Senise, 27.3.1941, ACS, MI, DGPS/DAGR 1941 (Cat.K1B N.15), bundle 53.

183 Giovanni Lauricella (Questore, Palermo) to Senise, 10.2.1941 (with comment), ACS, MI, DGPS/SCP, Senise, bundle 2; on Lauricella, see Senise, *Polizia,* p. 187.

184 Questore, Venice, to Senise, 22.12.1940, ACS, MI, DGPS/DAGR 1941 (Cat.K1B N.15), bundle 58.

185 See the many references to the speech in ACS, MI, DGPS/SCP, Senise, bundle 2, and DGPS/DAGR 1941 (Cat.K1B N.15), bundles 48–58; De Bono diaries, 24.2.1941, notebook 44, ACS.

186 See OVRA, Verona, to OVRA, Milan, 14.2.1940, and Questore, Venice, to Senise, 18.2.1941, ACS, MI, DGPS/SCP, Senise, bundle 2.

187 Informant report, Milan, 20.4.1941, ACS, PNF/SPP, bundle 6.

188 Halder, II, p. 212.

189 Puntoni, *Parla Vittorio Emanuele,* p. 225; KTB/OKW, pp. 182–3, 223.

190 Roatta letters, 16.11.1941; KTB/OKW, pp. 183, 196; Halder, II, pp. 191–3.

191 ADAP,D,XI,417; KTB/OKW, pp. 200, 221; Heeren to AA, 846, 24.11.1940, GFM 449/222932; Heeren to AA, 865, 3.12.1940, GFM B14/B002400; ADAP,D,XI,465; Kramarz minute, 8.12.1940, GFM 449/222972; also Breccia, *Jugoslavia,* pp. 381–405.

192 ADAP,D,XI,453, 450; Mackensen to AA, No. 2233, 6.12.1940, GFM B14/B002413–14; Mackensen to AA, No. 2240, 7.12.1940, GFM 2281/480821–22; Alfieri, *Due dittatori,* p. 106; Ciano, 4.12.1940.

193 All from Lanza, *Berlino,* pp. 187–8; also Alfieri, *Due dittatori,* pp. 105–7. No German minute has survived.

194 ADAP,D,XI,477; Halder II, pp. 214, 220.

195 See SD report (submitted to Hitler), 6.12.1940, GFM 4456/E086828–33; Schramm-von Thadden, *Griechenland,* pp. 140–1, 217–18; Koliopoulos, *Greece,* pp. 189–90; and Martin, Friedensinitiativen, pp. 393–407.

196 Eden, in meeting of the War Cabinet, 2.1.1941, PRO CAB 65.

197 SD report, 19.12.1940, PA Bonn, Inland II Geheim, Bd. 391 (Griechenland); Metaxas diary entries in Schramm-von Thadden, *Griechenland,* p. 150.

198 All from ADAP,D,XI,511 (emphasis in original) and 532.

199 See Hillgruber, "Der Faktor Amerika," pp. 14–15.

200 Armellini, *Diario,* p. 219, 221; ADAP,D,XI, p. 686, n. 8, and 499; Lanza, *Berlino,* p. 188; KTB/OKW, p. 225; Alfieri, *Due dittatori,* p. 110.

201 Lanza, *Berlino,* p. 189; Ciano to Alfieri, 17.12.1940, Ciano, *L'Europa,* pp. 618–22; KTB/OKW, p. 241; Cavallero, *Comando Supremo,* pp. 26–7.

202 Italian minute, 20.12.1940, AUSE, Marras report file.

203 Rintelen to OKW, OKH, g.Ks. 317/40, 20.12.1940; Löwisch to OKM, B.

Nr. gKdos. 399/40, 23.12.1940, GNR PG 45178; ADAP,D,XI,541; see also Roatta to Cavallero, Guzzoni, 40900, 17.12.1940, NARS T-821/127/000651–54.

204 ADAP,D,XI,538, 554; Armellini, *Diario,* pp. 231, 238–9.

205 Marras to Guzzoni, 2592/A, 31.12.1940, AUSE, Marras report file; Armellini, *Diario,* p. 246; minutes, 30.12.1940, NARS T-821/142/000269ff; ADAP, D,XI,619, 726; XII,19, 27.

206 KTB/OKW, p. 244; Marras to Guzzoni, 2592/A, 31.12.1940, AUSE, Marras report file; Lanza, *Berlino,* p. 194; Mussolini to Cavallero, 31.12.1940, NARS T-821/127/000007.

207 Marras to Guzzoni, 2648/A, 4.1.1941, NARS T-821/129/000067–71; Lanza, *Berlino,* pp. 196–7.

208 Ciano, 5.1.1941; Lanza, *Berlino,* p. 200; ADAP,D,XI,586; KTB/OKW, pp. 251–2; Rintelen, *Mussolini als Bundesgenosse,* p. 120.

209 ADAP,D,XI,635; Mussolini to Cavallero, 10.1.1940; Cavallero, "Appunto per il Duce," 14.1.1941, NARS T-821/129/000072, 000050–52.

210 Roatta memorandum, 372, 16.1.1941, NARS T-821/129/000040–43; Roatta to Graziani, 19.1.1941, ACS, Graziani, bundle 40/B; Marras to Guzzoni, 13.1.1941, AUSE, Marras report file; Ciano, 16.1.1941.

211 Fricke minute, 8–9.1.1941, Wagner, ed., *Lagevorträge,* p. 181.

212 See particularly meeting of the War Cabinet, 19.11.1940, PRO CAB 65; OKW (Abwehr) to AA, 11.10.1940, NARS T-77/934/658426–27; SD report, 7.12.1940 (marked "F[ührer]"), GFM F20/053–54; SD reports, 13.12.1940, 8.1.1941, GFM 850/284010–11, 284044; ADSS,IV,216.

213 ADSS,IV,116; in general, Martin, *Friedensinitiativen,* pp. 355, 387–8.

214 Cadogan, Diaries, p. 339; meetings of the chiefs of staff committee, 25.11, 17.12, 30.12, 31.12.1940, PRO CAB 79/8; Churchill to Ismay for chiefs of staff, 6.1.1941, Churchill, *The Grand Alliance,* p. 9; Mussolini to Graziani, 9.1.1941, USE, *La prima offensiva britannica,* p. 330.

215 Koliopoulos, *Greece,* pp. 204–13; Woodward, *British Foreign Policy,* I, pp. 518–19; Creveld, "Prelude to Disaster," pp. 74–9; Butler, *Grand Strategy,* II, pp. 377–8.

216 ADSS,IV,206, 229; Rendel to Eden, 24.12.1940, PRO FO 371/24965, R 8942, and meeting of the War Cabinet, 30.12.1940, PRO CAB 65; also Martin, *Friedensinitiativen,* pp. 387–8.

217 ADSS,IV,252; Sir R. Campbell to Eden, No. 37, 15.1.1941, PRO FO 371/24943, R 414; (the "next paper" on these contacts is apparently "closed until 2017"); Loraine to Halifax, 25.11.1940, PRO FO 800/320.

218 Fricke minute, 8–9.1.1941, Wagner, ed., *Lagevorträge,* pp. 181–2 and Jodl (retrospectively), KTB/OKW, pp. 282–3; see also ADAP,D,XI,642.

219 Roatta to Graziani, 370, 13.1.1940, ACS, Graziani, bundle 42.

220 See Toscano, *Designs in Diplomacy,* pp. 191–244.

221 Ciano, 18–21.1.1941; ADAP,D,XI,672; for Laval's dismissal, Warner, *Laval,* pp. 253–60, and Paxton, *Vichy France,* pp. 92–101.

222 For what follows, Italian minute, 19.1.1941, NARS T-821/142/000239–44.

223 KTB/OKW, pp. 270, 274; ADAP,D,XI,683; Cavallero, *Comando Supremo,* p. 66; Mussolini to Cavallero, 2.1.1941, NARS T-821/129/000091, and his remarks in Gorla, *L'Italia nella seconda guerra mondiale,* pp. 121, 129.

224 Ciano, 18–21.1.1941.

225 ADAP,D,XI,679; see also KTB/OKW, pp. 274-7.

226 Ciano, 18–21.1.1941; also Rintelen, *Mussolini als Bundesgenosse*, p. 126; Armellini, *Diario*, p. 288.

227 Rintelen to OKH, OKW, No. 81/41, 29.1.1941, NARS T-78/359/ 6319227-34; KTB/OKW, pp. 281, 293-4; ADAP,D,XII,24; Engel, *Heeresadjutant bei Hitler*, pp. 93-4.

228 KTB/OKW, pp. 300-2; also Rintelen, *Mussolini als Bundesgenosse*, pp. 128-9, who unjustifiedly accuses Hitler of indecision.

229 ADAP,D,XII,17, 24, and Rintelen, *Mussolini als Bundesgenosse*, pp. 28-9.

230 Rintelen–Guzzoni–Marras–Mussolini–Graziani correspondence, 2.2–10.2. 1940, USE, *La prima offensiva britannica*, pp. 243-7, 364-7.

231 ADAP,D,XII,35; Rintelen, *Mussolini als Bundesgenosse*, p. 130; USE, *La prima offensiva britannica*, pp. 290-1, 368-9, 371-2.

232 On the Merano meeting, Salewski, *Seekriegsleitung*, I, pp. 323-9 and Schreiber, *Weltmachtstreben*, pp. 300-9; on the battle, USMM, *Le azioni navali*, ch. 13, and Cunningham, *A Sailor's Odyssey*, ch. 26; on signals intelligence, Hinsley, *British Intelligence*, I, pp. 403-5.

233 For Italian military planning and propaganda agitation against France after Pétain's dismissal of Laval in December made German action against Vichy seem possible, see Roatta to Graziani, 370, 13.1.1940, ACS, Graziani, bundle 42, and Prefect, Imperia, to Ministero dell'Interno, 47906, 22.12.1940, ACS, MI, Ufficio Cifra, Telegrammi in Arrivo (Mussolini ordered Ezio Garibaldi to form irredentist "Nice action groups"); Löwisch to Mackensen, 9.1.1941, GFM 449/E066998-7000; Armellini, *Diario*, p. 233; Caracciolo, *E poi?.*, pp. 71-2.

234 Löwisch memorandum, 19.1.1941, GFM 2281/481096-98, and Raeder minute, 18.3.1941, Wagner, ed., *Lagevorträge*, p. 203.

235 See the admirable reconstruction of Creveld, "Prelude to Disaster"; also Woodward, *British Foreign Policy*, I, pp. 524-36, and Koliopoulos, *Greece*, ch. 8.

236 See Creveld, "Prelude to Disaster," pp. 91-2. The chiefs of staff were as responsible as anyone for this major strategic error; see their disastrous memorandum of 10 February 1941, WM(41)32(0), PRO CAB 56/80, which dismissed a prescient suggestion from Leo Amery that Wavell press on to Tripoli before the *Luftwaffe* and a "stiffening of German troops" arrived to save the Italians.

237 Jodl, in Halder, II, p. 301.

238 Marras to Guzzoni, 813/A, 26.2.1941, NARS T-821/129/000022; for Greco-German contacts, Schramm-von Thadden, *Griechenland*, pp. 169-70, and Martin, *Friedensinitiativen*, pp. 404-5.

239 Guzzoni to Marras, 28.2.1941, NARS T-821/129/000021; ADAP,D,XII, 111; Lanza, *Berlino*, pp. 211-12.

240 Marras to Guzzoni, 990/A, 991/A, 5.3, 7.3.1941, NARS T-821/129/ 000010-11; Marras to Guzzoni, 957/17, 5.3.1941, AUSE, Marras report file; Lanza, *Berlino*, p. 212. OKW indeed hoped that the Greeks would not resist a German occupation: KTB/OKW, pp. 348, 352; Halder, II, pp. 299, 301.

241 ADAP,D,XII,114; *Weizsäcker-Papiere*, pp. 233, 236, 239; Schramm-von Thadden, *Griechenland*, p. 220.

242 See Breccia, *Jugoslavia*, pp. 435-49, 479-83.

243 Mussolini memorandum, 4.2.1941, in *ibid.*, p. 447 n. 110.
244 ADAP,D,XII,85, 97; Woermann minute, 3.3.1941, GFM 230/152534; see also ADAP,D,XII,174, 175, 178, 182.
245 See Klaus Olshausen, *Zwischenspiel auf dem Balkan* (Stuttgart, 1973), pp. 75–9, 100–7, and Creveld, *Hitler's Strategy,* ch. 6 (which also disposes of the myth Hitler later propagated that the Balkan campaigns his Italian allies forced on him delayed *Barbarossa* and led to German defeat). For German domination of Italian strategy from 1941 on, see Ceva, *La condotta italiana della guerra,* especially ch. 3.

CONCLUSION
THE MEANING OF FASCIST ITALY'S LAST WAR

1 Ciano to Victor Emmanuel III (copy), 23.12.1943, ACS, V. E. Orlando, box 3; also Ciano's preface to his diaries, 23.12.1943. For the quotation on the preceding page, Mario Pellegrinotti, *Sono stato il carceriere di Ciano* (Milan, 1975), p. 96.
2 For the phrase, see Ceva, "Monografie dell'Ufficio storico dell'esercito sulla guerra in Africa Settentrionale (1940–1943)," *Italia Contemporanea,* No. 119, pp. 111 (see also chapter 4.2).
3 De Luna, *Benito Mussolini,* p. 129; *idem, Badoglio,* p. 197.
4 Hewel diary, 29.5.1941, quoted in Thies, *Architekt der Weltherrschaft,* p. 175; Henry Picker, *Hitlers Tischgespräche im Führerhauptquartier 1941–1942* (Stuttgart, 2nd rev. ed., 1965), p. 466.
5 Hillgruber, "Der Faktor Amerika," pp. 15–17, and draft Führer Directive, 11.6.1941, "Vorbereitung für die Zeit nach Barbarossa," ADAP,D,XII,617.
6 Even in September 1941, when the triumphant German advance in Russia made a swift, victorious end to the war appear possible (see Puntoni, *Parla Vittorio Emanuele,* p. 73).
7 See informant report, 20.8.1941, ACS, Ambasciata tedesca, folder 1, D.
8 See De Felice, "Alcune osservazioni sulla politica estera mussoliniana," p. 58.
9 The literature on the subject is too vast for summary here; Hans-Ulrich Wehler, *Bismarck und der Imperialismus* (Cologne, Berlin, 1969) is a convenient starting point. For a brilliant critique of attempts to apply the theory to Hitler's Germany, see Hildebrand, "Le forze motrici."
10 Gambino, *Storia del PNF,* p. 173. Gambino goes too far in suggesting that Mussolini feared the Party would "necessarily have crumbled" without war. Petersen ("Gesellschaftssystem, Ideologie und Interesse in der Aussenpolitik des Faschistischen Italien," *Quellen und Forschungen aus italienischen Archiven und Bibliotheken,* Bd. 54, 1974, pp. 428–70) has used Gambino's thesis to analyze the decision for war in terms of "ideology" and "interests." He concludes, along with contemporaries ranging from some anti-Fascists to those supporters and "flankers" of the regime who repented in defeat, that Mussolini's foreign policy was "powered by particular ideological premises, and served the interests of the Fascist regime, not those of the Italian Nation."
   Actually, "ideology," "interests," and the line between them are subjective constructions; everything depends on one's point of view. To Mussolini, his expansionist vision and the ultimate interests of the nation were identical. The

only distinction of this sort one might sustain is between Mussolini's vision as an "imperial ideology" (in the specialized sense of Franz Schurmann's brilliant though idiosyncratic *The Logic of World Power*, New York, 1974, pp. 16–17) and Italy's narrower national interest. But here again one would have to explain why both public and elites, those stern guardians of the "permanent national interest" according to the pedantic standards of 19th-century diplomacy, backed Mussolini until defeat.

11 On this issue, see Timothy W. Mason, *Arbeiterklasse und Volksgemeinschaft* (Opladen, 1975), pp. 165–6.

12 The framework of this book does not permit doing justice to the complexities of the issue, although I hope to deal with it elsewhere. The best guide to the various interpretations is De Felice, *The Interpretations of Fascism*.

13 See Hildebrand, "Le forze motrici," pp. 218–21, and *The Foreign Policy of the Third Reich*, pp. 135ff. Both Hildebrand and Hillgruber (in his review of Petersen's *Hitler-Mussolini* [*Historische Zeitschrift* 219:3, 1974, p. 698]) push the distinction too far in asserting that Mussolini's aims were "conventionally imperialistic." The internal revolutionary dimension of his expansionism saves him from that demeaning category.

APPENDIX I
THE DIARIES OF COUNT GALEAZZO CIANO

1 See Toscano, *The History of Treaties and International Politics* (Baltimore, 1966), pp. 456–7.

2 See particularly Duilio Susmel, *Vita sbagliata di Galeazzo Ciano* (Milan, 1962), pp. 77–8.

3 Hillgruber, *Hitlers Strategie*, p. 282 n. 17; Irving, *Hitler's War*, p. xx. The passage runs: "A catastrophic telegram of Graziani's has arrived, a mixture of bravado, literary flourishes, and fears. He plans to retire to Tripoli 'to keep flying on that citadel at least the banner of Italy,' but he is first of all concerned to accuse Rommel – in other words Mussolini – of having compelled him to fight the war 'of flea against elephant.' " Graziani's original (Chapter 6.2) blamed Rome, not Rommel. Regrettably, De Felice's recent edition of the diaries misdates the entry (as 13.12.1940), and prints the word as "Roma" even though the handwritten "Rommel" is unmistakable.

4 On the filming of the diaries, see Smyth, *Secrets of the Fascist Era*, pp. 57–72.

A note on sources

To list all archival material and published works consulted would be otiose. What follows is a brief survey of the most useful document collections. For published materials, readers should consult both the Abbreviations and the alphabetical list of Frequently Cited Works. For general bibliography, Geneviève Bibes, "Le fascisme italien, état des travaux depuis 1945," *Revue française de science politique* (December 1968), pp. 1191–1244, and Josef Schröder, *Italien im Zweiten Weltkrieg. Eine Bibliographie* (Munich, 1978), are convenient starting points.

Italian archival material is rich but uneven; most of the useful documents were available at the hospitable and generally well-organized Archivio Centrale dello Stato, Rome. Mussolini's surviving confidential files (Segreteria Particolare del Duce, Carteggio Riservato) are indispensable for any study of the man's *modus operandi*. Most are also available on film (NARS Microcopy T-586) at the U.S. National Archives, although some items among the originals in Rome were not filmed, and some filmed items are no longer among the originals. For a general description of the collection, readers should consult Howard McGaw Smyth's *Secrets of the Fascist Era* (Carbondale, Illinois, 1975). The vast mass of Mussolini's ordinary correspondence (Carteggio Ordinario) in Rome is difficult to sift, but contains occasional items of value. After the Segreteria Particolare, the files of the Ministero dell' Interno, Direzione Generale Pubblica Sicurezza, Divisione Affari Generali e Riservati, Divisione Polizia Politica, and Segreteria del Capo della Polizia are indispensable for internal politics and public opinion. Also important for opinion and Party activities are the PNF files on the *"Situazione politica ed economica delle Provincie."* Finally, the press directives, which are unfortunately missing for 1940, and the malicious but fascinating private intelligence reports to the chief of the Stefani news agency, all in the Agenzia Stefani/Manlio Morgagni collection, are valuable on internal affairs, as are the documents of the Ministero della Cultura Popolare.

For the military, the Navy and Air Force Ministry files at the Archivio Centrale are indispensable, particularly on prewar military preparations. Unfortunately, no similar Army collection exists, although the Ministero della Real Casa, Primo Aiutante di Campo documents contain occasional items of interest. Graziani's vast correspondence (Carte Graziani) fills some of the gap, particularly on colonial military policy. It is also invaluable for the North African campaign and for Italian strategy in 1940; Roatta's diary-letters (Carte Graziani, bundle 42) from Rome to Graziani in North Africa are vital and as yet more or less unexploited. Finally, the crabbed and sometimes less than coherent diaries of Marshal Emilio de Bono frequently throw light on Mussolini's attitudes, as well as on rivalries within the regime.

Other Rome archives were less forthcoming than the Archivio Centrale. The Navy archive (Archivio dell'Ufficio Storico della Marina Militare) is open to those with suitable recommendations on a case-by-case and file-by-file basis. Although I am grateful for what I was allowed to see, I cannot help feeling that the Navy would better serve its own interests, as well as the impartial evaluation of the past, with less restrictive policies. The Army files (Archivio dell'Ufficio Storico dell'Esercito) are even harder to consult, although lack of archival space seems to be primarily responsible; I was able to read, among other items, an important file of General Efisio Marras's reports from Berlin. Finally, I had insuperable difficulties at the archive of the Ministry of Foreign Affairs, which refused me access in 1973–4 because of an unevenly applied and idiosyncratically interpreted "fifty-year rule." During my next visit, in the summer of 1977, the director of the Ufficio Studi e Documentazione of the Ministry, Dr. Enrico Serra, very kindly saw to the lifting of the earlier ban. Unfortunately, the archive's summer schedule and my subsequent teaching obligations prevented me from actually consulting documents. But the voluminous and well-edited *Documenti diplomatici italiani* cover the 23 May 1939–28 October 1940 period in great detail, making work in the original files less necessary than it would otherwise be.

Outside Italy, the U.S. National Archives have the already mentioned films of the Segreteria Particolare, as well as a large but uneven collection of Ministero della Cultura Populare files and other documents assembled in 1943–5 (all on NARS Microcopy T-586). At least as important is the wide selection of *Comando Supremo* and Army material the *Wehrmacht* captured in 1943 and subsequently surrendered to the Allies (NARS Microcopy T-821); the documents are basic for any work on the Italian military in the 1938–43 period.

On the German side, the original files of the Auswärtiges Amt, particularly those of the office of the state secretary, Baron Ernst von Weizsäcker, are of the greatest importance; the editors of the printed German collection (ADAP,D) naturally sought first of all to select for publication documents elucidating German foreign policy, rather than that of Fascist Italy. Auswärtiges Amt files are available on film (but filmed selectively) on NARS Microcopy T-120. Some interesting unfilmed items are available at the Politisches Archiv des Auswärtigen Amts, Bonn. For a description of the collection, readers should consult George O. Kent, *A Catalog of the Files and Microfilms of the German Foreign Ministry Archives,* v. III, IV (Stanford, California, 1966–72). From the military, many *Wehrmacht* and army high command files, including some of the reports of General von Rintelen, are on NARS Microcopies T-77 and 78. Another file of Rintelen reports is available at the Imperial War Museum, London, Item AL 1007. The German naval archives, captured intact at Schloss Tambach in 1945, are almost equally useful, particularly the files and war diary of the German naval attaché (Rome), the German liaison staff to the Italian naval high command, and the operations section of the German naval high command. These items are available either on film (NARS Microcopy T-1022) or at the Bundesarchiv/Militärarchiv, Freiburg im Breisgau. Unfortunately, some files are only available at *one* of those locations. Few *Luftwaffe* documents of any use for this period seem to have survived the war. Finally, the papers of the personal staff of the

Reichsführer SS (NARS Microcopy T-175) contain some as yet unexploited documents on the Alto Adige question, while the collections of reporters' notes from the press briefings of the Ministerium für Volksaufklärung und Propaganda, now at the Bundesarchiv, Koblenz (particularly the Sammlung Brammer, Z. Sg. 101) throw interesting light on German policy toward Italy and on the Germans' view of their allies.

Outside the Axis, the most important archival source for Italian foreign and military policy, and for its context, is the vast and exceedingly well-organized hoard of Cabinet Office and Foreign Office documents at the Public Record Office, London. The minutes of the Cabinet and War Cabinet (Cab 23, Cab 65), the various series of Cabinet Papers, the Premier papers, the files and minutes of the Committee of Imperial Defence, the Chiefs of Staff Committee, the Joint Planning Committee, and so on, are all of great interest. The Foreign Office registry series (FO 371) is absolutely indispensable for the period after 3 September 1939, when published British documents cease. Even before that date, the richness of detail and the frequently pungent unpublished minutes make it exciting reading. The papers of Lord Halifax (FO 800) also contain documents of interest. Unfortunately, the British collection contains frequent gaps. Items known from other sources do not appear, and pages in many of the looseleaf volumes of documents are blank and stamped "closed until 2015." It is difficult to see what purpose such restrictions serve at this late date.

In Washington, the "decimal files" of the United States Department of State, particularly "740.0011 European War 1939," are full of interesting and often acute reporting – reporting that presumably sank without trace into the rat's nest of the department's filing system.

Frequently cited works

Alfieri, Dino, *Due dittatori di fronte* (Milan, 1946).

Allianz Hitler-Horthy-Mussolini. Dokumente zur ungarischen Aussenpolitik (1933 bis 1945), ed. Lajos Kerekes (Budapest, 1966).

Aloisi, Pompeo. *Journal (25 juillet 1932–14 juin 1936)* (Paris, 1957).

André, Gianluca. *La guerra in Europa 1939–1941. Annuario di politica internazionale (1939–1945)*, v. VI, t. I (Milan, 1964).

Anfuso, Filippo. *Dal Palazzo Venezia al Lago di Garda* (Bologna, 1957).

Aquarone, Alberto. "Nello Quilici e il suo 'diario di guerra,' " *Storia Contemporanea*, 6:2 (1975), pp. 305–58.

L'organizzazione dello Stato totalitario (Turin, 1965).

"Public Opinion in Italy Before the Outbreak of World War II," in Roland Sarti, ed., *The Ax Within. Italian Fascism in Action* (New York, 1974), pp. 209–20.

Armellini, Quirino. *Diario di guerra. Nove mesi al Comando Supremo* (Milan, 1946).

Badoglio, Pietro. *L'Italia nella seconda guerra mondiale* (Verona, 1946).

Bastianini, Giuseppe. *Uomini, cose, fatti. Memorie di un ambasciatore* (Milan, 1959).

Bédarida, François. *La stratégie secrète de la drôle de guerre* (Paris, 1979).

Bell, P. M. H. *A Certain Eventuality. Britain and the Fall of France* (n.p., 1974).

Benigno, Jo' di. *Occasioni mancate. Roma in un diario segreto 1943–44* (Rome 1945).

Bocca, Giorgio. *Storia d'Italia nella guerra fascista* (Milan, 1969).

Bosworth, R. J. B. *Italy, the Least of the Great Powers: Italian Foreign Policy Before the First World War* (London and New York, 1979).

Bottai, Giuseppe. *Vent'anni e un giorno (24 luglio 1943)* (Milan, 1949).

Breccia, Alfredo. *Jugoslavia 1939–1941. Diplomazia della neutralità* (Milan, 1978).

Butler, J. R. M. *Grand Strategy*, v. II (London, 1957).

Cadogan, Alexander, *The Diaries of Sir Alexander Cadogan, 1938–1945*, ed. David Dilks (London, 1971).

Canevari, Emilio. *La guerra italiana. Retroscena della disfatta*, 2 v. (Rome, 1948–9).

L'Italia, 1861–1943. Retroscena della disfatta (Rome, 1965).

Caracciolo di Feroleto, Mario. *E Poi? La tragedia dell'esercito italiano* (Rome, 1946).

Carboni, Giacomo. *Memorie segrete, 1935–1948. Più che il dovere* (Florence, 1955).

Carocci, Giampiero. *La politica estera dell'Italia fascista (1925–1928)* (Bari, 1969).

Cassels, Alan. *Mussolini's Early Diplomacy* (Princeton, N.J., 1970).

Castronovo, Valerio. *Giovanni Agnelli* (Turin, 1971).

Cavagnari, Domenico. "La marina nella vigilia e nel primo periodo della guerra," *Nuova Antologia,* 357 (August 1947), pp. 370–86.

Cavallero, Ugo. *Comando supremo. Diario 1940–1943 del Capo di S.M.G.* (Bologna, 1948).

Caviglia, Enrico, *Diario (aprile 1925-marzo 1945)* (Rome, 1952).

Cervi, Mario. *The Hollow Legions. Mussolini's Blunder in Greece, 1940–1941* (Garden City, N.Y., 1971).

Ceva, Lucio. "Appunti per una storia dello Stato Maggiore generale fino alla vigilia della 'non-belligeranza,' " *Storia Contemporanea* 10:2 (1979), pp. 207–52.

La condotta italiana della guerra. Cavallero e il Comando Supremo 1941/1942 (Milan, 1975).

"L'incontro Keitel-Badoglio del novembre 1940 nelle carte del Generale Marras," *Il Risorgimento* (Milan), 29:1–2 (1977), pp. 1–44.

"Un intervento di Badoglio e il mancato rinnovo delle artiglierie italiane," *Il Risorgimento* (Milan) 28:2 (1976), pp. 117–72.

Chiavarelli, Emilia. *L'opera della marina italiana nella guerra italo-etiopica* (Milan, 1969).

Churchill, Winston S. *The Grand Alliance* (New York, paperback ed., 1962).

Their Finest Hour (New York, paperback ed., 1962).

Cianca, Ernesto. *Nascita dello Stato imprenditore in Italia* (Milan, 1977).

Ciano, Galeazzo. *Diario 1937–1943,* ed. Renzo De Felice (Milan, 1980).

L'Europa verso la catastrofe (Verona, 1948).

Cliadakis, Harry. "Neutrality and War in Italian Policy, 1939–1940," *Journal of Contemporary History,* 9:3 (1974), pp. 171–90.

Conti, Ettore, *Dal taccuino di un borghese* (Milan, 1946).

Coverdale, John F. *Italian Intervention in the Spanish Civil War* (Princeton, N.J., 1975).

Creveld, Martin van. *Hitler's Strategy, 1940–1941. The Balkan Clue* (Cambridge, 1973).

"Prelude to Disaster: the British Decision to Aid Greece, 1940–1941," *Journal of Contemporary History,* 9:3 (1974), pp. 65–92.

"25 October 1940: a Historical Puzzle," *Journal of Contemporary History,* 6:3 (1971), pp. 87–96.

Cunningham of Hyndhope, Viscount Andrew. *A Sailor's Odyssey* (New York, 1951).

D'Amoja, Fulvio. *La politica estera dell'Impero* (Padua, 1967).

Deakin, F. W. *The Brutal Friendship. Mussolini, Hitler, and the Fall of Italian Fascism* (New York, rev. ed., 1966).

De Biase, Carlo. *L'Impero di "faccetta nera"* (Milan, 1966).

De Felice, Renzo. "Alcune osservazioni sulla politica estera mussoliniana," in *idem,* ed., *L'Italia fra tedeschi e alleati. La politica estera fascista e la seconda guerra mondiale* (Bologna, 1973), pp. 57–74.

The Interpretations of Fascism (Cambridge, Mass., 1977).

Mussolini il rivoluzionario, 1883–1920 (Turin, 1965).

Mussolini il fascista, I, La conquista del potere, 1921–1925 (Turin, 1966).

Mussolini il fascista, II, L'organizzazione dello Stato fascista, 1925–1929 (Turin, 1968).

Mussolini il duce, I, Gli anni del consenso, 1929–1936 (Turin, 1974).

Il problema dell'Alto Adige nei rapporti italo-tedeschi dall'Anschluss alla fine della seconda guerra mondiale (Bologna, 1973).

Storia degli ebrei italiani sotto il fascismo (Turin, 3rd rev. ed., 1972).

Delhaes-Guenther, Dietrich von. "Die Bevölkerungspolitik des Faschismus," *Quellen und Forschungen aus italienischen Archiven und Bibliotheken*, 59 (1979), pp. 392–420.

De Luna, Giovanni. *Badoglio. Un militare al potere* (Milan, 1974).

Benito Mussolini. Soggettività e pratica di una dittatura (Milan, 1978).

Delzell, Charles F. "Pius XII, Italy, and the Outbreak of War," *Journal of Contemporary History*, 2:4 (1967), pp. 137–61.

Domarus, Max, ed. *Hitler: Reden und Proklamationen*, 2 v. (Munich, 1965).

Engel, Gerhard. *Heeresadjutant bei Hitler 1938–1943. Aufzeichnungen des Majors Engel*, ed. Hildegard von Kotze (Stuttgart, 1974).

Faldella, Emilio. *L'Italia e la seconda guerra mondiale. Revisione di giudizi* (Bologna, 2nd rev. ed., 1960).

Fanizza, Ruggero. *De Vecchi – Bastico – Campioni. Ultimi Governatori dell'Egeo* (Forlì, n.d.).

Favagrossa, Carlo. *Perché perdemmo la guerra. Mussolini e la produzione bellica* (Milan, 1946).

Federzoni, Luigi. *L'Italia di ieri per la storia di domani* (Milan, 1967).

Fischer, Fritz. *Germany's Aims in the First World War* (New York, 1967).

Gabriele, Mariano. *Operazione C 3: Malta* (Rome, 1965).

Gambino, Antonio. *Storia del PNF* (Milan, 1962).

Gorla, Giuseppe. *L'Italia nella seconda guerra mondiale* (Milan, 1959).

Graziani, Rodolfo. *Ho difeso la patria* (Milan, 1947).

Africa Settentrionale, 1940–41.

Grazzi, Emanuele. *Il principio della fine (l'impresa di Grecia)* (Rome, 1945).

Grifone, Pietro. *Il capitale finanziario in Italia* (Turin, 2nd ed., 1971).

Guariglia, Raffaele. *Ricordi 1922–1945* (Naples, 1949).

Guarneri, Felice. *Battaglie economiche tra le due grandi guerre.* 2 v. (Milan, 1953).

La guerre en Méditerranée, 1939–1945 (Paris, 1971).

Guerri, Giordano Bruno. *Galeazzo Ciano. Una vita, 1903/1944* (Milan, 1979).

Giuseppe Bottai, un fascista critico (Milan, 1976).

Halder, Franz. *Kriegstagebuch. Tägliche Aufzeichnungen des Chefs des Generalstabes des Heeres 1939–1942*, 3 v. (Stuttgart, 1962–4).

Hildebrand, Klaus. *The Foreign Policy of the Third Reich* (Berkeley, Los Angeles, 1973).

"Le forze motrici di politica interna agenti sulla politica estera nazionalsozialista," *Storia Contemporanea*, 5:2 (1974), pp. 201–22.

Hillgruber, Andreas. "Der Faktor Amerika in Hitlers Strategie 1938–1941," *Aus Politik und Zeitgeschichte*, B.19/66, 11.5.1966, pp. 3–21.

Hitler, König Carol, und Marschall Antonescu. Die deutsch-rumänischen Beziehungen 1938–1941 (Wiesbaden, 1954).

Hitlers Strategie. Politik und Kriegführung 1940–1941 (Frankfurt a. M., 1965).

Hinsley, F. H. *British Intelligence in the Second World War*, v. 1 (London, 1979).

Hoptner, Jacob B. *Yugoslavia in Crisis, 1934–1941* (New York, 1964).

Hore-Belisha, Leslie. *The Private Papers of Hore-Belisha*, ed. R. J. Minney (London, 1960).

Jacobsen, Hans-Adolf. *Fall "Gelb." Der Kampf um den deutschen Operationsplan zur Westoffensive 1940* (Wiesbaden, 1957).

Jacomoni di San Savino, Francesco. *La politica dell'Italia in Albania nelle testimonianze del Luogotenente del Re Francesco Jacomoni di San Savino* (Bologna, 1965).

Jäckel, Eberhard. *Frankreich in Hitlers Europa* (Stuttgart, 1966).

Jodl, Alfred. Diary, printed in part in International Military Tribunal, *Trial of the Major War Criminals* (Nuremberg, 1947–9), v. XXVIII.

Knox, MacGregor. "1940. Italy's 'Parallel War,' Part I. From Non-Belligerence to the Collapse of France" (diss., Yale University, 1976).

Koliopoulos, John S. *Greece and the British Connection, 1935–1941* (Oxford, 1977).

Kordt, Erich. *Nicht aus den Akten* (Stuttgart, 1950).

Langer, William L. and Gleason, S. Everett. *The Challenge to Isolation, 1937–1940* (New York, 1952).

The Undeclared War, 1940–1941 (New York, 1953).

Lanza, Michele (pseud. Leonardo Simoni). *Berlino, Ambasciata d'Italia, 1939–1943* (Rome, 1946).

Larminat, Edgard de. *Chroniques irrévérencieuses* (Paris, 1962).

Leeb, Wilhelm von. *Tagebuchaufzeichnungen und Lagebetrachtungen aus zwei Weltkriegen* (Stuttgart, 1976).

Lessona, Alessandro. *Memorie* (Florence, 1958).

Un ministro di Mussolini racconta (Milan, 1973).

Leto, Guido. *OVRA. Fascismo – Antifascismo* (Bologna, 1952).

Long, Gavin. *To Benghazi* (Canberra, 1952).

Lowe, C. J. and Marzari, Frank. *Italian Foreign Policy, 1870–1940* (London, 1975).

Luciolli, Mario (pseud. Donosti). *Mussolini e l'Europa. La politica estera fascista* (Rome, 1945).

Mack Smith, Denis. *Italy. A Modern History* (Ann Arbor, 1959).

"Mussolini, Artist in Propaganda. The Downfall of Fascism," *History Today,* 9 (1959), pp. 223–32.

Mussolini's Roman Empire (New York, 1976).

Marder, Arthur. "The Royal Navy and the Ethiopian Crisis of 1935–36," *American Historical Review,* 75:5 (1970), pp. 1327–56.

Martin, Bernd. *Friedensinitiativen und Machtpolitik im Zweiten Weltkrieg 1939–1942* (Düsseldorf, 1974).

Marzari, Frank. "Projects for an Italian-led Balkan Bloc of Neutrals, September-December 1939," *Historical Journal,* 13:4 (1970), pp. 767–88.

Matteini, Claudio. *Ordini alla stampa. La politica interna ed estera del governo fascista nelle "disposizioni" emanate ai giornali dal Ministero della Cultura Popolare* (Rome, 1945).

Medlicott, W. N. *The Economic Blockade,* v. I (London, 1952).

Melograni, Piero. *Gli industriali e Mussolini. Rapporti tra Confindustria e fascismo dal 1919 al 1929* (Milan, 1972).

Michaelis, Meir. *Mussolini and the Jews* (Oxford, 1978).

Minniti, Fortunato. "Due anni di attività del 'Fabbriguerra' per la produzione bellica," *Storia Contemporanea,* 6:4 (1975), pp. 849–79.

"Il problema degli armamenti nella preparazione militare italiana dal 1935 al 1943," *Storia Contemporanea,* 9:11 (1978), pp. 5–61.

Paxton, Robert O. *Vichy France. Old Guard and New Order, 1940–1944* (New York, 1972).

Petersen, Jens. *Hitler-Mussolini. Die Entstehung der Achse Berlin-Rom 1933–1936* (Tübingen, 1973).

"La politica estera del fascismo come problema storiografico," in Renzo De Felice, ed., *L'Italia fra tedeschi e alleati. La politica estera fascista e la seconda guerra mondiale* (Bologna, 1973), pp. 11–55.

Phillips, William. *Ventures in Diplomacy* (Boston, 1952).

Pieri, Piero. "La stratégie italienne sur l'échiquier Méditerranéen," in *La guerre en Méditerranée 1939–1945* (Paris, 1971), pp. 61–78.

Playfair, I. S. O. *The Mediterranean and Middle East,* v. 1, *The Early Successes Against Italy (to May 1941)* (London, 1954).

Pricolo, Francesco. *La Regia Aeronautica nella seconda guerra mondiale (novembre 1939-novembre 1941)* (Milan, 1971).

Puntoni, Paolo. *Parla Vittorio Emanuele III* (Milan, 1958).

Puppo, Franca Avantaggiato. *Gli armistizi francesi del 1940* (Milan, 1963).

Quartararo, Rosaria. "Il 'canale' segreto di Chamberlain," *Storia Contemporanea* 7:4 (1976), pp. 648–716.

Quazza, Guido, ed. *Fascismo e società italiana* (Turin, 1973).

Rintelen, Enno von. *Mussolini als Bundesgenosse. Erinnerungen des deutschen Militärattachés in Rom 1936–1943* (Tübingen, 1951).

Roatta, Mario. *Otto milioni di baionette. L'esercito italiano in guerra dal 1940 al 1944* (Verona, 1946).

Rochat, Giorgio. "L'attentato a Graziani e la repressione italiana in Etiopia nel 1936–37," *Italia Contemporanea,* No. 118 (1975), pp. 5–37.

"L'esercito e il fascismo," in Guido Quazza, ed., *Fascismo e società italiana* (Turin, 1973), pp. 91–123.

L'esercito italiano da Vittorio Veneto a Mussolini (Bari, 1967).

Militari e politici nella preparazione della campagna d'Etiopia. Studio e documenti 1932–1936 (Milan, 1971).

"Mussolini, chef de guerre," *Revue d'histoire de la deuxième guerre mondiale,* No. 100 (1975), pp. 43–66.

"Mussolini e le forze armate," *Il Movimento di Liberazione in Italia,* No. 95 (1969), pp. 3–22.

"La repressione della resistenza araba in Cirenaica (1930–31)," *Il Movimento di Liberazione in Italia,* No. 110 (1973), pp. 3–39.

Rochat, Giorgio and Pieri, Piero. *Pietro Badoglio* (Turin, 1974).

Rossi, Francesco. *Mussolini e lo stato maggiore. Avvenimenti del 1940* (Rome, 1951).

Salewski, Michael. *Die deutsche Seekriegsleitung 1933–1945,* v. 1, *1933–1941* (Frankfurt a. M., 1970).

Salvemini, Gaetano. *Preludio alla seconda guerra mondiale* (Milan, 1967).

Santarelli, Enzo. *Storia del fascismo,* 3 v. (Rome, 1973).

Santoro, Giuseppe. *L'aeronautica italiana nella seconda guerra mondiale,* 2 v. (Rome, 1957).

Sarti, Roland. *Fascism and the Industrial Leadership in Italy* (Berkeley, Los Angeles, 1971).

Schmidt, Paul (Otto). *Statist auf diplomatischer Bühne 1923–1945. Erlebnisse des Chefdolmetschers im Auswärtigen Amt mit den Staatsmännern Europas* (Bonn, 1949).

Schramm-von Thadden, Ehrengard. *Griechenland und die Grossmächte im Zweiten Weltkrieg* (Wiesbaden, 1955).

Schreiber, Gerhard. *Revisionismus und Weltmachtstreben. Marineführung und deutsch-italienische Beziehungen 1919 bis 1944* (Stuttgart, 1978).

Senise, Carmine. *Quando ero Capo della Polizia* (Rome, 1946).

Siebert, Ferdinand. *Italiens Weg in den Zweiten Weltkrieg* (Frankfurt a.M./Bonn, 1962).

Smyth, Howard McGaw. *Secrets of the Fascist Era* (Carbondale, Illinois, 1975).

Sommer, Theo. *Deutschland und Japan zwischen den Mächten 1935–1940* (Tübingen, 1962).

Sullivan, Brian R. "A Thirst for Glory: Mussolini, the Italian Military, and the Fascist Regime, 1922–1940" (diss., Columbia University, 1981).

Sylos Labini, Paolo. *Saggio sulle classi sociali* (Bari, 1974).

Taylor, Telford. *The March of Conquest. The German Victories in Western Europe, 1940* (New York, 1958).

Thies, Jochen. *Architekt der Weltherrschaft. Die "Endziele" Hitlers* (Düsseldorf, 1976).

Thorne, Christopher. *The Approach of War, 1938–39* (London, 1967).

Toscano, Mario. *Designs in Diplomacy* (Baltimore, 1971).

The Origins of the Pact of Steel (Baltimore, 1967).

Trevor-Roper, H. R., ed. *Hitler's Secret Conversations, 1941–1944* (New York, 1953).

Truchet, André. *L'Armistice de 1940 et L'Afrique du Nord* (Paris, 1955).

Ufficio Storico, Stato Maggiore Esercito (USE). *In Africa Settentrionale. La preparazione al conflitto. L'avanzata su Sidi el Barrani* (Rome, 1955).

La battaglia delle Alpi occidentali (giugno 1940) (Rome, 1947).

L'esercito italiano tra la 1ª e la 2ª guerra mondiale (novembre 1918-giugno 1940) (Rome, 1954).

La guerra in Africa Orientale (giugno 1940-novembre 1941) (Rome, 1971).

La prima offensiva britannica in Africa Settentrionale (Rome, n.d.).

Ufficio Storico della Marina Militare (USMM). *Le azioni navali in Mediterraneo dal 10 giugno 1940 al 31 marzo 1941* (Rome, 1970).

La difesa del traffico con l'Albania, la Grecia, e l'Egeo (Rome, 1965).

I mezzi d'assalto (Rome, 1972).

L'organizzazione della Marina durante il conflitto, t. I, *Efficienza all'apertura delle ostilità* (Rome, 1972).

I sommergibili in Mediterraneo (Rome, 1972).

Visconti Prasca, Sebastiano. *Io ho aggredito la Grecia* (Milan, 1946).

Wagner, Gerhard, ed. *Lagevorträge des Oberbefehlshabers der Kriegsmarine vor Hitler 1939–1945* (Munich, 1972).

Watt, Donald C. "The Rome-Berlin Axis, 1936–1940, Myth and Reality," *The Review of Politics*, 22 (1960), pp. 519–42.

Weizsäcker, Ernst von. *Die Weizsäcker-Papiere 1933–1950*, ed. Leonidas Hill (Frankfurt a. M., 1974).

Woodward, Sir Llewellyn. *British Foreign Policy in the Second World War*. v. I (London, 1970).

Woolf, Stuart J. "Inghilterra, Francia e Italia: settembre 1939-giugno 1940," *Rivista di Storia Contemporanea*, 3:4 (1972), pp. 477–95.

Index